Lecture Notes in Computer Science 12583

More information about this subseries at http://www.springer.com/series/7410

Ilsun You (Ed.)

Information Security Applications

21st International Conference, WISA 2020
Jeju Island, South Korea, August 26–28, 2020
Revised Selected Papers

 Springer

Editor
Ilsun You (ID)
Soonchunhyang University
Asan, Korea (Republic of)

ISSN 0302-9743   ISSN 1611-3349   (electronic)
Lecture Notes in Computer Science
ISBN 978-3-030-65298-2   ISBN 978-3-030-65299-9   (eBook)
https://doi.org/10.1007/978-3-030-65299-9

LNCS Sublibrary: SL4 – Security and Cryptology

This Springer imprint is published by the registered company Springer Nature Switzerland AG
The registered company address is: Gewerbestrasse 11, 6330 Cham, Switzerland

Preface

Over the past decades, many advances in information technologies that include artificial intelligence (AI), 5G, blockchain, Internet of Things (IoT), and many more provided beneficial effects on various aspects of our lives. However, these advancements are accompanied with even more sophisticated threats to individuals, businesses, and government's most valuable data assets. Cybercriminals are also exploiting such technologies to find vulnerabilities and develop more sophisticated attacks. Therefore, it is of paramount importance to continuously study, inform, and develop new techniques to ensure information security.

World Conference on Information Security Application (WISA) is one of the main security research venues hosted by the Korea Institute of Information Security and Cryptography (KIISC) and sponsored by the Ministry of Science, ICT and Future Planning (MSIP), and co-sponsored by the Electronics & Telecommunication Research Institute (ETRI), the Korea Internet & Security Agency (KISA), and the National Security Research Institute (NSR). Especially in 2020, WISA celebrated the 31st anniversary for KIISC while going toward its new position as the best contributor to information security. Additionally, due to inevitable social changes caused by the COVID-19 pandemic, WISA took a new path in holding the 21st World Conference on Information Security Applications (WISA 2020). Despite the challenges, WISA continued to provide an open forum for exchanging and sharing common research interests through both live and recorded online presentations. The challenges lead to another opportunity for WISA to provide a platform for sharing results of on-going research, developments, and application on information security areas.

This volume is composed of the extended version of papers presented at WISA 2020, held at Jeju Island, South Korea during August 26–28, 2020. The primary focus of WISA 2020 is on systems and network security, including all other technical and practical aspects of security application. In particular, this year's conference invited researchers working on 5G/6G, AI, blockchain, V2X, and advanced IoT who are keen on bringing the latest open security challenges.

A total of 31 outstanding papers, covering areas such as AI and intrusion detection, steganography and malware, cryptography, cyber security, application, systems, and hardware security were accepted for presentation at WISA 2020. This year, WISA 2020 specially included poster presentations which composed of 39 posters. Moreover, invited keynote talks by Prof. Matt Bishop (University of California, USA), and Prof. Suman Jana (Columbia University, USA), as well as tutorial talks by Prof. Dan Dongseong Kim (The University of Queensland, Australia), and Dr. SeongHan Shin (National Institute of AIST, Japan) augmented the conference.

The great effort and countless dedication of the Organizing Committee and reviewers, support of the sponsor and co-sponsor, and active participation of all the participants led to another success story for WISA 2020. We would like to acknowledge the contribution of each individual Program Committee member. As well as our sincere gratitude to all the reviewers, authors, and participants around the world for their unending support.

October 2020   Ilsun You

Organization

General Chair

Souhwan Jung   Soongsil University, South Korea

Program Committee Chair

Ilsun You   Soonchunhyang University, South Korea

Program Committee

Pelin Angin	Middle East Technical University, Turkey
Joonsang Baek	University of Wollongong, Australia
Sang Kil Cha	KAIST, South Korea
Xiaofeng Chen	Xidian University, China
Jin-Hee Cho	Virginia Tech, USA
Dooho Choi	ETRI, South Korea
Swee-Huay Heng	Multimedia University, Malaysia
Hsu-Chun Hsiao	National Taiwan University, Taiwan
Qiong Huang	South China Agricultural University, China
Eul Gyu Im	Hanyang University, South Korea
Yeongjin Jang	Oregon State University, USA
Hiroaki Kikuchi	Meji University, Japan
Dongseong Kim	The University of Queensland, Australia
Jong Kim	POSTECH, South Korea
Jongkil Kim	University of Wollongong, Australia
Jonghoon Kwon	ETH Zurich, Switzerland
Byoungyoung Lee	Seoul National University, South Korea
Kyu Hyung Lee	University of Georgia, USA
Shengli Liu	Shanghai Jiao Tong University, China
Aziz Mohaisen	University of Central Florida, USA
Kirill Morozov	University of North Texas, USA
Masakatsu Nishigaki	Shizuoka University, Japan
Jason Nurse	University of Kent, UK
Kazumasa Omote	University of Tsukuba, Japan
Ki-Woong Park	Sejong University, South Korea
Marcus Peinado	Microsoft, USA
Junghwan Rhee	NEC Laboratories, USA
Ulrich Rührmair	LMU Munich, Germany
Kouichi Sakurai	Kyushu University, Japan
Junji Shikata	Yokohama National University, Japan
Dongwan Shin	New Mexico Tech, USA

Sang Uk Shin	Pukyong National University, South Korea
SeongHan Shin	AIST, Japan
Amril Syalim	University of Indonesia, Indonesia
Gang Tan	Penn State University, USA
Samuel Woo	Dankook University, South Korea
Toshihiro Yamauchi	Okayama University, Japan
Naoto Yanai	Osaka University, Japan
Siu Ming Yiu	The University of Hong Kong, Hong Kong
Taek-Young Youn	ETRI, South Korea
Mengyu Yu	Roosevelt University, USA

Organizing Committee Chair

Jung-Hyouk Lee	Sejong University, South Korea

Organizing Committee

Hyo-Beom Ahn	Kongju National University, South Korea
Soonjoung Byun	KISA, South Korea
Byung-Chul Choi	ETRI, South Korea
Yangseo Choi	ETRI, South Korea
KyengHwa Do	Konkuk University, South Korea
Dong-Guk Han	Kookmin University, South Korea
Hyoung Chun Kim	NSR, South Korea
Jin Cheol Kim	ETRI, South Korea
Jonghyun Kim	ETRI, South Korea
Jongsung Kim	Kookmin University, South Korea
JungHee Kim	KISA, South Korea
Tai Hyo Kim	Formal Works Inc., South Korea
Woo-Nyon Kim	NSR, South Korea
Young-Gab Kim	Sejong University, South Korea
Jin Kwak	Ajou University, South Korea
Changhoon Lee	Seoul National University of Science and Technology, South Korea
Deok Gyu Lee	Seowon University, South Korea
Manhee Lee	Hannam University, South Korea
Seoklae Lee	KISA, South Korea
Daesub Park	Sejong University, South Korea
Ki-Woong Park	Sejong University, South Korea
Youngho Park	Sejong Cyber University, South Korea
Jungtaek Seo	Soonchunhyang University, South Korea
Ji Sun Shin	Sejong University, South Korea
Kangbin Yim	Soonchunhyang University, South Korea
Joobeom Yun	Sejong University, South Korea

Contents

AI Security and Intrusion Detection

Steganography and Malware

Application, System, and Hardware Security

Cryptography

Advances in Network Security and Attack Defense

Cyber Security

AI Security and Intrusion Detection

Spatially Localized Perturbation GAN (SLP-GAN) for Generating Invisible Adversarial Patches

Yongsu Kim[iD], Hyoeun Kang[iD], Afifatul Mukaroh[iD], Naufal Suryanto[iD], Harashta Tatimma Larasati[iD], and Howon Kim[✉][iD]

Pusan National University, Busan, Republic of Korea
dkgoggog0329@gmail.com, hyoeun405@gmail.com, afifatul.mukaroh@gmail.com, naufalsuryanto@gmail.com, tatimmaharashta@gmail.com, howonkim@gmail.com

Abstract. Deep Neural Networks (DNNs) are very vulnerable to adversarial attacks because of the instability and unreliability under the training process. Recently, many studies about adversarial patches have been conducted that aims to misclassify the image classifier model by attaching patches to images. However, most of the previous research employs adversarial patches that are visible to human vision, making them easy to be identified and responded to. In this paper, we propose a new method entitled Spatially Localized Perturbation GAN (SLP-GAN) that can generate visually natural patches while maintaining a high attack success rate. SLP-GAN utilizes a spatially localized perturbation taken from the most representative area of target images (i.e., attention map) as the adversarial patches. The patch region is extracted using the Grad-CAM algorithm to improve the attacking ability against the target model. Our experiment, tested on GTSRB and CIFAR-10 datasets, shows that SLP-GAN outperforms the state-of-the-art adversarial patch attack methods in terms of visual fidelity.

Keywords: Adversarial patch · Generative Adversarial Networks · Spatially localized perturbation

1 Introduction

Deep neural networks (DNNs) have been extensively used in various intelligent systems such as facial recognition, object classification, and disease diagnosis.

This work was supported by Institute of Information and Communications Technology Planning and Evaluation (IITP) grant funded by the Korea government(MSIT) (2019-0-01343, Regional strategic industry convergence security core talent training business). This research was supported by the MSIT(Ministry of Science and ICT), Korea, under the ITRC(Information Technology Research Center) support program(IITP-2020-0-01797) supervised by the IITP(Institute of Information & Communications Technology Planning & Evaluation).

© Springer Nature Switzerland AG 2020
I. You (Ed.): WISA 2020, LNCS 12583, pp. 3–15, 2020.
https://doi.org/10.1007/978-3-030-65299-9_1

However, recent works have shown that DNNs are vulnerable to adversarial attacks, which leads to deep learning models to misbehave in unexpected ways.

The study of adversarial attacks began with adversarial perturbation with small magnitude added to an image that can cause to be misclassified by DNNs. In the past years, various works of adversarial perturbation have been developed using a number of optimization strategies such as Fast Gradient Sign Method (FGSM) [3], Projected Gradient Descent (PGD) [12], and Carlini & Wagner (C&W) Attack [2]. However, these methods have limitations that are applicable only to the digital domain (e.g., security camera systems) because they mainly focus on directly manipulating the pixels of the input images.

Compared to adversarial perturbation, an adversarial patch is introduced as an alternative and practical approach to physical domain attacks. Brown et al. [1] introduced to generate "universal adversarial patches" that can be physically printed out and put on any images. However, these adversarial patches can be easily recognized by human vision since they focus only on attack performance, not visual fidelity.

Liu et al. [10] propose a perceptual-sensitive GAN (PS-GAN) to generate adversarial examples using generative adversarial networks (GANs), which can learn and approximate the distribution of original instances [4]. PS-GAN can simultaneously enhance the visual fidelity and the attacking ability for the adversarial patch using a patch-to-patch translation and an attention mechanism. Even though the visual fidelity of adversarial patches is improved, they may still not have a natural appearance compared to the original image.

To address the problem, our paper proposes a new method called Spatially Localized Perturbation GAN (SLP-GAN) to generate invisible adversarial patches. Our SLP-GAN can generate spatially localized perturbations as adversarial patches that are visually natural with the original images. The patch region is taken from the most representative area of the input image (i.e., attention map) using the Grad-CAM algorithm [16] to improve the attacking ability. To evaluate the effectiveness of our SLP-GAN, we conduct the experiments on GTSRB [18] and CIFAR-10 [9] datasets using different target models, under white-box and black-box attack settings. We also demonstrate a physical-world attack experiment on Korean traffic sign mockups. The experimental results show that our SLP-GAN outperforms the state-of-the-art adversarial patch attack methods in terms of visual fidelity, maintaining a high attack success rate.

2   Related Work

The attack in Deep Neural Network (DNN) has raised concern for many researchers due to its fatal impact. Even a slight perturbation added to an image may cause to be misclassified. In this section, we provide an overview of adversarial perturbation and adversarial patches which is related to our work, and the overview of Generative Adversarial Networks (GANs), which recently has gained interest for use as generation methods of adversarial attacks.

2.1   Adversarial Perturbation

Adversarial perturbation is tiny perturbation added to the image that can cause to be misclassified by the target model with high confidence [19]. Suppose that a trained model M can classify an original image x correctly as $M(x) = y$; by adding slight perturbation η that could not be recognized by human eyes to x, an adversary can generate an adversarial example $x' = x + \eta$ so that $M(x') \neq y$.

Qiu et al. [14] and Yuan et al. [22] provide a review of the current attack and defense technologies based on adversarial perturbation. According to their reviews, adversarial attacks can be categorized into white-box attack and black-box attack based on the adversary's knowledge.

– White-box attacks: Adversary knows all the structure and parameters of the target model, including training data, model architectures, hyper-parameters, and model weights. L-BFGS [19], FGSM [3], Deepfool [13] are popular techniques for generating the adversarial examples based on white-box attack.
– Black-box attacks: Adversary has no knowledge about the target model and considers the target as a black-box system. Adversary analyses the target model by only observing the output based on a given series of adversarial examples. Most adversarial attacks are based on a white-box attack, but they can be transferred to a black-box attack due to the transferability of adversarial perturbation [23].

2.2   Adversarial Patch

Adversarial perturbation is typically applicable to the digital domain in the real-world attack scenario. In contrast, an adversarial patch is feasible in the physical domain because it can be attached to the specific location of the real object. Brown et al. [1] introduce a method to create a universal, robust, targeted adversarial patch in real-world applications. The patch can successfully fool a classifier with a variety of scenes, transformations, and output to any target class.

Another proposal is a black-box adversarial-patch-based attack called DPatch. It can fool mainstream object detectors (e.g., Faster R-CNN and YOLO) that can not be accomplished by the original adversarial patch [11]. They simultaneously attack the bounding box regression and object classification.

Both of the adversarial patch methods produce a visible patch that can be easily recognized by human vision. Therefore, we will focus on the invisibility of the patch while keeping the applicability in a real-world implementation.

2.3   Generative Adversarial Networks (GANs)

Recent studies have shown that most of the adversarial perturbations and patches generations rely on optimization schemes. To generate a more perceptually realistic perturbation efficiently, many variants of Generative Adversarial Networks (GANs) [4] have been commonly proposed by researchers.

Earlier, Goodfellow et al. [4] introduce a framework for estimating generative models via an adversarial process, which simultaneously trains two models: a generative model G that captures the data distribution and a discriminative model D that estimates the probability that a sample came from the training data rather than G. This discovery, coined as Generative Adversarial Network (GAN), has since been a big impact in data generation.

In the context of adversarial perturbation generation, Xiao et al. [21] propose AdvGAN to generate adversarial perturbation with generative adversarial networks (GANs). It can learn and approximate the distribution of original instances. Once the generator is trained, it can generate perturbations efficiently for any instance, so as to potentially accelerate adversarial training as defenses. The attack has placed the first with 92.76% accuracy on a public MNIST black-box attack challenge.

Liu et al. [10] propose a perceptual-sensitive GAN (PS-GAN) that can simultaneously enhance the visual fidelity and the attacking ability for the adversarial patch. To improve the visual fidelity, the authors treat the patch generation as a patch-to-patch translation via an adversarial process, feeding seed patch and outputting a similar adversarial patch with fairly high perceptual correlation with the attacked image. To further enhance the attacking ability, an attention mechanism coupled with adversarial generation is introduced to predict the critical attacking areas for placing the patches. The limitation of PS-GAN is that it uses a seed patch that is quite different from the original image, so it may still not seem visually natural.

Our proposed method is to generate a patch from the original input image using an attention map that maximizes the attack rate while maintaining high visual fidelity.

3   Spatially Localized Perturbation GAN

In this section, we describe the problem definition and introduce the Spatially Localized Perturbation GAN (SLP-GAN) framework for generating invisible adversarial patches.

3.1   Problem Definition

Suppose $\mathcal{X} \subseteq \mathcal{R}^n$ is a feature space with n number of features. Assume (x_i, y_i) is the ith instance in the training dataset with feature vector $x_i \in \mathcal{X}$ and $y_i \in \mathcal{Y}$ corresponding to true class labels. DNN attempts to learn the classification function $F : \mathcal{X} \rightarrow \mathcal{Y}$. The purpose of the adversarial attack in our study is to generate the adversarial example x_A, which satisfies the equation $F(x_A) \neq y$, where y is the true label of x. Additionally, x_A should also be similar to the original instance x in terms of visual fidelity. The adversarial example x_A is created by attaching a spatially localized patches p to the original data x, expressed as the equation $x_A = x + p$. Spatially localized itself, in our term, is defined as the characteristic of perturbation, which is only applied only to some specific part instead of the whole image. In the next section, we elaborate on our proposed method for creating adversarial patches which satisfy the above criteria.

3.2 SLP-GAN Framework

SLP-GAN. Our proposed structure SLP-GAN is mainly composed of three parts; a generator G, a discriminator D, and the target model T. In the first step, our mechanism is similar to the proposal of [21] for generating adversarial examples with adversarial networks. Generator G takes the original data x as input and generates perturbation throughout the entire area. Unlike previous proposals, our method employs additional steps of performing spatially localized perturbation to create adversarial patches that can be attached to a specific area. We leverage the Grad-CAM algorithm [16] to extract patch regions and apply the generated perturbation only to the extracted region. As a result, the spatially localized perturbation can be treated as adversarial patches p.

The role of discriminator D is to distinguish the original data x and adversarial example $x_A = x + p$. D encourages G to generate perturbation similar to the original data. Furthermore, G should have the ability to deceive the target model T. So, the whole structure of SLP-GAN mainly has three loss functions, the adversarial loss L_{GAN}, the attacking ability loss L_{atk}, the perturbation loss L_{ptb}. The adversarial loss L_{GAN} can be written as:

$$L_{GAN} = \mathbb{E}_x \log D(x) + \mathbb{E}_x \log(1 - D(x_A)). \tag{1}$$

The above equation shows that the discriminator D aims to distinguish the adversarial example x_A from the original data x. Note that D encourages G to generate perturbation with visual fidelity due to the above equation. The loss of attacking the target model T can be defined as follows:

$$L_{atk} = -\mathbb{E}_x \ell_T(x_A, y), \tag{2}$$

where y is the true class of original data x and ℓ_T is the loss function (e.g., cross-entropy loss) applied to the target model T. We apply the trick to take the negative of the target model loss function so that the target model cannot classify the adversarial example x_A to the real class y of the original data x. Additionally, we define the perturbation loss L_{ptb} using a soft hinge loss [8] on the L_2 norm to bound the magnitude of the generated perturbation:

$$L_{ptb} = \mathbb{E}_x \max(0, \|x_A\|_2 - c), \tag{3}$$

where c represents the user-specified bound and serves to stabilize the GAN's training. Finally, SLP-GAN loss function combined with the above visual fidelity and attacking ability for the target model can be expressed as:

$$L = L_{GAN} + \alpha L_{atk} + \beta L_{ptb}, \tag{4}$$

Algorithm 1. Training process of SLP-GAN Framework

Input: training image set $X_{image} = \{x_i \mid i = 1, \ldots, n\}$
Output: spatially localized patches $P = \{p_i \mid i = 1, \ldots, n\}$
for the number of training epochs **do**
    for k steps **do**
        sample minibatch of m images $\phi_x = \{x_1, \ldots, x_m\}$.
        generate minibatch of m adversarial perturbations $\phi_x^G = \{G(x_1), \ldots, G(x_m)\}$.
        obtain activation maps $M(\phi_x)$ by *Grad-CAM*.
        extract spatially localized patches $P = \{G(x_i)_{M(x_i)} \mid i = 1, \ldots, n\}$.
        create adversarial examples $x_A = \{x_i + p_i \mid i = 1, \ldots, n\}$.
        update D to $\max_D L$ with G fixed.
    end for
    sample minibatch of m images $\phi_x = \{x_1, \ldots, x_m\}$.
    create adversarial examples x_A (same as above).
    update G to $\min_G L$ with D fixed.
end for

---

where $\alpha > 0$ and $\beta > 0$ control the contribution of each loss function. The generator G and the discriminator D in our SLP-GAN are trained by solving the minimax game represented by the equation $\min_G \max_D L$. As a result, the generator G can generate a spatially localized perturbation that can be used as adversarial patches that satisfy both visual fidelity and attacking ability. Figure 1 illustrates the overall architecture of SLP-GAN, and Algorithm 1 describes the training process of SLP-GAN framework.

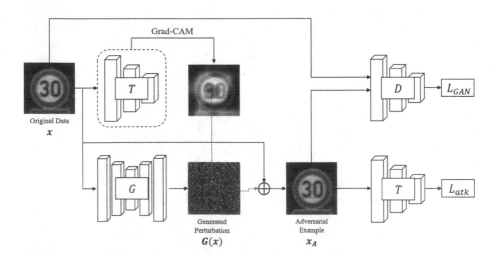

Fig. 1. The SLP-GAN framework consists of the generator G, the discriminator D, and the target model T.

Spatial Localization. As the attention method to extract a representative area of the input image, Grad-CAM can lead to good performance [16]. Grad-CAM produces "visual explanations" from image classification models. It uses the gradients of any target label flowing into the final convolutional layer to produce a localization map highlighting the important regions in the input image. To obtain a class-discriminative localization map, a gradient of the score for class y^c with respect to feature map activation A^k of the target layer.

$$\alpha_k^c = \frac{1}{Z} \sum_i \sum_j \frac{\partial y^c}{\partial A_{ij}^k} \tag{5}$$

α_k^c indicates the neuron importance weight of the feature map k for the target class c. We take a weighted sum of forward activation maps, A, with weights α_k^c, and follow it by a ReLU to obtain counterfactual explanations that have a positive influence on the class of interest.

$$L_{Grad-CAM}^c = ReLU(\sum_k \alpha_k^c A^k) \tag{6}$$

After localizing with class activation mapping (CAM), we take out the bounding boxes in the activated parts by filtering only the value, which is over 80% of the intensity of CAM. The acquired bounding boxes are the most representative area of the target model decision for the input image. In Fig. 2, we get Grad-CAM visualizations with bounding boxes for traffic signs of the VGG16 model.

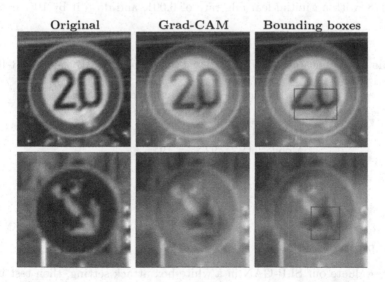

Fig. 2. Samples of Grad-CAM visualizations and bounding boxes on GTSRB datasets.

4   Experiments

4.1   Experiment Setup

Model Structure To configure our SLP-GAN framework, we utilize similar structures for the generator G and the discriminator D with image-to-image translation as in [8] and [24]. Specifically, the generator G consists of the U-Net structure, which has an encoder-decoder network. This structure has an advantage for generating high-resolution images by adding skip connections between each layer. The discriminator D uses modules in the form of convolution-BatchNorm-ReLU that increases the generation ability.

Datasets. We use two datasets, GTSRB [18] and CIFAR-10 [9], to evaluate our SLP-GAN framework. The German Traffic Sign Benchmark (GTSRB) is a large and lifelike database that contains photos of physical traffic signs with 43 classes and 50,000 images. CIFAR-10 is also a popular real-world dataset. There are 32×32 color images with ten categories, such as cats and ships.

Target Models. In our experiment, we use VGG16 [17], SqueezeNet1.1 [7], MobileNetV2 [15], ResNet34 [5], which have good performance in image classification problems, as target models. We train these target models with GTSRB and CIFAR-10 respectively. Table 1 shows the classification accuracy of target models on GTSRB and CIFAR-10.

Implementation Details. We use PyTorch for the implementation and test on an NVIDIA Titan Xp cluster. We train SLP-GAN for 250 epochs with a batch size of 128, with an initial learning rate of 0.001, and drop it by 10% every 50 epochs.

Table 1. Classification accuracy of target models on GTSRB and CIFAR-10.

Target model	Classification accuracy	
	GTSRB	CIFAR-10
ResNet34	92.1%	94.8%
MobileNetV2	92.3%	94.5%
VGG16	91.9%	92.3%
SqueezeNet1.1	90.8%	91.2%

4.2   Experiment Result

We first evaluate our SLP-GAN in a white-box attack setting, then test it in a black-box attack setting using the transferability. We also implement in a real physical environment on Korean traffic sign mockups.

White-Box Attack. In a white-box attack setting, an adversary knows about the structure and parameters of the target model to generate adversarial patches using the Grad-CAM algorithm. To evaluate the attacking ability and the visual fidelity for our SLP-GAN, we conduct a comparative experiment to AdvGAN [21], GoogleAP [1], and PS-GAN [10]. We choose these methods for comparison since AdvGAN and GoogleAP are the representative methods of the adversarial example and the adversarial patch, respectively, and PS-GAN is the most similar method to our SLP-GAN for generating adversarial patches. Firstly, we estimate the attacking performance of each target model on GTSRB and CIFAR-10. We also measure the SSIM [20] to show how our method satisfies visual fidelity. SSIM is based on the degradation of structural information, hence performs better than other simpler metrics such as the mean squared error (MSE) for the case of assessing the perceived visual quality [6].

Table 2. The comparative experiment result of classification accuracy and SSIM on GTSRB and CIFAR-10 in the white-box attack setting.

	SLP-GAN		AdvGAN		GoogleAP		PS-GAN	
	Acc	SSIM	Acc	SSIM	Acc	SSIM	Acc	SSIM
GTSRB	**16.3%**	**0.963**	14.1%	0.925	6.3%	0.824	12.5%	0.871
CIFAR-10	**9.2%**	**0.987**	6.7%	0.931	2.7%	0.839	4.9%	0.895

Table 2 shows the classification accuracy of each method for the adversarial attack about each dataset, and also SSIM between the original data x and the adversarial example x_A to represent the visual fidelity of our adversarial examples. The classification accuracy means the degree to which each target model classifies according to the true label of the adversarial example x_A. From this point of view, the lower the classification accuracy, the higher the attack success rate. We calculated the classification accuracy and SSIM as the average of each target model: VGG16, SqueezeNet1.1, MobileNetV2, and ResNet34. From the table, we can conclude that the attacking performance of our SLP-GAN is not much lower than other methods such as AdvGAN, GoogleAP, and PS-GAN. Since our method is to add small perturbation to a part of the image, it is obvious that the attack success rate is slightly lower than other methods. Note that our SLP-GAN has the highest SSIM value among methods for adversarial attacks. This indicates our method can generate adversarial patches that satisfy the visual fidelity, which means humans will have more difficulty to identify our patches in the original data. Figure 3 shows the adversarial patches generated by GoogleAP, PS-GAN, and SLP-GAN on GTSRB against VGG16 model. All of these adversarial examples are misclassified by the target model.

Black-Box Attack. In contrast to the white-box attack, an adversary doesn't know about the target model information in a black-box attack setting. We use

Fig. 3. Adversarial patches generated by GoogleAP, PS-GAN, and SLP-GAN on GTSRB.

the transferability to evaluate our SLP-GAN in a black-box attack instead of using the target model directly. Table 3 shows the classification accuracy of each target model using the transferability on GTSRB. We first generate adversarial patches for source models and then use these patches to attack all other target models. Note that adversarial examples generated to attack other source models also significantly reduces the classification accuracy of target models. It means that our SLP-GAN can encourage transferability among different target models so that it can perform quite well in a black-box attack setting.

Table 3. Classification accuracy of each target model using the transferability on GTSRB.

		Target models			
		VGG	SqueezeNet	MobileNet	ResNet
Source models	VGG	**18.7%**	27.3%	34.7%	31.2%
	SqueezeNet	21.8%	**14.9%**	26.5%	28.4%
	MobileNet	30.6%	23.8%	**17.1%**	26.2%
	ResNet	27.9%	31.1%	24.4%	**14.5%**

Physical-World Attack. We conduct a physical-world attack experiment to verify that our SLP-GAN is actually applicable. We use Korean traffic sign mockups with a size of about 15×15 cm and ten classes. We first take 100 pictures for each traffic sign mockup with varying distances and angles and then train the ResNet18 as a target model using these images. The classification accuracy of the target model on these images is 97.8% after training. We take 100 pictures randomly and generate adversarial patches for each image through SLP-GAN. After printing these patches, we attach them to the traffic sign mockups and take photos again for each mockup with the patch attached. Table 4 shows the physical-world attack result of traffic sign mockups with and without adversarial patches and the classification results. The adversarial patches generated by

SLP-GAN decrease the classification accuracy of the target model from 97.8% to 38.0% on average. Although the results show that the physical-world attack works quite well using our SLP-GAN, it can be seen that the attack performance is slightly lower compared to the white-box attack because of real-world distortion due to lighting conditions, various distances and angles.

Table 4. The physical-world attack result of traffic sign mockups with and without adversarial patches generated by SLP-GAN.

Original	Adversarial	Original	Adversarial
Roadworks	Danger	School Zone	No Jaywalking
No Jaywalking	Motorway	Bike path	Curfew

5 Conclusion

In this paper, we propose a spatially localized perturbation GAN (SLP-GAN) for generating invisible adversarial patches. We extract the target region to place an adversarial patch that can maximize the attack success rate by using the Grad-CAM algorithm. The experimental results show that SLP-GAN generates robust adversarial patches with high attack performance and a visually natural property under white-box and black-box attack settings. Validation of our model on GTSRB and CIFAR-10 datasets in the white-box attack implies that in terms of visual fidelity, SLP-GAN surpasses the performance of other patch attack methods by 13.9% and 3.8% compared to AdvGAN and GoogleAP, respectively. Additionally, our method can also perform quite well in a black-box attack and physical-world attack since it can encourage transferability and generality, as can be seen from the experimental results. In future work, we plan to complement our SLP-GAN to be robust enough to increase the physical-world attack success rate and survive real-world distortions due to various angles, distances, and lighting conditions.

References

1. Brown, T.B., Mané, D., Roy, A., Abadi, M., Gilmer, J.: Adversarial patch. CoRR abs/1712.09665 (2017). http://arxiv.org/abs/1712.09665
2. Carlini, N., Wagner, D.: Towards evaluating the robustness of neural networks (2016)
3. Goodfellow, I., Shlens, J., Szegedy, C.: Explaining and harnessing adversarial examples. In: International Conference on Learning Representations (2015). http://arxiv.org/abs/1412.6572
4. Goodfellow, I.J., et al.: Generative adversarial nets. In: Proceedings of the 27th International Conference on Neural Information Processing Systems, NIPS 2014, Cambridge, MA, USA, vol. 2, pp. 2672–2680. MIT Press (2014)
5. He, K., Zhang, X., Ren, S., Sun, J.: Deep residual learning for image recognition (2015)
6. Hore, A., Ziou, D.: Image quality metrics: PSNR vs. SSIM. In: 2010 20th International Conference on Pattern Recognition, pp. 2366–2369. IEEE (2010)
7. Iandola, F.N., Han, S., Moskewicz, M.W., Ashraf, K., Dally, W.J., Keutzer, K.: Squeezenet: Alexnet-level accuracy with 50x fewer parameters and ¡0.5mb model size (2016)
8. Isola, P., Zhu, J., Zhou, T., Efros, A.A.: Image-to-image translation with conditional adversarial networks. CoRR abs/1611.07004 (2016). http://arxiv.org/abs/1611.07004
9. Krizhevsky, A., Nair, V., Hinton, G.: Cifar-10 (canadian institute for advanced research). http://www.cs.toronto.edu/~kriz/cifar.html
10. Liu, A., et al.: Perceptual-sensitive GAN for generating adversarial patches. In: Proceedings of the AAAI Conference on Artificial Intelligence, vol. 33, pp. 1028–1035, July 2019. https://doi.org/10.1609/aaai.v33i01.33011028
11. Liu, X., Yang, H., Song, L., Li, H., Chen, Y.: Dpatch: attacking object detectors with adversarial patches. CoRR abs/1806.02299 (2018). http://arxiv.org/abs/1806.02299
12. Madry, A., Makelov, A., Schmidt, L., Tsipras, D., Vladu, A.: Towards deep learning models resistant to adversarial attacks. arXiv preprint arXiv:1706.06083 (2017)
13. Moosavi-Dezfooli, S., Fawzi, A., Frossard, P.: Deepfool: a simple and accurate method to fool deep neural networks. CoRR abs/1511.04599 (2015). http://arxiv.org/abs/1511.04599
14. Qiu, S., Liu, Q., Zhou, S., Wu, C.: Review of artificial intelligence adversarial attack and defense technologies. Appl. Sci. 9(5) (2019). https://doi.org/10.3390/app9050909, https://www.mdpi.com/2076-3417/9/5/909
15. Sandler, M., Howard, A., Zhu, M., Zhmoginov, A., Chen, L.C.: Mobilenetv 2: Inverted residuals and linear bottlenecks (2018)
16. Selvaraju, R.R., Das, A., Vedantam, R., Cogswell, M., Parikh, D., Batra, D.: Gradcam: why did you say that? visual explanations from deep networks via gradient-based localization. CoRR abs/1610.02391 (2016). http://arxiv.org/abs/1610.02391
17. Simonyan, K., Zisserman, A.: Very deep convolutional networks for large-scale image recognition (2014)
18. Stallkamp, J., Schlipsing, M., Salmen, J., Igel, C.: Man vs. computer: benchmarking machine learning algorithms for traffic sign recognition. Neural Networks: Official J. Int. Neural Network Soc. 32, 323–32 (2012). https://doi.org/10.1016/j.neunet.2012.02.016

19. Szegedy, C., et al.: Intriguing properties of neural networks. In: International Conference on Learning Representations (2014). http://arxiv.org/abs/1312.6199
20. Wang, Z., Bovik, A.C., Sheikh, H.R., Simoncelli, E.P.: Image quality assessment: from error visibility to structural similarity. IEEE Trans. Image Process. **13**(4), 600–612 (2004)
21. Xiao, C., Li, B., Zhu, J., He, W., Liu, M., Song, D.: Generating adversarial examples with adversarial networks. CoRR abs/1801.02610 (2018). http://arxiv.org/abs/1801.02610
22. Yuan, X., He, P., Zhu, Q., Li, X.: Adversarial examples: Attacks and defenses for deep learning. IEEE Trans. Neural Networks Learn. Syst. **30**(9), 2805–2824 (2019). https://doi.org/10.1109/TNNLS.2018.2886017
23. Zhang, J., Jiang, X.: Adversarial examples: opportunities and challenges. CoRR abs/1809.04790 (2018). http://arxiv.org/abs/1809.04790
24. Zhu, J.Y., Park, T., Isola, P., Efros, A.: Unpaired image-to-image translation using cycle-consistent adversarial networks, pp. 2242–2251 (2017). https://doi.org/10.1109/ICCV.2017.244

Detecting Block Cipher Encryption for Defense Against Crypto Ransomware on Low-End Internet of Things

Hyunji Kim, Jaehoon Park, Hyeokdong Kwon, Kyoungbae Jang,
Seung Ju Choi, and Hwajeong Seo[✉]

IT Department, Hansung University, Seoul, South Korea
khj930704@gmail.com, p9595jh@gmail.com, korlethean@gmail.com,
starj1023@gmail.com, bookingstore3@gmail.com, hwajeong84@gmail.com

Abstract. A crypto ransomware usually encrypts files of victims using block cipher encryption. Afterward, the ransomware requests a ransom for encrypted files to victims. In this paper, we present a novel defense against crypto ransomware by detecting block cipher encryption for low-end Internet of Things (IoT) environment. The proposed method analyzes the binary code of low-end microcontrollers in the base-station (i.e. server) and it is classified in either ransomware virus or benign software. Block cipher implementations from Lightweight block cipher library (i.e. FELICS) and general software from AVR packages were trained and evaluated through the deep learning network. The proposed method successful classifies the general software and potential ransomware virus by identifying the cryptography function call, which is evaluated in terms of recall rate, precision rate and F-measure.

Keywords: Ransomware virus · Deep learning network · Block cipher encryption · Static analysis

1 Introduction

In 2017, WannaCry ransomware virus spread to Microsoft Windows users through the vulnerability of file sharing protocol [1]. The Wannacry ransomware attack was one of the largest attack, which was estimated to have affected more than 200,000 computers across 150 countries.

The ransomware is largely classified into two sets, including locker ransomware and crypto ransomware. The locker ransomware locks the victim's device, which is unable to use the device anymore [2]. However, the data is not modified. For this reason, the data can be recoverable by copying the data to other devices.

The crypto ransomware encrypts files of victim's devices. Since the cryptography algorithm is designed to be secure theoretically, there is no way to recover the file without valid secret key. In order to receive the secret key, the victim need to pay the ransom to the hacker. With this secret key, the victim retrieve

I. You (Ed.): WISA 2020, LNCS 12583, pp. 16–30, 2020.
https://doi.org/10.1007/978-3-030-65299-9_2

original files. The ransomware virus has became a massive threat of people with digital devices, as every user is moving towards digitization. To prevent from these cyber threats, many researchers have published the ransomware recovery and detection methods.

In [3], four most common crypto ransomwares were analyzed. They identified all ransomware viruses relied on system tools available on the target system. By generating shadow copies during execution of tools, the file recovery process is available.

The ransomware detection is simply classified in network traffic analysis and function call analysis. For the accurate detection, the machine learning method is actively studied for the ransomware detection. In [4], they analyzed the ransomware network behavior and packet selection to identify the ransomware virus. In [5], they evaluated shallow and deep networks for the detection and classification of ransomware. To characterize and distinguish ransomware over benign software and ransomware virus, they analyzed the dominance of Application Programming Interface (API). In [6], they presented a multi-level big data mining framework combining reverse engineering, natural language processing and machine learning approaches. The framework analyzed the ransomware at different levels (i.e., Dynamic link library, function call and assembly instruction level) through different supervised ML algorithms.

Due to the nature of crypto ransomware, many works focused on the cryptography function. In [7], they performed fine-grained dynamic binary analysis and used the collected information as input for several heuristics that characterize specific, unique aspects of cryptographic code. In [8], they presented a novel approach to automatically identify symmetric cryptographic algorithms and their parameters inside binary code. Their approach is static and based on Data Flow Graph (DFG) isomorphism. In [9], they targeted public key cryptographic algorithms performed by ransomware. By monitoring integer multiplication instructions of target system, the public key encryption by ransomware was detected.

However, previous works paid little attention on the architecture of block cipher and there are not many works on the defense against ransomware on low-end Internet of Things (IoT) environment. In this paper, we present a novel defense against crypto ransomware by detecting block cipher encryption on low-end IoT environment. The proposed method analyzes the binary code of low-end microcontrollers and the binary code is classified in either potential ransomware virus or benign software. Block ciphers from Lightweight block cipher library (i.e. FELICS) and general software from AVR packages for low-end microcontrollers were trained and evaluated through the deep learning network. The proposed method successful classifies the benign software and potential ransomware virus, which is evaluated in terms of recall rate, precision rate and F-measure. Detailed contributions are as follows:

1.1   Contribution

Deep Learning Based Crypto Ransomware Detection for Low-End Microcontrollers. By classifying the cryptographic function code and general code, the potential ransomware virus is efficiently detected. In order to apply the deep learning network, the binary file is transformed to the image file, where the deep learning network has a strength in image classification.

Experiments with Several Options for High Accuracy. In order to achieve the high accuracy for the classification, several options are evaluated. Instruction and opcode based binary extraction are compared to show the performance. Afterward, each GCC optimization option is evaluated to find the proper option.

In-Depth Analysis of Instruction Sets for Block Cipher Implementation on Microcontrollers. There are a number of block ciphers. We classify block cipher algorithms into two sets, including SPN structure and ARX structure, by observing distinguished features between them. This classification rule improved the performance, significantly.

The remainder of this paper is organized as follows. In Sect. 2, the background of crypto ransomware detection techniques for low-end microcontrollers is covered. In Sect. 3, we present a novel approach to defense against crypto ransomware by detecting block cipher encryption. In Sect. 4, the performance of proposed methods in terms of detection accuracy is evaluated. Finally, Sect. 5 concludes the paper.

2   Related Works

2.1   Ransomware on IoT World

With the rapid development of Internet of Things (IoT), strengthening the security and preventing ransomware virus have become a fundamental building block for success of services [10]. There are many works to be secure the IoT environment. In [11], they presented a machine learning based approach to detect ransomware attacks by monitoring power consumption of Android devices. The method monitors the energy consumption patterns of different processes to classify ransomware from benign applications. In [12], they presented a deep learning based method to detect Internet Of Battlefield Things (IoBT) malware through the device's opcode sequence. They converted opcodes into a vector space and apply a deep Eigenspace learning approach to classify ransomware and benign application. In [13], they presented a Cryptowall ransomware attack detection model based on the communication and behavioral of Cryptowall for IoT environment. The model observes incoming TCP/IP traffic through web proxy server then extracts TCP/IP header and uses command and control (C&C) server black listing to detect ransomware attacks. In [14], they presented the method to transform the sequence of executable instructions into a grayscale image. Afterward,

Table 1. Comparison of ransomware detection techniques based on cryptographic function call.

Features	Gröbert et al. [7]	Lestringant et al. [8]	Kiraz et al. [9]	This Work
Target	Block & PKC	Block Cipher	PKC	Block Cipher
Analysis	Dynamic	Static	Dynamic	Static
Method	Heuristics	Data graph flow	System monitor	Deep learning
Machine	Desktop	Desktop	Desktop	Microcontroller

the statistical method is used for separating two or more classes along with dimension reduction.

However, previous ransomware detection focused on high-end IoT devices. A number of IoT devices are equipped with low-end microcontrollers, which collect the data in distance. This is one of the most important role of IoT applications. For this reason, the ransomware detection mechanism for low-end IoT devices should be considered. In this paper, we present the novel ransomware detection mechanism for low-end microcontrollers. In order to classify the ransomware, we transform the binary code into image file. Afterward, the image is classified through deep learning network.

2.2 Previous Ransomware Detection Techniques Based on Cryptographic Function Call

Ransomware encrypts victim's files with cryptographic function. For this reason, classifying the cryptographic function is important for ransomware detection.

In Table 1, the comparison of ransomware detection techniques based on cryptographic function call is given. In [7], block cipher and public key cryptography are detected by analyzing features of cryptographic functions. The method is heuristics depending on the implementation. In [8], the data graph flow is extracted from binary code. Sub-graph isomorphism is utilized to identity the cryptographic function call. In [9], public key cryptography, such as RSA, is detected by monitoring the multiplication instruction, which is heavily called in RSA algorithm. However, previous works do not explore the deep learning based ransomware detection. Recently, the work by [15] shows that deep-learning algorithm can improve the malware detection. However, the method is not targeting for ransomware and target platform is desktop. In this work, we firstly present the crypto ransomware detection for microcontrollers.

2.3 Block Cipher Implementation on Microcontrollers

A benchmarking framework of software based block cipher implementations named Fair Evaluation of Lightweight Cryptographic Systems (FELICS) was introduced by Luxembourg University in 2015 [16]. More than one hundred block cipher implementations on low-end IoT devices were submitted to FELICS by world-wide cryptographic engineers. In this paper, we utilized block cipher implementations of FELICS. The target low-end microcontroller is 8-bit AVR ATmega128, which is the most low-end IoT platform. The microcontroller is an 8-bit single chip based on the modified Harvard architecture developed by Atmel. The unit size of its registers and instructions is 8-bit wise. The block cipher can be largely categorized in Substitution-Permutation-Network (SPN) and Addition, Rotation, and bit-wise eXclusive-or (ARX). International block cipher standard, namely AES, is based on SPN architecture, while lightweight block ciphers, such as LEA, HIGHT, SIMON, and SPECK, follow ARX architecture due to high performance and simple design [17–20]. In this paper, we utilized distinguished features of both architectures to classify the binary code.

3   Proposed Method

This paper describes a method for detecting ransomware through binary files for low-end IoT-based embedded systems. Generally, the structure of sensor network is based on tree-structure [21]. The powerful root-node (i.e. base station) manages the structure and the leaf node (low-end IoT) collects the sensor data. The base station regularly updates the firmware of leaf nodes. When the hacker intercepts the packet between base station and firmware server and installs crypto ransomware to the firmware, the base station should detect the ransomware before deployment. In this scenario, the proposed method detects ransomware by classifying the binary file of the supplied firmware through a convolutional neural network. This approach distinguishes crypto ransomware from benign firmware depending on the existence of an encryption process. We can extend this approach to self-defense on the middle-end IoT, such as raspberry pi. The device can perform CNN on its machine through tensorflow[1].

The proposed system configuration for ransomware detection is shown in Fig. 1. Assembly instructions and the opcodes are extracted from the binary file and converted into image for deep learning training. In the test phase, if the encryption process is detected, it is classified as crypto ransomware. Overall, the proposed method consists of creating an image from binary code and two phases of deep learning.

3.1   Binary Code Based Image Generation

Instructions for images to be used for training are obtained by analyzing the binary files. Assembly instructions are a combination of opcode and operand, and operand area may specify different registers each time even though the same source code is compiled. In Fig. 2, the opcode is extracted from the instruction. Afterward, the extracted opcode is converted into an image file to generate data for training.

Since the binary code varies depending on the optimization option, data sets are created by compiling for each option. If the pattern of the opcode are similar, similar characteristics will be created. These features are trained in the deep learning phase.

---

[1] https://www.tensorflow.org/install/source_rpi?hl=ko.

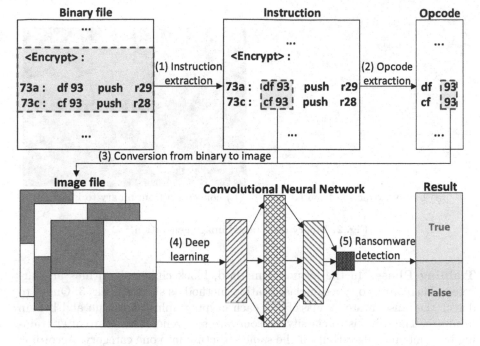

Fig. 1. System configuration for proposed method.

Table 2. Deep learning training hyperparameters.

Hyperparameters	Descriptions	Hyperparameters	Descriptions
pretrained model	Inception-v3	epochs	20
loss function	Categorical crossentropy	steps per epoch	10
optimizer	RMSprop(lr = 0.001)	batch size	5
active function	ReLu, Softmax	train, validation and test ratio	0.7, 0.2, 0.1

3.2 Deep Learning

The deep learning phase is divided into training phase and detection phase. A convolutional neural network known for its excellent image classification performance is used as a deep learning model. Inception-v3 is used as a pre-trained model, and this model performs well even on small data sets. Three fully connected layers are added to pre-trained weights to adjust the classification problem. In addition, a suitable model that is not over-fitting to a specific data set is selected through 10-fold cross validation. Grid search is performed on the selected model to tune to the optimal hyperparameter for the model and dataset. The detailed values are given in Table 2. Since it is a multi-class classification, the Softmax activation function is used in the output layer. ReLU is used, which is mainly used in hidden layers and is faster than other activation functions.

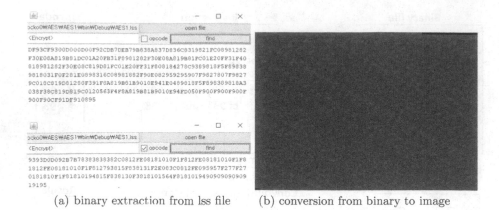

(a) binary extraction from lss file   (b) conversion from binary to image

Fig. 2. Binary code based image generation.

Training Phase. In the proposed method, block cipher algorithms are targeted. There are two types of classification method as shown in Fig. 3. One is to detect the ransomware by classifying each cryptographic algorithm and benign firmware. The other is to classify ransomware and general firmware after training by combining algorithms of the same structure into one category. According to previous methods, a data directory is configured, and the data is reshape to 150×150 pixels through pre-processing before being used as input data to the convolutional neural network.

The input layer and the hidden layer have a structure in which the convolution layer and the pooling layer are repeated. In the two dimensional convolution layer, the filter and the input image perform a convolution operation to extract features for the input image. In the max pooling layer, the output of the previous layer is divided into a window size, and the maximum value for each area is selected. By repeating the feature extraction process, the feature of the cryptographic algorithm included in each image is learned. Then, it is transferred to a fully-connected layer. Afterward, it is transformed into a one-dimensional array. Finally it enters into a classification phase for detection.

Ransomware Detection Phase. It is a phase to classify into labels for each input image by the Softmax activation function. The result of the classification is the probability value for each class. The input image is finally classified as the top-1 class with the highest probability.

Before checking the classification results of untrained test data, the performance of the validation data should be measured. If it is verified that it is an appropriate model, test data set not used for training is inputted to a trained CNN model. Test images are generated from a binary file of a block cipher or general program.

For the block cipher program, the test data has characteristics similar to the training data by the pattern of the instruction used and the repetition of rounds.

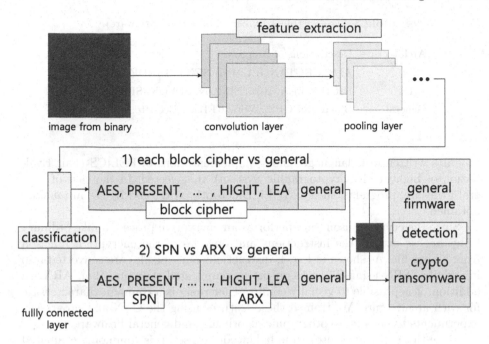

Fig. 3. Detailed deep learning phase for proposed method

As mentioned earlier, such characteristics can be classified by cryptographic structure (SPN and ARX) or each cryptographic algorithm. If it is classified as a cryptographic algorithm, it is judged as ransomware. It can block the installation to IoT devices. In other words, block ciphers and general programs are classified by weight values trained by image-based deep learning. Through the proposed framework, we can detect the potential ransomware virus for low-end IoT devices.

4 Evaluation

For the experiment, Google Colaboratory, a cloud-based service, was utilized. It runs on Ubuntu 18.04.3 LTS and consists of an Intel Xeon CPU with 13 GB RAM and an Nvidia GPU (Tesla T4, Tesla P100, or Tesla K80) with 12 GB RAM. In terms of programming environment, Python 3.6.9, tensorflow 2.2.0-rc and Keras 2.3.1 version are used. In order to create the dataset required for the experiment, we created a program that extracts instructions and opcodes of specific functions from the lss file. And instruction and opcode were converted to BMP image files using open source on github[2].

In Table 3, the experiment targets binary files of general firmware and block ciphers (e.g., SPN and ARX) in low-end embedded environment. Cryptographic

---

[2] https://github.com/Hamz-a/txt2bmp.

Table 3. Dataset (block ciphers and general firmware).

Architecture	Descriptions of programs
SPN	AES, RECTANGLE, PRESENT, PRIDE, PRINCE
ARX	HIGHT, LEA, RC5, SIMON, SPECK, SPARX
General	Bluetooth, GPS, WiFi, RFID, XBee, etc.

modules written in C language among implementations of FELICS (Fair Evaluation of Lightweight Cryptographic System) are selected. In the case of general firmware, programs, such as WiFi, Bluetooth, xBee, and RFID, are mainly obtained.

Since the crypto ransomware performs an encryption process unlike ordinary firmware, we extract the instructions and opcodes of the encryption function from binary file. As shown in Fig. 4, instructions and opcodes are converted into image files. SPN using S-box has a more complicated structure than ARX. In addition, it is possible to visually confirm that there is a common characteristic for each architecture. We trained these features using the CNN and progressed experiments to classify cryptographic algorithms and general firmware.

Since this experiment uses an unbalanced data set, it is commonly evaluated through the F-measure, which is a harmonic mean of precision and recall rather than accuracy. There are micro averaged and macro averaged in the F-measure. The micro averaged method considers the number of data belonging to each class. The macro averaged method considers all classes with the same weight. Therefore, results of macro method are a slightly lower measurement in the case of an unbalanced dataset.

4.1 Instruction-Based vs Opcode-Based

Since our proposed system classifies each cryptographic module according to the instruction (e.g. pattern of operation type and number of times) performed by encryption, the method of extracting the encryption part from the binary file is largely based on instruction and opcode. In the case of instruction-based, the opcode and operand are extracted together. In order to compare the performance, only opcode part, which is the actual operation, is extracted.

As shown in Fig. 5, training loss and validation loss decreases smoothly without significant difference. The training data has not been over-fitted. In the case of opcode based, the overall loss value was calculated less than instruction based approach.

After verifying the model with the data used in the training, the test data, which was not used in the training through the model is predicted. In Table 4, detailed results are given. By classifying with the test set, the instruction-based performance was slightly better. However, in the case of opcode-based, the standard deviation is 0.12, which has more stable performance. It indicates that the

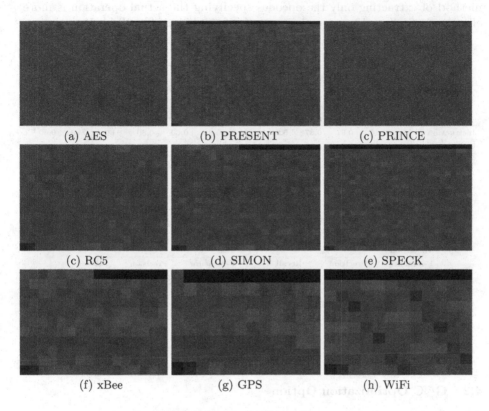

(a) AES   (b) PRESENT   (c) PRINCE

(c) RC5   (d) SIMON   (e) SPECK

(f) xBee   (g) GPS   (h) WiFi

Fig. 4. Images of binary files.

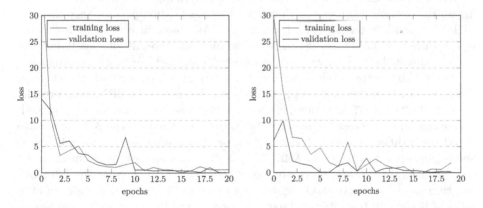

Fig. 5. Training and validation loss depending on instruction and opcode; left: instruction, right: opcode.

method of extracting only the opcodes specifying the actual operation is more effective in finding the instruction pattern of the binary file (Table 5).

Table 4. Validation and test on instruction and opcode.

Target	Validation						Test					
	F-measure		Precision		Recall		F-measure		Precision		Recall	
	micro	macro	micro	macro	micro	macro	micro	macro	micro	macro	micro	macro
Instruction	0.91	0.84	0.91	0.87	0.91	0.95	0.80	0.60	0.80	0.60	0.80	0.60
Opcode	0.96	0.93	0.96	0.92	0.96	0.94	0.77	0.58	0.77	0.59	0.77	0.60

Table 5. Validation and test on GCC optimization options.

Op.	Validation						Test					
	F-measure		Precision		Recall		F-measure		Precision		Recall	
	micro	macro	micro	macro	micro	macro	micro	macro	micro	macro	micro	macro
O0	0.96	0.93	0.96	0.92	0.96	0.94	0.77	0.58	0.77	0.59	0.77	0.60
O1	0.90	0.81	0.90	0.80	0.90	0.85	0.85	0.79	0.85	0.82	0.85	0.81
O2	0.92	0.89	0.92	0.90	0.92	0.9	0.81	0.67	0.81	0.69	0.81	0.68

4.2 GCC Optimization Option

After compiling with optimization option for each encryption algorithm, an opcode-based classification experiment was performed. For the experiment, the GNU AVR-GCC compiler and O0, O1 and O2 options were used.

Binary files used in the experiment were not changed significantly depending on the optimization option. However, the classification performance changed slightly depending on the optimization level. As shown in Fig. 6, the loss value was reduced without over-fitting as a whole. As a result of classifying the untrained test data, the optimization option O1 showed the best performance.

Table 6 shows the result of sorting the command used for each structure in the order in which they are used frequently. In the case of the SPN structure, the pattern of LD-XOR-ST is common in the part where S-box operation is performed, and operations to access the memory frequently occurred. In the ARX structure based on addition, rotation and exclusive-or operation, the ratio of arithmetic and logical operations, such as ADD, XOR, SUB were frequently performed. In the case of general firmware, there are many instructions to activate the interrupt function and to access the I/O register, not found in the encryption code, and the ratio of branch statements was largest among them. When applying the higher optimization option, it seems that the instruction pattern, count, and order that are effective for classifying each algorithm through the CNN model have changed slightly, affecting classification performance.

Cryptography algorithms of the same structure share similar instruction patterns. Since block cipher algorithms repeat rounds, certain patterns are repeated. Therefore, the BMP image generated based on the opcode also has a pattern. For this reason, cryptographic algorithm is successfully classified through the proposed approach.

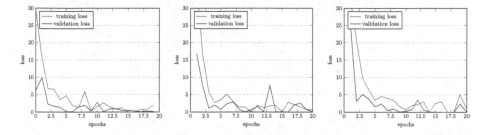

Fig. 6. Training and validation loss depending on optimization option; left: 00, middle: 01, right: 02.

Table 6. Frequently used instructions for each architecture.

Architecture	Ordered by frequency in program							
	1	2	3	4	5	6	7	8
SPN	LD	ST	MOV	XOR	ADD	SUB	AND	SWAP
ARX	LD	ADD	XOR	MOV	ST	SUB	ROR	RJMP
General	LD	RJMP	BNE	CP	OUT	NOP	MOV	SEI

4.3 Block Cipher Vs General

In this experiment, block cipher algorithms are divided in two design groups (i.e. SPN and ARX) to classify ransomware or general firmware.

In Table 7, F-measure for each option is given. The CNN model is properly fitted at high speed. The loss value decreases. When the epoch exceeds 10, the loss value converges to almost 0.00 (See Fig. 7).

The previous experiment does not properly classify, because the instructions used in cryptographic algorithms of the same architecture have similar patterns. By dividing the block cipher into two structures (i.e. SPN and ARX), the proposed method achieved better performance than classifying each block cipher module. Among the test data, the recognition of cryptographic algorithm as general firmware occurred once in the case of optimization options 00 and 02, respectively. The recognition of general firmware as cryptographic algorithm occurred once in 00. It accurately predicted test data in optimization option 01. The ransomware can be detected with a high overall probability for all optimization options.

Table 7. Validation and test depending on architectures (SPN, ARX, or general).

Op.	Validation						Test					
	F-measure		Precision		Recall		F-measure		Precision		Recall	
	micro	macro	micro	macro	micro	macro	micro	macro	micro	macro	micro	macro
00	0.99	0.99	0.99	0.99	0.99	0.99	0.94	0.91	0.94	0.91	0.94	0.95
01	1.00	1.00	1.00	1.00	1.00	1.00	1.00	1.00	1.00	1.00	1.00	1.00
02	1.00	1.00	1.00	1.00	1.00	1.00	0.98	0.99	0.98	0.99	0.98	0.99

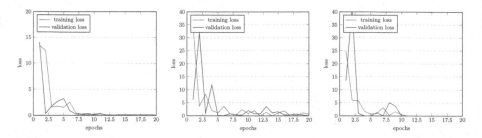

Fig. 7. Training and validation loss depending on classification rule and (i.e. SPN, ARX, and general program) optimization option; left: 00, middle: 01, right: 02.

5 Conclusion

In this paper, we presented a novel approach to detect ransomware virus through classification of block cipher module for low-end microcontrollers. The binary code is converted to image file and deep learning network is applied. By observing the specific features of SPN and ARX architectures, block cipher classification is divided into two categories. This approach significantly improved the accuracy.

Acknowledgement. This work was partly supported as part of Military Crypto Research Center (UD170109ED) funded by Defense Acquisition Program Administration(DAPA) and Agency for Defense Development(ADD) and this work was partly supported by Institute for Information & communications Technology Promotion (IITP) grant funded by the Korea government (MSIT) (No. 2018-0-00264, Research on Blockchain Security Technology for IoT Services) and this work was partly supported by the National Research Foundation of Korea (NRF) grant funded by the Korea government(MSIT) (No. NRF-2020R1F1A1048478).

References

1. Mohurle, S., Patil, M.: A brief study of Wannacry threat: Ransomware attack 2017. Int. J. Adv. Res. Comput. Sci. **8**(5) (2017)
2. Kharaz, A., Arshad, S., Mulliner, C., Robertson, W., Kirda, E.: UNVEIL: a large-scale, automated approach to detecting ransomware. In: 25th USENIX Security Symposium (USENIX Security 16), pp. 757–772 (2016)

3. Weckstén, M., Frick, J., Sjöström, A., Järpe, E.: A novel method for recovery from Crypto Ransomware infections. In: 2016 2nd IEEE International Conference on Computer and Communications (ICCC), pp. 1354–1358. IEEE (2016)
4. Tseng, A., Chen, Y., Kao, Y., Lin, T.: Deep learning for ransomware detection. IEICE Tech. Rep. **116**(282), 87–92 (2016)
5. Vinayakumar, R., Soman, Velan, K.S., Ganorkar, S.: Evaluating shallow and deep networks for ransomware detection and classification. In: 2017 International Conference on Advances in Computing, Communications and Informatics (ICACCI), pp. 259–265. IEEE (2017)
6. Poudyal, S., Dasgupta, D., Akhtar, Z., Gupta, K.: A multi-level ransomware detection framework using natural language processing and machine learning. In: 14th International Conference on Malicious and Unwanted Software" MALCON (2019)
7. Gröbert, F., Willems, C., Holz, T.: Automated identification of cryptographic primitives in binary programs. In: Sommer, R., Balzarotti, D., Maier, G. (eds.) RAID 2011. LNCS, vol. 6961, pp. 41–60. Springer, Heidelberg (2011). https://doi.org/10.1007/978-3-642-23644-0_3
8. Lestringant, P., Guihéry, F., Fouque, P.-A.: Automated identification of cryptographic primitives in binary code with data flow graph isomorphism. In: Proceedings of the 10th ACM Symposium on Information, Computer and Communications Security, pp. 203–214 (2015)
9. Kiraz, M.S., Genç, Z.A., Öztürk, E.: Detecting large integer arithmetic for defense against crypto ransomware. Technical report (2017)
10. Yaqoob, I., et al.: The rise of ransomware and emerging security challenges in the Internet of Things. Comput. Networks **129**, 444–458 (2017)
11. Azmoodeh, A., Dehghantanha, A., Conti, M., Choo, K.-K.R.: Detecting crypto-ransomware in IoT networks based on energy consumption footprint. J. Ambient Intell. Humaniz. Comput. **9**(4), 1141–1152 (2018)
12. Azmoodeh, A., Dehghantanha, A., Choo, K.-K.R.: Robust malware detection for internet of (battlefield) things devices using deep eigenspace learning. IEEE Trans. Sustain. Comput. **4**(1), 88–95 (2018)
13. Zahra, A., Shah, M.A.: IoT based ransomware growth rate evaluation and detection using command and control blacklisting. In: 2017 23rd International Conference on Automation and Computing (ICAC), pp. 1–6. IEEE (2017)
14. Karimi, A., Moattar, M.H.: Android ransomware detection using reduced opcode sequence and image similarity. In: 2017 7th International Conference on Computer and Knowledge Engineering (ICCKE), pp. 229–234. IEEE (2017)
15. Kumar, R., Xiaosong, Z., Khan, R.U., Ahad, I., Kumar, J.: Malicious code detection based on image processing using deep learning. In: Proceedings of the 2018 International Conference on Computing and Artificial Intelligence, pp. 81–85 (2018)
16. Dinu, D., Biryukov, A., Großschädl, J., Khovratovich, D., Le Corre, Y., Perrin, L.: FELICS-fair evaluation of lightweight cryptographic systems. In: NIST Workshop on Lightweight Cryptography, vol. 128 (2015)
17. Daemen, J., Rijmen, V.: AES proposal: Rijndael (1999)
18. Hong, D., Lee, J.-K., Kim, D.-C., Kwon, D., Ryu, K.H., Lee, D.-G.: LEA: a 128-bit block cipher for fast encryption on common processors. In: Kim, Y., Lee, H., Perrig, A. (eds.) WISA 2013. LNCS, vol. 8267, pp. 3–27. Springer, Cham (2014). https://doi.org/10.1007/978-3-319-05149-9_1
19. Hong, D., et al.: HIGHT: a new block cipher suitable for low-resource device. In: Goubin, L., Matsui, M. (eds.) CHES 2006. LNCS, vol. 4249, pp. 46–59. Springer, Heidelberg (2006). https://doi.org/10.1007/11894063_4

20. Beaulieu, R., Shors, D., Smith, J., Treatman-Clark, S., Weeks, B., Wingers, L.: SIMON and SPECK: Block ciphers for the internet of things. IACR Cryptology ePrint Archive **2015**, 585 (2015)
21. Williams, J.L., Fisher, J.W., Willsky, A.S.: Approximate dynamic programming for communication-constrained sensor network management. IEEE Trans. Signal Process. **55**(8), 4300–4311 (2007)

CAPTCHAs Are Still in Danger: An Efficient Scheme to Bypass Adversarial CAPTCHAs

Dongbin Na, Namgyu Park, Sangwoo Ji, and Jong Kim[✉]

Pohang University of Science and Technology, Pohang, South Korea
{dongbinna,namgyu.park,sangwooji,jkim}@postech.ac.kr

Abstract. Completely Automated Public Turing test to tell Computers and Humans Apart (CAPTCHA) is a challenge that is used to distinguish between humans and robots. However, attackers bypass the CAPTCHA schemes using deep learning (DL) based solvers. To defeat the attackers, CAPTCHA defense methods utilizing adversarial examples that are known for fooling deep learning models have been proposed.

In this paper, we propose an efficient CAPTCHA solver that periodically retrain the solver model when its accuracy drops. The proposed method uses incremental learning that requires a small amount of data while achieving high accuracy. We demonstrate that the proposed solver bypasses the existing defense methods based on a text-based CAPTCHA scheme and an image-based CAPTCHA scheme.

Keywords: CAPTCHAs · Adversarial examples · Adversarial training · Incremental learning · ML security

1 Introduction

Completely Automated Public Turing test to tell Computers and Humans Apart (CAPTCHA) systems produce challenges that are easy to solve for humans but difficult for robots. The most common and widely used CAPTCHA schemes are text-based and image-based CAPTCHAs, and these schemes are widely used in popular websites.

Text-based CAPTCHAs have been the most commonly used before the era of deep learning. The major websites have adopted these text-based schemes to filter out spam robots. However, a number of recent studies demonstrated that deep learning (DL) based solvers can easily bypass text-based CAPTCHA schemes [2,20,21]. Despite the text-based CAPTCHA schemes are vulnerable to DL-based solvers, many major websites are still using their own text-based CAPTCHA schemes. Meanwhile, image-based CAPTCHA schemes such as Google's reCAPTCHA v2 also have adopted by major websites. Recent studies showed DL-based object detection techniques can bypass the reCAPTCHA v2 [8,17]. Those DL-based automated solvers can solve

© Springer Nature Switzerland AG 2020
I. You (Ed.): WISA 2020, LNCS 12583, pp. 31–44, 2020.
https://doi.org/10.1007/978-3-030-65299-9_3

CAPTCHA problems with higher efficiency than human labor solver services on both text-based and image-based CAPTCHA schemes [8].

To defend against the DL-based solvers, defense studies have focused on the ways to improve security while maintaining the usability of existing CAPTCHA schemes. The *DeepCAPTCHA* algorithm utilizes the IAN generation method for misleading DL-based solvers [12]. The IAN generation method is fast enough to be used in a real-time CAPTCHA generation system and sufficient to disrupt attackers who are based on pre-trained DL models. The *Adversarial CAPTCHAs* framework proposed also the ways to insert more powerful adversarial examples into CAPTCHA schemes [16]. These defense methods dynamically change the distribution of the CAPTCHA images using adversarial examples to defeat attackers using pre-trained models.

In this paper, we propose an efficient and robust DL-based solver using the incremental learning process. The proposed method retrains a DL model when a significant accuracy drop is observed. The significant accuracy drop implies that the distribution of CAPTCHA images is changed. We use the incremental learning process to retrain the solver to preserve accuracy on both of the original distribution and the changed distribution. The incremental learning process requires a small amount of additional data which is only 2% of the number of the original training dataset.

We evaluate the proposed method with accuracy on two datasets: original CAPTCHAs and adversarial CAPTCHAs. For text-based CAPTCHAs, the proposed method demonstrates 86.49% accuracy for the original dataset and 70.14% accuracy for the adversarial dataset. For image-based CAPTCHAs, the proposed method demonstrates 87.37% accuracy for the original dataset and 78.19% accuracy for the adversarial dataset. Compared with two previous works, the proposed method shows higher accuracy on the original dataset than the preprocessing method [12] and higher accuracy on the adversarial dataset than the adversarial training method [16]. Moreover, the proposed method requires about 5.5 times smaller training time overhead compared with the adversarial training [16].

Our paper achieves the following contributions:

- We propose an efficient CAPTCHA solver using the incremental learning process. To the best of our knowledge, we are the first to demonstrate incremental learning for the DL-based solvers against adversarial CAPTCHAs.
- We conduct extensive experiments on a well-known CAPTCHA library and image recognition tasks equipped with the existing solver defense methods.

2 Background

2.1 CAPTCHA Schemes

There exist various CAPTCHA schemes such as text-based, image-based, audio-based, and game-based CAPTCHAs. Among them, we focus on the most commonly used text-based and image-based CAPTCHAs (see Fig. 1) [17,18,21].

Text-based CAPTCHA   Image-based CAPTCHA

Fig. 1. Examples of CAPTCHA schemes.

Text-Based CAPTCHA. A text-based CAPTCHA is the first introduced scheme to block automated robots. It presents an image including several characters, then users have to type the characters correctly to prove that they are not robots. However, text-based schemes are vulnerable to DL-based attacks, even to widespread optical character recognition (OCR) tools. To make this scheme robust, many defense methods such as character overlapping, hollow the line, and character rotation have been proposed [3]. Attackers have developed DL-based solvers to break through these defenses. A simple convolution neural network (CNN) can defeat fixed-size text-based CAPTCHA, and the long short-term memory (LSTM) network can also be used for bypassing variable-sized text-based CAPTCHA [14,22].

Image-Based CAPTCHA. An image-based CAPTCHA is motivated by the vulnerability of text-based CAPTCHA schemes. This scheme requires users to select one or more images with specific semantic meanings from several candidate images. Recognizing the semantic of images is more difficult than that of text, thus it was more resilient to automated attacks. However, as the performance of neural networks explodes, recent studies have demonstrated that CNN and R-CNN can respectively bypass image classification CAPTCHAs and object detection CAPTCHAs [8,17].

2.2 Adversarial Attacks

As the processing power of a GPU grows, deep learning based methods have led to impressive performances on various challenging perceptual tasks, especially image classification and image recognition. DL-based methods are, however, vulnerable to adversarial examples. Inputs with a subtle perturbation can be correctly recognized by humans but make the machine learning model fooled.

Fast Gradient Sign Method. Goodfellow *et al.* showed that misclassification of adversarial examples can be caused by the linear nature of neural networks and high dimensional input space [5]. They propose a simple adversarial attack called Fast Gradient Sign Method (FGSM).

$$x^* = x + \epsilon \cdot sign(\bigtriangledown_x J(\theta, x, y))$$

In this equation, θ denotes the parameters of a model, x denotes the input to the model, y denotes the original target class, $J(\theta, x, y)$ denotes the cost used to train the network. The FGSM only computes the gradients for once, thus this method generates adversarial examples quickly.

Projected Gradient Descent. Madry *et al.* demonstrated that the Projected Gradient Descent (PGD), a multi-step variant of FGSM, can make the adversarial attack more powerful [10].

$$x^{t+1} = \Pi_{x+S}(x^t + \alpha \cdot sign(\bigtriangledown_x J(\theta, x, y)))$$

In this equation, S denotes a feasible perturbation set, and this multi-step approach can maximize the inner part of the saddle point problem in adversarial training formulation. Madry *et al.* demonstrated PGD is competitive compared with other state-of-the-art attacks such as CW attack [4], thus PGD can be used for adversarial training.

Adversarial attacks can be divided into two types. The first type is a white-box attack, where an attacker has full knowledge of the target neural network model's architecture and weight values. In a white-box manner, the attacker uses the model weights to generate adversarial examples. The second type is a black-box attack, where an attacker can only query the model without accessing the weights of the target model. Prior work has shown we can train a substitute model with given black-box access to a target model, and by attacking the substitute model, we can then transfer these attacks to the target model [13].

2.3   Adversarial CAPTCHAs

Recently, popular websites have adapted improved CAPTCHA systems such as Google's reCAPTCHA v2 that use adversarial examples or artificial noises to defend against automated attacks using DL-based solvers [8].

IAN Generation. Osadchy *et al.* proposed a method called IAN generation for producing powerful adversarial CAPTCHAs to defeat DL-based solvers [16]. This method is based on gradient descent technique and optimizes a perturbation using L_∞ distance metric. The algorithm of IAN generation is similar to the PGD attack as small perturbation continuously to be mixed. Thus, the produced adversarial CAPTCHAs can deceive the DL-based solvers with a median filter.

$$argmin \ \|\epsilon\|^2 \ s.t. \ Net(Median(x + \epsilon)) \neq C$$

For solving this optimization problem, IAN generation leverages a FGSM variant, as the perturbations of adversarial examples can remain after a median filter preprocessing. In the formula, ϵ denotes a perturbation, Net denotes a neural network, and C denotes the original class. However, IAN is designed for only defeating DL-based solvers who use preprocessing techniques. In this paper, we assume CAPTCHA defense schemes produce adversarial CAPTCHAs using the PGD method which can respond to various DL-based solvers.

2.4 Defending Against Adversarial Examples

To correctly classify adversarial examples, Goodfellow *et al.* proposed adversarial training [5]. Adversarial training is one of the most effective methods to defend against adversarial examples by training a model on original images and adversarial examples in appropriate proportions [5,10]. The key point of this defense technique is to generalize the model by increasing the size and diversity of the dataset through producing adversarial examples and make the model learn the distributions of adversarial examples. However, this technique requires more data and time than normal training methods [15].

On the other hand, recent studies have proposed the preprocessing methods that can defend against adversarial examples. The key point of this technique is to change perturbed input to refined input by eliminating adversarial perturbation before the model inference [6,9,19]. This method is time efficient since it does not need to retrain the model. However, they are vulnerable to attackers who know the preprocessing technique in a white-box manner [1].

2.5 Incremental Learning

The incremental learning is a training method that extends existing model knowledge by continuously using new input data [7]. The goal of incremental learning is to produce a well-generalized model adapted to new data without forgetting existing knowledge. It does not need to retrain the whole model, and by using only a little bunch of new data, the model can learn fresh information.

3 CAPTCHA Solver Methods

In this section, we show three types of CAPTCHA solver methods for bypassing adversarial CAPTCHA schemes. We first explain two adversarial CAPTCHA solver methods previously mentioned in other research. We will then introduce our proposed solver method and its hyperparameter setting.

3.1 Preprocessing for CAPTCHA Solvers

The traditional OCR-based text CAPTCHA solver tools provide filtering methods to eliminate a variety of noises. The filtering method can increase the accuracy of text-based CAPTCHA solver since the CAPTCHA image contains a lot of artificial noises. The DL-based solver also can preprocess CAPTCHA instances to remove effects from adversarial perturbations. Osadchy *et al.* found that the median filter is one of the most successful preprocessing methods to revert the noise for image-based CAPTCHAs [12]. Therefore we utilize the various sizes of median filters for preprocessing inputs to baseline DL-based models.

3.2 Adversarial Training for CAPTCHA Solvers

For DL-based solvers, an attacker can perform adversarial training to achieve high accuracy on adversarial CAPTCHAs. Shi *et al.* showed that the adversarial training achieves high accuracy for text-based CAPTCHAs [16]. Therefore we also adopt the adversarial training method for CAPTCHA solvers to compare performance with our method.

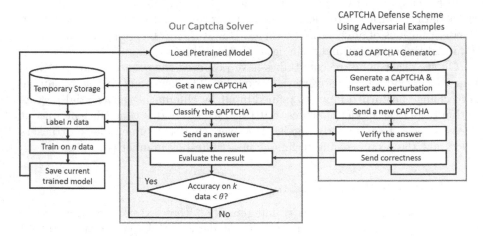

Fig. 2. Process flow diagram of a CAPTCHA defense scheme using adversarial examples (right) and our CAPTCHA solver scheme (middle).

3.3 Proposed Method: Incremental Learning for CAPTCHA Solvers

We propose a CAPTCHA solver using an incremental learning process. The simplified workflow of our proposed method is summarized in Fig. 2. This workflow consists of two components, our CAPTCHA solver and a defense method utilizing adversarial CAPTCHAs. In the attack process, our method incrementally trains a single DNN model instance. Our algorithm repeatedly verifies that the current model instance achieves high accuracy on recent CAPTCHAs. When necessary, our method trains the model on a small number of n recent CAPTCHAs. Using incremental learning, the attacker can classify new CAPTCHAs from the changed distribution, while preserving high accuracy on original CAPTCHAs.

Learning Process. In the beginning, the solver trains a model on original CAPTCHAs, and the model is referred to as a basic model. The solver then uses the basic model to solve CAPTCHAs repeatedly. Most CAPTCHA schemes immediately inform a client whether the client's answer is correct or not. Therefore, the attacker can measure the accuracy on the most recently collected k CAPTCHAs. If the accuracy is less than the threshold θ, the solver trains the model instance on the most recently collected n CAPTCHAs. In this process, humans manually label n CAPTCHAs for training in text-based and image-based CAPTCHA schemes.

Hyperparameter Setting. The proposed method has three hyperparameters to control a way to train a model. We can change k to set how fast our solver responds to changes of the CAPTCHA schemes. If the value of k is small, the solver becomes sensitive to the change of the CAPTCHA distribution. With a small k, the solver immediately performs incremental learning when the CAPTCHA scheme presents adversarial CAPTCHAs.

An accuracy threshold for determining the necessity of incremental learning is referred to as θ. Previous work showed that even if a solver shows only 1% accuracy (θ value of 0.01), the solver effectively automates the desired work on the target website [11]. In this paper, we set the θ value to 0.5 (50% accuracy), preserving the attack success rate high enough.

The n denotes the number of CAPTCHAs to conduct the incremental learning process. According to our experiment, when the basic model is trained on 120,000 CAPTCHAs, newly collected 2,400 CAPTCHAs (n) are enough to train a robust model using the incremental learning process. We empirically demonstrate n should be larger than 0.5% of the number of train dataset of the basic model to retrain the robust solver with more than the 50% accuracy threshold.

4 Experiments

This section addresses the evaluation results of the proposed method against the defense method using adversarial CAPTCHAs. We first introduce the dataset for the experiments and the DNN architecture used for solvers. We then present the advantages of our incremental learning method compared with the methods of adversarial training and pre-processing, which are previously suggested countermeasures for adversarial CAPTCHAs [12,16].

4.1 Experiment Setting

Original CAPTCHA Dataset. We construct a text-based and image-based CAPTCHA dataset for the experiment. For text-based schemes, we generate 4-character text CAPTCHAs using the *captcha* library of Python. Each letter in the text-based CAPTCHA image is an alphabetical capital or numeral, representing one of 36 classes. The dataset of the text-based scheme consists of a total of 180,000, which are split into 150,000 train data and 30,000 test data.

Moreover, we adopted the CIFAR-10 dataset for image-based CAPTCHAs, since the image-based CAPTCHA schemes are similar to the image recognition tasks. Traditional image-based CAPTCHA schemes present about 10 images and then require the user to classify images into the correct label [17]. CIFAR-10 dataset is a widely used image classification dataset consisting of 50,000 train data and 10,000 test data.

In text-based schemes, we determine the answer of the solver as correct only if all the 4 characters in the answer are correct. In image-based schemes, we determine the answer of the solver as correct only if the selected class of the answer for the single image instance is the same as the ground-truth class.

Adversarial CAPTCHA Dataset. To evaluate the accuracy of the solvers after CAPTCHA defense schemes change the distribution of images, we generate an adversarial CAPTCHA dataset. We first divide the original train dataset into $Train_1$ and $Train_2$ datasets, then train a baseline model only on $Train_1$ for text-based CAPTCHA and image-based CAPTCHAs.

We assume the defense methods produce adversarial CAPTCHAs using their own solver model to transfer adversarial perturbation to CAPTCHA solvers. Therefore, we generate the adversarial CAPTCHA dataset by inserting adversarial perturbations to $Train_2$ using the model. The generated adversarial CAPTCHA dataset is referred to as $Train_{adv}$. When producing adversarial perturbations, we use the PGD method, since PGD is a powerful and general method for producing adversarial examples [10].

For text-based CAPTCHA, we split the 150,000 original train data into 120,000 for $Train_1$ and 30,000 for $Train_2$. We then train a ResNet-18 model on $Train_1$ and generate 30,000 adversarial train data ($Train_{adv}$) by perturbing $Train_2$. In the same way, we generate 30,000 adversarial test data ($Test_{adv}$) by perturbing 30,000 original test data. All the text-based adversarial CAPTCHAs are constructed with $\epsilon = 0.1$, step size of 0.03, and 7 steps.

For image-based CAPTCHA, we split the 50,000 original train data into 40,000 for $Train_1$ and 10,000 for $Train_2$. We then train a ResNet-18 model on $Train_1$ and generate 10,000 adversarial train data ($Train_{adv}$) by perturbing $Train_2$. In the same way, we generate 10,000 adversarial test data ($Test_{adv}$) by perturbing 10,000 original test data. All the image-based adversarial CAPTCHAs are constructed with $\epsilon = 0.0314$, step size of 0.00785, and 7 steps, which are the same parameters in the original paper proposing the PGD method [10].

Architecture of CAPTCHA Solver Suppose that the attacker leverages the state-of-the-art CNN architecture, ResNet-18, for both image-based and text-based CAPTCHA schemes (see Fig. 3). We find that the solver based on ResNet-18 is sufficient to bypass the defense methods and outperforms other architectures such as AlexNet, VGGNet, and GooLeNet for benign 4-character text-based CAPTCHAs. For text-based schemes, we set the number of the output layer's neuron to 144 in ResNet-18, since we use each set of 36 neurons to

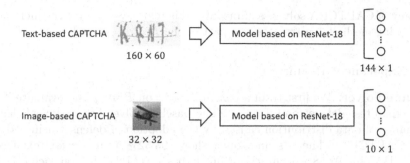

Fig. 3. The architectures of our CAPTCHA solver for experiments.

represent a single character. The image-based CAPTCHA solver is also based on ResNet-18 with 10 dimensions of the output layer for classifying the CIFAR-10 dataset (see Fig. 3).

In the training process, we train a ResNet-18 model using 50 epochs for text-based CAPTCHA and 200 epochs for image-based CAPTCHAs setting the batch size to 128 for both of them. For the text-based CAPTCHA solver, we fix the learning rate to 0.0005, while we adjust learning rates from 0.1 to 0.001 for the image-based CAPTCHA solver.

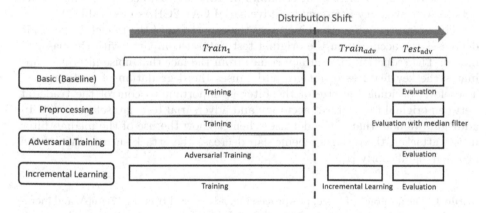

Fig. 4. The experiment setting for comparison between CAPTCHA solvers.

We assume all the CAPTCHA solvers want to not only classify original CAPTCHA images (original test dataset) and but also adversarial CAPTCHA images ($Test_{adv}$). We, therefore, train all CAPTCHA solvers on $Train_1$, and then evaluate on the original test dataset and $Test_{adv}$. We note that previous works have assumed the CAPTCHA solver utilizing proprocessing or adversarial training simply uses only a statically fixed classification model [12,16]. However, we demonstrate only a small number of newly collected train data can boost the accuracy of CAPTCHA solvers significantly. Therefore, we assume the incremental learning method can train on the part of the $Train_{adv}$ (see Fig. 4).

4.2 Experiment Results

Baseline Solver. We first train a baseline solver on $Train_1$ and evaluate it on the original test dataset and $Test_{adv}$. The baseline solver has no knowledge of the change of data distribution caused by the adoption of defenses using adversarial CAPTCHAs. The baseline solver shows 93.32% accuracy for text-based CAPTCHAs and 92.58% accuracy for image-based CAPTCHAs on each original test datasets (see Table 1). Meanwhile, the baseline solver shows 7.19% accuracy for text-based CAPTCHAs and 4.28% accuracy for image-based CAPTCHAs on each adversarial datasets ($Test_{adv}$). The results indicate that the baseline solvers are inappropriate to solve adversarial CAPTCHAs.

Preprocessing Solver. We demonstrate the attack success rate of the preprocessing method by adding a median filter to the baseline model. This model preprocesses all the image inputs with a median filter (median blur) in inference time [12]. For text-based CAPTCHAs, our ResNet-18 model with a 5×5 median filter shows 85.41% original accuracy. This model gets 24.42% adversarial accuracy for adversarial CAPTCHAs. For image-based CAPTCHAs, our ResNet-18 model with a 3×3 median filter shows 82.13% original accuracy. This model gets 61.47% accuracy accuracy for adversarial CAPTCHAs (see Table 1).

The preprocessing method increases the robustness of the model, however, it decreases the accuracy on the original test dataset compared with the baseline model. The reduction of accuracy comes from the fact that noise filtering eliminates the key features of images and causes the degradation of performance. Therefore, deciding the size of the filter is important to control the trade-off between original test dataset accuracy and adversarial test dataset accuracy. In addition, we note that if the defense schemes know the use of the median filter in the attacker, the defense scheme can decrease the attack success rate of the attacker significantly [1].

Table 1. The accuracy of basic, pre-processing, adversarial training (7-step), and incremental learning (with 2% more adversarial CAPTCHA images) ResNet-18 solver models against CAPTCHA defense schemes.

	Basic		Preprocessing [12]		Adv. Training [16]		Inc. Learning	
	Original	Adver.	Original	Adver.	Original	Adver.	Original	Adver.
Text-based	93.32%	7.19%	85.41%	24.42%	63.68%	60.74%	**86.49%**	**70.14%**
Image-based	92.58%	4.28%	82.13%	61.47%	81.32%	79.54%	**87.37%**	**78.19%**

Adversarial Training Solver. We experimented on the text-based and image-based CAPTCHA dataset for evaluating the effect of adversarial training. The attack success rate of the adversarially trained model is competitive since the CAPTCHA defense schemes should attack the adversarially trained model in a black-box manner. The adversarial training solver shows 63.68% for text-based CAPTCHAs and 81.32% for image-based CAPTCHAs on each original test datasets (see Table 1). Moreover, the adversarial training solver shows 60.74% for text-based CAPTCHAs and 79.54% for image-based CAPTCHAs on each adversarial test datasets ($Test_{adv}$). We note that the adversarially trained solver can be still efficient even if the defense schemes know the exact architecture of the solver model in a white-box manner.

However, adversarial training for robust CAPTCHA solvers has the following two shortcomings. First, adversarial training can reduce the accuracy on original images. Second, adversarial training takes a lot of time. In our experiment, 7-step PGD adversarial training takes about 5.5 times more than basic training for both text-based and image-based solvers.

Incremental Learning Solver. We demonstrate our incremental learning process is an effective method for creating a robust CAPTCHA solver compared to the adversarial training and pre-processing. In our proposed method, the CAPTCHA solver can improve accuracy quickly through incremental learning, when the CAPTCHA defense schemes present adversarial examples. For the incremental learning, we set the learning rate to 0.0005 and 0.001 for text-based solver and image-based solver individually, then retrain the models by 50 epochs with batch size 128.

Table 2 shows the results of our incremental learning. Without incremental learning, CAPTCHA solver has only 7.19% accuracy for text-based and 4.28% accuracy for image-based CAPTCHA schemes using adversarial perturbations. However, if we leverage incremental learning with a small number of new perturbed CAPTCHA images, the accuracy of the CAPTCHA solver can increase high enough again. For text-based CAPTCHAs, with only 600 (0.5% of the number of the original training dataset $train_1$) new adversarial CAPTCHA images, the accuracy of the CAPTCHA solver reaches the adversarial accuracy of 57.78% by performing incremental learning. For image-based CAPTCHAs, only 200 (0.5% of the number of the original training dataset $train_1$) new adversarial CAPTCHA images can make the CAPTCHA solver reach the adversarial accuracy of 69.84%. From Table 2, we are able to see that the accuracy is enhanced as the learning model includes more adversarial CAPTCHA data in its incremental learning process. We empirically demonstrated if n is larger than 0.5% of the number of train dataset of the basic model, we can retrain the robust solver achieving more than the 50% accuracy threshold again.

Our experimental results show that incremental learning is more efficient than adversarial training and noise filtering for CAPTCHA solver. The incremental learning solver outperforms preprocessing and adversarial training with a small amount of additional perturbed data which is only 2% (2,400 of 120,000 for text-

Table 2. The accuracy of text-based and image-based CAPTCHA solvers with incremental learning.

(a) Text-based CAPTCHA solver

ratio	0%	0.1%	0.2%	0.5%	1.0%	**2.0%**	4.0%	8.0%	15.0%	25.0%
Original dataset (%)	93.32	88.95	89.43	88.17	87.23	**86.49**	86.35	86.41	87.23	89.16
Adversarial dataset (%)	7.19	42.61	49.35	57.78	63.97	**70.14**	76.37	84.13	89.76	92.87
Required time (second)	0	22	31	74	110	**174**	394	831	1256	2374

(b) Image-based CAPTCHA solver

ratio	0%	0.1%	0.2%	0.5%	1.0%	**2.0%**	4.0%	8.0%	15.0%	25.0%
Original dataset (%)	92.58	88.27	89.54	88.15	87.55	**87.37**	87.87	88.28	89.01	89.39
Adversarial dataset (%)	4.28	45.92	55.70	69.84	75.20	**78.19**	79.62	81.42	82.92	84.59
Required time (second)	0	8	11	19	26	**45**	93	143	348	578

based and 800 of 40,000 for image-based) of the number of train data initially required. Moreover, our method is 5.5 times faster than the adversarial training, since the required time for incremental learning is significantly small (can be ignored) than the training time for baseline solvers which requires more than 4 h with a single NVIDIA Titan Xp graphics card (12 GB) in our experiments.

5   Discussion

The experimental results show that our simple incremental learning process works better than previously suggested techniques. We note that these results are caused by limitations of current CAPTCHA defense schemes.

First, CAPTCHA schemes should generate challenges every time a user requests access. Therefore, a malicious user can simply get new train data from CAPTCHA schemes. Second, CAPTCHA schemes using adversarial examples assume static CAPTCHA solvers who only use a fixed pre-trained model. Hence, they generate adversarial CAPTCHA images against fixed CAPTCHA solvers and transfer these images to the solver model in a black-box manner. It is challenging to fool attackers who periodically train DL-based solvers with newly collected data. These restrictions make the process of finding optimal adversarial perturbation for current CAPTCHA solvers extremely hard.

In this restriction of current CAPTCHA defense schemes, our incremental learning process is suitable to bypass the adversarial CAPTCHAs with a small amount of new train data. Our method requires more labeling works than adversarial training and preprocessing methods. However, we demonstrate attackers can be strong enough by training on a small amount of additional perturbed data which is only 2% of the number of train data initially required.

6 Conclusion

Our work demonstrates that a CAPTCHA solver using incremental learning with the small dataset is strong enough to break existing defense methods for CAPTCHA systems. We show that just utilizing adversarial examples in CAPTCHA schemes is not effective for our adaptive CAPTCHA solver. Thus, for a more accurate evaluation of CAPTCHA defense methods, an adaptive attacker should be considered. We hope our incremental learning method can be used as a baseline attacker for future CAPTCHA defense studies.

Acknowledgement. This work was supported by Institute of Information & communications Technology Planning & Evaluation (IITP) grant funded by the Korea government(MSIT) (No. 2018-0-01392).

References

1. Athalye, A., Carlini, N., Wagner, D.: Obfuscated gradients give a false sense of security: circumventing defenses to adversarial examples. arXiv preprint arXiv:1802.00420 (2018)
2. Bursztein, E., Aigrain, J., Moscicki, A., Mitchell, J.C.: The end is nigh: generic solving of text-based captchas. In: 8th {USENIX} Workshop on Offensive Technologies ({WOOT} 14) (2014)
3. Bursztein, E., Martin, M., Mitchell, J.: Text-based captcha strengths and weaknesses. In: Proceedings of the 18th ACM conference on Computer and communications security. pp. 125–138. ACM (2011)
4. Carlini, N., Wagner, D.: Towards evaluating the robustness of neural networks. In: 2017 IEEE Symposium on Security and Privacy (SP), pp. 39–57. IEEE (2017)
5. Goodfellow, I.J., Shlens, J., Szegedy, C.: Explaining and harnessing adversarial examples. arXiv preprint arXiv:1412.6572 (2014)
6. Guo, C., Rana, M., Cisse, M., van der Maaten, L.: Countering adversarial images using input transformations. In: International Conference on Learning Representations (2018), https://openreview.net/forum?id=SyJ7ClWCb
7. Guo, H., Wang, S., Fan, J., Li, S.: Learning automata based incremental learning method for deep neural networks. IEEE Access **7**, 41164–41171 (2019)
8. Hossen, M.I., Tu, Y., Rabby, M.F., Islam, M.N., Cao, H., Hei, X.: Bots work better than human beings : An online system to break Google's image-based Recaptcha v2 (2019)
9. Liao, F., Liang, M., Dong, Y., Pang, T., Hu, X., Zhu, J.: Defense against adversarial attacks using high-level representation guided denoiser. In: Proceedings of the IEEE Conference on Computer Vision and Pattern Recognition, pp. 1778–1787 (2018)
10. Madry, A., Makelov, A., Schmidt, L., Tsipras, D., Vladu, A.: Towards deep learning models resistant to adversarial attacks. arXiv preprint arXiv:1706.06083 (2017)
11. Makris, C., Town, C.: Character segmentation for automatic captcha solving. Open Computer Science Journal **1**(1) (2014)

12. Osadchy, M., Hernandez-Castro, J., Gibson, S., Dunkelman, O., Pérez-Cabo, D.: No bot expects the deepcaptcha! introducing immutable adversarial examples, with applications to captcha generation. IEEE Trans. Inf. Forensics Secur. **12**(11), 2640–2653 (2017)

13. Papernot, N., McDaniel, P., Goodfellow, I.: Transferability in machine learning: from phenomena to black-box attacks using adversarial samples. arXiv preprint arXiv:1605.07277 (2016)

14. Rui, C., Jing, Y., Rong-gui, H., Shu-guang, H.: A novel lstm-rnn decoding algorithm in captcha recognition. In: 2013 Third International Conference on Instrumentation, Measurement, Computer, Communication and Control, pp. 766–771. IEEE (2013)

15. Schmidt, L., Santurkar, S., Tsipras, D., Talwar, K., Madry, A.: Adversarially robust generalization requires more data. In: Advances in Neural Information Processing Systems, pp. 5014–5026 (2018)

16. Shi, C., et al.: Adversarial captchas. arXiv preprint arXiv:1901.01107 (2019)

17. Sivakorn, S., Polakis, I., Keromytis, A.D.: I am robot:(deep) learning to break semantic image captchas. In: 2016 IEEE European Symposium on Security and Privacy (EuroS&P), pp. 388–403. IEEE (2016)

18. Stark, F., Hazırbas, C., Triebel, R., Cremers, D.: Captcha recognition with active deep learning. In: Workshop new challenges in neural computation. vol. 2015, p. 94. Citeseer (2015)

19. Tian, S., Yang, G., Cai, Y.: Detecting adversarial examples through image transformation. In: Thirty-Second AAAI Conference on Artificial Intelligence (2018)

20. Wang, Y., Lu, M.: An optimized system to solve text-based captcha. arXiv preprint arXiv:1806.07202 (2018)

21. Ye, G., et al.: Yet another text captcha solver: A generative adversarial network based approach. In: Proceedings of the 2018 ACM SIGSAC Conference on Computer and Communications Security, pp. 332–348. ACM (2018)

22. Zhang, L., Huang, S.G., Shi, Z.X., Hu, R.G.: Captcha recognition method based on rnn of lstm. Pattern Recogn. Artif. Intell. **24**(1), 40–47 (2011)

Unsupervised Intrusion Detection System for Unmanned Aerial Vehicle with Less Labeling Effort

Kyung Ho Park, Eunji Park, and Huy Kang Kim[✉]

School of Cybersecurity, Korea University, Seoul, South Korea
{kyungho96,epark911,cenda}@korea.ac.kr

Abstract. Along with the importance of safety, an IDS has become a significant task in the real world. Prior studies proposed various intrusion detection models for the UAV. Past rule-based approaches provided a concrete baseline IDS model, and the machine learning-based method achieved a precise intrusion detection performance on the UAV with supervised learning models. However, previous methods have room for improvement to be implemented in the real world. Prior methods required a large labeling effort on the dataset, and the model could not identify attacks that were not trained before.

To jump over these hurdles, we propose an IDS with unsupervised learning. As unsupervised learning does not require labeling, our model let the practitioner not to label every type of attack from the flight data. Moreover, the model can identify an abnormal status of the UAV regardless of the type of attack. We trained an autoencoder with the benign flight data only and checked the model provides a different reconstruction loss at the benign flight and the flight under attack. We discovered that the model produces much higher reconstruction loss with the flight under attack than the benign flight; thus, this reconstruction loss can be utilized to recognize an intrusion to the UAV. With consideration of the computation overhead and the detection performance in the wild, we expect our model can be a concrete and practical baseline IDS on the UAV.

Keywords: Unmanned aerial vehicle · Intrusion detection system · Unsupervised learning · Autoencoder

1 Introduction

The Unmanned Aerial Vehicle (UAV) is a promising future technology due to its various applications. The UAVs can deliver packages or medicines at the urgent medical circumstances, or ship goods and products rapidly in the urban areas [9]. Although the UAVs provide a wide range of benefits to the society, however, concerns on the safety and security still exist [5]. If the UAV's communication signals are intruded, UAVs without appropriate control might cause a severe

© Springer Nature Switzerland AG 2020
I. You (Ed.): WISA 2020, LNCS 12583, pp. 45–58, 2020.
https://doi.org/10.1007/978-3-030-65299-9_4

problem. UAVs under attack might not be able to come back to their base station, or they could fail to land on the safe zone under the emergency. Along with the safety concerns, it has become a significant task to identify whether the UAV is intruded or not; thus, an intrusion detection system (IDS) has emerged into the academia and the industry.

An IDS is a security technology that recognizes an intrusion into the computer system [3]. An IDS on the UAV especially recognizes abnormal patterns or unauthorized activities at the UAV by analyzing activity logs [5]. As the IDS can identify abnormal UAV activities during the flight, several studies it has been researched from the past. The first approach of the IDS on the UAV was a rule-based model. Prior studies analyzed the pattern of UAVs during the flight under attack, and extracted features which describe an abnormal status. The proposed rule-based models achieved a concrete baseline of the IDS on the UAV; however, the model performance was not precise enough to be deployed in a real world. If an abnormal pattern of the UAV is not identified by the detection rules, the proposed models could not recognize the status as an intrusion. Thus, it has become an essential task to increase the detection performance at various types of attacks.

To improve the limit of prior studies, a detection model with machine learning models have been proposed. Numerous machine learning models precisely learn the pattern of UAVs during the flight; thus, presented machine learning-based models achieved a significant detection performance. Although proposed models improved the detection performance from the past, there existed a labeling problem. As prior approaches leveraged supervised machine learning models, a practitioner must provide a well-labeled training data into the model. Under supervised learning, the practitioner should collect and label the flight data under attack, and this data collection process accompanies an enormous cost and effort. Furthermore, a detection model with supervised learning cannot identify non-trained patterns of attack. If a malicious intruder performs non-trained attacks into the UAV, the IDS cannot identify the attack; thus, we analyzed the IDS on the UAV should be implemented without supervised learning.

In this study, we propose a novel IDS for UAVs leveraging unsupervised learning. We presented a series of analyses to extract features from the raw log data and how we transformed it into an effective form. We designed the detection model with an autoencoder, a deep neural network of unsupervised learning, and trained the model with the benign flight data only. Lastly, we validated the model precisely recognizes two types of attack (DoS attack, GPS Spoofing attack) from the benign status. Throughout the study, key contributions are described below:

- We designed an intrusion detection model leveraging unsupervised learning with the benign flight data only; thus, our approach reduces a labeling effort.
- The proposed intrusion detection model effectively recognized the difference between the benign flight and the flight under two types of attack: DoS attack and GPS Spoofing attack.
- Our study illustrated a series of analysis to produce essential features from raw log data, and extracted features can be applied into the common UAVs.

2   Literature Review

Researchers have proposed various IDS approaches on the UAV. Prior works can be categorized into two streams as shown in Table 1: a rule-based approach and the machine learning-based approach.

Table 1. Prior researches of the IDS on UAVs

Category	Intrusion type	Key model	Reference
Rule-based approach	SYN flooding, Password guessing, Buffer overflow, scanning	Behavioral rules	[8]
	Spoofing, Gray/Blackhole attacks false information dissemination, Jamming	Hierarchical scheme	[12]
	Constant flash-crowd attack progressive flash-crowd attack	Spectral analysis	[14]
Machine learning approach	SYN flooding, Password guessing, Buffer overflow, Scanning	PSO-DBN	[13]
	Spoofing, Jamming	STL and SVM	[2]
	Spoofing	SVM	[10]

Mitchell and Chen [8] analyzed attackers' behaviors according to their recklessness, randomness, and opportunistic characteristic and derived a set of behavior rules to identify attacks on the UAV. The proposed model achieved a promising detection accuracy. Moreover, it provided the capability to adjust detection strength, which allowed them to trade false-positive and false-negative rates. Sedjelmaci et al. [12] designed rule-based algorithms for five most lethal attacks to UAV network. They investigated how each attack impacted the network indicators, such as the signal strength intensity (SSI) or the number of packets sent (NPS). Four rule-based detection models were implemented, and they showed a precise detection ability with low false positives in a simulated environment. Zhang et al. [14] suggested an IDS as a hybrid model of spectral analyses. They used wavelet analysis to leverage spectral characteristics of the network traffic. They also proposed a controller and an observer tracking the traffics of the attacker to establish a precise IDS on the UAV. However, rule-based approaches were not sustainable in a different environment. Proposed methods could not sustain its detection performance when the platform or the system configuration changes. If the UAV gets updated, several rules might not be suitable for the new system. Furthermore, the detection model necessitates a more precise performance to be implemented in the real world.

To overcome the drawback, several studies applied machine learning models to detect intrusions on the UAV. Tan *et al.* [13] applied a Deep Belief Network (DBN) with Particle Swarm Optimization (PSO). They interpreted an intrusion detection task as a massive and complicated problem. They trained a classifier with the DBN and utilized the PSO optimizer to obtain an optimal number of hidden layer nodes for the classification. DBN-PSO effectively leveraged the machine learning model and showed a significant performance rather than prior approaches. Arthur [2] discovered the connection of the UAV often became intermittent and left a non-linear log data. The model employed a Self-Taught Learning (STL) to gain a set of features from the flight data and utilized the Support Vector Machine (SVM) as a classifier. The proposed IDS verified its efficiency with a significant detection performance. Panice *et al.* [10] utilized a SVM on the estimated state of the UAV to detect GPS spoofing attacks on UAVs. They utilized estimated states of the UAV as key features and classified the UAV status into two cases: safe status and unsafe. They achieved a promising intrusion detection performance through the binary classification of safe status and unsafe status.

The machine learning approaches demonstrated their efficacy in many studies, but they accompanied the limit of supervised learning. As proposed machine learning approaches employed supervised learning models, the practitioner must provide a well-labeled data at the training phase. In the context of the IDS on the UAV, labels indicate whether the flight data is benign or under attack, and the type of attack techniques. However, labeling every flight data requires an enormous effort and the cost. Furthermore, an IDS with supervised learning cannot recognize attacks that were not trained before. As the supervised learning models can only identify learned attacks, the IDS might be neutralized with an unseen attack into the system.

Considering analyzed drawbacks of both rule-based and machine-learning-based approaches, we propose an IDS on the UAV with unsupervised learning. As unsupervised learning does not necessitate solid labels during the model training, it reduces the burden of labeling cost to the practitioner. Furthermore, unsupervised learning enables the model to detect various intrusions that are not labeled or not pre-known. The following sections further provide a detailed description of how we designed an IDS on the UAV leveraging the efficacy of unsupervised learning.

3   Proposed Methodology

3.1   Dataset

Description. We utilized Hardware-In-The-Loop (HITL) UAV DOS & GPS Spoofing Attacks on MAVLINK dataset [7] on the experiment. The dataset contains system logs along with the simulated flight. These system logs are collected under the simulated environment, which follows standard jMAVSim setup. The dataset contains system logs at the UAV under three circumstances described below:

- **Benign Flight**: A log data during the flight without any attacks on the system
- **DoS Attack**: A log data during the flight with Denial-of-Service (DoS) attack for 11 s
- **GPS Spoofing Attack**: A log data during the flight with GPS Spoofing attack for 28 s

Our key takeaway of the study is utilizing the benign flight data only at the model training stage, and whether the trained model can recognize the intrusion unless attacks are not trained before. As the dataset includes both the benign flight and the flight under attacks, we analyzed we can utilize the dataset to train the model with the benign flight and validate the model with logs under two attacks: DoS attack and GPS Spoofing attack.

Ground-Truth Confirmation. We confirmed the ground-truth of the dataset by checking the timestamp of the log data. As HITL DOS & GPS Spoofing Attacks dataset provides a particular timestamp of attack, we labeled the log between attack start time and the attack end time as the flight under attack. The log from the benign flight does not contain both attack start time and the attack end time as the flight does not include any intrusions to the system. Detailed timestamps are described in Table 2.

Table 2. Particular timestamps of the dataset

Dataset	Flight start time	Attack start time	Attack end time	Flight end time
Benign flight	14:00:52	-	-	14:25:50
DoS attack	15:29:06	15:54:09	15:54:20	15:55:09
GPS spoofing attack	15:58:19	16:24:14	16:24:42	16:26:25

3.2 Feature Extraction

The dataset contains a wide range of features related to the UAV. These features are written in a system log to record the status of the UAV during the flight. We categorized every features of the dataset into five types as summarized in Table 3.

From the five categories of the feature, we extracted features that can effectively recognize abnormal patterns of the UAV during the flight under attack. We established two rules for feature extraction. First and foremost, we considered a hardware generality to select the category of the feature. Furthermore, we investigated sensor stability to choose particular features under the category. A detailed explanation is elaborated below.

Table 3. Five categories of features in the dataset

Category	Description
Location	A set of features related to the location of the UAV. A particular coordinates of the location is described along with the Global Positioning System (GPS)
Position & Orientation	A set of features related to the position and the orientation of the UAV
Internal measurements	A set of features extracted from the Internal Measurement Units (IMUs)
System status	A set of features related to the system management such as on-board sensors
Control	A set of features illustrating an input toward the actuator to move the UAV

Hardware Generality. We analyzed features shall exist regardless of the type of the UAV; thus, we extracted features related to the geographic properties and physical properties. One of the key takeaways of our study is a generality; that our models can be easily established regardless of the hardware. If a particular feature exists only at our employed UAV, the proposed model cannot be utilized at other types of UAVs. Therefore, we excluded every unique feature which only exists at our UAV (MAVLINK). For instance, we excluded features in a control category as the control input varies along with the hardware. As an input toward the actuator differs from the hardware configuration, we analyzed features in the control category that cannot be widely utilized. Instead, we selected features related to the geographic properties and physical properties as we intuitively inferred most UAV systems measure these properties during the flight. Therefore, we employed features in a geographic category - location - and physical category - position & orientation, internal measurements, and system status.

Sensor Stability. We inferred selected features should not be frequently lost during the flight; therefore, we employed features that do not contain any failure from the sensor. The absence of a particular feature causes damage to the model. If a particular feature contains any missed values, this feature exercises a negative influence on the model training and inference. Moreover, a feature without any changes can blur the pattern of UAVs during the flight. The model should learn unique characteristics of benign flight; however, a tranquil feature without any changes would blur these characteristics. Therefore, we established two conditions described below and dropped every feature under any of the illustrated conditions.

- **Missing Value:** A feature contains any missing values during the flight at both benign flights and the flight under attack (i.e., Null)
- **Tranquil Value:** A feature only includes the same value without any changes at both benign flights and the flight under attack

By considering the aforementioned hardware generality and the sensor stability, we extracted features from the dataset. The used features are described at the Table 4.

3.3   Feature Engineering

Although we extracted essential features from the dataset, we figured out two obstacles to provide the data into the model: Different scales of each feature and different periods of each feature. A different scale and periods of each feature cause a negative influence at training deep neural networks. We mitigated these two obstacles with the following feature engineering steps: Feature scaling and timestamp pooling.

Feature Scaling. We transformed the values of each feature under the same scale. As each feature has a different magnitude of the scale, a deep neural networks-based model would get confused easily when it optimizes parameters. If several features have much larger value than other features, the loss cannot be minimized along with the training steps; thus, it creates an obstacle at the model training. By applying the scaling function elaborated in Eq. (1), we scaled each feature under the same scope and mitigated different scales of each feature.

$$X_{scaled} = \frac{X_i - Min(X_i)}{Max(X_i) - Min(X_i)} \tag{1}$$

Timestamp Pooling. We unified the length of each feature through the timestamp pooling. Following the characteristic of UAV, each feature is recorded in a different period, as visualized in Fig. 1. (a). Referring the Fig. 1. (a), Feature A, B, and C have different periods of data recording under the same time window. When we transform these features during a particular time window, the length of feature vectors varies. During the same time window, the number of data points at each feature is 6, 4, 2 for Feature A, B, C, respectively. As the intrusion detection system identifies the attack per timestamp, a different number of data points during the same time window become an obstacle against the model training. We interpret that each feature necessitates a transformation process with the same number of data points during the fixed time window.

To fulfill this requirement above, we applied a timestamp pooling, which is selecting a single value from the values during a fixed time window. We randomly sampled a single value from each feature, and inferred randomly-selected value can be a representative value during the fixed time window. We set the time window as 500 ms and applied a timestamp pooling to every feature. If we apply the timestamp pooling at the example as mentioned earlier, the result is displayed in Fig. 1. (b). Each feature has a single value during 500 ms; thus, each feature's length has become unified. Therefore, we mitigated a different period of each feature by applying the timestamp pooling.

Throughout two feature engineering processes, we transformed raw log data into the trainable feature vector. The feature vectors have the same scope of

Table 4. Features used in the analysis

Category	Feature name	Description
Location	Latitude	A value of latitude from the virtual GPS system
	Longitude	A value of longitude from the virtual GPS system
	Altitude	A value of altitude from the virtual GPS system
	EPH	A hotizontal dilution of the position at the virtual GPS system
	EPV	A vertical dilution of the position at the virtual GPS system
	Velocity	A ground speed at the virtual GPS system
	Course Over Ground	A direction of the movement recorded in the angular degree
Position & Orientation	Local Position (x,y,z)	Local position of the UAV in the local coordinate frame along with the axis x,y,z, respectively
	Ground Speed X	Ground X speed toward the latitude, positive north
	Ground Speed Y	Ground Y speed toward the longitude, positive east
	Ground Speed Z	Ground Z speed toward the altitude, positive down
	Roll	A roll angle
	Pitch	A pitch angle
	Yaw	A yaw angle
	Roll Speed	An angular speed at the roll
	Pitch Speed	An angular speed at the pitch
	Yaw Speed	An angular speed at the speed
	Relative Altitude	An altitude above the home position
	Local Altitude	An altitude in the local coordinate frame
	Quaternion (1,2,3,4)	Quaternion component of w,x,y,z, respectively
IMUs	Acceleration (x,y,z)	An acceleration at axis x,y,z, respectively
	Angular speed (x,y,z)	An angular speed around axis x,y,z, respectively
	Magnetic field (x,y,z)	A value of magnetic field at at axis x,y,z, respectively
	Absolute pressure	An absolute pressure at the UAV
	Pressure altitude	A value of the altitude calculated from the pressure
System status	Temperature	A temperature of the battery
	Air speed	Current indicated airspeed
	Heading	Current heading in a compass units scaled in 0 to 360
	Throttle	Current setting of the throttle scaled in 0 to 100
	Climb rate	Current level of the climb rate

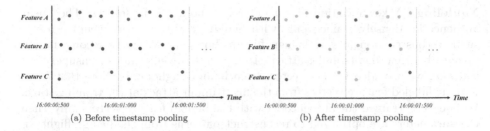

(a) Before timestamp pooling   (b) After timestamp pooling

Fig. 1. Timestamp pooling

scale and the same length; thus, we analyzed deep neural networks based model can effectively learn the pattern of the UAV.

3.4 Unsupervised Intrusion Detection Model

Our key intuition of the intrusion detection model is training the autoencoder to learn the dynamics of benign flights only. Then, the autoencoder trained only with benign patterns generates a low reconstruction loss toward the benign flight and high reconstruction loss with the flight under attack.

Autoencoder. The autoencoder is a deep neural network which learns the representation of feature vectors by iterating an encoding phase and a decoding phase. The encoder optimizes its parameters to find effective representations of feature vectors while the decoder optimizes its parameters to reconstruct the original input vector from the created representation [11]. A loss function of the autoencoder is defined as the difference between the original input vector and the reconstructed input vector. The autoencoder optimizes its parameters to minimize the loss; thus, a well-trained autoencoder reconstructs the input vector without much loss. In this study, we employed a linear autoencoder in which the encoder and the decoder are designed with linear neurons, and the activation function as ReLU function [1]. For a clear elaboration of the model, we described a single layer of the encoder, single layer of the decoder, reconstruction loss (loss function), and the objective function at (2), (3), (4), and (5), respectively.

$$Encoder : e(x) = ReLU(W_{enc}x + b_{enc}) \tag{2}$$

$$Decoder : d(r) = ReLU(W_{dec}r + b_{dec}) \tag{3}$$

$$Loss : L(x, y) = ||f_\theta(x) - y||^2 where f_\theta(x) = d^n(e^n(x)) \tag{4}$$

$$\theta^* = argmin_\theta(\sum_{x \in D} L(x, y)) \tag{5}$$

Modeling. A key intuition of our detection models is as follows: The linear autoencoder densely trained only with benign feature vectors would produce small reconstruction loss at benign flights, but generate large reconstruction loss at abnormal flights under attack. To leverage the efficiency of unsupervised learning, we provided feature vectors from benign flights only. Note that there were no labeled feature vectors from the flight under attack at the training stage. We 'densely' trained the autoencoder with the benign feature vectors only, then the parameters are optimized to reconstruct patterns from the benign flight. In other words, a well-trained autoencoder reconstructs benign feature vectors without much loss. On the other hand, the trained autoencoder will produce larger reconstruction loss with feature vectors under attack. As the autoencoder did not learn patterns of the attack, parameters are not optimized to feature vectors under attack; thus, the model produces a large reconstruction loss. Following the aforementioned intuition, we inferred the difference in reconstruction loss could be utilized to recognize the intrusion. If the data point from a particular time window records a large reconstruction loss, we can identify the existence of intrusion. Along with the experiments described in a further Section, we proved the trained autoencoder generates small reconstruction loss with benign feature vectors while it produces large reconstruction loss at feature vectors under attack.

4   Experiment

Our experiment's objective is to validate whether the proposed methodology effectively recognizes the intrusion from the benign flight. Throughout the experiment, we aimed to validate two key takeaway. First, we checked whether the trained model provides a larger reconstruction loss during the flight under attack rather than the benign flight. Second, we explored the difference between reconstruction losses from both the benign flight and the flight under attack. The following contents describe how we configured the experiment, and the experiment results showed the proposed model can be utilized to detect intrusion on the UAV.

4.1   Setup

We leveraged three log data (benign flight, DoS attack, and GPS Spoofing attack) from the dataset. As our approach highlights the advantage of unsupervised learning, we configured the training set only with the feature vectors from the benign flight. On the other hand, we configured two test sets from the DoS attack log data and GPS Spoofing log data. We randomly selected a particular timestamp as a starting point for the test set configuration, where the chosen timestamp is located before the attack. From this starting point, we extracted every log data until the attack ends. In this way, we configured the test set to include patterns from both benign status and the status under attack. In other words, two test sets - DoS attack and GPS Spoofing attack - have patterns from the benign status and the status under attack at the same time. After we set the training set and the test set, we applied the aforementioned feature engineering process. Note that we scaled features in the test set with the scaler used in the training set.

4.2   Experiment Result

We trained a linear autoencoder with the training set, which is composed of the benign feature vectors only. To fit benign patterns into the model, we leveraged several techniques toward the model training. A batch normalization is applied toward the encoder and the decoder. We utilized both L1 regularizer [15] and L2 regularizer [6] to evade an overfitting problem, and parameters are optimized with Adam optimizer for an effective model training. After the model is fully trained, we provided two test sets to the model and collected reconstruction losses. The experiment results from the test of DoS attack, and the GPS Spoofing attack is described in Fig. 2 and Fig. 3.

Figure 2 explains the first takeaway of our experiment. The blue part of the figure implies a reconstruction loss under the benign status, and the red part of the figure stands for the loss under attack. We figured out the reconstruction losses excessively rise when the flight is under attack at both DoS attack and the GPS Spoofing attack. The reconstruction loss increases in a large amount when the feature vector from the flight under attack is provided—furthermore, Fig. 3 shows the second takeaway of the experiment is also valid. Figure 3 illustrates a distribution of reconstruction losses at both benign status and the status under attack. The reconstruction loss distributes such far from the benign status at both DoS attack and GPS Spoofing attack. A significant difference implies a large difference in a pattern; thus, we discovered our model effectively learned the dynamics of benign patterns and recognized any abnormal patterns on the UAV. Despite a significant performance of our model, however, we figured out a room for improvement with the consideration of real-world deployment. Detailed contents are elaborated in the following section.

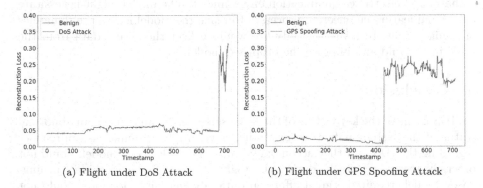

(a) Flight under DoS Attack   (b) Flight under GPS Spoofing Attack

Fig. 2. Experiment result at two simulated flights: a flight under DoS attack and the flight under GPS spoofing attack

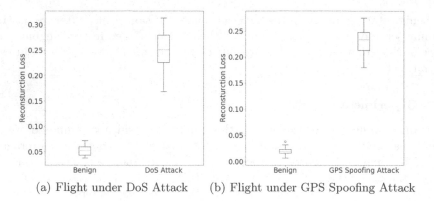

(a) Flight under DoS Attack   (b) Flight under GPS Spoofing Attack

Fig. 3. Reconstruction losses at both normal status and intruded status

5   Discussions

Computation Overhead. First, future studies can consider the computation overhead of the proposed model. Although our model produced a precise intrusion detection result, it should accompany small computing resources. Under the heavy computation overhead, the model cannot be deployed into individual UAVs as the computing environment of the UAVs is not sufficient. If the model requires substantial computing resources, it can be transformed into a lightweight. We expect future studies to reduce the computation overhead by minimizing the size of feature vectors or applying model compression techniques [4] into the proposed model.

Model Improvement in the Wild. The model shall be improved with the actual flight data. As our model is trained and validated with a simulated dataset, log data would have fewer noises rather than the actual data. We expect an actual flight would be interfered with by various factors such as sensor errors, climate, and electric communication environment. The model might necessitate additional feature engineering processes to make the model learns the dynamics of benign flight. In a future study, we would collect the actual data from the UAV in the wild and improve the proposed model.

6   Conclusion

An IDS is one of the key factors of the UAV safety, as it can identify an abnormal status of the system at first. Prior studies have proposed numerous approaches regarding the IDS, but they accompany limits. The rule-based models could not precisely recognize attacks during the flight. Moreover, the machine learning-based models required a great effort on data labeling, and the model could not recognize the attack which was not trained. These limits were a room for the improvement to build a practical IDS on the UAV.

We presented a novel IDS on the UAV to improve the limits of previous studies. Our study proposed an IDS leveraging an autoencoder, a deep neural network of unsupervised learning. Throughout the study, we presented a series of analyses to extract features from the raw UAV flight data. Furthermore, we trained the model only with the benign flight data and validated the model effectively recognize DoS attacks and GPS Spoofing attack though these patterns are not trained. Our model with the unsupervised learning provided two advantages. First, the model does not necessitate a heavy effort on data labeling. Second, our model can identify attacks during the flight, although the model did not learn the dynamics of the flight under attack. We expect our study can be a concrete base in the pursuit of safe utilization of UAVs in the real world.

Acknowledgement. This work was supported by Institute of Information & communications Technology Planning & Evaluation (IITP) grant funded by the Korea government (MSIT) (No.2018-0-00232, Cloud-based IoT Threat Autonomic Analysis and Response Technology).

References

1. Agarap, A.F.: Deep learning using rectified linear units (relu) (2018). arXiv preprint arXiv:1803.08375
2. Arthur, M.P.: Detecting signal spoofing and jamming attacks in UAV networks using a lightweight ids. In: 2019 International Conference on Computer, Information and Telecommunication Systems (CITS), pp. 1–5. IEEE (2019)
3. Biermann, E., Cloete, E., Venter, L.M.: A comparison of intrusion detection systems. Comput. Secur. **20**(8), 676–683 (2001)
4. Cheng, Y., Wang, D., Zhou, P., Zhang, T.: A survey of model compression and acceleration for deep neural networks (2017). arXiv preprint arXiv:1710.09282
5. Choudhary, G., Sharma, V., You, I., Yim, K., Chen, R., Cho, J.H.: Intrusion detection systems for networked unmanned aerial vehicles: a survey. In: 2018 14th International Wireless Communications & Mobile Computing Conference (IWCMC), pp. 560–565. IEEE (2018)
6. Cortes, C., Mohri, M., Rostamizadeh, A.: L2 regularization for learning kernels (2012). arXiv preprint arXiv:1205.2653
7. El-Khatib, J.W.T.S.O.M.A.A.K.: Hitl UAV dos & gps spoofing attacks (mavlink) (2020). https://doi.org/10.21227/00dg-0d12
8. Mitchell, R., Chen, R.: Adaptive intrusion detection of malicious unmanned air vehicles using behavior rule specifications. IEEE Trans. Syst. Man Cybern. Syst. **44**(5), 593–604 (2013)
9. Pajares, G.: Overview and current status of remote sensing applications based on unmanned aerial vehicles (uavs). Photogram. Eng. Remote Sens. **81**(4), 281–330 (2015)
10. Panice, G., et al.: A SVM-based detection approach for GPS spoofing attacks to UAV. In: 2017 23rd International Conference on Automation and Computing (ICAC), pp. 1–11. IEEE (2017)
11. Schmidhuber, J.: Deep learning in neural networks: an overview. Neural Netw. **61**, 85–117 (2015)

12. Sedjelmaci, H., Senouci, S.M., Ansari, N.: A hierarchical detection and response system to enhance security against lethal cyber-attacks in UAV networks. IEEE Trans. Syst. Man Cybern. Syst. **48**(9), 1594–1606 (2017)
13. Tan, X., Su, S., Zuo, Z., Guo, X., Sun, X.: Intrusion detection of UAVs based on the deep belief network optimized by PSO. Sensors **19**(24), 5529 (2019)
14. Zhang, R., Condomines, J.P., Chemali, R., Larrieu, N.: Network intrusion detection system for drone fleet using both spectral analysis and robust controller/observer (2018)
15. Zou, H., Hastie, T.: Regularization and variable selection via the elastic net. J. R. Stat. Soc. Series B (statistical methodology) **67**(2), 301–320 (2005)

Entropy-Based Feature Grouping in Machine Learning for Android Malware Classification

Hyunseok Shim[1] and Souhwan Jung[2]

[1] Department of Information and Communication Convergence, Soongsil University, Seoul, South Korea
ant_tree@naver.com
[2] School of Electronic Engineering, Soongsil University, Seoul, South Korea
souhwanj@ssu.ac.kr

Abstract. In this paper, we have developed a tool to perform an analysis for all APIs over an APK and all APIs of every version of Android, to solve problems of overfitting in machine-learning-based malware classification. The tool is Java-based software consisting of approximately 2,000 lines, performing frequency analysis for the entire API or performing frequency analysis based on the decompiled APK. For frequency analysis, we split all API signatures into word units and grouped them according to their entropy, which is calculated by the number of the emergence of each unit words. As a result, the tool reduces 39,031 methods to 4,972 groups and 12,123 groups when including classes. This shows an approximately 69% feature reduction rate. For classification using machine learning, 14,290 APKs from 14 different categories are collected and trained with 10,003 APKs and tested with 4,287 APKs among them. As a result, we got 98.83% of true positive rate and 1.16% of false positive rate on average, with 98.8% of F-measure score.

Keywords: Feature grouping · Feature manipulation · Machine learning · Android · Android malware · Classification

1 Introduction

The most widely used OS for smartphones and tablets in recent years is Android, which takes part for 76% of mobile OS in 2019 [1]. And many experts expect the continuous growth of the Android platform in market share until 2023 [2]. Despite

This work was supported by Institute of Information & communications Technology Planning & Evaluation (IITP) grant funded by the Korea government(MSIT) (No. 2019-0-00477, Development of android security framework technology using virtualized trusted execution environment) and this work was supported by Institute of Information & communications Technology Planning & Evaluation (IITP) grant funded by the Korea government(MSIT) (No.2020-0-00952, Development of 5G Edge Security Technology for Ensuring 5G+ Service Stability and Availability).

© Springer Nature Switzerland AG 2020
I. You (Ed.): WISA 2020, LNCS 12583, pp. 59–72, 2020.
https://doi.org/10.1007/978-3-030-65299-9_5

the market share of Android OS, vulnerabilities are widespread across most categories of application [3]. According to threat report from NOKIA, Android malware samples are keep increasing since 2012 until 2019, and increased approximately 30% and more compare to previous year [4]. For Android malware, it is difficult to analyze due to the complicated source code structure and an enormous amount of resources. In order to analyze android malware, a number of researches are conducted and the major two methods are static analysis and dynamic analysis. While dynamic analysis is mainly based on ART environment, the static analysis aims to analyze without executing the APK. Most of the static analysis methods are based on op-code, manifest file, and API calls, and nowadays researches are based on machine learning and deep learning. To leverage machine learning for static analysis, the feature set is one of the most important parts. Previous researches using machine learning and deep learning already discovered that too many or too small numbers of features could be a problem [5]. If we use too many features, it tends to cause overfitting to training data, which cannot deal with new types of data [6]. And if we use too small feature set, it tends to cause underfitting, which cannot be trained as intended [7]. To address these problems, previous researches [8–10] suggested methods such as feature reduction or normalization. These methods can be used for specific categories of classification, yet inappropriate for Android malware analysis, or even purge general features. In this paper, we present the feature selection and grouping method for Android malware classification. This method divides each Android API name into unit words and groups each unit word based on entropy. This allows all APIs within APK to be considered without generating all APIs to feature set. Finally, we evaluated our approach using 14,290 APKs from 14 categories of malware, 10,003 APKs for training, and 4,287 APKs for testing. In summary, our paper makes the following contribution:

- Analyze APIs used within Android and identified their problems.
- Analyze the feature set for Android malware categorization and its limitations in the previous study.
- Proposal of a new feature manipulation method that can consider all APIs in Android platform for malware classification.
- Results of a machine learning-based categorization to evaluate the performance of the methods presented.

The rest of the paper is organized as follows. The next section shows the motivating example of this work. In Sect. 3, we describe our design. Section 4 presents the method and approaches for our work. In Sect. 5, we evaluate the effectiveness of the feature grouping method proposed in this paper. Finally, Sect. 6 shows the conclusions obtained by the experiment and discuss limitation with future work to be carried out.

2 Motivation

2.1 Android API Version

Android provides software development kits (SDKs) for each version, and developers can designate development environments by using them. Moreover, the Android platform manages code such as the version of user applications and version of the system itself SDK through API level. Since 2008, Android releases total of 29 versions from Android versions 1 to 29. Android releases about three versions per year on average, showing rapid development and distribution trends. These characteristics also affect the development environment and user experience. For example, for each version, they change, add, and deprecate several APIs. As consequence, it leads to a security policy change or restrain existing functions.

Table 1 shows changes in the number of classes and methods of each API level. This covered only changes from API level 14, with an average of 82 classes added, five classes deprecated, 795 methods added, and 30 deprecated. Compare to the total 39,031 numbers of APIs, and these changes may seem small. However, when we consider a specific API version only, we may miss some of the important APIs that are changed. For example, if we target API levels with version code N, we may consider the newly added APIs before version code O, which are 8,351 numbers of APIs. However, since version code O, 2,785 methods are newly added, and they will be ignored for the target API level. On the other hand, it is also inappropriate to target the newest version of API, due to deprecated or deleted APIs during the update. Therefore, it is inappropriate to analyze the Android APK based on a specific version, and we should consider total APIs through versions to take differences into account.

Table 1. Android API changes in number.

Version Code	Class		Method	
	Added	Deleted	Added	Deleted
I (API level 14 - 15)	87	2	641	23
J (API level 16 - 18)	134	6	1,561	100
K (API level 19 - 20)	107	0	836	26
L (API level 21 - 22)	246	21	2,532	76
M (API level 23)	130	7	36	93
N (API level 24 - 25)	200	24	2,745	38
O (API level 26 - 27)	243	10	2,785	63
Total	1,147	70	11,136	419

2.2 Feature Selection

Previously, many researches were conducted to create a feature through data such as permission and version codes within AndroidManifest.xml as well as API [11, 12]. However, these researches target only certain API levels and did not consider changes from earlier or later versions' APIs, making it difficult to consider the characteristics of all versions of APK. In addition, it was found that the false-negative rate was high that it reached over 17.3% when considering API only without manipulate the features.

On the other hand, among existing researches, we were able to find researches that generate features from API and permission and manipulates for better performance [13, 14]. They generate a feature set and then manually analyze it to select specific features, which are not guaranteed to consider all API characteristics. These researches also considered only certain functions and their APIs, and cannot respond if malicious apps with different behaviors emerge or if the signature of those APIs changes. In addition, there is research that takes a similar approach with this paper [15], which split the list of permissions and APIs used in APK to a list of unit words and manipulated the feature. However, this research has the same limitation as previous researches due to criteria to select the main unit word that was chosen empirically.

3 Related Works

Previously, many works focused on detecting or classifying Android malware based on machine learning or deep learning [16–18]. As proposed in those works, in order to apply machine learning and deep learning on purpose, the popular way to generate feature is using signatures and permissions. However, the Android platform provides over 39,000 numbers of APIs currently, so considering all those APIs as a feature is way too huge, so other works tried to reduce the feature set [15, 19, 20].

The feature selection method is one of the most commonly used methods for feature reduction in the area of Android malware detection or classification. Although most of these methods have their own way of selection such as ranking APIs used primarily in training data, it has not been proven whether the criteria for selection is correct. While training the model, those feature selection method may exclude some of APIs that are used less frequently, but decisive API to detect or classify the Android malware.

4 System Design

To automatically group the features and perform the Android malware classification, we design the system, as shown in Fig. 1. Architecture is mainly divided into two parts, one for the preprocessing part and the other is the machine learning part. In the preprocessing part, the system requires a full API list of every version and categorized APK data to train the model. From the API list collected, we split each API's signature and store them as a form of unit word array. As each API's signature has been split into words, we can calculate the frequency of each word for every word array of every APIs. This step is called the frequency analysis step, and in this step, we choose the root word for API that is most unpopular (has the smallest frequency) in the word frequency map. In the end, we obtain mapping between API and its root word.

Meanwhile, categorized APKs will be decompiled, and APIs used in each APK will be collected individually. For those collected APIs, we match each API to API - root word map, and the APIs will be converted into root word with frequency. This is API – root word matching step, and the final result of this step is grouped feature data set, which will be the training data for our classifier.

After generating the feature data set from the preprocessing step, the next part will perform machine learning against collected training data. For all the data collected, we will test with different machine learning algorithms and compare the result with each other.

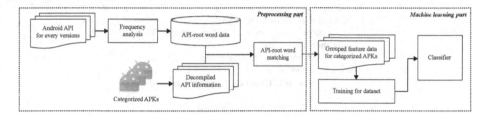

Fig. 1. Overall system design (analysis pipeline)

5   Feature Generation and Grouping

5.1   Feature Map Generation

For feature map generation, we collected all the APIs of each version from 1 to 29. Based on the list of APIs, we generated the feature map, which is consists of the root word and corresponding APIs. All features are mainly based on the feature map and will be collected for all the target APKs. Figure 2 presents the algorithm to generate a feature map.

The algorithm is consists of 3 steps, and the final output is the feature map of all APIs. The first step is about splitting the API signature into word array to obtain a word map. For all the APIs, the method name will be split into word array by regular expression. By the code convention of JAVA, Android's method name follows the camel case. For this reason, it is possible to get the array of unit words by splitting with capital letters. For example, *numberToCalledPartyBCD* from *android.telephony.PhoneNumberUtils* has 5 unit words, which are {number, to, called, party, BCD}. In this case, BCD should be treated as 1 unit word. In order to satisfy this condition, regular expression with pattern

ALGORITHM 1. Generate feature map
Define :
FM = {API, rootWord} //Feature Map
WM = {rootWord, frequency} //Word Map
Ensure :
apiList avoids duplicate

```
1     function generateFeatureMap
2         apiList = {Version, Signature}
3         for all api ∈ apiList do
4             wordArray = splitWordMap(api)
5             frequencyMap = {word, frequency}
              = calculateFrequency(wordArray, frequencyMap)
6             add frequencyMap to wordMap
7         for all api ∈ apiList do
8             add {api, getRootWord(api, frequencyMap)} to featureMap


10    function splitWordMap(apiSignature)
11        wordArray = split method name with discontinuous capital letter
12        return wordArray
                      ⇒ Step 1: Split signature to word array


13    function calculateFrequency(wordArray, frequencyMap)
14        for all word ∈ wordArray do
15            if word in frequencyMap then
16                replace {word, frequency+1} to frequencyMap
17            else then
18                add {word, 1} to frequencyMap
19        return frequencyMap
                      ⇒ Step 2: Generate frequency map of words


20    function getRootWord(api, frequencyMap)
21        wordArray = splitWordMap(api)
22        for all word ∈ wordArray do
23            frequency = get frequency from frequencyMap
24            if frequency is lower than current rootWord frequency then
25                rootWord = word
          return rootWord
                      ⇒ Step 3: Get root word from API
```

Fig. 2. Algorithm for feature map generation

```
(?<!(^|A-Z]))(?=[A-Z])|(?<!^)(?=[A-Z][a-z])
```

will be used so that we can consider the unit word with continuous capital letters.

The second step is calculating the frequency and generate a word map of words. In this step, we gather all the unit word array of signature from step 1, and accumulate the frequency by counting the emerge of each word. It is slightly different from the feature map, and the feature map will be generated with a frequency map. The frequency map provides information on the popularity of each API.

In the final step, we get the root word from each API and store it in the form of a map. We call this map the feature map. This step is performed after the second step is completely over.

From the frequency map and word array of each API, the root word will be selected with the most unpopular word from the word map. This is due to information gain and entropy, that when a low-probability event occurs, the event carries more information than when the data source produces a high-probability value.

As the final step is over, we obtain the feature map that can reproduce the API signature into a single word. And by the nature that we generate the features with the unit word in lowest probability, generated features will have maximum information with grouped root words. With this feature map, we were able to group 39,031 APIs from all versions into 5,086 numbers of root words.

5.2   Feature Grouping

The feature grouping step is much more simple than the feature generation step. Firstly, for all the target APKs collected, we decompile them to get an API usage map over all the APIs. For 39,031 numbers of total APIs, each API with a number of emergences will be counted. And for the APIs that do not exist will be counted as zero. This will be the initial feature set, and will be manipulated.

For manipulation, we use a feature map generated from the previous step. Each of API that emerged more than once will be recalculated according to a feature map. Fig 3 depicts this process. Finally, to avoid the situation that same method names from the different classes to be treated as one, we added the part of the class name to distinguish each. As we added the part of the class name to the duplicated method names, we obtained a feature set with 12,123 numbers of features, which is 69% smaller than the original.

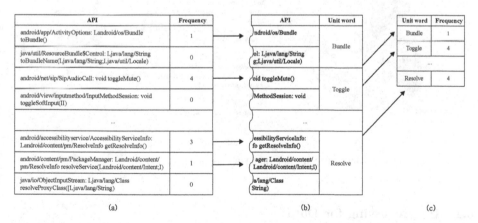

(a)   (b)   (c)

Fig. 3. Procedure of converting API frequency map into root word frequency map. (a) shows API frequency map, which is from a single APK and used to be the initial feature for machine learning. (b) the table is API – root word relationship map that groups API to root word. (c) According to API – root word map, API can be grouped as root word – frequency relationship map

5.3   APK Decompile and Preprocessing as Data

To collect the API from APK, firstly, we have to decompile the APK. There are several existing tools for APK decompiling, such as APKTool [21], AmanDroid [22]. To take advantage of modification, we decided to utilize Soot [23], analyze, and optimization framework for Java. Soot supports the function to convert bytecode of APK into Java-readable data so that we can read and manipulate as we intend. For these reasons, our tool is built on top of the Soot framework.

For further analysis, our tool outputs the decompiled result as a form of Json and store it. After we decompile all the given APKs, we read all the results again and analyze them. Before this step, we already have an API – root word map for all versions of API. Therefore we match all the APIs declared in each APK and reproduce them as a frequency of root word. Final results will be stored as CSV format, which is one of the input formats for WEKA [24] library.

6   Evaluation

For evaluation, we collected 14,290 numbers of each different 14 categories. Source of APK is AMD dataset [25], which contains 24,553 samples. As training data should be enough and bigger the better [26], among the samples, we selected the categories with more than 100 APKs. Each portion for categories is depicted as Fig 4.

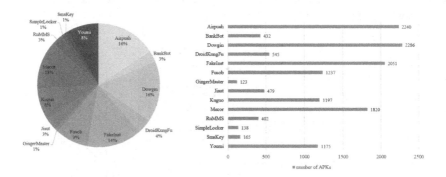

Fig. 4. Number of APKs for each category

6.1   Preprocessing for Data

Before using a machine learning algorithm for building a classifier, we have to process the original API call data into a form grouped feature dataset. As mentioned in Sect. 4, we applied the entropy rule to get the dataset with the highest information value. Meanwhile, we had to prove that this entropy-based feature grouping has the best performance than other strategies, such as reverse-entropy that arrange the word map from the highest frequency and group the feature from it. Therefore we decided to process the data into three different types, ORI, ENT and RENT, which represent original, entropy-based, and reverse-entropy-based grouped features, respectively. Original here means the feature produced from 39,031 numbers of APIs with its frequency. As the ORI type feature set has too huge dimension, we visualized grouped feature sets, and the results of each strategy are depicted as Fig 5. As we can see from the visualized results of each strategy, ENT data seems much more diverse than RENT data. RENT data is biased to some or one of the root words, and some data has high value regardless of category. When we choose a root word for each APIs, some of the words that have high frequency will group almost all the APIs, and in the end, it will produce API - root word map with small diversity.

Fig. 5. (Left) Visualization of entropy-based grouped features in average value, (Right) Visualization of reverse-entropy-based grouped features in average value.

6.2   Machine Learning for Classification

After we refine the data, we applied machine learning for all categories. Among 14,290 samples, only 70% of samples are used as training data. Training data is randomly selected, and the rest of the data, which takes 30% of total samples are used as test data. Therefore, as we mentioned in the previous section, we trained and tested using four algorithms and compared the results. To compare the result, we mainly focused on the F-measure score with true/false positive rates. One of the objectives that we aimed for is reducing the false positive rates. In addition, after we test with all 4 algorithms, we will visualize the result with the algorithm that has the highest performance and analyze based on it.

Table 2. Classification results for 4 algorithms with ORI, ENT and RENT type features.

Feature type	Algorithm	TP rate	FP rate	F-measure
ORI	RandomForest	98.68%	1.32%	98.7%
	J48	98.58%	1.41%	98.6%
	SMO	98.76%	1.23%	98.8%
	NaiveBayes	89.69%	10.31%	89.8%
ENT	RandomForest	98.16%	1.84%	98.1%
	J48	97.53%	2.47%	97.5%
	SMO	98.83%	1.16%	98.8%
	NaiveBayes	93.33%	6.67%	93.3%
RENT	RandomForest	97.08%	2.92%	97.0%
	J48	96.20%	3.80%	96.2%
	SMO	97.60%	2.40%	97.6%
	NaiveBayes	90.39%	9.61%	90.7%

For 4 algorithm, the results of each are shown in Table 2. While training the model, it took about 136.34, 224.63, 112.41, 15.11 s, respectively, for Random forest, J48, SMO, NaiveBayes. In this case, NaiveBayes seems much effective in the aspect of speed, however, it took 138.81 s for testing while the other's average testing time was only 6.44 s. According to the results in Table 2, as we expected, ENT type is higher in accuracy than the RENT type for every algorithm. This is because, ENT type has more diversity in RENT type, while RENT type has been biased to some of the root words. In other words, the ENT type has more diversity and rich of information.

When comparing ENT type result with ORI type result, even though the number of features has been reduced to 31%, overall accuracy has not been decreased much. For the ORI type feature set, about 0.52% and 1.05% of TP rate have been increased, and only an average 0.85% of F-measure has been increased for tree-based algorithms. And for SMO, it is slightly lower or the same for all the metrics we decided. Moreover, for bayes type algorithms such as NaiveBayes, accuracy decreased, and the false positive rate increased by 3.64%. Due to the dataset to train the model, which is consists of 39,031 columns with 10,003 rows, it took about four times longer to train the model. For these reasons, we can see that feature grouping contributes to overall performance.

Among the results of each algorithm, There are differences in accuracy and false positive rates. For our dataset, each algorithm showed a higher true positive rate has a lower false positive rate. For example, the Random forest and J48 algorithm are ranked as 2nd and 3rd in performance. And as Random forest is higher in true positive rate than J48 algorithm, Random forest shows a lower false positive rate than J48. The algorithm that showed the highest accuracy with the lowest false rate is SMO, which has 98.83% of true positive rate with 1.16% of the false positive rate, and 98.8% of the F-measure score. In contrast, the NaiveBayes algorithm showed the worst performance with the highest false rates. It showed over 6.67% of false positive rate with 93.33% of the true-positive rate.

Finally, as we confirmed that SMO is best in performance, we visualized our results of classification done by SMO (See Fig 6). In addition, SMO showed the highest performance in RENT type either, we visualized the result of RENT type. Both with ENT type and RENT type showed a massive false rate in RuMMS, which is consists of 402 numbers of APKs. Our trained model confuses

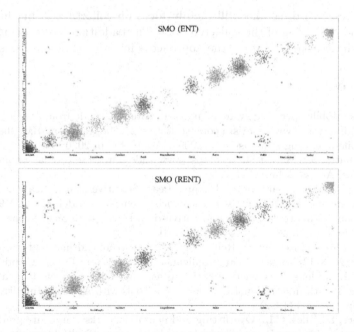

Fig. 6. (Left) SMO classification result with ENT(Entropy) based grouped feature (Bottom) SMO classification result with RENT(Reverse-Entropy) based grouped feature

RuMMS category APKs with BankBot category APKs. In fact, the RuMMS category showed 80.3% of true positive rate, which is the worst performance of all categories. Since RuMMS has similar characteristics with BankBot, they both have a small number of the dataset. Therefore, when a larger dataset is available, we can expect better performance.

7   Conclusion

In this paper, we propose a new feature grouping method for the machine learning approach of Android malware classification. In our approach, we first collected all the APIs of Android and generate the API – root word map to group the API into smaller groups. After generating a map, we match the APIs of target APKs to convert the APIs into grouped features, and performed machine learning-based classification and achieved 98.8% of F-measure score with 1.16% of false positive rate.

Until now, this approach can only be applied to Android malware classification. However when we can collect the samples from other frameworks such as Spring or other Java-based frameworks, it is possible to apply on them either. Moreover, even though there are a lot more categories or family to distinguish Android malware, but it is hard work to get a dataset according to them. In order to consider wider categories into our system, it is necessary to collect plenty of data.

Future research directions will mainly focus on collecting as much data as possible and processing of the collected data. Then additional processing will be performed if necessary, to apply the approaches introduced on our paper.

References

1. Statista, Mobile operating systems' market share worldwide from January 2012 to July 2019. https://www.statista.com/statistics/272698/global-market-share-held-by-mobile-operating-systems-since-2009/. Accessed Jan 2020
2. IDC, Smartphone Market Share. https://www.idc.com/promo/smartphone-market-share/os. Accessed Jan 2020
3. Forbes, Many Popular Android Apps Leak Sensitive Data, Leaving Millions Of Consumers At Risk https://www.forbes.com/sites/ajdellinger/2019/06/07/many-popular-android-apps-leak-sensitive-data-leaving-millions-of-consumers-at-risk/#69643a7b521e. Accessed Jan 2020
4. Nokia, Threat Intelligence Report 2019. https://blog.drhack.net/wp-content/uploads/2018/12/Nokia_Threat_Intelligence_Report_White_Paper_EN.pdf
5. Vafaie, H., De Jong, K.: Genetic algorithms as a tool for feature selection in machine learning. In: 4th International Conference on Tools with Artificial Intelligence TAI 1992, pp. 200–203 (1992)
6. Lawrence, S., Giles, C.L.: Overfitting and neural networks: conjugate gradient and backpropagation. In: Proceedings of the IEEE-INNS-ENNS International Joint Conference on Neural Networks (IJCNN 2000), vol. 1, pp. 114–119 (2000)
7. Goodfellow, I., Bengio, Y., Courville, A.: Deep Learning. MIT Press, Cambridge (2016)

8. Graf, A.B.A., Smola, A.J., Borer, S.: Classification in a normalized feature space using support vector machines. IEEE Trans. Neural Netw. **14**(3), 597–605 (2003)
9. Kolter, J.Z., Ng, A.Y.: Regularization and feature selection in least-squares temporal difference learning. In: 26th Annual International Conference on Machine Learning (ICML 2009), pp. 521–528 (2009)
10. Mukherjee, S., Sharma, N.: Intrusion detection using Naive Bayes classifier with feature reduction. In: 2nd International Conferences on Computer, Communication, Control and Information Technology (C3IT- 2012), pp. 119–128 (2012)
11. Peiravian, N., Zhu, X.: Machine learning for android malware detection using permission and API calls. In: 2013 IEEE 25th International Conference on Tools with Artificial Intelligence, pp. 300–305 (2013)
12. Grace, M., Zhou, Y., Wang, Z., Jiang, X.: Systematic detection of capability leaks in stock android smartphones. In: 19th Network and Distributed System Security Symposium (NDSS), pp. 1–15 (2012)
13. Kim, D., Kim, J., Kim, S.: A malicious application detection framework using automatic feature extraction tool on Android market. In: 3rd International Conference on Computer Science and Information Technology (ICCSIT 2013), pp. 1–4, 2013
14. Yang, M., Wen, Q.Y.: Detecting android malware with intensive feature engineering. In: 2016 7th IEEE International Conference on Software Engineering and Service Science (ICSESS), pp. 157–161 (2016)
15. Ugur, P., Nuray, B., Cengiz, A., Nazife, B.: The analysis of feature selection methods and classification algorithms in permission based Android malware detection. In: 2014 IEEE Symposium on Computational Intelligence in Cyber Security (CICS), pp. 1–8 (2014)
16. Alam, M.S., Vuong, S.T.: Random forest classification for detecting android malware. In: 2013 IEEE International Conference on Green Computing and Communications and IEEE Internet of Things and IEEE Cyber, Physical and Social Computing, pp. 663–669 (2013)
17. Yerima, S.Y., Sezer, S., McWilliams, G., Muttik, I.: A new Android Malware detection approach using Bayesian classification. In: 2013 IEEE 27th International Conference on Advanced Information Networking and Applications (AINA), pp. 121–128 (2013)
18. McLaughlin, N. et al.: Deep android malware detection. In: Proceedings of the Seventh ACM on Conference on Data and Application Security and Privacy, CODASPY 2017, pp. 301–308 (2017)
19. Hyo-Sik H., Mi-Jung, C.: Analysis of android malware detection performance using machine learning classifiers. In: International Conference on ICT Convergence (ICTC), pp. 490–495 (2013)
20. Crussell, J., Gibler, C., Chen, H.: Attack of the clones: detecting cloned applications on android markets. In: Foresti, S., Yung, M., Martinelli, F. (eds.) ESORICS 2012. LNCS, vol. 7459, pp. 37–54. Springer, Heidelberg (2012). https://doi.org/10.1007/978-3-642-33167-1_3
21. Wiśniewski, R., Tumbleson, C.: APKtool (2020). https://ibotpeaches.github.io/Apktool/install/. Accessed Mar 2020
22. Wei, F., et al.: Amandroid: a precise and general inter-component data flow analysis framework for security vetting of android apps. ACM Trans. Priv. Secur. **21**(3), 1–32 (2018)
23. Vallée-Rai, R. et al.: Soot: a java bytecode optimization framework. In: CASCON First Decade High Impact Papers, pp. 214–224 (2010)
24. University of Waikato, Weka3 - Data Mining with Open Source Machine Learning Software in Java. https://www.cs.waikato.ac.nz/ml/weka/. Accessed Mar 2020

25. Wei, F. et al.: Deep ground truth analysis of current android malware. In: International Conference on Detection of Intrusions and Malware, and Vulnerability Assessment (DIMVA 2017), pp. 252–276 (2017)
26. Banko, M., Brill, E.: Scaling to very very large corpora for natural language disambiguation. In: 39th Annual Meeting on Association for Computational Linguistics (ACL 2001), pp. 26–33 (2001)

DLDDO: Deep Learning to Detect Dummy Operations

JongHyeok Lee[1] and Dong-Guk Han[1,2](✉)

[1] Department of Financial Information Security, Kookmin University, Seoul, Korea
{n_seeu,christa}@kookmin.ac.kr
[2] Department of Information Security, Cryptography and Mathematics,
Kookmin University, Seoul, Korea

Abstract. Recently, research on deep learning based side-channel analysis (DLSCA) has received a lot of attention. Deep learning-based profiling methods similar to template attacks as well as non-profiling-based methods similar to differential power analysis have been proposed. DLSCA methods have been proposed for targets to which masking schemes or jitter-based hiding schemes are applied. However, most of them are methods for finding the secret key, except for methods for preprocessing, and there are no studies on the target to which the dummy-based hiding schemes or shuffling schemes are applied. In this paper, we propose a DLSCA for detecting dummy operations. In the previous study, dummy operations were detected using the method called BCDC, but there is a disadvantage in that it is impossible to detect dummy operations for commercial devices such as an IC card. We consider the detection of dummy operations as a multi-label classification problem and propose a deep learning method based on CNN to solve it. As a result, it is possible to successfully perform detection of dummy operations on an IC card, which was not possible in the previous study.

Keywords: Hiding countermeasure · Deep learning · Multi-label classification · IC card · Dummy operation

1 Introduction

Electronic devices such as smart watches, air conditioners, and refrigerators used to perform simple manipulations have recently begun to deal with personal data by providing a variety of features, such as being able to make phone calls by starting to be interconnected. Accordingly, the security of these devices must be carefully considered. Side-Channel Analysis (SCA) is the most representative of potential attacks, and it recovers secret information using physical properties such as power consumption [7] or electromagnetic emissions [1].

This work was supported as part of Military Crypto Research Center (UD170109ED) funded by Defense Acquisition Program Administration (DAPA) and Agency for Defense Development (ADD).

I. You (Ed.): WISA 2020, LNCS 12583, pp. 73–85, 2020.
https://doi.org/10.1007/978-3-030-65299-9_6

Deep learning, which was not under consideration at the beginning of the proposal, has seen rapid progress in recent years due to the advent of big data and the gradual enhancement of computing power over the past decade. Recently, deep learning has been used in various fields such as image recognition, speech recognition, and natural language processing. In side-channel analysis, deep learning will also come to play an important role. Beginning with the case of leakage characterization using multi-layer perceptron (MLP) [19], deep learning-based SCA (DLSCA) was conducted using convolutional neural network (CNN), autoencoder, long short-term memory (LSTM), etc. [14]. Analysis was also performed in the case of using a masking scheme and jitter-based hiding schemes [11]. In addition, a DLSCA method based on non-profiling has been proposed recently [18].

Of the various DLSCA methods that have been studied, the majority have been for the purpose of revealing a secret key. In the end, they mention that they succeeded in analyzing only those targets to which the jitter-based hiding schemes, which have relatively weak strength, were applied. To the best of our knowledge, we haven't seen cases of successful secret key recovery with DLSCA for targets with dummy-based hiding schemes or shuffling scheme. Designers intend to increase attack complexity by simultaneously using the shuffling scheme and the random insertion of dummy operation schemes. For example, if the designer adds up to d dummy operations to n sbox operations and apply the shuffling scheme, $\alpha \times (n+d)^2$ traces are needed to recover a one-byte of secret key. Here, α is the number of traces needed to recover the one-byte secret key when hiding schemes are not applied. However, if the dummy operations are filtered out, the number of required traces is reduced to $\alpha \times n^2$. When $n = d = 16$, the reduction rate is 75%, which is very dangerous. Therefore, even if the secret key cannot be recovered from a target to which the shuffling scheme or dummy-based hiding schemes are applied, there is a need for research on a method of neutralizing them.

Our Contributions. In the previous work [10], they proposed a technique to detect dummy operations using the method BCDC (Bounded Collision Detection Criterion) [4]. However, in order to calculate BCDC values, it is necessary to specify a suitable reference area, which is very empirical. So we were wondering if there is a way to automatically distinguish dummy operations. Research has already been conducted using CNN to detect fake face images, fake news, and fake data transmission [15,16,20]. Inspired by these existing studies, we thought that CNN could be used to detect dummy operations in side-channel traces. In this paper, we propose a method of detecting dummy operations using deep learning. The proposed method can detect dummy operations very well even though it takes different devices for training and testing. In addition, this method can detect dummy operations even for commercial devices such as an IC card, which the previous method could not.

Outline. The rest of this paper is structured as follows. In Sect. 2, Deep Learning and Deep Learning-based Side-Channel attacks are introduced. It also discusses hiding schemes, one of the countermeasures against side-channel attacks. Section 3 covers the previous work and the proposed methodology to detect dummy operations. We describe experiment results performed on an IC card in Sect. 4 along with the experiment setup. Finally, in Sect. 5, we conclude this paper and comment on future research.

2 Preliminaries

2.1 Deep Learning

Deep learning is a type of machine learning and makes computational models consisting of multiple processing layers to learn representations of data with multi-level abstraction [8]. Recent works have shown that deep learning successfully applied to many fields such as image recognition, speech recognition, and natural language processing. In this chapter, we describe deep learning by taking deep learning for data classification as an example. A neural network for data classification is a function $\mathtt{Net} : \mathbb{R}^D \to \mathbb{R}^{|\mathcal{Z}|}$. $\mathtt{Net}$ is trained to classify some data $x \in \mathbb{R}^D$ into their labels $z(x) \in \mathcal{Z}$, where D is the dimension of the data and $\mathcal{Z}$ is the set of labels.

Multilayer Perceptron. A multilayer perceptron (MLP) is a kind of neural network composed of several perceptron layers [2]. A perceptron $\mathtt{P} : \mathbb{R}^D \to \mathbb{R}$ takes $x \in \mathbb{R}^D$ as input and calculates the output as follows:

$$\mathtt{P}(x) = A\left(b + \sum_{i=1}^{D} w_i x_i\right)$$

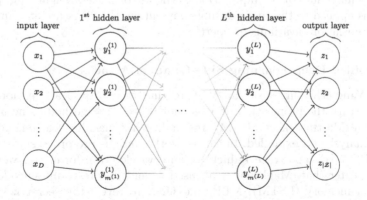

Fig. 1. Multilayer perceptron of a $(L + 1)$-layer perceptron with D input units and $|\mathcal{Z}|$ output units. The lth hidden layer contains $m^{(l)}$ hidden units.

where A is an *activation function*, w_i are *weights*, and b is the *bias*. The activation function serves to determine which neurons are triggered in each layer, and sigmoid function, Rectified Linear function (relu), or Hyperbolic Tangent function (tanh) are typically used.

A MLP is a neural network which is a combination of many perceptron units organized in layers as shown in Fig. 1. A MLP consists of an input layer, intermediate layers called *hidden layers* and an output layer. The weights and biases of the MLP are adjusted as learning progresses.

Convolutional Neural Network. Convolutional Neural Networks (CNN) is a type of neural network composed of a mixture of *Convolutional* layers and *Pooling* layers [9].

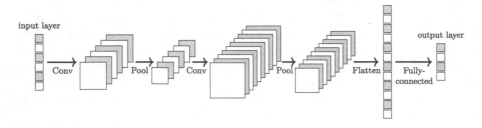

Fig. 2. Convolutional neural networks architecture.

The general structure of CNN is shown in Fig. 2. The CNN architecture is composed of a mixture of convolutional layers and pooling layers, and then fully-connected layers are attached. The convolutional layer slides a set of *filters* to apply a convolution operation to the input. The pooling layers is a nonlinear layer that slides a window over the input and outputs a local summary, such as the average or maximum of the input. Due to the use of shared weights and pooling operations applied to the space during convolution, the CNN architecture has a natural translation-invariance property.

2.2   Profiled Deep Learning Side-Channel Attacks

In 2011, Yang et al. first used an MLP to characterize the leakage model [19]. Beginning with the proposition of a secret key recovery method using a neural network by Martinasek et al. [14], research using machine learning for side-channel analysis has exploded. In earlier works, various pre-processing methods such as PCA, average trace reduction, and wavelet transformation were used [5,13,17]. After that, Maghrebi et al. used a random forest, autoencoder, long short-term memory (LSTM), MLP, and CNN to reveal the secret key of the unprotected or first-order masked AES [11].

While an MLP pays attention to numerical values in traces, a CNN focuses on the shape of traces. Therefore, it is mainly used for image recognition that must be resistant to distortion. Cagli et al. first used a CNN to defeat jitter-based hiding countermeasure [3]. However, as far as we know, no results have been applied to hiding schemes using dummy operations.

2.3 Hiding Schemes

Traditional side-channel analysis methods such as differential power analysis or template attacks are applied to aligned side-channel traces. Attackers must process side-channel traces using pre-processing methods such as domain transformation to improve performance when the traces are not aligned. Hiding schemes are used to artificially disrupt the alignment. Eventually, designers can break the association between intermediate values and side-channel traces. Time-domain de-synchronization and changing the vertical values are typical features of a hiding scheme. When the time-domain de-synchronization is applied, it is difficult for an attacker to identify when the target operations are performed.

Random insertion of dummy operations scheme is the first approach of the time-domain de-synchronization. This approach randomly inserts dummy operations, which are meaningless operations that are not related to encryption and decryption, into the middle of real operations. The second method is a shuffling scheme that randomly reorganizes the order of operations. These two methods make an attacker hard to detect when real operations are being performed.

3 Detection of Dummy Operations

In this section, we describe the previously proposed dummy operation detection method [10] and the method we propose. Since our method is based on profiling-based DLSCA, it explains how to make labels corresponding to profiling traces and the model configuration used.

3.1 Detection of Dummy Operations Using BCDC

In a previous study [10], they used the BCDC value [4] as a reference to detect dummy operations. The BCDC is a measure of similarity between two groups and is defined as follows:

$$BCDC\left(T_1, T_2\right) = \frac{1}{\sqrt{2}} \times \frac{\sigma_{(T_1-T_2)}}{\sigma_{(T_1)}}$$

where T_1 and T_2 denote the reference area and the target area, respectively. $\sigma_{(T_1)}$ is the standard deviation of T_1. If a BCDC value close to zero is calculated, it means that the two groups are similar.

An attacker sets a part of the section as the reference area T_1 to determine whether it is a dummy operation or a real operation. It does not matter if it is actually a dummy or real operation. Then, the BCDC value is calculated by shifting the target area T_2 of the same length as T_1 by one point from the start of the trace. The attacker sequentially acquires the desired number of sections having the lowest value from the calculated BCDC values. The acquired sections may be real operations or dummy operations. If these are dummy operations, the attacker can take the sections that have not been acquired.

3.2 DLDDO

Label. For supervised learning, corresponding labels of an input trace are needed. Models for revealing a secret key used labels as expected values such as outputs of Sbox or its Hamming Weight values. However, the purpose of our model is to determine if this is a real operation or a dummy operation. Moreover, there is not only one operation to judge. Therefore, we use a multi-label classification problem. For example, if the following index of the real operations were performed:

$$[2, 3, 5, 6, 8, 10, 14, 16, 17, 18, 19, 24, 26, 27, 30, 31],$$

we can construct the following 32 labels:

$$[0, 0, 1, 1, 0, 1, 1, 0, 1, 0, 1, 0, 0, 0, 1, 0, 1, 1, 1, 1, 0, 0, 0, 0, 1, 0, 1, 1, 0, 0, 1, 0].$$

Here, 0 means the dummy operation and 1 means the real operation.

Algorithm 1. Generate labels for dummy operation detection

Input: Index of real operations $\mathbf{I} = [i_0, i_1, \ldots, i_{15}]$ where $i_j \in \{0, 1, \ldots, 31\}$
Output: Label $\mathbf{L} = [l_0, l_1, \ldots, l_{31}]$ where $l_j \in \{0, 1\}$
 1: Initialize $\mathbf{L}$ to zero array   ▷ size of $\mathbf{L} = 31$
 2: **for** $j \leftarrow 0$ to 16 **do**
 3:     $\mathbf{L}[\mathbf{I}[j]] = 1$
 4: **return** $\mathbf{L}$

Algorithm 1 describes how to generate labels for dummy operation detection. For each profiling trace, an attacker can generate corresponding labels using Algorithm 1. Although we are going to experiment with the number of dummy operations inserted set at 16 in Sect. 4, even if the number of inserted dummy operations is variable, Algorithm 1 can be used through modification such as setting the value of trailing labels, which are equal to the number of dummy operations not inserted, to 0. If the number of dummy operations inserted is less than the maximum value, we can determine whether the real Sbox operation is performed on side-channel traces corresponding to ShiftRows or MixColumns functions. Therefore, it makes sense to set the label value corresponding to the ShiftRows and MixColumns part of the side-channel trace to 0 because the ShiftRows and MixColumns part of the side-channel trace is not a real Sbox operation, just like a dummy operation from the attacker's perspective.

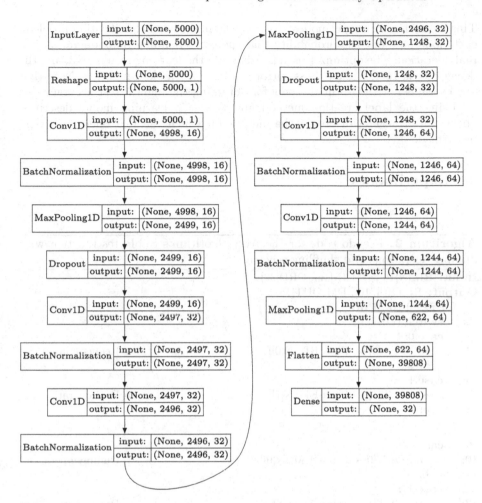

Fig. 3. CNN model for dummy operation detection

Deep Learning Model. We use a CNN model for dummy operation detection due to the possibility of side-channel traces being shaken. Figure 3 shows the full construction process for our model. All convolutional layers use small sized kernels like 2 or 3 with a stride size 1 and "valid" padding. In order to minimize the number of trainable parameters, this model has been constructed by using a lot of convolutional layers and one dense layer. As the activation function, relu and sigmoid functions are used for convolutional layers and the dense layer, respectively. The sigmoid function is used for binary classification and the softmax function is used for multiple classification. In the multi-label classification used in this model, since each label is used for binary classification, the activation function of the output layer is used as the sigmoid function. The dropout ratio is 0.25, and He initializer is used as a kernel initializer in the dense layer.

This model has 32 output nodes. To solve the multi-label classification problem, each node puts out the probability that the corresponding Sbox operation is a real operation. The optimizer used is Adam [6], the learning rate is 1e-3, and the decay rate is 1e-4. Binary cross-entropy is used as the loss function. Note that our model is not the optimal model for obtaining the highest test accuracy.

Using the label creation method and the deep learning model described above, an attacker can obtain the indexes on which the real operations were performed.

4   Experiments

Algorithm 2. Pseudo code for the AES algorithm's SubBytes function with dummy operations and shuffling scheme

---

Input: RL_IN[16], DM_IN[16], ORD[32]
Output: RL_OUT[16], DM_OUT[16]
1: **for** $i \leftarrow 0$ **to** 31 **do**
2:     **switch** (ORD[i])
3:     **case 0:**
4:         RL_OUT[0] $\leftarrow$ Sbox[RL_IN[0]]   ▷ Real operation
5:         break
6:     **case 1:**
7:         RL_OUT[1] $\leftarrow$ Sbox[RL_IN[1]]   ▷ Real operation
8:         break
          ⋮
9:     **case 16:**
10:        DM_OUT[0] $\leftarrow$ Sbox[DM_IN[0]]   ▷ Dummy operation
11:        break
12:    **case 17:**
13:        DM_OUT[1] $\leftarrow$ Sbox[DM_IN[1]]   ▷ Dummy operation
14:        break
          ⋮
15:    **end switch**

In the previous work [10], we classified the implementation method of the hiding scheme using one of four types of dummy operations according to the type of variables used in the dummy operations. We named them local variable, global variable, separate function argument, and combined function argument. We took the target algorithm using the switch-case statement as Algorithm 2. The above four variable types were applied to DM_IN and DM_OUT. In addition, the countermeasure was also presented in the previous paper. This countermeasure is configured to select the variable index of the Sbox operation by referring to the ORD variable in which the shuffled operation order is stored instead of using the switch-case statement as in Algorithm 3.

Algorithm 3. Pseudo code for the countermeasure [10]

Input: IN[32], ORD[32]
Output: OUT[32]
1: **for** $i \leftarrow 0$ to 31 **do**
2:    OUT[ORD[i]] = Sbox[IN[ORD[i]]]

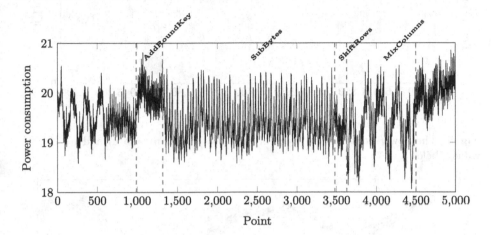

Fig. 4. A power consumption trace of an IC card

The model number of our target IC card is S3FJ9SK which is made by Samsung. The number of dummy operations used is fixed at 16, and four implementation methods are pushed on the smart card. The power consumption trace of the implementation using `local variable` is shown in Fig. 4. The power consumption traces for the other three implementations are similar to Fig. 4. After measuring the trace with 500M sampling, the trace was compressed using 50 units of Raw Integration method [12]. We used two IC cards of the same model to apply to DLDDO, our proposed method. For training the deep learning model, 10,000 traces were collected from the profile card and 1,000 traces were collected from the other card for testing.

4.1 Using BCDC

We attempted to detect dummy operations by setting a portion of the first Sbox operation area as reference area T_1 in the trace in Fig. 4. No matter how much the reference area was changed, dummy operations could not be detected with a high success rate. Figure 5 shows the result of one of the attempts to distinguish dummy operations using BCDC. The above graph is the power consumption trace of the SubBytes function and the graph below is the calculated BCDC trace. For each of the 32 areas, each one is represented by **R** in case of real operations and **D** in case of dummy operations. We set the reference area for calculating BCDC values as part of the first dummy operation and compute the

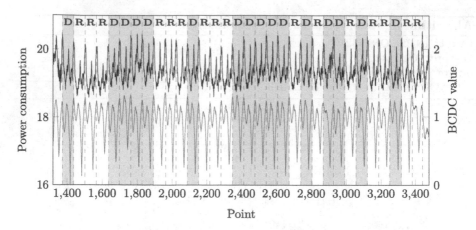

Fig. 5. The power consumption trace of SubBytes function (above) and its BCDC values (below).

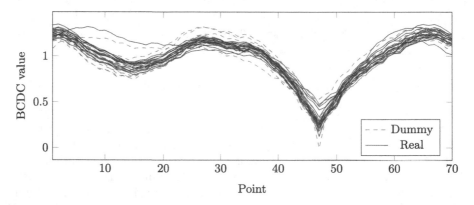

Fig. 6. Blue lines are BCDC traces of real operations and red dashed lines are BCDC traces of dummy operations. (Color figure online)

BCDC trace. We splitted the BCDC trace into each operation, then overlapped the pieces of operation as shown in Fig. 6. However, we cannot set any threshold to distinguish the dummy operations from the real operations. At best, the success rate was only about 50%. The problem of determining whether each Sbox is a real operation or a dummy operation is the same as the problem of choosing the front or back of a coin. Therefore, if the method is not capable of distinguishing dummy operations, the accuracy should be about 50%.

4.2   Using DLDDO

We used a profiling card to train the neural network and a test card to check if we could extract dummy operations from other cards with the trained neural network. Both cards use the same model IC chip. 10,000 power consumption traces were collected from the profiling card, of which 9,000 were used for the training phase and 1,000 were used for the validation phase.

1,000 power consumption traces were collected from the test card. Through the trained neural network, the probabilities that each of the 32 Sbox operations were real operations were calculated. The 16 indexes having the highest probability are judged to be the indexes on which the real operation was performed. For example, the output values of the trained neural network are

$$[0.87, 0.53, 0.96, 0.97, 0.02, 0.89, 0.99, 0.32,$$
$$0.96, 0.20, 0.88, 0.02, 0.35, 0.52, 0.90, 0.19,$$
$$0.99, 0.99, 0.99, 0.91, 0.50, 0.50, 0.29, 0.01,'$$
$$0.96, 0.09, 0.92, 0.94, 0.62, 0.29, 0.99, 0.95]$$

we judge indexes of real operations are

$$[2, 3, 5, 6, 8, 10, 14, 16, 17, 18, 19, 24, 26, 27, 30, 31].$$

Table 1. Test accuracies according to variable types

Variable types	Test accuracy
Local variables	95.4125%
Global variables	82.4375%
Separate function arguments	96.1875%
Combined function arguments	74.4375%
Countermeasure	50.0906%

As a result of estimating the real operation indexes of the test traces with the trained neural networks, the accuracies are shown in Table 1. Using the DLDDO method, we were able to detect dummy operations when targeting dummy operations of power consumption traces collected from the IC card for all four types of variables used for the dummy operations. It has been confirmed that the dummy operations cannot be detected when the countermeasure proposed in the previous paper is still applied.

For the BCDC value to convert to 0, the standard deviation of the point-wise subtraction of the two areas must converge to 0. This means that the two areas are well aligned and there is little variation due to noise. Therefore, in the previous work [10], they succeeded in distinguishing dummy operations using BCDC for the ChipWhisperer-Lite board which has low noise and good alignment. However, the target white card in this paper is noisier and misaligned than the ChipWhisperer-Lite board, and the time during which each operation is performed can vary. It is obvious that it is impossible to distinguish dummy operations of the white card using BCDC for these reasons. On the other hand, our proposed DLDDO uses a convolutional network used in image recognition, making it resistant to alignment and noise issues. The reason DLDDO can do what BCDC cannot do is the same reason CNN does image recognition better than MLP.

5   Conclusion

In this paper, we propose the deep learning method DLDDO for detecting dummy operations. The previous work, which used BCDC to detect dummy operations, has the disadvantage that empirical reference area setting is required. Also, detection of dummy operations was possible only when the noise was relatively small on the side-channel traces. We solved these drawbacks by applying the CNN model and the multi-label classification problem. In addition, it was possible to detect dummy operations even in a situation where a profile device and a test device were used differently.

DLDDO is a supervised learning method for solving multi-label classification problems. As a recent successful case of image classification problem solving through unsupervised learning was proposed, it seems to be applicable to dummy operation detection. We targeted a cryptographic algorithm that was applied by combining a random dummy operation insertion scheme and a shuffling scheme. On this target, we have succeeded in detecting dummy operations, but the shuffling scheme has not been neutralized. There is also a need for research on how to neutralize the shuffling technique using various deep learning algorithms.

References

1. Agrawal, D., Archambeault, B., Rao, J.R., Rohatgi, P.: The EM side—channel(s). In: Kaliski, B.S., Koç, K., Paar, C. (eds.) CHES 2002. LNCS, vol. 2523, pp. 29–45. Springer, Heidelberg (2003). https://doi.org/10.1007/3-540-36400-5_4
2. Bishop, C.M., et al.: Neural Networks for Pattern Recognition. Oxford University Press, Oxford (1995)
3. Cagli, E., Dumas, C., Prouff, E.: Convolutional neural networks with data augmentation against jitter-based countermeasures. In: Fischer, W., Homma, N. (eds.) CHES 2017. LNCS, vol. 10529, pp. 45–68. Springer, Cham (2017). https://doi.org/10.1007/978-3-319-66787-4_3
4. Diop, I., Liardet, P.Y., Linge, Y., Maurine, P.: Collision based attacks in practice. In: 2015 Euromicro Conference on Digital System Design, pp. 367–374. IEEE (2015)
5. Gilmore, R., Hanley, N., O'Neill, M.: Neural network based attack on a masked implementation of AES. In: 2015 IEEE International Symposium on Hardware Oriented Security and Trust (HOST), pp. 106–111. IEEE (2015)
6. Kingma, D.P., Ba, J.: Adam: a method for stochastic optimization. arXiv preprint arXiv:1412.6980 (2014)
7. Kocher, P., Jaffe, J., Jun, B.: Differential power analysis. In: Wiener, M. (ed.) CRYPTO 1999. LNCS, vol. 1666, pp. 388–397. Springer, Heidelberg (1999). https://doi.org/10.1007/3-540-48405-1_25

8. LeCun, Y., Bengio, Y., Hinton, G.: Deep learning. Nature **521**(7553), 436–444 (2015)
9. LeCun, Y., Bengio, Y., et al.: Convolutional networks for images, speech, and time series. Handb. Brain Theory Neural Netw. **3361**(10), 1995 (1995)
10. Lee, J., Han, D.G.: Security analysis on dummy based side-channel countermeasures-case study: AES with dummy and shuffling. Appl. Soft Comput. **93**, 106352 (2020). https://doi.org/10.1016/j.asoc.2020.106352
11. Maghrebi, H., Portigliatti, T., Prouff, E.: Breaking cryptographic implementations using deep learning techniques. In: Carlet, C., Hasan, M.A., Saraswat, V. (eds.) SPACE 2016. LNCS, vol. 10076, pp. 3–26. Springer, Cham (2016). https://doi.org/10.1007/978-3-319-49445-6_1
12. Mangard, S., Oswald, E., Popp, T.: Power Analysis Attacks. Springer, Boston (2007). https://doi.org/10.1007/978-0-387-38162-6
13. Martinasek, Z., Hajny, J., Malina, L.: Optimization of power analysis using neural network. In: Francillon, A., Rohatgi, P. (eds.) CARDIS 2013. LNCS, vol. 8419, pp. 94–107. Springer, Cham (2014). https://doi.org/10.1007/978-3-319-08302-5_7
14. Martinasek, Z., Zeman, V.: Innovative method of the power analysis. Radioengineering **22**(2), 586–594 (2013)
15. Mo, H., Chen, B., Luo, W.: Fake faces identification via convolutional neural network. In: Proceedings of the 6th ACM Workshop on Information Hiding and Multimedia Security, pp. 43–47 (2018)
16. Pan, J., Liu, Y., Zhang, W.: Detection of dummy trajectories using convolutional neural networks. Secur. Commun. Netw. **2019** (2019)
17. Saravanan, P., Kalpana, P., Preethisri, V., Sneha, V.: Power analysis attack using neural networks with wavelet transform as pre-processor. In: 18th International Symposium on VLSI Design and Test, pp. 1–6. IEEE (2014)
18. Timon, B.: Non-profiled deep learning-based side-channel attacks with sensitivity analysis. IACR Trans. Cryptogr. Hardw. Embed. Syst. **219**, 107–131 (2019)
19. Yang, S., Zhou, Y., Liu, J., Chen, D.: Back propagation neural network based leakage characterization for practical security analysis of cryptographic implementations. In: Kim, H. (ed.) ICISC 2011. LNCS, vol. 7259, pp. 169–185. Springer, Heidelberg (2012). https://doi.org/10.1007/978-3-642-31912-9_12
20. Yang, Y., Zheng, L., Zhang, J., Cui, Q., Li, Z., Yu, P.S.: TI-CNN: convolutional neural networks for fake news detection. arXiv preprint arXiv:1806.00749 (2018)

Steganography and Malware

3-Party Adversarial Steganography

Ishak Meraouche[1(✉)], Sabyasachi Dutta[2], and Kouichi Sakurai[1]

[1] Faculty of Information Science and Electrical Engineering,
Kyushu University, Fukuoka, Japan
meraouche.ishak.768@s.kyushu-u.ac.jp, sakurai@inf.kyushu-u.ac.jp
[2] Department of Computer Science, University of Calgary, Calgary, Canada
saby.math@gmail.com

Abstract. Steganography enables a user to hide information by embedding secret messages within other non-secret texts or pictures. Recently, research along this direction has picked a new momentum when Hayes & Danezis (NIPS 2017) used *adversarial learning* to generate steganographic images. In adversarial learning, two neural networks are trained to learn to communicate securely in the presence of eavesdroppers (a third neural network). Hayes–Danezis forwarded this idea to steganography where two neural networks (Bob & Charlie) learn "embed" and "extract" algorithms by exchanging images with hidden text in presence of an eavesdropping neural network (Eve). Due to non-convexity of the models in the training scheme, two different machines may not learn the same embedding and extraction model even if they train on the same set of images. We take a different approach to address this issue of "robustness" in the "decryption" process. In this paper, we introduce a third neural network (Alice) who initiates the process of learning with two neural networks (Bob & Charlie). We implement and demonstrate through experiments that it is possible for Bob & Charlie to learn the same embedding and extraction model by using a new loss function and training process.

Keywords: Deep learning · Neural networks · Steganography

1 Introduction

1.1 Background

Cryptographic techniques are highly relied on nowadays for resolving security threats. Provably secure cryptographic protocols have been useful for securing

Ishak Meraouche is financially supported by the Ministry of Education, Culture, Sports, Science and Technology (MEXT), Japan for his studies at Kyushu University.
Sabyasachi Dutta was financially supported by the National Institute of Information and Communications Technology (NICT), Japan, under the NICT International Invitation Program during his stay at Kyushu University where the initial phase of the research work was carried out.

© Springer Nature Switzerland AG 2020
I. You (Ed.): WISA 2020, LNCS 12583, pp. 89–100, 2020.
https://doi.org/10.1007/978-3-030-65299-9_7

communication protocols as TCP or FTP where the connection is insecure. But as these protocols were not invented with the security in mind, implementing them with provable security incurs a huge overhead and a larger size of the data exchanged. Several lighter and faster cryptographic algorithms are proposed but in most cases they are not provably secure and often they are broken. A new direction is added in the realm of cryptography which uses artificial neural networks. It is a relatively new field and much remains to be explored. Some works proposed in the past encryption methods that use neural networks (NN) e.g. [8,14,16] and also attacks [10]. Although the idea of using artificial neural networks for securing communication has been a buzzword for the last two decades, a recent work by the Google Brain researchers [1] has drawn a lot of attention.

In the model shown in [1], two neural networks train to protect a communication in the presence of a third eavesdropping neural network. Many contributions followed the work done in [1]; For example in [2] where the researchers propose a better model that improves the security in [1] and making it resistant to probabilistic attacks. These contributions originate from the idea done by Goodfellow et al. in [4,5]. A study and analysis of the security of the encryption method learned by the neural networks was done by Zhou et al. in [18] which states that the neural networks are weak against probabilistic attacks. The work done in [18] also shows other training models and scenarios that improve the security. The tests done in [18] include several statistical tests e.g. χ^2 test, Kolmogorov-Smirnov test.

GAN (Generative Adversarial Neural Network). In a generative adversarial network (GAN), two neural networks contest each other in an adversarial game. One network is a `generator` and the other is a `discriminator`. Broadly speaking, task of the generator is to generate "fake samples" of a data distribution and the discriminator distinguishes samples produced by the generator from the true data distribution. Goal of the training process is to enable the generator to produce a synthetic data distribution which is "close" to the real data distribution *i.e.* the error rate of the discriminator is maximized and it cannot distinguish between the synthetic data distribution from the true distribution.

ReLU, Sigmoid, Tanh. ReLU, Sigmoid and Tanh are all activation functions used in deep learning and they help get the output from a neural network in a specific format. ReLU is widely used in convolutional neural networks as it has faster speed in converging the stochastic gradient descent when compared to Tanh and Sigmoid [11]. Tanh is used in this work in order to get values in $[-1, 1]$ which help map our binary output.

1.2   Related Works

Adversarial Cryptography. First adversarial cryptography (symmetric key encryption) scheme was introduced in [1]. In their proposed model, Three neural networks with the same structure are competing in a GANs setup, Alice and Bob are neural networks that share a secret key and their goal is to exchange messages with the presence of an eavesdropper Eve which has not access to the secret key K. Implementing public-key encryption has been a challenging issue – some attempts were made in [1,19], however the results are not satisfying as the neural networks were not able to synchronize in the majority of attempts. In another recent work [17], a secret sharing scheme based on GANs is proposed which was done in order to work around main problems including the hard recovery of lost keys, low communication efficiency etc. in blockchain.

Adversarial Privacy. Adversarial Privacy was derived from Adversarial Cryptography [1], the authors in [7] built a model called Generative Adversarial Privacy (GAP) that can anonymize data and remove any potential information that can lead back to the original user. The model is composed of two learning blocks: A privatizer that learns to process the public data and output a sanitized version of it and an adversary that tries to learn private data from the public data. This is done through competing in a constrained minimax zero-sum game. The privatizer trains on minimizing the adversary's performance and the adversary tries to find the best strategy to maximize its performance. A loss function is used to measure the efficiency of the adversary.

Adversarial Steganography. Adversarial steganography was also derived from adversarial cryptography. It aims to hide information inside an image. The setup is the same but the goal is to hide a plaintext inside an image. Alice hides a plaintext P inside a cover image and sends the image to Bob. Bob has to extract the original plaintext and Eve tells whether the image he intercepted contains a secret message or not.

Recent works show that it is also possible to steganography based on GANs as in [9] where the neural networks learn to generate secret message without modying the original message or in [6] where the neural networks learn to hide a text inside an image instead of encrypting the plain text in [1]. Multiple agent diverse GAN was considered in [3] which had taken into account multiple generators and one discriminator for developing MAD-GAN (A Multivariate Anomaly Detection for Time Series Data with Generative Adversarial Networks). Another variant of Adversarial Steganography is in the work done in [15]. In their work, Alice and Bob are sharing a key K (Whereas there is no key used in [6]) and exchanging steganographic images in the presence of an eavesdropper. Alice must trains to hide random messages inside a cover image in a way that only Bob can extract those messages.

Motivation and Challenging Issues. It was mentioned (and also a known fact) in [6] that due to the non-convexity of the training models, two different parties training on learning the model on different machines are not guaranteed to learn the same embedding and extraction model. [6] made a workaround by training one party with Alice and then sending an encrypted version of the trained parameters to the other party to allow it to have the same model and be able to extract the plaintext from the images correctly. But this requires an additional (encryption) process which is not desirable. Therefore, we ask the following question: is it possible to learn the same model while simultaneously training on different machines in order to avoid sending an encrypted version of the parameters to the second machine? One of our motivations for this work is to solve the problem stated in section 4.4 in [6] and to enable multiple parties to learn the same embedding and extraction model through training. We perform the experiments by adding one more party and test it in the first scenario. The results show that it is possible for two different parties to train with Alice and be able to extract the same plaintext no matter who sends the image.

1.3 Our Contribution

To answer the question of the learnability of the same model on different machines, we implemented in the first scenario a case where Alice, Bob and Charlie are three neural networks in different machines exchanging steganographic images; and we will see if it is possible for Bob and Charlie to learn the same embedding and extraction model.

We show that in our method (presented in Sect. 4.1), two different parties can learn the same model and are able to extract the same plaintext to solve the problem stated in Section 4.4 in [6] where multiple parties are not guaranteed to learn the same model when being on different machines. We did a similar work previously in [13] where we do a study on the extension to multiple parties; The concept is an analogy to this work however the main difference is the neural network structure, training process and the loss functions especially for Eve.

The next two scenarios viz. scenario 2 and scenario 3 (presented in Sect. 4.2) show that different 3-party steganographic communications are achievable with similar training time and extraction accuracy as the two-party case. Although, they do not allow all parties to communicate with each other but they can be useful when multi-hop communications are allowed where we allow a party to act as an intermediary.

2 Neural Network Structure Used

Similar to the scenarios in [6] and in [1], for Alice we use a random cover image and a random n-bit bit-stream (The secret message) as input. We flatten the cover image and concatenate it with the secret message which is then fed into the neural network. The first layer is a fully connected layer so that the message is mixed with the image. It is then reshaped to a $4 \times 4 \times I * 8$ where I is the width of the cover image. Then we follow with a sequence of four layers which consist of a sequence of convolutions, normalization and ReLU except for the final layer where tanh is used as the activation function. Bob and Charlie use the image output by Alice as their input, their structure consists of four consecutive and fractionally-strided convolutions. All the layers use Leaky ReLU except the final one, which uses $tanh$ in order to get a binary output. Eve has the same structure as Bob and Charlie except in the final layer where he has sigmoid in order to output probabilities whether what he was fed is a normal or steganographic image.

3   Training Process and Loss Functions

In order to allow multiple neural networks to learn the same model on different machines, we choose one machine that will act as a leader (Alice), and all of the other machines will train with that leader which is be better than training Bob and Charlie with a local Alice running on their own machine. Sharing a leading machine is what allows multiple parties to learn the same model. In this paper, we only focus on communicating among three parties to reduce training time. When training is complete, the three neural network will learn the same embedding and extraction algorithm (i.e the steganography algorithm).

The parameters used to train the neural networks are as follow: θ_A for Alice, θ_B for Bob, θ_C for Charlie and θ_E for Eve. The function $E_A(\theta_A, M, P)$ represents the embedding function on the image M and the plaintext P for Alice and with a steganographic image as output and $D_B(\theta_B, S)$ represents the extraction algorithm of Bob on the steganographic image S with output as $\mathbf{P_{Bob}}$. The loss function for Eve is as follow: $D_E(\theta_E, M, S)$ where M is a normal image and S is the steganographic image. Eve's output on an image is the probability of it being a steganographic image.

The distance between the original plaintext and each extracted text is calculated in order to tell how accurate each neural networks is:

$$d(P, P') = \sum_{i=0}^{N} \mid P_i - P'_i \mid$$

The definition of the loss function for Bob is the euclidean distance d between Bob's output and the Original plaintext:

$$L_B(\theta_A, \theta_B, M, C) = d(P, D_B(\theta_B, E_A(\theta_A, M, C)))$$

When adding Charlie, the third neural network, he will have the same structure as Bob and therefore the same loss function:

$$L_C(\theta_A, \theta_C, M, C) = d(P, D_C(\theta_C, E_A(\theta_A, M, C)))$$

The loss function for Eve is the sigmoid cross entropy loss:

$$L_E(\Theta_A, \Theta_E, M, S) = -y \cdot \log(E(\Theta_E, x)) - (1 - y) \cdot \log(E(1 - \Theta_E, x))$$

where $y = 0$ if $x = S$ and $y = 1$ if $x = M$.

As in [6]. Alice's loss is the weighted sum of Bob's, Charlie's and Eve's loss on steganographic images, combined with an additional loss term:

$$L_E(\Theta_A, \Theta_E, M, S) = \lambda_A \cdot d(S, M) + \lambda_B \cdot L_B + \lambda_C \cdot L_C + \lambda_E \cdot L_E(\Theta_E, S)$$

where $\Theta_A, \Theta_B, \Theta_C, \Theta_E \in \mathbb{R}$ represent the weight given to each of the respective loss terms. Note that it is mandatory to add the parameters of Charlie or any additional party to the above equation so that they all can learn the same model.

To summarize, the main idea behind hiding and extracting the plain text consists of concatenating the image with the plaintext (secret message of Alice) and passing it through Alice's neural network. The output from Alice's neural network is sent to Bob and Charlie which will again go through their neural networks respectively. The outputs of Bob and Charlie are plaintexts and the neural networks are trained until the plaintexts become equal to Alice's secret message.

4 Main Results

Our goal is to train the three neural networks and synchronize them in a way that they learn the same embedding and extraction algorithm. Our three communicating neural networks with the same structure are Alice, Bob and Charlie and Eve will play the role of the eavesdropper. We use the CelebA data set [12] to train the neural networks, a new image and plaintext are used in every step of training.

4.1 First Scenario

In this scenario we solve the issue mentioned in Section 4.4 of [6] to allow multiple parties to learn the same embedding and extraction model simultaneously.

Training Process I. We have Alice, Bob, Charlie in three different machines and Alice will embed random plaintexts inside images from CelebA data set. We see that after around 200 epochs Bob and Charlie will synchronize and extract the same plaintext. The training process is presented in Algorithm 1.

Algorithm 1 Training Process I.

1: *image_array* ← CelebADataSetImages *// loads the image data set into an array*
   // n refers to the number of images in the data set and synchronized *is a Boolean variable that indicates if synchronized or not*

2: initialize: $i = 0$

3: **while** i $<=$ n *or* synchronized **do**

4:   AliceGetNextImage(i) *//Alice gets the next image from the dataset*

5:   AliceGenerateBitstream(100) *//Alice generates a random bitstream of* 100 *bits*

6:   AliceGenerateStegoImage(i) *//Alice generates the steganographic image*

7:   BobCharlieExtractBitstream($stegoImage$) *//Bob and Charlie extract the bitstream from the steganographic image*

8:   EveAnalyzeImages($stegoImage, originalImage$) *//Eve tries to distinguish between steganographic and cover images*

9:   UpdateParameters($\Theta_A, \Theta_B, \Theta_C, \Theta_E$) *//update the parameters*

10: **end**

Algorithm Explanation. In this algorithm, we load the training data set and we enter a loop that only stops when there is no more images or that the neural networks are synchronized. In the body of the loop, we get the first image, generate a bitstream which will be the plaintext we will hide, feed it into the neural network of Alice in order to generate the steganographic image. Bob and Charlie will then extract the text from the stego image and Eve will analyse the image and output either 1 if she thinks that the image is steganographic or 0 if it is a cover image. After getting the output, the loss function is verified and if it is not satisfied yet, we will jump to the next iteration.

Experiment I. In the first experiment, Alice generates a random 100 bits plaintext P, and hides it inside a sequentially picked cover image from CelebA data set and sends it to Bob and Charlie

Bob and Charlie extract the hidden text and output $P_{Bob}, P_{charlie}$. As Eve has access to the communication, he intercepts the cover image and tells if it's a cover image or a steganographic image by outputting either 1 or 0 as P_{eve}.

In every iteration, we calculate the loss of each neural network as well as the minimum distance between the original plaintext and the extracted ones respectively: $P_{Bob}, P_{Charlie}$. Figure 1 shows the plotted loss made by each neural network during training.

Analysis I. In Experiment I, we can see in Fig. 1 that Bob and Charlie have a loss of about 0.5 at the beginning of the experiment but reach 0 loss after around 175 epochs. We also see that they learned the same extraction algorithm.

To make sure they learned the same embedding and extraction algorithms, we also make Bob & Charlie generate a random plaintext and hide it inside a random image; Bob will send its image to Charlie for extraction and vice versa. We will not update the parameters in exchanges between Bob and Charlie in order to only learn when exchanging with Alice.

Figure 2 shows the accuracy of Charlie while extracting images received from Bob, and Fig. 3 shows the accuracy of Bob when extracting images received from Charlie. We can see that after around 160 epochs, they both have 100% accuracy when extracting messages and this therefore proves that they all learned the same embedding and extraction algorithms.

4.2   Second and Third Scenario

Second Scenario

Training Process II. In the Second Scenario, we split the neural networks into two communicating pairs. Concretely, Alice will communicate with Bob and Bob will communicate with Charlie. And Alice cannot communicate directly with Charlie. This can be useful in IoT devices where two devices are too far from each other and need another device as a bridge.

Experiment II. In this scenario, Alice generates a steganographic image and sends it to Bob. Bob extracts the hidden text, hides it again in another image through its neural network and the new steganographic image is sent to Charlie.

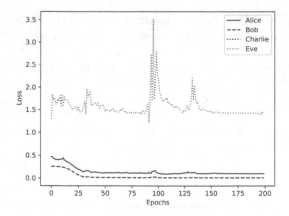

Fig. 1. Test results of experiment 1

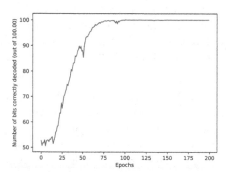

Fig. 2. Charlie's accuracy when extracting from Bob in scenario I

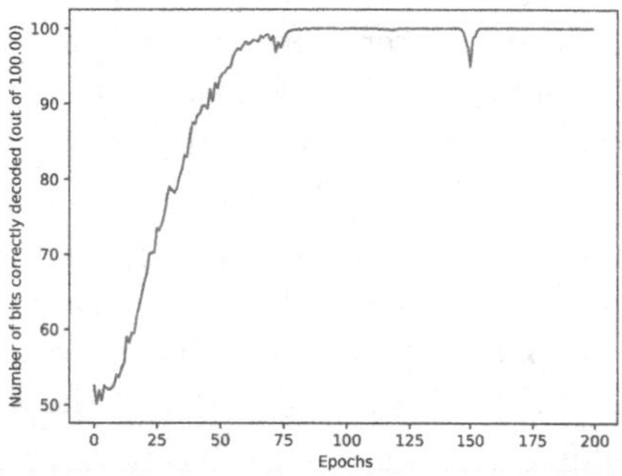

Fig. 3. Bob's accuracy when extracting from Charlie in scenario I.

Charlie will extract the hidden text from the image received from Bob in order to output P_{Charlie}. Eve can intercept any of the images exchanged between the neural networks. At every step of the training, we calculate the distance between the original plain texts and the extracted texts, we also calculate the loss of every neural network. The loss of the neural networks are plotted in Figs. 4 and 5.

Analysis II. Similarly to the first scenario, we can see that Alice, Bob and Charlie converge to 0 loss in around 200 epochs. However the communication between Charlie and Alice is not possible and the accuracy was around 50% during our tests Therefore they will need to use Bob as a bridge to communicate.

Third Scenario

Training Process III. In this scenario, Alice's synchronization with Bob and Charlie is done in an independent way; In other words, Alice will use one unique set of parameters for the communication with Bob and another unique set of parameters with Charlie. Therefore, a communication between Bob and Charlie would require the use of Alice as a bridge.

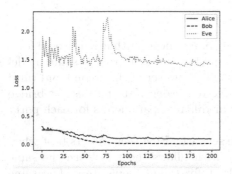

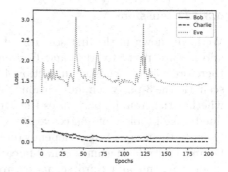

Fig. 4. Loss in the communication between Alice and Bob in Exp. II

Fig. 5. Loss in the communication between Bob and Charlie in Exp. II

Experiment III. Two sets of unique parameters are generated by Alice in this scenario; When generating a steganographic image by Alice, if the image is sent to Bob, the first set of parameters is used and when sending the steganographic image to Charlie, the second set of parameters is used. We record the loss of every neural network and we plot it in Fig. 6 and Fig. 7.

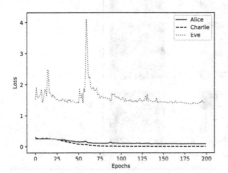

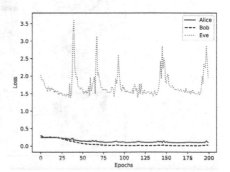

Fig. 6. Loss in the communication between Alice and Charlie in Exp. III

Fig. 7. Loss in the communication between Alice and Bob in Exp. III

Analysis III. We can see that Bob and Charlie start with a loss of around 0.5 but the loss quickly decreases and we get a nearly perfect accuracy. Eve's loss was between 2.0 and 3.5. Which means that each pair of neural networks is synchronized. But the communication between Charlie and Bob is not possible and Alice must be used as a bridge.

4.3   Discussions

We have shown in the first scenario of the communication that it is possible to add a third party to Alice and Bob and enable them to learn the same model therefore solving the issue in Section 4.4 in [6]. However in the second and third scenario the 3-party communication will need to use one of the parties as a bridge whether the training party uses the same or different parameters for each party due to the problem of non-convexity.

Overall, the usage of cases depends on the scenario. First scenario fits best when having multiple machines communicating as it allows them to learn the same model. Second and third scenarios are best for talking separately. The same applies in the case of multiple parties communication.

After training our neural networks, we tried feeding them the same set of images and see the output. Figure 9 and Fig. 10 show the images generated by Alice at the beginning and end of training respectively. Figure 8 shows the set of original images.

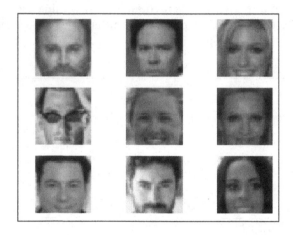

Fig. 8. Original image

The extension to a multi-party scheme is possible by just adding as many parties as needed and including their parameters in the main loss function in order to enable them to learn the same model. However the training time should be taken into consideration as it will rise significantly when more parties are added to the scheme.

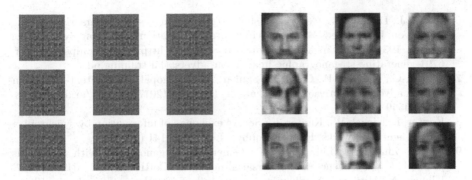

Fig. 9. Images generated by Alice before training

Fig. 10. Images generated by Alice after training

5   Conclusion and Future Work

We proposed a methodology to enable more than two parties to learn the same steganography model (with a 3-party example) based on Google's Adversarial Cryptography model [1] and 2-Party Steganography model [6]. We took a novel approach by training several machines altogether with respect to one (leader) machine. We also showed (in Scenario 2 & 3) that it is not always possible to learn the same steganography model by introducing a third machine.

Several interesting future works are in order. For example, scrutinize the (concrete) implementation of the scheme for more than three parties; perform concrete (standardized) steganalysis attacks on these extended versions. One may consider achieving resistance against more concrete adversaries (e.g. chosen plaintext attack) in order to improve the security.

References

1. Abadi, M., Andersen, D.G.: Learning to protect communications with adversarial neural cryptography. CoRR abs/1610.06918 (2016)
2. Coutinho, M., de Oliveira Albuquerque, R., Borges, F., García-Villalba, L.J., Kim, T.: Learning perfectly secure cryptography to protect communications with adversarial neural cryptography. Sensors **18**(5), 1306 (2018)
3. Ghosh, A., Kulharia, V., Namboodiri, V.P., Torr, P.H., Dokania, P.K.: Multi-agent diverse generative adversarial networks. In: The IEEE Conference on Computer Vision and Pattern Recognition (CVPR) (June 2018)
4. Goodfellow, I., et al.: Generative adversarial nets. In: Ghahramani, Z., Welling, M., Cortes, C., Lawrence, N.D., Weinberger, K.Q. (eds.) Advances in Neural Information Processing Systems, vol. 27, pp. 2672–2680. Curran Associates, Inc. (2014). http://papers.nips.cc/paper/5423-generative-adversarial-nets.pdf
5. Goodfellow, I.J., Shlens, J., Szegedy, C.: Explaining and harnessing adversarial examples. In: 3rd International Conference on Learning Representations, ICLR 2015, Conference Track Proceedings, San Diego, CA, USA, May 7–9, 2015 (2015)

6. Hayes, J., Danezis, G.: Generating steganographic images via adversarial training. In: Guyon, I., et al. (eds.) Advances in Neural Information Processing Systems, vol. 30, pp. 1954–1963. Curran Associates, Inc. (2017). http://papers.nips.cc/paper/6791-generating-steganographic-images-via-adversarial-training.pdf
7. Huang, C., Kairouz, P., Chen, X., Sankar, L., Rajagopal, R.: Context-aware generative adversarial privacy. CoRR abs/1710.09549 (2017). http://arxiv.org/abs/1710.09549
8. Kanter, I., Kinzel, W., Kanter, E.: Secure exchange of information by synchronization of neural networks. EPL (Europhys. Lett.) 57, 141 (2002)
9. Ke, Y., Zhang, M., Liu, J., Su, T.: Generative steganography with Kerckhoffs' principle based on generative adversarial networks. CoRR abs/1711.04916 (2017)
10. Klimov, A., Mityagin, A., Shamir, A.: Analysis of neural cryptography. In: Zheng, Y. (ed.) ASIACRYPT 2002. LNCS, vol. 2501, pp. 288–298. Springer, Heidelberg (2002). https://doi.org/10.1007/3-540-36178-2_18
11. Krizhevsky, A., Sutskever, I., Hinton, G.E.: ImageNet classification with deep convolutional neural networks. Commun. ACM 60(6), 84–90 (2017). https://doi.org/10.1145/3065386
12. Liu, Z., Luo, P., Wang, X., Tang, X.: Deep learning face attributes in the wild. In: Proceedings of International Conference on Computer Vision (ICCV) (December 2015)
13. Meraouche, I., Dutta, S., Sakurai, K.: 3-party adversarial cryptography. In: Barolli, L., Okada, Y., Amato, F. (eds.) EIDWT 2020. LNDECT, vol. 47, pp. 247–258. Springer, Cham (2020). https://doi.org/10.1007/978-3-030-39746-3_27
14. Wang, X., Yang, L., Liu, R., Kadir, A.: A chaotic image encryption algorithm based on perceptron model. Nonlinear Dyn. 62, 615–621 (2010)
15. Yedroudj, M., Comby, F., Chaumont, M.: Steganography using a 3 player game. CoRR abs/1907.06956 (2019)
16. Yu, W., Cao, J.: Cryptography based on delayed chaotic neural networks. Phys. Lett. A 356(4), 333–338 (2006)
17. Zheng, W., Wang, K., Wang, F.: GAN-based key secret-sharing scheme in blockchain. IEEE Trans. Cybern. 1–12 (2020)
18. Zhou, L., Chen, J., Zhang, Y., Su, C., James, M.A.: Security analysis and new models on the intelligent symmetric key encryption. Comput. Secur. 80, 14–24 (2019)
19. Zhu, Y., Vargas, D.V., Sakurai, K.: Neural cryptography based on the topology evolving neural networks. In: 2018 Sixth International Symposium on Computing and Networking Workshops (CANDARW), pp. 472–478 (2018)

Accessibility Service Utilization Rates in Android Applications Shared on Twitter

Shuichi Ichioka[1]([✉]), Estelle Pouget[1,2], Takao Mimura[3], Jun Nakajima[3],
and Toshihiro Yamauchi[1] [iD]

[1] Graduate School of Natural Science and Technology,
Okayama University, Okayama, Japan
ichioka@s.okayama-u.ac.jp, yamauchi@cs.okayama-u.ac.jp
[2] Grenoble INP - Esisar, Valence, France
[3] SecureBrain Corporation, Tokyo, Japan

Abstract. The number of malware detected has been increasing annually, and 4.12% of malware reported in 2018 attacked Android phones. Therefore, preventing attacks by Android malware is critically important. Several previous studies have investigated the percentage of apps that utilize accessibility services and are distributed from Google Play, that have been reportedly used by Android malware. However, the Social Networking Services (SNSs) that are used to spread malware have distributed apps not only from Google Play but also from other sources. Therefore, apps distributed from within and outside of Google Play must be investigated to capture malware trends. In this study, we collected apps shared on Twitter in 2018, which is a representative SNS, and created a Twitter shared apps dataset. The dataset consists of 32,068 apps downloaded from the websites of URLs collected on Twitter. We clarified the proportion of apps that contained malware and proportion of apps utilizing accessibility services. We found that both, the percentage of malware and percentage of total apps using accessibility services have been increasing. Notably, the percentages of malware and un-suspicious apps using accessibility services were quite similar. Therefore, this problem cannot be solved by automatically blocking all apps that use accessibility services. Hence, specific countermeasures against malware using accessibility services will be increasingly important for online security in the future.

Keywords: Accessibility service · Android app · Malware · SNS

1 Introduction

The number of malware detected has increased annually, with 4.12% of malware found in 2018 reportedly attacking Android phones [6]. A 2018–19 security report by AV-TEST found a total of 5,490,000 Android malware attacks in 2018 [6].

© Springer Nature Switzerland AG 2020
I. You (Ed.): WISA 2020, LNCS 12583, pp. 101–111, 2020.
https://doi.org/10.1007/978-3-030-65299-9_8

Contrarily, WeLiveSecurity has reported that the number of Android malware is actually decreasing [18]. Either way, the number of Android malware is still large and this poses a significant problem that warrants investigation and prevention.

In 2017, Dr. Web has reported accessibility service (AS) utilization as a recent trend for mobile malware [9]. These services are an Android feature intended for use by people with disabilities, but they have been reportedly used by Android malware as well. For example, a malware called Skygofree, which uses AS to eavesdrop on information on user screens was reported in 2018 [14]. Additionally, in 2019 a malware called Gustuff reportedly used AS to send money unintended by users [11]. Clearly, there have been many malware attacks that exploit these well-intentioned AS.

It is therefore important to investigate the utilization rates of AS by Android applications (apps). There have been reports on the AS utilization rate, specifically by apps that were distributed by Google Play. In November 2017, it was announced that any apps that were using AS for purposes other than supporting users with disabilities would be deleted from Google Play [4]. According to the AS documentation [3]:

> "Although it's beneficial to add accessibility features in your app, you should use them only for the purpose of helping users with disabilities interact with your app."

Therefore, developers could not use Google Play to distribute apps that use AS, except those intended to help users with disabilities. However, many apps that use AS could be distributed by methods other than Google Play, so surveys targeting only Google Play apps are insufficient to investigate the actual distribution of such apps. We must, therefore, investigate the distribution of apps that use AS from all sources to evaluate the overall utilization of AS in malware.

Malware and fake websites have been widely shared on Social Networking Services (SNSs) [13], where many cybercrimes have also occurred [7]. It is therefore important to investigate the true situation around Android apps that use AS so that malware trends can be accurately characterized.

In this study, we collected URLs obtained from Twitter, which is a representative SNS, accessed these URLs, and collected the Android apps that could be downloaded to explore apps distributed from sources other than Google Play. We created a Twitter shared apps dataset that consists of 32,068 apps downloaded from the websites of URLs collected on Twitter. We clarified the proportion of apps that contained malware and proportion of apps utilizing AS.

We used this data to identify the proportion of the total number of shared apps that used AS. This revealed both the threat level presented by apps shared on Twitter and the danger of allowing AS for SNS distributed apps.

In summary, our study makes the following contributions:

- We created a dataset that consists of apps downloaded from the websites of URLs collected on Twitter. As far as we know, there is no dataset that focuses on apps distributed by URLs via Twitter.

```
<service android:permission="android.permission.BIND_ACCESSIBILITY_SERVICE">
    <intent-filter>
        <action android:name="android.accessibilityservice.AccessibilityService"/>
    </intent-filter>
    <meta-data android:name="android.accessibilityservice" android:resource="@xml/accessibility_config"/>
</service>
```

Fig. 1. Extract of manifest declaring AS use

- We analyzed the rate at which Android apps shared on Twitter use AS. Focusing on these apps, which are distributed from third party app stores or websites, we identified an accurate summary of apps distributed from these sources in 2018.
- We show that the proportion of malware is increasing for apps shared on Twitter.
- We find increasing AS usage rates for Android apps shared on Twitter.
- We show some countermeasures that mitigate the threats of apps utilizing AS. We believe that the increasing trend of apps utilizing AS will continue, thus we should carefully check the apps that require AS and their required permissions.

2   Accessibility Services Overview

Following the AccessibilityEvents documentation [1]:

Accessibility services should only be used to assist users with disabilities in using Android devices and apps. They run in the background and receive callbacks by the system when AccessibilityEvents are fired. Such events denote some state transition in the user interface, for example, the focus has changed, a button has been clicked, etc. Such a service can optionally request the capability for querying the content of the active window.

Notably, apps that use AS can read string data that is displayed on screens and operate other apps [2], making them particularly powerful and potentially dangerous.

For an app to use AS, two things must occur. First, it must be declared in AndroidManifest.xml, an example of which is shown in Fig. 1. Second, the user must allow AS in the app settings. A sample settings screen for Android users is shown in Fig. 2. When utilizing AS, users must change their settings, as the AS cannot be engaged unless the user permits it.

Malware have been reported to exploit AS. According to Kaspersky, a malware named Skygofree used AS to eavesdrop on messages received by chat apps [14]. Skygofree also hid AS permission requests behind other requests to trick users [14]. Additionally, Group IB reported a malware called Gustuff that automatically filled forms using AS, in mobile banking app, and was thus able to steal money from users [11]. Generally, malware that exploit AS can obtain sensitive information displayed on user screens such as passwords [10]. Further, malware can operate Android phones automatically to download other applications from

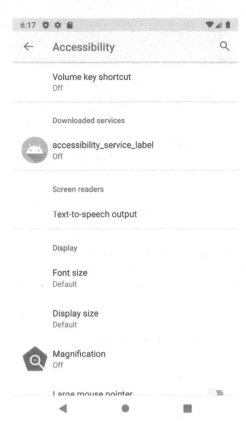

Fig. 2. Sample AS settings screen

Google Play and post reviews [15]. Often, attackers trick users into granting access to AS to take advantage of these capabilities.

3   Investigation of the Ratio of Malicious Apps and Their Accessibility Service Utilization Rates

3.1   Purpose of Investigation

Our purpose herein is to investigate the actual AS usage rates of the distributed apps. To this end, we investigated apps shared on SNS, specifically Twitter. We selected Twitter because users can use it anonymously, and a single user can have multiple accounts, making it particularly vulnerable to criminal misuse.

3.2   Method for Collecting Apps on Twitter

As a result of searching for "apk" as a keyword in the public streaming application programming interface (API) [17] of Twitter, we collected the uniform

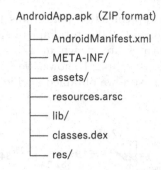

Fig. 3. Android app file structure

Table 1. Number of apps

Month	Number of apps	Number of different certificates
Jan.	3,499	1,220
Feb.	2,702	1,088
Mar.	2,399	936
Apr.	2,848	1,072
May	4,563	1,201
Jun.	2,815	855
Jul.	2,817	988
Aug.	2,384	959
Sep.	1,256	513
Oct.	1,653	631
Nov.	2,913	987
Dec.	2,397	771

resource locators (URLs) included in all acquired text. We selected "apk" as a keyword because "apk" is used as the file extension for Android apps. We obtained the contents from the websites of the URLs collected from Twitter as well as the contents from the websites contained in the links included on the websites. Android apps include files with unique names such as those shown in Fig. 3. Hence, we collected files that met all of the following conditions, which indicate that the file is indeed an app.

A) It is in ZIP format.
B) It includes class.dex and AndroidManifest.xml.
C) It includes a directory named META-INF.

For the identified apps, we used VirusTotal to determine whether each was suspicious and to obtain a list of "detected" warnings for users from multiple virus scanners. In this research, one or more "detected" readings determined that the app was suspicious. The app collection period was 1 year, spanning January 1, 2018 to December 31, 2018, and 32,068 total apps were analyzed. The number of apps and different certificates are shown in Table 1. Different certificates indicate different developers. As Table 1 shows, we have collected many apps with different certificates to ensure we obtained a wide range of apps.

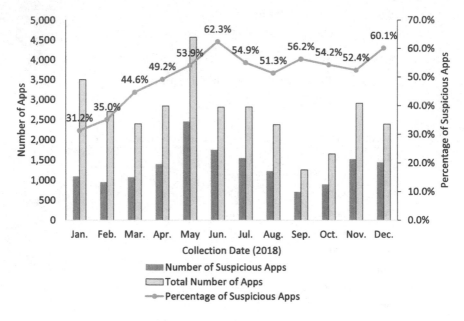

Fig. 4. Percentage of suspicious apps shared on Twitter

3.3   Investigation Method

The flow for analyzing AS usage rates is shown below:

(1) Extract AndroidManifest.xml from the app using Apktool [5].
(2) Search for the following in AndroidManifest.xml:
    android.permission.BIND_ACCESSIBILITY_SERVICE
(3) If a character string is found as a result of this search, the app is determined to use AS. Apps exhibiting technical issues such as Apktool that abnormally terminated, were excluded from the AS usage rate survey.

This analysis allowed us to collect apps according to their trend of being shared on Twitter. In addition, analyzing AndroidManifest.xml revealed the percentage of apps that can use AS. Therefore, the ratios of suspicious apps shared on Twitter and apps using AS could be clarified.

3.4 Investigation Results

Investigating the Ratio of Suspicious Apps. In Fig. 4, the percentage of suspicious apps identified in each month of 2018 is shown, which exhibits an overall increasing trend.

We can infer from these results that the proportion of malware in the apps distributed on Twitter is also increasing. Specifically, the average percentage of suspicious apps was 49.8%. If we generalize this result, we can conclude that about half of all SNS-distributed apps are suspicious, and installing them is dangerous and not recommended.

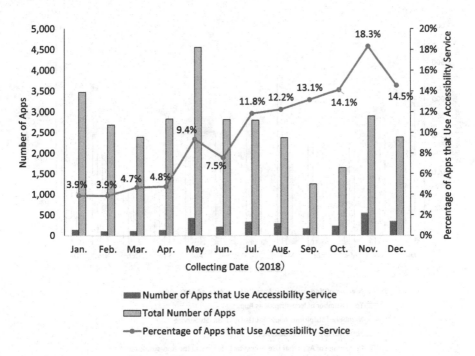

Fig. 5. Percentage of apps that use AS

Investigating the Percentage of Apps that Use Accessibility Services. In Fig. 5, the AS usage rates for apps shared on Twitter are shown. The rate increased from 3.9% in January 2018 to 14.5% in December 2018, for an overall 3.7 fold increase in 2018. Therefore, we concluded that AS utilization in apps shared on Twitter was on the rise.

Notably, the 2018 AS usage rate for apps distributed on Google Play was reported to be 0.37% [8], while it was 9.4% (3,015/32,068) for the apps collected in our study. Thus, the utilization rate found here is quite high. This implies that the AS utilization rates for apps shared on Twitter is higher than that for apps on Google Play. We can thus infer that the proportion of apps that use AS increases for app distribution sources without any AS use restrictions such as those imposed by Google Play.

Analyzing the Ratio of Apps that Use as for Suspicious Activity. Figure 6 shows usage rates, classified by whether they correspond to suspicious apps. From Fig. 6, we observe almost no difference in the AS usage rate depending on whether or not an app is suspicious. Therefore, the use of AS cannot on its own be used to identify an app as malware. In fact, the number of suspicious and benign apps that use AS were very similar. However, as the ratio of suspicious apps to all those that use AS was high, about 52.8% (1,591/3,015), we can clearly state that apps shared on Twitter that require AS should not be installed without considering the significant risk of malware.

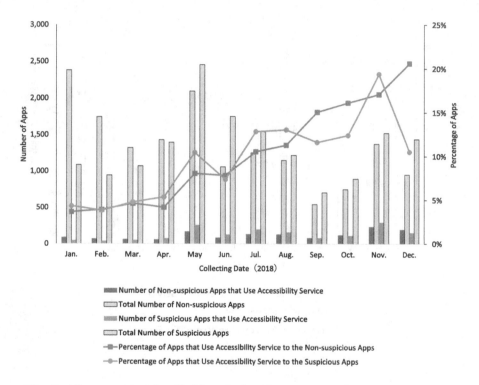

Fig. 6. AS usage rates classified by whether they correspond to suspicious apps

4   Discussion

As described in Sect. 3.4, the overall prevalence of malware and overall AS usage rates have been increasing. Thus, the malware risk associated with apps distributed from third-party stores or developer websites has increased accordingly. These are common sources for apps that use AS, likely because Google Play prohibits the distribution of apps that use AS with any intention other than supporting app usage by people with disabilities. Figure 6 clearly indicates that apps that use AS are not necessarily suspicious. Therefore, all apps that use AS cannot automatically be blocked. Therefore, specific countermeasures against malware will become increasingly important for online security in the future.

We believe these countermeasures may include:

- Checking the app developer
  When installing an SNS distributed app, it is important to ensure that the app developer is trust worthy to avoid unintentionally installing malware. Contaminated apps may be repackaged and distributed, so it is imperative to check with the original developers.
- Allow AS only when needed
  Confirm the reason that an app requires AS, before permitting the AS use. This is expected to reduce AS-exploiting attacks.
- Check permissions required with AS
  Users should check the permissions required with AS, as attacks could be prevented by denying these permissions that may leak information.

5   Related Work

5.1   Identifying AS Vulnerabilities

Kalysch et al. [12] showed that AS could be used to eavesdrop on sensitive user information. They also surveyed the top 1,100 apps on Google Play and found that 99.25% were vulnerable to this type of exploitation. Furthermore, Fratantonio et al. [10] showed that by combining AS with SYSTEM_ALERT_WINDOW, which grants permissions to display on top of other apps, an attacker could perform tasks such as clickjacking, keylogger, and password stealing. Additionally, McAfee [15] introduced Click Farm, which uses AS to send fake reviews from devices infected with malware. Collectively, these studies prove that AS can be abused and exploited, highlighting the importance of investigating AS usage among real Android Apps distributed on SNSs. In addition, unsuspicious apps use AS. Thus, it is important to make clear the differences in the AS usage ratios of suspicious and unsuspicious apps.

5.2   Survey of AS Usage Rates

Wenrui et al. [8] investigated apps distributed by Google Play, and Mohammad et al. [16] reported that 2,815 of these 4,155,414 apps used AS, after investigating their dataset. While these studies investigated AS usage in apps distributed from Google Play, they did not address those from other sources, such as SNS, third-party app stores, and developer websites.

6   Conclusion

We collected URLs from the Twitter streaming API, which is a representative SNS. We then accessed these URLs and collected the Android apps that could be downloaded to investigate apps distributed from sources other than Google Play. We created a data set of the 32,068 apps shared on Twitter in 2018 and showed that 49.8% of these apps are suspicious. Our results also indicate that the proportions of suspicious apps and apps that use AS had been increasing. Installing these apps is dangerous and not recommended. In addition, we showed some countermeasures. The 2018 AS usage rate for apps distributed on Google Play was reported to be 0.37% [8], but it was 9.4% for the apps collected in our study. This implies that the AS utilization rates for apps shared on Twitter is higher than that for apps on Google Play. Further, the AS usage rates for suspicious apps and benign apps are very similar, demonstrating the increasing importance of malware specific countermeasures in the future of online security.

In future works, malware utilizing AS must be analyzed in detail, and specific countermeasures should be considered and outlined.

Acknowledgement. The research results have been achieved by "WarpDrive: Web-based Attack Response with Practical and Deployable Research InitiatiVE," the Commissioned Research of National Institute of Information and Communications Technology (NICT), Japan.

References

1. Android Developers: AccessibilityService. https://developer.android.com/reference/android/accessibilityservice/AccessibilityService. Accessed 22 Apr 2020
2. Android Developers: Create your own accessibility service. https://developer.android.com/guide/topics/ui/accessibility/service. Accessed 26 Apr 2020
3. Android Developers: Build more accessible apps. https://developer.android.com/guide/topics/ui/accessibility. Accessed 22 Apr 2020
4. Android Police: Google will remove play store apps that use accessibility services for anything except helping disabled users. https://www.androidpolice.com/2017/11/12/google-will-remove-play-store-apps-use-accessibility-services-anything-except-helping-disabled-users/. Accessed 19 Apr 2020
5. Apktool. https://ibotpeaches.github.io/Apktool/. Accessed 28 Apr 2020
6. AV-TEST: Security report 2018/19. https://www.av-test.org/fileadmin/pdf/security_report/AV-TEST_Security_Report_2018-2019.pdf. Accessed 24 Apr 2020
7. Bromium: Report: social media platforms and the cybercrime economy. https://www.bromium.com/resource/report-social-media-platforms-and-the-cybercrime-economy/. Accessed 19 Apr 2020
8. Diao, W., et al.: Kindness is a risky business: on the usage of the accessibility APIs in Android. In: 22nd International Symposium on Research in Attacks, Intrusions and Defenses (RAID 2019), pp. 261–275. USENIX Association, Beijing (September 2019). https://www.usenix.org/conference/raid2019/presentation/diao
9. Doctor Web: Mobile malware review for 2017. https://news.drweb.com/show/review/?i=11671&lng=en. Accessed 30 Mar 2020
10. Fratantonio, Y., Qian, C., Chung, S.P., Lee, W.: Cloak and dagger: from two permissions to complete control of the UI feedback loop. In: 2017 IEEE Symposium on Security and Privacy (SP), pp. 1041–1057 (2017)
11. Gustuff: Weapon of mass infection. https://www.group-ib.com/blog/gustuff. Accessed 30 Mar 2020

12. Kalysch, A., Bove, D., Müller, T.: How Android's UI security is undermined by accessibility. In: Proceedings of the 2nd Reversing and Offensive-Oriented Trends Symposium. ROOTS 2018. Association for Computing Machinery, New York (2018). https://doi.org/10.1145/3289595.3289597
13. Kaspersky Daily: No, you have not won two free airline tickets. https://usa. kaspersky.com/blog/free-airline-tickets-scam/11533/. Accessed 19 Apr 2020
14. Kaspersky Daily: Skygofree - a Hollywood-style mobile spy. https://usa.kaspersky. com/blog/skygofree-smart-trojan/14418/. Accessed 30 Mar 2020
15. McAfee Mobile Threat Report Q1, 2020. https://www.mcafee.com/content/dam/ consumer/en-us/docs/2020-Mobile-Threat-Report.pdf. Accessed 25 Apr 2020
16. Naseri, M., Borges, N.P., Zeller, A., Rouvoy, R.: Accessileaks: investigating privacy leaks exposed by the android accessibility service. Proc. Priv. Enhanc. Technol. **2019**(2), 291–305 (2019).   https://content.sciendo.com/view/journals/popets/ 2019/2/article-p291.xml
17. Twitter Developers: POST statuses/filter. https://developer.twitter.com/en/docs/ tweets/filter-realtime/api-reference/post-statuses-filter. Accessed 27 Apr 2020
18. WeLiveSecurity: Semi-annual balance of mobile security 2019. https://www. welivesecurity.com/2019/09/05/balance-mobile-security-2019/. Accessed 25 Apr 2020

Novel Reversible Acoustic Steganography Based on Carrier Orthogonality

Hung-Jr Shiu[1], Fang-Yie Leu[1(✉)], Chun-Ming Lai[1], and Yu-Chun Huang[2]

[1] Department of Computer Science, Tunghai University, Taichung, TW 407302,
Republic of China
leufy@thu.edu.tw
[2] LUXSHARE-ICT, Zhubei, TW 30273, Republic of China

Abstract. **A well-known technology called** steganography is a strategy of hiding secrets that nobody will suspect the existence of secrets in cover medium. This paper indicates a novel and reversible steganographic protocol based on transformation of secrets to be transmitted covertly in high-frequencies waves carried by a public audio. In principle: a secret is first turned into a digital wave, and then lifted to a radio frequency. The radio-frequency signal is out of the threshold corresponding to human beings' awareness and will be put onto an audio that could be downloaded by receivers legally. A receiver can lift down the radio-frequency wave and drain out the secret. The proposed technology decreases the risk greatly about preventing secrets from explosion during a transition. Experiments, comparisons and analyses are also performed to investigate practicability and superior performance compared with state-of-the-art steganographic schemes.

Keywords: Reversible · Acoustic · Steganography · Secrets · Radio-frequency signals

1 Introduction

In recent years, people accessing different data on the Internet have been frequent. Therefore, it is important to protect and secure the information. Many state-of-the-art techniques were designed to maintain the confidentiality consequently. Among lots kinds of data protection schemes available nowadays, various forms of steganography have been prevalent. Steganography is a data hiding technique in which a secret is embedded on medium, known as the 'cover media'. If the contents of cover medium are modified with secrets, resultant medium becomes 'stego-medium'. Only authorized receivers are able to obtain secrets by recovering them from stego-medium. There are also other cover media like text [1], DNA sequences [2] and physiological signals [3].

Lots numbers of data are able to be hidden on acoustics, and many published papers described how to hide secret data in these signals [4–24]. Bender [4] concluded four principle steganographic strategies in acoustics including LSB, spread spectrum, phase coding and echo data hiding.

© Springer Nature Switzerland AG 2020
I. You (Ed.): WISA 2020, LNCS 12583, pp. 112–123, 2020.
https://doi.org/10.1007/978-3-030-65299-9_9

The main meaning of LSB strategy is that the data will be hidden by replacing the least significant bits of cover medium [5]. It is easy to deploy and manipulate. However, it is also easy to be aware of the modified parts. Further, its applications are restricted only on digital data.

Spreading data via different frequency spectrums are designed by segmenting secrets in many pages and spreading secrets across as many frequency bands. The benefit is ensuring signal integrity and reception, even though there are lots of existing interferences [6].

The main idea of phase coding is substituting phases of initial acoustic segments by referencing phases which represent data. Phases of successive blocks being adjusted are set to preserve relative phases of blocks. When phases' relationship of frequencies is changed dramatically, obvious phase dispersions occur. As this is effective by means of signal-to-perceived noise ratio, it is hard to detect in host medium.

One strategy is psychoacoustic masking [7]. Secrets are embedded after replacing of high and low frequencies of cover medium. The cover medium obtains some ratio frequencies out of the threshold on human ears, and the frequencies are available to embed messages.

One strategy is called Echo data hiding which hides secrets into cover medium by inserting echoes [8]. Human ears are not able to distinguish pure echoes and those carrying secrets. Echoes are either derived from cover medium or available on cover medium. Echoes derived from cover medium increase capacity of a host when embedding secret messages while it is not easy to ensure artificial echoes not to be noticed.

The article is organized as follows. Section 2 describes the proposed protocol. Section 3 presents an experiment and simulation of the proposed scheme to demonstrate the practicability. Section 4 compares robustness of some related work and gives theoretical analysis of capacity and security. Conclusions are addressed in Sect. 5.

2   The Scheme

The workflow of the proposed protocol: First, transform a bit stream with embedded secrets to acoustic signals and lifts the signals into very high frequencies. Then, embed the high frequency signals on a public cover acoustic. Also, reveal the corresponding process of data recovery.

The overview of the proposed strategy runs as follows (the process of data hiding):

(1) Turn the secret S into a bit stream S'.
(2) Transform S' to a digital wave M.
(3) Adopt a frequency lifting onto M and M changes to a radio-frequency wave M'.
(4) Put the radio-frequency wave M', which cannot be heard, onto a public music audio P, that is low-frequency and auditable to generate an audio P'. Process of data recovery works in the following:
(5) Legal receivers download audio P' which is composed of a low-frequency audio P and the radio-frequency secrets M'.
(6) Legal receivers lift radio-frequency audio M' down and recover M.

(7) Legal receivers turn M to a digital bit stream S'.
(8) Legal receivers recover S and check the correctness of S by referencing P.

This scheme uses a special property of communications and brings the best effects to make transmitted contents unnoticeable. A translated bit stream S' will be first turned to be an audio wave $n(t)$ by using the coming operations:

(a) Cut S' into blocks of equal size w until the size of the last block is not larger than w. Thus, $S' = S_1'S_2'...S_i'S_{i+1}'$, i is equal to $|S|/w$ and $|S_{i+1}'| \le w$.
(b) If $|S_{i+1}'| \le w$, pad zeros after S_{i+1}' until $|S_{i+1}'| = w$.
(c) Assume that the number of padding zeros after S_{i+1}' is x, produce a bit stream S_{i+2}', where $|S_{i+2}'| = w$ which denotes the value of x in binary, and appends it after S_{i+1}'.

For instance, a bit stream $S' = 1001011001011010100010101010101001010$. Based on the procedure, suppose $l = 8$ and S' will be first divided as $S1'S2'S3'S4'S5'$ where $S_1' = 10010110, S_2' = 01011010, S_3' = 10001010, S_4' = 10101010, S5' = 01010$. The last segment should be extended by adding 0 after it until its size is equal to l and it shall be $S_5' = 01010000$ in this case. There are three zeros added to S_5' such that $S_6' = 00000011$ should be created to point out the number of zeros added after S_5'. l should be given to legal receivers. S_1', $S_2'...S_6'$ are used to compose an acoustic wave $n(t)$. Then, lift $n(t)$ to be a radio- frequency wave $n'(t)$. The exploited frequency lifting will be discussed in the following subsections. Finally, choose a public known music $P(t)$ and append $n'(t)$ on $P(t)$ to produce $P'(t)$. $P'(t)$ will be put in a public music database and downloaded by authorized receivers. Notice that senders do not need to deliver the stego-audio $P'(t)$ while senders and authorized receivers negotiate for the cover medium under a secure channel.

The procedure of data recovery works as follows: when authorized receivers receive a public acoustic $P'(t)$, the first process is to use a high-pass filter (HPF) to strain the radio-frequency wave $n'(t)$ and the public music $P(t)$ out. It is sure that legal receivers know all frequencies of the lifting in the process of hiding secret. Then, lift down the radio-frequency wave $n'(t)$; it is doubtless that authorized receivers can obtain $n(t)$ via the operations of communication. The detail procedure of the operations will also be described later. After obtaining $n(t)$, receivers then transform $n(t)$ to a digital, meaningful data. It works like the following:

(d) An authorized receiver uses the information of block size l to derive the number of blocks in sampled wave $n(t)$, suppose it is $i + 1$, then it will obtain a group of binary streams S_1', S_2',..., S_i', S_{i+1}'.
(e) According to the transformation, the value of S_{i+1}' represents the number of zeros padded after S_i', suppose it is d.
(f) After deleting d zeros from the tail of S_i', the collecting of bit stream S_1', S_2', ..., S_{i-1}' and the S_i' could be concatenated one by one as a bit stream S'.

If an authorized receiver successfully turns $n(t)$ to a bit stream, it means the transformed output is S'. Finally, turn the bit stream S' to rebuild a meaningful content S. Receivers could identify the rebuilt data and judge that S is the correct one or not. The identification procedure is to compare the public audio $P(t)$ and others which contain the same meanings. The exhaustion will not need to be considered because all procedures are done by mathematical simulations.

2.1 Properties and Operations

The basic design of the scheme is on the characteristics of human-hearing system by psychoacoustics that humans are not able to hear radio-frequency (over 16,000 Hertz) signals [25]. If the frequency of a human voice can be lifted to a very-high-frequency band, the generated signals will not be heard by humans. In communication systems, it is necessary to lift up frequencies of signals because of long antennas corresponding to low-frequency signals. Long antennas are not feasible for delivering signals. In the following section, a frequency lifting which lifts up frequencies effectively is introduced [25]. We will describe how to use this technique steganography lately.

2.2 DSB-SC (Double-Sideband Suppressed Carrier)

Suppose there is a carrier sinusoidal wave $f(t)$ defined as $f(t) = Ac\ \cos(2\pi f ct)$, where t represents time in second, A_c is a carrier wave and f_c is a carrier frequency. Let $n(t)$ be the candidate signal (baseband signal). The DSB-SC wave $r(t)$ (delivering signal) is defined as $r(t) = Acn(t)\cos(2\pi fct)$. It is no doubt that the lifting process increases the frequency of a baseband. Also, F.T. (Fourier transform) of a periodic wave $a(t) = \cos 2\pi f0t$ according to frequency f_0 can be computed as

$$A(f) = F\{\cos(2\pi f_0 t)\} = F\{(1/2)(e^{2\pi f_0 t} + e^{-2\pi f_0 t})\} = (1/2)F(e^{2\pi f_0 t}) + (1/2)F(e^{-2\pi f_0 t})$$
$$= (1/2)(\delta(f - f_0) + \delta(f + f_0) \tag{1}$$

According to the Eq. (1), the F.T. of $c(t)$ is $(Ac/2)[\delta(f\text{-}fc) + \delta(f + fc)]$.

Let the F.T. of $a(t)$, $b(t)$ and $c(t)$ be denoted as $A(t)$, $B(t)$ and $C(t)$, respectively. Let $c(t) = a(t)b(t)$. Then follow the rule:

$$c(t) = a(t)b(t) \underset{\leftarrow}{\overset{\rightarrow}{\ }} C(f) = A(f) * B(f)$$

where $\rightarrow$ and $\leftarrow$ denotes Fourier and inverse Fourier transforms and $*$ represents convolution denoted as $A(f) * B(f) = \int_{-\infty}^{\infty} A(v)B(f - v)dv$. In this case, $a(t) = n(t)$, it indicates $A(f) = N(f)$ and $b(t) = \cos(2\pi f_c t)$ is also obtained. According to Eq. (1), it is known that $B(f) = (1/2)[\delta(f\text{-}f_c) + \delta(f + f_c)]$ and $B(f\text{-}v) = (1/2)[\delta(f\text{-}v\text{-}f_c) + \delta(f\text{-}v + f_c)]$. Thus,

$$A_c A(f) * B(f) = (A_c/2)\int_{-\infty}^{\infty} N(v)[\delta(f - v - f_c) + \delta(f - v + f_c)]dv =$$
$$(A_c/2)[N(f - f_c) + N(f + f_c)] \tag{2}$$

Equation (2) indicates that a base-band signal-frequency spectrum $N(t)$ is now lifted up to $N(f\text{-}f_c)$ and $N(f + f_c)$. Assume the signal $n(t)$ is band-limited to $[W, W]$. For instance, the F.T. of $N(f)$ is zero for $|f| > W$. Bandwidth of the message wave is then defined as W. For instance, a voice may have spectrum concentrated within 3 k Hertz. Its bandwidth is therefore $W = 3$ kHz. Components $N(f-f_c)$ and $N(f + f_c)$ are corresponding to higher frequencies. The lifted signal then consists of a spectrum concentrated around f_c, i.e., from $f_c - W$ to $f_c + W$. Bandwidth of the lifted signal is therefore $2W$. Note that the raising of frequencies of baseband signals to higher ones is the main purpose of the proposed protocol.

The system will recover signal $n(t)$ from DSB-SC signal and the lifting down works as follows. A lock oscillator produces a local sinusoidal waveform $\cos(2\pi fct)$ with the same frequency and phase as those of the transmitted carrier. The signal $r'(t) = r(t)\cos(2\pi fct)$ can be expressed as:

$$r'(t) = r(t)\cos(2\pi f_c t) = Acn(t)\cos^2(2\pi f_c t) = (A_c/2)n(t) + (A_c/2)n(t)\cos(2\pi(2f_c)t) \quad (3)$$

First term of Eq. (3) is a low-frequency part of $n(t)$. Second term of the Eq. (3) is a high-frequency part that is equivalent to a DSB-SC wave with carrier $2fc$. Signal $r'(t)$ will pass over a low-pass filter. A low-pass filter will only permit a low-frequency part which is $n(t)$ to pass and strain over a high-frequency part in the DSB-SC wave. Therefore, the lifted down output of a low-pass filter obtains only $(Ac/2)n(t)$. This indicates the $n(t)$ is recovered.

2.3 Carrier Orthogonality and Steganography

According to the previous properties, the authors proposed a protocol to hide secrets $N(t)$ into an acoustic $P(t)$ and then put in a voice/speech storage. Intruders who try to crack needs to brute force trying numerous public music in the database while authorized receivers are able to recover $N(t)$ according to the pre-shared information (cover medium and the carriers). The proposed protocol consists of the coming 3 steps:

(1) Multiply $N(t)$ and $\cos(2\pi fct)$ where fc is a very high frequency. It will lift all frequencies contained in $N(t)$ to radio frequency bands, namely surrounding fc. Define the lifted signal $N'(t)$. Since fc is very high, no one can hear the lifted wave $N'(t)$.
(2) Add $P(t)$ and $N'(t)$ to produce $P'(t)$. Any interceptor can hear $P(t)$ and would not be suspicious to embedded secrets.
(3) Authorized receivers use a high pass filter to strain out $N'(t)$ and then they will recover $N(t)$ after multiplying $N'(t)$ and $\cos(2\pi fct)$.

2.4 Entire Schemes

In the process of the secret hiding, suppose the secrets are $S1, S2, ..., Sn$. The first action is to turn the secrets to bit stream $S'1, S'2, ..., S'n$. However, the next operation is an frequency lifting and it is necessary to transform $S'1, S'2, ..., S'n$ to acoustic signals. The transformed signals are $n1(t), n2(t), ..., nn(t)$ and then transformed as high-frequency signals of lifting by high frequencies. At the end, the acoustic $P(t)$ is also embedded secrets to produce $P'(t)$. The sender provides the stego-acoustic $P'(t)$

in a public multimedia storage and authorized receivers are permitted to download. In the process of data recover, when authorized receivers download $P'(t)$, they adopt the recovering process to strain out waves $n'_1(t)$, $n'_2(t)$, ..., $n'_n(t)$ and turn them to bit streams. $S'1$, $S'2$, ..., $S'n$. Authorized receivers finally turn $S'1$, $S'2$, ..., $S'n$ to secret $S1$, $S2$, ..., Sn. Notice that there is pre-shared information, such as the translation of meaningful data and bit streams, the information of bit streams, acoustic waves and carrier frequencies, that should be given to authorized receivers. The regular data hiding and recovery procedures are given below.

Procedure of Embedding Secrets

Input: selected secrets $S1$, $S2$, ..., Sn, the translation rule translating secrets to binary strings, transformation rule transforming bit stream to acoustic waves, the cover acoustic $P(t)$, and carrier frequencies $f1, f2, ..., fn$.
Output: the stego-acoustic $P'(t)$.
Step 1:   use the translation rule to translate the secrets $S1$, $S2$, ..., Sn to bit streams $S'1$, $S'2$, ..., $S'n$.
Step 2:   use the transformation rule to transform bit streams $S'1, S'2, ..., S'n$ to acoustic waves $n1(t)$, $n2(t)$, ..., $nn(t)$.
Step 3:   Calculate $\cos(2\pi f\ 1t)$, $\cos(2\pi f\ 2t)$, ..., $\cos(2\pi fnt)$.
Step 4:   Multiply $n1(t)$, $n2(t)$, ..., $nn(t)$ by $\cos(2\pi f\ 1t)$, $\cos(2\pi f\ 2t)$, ..., $\cos(2\pi fnt)$ individually and generate $n'1(t)$, $n'2(t)$, ..., $n'n(t)$.
Step 5:   Summarize $n'1(t)$, $n'2(t)$, ..., $n'n(t)$, the result is $sum(t)$.
Step 6:   sum up $sum(t)$ and $P(t)$ to $P'(t)$

Procedure of Recovery Secrets

Input: received cover acoustic $P'(t)$, carrier frequencies $f1, f2, ..., fn$, HPF (high pass filter), LPF (low pass filter), transformation rule transforming acoustic waves to bit streams and the translation rule translating bit streams to secrets.
Output: secrets $S1$, $S2$, ..., Sn.
Step 1:   calculate $\cos(2\pi f\ 1t)$, $\cos(2\pi f\ 2t)$, ..., $\cos(2\pi fnt)$.
Step 2:   use HPF on $P'(t)$, the resulting wave is $sum'(t)$.
Step 3:   multiply $sum'(t)$ and individual of $\cos(2\pi f\ 1t)$, $\cos(2\pi f\ 2t)$, ..., and $\cos(2\pi fnt)$, it obtains $n11(t)$, $n21(t)$, ..., $nn1(t)$, respectively.
Step 4:   use LPF on $n11(t)$, $n21(t)$, ..., $nn1(t)$ to acquire the lifted down waves $n12(t)$, $n22(t)$, ..., $nn2(t)$, respectively.
Step 5:   adopt transformation rule to transform $n12(t)$, $n22(t)$, ..., $nn2(t)$ to bit streams $S'1$, $S'2$, ..., $S'n$
Step 6:   translate and recover secrets $S1$, $S2$, ..., Sn

3   Implementation and Experiment

A practical experiment which includes HPF, LPF and carrier lifting are simulated by using MATLAB 2010 in this section. Input secrets could be text or images. In this experiment, a text is the first secret and an image is the second secret. The data of the text file is **Revelation**, the last chapter of the **BIBBLE**. It will be transformed to binary value by ASCII. The image file is a 256×256 pixel PGM file, called Lena.pgm, which represents a famous testing file in image processing. Figure 1 is the description of "Lena.pgm". Figure 2 is the time-domain spectrum of a public voice $P(t)$.

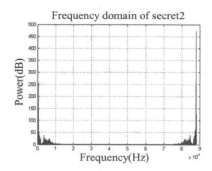

Time domain of the host audio

Fig. 1. Lena.pgm.

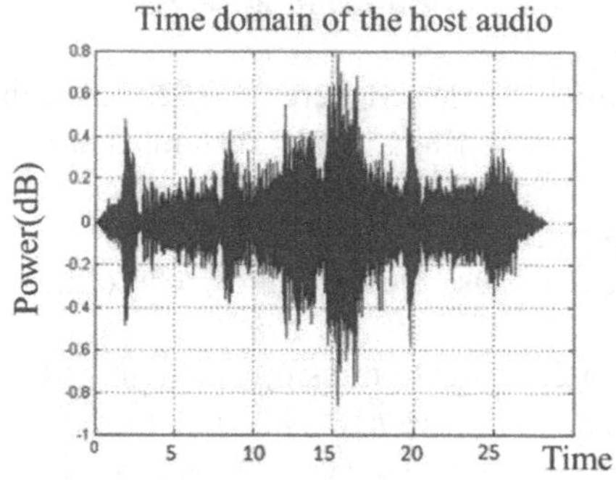

Fig. 2. The time domain of $P(t)$.

Each binary value will be processed to be a sampled value in time domain. Here the digital signal of the text and the image are denoted as $n_1(t)$ and $n_2(t)$, respectively. Figure 3 (Fig. 4) is the frequency domain of $n_1(t)$ ($n_2(t)$). Both of $n_1(t)$ and $n_2(t)$ are set up as 16 bits, 8000 Hzsignals.

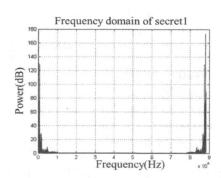

Fig. 3. The frequency spectrum of $n_1(t)$.

Fig. 4. The frequency spectrum of $n_2(t)$.

Consult to the data hiding process, $n_1(t)$ and $n_2(t)$ should be lifted to higher frequency, named $n'_1(t)$ and $n'_2(t)$. Figures 5 and 6 demonstrate their frequency domains after lifting to 18,000 Hz and 3,9000 Hz. The last step is to sum up $n'_1(t)$, $n'_2(t)$ and $P(t)$ to generate $P'(t)$ as shown in Fig. 7.

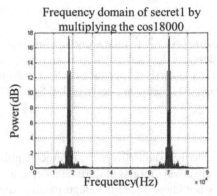

Fig. 5. Frequency spectrum of $n'_1(t)$.

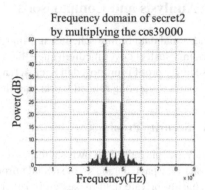

Fig. 6. Frequency specturm of $n'_2(t)$.

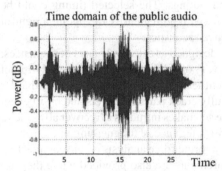

Fig. 7. Time series of $P'(t)$.

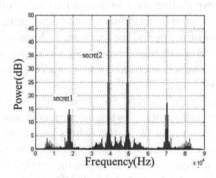

Fig. 8. Frequency spectrum of $sum(t)$.

In the recovery procedure, Fig. 8 demonstrates the frequency domain of the summation $sum(t)$ according to secrets $n'_1(t)$ and $n'_2(t)$ after applying HPF to $P'(t)$. Then multiply $\cos(2\pi f_1 t)$ and $\cos(2\pi f_2 t)$ which are carrier frequencies of $n_1(t)$ and $n_2(t)$, respectively. Figure 9 and Fig. 10 show the lifted-down secrets and after using low pass filter, respectively. It is clear that $n_1(t)$ and $n_2(t)$ have been successfully recovered.

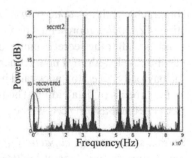

Fig. 9. Frequency spectrum of recovered $n_1(t)$.

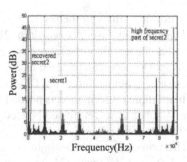

Fig. 10. Frequency spectrum of $n_2(t)$.

4 Analysis and Comparisons

Traditional data hiding schemes use images as the host file to hide secrets, while it will certainly distort cover medium such that intruders can detect the distortion and attack it. A security proof is proposed in Sect. 4.1, a capacity analysis is introduced in Sect. 4.3 and comparisons among related works and the proposed scheme are described in Sect. 4.3.

4.1 Security Proof

Today, people have their own databases referring to the availability of the Internet. Unlike those in the past, databases of special purposes are always targets of intruders. Popularity of sharing private data makes an intruder does not know where the stego-medium are. The proposed protocol is a primal steganographic scheme. It has different versions based on requirements of users. For example, senders can make appointments to receivers for downloading the modified audio in permitted timings. The selected timing could be encrypted by hash functions or other principles, with no regularity to appoint a rightful short-time period for receivers to download cover acoustics.

Besides, the secrets $S_1, S_2, ..., S_n$ could be designed as a dependent set of sequences: S_2 cannot be recovered without successful recovery of S_1, S_3 cannot be recovered without correct recovery of S_2, ..., and so on. A dependent set of sequences makes intruders harder to crack all secrets. An intruder may successfully crack parts of secrets and try to guess the entire contents, while a dependent sequence set makes intruders to recover all of them. According to [2, 3], the authors gave possibilities for successful guessing or recovering of secrets, meaning $P_r(S_i)$ which corresponds to brute force analysis on the composition of a sequence. In this paper, the above measurements are also provided while they are different. The probability $P_r(S_i)$ is composed of three probabilities: $P_{rBT}(S_i)$, $P_{rSM}(S_i)$ and $P_{rCL}(S_i)$. $P_{rBT}(S_i)$ defines the probabilities of cracking bit translation from secret S_i to bit streams S'_i. $P_{rSM}(S_i)$ represents the probability of cracking S'_i to $n_i(t)$. $P_{rCL}(S_i)$ is the probability of cracking the carrier frequencies which are used to lift the secrets to high frequencies from $n_i(t)$ to $n'_i(t)$. Obviously, $P_r(S_i) = P_{rBT}(S_i) \times P_{rSM}(S_i) \times P_{rSM}(S_i)$, and the probability of breaking a dependent set of sequences is $\prod_{i=1}^{n} Pr(S'_i)$.

4.2 Capacity Analysis

Other considerations in the research field of steganography such as *capacity*, *payload* and *bpn* should be issued. Consult to [2], the definition of *capacity*, represented by *CA* is defined as the length of the increased-referencing sequence after the secret is embedded within it. The *payload*, denoted as *PA*, is defined as the rest length of a new sequence after straining out a referencing DNA sequence. The payload is used to understand how much additional information is needed to append in the process of data hiding. The *bpn* as the number of secret bits embedded per character is defined as $|M|/CA$, where M is the number of secret bits.

The proposed protocol might contain many secrets such that the *capacity* $C_M = \frac{|P(t)|}{2} + \sum_{i=1}^{n} CA_i$. (each CA_i is a *capacity* generated after hiding a secret in $P(t)$) if there are n secret bits embedded in the cover audio $P(t)$. Note that $\frac{|P(t)|}{2}$ is the character size of $P(t)$ because all CA_i's are in character form. The *payload* $PA_M = \sum_{i=1}^{n} PA_i$ is the summation of all PA_i's of secrets. The *bpn* is equal to $\frac{\sum_{i=1}^{n}|M_i|}{CA_M}$, where $|M_i|$ is the size of a secret hidden in one of the secrets. It is obvious that the size of $P(t)$ does not restrict the capacity of the proposed protocol. It can be said that if the number of secrets is large enough or $|P(t)|$ is quite small, *bpn* will be nearly equal to $\frac{\sum_{i=1}^{n}|M_i|}{\sum_{i=1}^{n}CA_i}$.

4.3 Comparisons

This section compares related works [8, 10] and the proposed scheme. Audio steganography focuses on bit error ratio under signal-processing attack including filtering (high/low pass), direct current (DC) padding, re-quantization (such 16 to 8bits or 8 to 16 bits), random noise padding and echo injection [10]. Bit error ratio denoted by *BER* is defined as the percentage of correct numbers of secrets under attack. Echo, DC and random noise intervention utilize noise with low frequency to distort the stego-acoustic. HPF (High pass filter) will not affect the secrets of the proposed scheme because they are all lifted to high frequencies. Re-quantization will not affect the proposed scheme because the secrets are all used as eight-bits data. Table 1 points out the performance when the proposed protocol is under each kind of attacks. The results confirm the presented scheme outperforms other methods.

Table 1. Comparisons of bit error ratio (*BER*) under some types of attacks.

Schemes	Attacks				
	Direct current	High pass filter (8 kHz)	Re-quantization (16 to 8 bits)	Noise (25 dB)	Echo
The proposed scheme	0.0%	0.0%	0.0%	0.3%	0.1%
[8]	4.5%	4.2%	11.9%	22.8%	7.2%
[10]	0.0%	0.0%	0.0%	1.0%	12.0%

Ø: not proposed

Table 2 demonstrates numbers of data which can be embedded by adopting LSB (least significant bit), spread spectrum and the proposed scheme. A selected cover audio with size equal to two hundred kilo-bits and secret with size of thirty kilo-bits are used. The LSB strategy only has 1/8 space of selected cover signal, i.e., 25,000 bits, which is replaced by the secret. Spread spectrum will be used to hide all data in a cover signal, while available space might be less than the secret. The proposed protocol will not be restricted by the size of the cover signal, that is, all secrets can be embedded via giving enough carrier frequencies and making sure all given frequencies are orthogonal to each other.

Table 2. Available spaces of different strategies.

Variables	Strategy		
	Spread spectrum (bits)	LSB (bits)	Proposed scheme
$P(t)$	200,000	200,000	200,000
$|M|$	<30,000	25,000	30,000

5 Conclusions

In this paper, a steganography based carrier orthogonality is proposed. Secrets are first transformed to acoustic waves and embedded in an acoustic via frequency lifting. The strategy proposed here adds a hiding audio to make illegal intruders unaware of the secrets and the transmission restriction is also neglected. Unlike previous studies, the popularity of a cover audio will make intruders ignore suspicious files with secrets hidden inside, and numerous secrets are allowed to be delivered via once transmission. Different multimedia could be embedded in cover acoustics and delivered by respectively lifting them to different radio frequencies and these radio signals do not mutually interfere with others due to using accurate carrier frequencies to extract them out correctly. The property is so called carrier orthogonality. Also, it obtains high security even if the intruders know that those secrets are presented in a stego-acoustic. It will be impossible for the stego-acoustic being successfully recovered by intruders. In the last step, a widely-used personal database on Internet can be selected to store the stego-audio which can then be downloaded by legal users actively. It will certainly decrease risks on exposing the secrets via a transition. Furthermore, legal receivers will not be induced by identifying the recovered host audio. In addition, high capacity will be still practical if the sender uses a cover medium of small size. At the end, the proposed protocol is easily changed to further reduce the cracking probability by adding the time constraint.

References

1. Shiu, H.J., Lin, B.S., Lin, B.S., Huang, P.Y., Huang, C.H., Lei, C.L.: Data hiding on social media communications using text steganography. In: Cuppens, N., Cuppens, F., Lanet, J.L., Legay, A., Garcia-Alfaro, J. (eds.) CRiSIS 2017. LNCS, vol. 10694, pp. 217–224. Springer, Cham (2018). https://doi.org/10.1007/978-3-319-76687-4_15
2. Hsu, H.Z., Lee, R.C.T.: DNA based encryption methods. In: The 23rd workshop on combinatorial mathematics and computation theory, pp. 545 (2006)
3. Shiu, H.J., Lin, B.S., Huang, C.H., Chiang, P.Y., Lei, C.L.: Preserving privacy of online digital physiological signals using blind and reversible steganography. Comput. Methods Programs Biomed. **151**, 159–170 (2017)
4. Bender, W., Morimoto, N., Lu, A.: Techniques for data hiding. IBM Syst. J. **35**(3/4), 313–336 (1996)
5. Swanson, M.D., Zhu, B., Tewfik, A.H., Boney, L.: Robust watermarking using perceptual masking. Sig. Process. **66**(3), 337–355 (1998)

6. Cox, I.J., Kilian, J., Leighton, T., Shamoon, T.: Secure spread spectrum watermarking for multimedia. IEEE Trans. Image Process. **6**(12), 1673–1687 (1997)
7. Wu, S., Huang, J., Huang, D., Shi, Y.Q.: Efficiently self-synchronized audio watermarking for assured audio data transmission. IEEE Trans. Broadcast. **151**(1), 69–76 (2005)
8. Chen, O.T.-C., Wu, W.-C.: Highly robust, secure, and perceptual-quality echo hiding scheme. IEEE Trans. Audio, Speech, Lang. Process. **16**(3), 629–638, March 2008
9. Shiu, H.J., Lin, B.S., Cheng, C.W., Huang, C.H., Lei, C.L.: High-capacity data-hiding scheme on synthesized pitches using amplitude enhancement-a new vision of non-blind audio steganography. Symmetry **9**(6), 92 (2017)
10. Akhaee, M.A., Saberian, M.J., Feizi, S., Marvasti, F.: Robust audio data hiding using corre-lated quantization with histogram-based detector. IEEE Trans. Multimedia **11**(5), 834–842 (2009)
11. Tian, H., Jiang, H., Zhou, K., Feng, D.: Transparency-orientated encoding strategies for voice-over-ip steganography. Comput. J. **55**(6), 702–716 (2011)
12. Tian, H., et al.: Improved adaptive partial-matching steganography for voice over IP. Comput. Commun. **70**, 95–108 (2015)
13. Tian, H., et al.: Optimal matrix embedding for voice-over-IP steganography. Sig. Process. **117**, 33–43 (2015)
14. Nishimura, A.: Reversible audio data hiding based on variable error-expansion of linear prediction for segmental audio and G.711 speech, IEICE Trans. Inf. Syst. **E99-D**(1), 83–91 (2016)
15. Xiang, S., Li, Z.: Reversible audio data hiding algorithm using noncausal prediction of alter-able orders. EURASIP J. Audio Speech Music Process. **2017**(1), 1–16 (2017). https://doi.org/10.1186/s13636-017-0101-9
16. Parthasarathi, M., Shreekala, T.: Secured data hiding in audio files using audio steganography algorithm. Int. J. Pure Appl. Math. **116**(21), 619–628 (2017)
17. Ali, A.H., George, L.E., Zaidan, A.A., Modhtar, M.R.: High Capacity, Transparent and Secure Audio Steganography Model Based on Fractal Coding and Chaotic Map in Temporal Domain, vol. 77, pp. 31487–31516 (2018)
18. X. Liu, H. Tian, Y. Huang and J. Lu, "A Novel Steganography Method for Algebraic-Code-Excited-Linear-Prediction Speech Streams Based on Fractional Pitch Delay Search," vol. 78, pp. 8447–8461, 2019
19. Dai, Y., Liu, W., Liu, G., Ji, X., Zhai, J.: An End-To-End Generative Network for Environmental Sound-Based Covert Communication, vol. 78, pp. 8635–8653 (2019)
20. Said, E.E.K., Noha, O.K., Marwa, H.E.S.: Highly Secured Image Hiding Technique in Stereo Audio Signal Based on Complete Complementary Codes, vol. 78, pp. 34373–34395 (2019)
21. Javad, C., Mohammad, M., Saeed, R.H.: A Novel Quantum Steganography-Steganalysis System for Audio Signals, Multimedia Tools and Applications (2020)
22. Su, Z., Li, W., Zhang, G., Hu, D., Zhou, X.: A steganographic method based on gain quantization for iLBC speech streams. Multimedia Syst. **26**, 223–233 (2020)
23. Wu, J., Chen, B.: Audio steganography based on iterative adversarial attacks against convolutional neural networks. IEEE Trans. Inf. Forensics Secur. **15**, 2282–2294 (2020)
24. Shiu, H., Lin, B., Lin, B., Lai, W.C., Huang, C.H., Lei, C.L.: A stereo audio steganography by inserting low-frequency and octave equivalent pure tones. In: Krömer, P., Alba, E., Pan, J.S., Snášel, V. (eds.) ECC 2017. AISC, vol. 682, pp. 244–253. Springer, Cham (2018). https://doi.org/10.1007/978-3-319-68527-4_27
25. Lee, R.C.T., Chiu, M.C., Lin, J.S.: Communications Engineering: Essentials for Computer Scientists and Electrical Engineers, Wiley, Asia (2007)

Application, System, and Hardware Security

Compact Implementation of CHAM Block Cipher on Low-End Microcontrollers

Hyeokdong Kwon, Hyunji Kim, Seung Ju Choi, Kyoungbae Jang, Jaehoon Park, Hyunjun Kim, and Hwajeong Seo[✉]

IT Department, Hansung University, Seoul, South Korea
korlethean@gmail.com , bookingstore3@gmail.com, starj1023@gmail.com , p9595jh@gmail.com, khj930704@gmail.com, hwajeong84@gmail.com

Abstract. In this paper, we presented an optimized implementation of CHAM block cipher on low-end microcontrollers. In order to accelerate the performance of the CHAM block cipher, the architecture of CHAM block cipher and the full specification of 8-bit AVR microcontrollers are efficiently utilized. First, the counter mode of operation for CHAM block cipher is optimized. A number of computations for round function are replaced to look-up table accesses. Second, multiple blocks of CHAM block cipher are computed in a parallel way for high throughput. With the parallel computation, we also presented the adopted encryption. This approach is efficient for long-length data handling. Third, the state-of-art engineering technique is fully utilized in terms of instruction level and register level. The partially unrolled 8-round based implementation is adopted, which avoids a number of word-wise rotation operations. With above optimization techniques, proposed CHAM implementations for counter mode of operation outperform the state-of-art implementations by 30.1%, 9.3%, and 10.0% for CHAM-64/128, CHAM-128/128, and CHAM-128/256, respectively.

Keywords: CHAM block cipher · Microcontroller · Counter mode of operation · Parallel computation · Round based encryption

1 Introduction

Internet of Things (IoT) becomes feasible services as the technology of embedded processors are developed. In order to provide user-friendly services, IoT applications need to analyze data which should be securely encrypted before packet transmission. However, the encryption is expensive for resource-constrained IoT devices with limited computation, energy, and storage. For this reason, block cipher algorithms should be implemented in an efficient manner under certain limitations.

In this paper, we introduce optimization techniques for CHAM block cipher on 8-bit AVR microcontrollers. Optimized counter mode of CHAM block cipher

© Springer Nature Switzerland AG 2020
I. You (Ed.): WISA 2020, LNCS 12583, pp. 127–141, 2020.
https://doi.org/10.1007/978-3-030-65299-9_10

and parallel computations are presented. To get compact results, we used platform-specific assembly-level optimizations for CHAM block ciphers (e.g. word size, number of registers, and instruction set). Proposed implementation techniques for CHAM block cipher can be used for other ARX based block ciphers, such as SPECK and SIMON, straightforwardly. Detailed contributions are as follows:

1.1 Contribution

Optimized Counter Mode of Operation for CHAM Block Cipher. The repeated input of counter mode of operation for CHAM block cipher can be optimized with the pre-computation. In total, 5 left rotation by 1-bit, 10 XOR, 3 ADD, and 3 left rotation by word-wise operations are replaced to 5 word-wise table accesses. The proposed method optimizes all CHAM parameters.

Parallel Implementation of CHAM-64/128. The lightweight version of CHAM block cipher (i.e. CHAM-64/128) is accelerated with the parallel computation. By utilizing all registers, multiple blocks of CHAM block cipher are computed, simultaneously. We also presented an adopted encryption with the parallel computation, which is efficient when the data length is long enough.

Highly Optimized Source Code and 8-Round Based Implementation. The state-of-art engineering technique is fully utilized with the available instruction sets and register files to achieve the high performance. The partially unrolled 8-round based implementation is adopted, which optimizes the left rotation by 8-bit wise operations.

The remainder of this paper is organized as follows. In Sect. 2, the basic specifications of CHAM block cipher and target AVR microcontrollers are described. In Sect. 3, the compact implementation of CHAM block cipher on AVR microcontrollers are described. In Sect. 4, the performance of proposed methods in terms of execution timing is evaluated. Finally, Sect. 5 concludes the paper.

2 Related Works

2.1 CHAM Block Cipher

Lightweight cryptography is a fundamental technology to optimize the hardware chip size and reduce the execution timing for low-end Internet of Things (IoT) devices. Recently, a number of block cipher algorithms have been designed for being lightweight features.

In ICISC'17, a family of lightweight block ciphers CHAM was announced by the Attached Institute of ETRI [1]. The family consists of three ciphers, including CHAM-64/128, CHAM-128/128, and CHAM-128/256. The CHAM block ciphers are of the generalized 4-branch Feistel structure based on ARX operations.

In ICISC'19, the revised version of CHAM block cipher was presented [2]. In order to prevent new related-key differential characteristics and differentials of CHAM using a SAT solver, the numbers of rounds of CHAM-64/128, CHAM-128/128, and CHAM-128/256 are increased from 80 to 88, 80 to 112, and 96 to 120, respectively.

2.2 Previous Block Cipher Implementations on 8-Bit AVR Microcontrollers

Table 1. Instruction set summary for efficient CHAM implementations on 8-bit AVR microcontrollers.

asm	Operands	Description	Operation	#Clock
ADD	Rd, Rr	Add without Carry	$Rd \leftarrow Rd + Rr$	1
ADC	Rd, Rr	Add with Carry	$Rd \leftarrow Rd + Rr + C$	1
EOR	Rd, Rr	Exclusive OR	$Rd \leftarrow Rd \oplus Rr$	1
LSL	Rd	Logical Shift Left	$C\|Rd \leftarrow Rd \ll 1$	1
ROL	Rd	Rotate Left Through Carry	$C\|Rd \leftarrow Rd \ll 1\|\|C$	1
MOV	Rd, Rr	Copy Register	$Rd \leftarrow Rr$	1
MOVW	Rd, Rr	Copy Register Word	$Rd + 1:Rd \leftarrow Rr + 1:Rr$	1
LDI	Rd, K	Load Immediate	$Rd \leftarrow K$	1
LD	Rd, X	Load Indirect	$Rd \leftarrow (X)$	2
LPM	Rd, Z	Load Program Memory	$Rd \leftarrow (Z)$	3
ST	Z, Rr	Store Indirect	$(Z) \leftarrow Rr$	2
PUSH	Rr	Push Register on Stack	$STACK \leftarrow Rr$	2
POP	Rd	Pop Register from Stack	$Rd \leftarrow STACK$	2

The low-end 8-bit AVR platform working at 8 MHz supports 8-bit instruction set, 128 KB FLASH memory, and 4 KB RAM. The number of available registers is 32. Among them, 6 registers (i.e R26–R31) are reserved for address pointers and the other registers are used for general purpose. The basic arithmetic instruction takes one clock cycle, while the memory access takes two clock cycles per byte. Detailed instruction set summary for efficient CHAM-CTR implementation is given in Table 1.

A number of works devoted to improve the performance of lightweight cryptography implementations on low-end microcontrollers (e.g. 8-bit AVR). The structure of block cipher is largely divided into two categories. First, Addition, Rotation, and eXclusive-or (ARX) based block ciphers were efficiently implemented on low-end microcontrollers.

In WISA'13, LEA block cipher was by the attached institute of ETRI [3]. First implementation of LEA-128 on the 8-bit AVR microcontroller achieved 190 clock cycles per byte for the encryption [3]. In WISA'15, speed-optimized and memory-efficient LEA implementations were presented [4]. In [5], the number of general purpose registers and the instruction set of the AVR microcontroller were fully utilized to optimize the LEA block cipher implementation. In WISA'18, general purpose registers are efficiently utilized to cache intermediate results of delta variables during the key scheduling of LEA [6].

In CHES'06, HIGHT block cipher was introduced [7]. The basic implementation of HIGHT was firstly introduced in [8]. The execution timing for encryption and decryption is 2,438 and 2,520 clock cycles per byte, respectively. In [5], efficient rotation operations were suggested and achieved high performance. In [9], speed-optimized and memory-efficient HIGHT implementations were presented.

In ICISC'17, the original CHAM on 8-bit AVR microcontrollers achieved 172, 148, and 177 clock cycles per byte for CHAM-64/128, CHAM-128/128, and CHAM-128/256, respectively [1]. In [10], 2-round based memory-efficient implementation was suggested. The work achieved 211, 187, and 223 clock cycles per bytes for CHAM-64/128, CHAM-128/128, and CHAM-128/256, respectively, with reasonably small memory footprint. In ICISC'19, revised CHAM was presented by modifying the round of CHAM [2]. AVR implementations achieved 188, 203, and 219 clock cycles per byte for CHAM-64/128, CHAM-128/128, and CHAM-128/256, respectively.

Second, Substitution Permutation Network (SPN) based block ciphers were also actively investigated. Among them, AES implementations received the high attention since the block cipher is international standard.

In [11], S-box pointer was maintained in Z address pointer for the fast memory access. The mix-column computation was efficiently handled with the conditional branch skip. In ICISC'19, the compact implementation of AES-CTR on microcontrollers (i.e. FACE-LIGHT) was presented [12]. With the newly designed cache table for low-end microcontrollers, implementations of AES-CTR achieved 138, 168, and 199 clock cycles per byte for 128-bit, 192-bit, and 256-bit security levels, respectively.

3   Proposed Method

3.1   Optimized CHAM-CTR Mode Encryption

We present the optimized CHAM-CTR mode encryption on 8-bit AVR microcontrollers. The counter mode utilizes nonce and counter as an input value. The nonce is a fixed value, and the counter indicates the order of blocks. Generally, the length of counter is set to a quarter of plaintext. CHAM-64/128, CHAM-128/128, and CHAM-128/256 assigned 16-bit, 32-bit, and 32-bit counter values, respectively. The remainder is set to nonce (i.e. 48-bit, 96-bit, and 96-bit for CHAM-64/128, CHAM-128/128, and CHAM-128/256, respectively)[1]. By utilizing the fixed nonce value, operations for several rounds are replaced to look-up table. Unlike the nonce value, the counter value increases in each encryption,

---

[1] 32-bit counter can be used for CHAM-64/128. In this case, pre-computed part is slightly reduced to half but still this leads to performance improvements over basic implementation.

which updates the intermediate result. For this reason, some intermediate results cannot be cached. In Fig. 1, the part affected by counter value is described.

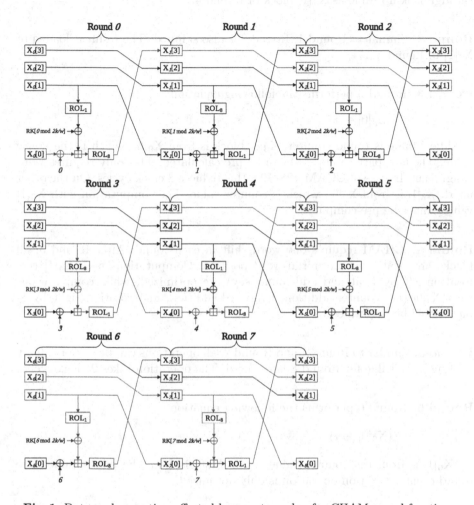

Fig. 1. Data and operation affected by counter value for CHAM round function.

Round 0. $X_0[0]$ block is counter value and the result cannot be pre-computed, while $X_0[1]$ block is nonce value and rotation to left by 1-bit and XOR operations can be pre-computed, which can be accessible through memory access. For better performance, LDI instruction is utilized, which directly assigns the 8-bit value in 1 clock cycles. This approaches reduces 2 clock cycles than memory access in each 8-bit assignment.

Round 1. Round 1 can be skipped because all inputs are fixed values, such as nonce, round key, and round counter. The result of this round is obtained through look-up table as $X_4[1]$ block of Round 4.

Round 2. Similar to Round 1, Round 2 is also skipped. The result is loaded to $X_5[1]$ of Round 5.

Round 3. Round 3 performs the following equation:

$$((X_3[0] \oplus i) \boxplus ((X_3[1] \lll 8) \oplus RoundKey[3]) \lll 1)$$

The i value is round counter. $X_3[0]$ block is from $X_0[3]$, which is the nonce value. The first part $(X_3[0] \oplus i)$ can be pre-calculated. This only requires word assignment. In case of CHAM-128/128, this reduces 8 clock cycles. On the other hand, $X_3[1]$ is from $X_0[0]$, which is counter value. The computation with $X_3[1]$ value cannot be pre-computed.

Round 4. CHAM requires one word shift in each round. After Round 3, all blocks are located in the initial word position. Computations with $X_4[1]$ (i.e. rotation left by 1-bit and add-round key) are optimized, while computations with $X_4[0]$ (i.e. counter-addition, two-word-addition, and rotation right by 8-bit) should be performed.

Round 5. Similar to Round 1 and Round 2, all operations can be skipped. Only loading $X_5[0]$ value for Round 8 is required. The operation takes 2 clock cycles.

Round 6. Round 6 performs the following equation:

$$((X_6[0] \oplus i) \boxplus ((X_6[1] \lll 1) \oplus RoundKey[6]) \lll 8)$$

$X_6[1]$ is from the counter value, while $X_6[0]$ is from the nonce value. The round counter addition operation is only optimized.

Round 7. Since all operations are originated from counter value, all operations should be implemented.

Round 8+. After Round 7, some operations are still pre-computed. In Round 8, $X_8[1]$ is not affected by counter value, which is represented in Fig. 1. XOR operation between $X_8[1]$ and round key part can be pre-computed. The optimization is only 0.6, 0.7, and 0.7 clock cycles per byte for CHAM64/128, CHAM-128/128, and CHAM-128/256 respectively. For this reason, this case is not considered in this paper. The optimized CHAM-CTR is given in Fig. 2. The green line indicates the pre-computed part. The proposed design shows that only 5 memory accesses for cache tables in Round 0, 3, 4, 6, and 7 are required.

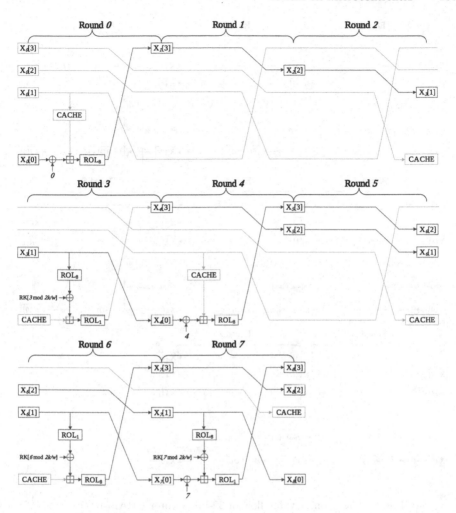

Fig. 2. Optimized CHAM-CTR mode encryption for round function. (Color figure online)

32-Bit Counter for CHAM-64/128. Originally, CTR mode of operation using 32-bit counter, but in this paper we implemented 16-bit counter CHAM-64/128, since CHAM-64/128 defines the block size as 16-bit. For compatibility with existing mode of operation, it needs to implement 32-bit counter CHAM-64/128. It can be implemented by storing counter value in two blocks. In Fig. 3, the counter value flow represented, the counter value is extended to $X_0[1]$ block as following figure. So we can see that some sections are no longer available pre-computation. It will result in slightly less performance than 16-bit counter CHAM-64/128.

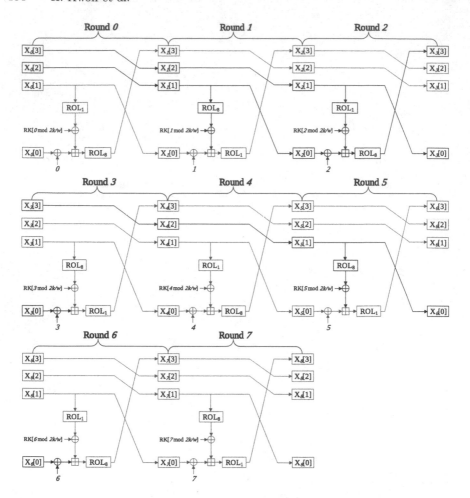

Fig. 3. The counter value flow of 32-bit counter CHAM-64/128.

Optimized Memory Access. The round key is stored in SRAM and accessed through LD instruction. This requires 2 clock cycles per byte. By aligning the round key in 8-bit wise, the offset is only controlled with lower byte. In order to access the pre-computed value, LDI instruction is utilized. This requires 1 clock cycle per byte and does not require memory pointer setting.

Round Counter and Pointer Address Optimization. In the optimized version, the round counter is only used in Round 0, 4, and 7. The round key is used in Round 3, 6, and 7. Thus round counter or pointer address value is assigned directly in each round. With this approach, 8 INC instructions for round counter are replaced to 1 INC and 2 LDI instructions. Five ADIW instructions for pointer address value are reduced to 2 ADIW. The ADIW instruction adds for pointer address in multiples of 2 and 4 for CHAM-64/128 and CHAM-128/128 or CHAM-128/256, respectively due to varied length of plaintext.

3.2   Parallel Implementations of CHAM Block Cipher

Parallel implementations generate multiple ciphertexts in one implementation. Two types of parallel implementations have been investigated (i.e. 2-parallel and 3-parallel). Since the implementation requires intermediate result caching, the register utilization should be optimized.

Target 8-bit AVR microcontrollers has 32 8-bit registers. For the CHAM-64/128 block cipher, 8 registers are needed. For the case of 2-parallel implementation, it requires 16 registers to save two plaintexts. In addition, the operation requires control variables, including round counter, round key, and address pointer for loading round keys and plaintexts storage. In Fig. 4 (a), the register utilization for 2-parallel implementation is given. In this case, all values can be maintained in registers.

On the other hand, 3-parallel implementation requires more registers than 2-parallel implementation. Twenty four registers are used for plaintexts. Since there are not enough registers, STACK memory is utilized and some registers are used for multiple purposes. Detailed optimization techniques are as follows:

- **Total round variable:** By using CPI instruction, total round value is not maintained in the register.
- **Plaintext block** Only part of plaintext (i.e. $X_i[0]$, and $X_i[1]$) is required to perform the round. Other plaintext values are temporarily stored in STACK memory.
- **Address pointer:** Round key and plaintext address pointers are required in computations. However, the address pointer for plaintext is not used throughout computations. The address pointer is stored in STACK.
- **Round Key:** Each round key access requires word-wise memory access. By accessing byte by byte, only one register is utilized to access round key.
- **Round counter** Round counter is XORed with data in each round. After the XOR operation, the round counter is stored in STACK.
- **ZERO:** R1 register is ZERO register. For 3-parallel implementation, R1 register is assigned for plaintext. Some registers are temporarily initialized to act as ZERO register.

In Fig. 4 (b), the register utilization for 3-parallel implementation is given.

The parallel computation of CHAM-64/128 is given in Algorithm 1. From Step 3 to 7, rotation operations are performed depending on the counter. In Step 8, round key addition is performed. With these round keys, multiple blocks are computed in parallel way. From Step 11 to 15, rotation operations are performed depending on the counter. From Step 16 to 19, the intermediate result is relocated by word-wise.

There are limitations to implement the parallel version of CHAM-128/128 and CHAM-128/256. CHAM-128/128 and CHAM-128/256 have twice much longer plaintext then CHAM-64/128. For this reason, parallel implementations for these algorithms are not considered.

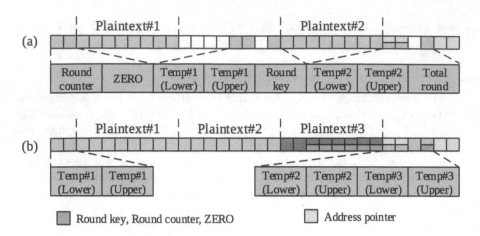

Fig. 4. Register alignment for (a) 2-parallel and (b) 3-parallel of CHAM-64/128 implementations. Each block represents one register. Two color in one register is used for various purposes. (Color figure online)

3.3   Adaptive Encryption of CHAM Block Cipher

The parallel computation is effective for huge data handling. The parallel computation can be applied to adaptive encryption [13]. The adaptive encryption performs parallel encryption operations when the length of data is long enough. When only one block is remained, single block encryption is performed. Detailed descriptions for 2-way adaptive encryption are given in Algorithm 2. The method performs 2-parallel computations. From Step 3 to 5, parallel computation is performed. Afterward, from Step 6 to 8, sequential computation is performed for remaining data.

3.4   Optimized Implementations of Primitive Operations

The implementation is based on 8-round based implementation. In every 8 round, the 8-bit rotation operation on data for CHAM-64/128 is optimized away. For CHAM-128/128 and CHAM-128/256, still 16-bit wise rotation operation is required. This is performed in 16-bit wise move operation MOVW. The other optimized 16/32-bit word rotation operations are given in Table 2.

4   Evaluation

Proposed implementations of CHAM block cipher were evaluated on low-end 8-bit AVR microcontrollers. The performance was measured in execution time (clock cycles per byte). The software was implemented over Atmel Studio 7 and the code was complied in -O2 option. Comparison result of CHAM block cipher is given in Fig. 5. Compared with previous works by [2], CHAM-64/128, CHAM-128/128, and CHAM-128/256 are improved by 11.7%, 6.5%, and 7.4%.

Algorithm 1. Parallel implementation of CHAM-64/128.

Input: Plaintext blocks $(X[0][0 \sim 3], ..., X[\#parallel - 1][0 \sim 3])$.
Output: Ciphertext blocks $(X[0][0 \sim 3], ..., X[\#parallel - 1][0 \sim 3])$.

1: **for** $i = 0$ to $\#round$ **do**
2: **for** $j = 0$ to $\#parallel$ **do**
3:   **if** i mod $2 == 0$ **then**
4:    $tmp[j][0] \leftarrow ROL_1(X[j][1])$
5:   **else**
6:    $tmp[j][0] \leftarrow ROL_8(X[j][1])$
7:   **end if**

8:   $tmp[j][1] \leftarrow tmp[j][0] \oplus RK[i \text{ mod } 16]$ `//round key access optimization`
9:   $tmp[j][2] \leftarrow X[j][0] \oplus i$
10: $tmp[j][3] \leftarrow tmp[j][1]tmp[j][2]$

11: **if** i mod $2 == 0$ **then**
12:   $tmp[j][4] \leftarrow ROL_8(tmp[j][3])$
13: **else**
14:   $tmp[j][4] \leftarrow ROL_1(tmp[j][3])$
15: **end if**

16: $X[j][0] \leftarrow X[j][1]$
17: $X[j][1] \leftarrow X[j][2]$
18: $X[j][2] \leftarrow X[j][3]$
19: $X[j][3] \leftarrow tmp[j][4]$
20: **end for**
21: **end for**

Table 2. Optimized 16/32-bit word rotation operations on 8-bit AVR microcontroller.

16-bit ROL_1	16-bit ROL_8	32-bit ROL_1	32-bit ROL_8

LSL LOW
ROL HIGH
ADC LOW, ZERO
	MOV TEMP, LOW
	MOV LOW, HIGH
	MOV HIGH, TEMP
		LSL R0
		ROL R1
		ROL R2
		ROL R3
		ADC R0, ZERO
			MOV TEMP, R3
			MOV R3, R2
			MOV R2, R1
			MOV R1, R0
			MOV R0, TEMP

3 cycles	3 cycles	5 cycles	5 cycles

The performance enhancement comes from the 8-round implementation and fast memory for round key. For the case of counter mode of operation, the implementation improved the performance further by 4.2%, 3.0%, and 2.8% for CHAM-64/128, CHAM-128/128, and CHAM-128/256, respectively. The implementation utilized the repeated data (i.e. nonce) to improve the performance. The parallel implementation of CHAM-64/128 shows 137.2 and 149 clock cycles per byte for

Algorithm 2. 2-way adaptive encryption for CHAM64/128.

Input: Number of blocks N, Plaintext blocks $P \in \{P_1, P_2, ..., P_N\}$.
Output: Ciphertext blocks
$\quad C \in \{C_1, C_2, ..., C_N\}$.

1: $n \leftarrow \frac{N}{2}$
2: $m \leftarrow N \bmod 2$

3: **for** $i = 0$ to n **do**
4: $\quad \{C_{2 \cdot i+1}, C_{2 \cdot i}\} \leftarrow ENC(\{P_{2 \cdot i+1}, P_{2 \cdot i}\})$ `//parallel computation`
5: **end for**

6: **if** m **then**
7: $\quad C_{2 \cdot n+2} \leftarrow ENC(P_{2 \cdot i+2})$ `//sequential computation`
8: **end if**
9: **return** C

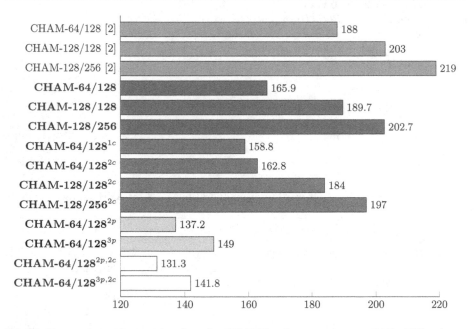

Fig. 5. Comparison of execution time for CHAM implementations on 8-Bit AVR micro-controllers under the fixed-key scenario in terms of clock cycles per byte, 1c: counter mode of operation (16-bit counter), 2c: counter mode of operation (32-bit counter), 2p: 2-parallel, 3p: 3-parallel.

2-parallel and 3-parallel versions, respectively. Due to limited number of registers, 2-parallel based implementation shows better performance than that of 3-parallel.

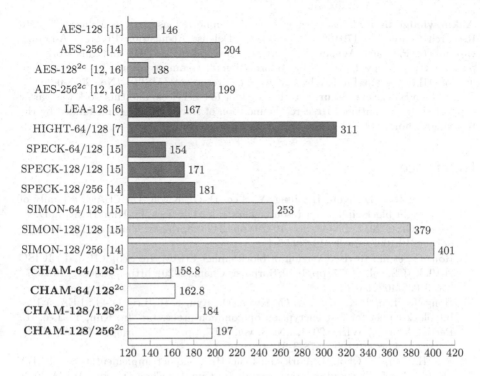

Fig. 6. Comparison of execution time for CHAM with other block ciphers on 8-Bit AVR microcontrollers in terms of clock cycles per byte, 1c: counter mode of operation (16-bit counter), 2c: counter mode of operation (32-bit counter).

We also compared the result with other block ciphers in Fig. 6. SPN based AES implementation achieved the highest performance among them, because AES is designed to fit into 8-bit word architecture. Among ARX implementations, SPECK shows the fastest performance. Second winner is proposed CHAM block cipher.

5 Conclusion

In this paper, we presented optimization implementations of lightweight CHAM block ciphers on low-end 8-bit AVR microcontrollers. Proposed techniques include pre-computed counter mode of operation, parallel implementation, and optimized primitive operations. We evaluated our implementations in terms of execution time. The result shows that our implementations achieved fast execution timing for practical IoT applications.

Future work is applying proposed method to other ARX–based block ciphers, such as SIMON and SPECK. Furthermore, other microcontrollers including 16-bit MSP and 32-bit ARM will be investigated.

Acknowledgement. This work was partly supported as part of Military Crypto Research Center (UD170109ED) funded by Defense Acquisition Program Administration (DAPA) and Agency for Defense Development (ADD) and this work was partly supported by Institute for Information & communications Technology Promotion (IITP) grant funded by the Korea government (MSIT) (No. 2018-0-00264, Research on Blockchain Security Technology for IoT Services) and this work was partly supported by the National Research Foundation of Korea (NRF) grant funded by the Korea government (MSIT) (No. NRF-2020R1F1A1048478).

References

1. Koo, B., Roh, D., Kim, H., Jung, Y., Lee, D.-G., Kwon, D.: CHAM: a family of lightweight block ciphers for resource-constrained devices. In: Kim, H., Kim, D.-C. (eds.) ICISC 2017. LNCS, vol. 10779, pp. 3–25. Springer, Cham (2018). https://doi.org/10.1007/978-3-319-78556-1_1
2. Roh, D., et al.: Revised version of block cipher CHAM. In: Seo, J.H. (ed.) ICISC 2019. LNCS, vol. 11975, pp. 1–19. Springer, Cham (2020). https://doi.org/10.1007/978-3-030-40921-0_1
3. Hong, D., Lee, J.-K., Kim, D.-C., Kwon, D., Ryu, K.H., Lee, D.-G.: LEA: a 128-bit block cipher for fast encryption on common processors. In: Kim, Y., Lee, H., Perrig, A. (eds.) WISA 2013. LNCS, vol. 8267, pp. 3–27. Springer, Cham (2014). https://doi.org/10.1007/978-3-319-05149-9_1
4. Seo, H., Liu, Z., Choi, J., Park, T., Kim, H.: Compact implementations of LEA block cipher for low-end microprocessors. In: Kim, H., Choi, D. (eds.) WISA 2015. LNCS, vol. 9503, pp. 28–40. Springer, Cham (2016). https://doi.org/10.1007/978-3-319-31875-2_3
5. Seo, H., Jeong, I., Lee, J., Kim, W.-H.: Compact implementations of ARX-based block ciphers on IoT processors. ACM Trans. Embed. Comput. Syst. (TECS) **17**(3), 1–16 (2018)
6. Seo, H., An, K., Kwon, H.: Compact LEA and HIGHT implementations on 8-bit AVR and 16-bit MSP processors. In: Kang, B.B.H., Jang, J.S. (eds.) WISA 2018. LNCS, vol. 11402, pp. 253–265. Springer, Cham (2019). https://doi.org/10.1007/978-3-030-17982-3_20
7. Hong, D., et al.: HIGHT: a new block cipher suitable for low-resource device. In: Goubin, L., Matsui, M. (eds.) CHES 2006. LNCS, vol. 4249, pp. 46–59. Springer, Heidelberg (2006). https://doi.org/10.1007/11894063_4
8. Eisenbarth, T., et al.: Compact implementation and performance evaluation of block ciphers in ATtiny devices. In: Mitrokotsa, A., Vaudenay, S. (eds.) AFRICACRYPT 2012. LNCS, vol. 7374, pp. 172–187. Springer, Heidelberg (2012). https://doi.org/10.1007/978-3-642-31410-0_11
9. Kim, B., Cho, J., Choi, B., Park, J., Seo, H.: Compact implementations of HIGHT block cipher on IoT platforms. Secur. Commun. Netw. **2019**, 10 (2019)
10. Seo, H.: Memory-efficient implementation of ultra-lightweight block cipher algorithm CHAM on low-end 8-bit AVR processors. J. Korea Inst. Inf. Secur. Cryptol. **28**, 545–550 (2018)
11. Osvik, D.A., Bos, J.W., Stefan, D., Canright, D.: Fast software AES encryption. In: Hong, S., Iwata, T. (eds.) FSE 2010. LNCS, vol. 6147, pp. 75–93. Springer, Heidelberg (2010). https://doi.org/10.1007/978-3-642-13858-4_5

12. Kim, K., Choi, S., Kwon, H., Liu, Z., Seo, H.: FACE–LIGHT: fast AES–CTR mode encryption for low-end microcontrollers. In: Seo, J.H. (ed.) ICISC 2019. LNCS, vol. 11975, pp. 102–114. Springer, Cham (2020). https://doi.org/10.1007/978-3-030-40921-0_6

13. Park, T., Seo, H., Lee, S., Kim, H.: Secure data encryption for cloud-based human care services. J. Sens. **2018**, 10 (2018)

14. Beaulieu, R., Shors, D., Smith, J., Treatman-Clark, S., Weeks, B., Wingers, L.: The SIMON and SPECK block ciphers on AVR 8-bit microcontrollers. In: Eisenbarth, T., Öztürk, E. (eds.) LightSec 2014. LNCS, vol. 8898, pp. 3–20. Springer, Cham (2015). https://doi.org/10.1007/978-3-319-16363-5_1

15. Beaulieu, R., Shors, D., Smith, J., Treatman-Clark, S., Weeks, B., Wingers, L.: Simon and speck: block ciphers for the internet of things. IACR Cryptol. ePrint Arch. **2015**, 585 (2015)

16. Kim, K., Choi, S., Kwon, H., Kim, H., Liu, Z., Seo, H.: PAGE–practical AES-GCM encryption for low-end microcontrollers. Appl. Sci. **10**(9), 3131 (2020)

The Gravy Value: A Set of Features for Pinpointing BOT Detection Method

Semi Park and Kyungho Lee[✉]

School of Cybersecurity, Korea University, 145 Anam-ro Seongbuk-gu,
Seoul 02941, Republic of Korea
{semi0502,kevinlee}@korea.ac.kr

Abstract. The critical success of online games has led the industry to global success, as the market size is expected to reach 18,194 USD by the year 2020. However, the success of the online game market has led to the growth of illegal activities, such as the use of game bots. Game bots are software applications capable of collecting game items, which are often banned from online game service providers. The illegal activities are not limited to tax evasion and money laundering. In order to help detect these bots, this study employs the dataset from an MMORPG called Aion. By detecting the bots using the server-side analysis, this paper analyzed user behavior and used features based on the experience, skill, and *gravy value* that represents the cost-efficiency. We experimented with machine learning algorithms such as MLP, SVM, and Random Forest. As a result, the F-score for detecting the total sum of the accounts that consists of the game bots and real users reached 0.9638. We believe our study may help online game service providers, future researchers, and governmental agencies to detect and classify the MMORPG game bots.

Keywords: BOT detection · Online game · MMORPG · Security · Machine learning

1 Introduction

The consumption values of online games can be attributed to the success of online games, as purchasing online game items and virtual items have been a huge part of the culture. By the year 2020, the global market for online games is expected to reach 18,194 USD [7]. In the realm of online games, 'time' is a resource and a fair commodity for everyone. However, purchasing online games have become an integral part of the gaming phenomena, as players aim to enhance the players'

This research was supported by the MSIT(Ministry of Science and ICT), Korea, under the ITRC(Information Technology Research Center) support program(IITP-2020-2015-0-00403)supervised by the IITP(Institute for Information & communications Technology Planning & Evaluation)
Following(or This research) was results of a study on the "HPC Support" Project, supported by the 'Ministry of Science and ICT' and NIPA.

ability in a short amount of time. As the consumption rate for online games has continuously increased during the past decades, the online game market has been forecasted to grow. Yet, with the increase in the demand for online games, the use of BOTs have been considered a problem for online game service providers.

Automated accounts have posed a threat as game BOTs are capable of repeating malicious tasks while creating obtrusive and distractive actions that are intolerable for a regular player [5,13]. Past studies have aimed to detect and prevent BOTs to diffuse the malicious behaviors. In addition, the items were cashed in using game items collected through game BOTs and used for tax evasion or money laundering. These BOTs are capable of disrupting and annoying users with relative deprivation. The complaint from the players has a correlation to the profit of the game company. As the number of dissatisfied users increases, the profit of the game will also simultaneously decrease. From the perspective of the gaming company, BOTs are considered a threat to the overall business. Various laws have been enforced by the Korean government to detect and prohibit the game BOT. Article 32 of the Game Industry Promotion Act was revised in 2018, which prevents game BOTs from operating in the game.

Past studies have focused on detecting the malicious activities of the game BOTs. As depicted in Table 1., BOT detection researches have been divided into three types: (i) client-side detection, (ii) server-side detection, and (iii) network-side detection [28].

Table 1. Three types of online game BOT detection: definitions, detection methods.

Category	Definition	Detection methods
Client-side detection	Detecting BoT with user PC level (e.g. XIGNCODE)	Human interaction
Network-side detection	Detecting BoT based on network information (e.g. DNS, IP, and VPN)	Network traffic
Server-side detection	Detecting BoT based on the user game log which was saved in server	In-game logOut-game log

The client-side analysis focuses on analyzing the user's PC that extracts the information from the user's PC. Yet, the drawback of the method is limited usability and weak security measures. While the client-side detection method is capable of detecting the BOTs patterns, the malicious actors are capable of easily bypassing the security measures. Network-side analysis can bypass BOTs usage by using only the low key values, and the usability of the client-side is poorly designed. However, there are limitations that require constant key changes and vulnerabilities due to simple encryption operation. Server-side based analysis is a way to classify differences between BOTs and real game users. Using server-side analysis, online game companies can block accounts using BOTs whenever they want. It has the advantage of detecting BOTs that were not detected by the client-side and considered usability. This is due to the development of big data analysis. Therefore, we used a method to detect BOTs in MMORPGs using the server-side analysis.

Massively Multiplayer Online Role-Playing Game (MMORPG) focuses on multi-users' gameplay by taking on various characters' roles. Often times in MMORPG, game BOTs are capable of gaining experiences by performing redundant tasks. The BOTs in the games can also break the balance in the game by acquiring items and credits in a short duration of time. In the case of online games in the MMORPG genre, each set of characters have different skills and stats. In our study, we suggested the *gravy value* based on these skills and the experience of the characters. Contrary to the previous research, this study implemented a set of data that consisted of real accounts. We applied features that were easy to apply for MMORPGs, instead of focusing on features that were optimized for a single game.

The contributions of this paper are as such:

- We used a machine learning model to classify BOTs against the users.
- We generated widely adaptable features in MMORPGs.
- The algorithms generated in the game provides features without requiring a specific domain knowledge.

The composition of this paper is as follows. Sect. 2 examines the existing studies related to this paper. We then, introduce the existing research related to methods of detecting server-side BOTs in the MMORPG. In Sect. 3, we introduced a methodology that detects BOTs through features made through user behavior-based features and *gravy value*. Section 4, we experimented with the methodology presented through the actual Aion dataset and analyzed the results. In the penultimate section, we provide our results in the discussion. Finally, we conclude the paper with the conclusion.

2   Related Works

Past researchers have conducted studies on BOT detection in three areas. The three categories of the game BOTs are client-side detection, network-side detection, and server-side detection, as shown in Table 1. Our study focuses on the server-side detection method. The server-side detection method has higher usability than other methods because it does not interfere with the user's game activity. This method does not waste system resources on the client-side, as the bot detection process is performed by analyzing the logs in the server. As such, we wanted to use a server-side detection method based on the game action log of the Aion dataset. Table 2. Depicts the research from the server-side BOT detection.

Table 2. Research on Server-side BOT Detection in MMORPGs.

Methods of analysis	Description	References
Game-play styles	Investigating user game style	[2,6,9]
Movement	Detecting the movement patterns of users within the game	[3,4,12]
Window event sequences	Evaluating the windows event sequence	[8,14]
Social networks	Comparing the users' social network activity	[10,11,21,27]
Similarity	Analyzing behavioral similarity	[15,18,25,26]
Trading network	Measuring the user's transaction pattern	[16,17,24]
Action sequence	Testing the user's action sequence	[19,20,23]

Prior studies have mainly analyzed the user behavior logs generated in the games. These studies mainly analyzed the differences in the game patterns between the game bots and real users, which is called the user behavior analysis. User behavior analysis is an anomaly detection method that defines the patterns of the bot as abnormal. We summarized the papers related to our research in the Table 2. In this study, we showed the server-side BOT detection as a data mining method. We have classified server-side detection methods into seven categories: game-play styles, movement, window event sequences, social networks, similarity, trading network, and action sequences. These methods analyzed patterns of bots and real users through data mining and statistical analysis based on game action logs. Lee et al. [17] and Song et al. [24] were analyzed based on the credits of the characters. They used the credits from the game to measure the fluctuations and one-way trading network analysis. Previous studies analyzed user behavior [2,6,9] and user behavior sequence [19,20,23]. They also analyzed differences in user movement patterns, such as in [3,4,12]. Prior studies were analyzed for similarity [15,18,25,26]. Past studies conducted studies on guild activities and social activities such as chatting and creating parties [10,11,21,27]. Gianvecchio et al. [8] and Kim et al. [14] used windows event sequences such as mouse click and keyboard input.

Existing research should be preceded by domain knowledge about the game, which may not be easy to analyze for analysts with limited domain expertise. There has been a lack of study that focuses on the MMORPGs characteristic's and character's skills. We conducted the server-side analysis to minimize the detection technique exposure to gold farming groups (GFGs) and bots makers. In particular, we created a cost-efficiency features for a user's behavioral action based on skill, which generates widely adaptable features in the MMORPGs. We used features that were easy to apply in various MMORPGs, instead of using features that were suitable for a single game.

3   Methodology

3.1   Datasets

We used the Game Bot Detection Challenge dataset, which was held on the 2019 Information Security R&D challenge [1]. The dataset contained the user activity logs from Aion for a total of 22 d. For the past decade, Aion is an MMORPG game that has been ranked 30th in South Korea. The duration of the dataset expands from 2010-04-16 to 2010-05-07. The dataset contained enough detailed information about each user. Sensitive information such as character names and personally identifiable information was removed from the original data log to avoid privacy issues. As such, there were fields in the dataset that were converted to other random values to avoid exposing the real account's information.

The dataset provided a label that helped validate the bots from the real accounts. We excluded all of the accounts that were active for less than 3 h during the log period. The banned list was provided by the game company to serve as the ground truth, and each banned user has been vetted and verified by human labor and active monitoring. We found 12,862 real users and 687 game bots in this dataset.

3.2   Experimental Environment

For our experiment, we used Windows 10 for the operating system and Python 3.6. We used scikit-learn [22] for our machine learning library. Our computational environment is 128 GB RAM with the Xeon CPU processor and over 20 TFLOPS GPU provided by NIPA. Since we have log data that spans across 22 d, we used 5-fold cross-validation for evaluating our model. When we used 10-fold cross-validation, the model cannot be trained to classify bots from real users, because of the highly imbalanced class in the dataset. So we used 5-fold cross-validation with randomly shuffled data.

3.3   Data Preprocessing

As we mentioned above, we had to pre-process all the dataset prior to training and classifying the bots from the real users. In this research, we tried to sort the bots from the real users based on the character's skill data and user experience. The data were prevalent for MMORPGs, so this approach was quickly adopted in other MMORPGs. Based on the log description, we extracted the user behavior log related to the game skills and experience.

3.4   Feature Extraction

With the preprocessed dataset, we made some features to classify between the game bots and the real users. We used `groupby` to generate the user's features from a single day. Based on the `groupby` command, we can easily calculate the pre-defined features. We made features based on the statistic approach: mean, sum, count, skewness, kurtosis, average, and standard deviation. The statistical approach is well known for extracting the distribution and attribution of the dataset for a set of features in a timely manner. Hence, we attempted to use the statistical approach that does not require the domain knowledge of the MMORPG. The following Table 3 represents the features and detailed descriptions. We wrap up all of the features used for this research in Table 3.

Table 3. Description of Feature sets and number of features used in the experiment.

Source	Feature	Num of feature	Description
Experience	Statistic method	7	Use statistic method to extract time series data e.g. mean, sum, count, standard deviation, kurtosis
	Count value	1	Count each day log related with experience data
Skill	Count value	200	The value consists of the top 200 frequent skills and count
Gravy value	Eq. 1	200	The value consists of the top 200 frequent skills
Total	-	409	-

Even if the account was identified as a bot, the account could play for more than a single day. Thus, we had to consider the situation that some users played on a certain set of days, while other users may play on a particular set of days. In this experiment, we composed an approach that is similar to max-pooling, which is widely used for deep learning. After we generated features for the players within a single day, we calculated a maximum value per each feature and user. We extracted the dataset of each account. We selected a single day with the highest activity for each account that would allow us to obtain a maximized feature within a day in a dataset. We also used the *gravy value* for the feature to classify bots and real users. The *gravy value* was the calculated value of how many actions were performed at the time in order to level up. This formula was based on the assumption that the bot could cost-effectively improve a certain set of skill levels. We defined as *gravy value* as follow:

$$Gravy\,value = \frac{1}{(index(skill_k, level_m) - index(skill_k, level_{m-1}))} \tag{1}$$

$$k \in \{Top\,200\,frequent\,skill\}, m \in \{1, 2\} \tag{2}$$

The $skill_k$ represents the set of skills within the games that are given a numerical value. The set consists of 200 skills with the most frequently used skill numbers. $level_m$ indicates the number of user action values in the list function. By finding the difference between the $level_m$ and $level_{m-1}$, and finding the number of actions, $skill_k$, required to level up will help solve the *gravy value*, as shown in Eq. (1). Based on Equation (1) we were able to derive to Eq. (1) can obtain the value of the user action required for $skill_k$ to level up. In this study, we experimented with a machine learning algorithm using the feature set in Table 3.

4   Experiments

We used three machine learning algorithms in the classification problem, as mentioned in the aforementioned section. We used Multi-Layer Perceptron (ML), Support Vector Machine (SVM), Random Forest to classify the game bots and real account users. We used the default parameter from the scikit-learn python library. The cross-validation made the average evaluation of the model.

Table 4. Machine learning results by feature set algorithm.

Feature set	Machine learning algorithm	Accuracy	Recall	F-score
Statistics (experience)	MLP	96.03%	54.00%	0.5801
	SVM	94.82%	22.41%	0.3052
	Random forest	96.34%	60.40%	0.6264
Skill counts	MLP	96.38%	53.27%	0.5990
	SVM	96.56%	38.71%	0.5330
	Random forest	96.54%	48.90%	0.5894
Gravy value	MLP	98.58%	72.05%	0.9927
	SVM	99.80%	98.10%	0.9810
	Random forest	99.80%	98.10%	0.9810
All	MLP	99.63%	95.19%	0.9638
	SVM	96.84%	43.08%	0.5809
	Random forest	99.57%	97.96%	0.9586

We used feature sets to find out which feature set was the most useful. Table 4 depicts the results from the experiments on the feature sets, which we made through three machine learning algorithms. We found that most of the feature set achieved over 96% accuracy when training and testing the Aion game datasets. MLP algorithm showed the highest score amongst the algorithms. Using all the features, we could get over 99.63% accuracy over 0.9638 of the F-score from the experiment. With the experimental result, we concluded that our approach to detect bots that ruins the MMORPG game environment was practical that was better than related works, in the aforementioned section. In Table 4., we can see that only using the *gravy value* method showed better performance than other features, even using all of the features which also contain the *gravy value* feature. We thought this result come from the model that had overfitted. Therefore, we decided that we should not have to rely on the *gravy value* feature and considered using other features to avoid overfitting. In this study, we adopted the results using the MLP algorithm using all feature sets. We detected the bots using machine learning using feature sets, and we confirmed that the experimental result was an F-score of 0.9638.

5   Discussion

In this study, we confirmed that the results of using the model we proposed are useful in classifying bots and real users. Through the results of this study, we confirmed that the bot and the real user had different behavioral characteristics. We posited that using the MLP algorithm would be the most effective. In order to verify the hypotheses, we evaluated the feature importance. Moreover, we evaluated the feature exploration to analyze the model fit. The MLP model does not have interaction power. Hence, we used the random forest model to find the model-agnostic interpretation. Even though we used MLP, we used the RF model to evaluate the model-agnostic interpretation.

We previously assumed that bots were more cost-effective than real users. We explored the skills and gravy value feature, which showed the most convincing performance in this research. Before we set up the experiment, we posit that bots are more efficient than human players. In order to test our hypothesis, we measured the skills and levels of the various accounts. When we experimented with the gravy value, we measured the efficiency of the bots against the real accounts. As shown in Table 4., the F-score was 0.99. We found that the gravy value was an accurate set of features to measure and detect the bots, which proved our hypotheses.

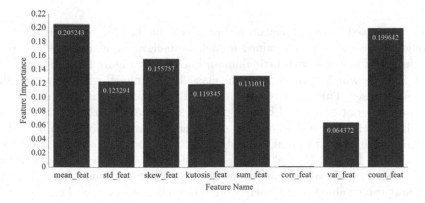

Fig. 1. Experience based on the Feature Importance.

We assumed that bots gain experience with fewer actions than real users. And we experimented to verify this. Figure 1. was about experience log-based feature importance results generated by statistic method. We founded that the most powerful feature as a means of experience day by day. The Count feature followed after the mean feature. In Fig. 1., the mean feature was mean_feat, and the count feature was count_feat. Since the mean was count/sum, it was found that the mean changed according to the count. The count was the number of actions, so the number of actions was significant. We confirmed through the experiment results that mean and count were important to distinguish bots from real users. The importance of features was an essential criterion for classifying bots and real users. As a result, the bot could get more experience with fewer actions than the real user.

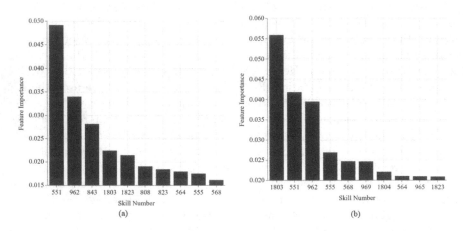

Fig. 2. Skills based upon the Feature Importance. (a) Skill Count Feature Importance. (b) Gravy Value Feature Importance.

We evaluated a set of features that could be helpful to game analysts. Through the use of the well-trained model, we believe game analysts may evaluate the set of features with little domain knowledge. Figure 2. (a). showed the top 10 features which have useful in the classification model when using the skill count feature set. This graph showed that skill number 551 had the most effective to discern bot and a real human. Figure 2. (b). showed the top 10 features which have useful in the classification model when using the gravy value feature set. This graph showed that skill number 1803 had the most effective to discern bot and a real human. 551, 962, 555 follows after the first. Showed both feature importance graphs, even if there were quite different between calculating skill count and gravy value feature, there were intersection areas. Based on the top 10 of each feature, we selected six features intersection. We decided this skill 551, 962, 1803, 555, 564, 568 were useful to classify bots and real users. This result will be useful information for analysts with little domain knowledge.

We did a feature exploration to make sure the model worked, and we analyzed feature distributions to check the hypothesis that bots and real users behave

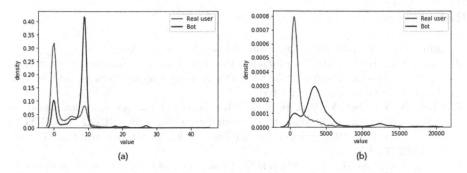

Fig. 3. Feature exploration results. (a) Different distribution in gravy value feature ($skill_k$: 1803). (b) Different distribution in sum of experience feature.

differently. As we expected above, in Fig. 3. (a). showed a different distribution of skill usage. This model can be useful knowledge for game bot analysts to feature engineering further. Also, we checked the statistical feature especially, the distribution of experiment values. We found in Fig. 3. (b). that the game bots got more mean of experiment values as we expected above. We thought that even game log analyst who did not have domain information about bots to give useful information about through feature exploration that comes from a well-trained model. Furthermore, we identified some data that were quite different from classifying bots and real human users.

6   Conclusion

In this study, we analyzed the user behavior log by using the server-side method, and our study employed the Aion dataset. The study analyzed the experience and skills from the user behavior log to see if the characteristics of the game bots and the real user were indeed different. We proposed a *gravy value*, a cost-effective feature. We experimented with three machine learning algorithms using feature sets such as the experiment, skills, and *gravy value*. As a result, the MLP algorithm classified game bots and real users with an F-score of 0.9638. This paper distinguished the bots from real users with high performance. Since we created the *gravy value* using a common set of features from the MMORPGs, future researchers and game developers can analyze these sets of features by applying it to various MMORPGs. This means that analysts who would want to differentiate between the bots and real users do not need to have in-depth domain knowledge in the MMORPGs realm. The methodology used in this study can be used as a useful reference for game service providers and government agencies. We have detected a BOT that interferes with the usual gameplay of the real user, and we can prevent various issues caused by the bots. For our future study, we would like to examine the user's churn rate using the set of features using in this study. Furthermore, one of the characteristics of the MMORPG 'stat', a value that gives a kind of specific ability value of a character, can be further analyzed and verified through data sets of various games.

References

1. Information Security R&D Challenge (2019). Accessed 1 Aug 2020
2. Chen, K.T., Hong, L.W.: User identification based on game-play activity patterns. In: Proceedings of the 6th ACM SIGCOMM Workshop on Network and System Support for Games, pp. 7–12 (2007)
3. Chen, K.-T., Liao, A., Pao, H.-K.K., Chu, H.-H.: Game bot detection based on avatar trajectory. In: Stevens, S.M., Saldamarco, S.J. (eds.) ICEC 2008. LNCS, vol. 5309, pp. 94–105. Springer, Heidelberg (2008). https://doi.org/10.1007/978-3-540-89222-9_11
4. Chen, K.T., Pao, H.K.K., Chang, H.C.: Game bot identification based on manifold learning. In: Proceedings of the 7th ACM SIGCOMM Workshop on Network and System Support for Games, pp. 21–26 (2008)
5. Chu, Z., Gianvecchio, S., Wang, H., Jajodia, S.: Detecting automation of twitter accounts: are you a human, bot, or cyborg? IEEE Trans. Dependable Secure Comput. **9**(6), 811–824 (2012)
6. Chung, Y., et al.: Game bot detection approach based on behavior analysis and consideration of various play styles. ETRI J. **35**(6), 1058–1067 (2013)
7. Forecast, S.M.: Online games-worldwide (2020). Accessed 1 Aug 2020
8. Gianvecchio, S., Wu, Z., Xie, M., Wang, H.: Battle of botcraft: fighting bots in online games with human observational proofs. In: Proceedings of the 16th ACM Conference on Computer and Communications Security, pp. 256–268 (2009)
9. Kang, A.R., Jeong, S.H., Mohaisen, A., Kim, H.K.: Multimodal game bot detection using user behavioral characteristics. SpringerPlus **5**(1), 1–19 (2016). https://doi.org/10.1186/s40064-016-2122-8
10. Kang, A.R., Kim, H.K., Woo, J.: Chatting pattern based game bot detection: do they talk like us? KSII Trans. Internet Inf. Syst. **6**(11), 2866–2879 (2012)
11. Kang, A.R., Woo, J., Park, J., Kim, H.K.: Online game bot detection based on party-play log analysis. Comput. Math. Appl. **65**(9), 1384–1395 (2013)
12. van Kesteren, M., Langevoort, J., Grootjen, F.: A step in the right direction: Botdetection in mmorpgs using movement analysis. In: Proceedings of the 21st Belgian-Dutch Conference on Artificial Intelligence (BNAIC 2009), pp. 129–136 (2009)
13. Kim, H., Yang, S., Kim, H.K.: Crime scene re-investigation: a postmortem analysis of game account stealers' behaviors. In: 2017 15th Annual Workshop on Network and Systems Support for Games (NetGames), pp. 1–6. IEEE (2017)
14. Kim, H., Hong, S., Kim, J.: Detection of auto programs for MMORPGs. In: Zhang, S., Jarvis, R. (eds.) AI 2005. LNCS (LNAI), vol. 3809, pp. 1281–1284. Springer, Heidelberg (2005). https://doi.org/10.1007/11589990_187
15. Kwon, H., Kim, H.K.: Self-similarity based bot detection system in MMORPG. In: Proceedings of the 3th International Conference on Internet, pp. 477–481 (2011)
16. Kwon, H., Mohaisen, A., Woo, J., Kim, Y., Lee, E., Kim, H.K.: Crime scene reconstruction: Online gold farming network analysis. IEEE Trans. Inf. Forensics Secur. **12**(3), 544–556 (2016)
17. Kwon, H., Woo, K., Kim, H.C., Kim, C.K., Kim, H.K.: Surgical strike: a novel approach to minimize collateral damage to game bot detection. In: 2013 12th Annual Workshop on Network and Systems Support for Games (NetGames), pp. 1–2. IEEE (2013)
18. Lee, E., Woo, J., Kim, H., Mohaisen, A., Kim, H.K.: You are a game bot!: uncovering game bots in mmorpgs via self-similarity in the wild. In: Ndss (2016)

19. Lee, J., Lim, J., Cho, W., Kim, H.K.: In-game action sequence analysis for game BOT detection on the big data analysis platform. In: Handa, H., Ishibuchi, H., Ong, Y.-S., Tan, K.-C. (eds.) Proceedings of the 18th Asia Pacific Symposium on Intelligent and Evolutionary Systems - Volume 2. PALO, vol. 2, pp. 403–414. Springer, Cham (2015). https://doi.org/10.1007/978-3-319-13356-0_32
20. Mishima, Y., Fukuda, K., Esaki, H.: An analysis of players and bots behaviors in MMORPG. In: 2013 IEEE 27th International Conference on Advanced Information Networking and Applications (AINA), pp. 870–876. IEEE (2013)
21. Oh, J., Borbora, Z.H., Sharma, D., Srivastava, J.: Bot detection based on social interactions in MMORPGS. In: 2013 International Conference on Social Computing, pp. 536–543. IEEE (2013)
22. Pedregosa, F., et al.: Scikit-learn: machine learning in python. J. Mach. Learn. Res. **12**, 2825–2830 (2011)
23. Platzer, C.: Sequence-based bot detection in massive multiplayer online games. In: 2011 8th International Conference on Information, Communications & Signal Processing, pp. 1–5. IEEE (2011)
24. Song, H.M., Kim, H.K.: Game-bot detection based on clustering of asset-varied location coordinates. J. Korea Inst. Inf. Secur. Cryptology **25**(5), 1131–1141 (2015)
25. Stefan, M., Christian, P., Christopher, K., Engin, K.: Server-side bot detection in massive multiplayer online games. IEEE Secur. Priv. **7**(3), 29–36 (2009)
26. Thawonmas, R., Kashifuji, Y., Chen, K.T.: Detection of MMORPG bots based on behavior analysis. In: Proceedings of the 2008 International Conference on Advances in Computer Entertainment Technology, pp. 91–94 (2008)
27. Varvello, M., Voelker, G.M.: Second life: a social network of humans and bots. In: Proceedings of the 20th International Workshop on Network and Operating Systems Support for Digital Audio and Video, pp. 9–14 (2010)
28. Woo, J., Kim, H.K.: Survey and research direction on online game security. In: Proceedings of the Workshop at SIGGRAPH Asia, pp. 19–25 (2012)

Impact of Optimized Operations $A \cdot B$, $A \cdot C$ for Binary Field Inversion on Quantum Computers

Kyoungbae Jang, Seung Ju Choi, Hyeokdong Kwon, Zhi Hu, and Hwajeong Seo[✉]

IT Department, Hansung University, Seoul, South Korea
starj1023@gmail.com, bookingstore3@gmail.com, korlethean@gmail.com, huzhi_math@csu.edu.cn, hwajeong84@gmail.com

Abstract. The inversion circuit based on the Itoh-Tsujii algorithm, used for many cryptography functions, requires a number of multiplication and squaring operations in circuits. In the past, the optimized inversion implementation has been actively studied in modern computers. However, there are very few works to optimize the inversion on the quantum computer. In this paper, we present the optimized implementation of binary field inversion in quantum circuits. Reversible and non-reversible multiplication circuits are finely combined to reduce the number of CNOT gate. In particular, we optimized the reversible circuit for $A \cdot B$ and $A \cdot C$ case in the inversion operation. Afterward, the multiplication and squaring routine efficiently initializes some of the qubits used for the routine into zero value. Lastly, the-state-of-art multiplication and squaring implementation techniques, such as Karatsuba algorithm and shift-based squaring are utilized to obtain the optimal performance. In order to show the effectiveness of the proposed implementation, the inversion is applied to the substitute layer of AES block cipher. Furthermore, the proposed method can be applied to other cryptographic functions, such as binary field inversion for public key cryptography (i.e. Elliptic Curve Cryptography).

Keywords: Quantum computers · Itoh-tsujii algorithm · Karatsuba algorithm · Binary field multiplication

1 Introduction

The binary field is a finite field of characteristic 2, which is a binomial polynomial consisting of an irreducible polynomials of n degrees. The binary field arithmetic is widely used in cryptographic applications. For the high performance of cryptography analysis, the optimized binary field arithmetic in the quantum circuit is a fundamental building block. Among binary field arithmetic operations, the most expensive operation is an inversion operation, which is a multiplicative computation of finding a^{-1} of element $a \in GF(2^m)$, such that $a \cdot a^{-1} = 1$.

© Springer Nature Switzerland AG 2020
I. You (Ed.): WISA 2020, LNCS 12583, pp. 154–166, 2020.
https://doi.org/10.1007/978-3-030-65299-9_12

The inversion operation is mainly used in both symmetric and asymmetric cryptography, such as the substitute layer of AES and inversion of Elliptic Curve Cryptography (ECC) [1]. A number of optimization methods have been proposed for computing the multiplicative inverse [2–4]. One of the well known algorithm is the Itoh-Tsujii multiplicative inverse algorithm [5], which is a inverse algorithm based on Fermat's Little Theorem (FLT).

When computing the binary field inversion, multiplication and squaring operations are required. The multiplication in binary field involves multiplying two polynomial multiplication and a modular reduction with an irreducible polynomial. The reduction operation is a relatively simpler operation than the polynomial multiplication, because the reduction consists of only eXclusive-or operations [6]. For this reason, an optimized polynomial multiplication for binary fields has been studied [7–9]. Among them, Karatsuba algorithm is widely used in practice. Karatsuba algorithm replaces the one n-bit multiplication operation into three $\frac{n}{2}$-bit multiplication operations. Although, Karatsuba multiplication requires several extra addition operations (i.e. eXclusive-or), the method significantly reduces the complexity of multiplication. By applying the Karatsuba algorithm to quantum computing, the computation complexity in quantum circuits is also optimized.

By using the Karatsuba multiplication for the Itoh-Tsujii inversion algorithm, the multiplication part of the inversion is optimized [10]. During the calculation, there is a multiplication routine that proceeds $A \cdot B$ and $A \cdot C$ in this pattern, where A, B, and C are operands for each operation. The value of A should be maintained during the computation since it gets reused in both $A \cdot B$ and $A \cdot C$ multiplications. Due to the nature of Karatsuba multiplication, operand A gets changed to other value after $A \cdot B$. For this reason, the direct reuse of operand A in following $A \cdot C$ is not available. Therefore, a reverse circuit must be added to revert the A value to its original value after $A \cdot B$ operation.

In this paper, we present a state-of-art multiplication based on [11] and squaring method to implement the Itoh-Tsujii algorithm. [11] minimizes the number of multiplications by recursively applying Karatsuba multiplication on quantum computers. However, only $A \cdot B$ multiplication is considered. In order to apply [11] in $A \cdot B$ and $A \cdot C$ multiplication, a additional reversible circuit is required to calculate the $A \cdot B$ and $A \cdot C$ multiplication. We have successfully enhanced the [11] multiplication. This can be applied to $A \cdot B$ and $A \cdot C$ multiplication in Karatsuba approach. $A \cdot B$ and $A \cdot C$ structures are optimized by omitting the reverse circuit. Furthermore, we proposed qubit re-use techniques for squaring and multiplication routine. By initializing qubits, the circuit is implemented with minimal circuit gates. Finally, the proposed technique is applied to the substitute layer of AES in order to show practicality and efficiency. The algorithm can be applied to other cryptographic functions, such as binary field inversion of Elliptic Curve Cryptography (ECC).

1.1   Research Contributions

- **Optimized implementation of binary field inversion** The quantum circuit for multiplicative inversion based on Itoh-Tsujii algorithm is optimized by utilizing the $A \cdot B$ and $A \cdot C$ pattern. By changing the reversible structure of the algorithm into non-reversible structure, the number of CNOT gate is optimized. Furthermore, the qubit of B is initialized with optimal routine. The initialized qubit gets used in the following operation, which reduces the total number of qubits required for the inversion operation. The binary field polynomial multiplication is optimized with the-state-of-art Karatsuba multiplication and shift-based squaring method, which reduced the total number of Toffoli and CNOT gates.
- **Optimized cryptographic primitives for AES and ECC** The proposed method can be applied to the substitute layer of AES and binary field inversion of ECC. We show the impact of proposed method by implementing the substitute layer. The proposed circuit significantly reduces the required resource in terms of CNOT gates and qubits.

1.2   Organization of the Paper

The organization of this paper is as follows. Section 2 presents the background of binary field inversion. In Sect. 3, the proposed inversion operation is presented. In Sect. 4, we evaluate the proposed inversion method for AES. Finally, Sect. 5 concludes the paper.

2   Related Work

2.1   Itoh-Tsujii Multiplicative Inverse Algorithm

Itoh-Tsujii multiplicative inverse algorithm is an exponentiation based algorithm for the inversion in binary field [5]. In a normal basis representation, it reduces the complexity of computing the inverse of a non-zero element in $GF(2^n)$ with the binary exponentiation method.

2.2   Karatsuba Multiplication

Karatsuba algorithm reduces the complexity of multiplication by additional addition operations. When multiplying the polynomial f and g of size n through $h = f \cdot g$, two input polynomials are divided into $s = n/2$ units as follows:

$$
\begin{aligned}
f = f_1 x^s + f_0 \\
g = g_1 x^s + g_0
\end{aligned}
\tag{1}
$$

After splitting two input polynomials, Karatsuba multiplication can be performed as follows:

$$
f_0 \cdot g_0 + \{(f_0 + f_1) \cdot (g_0 + g_1) + f_0 \cdot g_0 + f_1 \cdot g_1\} x^s + f_1 \cdot g_1 x^{2s}
\tag{2}
$$

With the Karatsuba multiplication, multiplication of $O(n^2)$ can be performed in $O(n^{\log_2 3})$ with a few addition operations.

2.3   Quantum Gates

Quantum computers have several gates that can represent the classical gates [12]. Two most representative gates are CNOT and Toffoli gates. The CNOT gate performs a NOT gate operation on the second qubit when the first input qubit of the two input qubits is one. This gate performs the same role as the add operation on the binary field. The circuit configuration is shown in left side of Fig. 1. The Toffoli gate receives three qubits. When the first and second qubits are one, the gate performs a NOT gate operation on the last qubit. This serves as an AND operation on the binary field, and the circuit configuration is shown in right side of Fig. 1.

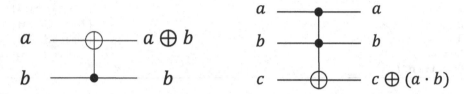

Fig. 1. Circuit configuration of the (left) CNOT and (right) Toffoli gate.

3   Proposed Method

In this paper, the Itoh-Tsujii algorithm for binary field inversion was optimized on the quantum computer. First, the multiplication of Itoh-Tsujii algorithm was optimized by applying the Karatsuba multiplication technique. Second, the quantum circuit is optimized by changing the reversible circuit to a non-reversible circuit when calculating $A \cdot B$ and $A \cdot C$ pattern in the Itoh-Tsujii algorithm with Karatsuba algorithm. Lastly, some of qubits are reuse during squaring and multiplication operations by using the initialization technique. Initialized qubits are used for following computations. With this technique, the total number of qubits required for the operation is optimized.

3.1   Optimization of $A \cdot B$, $A \cdot C$ Structure in Inversion

The proposed method optimized the $A \cdot B$ and $A \cdot C$ structure in inversion algorithm by using non-reversible circuits rather than reversible circuits. Itoh-Tsuji algorithm consists of squaring and multiplication operation. The squaring operation is designed with few CNOT gates on a quantum circuit [13]. Unlike the squaring operation, the multiplication operation is an expensive operation. Therefore, it is necessary to apply an efficient multiplication technique to achieve the optimal performance. There are a number of studies to implement the multiplication. Among them, one of the well known efficient multiplication method is the Karatsuba multiplication. When performing the two polynomial $f \cdot g$ multiplication on a quantum gate, the Karatsuba algorithm can reduce the usage

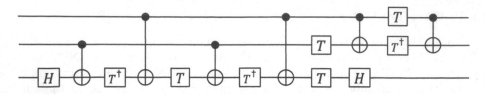

Fig. 2. Circuit configuration of the CNOT gate.

Algorithm 1. Itoh-Tsuji-based inversion for $p = x^8 + x^4 + x^3 + x + 1$

Require: Integer z satisfying $1 \leq z \leq p - 1$.
Ensure: Inverse $t = z^{p-2} \mod p = z^{-1} \mod p$.

1: $z_2 \leftarrow z^2 \cdot z$	{ cost: 1S+1M }
2: $z_3 \leftarrow z_2^2 \cdot z$	{ cost: 1S+1M }
3: $z_6 \leftarrow z_3^{2^3} \cdot z_3$	{ cost: 3S+1M }
4: $z_7 \leftarrow z_6^2 \cdot z$	{ cost: 1S+1M }
5: $t \leftarrow z_7^2$	{ cost: 1S }
6: **return** t	

of Toffoli gates while increasing the number of CNOT gates. The Toffoli gate consists of 6 CNOT gates and 9 single qubit gates as shown in Fig. 2. For this reason, it is important to design a circuit with a minimum number of Toffoli gates to implement the quantum algorithm.

In order to show the impact of proposed method, the substitute layer of AES is selected as an example, which uses $x^8 + x^4 + x^3 + x + 1$ as a target polynomial. The substitute layer requires binary field inversion operation of $x^8 + x^4 + x^3 + x + 1$. The inversion operation of AES is given in Algorithm 1.

In Step 1, the squaring operation is performed. The squaring operation can be obtained with 11 CNOT gates as shown in Fig. 3. The squaring directly reduces the result due to the nature of squaring on binary field [13]. After the squaring operation, a multiplication operation is performed on the squared value (i.e. z^2) and the input integer z. The integer z is reused in Step 2. This process follows $A \cdot B$, $A \cdot C$ structure (i.e $z = A, z_2 = B, z_2^2 = C$).

When the Karatsuba method is applied to the multiplication, the input value (i.e. z) is updated due to the operand addition step of Karatsuba. Generally, the operand is restored to the original z value for the following operation. The condition is described with an example on 2-bit case in Fig. 4. The circuit describes the condition after the 2-bit multiplication.

When the 2-bit multiplication operations on operands $A(a_0, a_1)$ and $B(b_0, b_1)$ are performed, a_1 and b_1 are changed to $a_0 + a_1$ and $b_0 + b_1$, respectively. If only the result of the multiplication is needed, reversible gates are not required. However, the value of $A(a_0, a_1)$ is used again in following calculations, (i.e. $A \cdot C$).

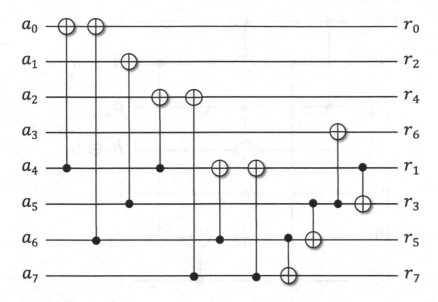

Fig. 3. Circuit configuration of the squaring operation on $x^8 + x^4 + x^3 + x + 1$.

For this reason, the reversible circuit should be performed for the operand A. The reversible gate is described in Fig. 5. In each n-bit multiplication, the reversible gate requires $(n - 1)$ CNOT gates for each operand.

In order to reduce this overhead, we present a non-reversible gate based $A \cdot B$ and $A \cdot C$ structure of inversion. Detailed descriptions for 2-bit case are given in Fig. 6.

First, the $a_0 \cdot c_0$ operation is calculated. When the operation of $a_0 \cdot c_0$ is completed, the a_0 value is no longer used in following operations, because the value will not affect the following calculation. The second qubit, $a_0 + a_1$, then performs a CNOT operation with a_0 to change the value of the first qubit to a_1. Afterward, $a1 \cdot c1$ operation gets calculated using c_1 with the a_1 value. The $(c_0 + c_1)$ is simply made through CNOT operation between c_0 and c_1. Finally, the $(a_0 + a_1) \cdot (c_0 + c_1)$ gets calculated.

In conclusion, it is possible to make the same result of $A \cdot B$ and $A \cdot C$, through $A \cdot B$ and $A' \cdot C$ structure, which excludes reversible circuits.

By using the proposed method, the inversion for $x^8 + x^4 + x^3 + x + 1$ is implemented. This implementation reduced the number of Toffoli gates used compared to the basic multiplication method. Generic multiplication uses 64 (n^2) Toffoli gates per multiplication, while Karatsuba only uses 27 Toffoli gates per multiplication. However, the Karatsuba method for the inversion operation uses 108 additional CNOT gates than the generic multiplication method. However the number of Toffoli gates should be considered than CNOT gates since the Toffoli gate consists of 6 CNOT gates with 9 one-gates.

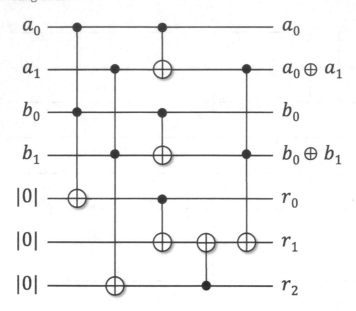

Fig. 4. Non-reversible multiplication of $A \cdot B$ with Karatsuba multiplication.

The Karachuba multiplication circuit of [11] is not designed to be reversible, and all of the remaining operators A, B and input qubits get treated as garbage qubits after multiplication, except for the qubits that contain the result of the operation. This is because the calculation of $A \cdot C$ was not considered which comes after $A \cdot B$ during multiplication of Itoh-Tsuji algorithm. Conventionally, in order to perform Itoh-Tsuji multiplication with Karatsuba, a reversible circuit is required to recover the original values of the operand. In the case of inversion for $x^8 + x^4 + x^3 + x + 1$, 14 CNOT gates are required for the reverse circuit for the Karatsuba algorithm. In the proposed method, the reverse process is omitted by utilizing the $A \cdot B$ and $A' \cdot C$ pattern, which optimizes 14 CNOT gates.

3.2   Reducing the Number of Qubits

In this section, we present the technique to reduce the total number of qubits required for the operation during the multiplication and squaring operation of Itoh-Tsujii's algorithm.

In Steps 1 and 2 of Algorithm 1, the value of B is the square of the A value (i.e. z on the algorithm) and the value C is created through the square of $A \cdot B$. Both B and C are originated from the value A.

The value of B is computed with the squaring operation as described in Fig. 3. The squaring operation is performing the left-shifting and modular operations on the input qubit. In other words, the value B is the result of left-shifting the qubit of A and the modular operation on it.

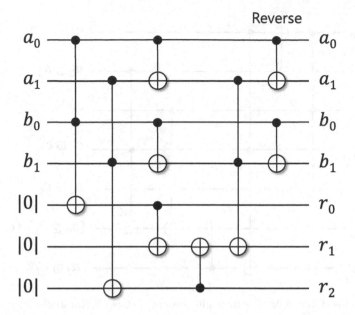

Fig. 5. Reversible multiplication of $A \cdot B$ with Karatsuba multiplication.

Using these features, some of the qubits are initialized to zero, which allows the calculation to use less qubits than original multiplication computation. Detailed descriptions of the method are presented in Fig. 7.

The first Step represents the value B, the second Step represents the value A, and the third Step represents the value C from $A \cdot B$, $A \cdot C$ multiplication of Itoh-Tsujii algorithm.

First, B value is formed from A value through the square operation. In Step 2, $A \cdot B$ multiplication is performed. After the multiplication, the values of B and A get changed into B' and A', respectively. The result of $A \cdot B$ calculation gets stored in the third row. A gets changed into A', because the calculation does not require the reverse circuit. In Step 3, $A \cdot B$ operation is calculated, and C value is formed with the result. In Step 4, values A' and C are multiplied. During the multiplication process of Step 4, the value of A' gets changed in order to proceed with the Karatsuba operation (i.e $A' \longrightarrow A''$). During this process, the changed value of multiplication (A'') forms the same value with B' during the multiplication process of $A' \cdot C$. By performing the CNOT operation on the same value between A'' and B', some of the qubits of B' is initialized back to zero (See Step 5). In Algorithm 1, the value B is not used again after the $A \cdot B$ operation. For this reason, we can utilize these qubits for other purposes. Initialized qubits of B are used as a extra qubit space during the following inversion operation.

Table 1 presents the values contained in the value B' after $A \cdot B$ multiplied by B and a formed through the squaring of A on $x^8 + x^4 + x^3 + x + 1$.

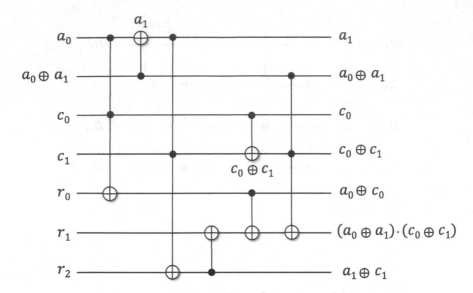

Fig. 6. Proposed non-reversible multiplication of $A \cdot C$ with Karatsuba multiplication.

Table 1. Combination of A values of B' after $A \cdot B$ computation on $GF(2^8)$.

k	B_k	k	B_k
0	$a_0 + a_2 + a_6 + a_7$	4	$a_2 + a_3 + a_4 + a_5 + a_7$
1	$a_4 + a_5 + a_7$	5	$a_5 + a_7$
2	$a_1 + a_3$	6	$a_3 + a_5 + a_6 + a_7$
3	$a_4 + a_5$	7	$a_6 + a_7$

As shown in Table 2, it can be seen that the value of B' after the operation of $A \cdot B$ consists of the addition of the A values. These combinations of A values are made through the Karatsuba operation. This combination is also observed in A'', which are values that get formed during $A' \cdot C$ multiplication. Values are shown in Table 2.

Using both Table 1 and Table 2, the combination can initialize the value of B to zero. For example, in Table 1, the element of k_0 is presented as $a_0 + a_6 + a_2 + a_7$. This value is initialized by using k_6 and k_{14} value from Table 2 which are $a_0 + a_2$ in red and $a_6 + a_7$ in orange, respectively. By performing the CNOT operation on B_0 with k_6 and k_{14}, B_0 is initialized into zero.

If the initialization is performed for multiplication with the conventional multiplication method, it would require 18 additional CNOT gates in order to form elements of k_n. However, the Karatsuba multiplication makes it possible to initialize the value of B to zero without having to take extra steps to form elements of k_n. During the multiplication process of Karatsuba, the elements

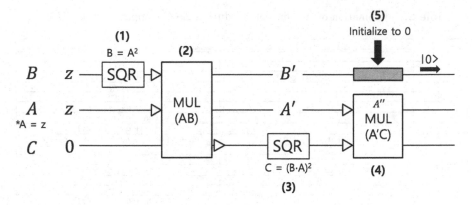

Fig. 7. Overview of proposed method for initializing some of the qubits during Karatsuba multiplication.

of k_n gets created eventually in order to be used as a multiplication factor. By utilizing this feature, we were able to initialize 8 qubits with 11 CNOT gates.

In the process of calculating the Step 3 of the Algorithm 1, the qubit can be reduced in a similar way. Unlike Steps 1 and 2 of the Algorithm 1, the Step 3 does not have a exact same structure of $A \cdot B$ and $A \cdot C$. However there is still a part that can initialize the qubit to zero. 8 additional qubits can be initialized to zero. Finally, 16 qubits can be initialized to zero and be used for the following calculation.

4   Evaluation

In order to evaluate quantum gates, we utilized the quantum computer emulator. We utilized the well-known IBM's ProjectQ framework for evaluation of the proposed method[1]. The framework provides quantum computer compiler and quantum resource estimator. This is useful for accurate evaluation. Proposed quantum gates are written in Python and follow the ProjectQ grammar.

We compare the number of Toffoli gates, CNOT gates, and qubit of implementation method based on $x^8 + x^4 + x^3 + x + 1$ inversion, which is used in the substitute layer of AES. The inversion operation of $x^8 + x^4 + x^3 + x + 1$ consists of 4 multiplications and 7 squaring operations using the Itoh-Tsuji's algorithm. We present two methods including CNOT reduction version and qubit recycle version. The CNOT reduction version performs $A \cdot B$ and $A \cdot C$ pattern with non-reversible multiplications. For the qubit recycle version, few CNOT gates are used more than CNOT reduction version but some qubits are recycled. The required quantum resources of proposed method is given in the Table 3. Compared with Karatsuba approach by [11], the number of Toffoli gates is identical. For the CNOT gate, CNOT reduction and qubit recycle versions reduces 14 and

---

[1] https://github.com/ProjectQ-Framework/ProjectQ.

Table 2. Combination of A values of A'' during $A \cdot C$ computation on $GF(2^8)$.

k	A_k	R_k
0	a_0	$a_0 c_0$
1	a_1	$a_1 c_1$
2	$a_0 + a_1$	$(a_0 + a_1)(c_0 + c_1)$
3	a_2	$a_2 c_2$
4	a_3	$a_3 c_3$
5	$a_2 + a_3$	$(a_2 + a_3)(c_2 + c_3)$
6	$a_0 + a_2$	$(a_0 + a_2)(c_0 + c_2)$
7	$a_1 + a_3$	$(a_1 + a_3)(c_1 + c_3)$
8	$a_0 + a_1 + a_2 + a_3$	$(a_0 + a_1 + a_2 + a_3)(c_0 + c_1 + c_2 + c_3)$
9	a_4	$a_4 c_4$
10	a_5	$a_5 c_5$
11	$a_4 + a_5$	$(a_4 + a_5)(c_4 + c_5)$
12	a_6	$a_6 c_6$
13	a_7	$a_7 c_7$
14	$a_6 + a_7$	$(a_6 + a_7)(c_6 + c_7)$
15	$a_4 + a_6$	$(a_4 + a_6)(c_4 + c_6)$
16	$a_5 + a_7$	$(a_5 + a_7)(c_5 + c_7)$
17	$a_4 + a_5 + a_6 + a_7$	$(a_4 + a_5 + a_6 + a_7)(c_4 + c_5 + c_6 + c_7)$
18	$a_0 + a_4$	$(a_0 + a_4)(c_0 + c_4)$
19	$a_1 + a_5$	$(a_1 + a_5)(c_1 + c_5)$
20	$a_0 + a_1 + a_4 + a_5$	$(a_0 + a_1 + a_4 + a_5)(c_0 + c_1 + c_4 + c_5)$
21	$a_2 + a_6$	$(a_2 + a_6)(c_2 + c_6)$
22	$a_3 + a_7$	$(a_3 + a_7)(c_3 + c_7)$
23	$a_2 + a_3 + a_6 + a_7$	$(a_2 + a_3 + a_6 + a_7)(c_2 + c_3 + c_6 + c_7)$
24	$a_0 + a_2 + a_4 + a_6$	$(a_0 + a_2 + a_4 + a_6)(c_0 + c_2 + c_4 + c_6)$
25	$a_1 + a_3 + a_5 + a_7$	$(a_1 + a_3 + a_5 + a_7)(c_1 + c_3 + c_5 + c_7)$
26	$a_0 + a_1 + a_2 + a_3 + a_4 + a_5 + a_6 + a_7$	$(a_0 + a_1 + a_2 + a_3 + a_4 + a_5 + a_6 + a_7)$ $(c_0 + c_1 + c_2 + c_3 + c_4 + c_5 + c_6 + c_7)$

3 CNOT gates, respectively. In particular, the qubit recycle version reduces the number of qubit by 8.

Table 3. Comparison of quantum resource for $A \cdot B$ and $A \cdot C$ computation on $GF(2^8)$.

Method	Toffoli gate	CNOT gate	Qubit
Kepley et al. [11]	54	252	70
This work (CNOT reduction)	54	**238**	70
This work (qubit recycle)	54	**249**	**62**

The proposed method can be applied to the Itoh-Tsuji-based inversion of binary field ECC. In Algorithm 2, the inversion algorithm for sect283k1 and sect283r1 is given. In Step 1, 5, 7, and 10, $A \cdot B$ and $A \cdot C$ pattern is observed. This case can be optimized by using the proposed method in terms of CNOT gates and qubits.

Algorithm 2. Itoh-Tsuji-based inversion for $p = x^{283} + x^{12} + x^7 + x^5 + 1$

Require: Integer z satisfying $1 \leq z \leq p - 1$.
Ensure: Inverse $t = z^{p-2} \bmod p = z^{-1} \bmod p$.

1: $z_2 \leftarrow z^2 \cdot z$	{ cost: 1S+1M }
2: $z_4 \leftarrow z_2^{2^2} \cdot z_2$	{ cost: 2S+1M }
3: $z_8 \leftarrow z_4^{2^4} \cdot z_4$	{ cost: 4S+1M }
4: $z_{16} \leftarrow z_8^{2^8} \cdot z_8$	{ cost: 8S+1M }
5: $z_{17} \leftarrow z_{16}^{2} \cdot z$	{ cost: 1S+1M }
6: $z_{34} \leftarrow z_{17}^{2^{17}} \cdot z_{17}$	{ cost: 17S+1M }
7: $z_{35} \leftarrow z_{34}^{2} \cdot z$	{ cost: 1S+1M }
8: $z_{70} \leftarrow z_{35}^{2^{35}} \cdot z_{35}$	{ cost: 35S+1M }
9: $z_{140} \leftarrow z_{70}^{2^{70}} \cdot z_{70}$	{ cost: 70S+1M }
10: $z_{141} \leftarrow z_{140}^{2} \cdot z$	{ cost: 1S+1M }
11: $z_{282} \leftarrow z_{141}^{2^{141}} \cdot z_{141}$	{ cost: 141S+1M }
12: $t \leftarrow z_{282}^{2}$	{ cost: 1S }
13: **return** t	

5 Conclusion

In this paper, we presented the optimized implementation of binary field inversion in quantum circuits for $A \cdot B$ and $A \cdot C$ structure. First, non-reversible circuits are used for $A \cdot B$ and $A \cdot C$ patterns. Second, qubit reuse technique is suggested. Both techniques reduce the required number of CNOT gates and qubits. The-state-of-art optimization techniques, such as Karatsuba algorithm and modular squaring, are also utilized to reduce the number of Toffoli gates and qubits. Finally, the quantum circuit for binary field inversion achieved the optimal number of Toffoli gates, CNOT gates and qubits. The proposed method is used to implement the substitute layer of AES. The result shows that proposed method uses lesser CNOT and qubits than previous Karatsuba based approach. Furthermore, the proposed method can be used for the binary field inversion of ECC.

The future work is going to find another arithmetic structures to optimize the quantum circuit for other cryptographic algorithms. In the inversion, the consecutive multiplication and squaring structure is frequently used. We will find the optimal computation routine for this structure.

Acknowledgement. This work was supported by Institute for Information & communications Technology Planning & Evaluation (IITP) grant funded by the Korea government(MSIT) (< Q | Crypton >, No.2019-0-00033, Study on Quantum Security Evaluation of Cryptography based on Computational Quantum Complexity). This work of Zhi Hu is supported by the Natural Science Foundation of China (Grants No. 61972420, 61602526) and Hunan Provincial Natural Science Foundation of China (Grants No. 2019JJ50827, 2020JJ3050).

References

1. Hankerson, D., Menezes, A.J., Vanstone, S.: Guide to Elliptic Curve Cryptography. Springer, New York (2006)
2. Abdul-Aziz Gutub, A., Tenca, A.F., Savaş, E., Koç, R.C.C.K.: Scalable and unified hardware to compute Montgomery inverse in GF(p) and $GF(2^n)$. In: Kaliski, B.S., Koç, K., Paar, C. (eds.) CHES 2002. LNCS, vol. 2523, pp. 484–499. Springer, Heidelberg (2003). https://doi.org/10.1007/3-540-36400-5_35
3. Yen, S.: Improved normal basis inversion in $GF(2^m)$. IEE Electron. Lett. **33**, 196–197 (1997)
4. Hasan, M.A.: Efficient computation of multiplicative inverses for cryptographic applications. In: 15th IEEE Symposium on Computer Arithmetic (2001)
5. Itoh, T., Tsujii, S.: A fast algorithm for computing multiplicative inverses in $GF(2^m)$ using normal basis. Inf. Comput. **78**, 171–177 (1988)
6. Kaminski, M., Bshouty, N.H.: Multiplicative complexity of polynomial multiplication over finite fields. J. ACM **36**(3), 150–170 (1989)
7. O. Karatsuba, "Multiplication of multidigit numbers on automata," in Soviet physics doklady, pp. 595–596, Springer, 1963
8. Bernstein, D.J.: Batch binary Edwards. In: Halevi, S. (ed.) CRYPTO 2009. LNCS, vol. 5677, pp. 317–336. Springer, Heidelberg (2009). https://doi.org/10.1007/978-3-642-03356-8_19
9. Cook, S.: On the minimum computation time of functions. Phd thesis, Harvard University (1966)
10. Schwabe, P., Westerbaan, B.: Solving binary $\mathcal{MQ}$ with grover's algorithm. In: Carlet, C., Hasan, M.A., Saraswat, V. (eds.) SPACE 2016. LNCS, vol. 10076, pp. 303–322. Springer, Cham (2016). https://doi.org/10.1007/978-3-319-49445-6_17
11. Kepley, S., Steinwandt, R.: Quantum circuits for $\mathbb{F}_{2^n}$-multiplication with subquadratic gate count. Quantum Inf. Process. **14**(7), 2373–2386 (2015). https://doi.org/10.1007/s11128-015-0993-1
12. Li, X., et al.: An all-optical quantum gate in a semiconductor quantum dot. Science **301**(5634), 809–811 (2003)
13. Muñoz-Coreas, E., Thapliyal, H.: Design of quantum circuits for Galois field squaring and exponentiation. In: 2017 IEEE Computer Society Annual Symposium on VLSI (ISVLSI), pp. 68–73 (2017)

Virtualization Technologies in the Android Framework and Compatibility with SEAndroid

Jaehyeon Yoon[1] , Tu Chau Ngoc[2] , Hoang Nguyen Huy[1] ,
and Souhwan Jung[2]([⊠])

[1] Department of Information and Communication Convergence, Soongsil University,
Seoul, South Korea
{yjh7593,hoangnh}@soongsil.ac.kr
[2] School of Electronic Engineering, Soongsil University, Seoul, South Korea
chaungoctu@soongsil.ac.kr, souhwanj@ssu.ac.kr

Abstract. Virtualization is used in various environments such as cloud
and network, but it was difficult to utilize it in mobile devices due
to computing resource problems. Technology such as containers that
are faster and lighter than traditional hypervisor-based virtualization is
being developed. In this paper, we implemented three virtualization technologies in the Android framework: hypervisor-based virtual machine,
lightweight hypervisor-based virtual machine, and container. In the process of implementation, we created and applied the SEAndroid policy
for each virtualization technology. In addition, we measured performance
by considering the boot time for the implemented virtual instance. As
a result of empirical experiments, the container showed the best performance, but it showed a problem with the compatibility of security
function SEAndroid. The lightweight hypervisor technology shows faster
performance than the legacy one and also provides safety by an additional kernel.

Keywords: Android · Virtualization · SEAndroid

1 Introduction

In the mobile market, the Android operating system is being used by various
vendors by taking advantage of open source. According to statistics, Android has
more than 70% share of the mobile device operating system market. As mobile
devices are closely related to the lives of users, personal financial information
and privacy are being used in Android, and the demand for security techniques
or additional functions to protect them is increasing. Various studies have been

This work was supported by Institute of Information & communications Technology
Planning & Evaluation (IITP) grant funded by the Korea government(MSIT) (No.
2019-0-00477, Development of android security framework technology using virtualized
trusted execution environment).

I. You (Ed.): WISA 2020, LNCS 12583, pp. 167–178, 2020.
https://doi.org/10.1007/978-3-030-65299-9_13

conducted to safely store the data of the app or to isolate the environment of a specific process. One of the methods is to utilize the advantage of the virtual environment by using a hypervisor in Android. Virtualization technology can minimize the impact on the entire operating system by running untrusted applications such as malware in isolated spaces. However, when applying a method using a traditional hypervisor-based virtual machine to a mobile device, a computing resource problem of the device was presented. Advancements in hardware and lightweight virtualization technologies, however, can solve these problems, and mobile devices now have enough computing power to realize a virtual environment.

The Android environment provides a closed environment compared to other operating systems such as Linux. Since Android applications are isolated from other applications and systems by Dalvik VM, it must perform the privileged tasks provided by system services through the Android API. Therefore, all virtualization technologies must be implemented at the software level because normal applications can't directly access the system or hardware. In order to solve these problems, some users are using a technique such as rooting to obtain the authority of the administrator, but this can cause a risk in terms of security [16].

In order to solve these problems, this paper proposed a method for implementing virtualization without affecting the Android security framework such as SEAndroid, and evaluated the performance of the implemented virtual environments simply. The following section describes virtualization technologies used in other environments, and Sect. 3 describes studies using virtual environments in Android. Section 4 describes methods for implementing a virtual environment on Android, and its evaluation is in Sect. 5. Section 6 considers the scope and limitations of existing security functions when applying a virtual environment, and finally concludes in Sect. 7.

2   Background

2.1   Virtualization Methods

Hypervisor-Based Virtual Machine. The most common way to implement a virtual environment is to use a hypervisor. The hypervisor emulates virtual hardware and loads the kernel and operating system to create a new virtual environment. There are two types of hypervisors: bare metal and hosted. In the case of a bare metal hypervisor, it runs directly on the hardware and can run the guest operating system directly without a host operating system. The hosted hypervisor runs on the host operating system and the administrator can manage guest operating systems through the executed hypervisor. It may cause a lot of overhead because all hardware is emulated and operated. KVM can be used together to utilize some kernel functions of the host operating system [6,7].

Container. Container technology, unlike hypervisors, implements a virtual environment that shares the host's kernel. Although it is actually a process, it uses the namespace and Cgroups provided by the Linux kernel to isolate the process from the host operating system [4]. Container implements the guest operating system in the form of a process without a hypervisor and a guest kernel. It has the advantage of low overhead. However, since the kernel is shared, some file systems (/proc, /dev, etc.) can be shared. And some kernel vulnerability may affect the isolation between the host OS and the guest OS [10,14]. Figure 1 shows the difference between a virtual machine and a container.

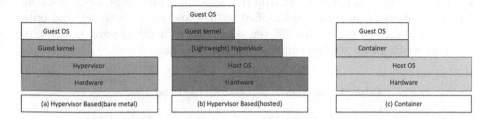

Fig. 1. Comparison of the virtual architectures

Lightweight Hypervisor-Based Virtual Machine. In order to solve the overhead of the hypervisor-based virtual machine and the security problem of the container, the concept of a lightweight hypervisor-based security container has appeared [17]. The representative tool, kata container, implements an isolated runtime environment using a lightweight hypervisor and enables container images such as dockers to be executed in the environment. The lightweight hypervisor virtualized only the essential hardware and shortened the boot time to reduce the overhead caused by hardware virtualization and implemented an isolated environment from the host operating system.

2.2 Differences Between Android Framework and Linux

Android was developed based on the Linux kernel, but it has a very different framework from normal Linux. Common Linux processes can easily communicate with other processes using Unix sockets, but Android applications require services to perform interprocess communication because they are isolated by Dalvik VM [3]. Android applications that are not system processes are executed by zygote, and each application is isolated from each other and does not affect the outside. Applications are designed to perform communication through a binder device using service APIs inherited through zygote [13].

For this reason, normal Android applications cannot perform any privileged tasks. In order to perform a privileged operation such as network or storage access, a request must be made to a service having the privilege and wait for the service to deliver the result of processing the task [5].

Another difference between Android and traditional Linux is the configuration of the file system. The Linux system has a file system configuration to support multi-users. Compared to Linux, Android may have executable files or configuration files stored in different directories. This difference should be corrected when applying programs provided as packages in Linux to Android.

Finally, one of the differences between Android and Linux is SELinux's policy. In the case of Linux, in order to provide an appropriate security policy for a multi-user operating system, files and processes are provided with labels in "user/role/type" order [15]. SEAndroid uses the same LSM mechanism as SELinux, but users and roles are unified with u and r, respectively, and only rules are managed by type. This difference makes it difficult to provide SELinux rules like existing Linux when running containers in the future.

Table 1. Differences between Android and Linux

Component	Linux App	Android App
IPC	Socket	Binder
Isolation	None	Dalvik VM
Parent process for Apps	Init or other process	Zygote
Permission for Apps	Linux DAC SELinux context	Android permission
User	Multi-user	Single user

2.3   SELinux and SEAndroid

One of the differences between Android and Linux is SELinux's policy. SELinux is one of the Linux Security Modules (LSM) provided by the Linux kernel. This SELinux consists of policies including context, domain, etc., and uses this to control access to specific objects by specific subjects. SELinux assigns context to each user, process, and file and performs access control using the policy related to the context. The SELinux context consists of user, role, and type [15]. User and role can be set to distinguish multiple users or groups, and type represents the authority of each object.

SEAndroid is a module modified to apply SELinux to the Android framework. It is based on the existing SELinux system, but due to the characteristics of the mobile phone, many parts have been omitted to be lightweight. SEAndroid does not need user and role roles for multiple users, so it is unified with u and r [20]. Most of the rules of policy are organized based on type. This difference makes it difficult to provide SELinux rules like existing Linux when running containers in the future.

3   Related Works

There have been many studies using virtualization technology on Android. Kevin et al., proposed a method of creating an isolated environment using a bare metal hypervisor and running the application for safe application execution on mobile devices [9]. This study uses a bare metal hypervisor instead of implementing a reliable operating system as part of the TCB in a mobile environment. This virtual environment consists of fewer lines of code than a typical OS, making it more suitable for TCB. This method provides a safe environment based on bare metal and can provide a TCB, but requires a firmware level modification.

Guillaume et al., classified the application's authority into four types of system, OS, Framework, and Application using a bare metal hypervisor, and developed a policy and system to manage it [1]. These methods use a bare-metal hypervisor and operate on the hardware directly in the form of TCB, thus cause the device dependency. Also, There wasn't an evaluation of performance.

Julian et al., proposed a method for encrypting RAM memory at the hypervisor level for small ARM devices [11]. Zhichao et al., proposed a method to virtualize the function of TrustZone, a hardware-based trust execution environment, and apply it to mobile devices [12]. These methods utilized a method of inheriting reliability from a hardware-based trust execution environment to modify the hypervisor and provide the reliability of the virtual environment in which the security function operates.

Dong et al., proposed a method to more safely isolate the guest operating system by utilizing Hyp mode, which can be used in ARM [19]. The newly developed H-binder hooks the Binder transaction to ensure the integrity and safety of data transmission.

The ARM architecture provides hardware-based functions for virtualization security. The HYP mode of ARM is a CPU mode that has higher privileges than the existing user interrupt, and is also called Eception level 2. Figure 2 shows the Exception mode in ARM architecture. When using this mode in a bare metal hypervisor, hypervisor codes that can control each guest OS arc executed in HYP mode, so that they can have more authority. However, in the case of a host-based hypervisor, the host operating system runs on EL1, and KVM also belongs to EL1. To solve this problem, Dall et al. modified the existing KVM for the virtualization support mode provided by the ARM architecture [6]. Among the existing KVM codes, the codes to be executed in HYP mode are made into a lowvisor and divided into highvisor and lowvisor. Figure 3 shows Highvisor and Lowvisor in ARM Exception mode. This HYP mode can be applied to make secure the VM of our idea. But we didn't mention it, because enabling the hyp mode is in firmware. And our goal is to find the best way to trigger the virtual environment from the application by checking the compatibility.

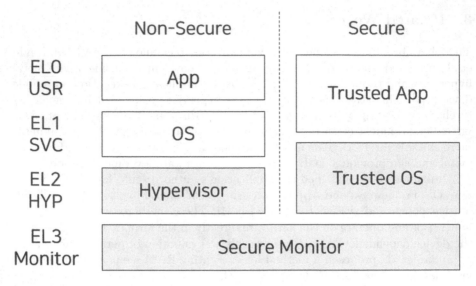

Fig. 2. HYP mode in ARM Exception Modes

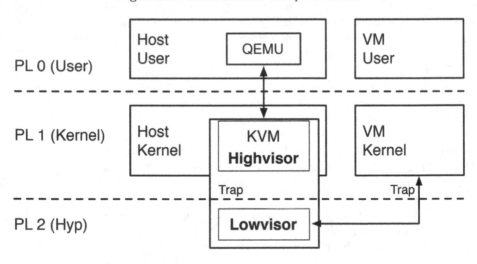

Fig. 3. KVM for ARM HYP mode by Dell et al.

4 Implementation

4.1 Environment Setup

As mentioned in Sect. 2.2, it is necessary to solve the dependency problem on libraries and configuration files in order to run a virtual environment program such as hypervisor on Android. To this end, all compilation work was performed with the static option that does not require an external library. We hard-coded the configuration values by modifying the parts that access and utilize the configuration file.

The hypervisor was based on QEMU, and the lightweight hypervisor utilized lkvm. In both cases, it was implemented using source code [2]. Container is implemented based on LXC container. All compiled files are located in the /system/bin directory, and the permissions are set so that test-app can access them.

As shown in the Fig. 4, the Android application sends a request for the virtualization to an authorized service(Virtual Environment Service) through the binder(a). The requested service executes QEMU, lkvm, or LXC according to the request. If there is an execution request for QEMU or lkvm, the KVM module of the host kernel can be utilized by trigger(b,c). When a request for LXC creation is received, the Virtual Environment Service can execute the container immediately(d).

Android App. The Android app needs the help of the VE service to run the virtual environment. There is no API related to the virtual environment in the API provided by the general Android SDK. The Android app uses the VE Service SDK developed to communicate with the VE service.

Virtual Environment Service. The virtual environment service can execute the virtual environment according to the request received from the application. This service operates as a system service. It runs QEMU, lkvm, lxc at the request of the application.

Virtual Environment Trigger. The virtual environment trigger consists of three executable binary files. QEMU, lkvm, lxc. Each executable binary file is located in the system directory. Applications can't directly access the executable file.

Virtual Environment. The run virtual environment was created for testing. We used a busybox-based image to remove various processes that could run inside and to evaluate the performance until each virtual environment runs.

4.2 Kernel Reconfiguration

The kernel used in Android was developed based on the Linux kernel, but over time, it includes additional new features, and features that have been used in Linux but are not used well in Android are not set [18]. In the case of QEMU, it is possible to operate without a KVM kernel module. In order to reduce overhead, a KVM module is essential when used in the form of QEMU-kvm [8]. lkvm, which will be used as a lightweight hypervisor, is also a program that can implement a simple virtual environment based on KVM. It is also implemented by adding the KVM function to the Android kernel. In addition, by enabling VitualIO-related

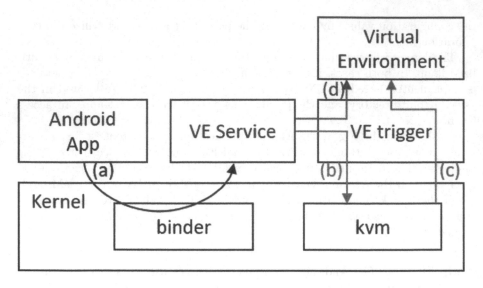

Fig. 4. Operation flow to create the virtual environment

modules to be used in communication between the virtual environment and the host, a virtual environment can be implemented. The kernel features needed to implement a container are typically namespaces and cgroups, and the features were applied through pre-compilation configuration.

4.3   SEAndroid Support for Virtualization

SELinux's policy is created using the Type Enforcement(TE) file to define the rule. In the case of SEAndroid, all relevant TE files for creating rules are included in the Android source code [20]. However, there are no rules for programs like QEMU or lkvm. As mentioned above, the rules used for QEMU and lkvm in SELinux do not work properly in the Android environment, so a new TE file must be created.

   In order to create a new TE file for the virtualization, the kernel parameter was changed to modify SEAndroid to permissive mode. In the permissive mode, there is no access control according to the policy, and only an audit can log. This allowed us to collect behaviors of virtualization technologies that are not allowed in existing SEAndroid policies. Since all the operations of the virtualization technique may not be performed, we have used the existing Linux rules to fill in additional necessary parts. We created new rules for virtualization using the generated audit log and existing Linux rules. The newly created rules are integrated into the Android source code to implement SEAndroid policies that can be virtualization function properly.

5   Evaluation

For evaluation in the same environment, QEMU, lkvm, and lxc were installed on one device. For compatibility with the Android operating system, the device utilizes Hikey960. The Android version used 10, and the device performance is shown in the following Table 2.

Table 2. Testbed hardware spec

Component	Spec
Model	Hikey 960
SoC	Kirin 960
CPU	4 Cortex A73 + 4 Cortex A53 Big.Little CPU architecture
RAM	3 GB LPDDR4 SDRAM
GPU	ARM Mali G71 MP8
Storage	32 GB UFS Flash Storage

In order to compare the performance of the implemented virtual environments, the timestamp when the shell was obtained from the virtual environment creation time was obtained and the difference was compared. The experiment was repeated 30 times, and after each experiment, the device rebooted and had sufficient idle time. Figure 5 shows the average time required. In the case of a container environment, it was confirmed that "init" immediately launched a shell, and the environment was configured in a very short time. In the case of QEMU and lkvm, we can see that it takes relatively more time to configure the environment and apply the kernel.

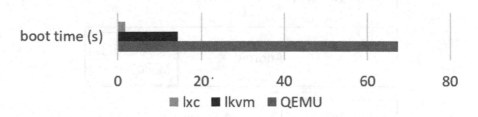

Fig. 5. Comparison of the boot time

6   Compatibility with SEAndroid

SEAndroid is a representative security module that can be used in Android. The technologies to be used in Android need to provide proper security in conjunction with SEAndroid. In the previous experiment, we experimented with porting virtualization techniques to Android. We created appropriate rules for virtualization techniques using permissive mode and Linux's SEAndroid rules. Hypervisor-based virtualization techniques were not directly affected by SEAndroid using an additional kernel. However, these techniques also require rules to communicate with some hardware of Android, so a new context is given to hardware files or additional rules are created.

However, as shown in Fig. 6, the container running on Android caused a functional crash. The container shares the kernel with the host operating system, and SEAndroid is one of the LSMs, which is a security module that provides functions in the kernel. The shared kernel is directly accessible inside Android and the container. All system calls executed in the container are executed through the same kernel. For this reason, all actions executed inside the container are controlled by the SEAndroid policy provided by Android.

In order to solve this problem, unlike hypervisor-based virtualization, all operations of specific processes running inside the container had to be specified in advance and rules had to be created. However, it is very difficult to predefine all the actions executed inside the container. Unlike SELinux, which is used in Linux, SEAndroid is compiled with the Android framework, and subsequent modifications are very difficult. In a recent version, a technique called Treble was introduced. Treble allows device vendors to compile additional rules at device boot time to create a single SEAndroid policy. However, this method is also very difficult because Android's vendor image must be created with SEAndroid rules.

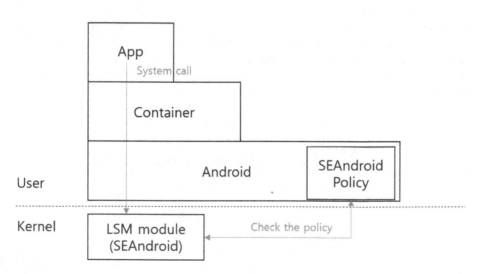

Fig. 6. Access control by SEAndroid for container

Container technology may be limited by security functions in that it shares the host and kernel. In the case of the Integrity Measurement Architecture(IMA) namespace, the LSM function between the container and the host can be separated [21]. However, it is still in the research level, so it is difficult to use it in most kernels. In addition, this study was developed in conjunction with Apparmor, and technology integrated with SELinux has not been developed yet, making it difficult to apply to the Android environment.

7 Conclusion

In this paper, we proposed how to apply a virtual environment without hardware dependency in the Android framework, and compared the boot time by implementing a hypervisor-based and lightweight hypervisor-based virtual machine and container environment. Also, when using a virtual environment, we described the compatibility of security mechanisms that can be used in existing Android. The hypervisor-based virtual machine showed a lot of overhead as expected. The container environment will need additional development due to the conflict with the existing Android security mechanism. The lightweight hypervisor was tested without optimization of the kernel. It is expected that if optimized work is done, it will provide less overhead and better security environments. As the computing power of the Android mobile device increases, various virtual environment-based security functions may be additionally utilized. Future research can be about the application using the lightweight hypervisor at the Android framework level.

References

1. Averlant, G.: Multi-level isolation for android applications. In: 2017 IEEE International Symposium on Software Reliability Engineering Workshops (ISSREW), pp. 128–131. IEEE (2017)
2. Bellard, F.: Qemu, a fast and portable dynamic translator. In: USENIX Annual Technical Conference, FREENIX Track. vol. 41, p. 46 (2005)
3. Bornstein, D.: Dalvik vm internals. Google I/O developer Conference **23**, 17–30 (2008)
4. Chau, N.T., Jung, S.: Dynamic analysis with android container: challenges and opportunities. Digital Investigation **27**, 38–46 (2018)
5. Chen, L., Zhang, C.: Design and implement of binder extension model based on android inter-process communication. J. Xi'an Univ. Posts and Telecommun. **3** (2013)
6. Dall, C., Nieh, J.: Kvm/arm: the design and implementation of the linux arm hypervisor. ACM Sigplan Notices **49**(4), 333–348 (2014)
7. Felter, W., Ferreira, A., Rajamony, R., Rubio, J.: An updated performance comparison of virtual machines and linux containers. In: 2015 IEEE International Symposium on Performance Analysis of Systems and Software (ISPASS), pp. 171–172. IEEE (2015)
8. Goto, Y.: Kernel-based virtual machine technology. Fujitsu Sci. Techn. J. **47**(3), 362–368 (2011)
9. Gudeth, K., Pirretti, M., Hoeper, K., Buskey, R.: Delivering secure applications on commercial mobile devices: the case for bare metal hypervisors. In: Proceedings of the 1st ACM workshop on Security and privacy in smartphones and mobile devices, pp. 33–38 (2011)

10. Hertz, J.: Abusing privileged and unprivileged linux containers. Whitepaper, NCC Group 48 (2016)
11. Horsch, J., Huber, M., Wessel, S.: Transcrypt: Transparent main memory encryption using a minimal arm hypervisor. In: 2017 IEEE Trustcom/BigDataSE/ICESS, pp. 152–161. IEEE (2017)
12. Hua, Z., Gu, J., Xia, Y., Chen, H., Zang, B., Guan, H.: vtz: Virtualizing {ARM} trustzone. In: 26th {USENIX} Security Symposium ({USENIX} Security 17), pp. 541–556 (2017)
13. Huang, J.: Android IPC mechanism. Southern Taiwan University of Technology (2012)
14. Lin, X., Lei, L., Wang, Y., Jing, J., Sun, K., Zhou, Q.: A measurement study on linux container security: attacks and countermeasures. In: Proceedings of the 34th Annual Computer Security Applications Conference, pp. 418–429 (2018)
15. Loscocco, P., Smalley, S.: Integrating flexible support for security policies into the linux operating system. In: USENIX Annual Technical Conference, FREENIX Track, pp. 29–42 (2001)
16. Nguyen-Vu, L., Chau, N.T., Kang, S., Jung, S.: Android rooting: an arms race between evasion and detection. Secur. Commun. Netw. **2017** (2017)
17. Randazzo, A., Tinnirello, I.: Kata containers: An emerging architecture for enabling mec services in fast and secure way. In: 2019 Sixth International Conference on Internet of Things: Systems, Management and Security (IOTSMS), pp. 209–214. IEEE (2019)
18. Shanker, A., Lai, S.: Android porting concepts. In: 2011 3rd International Conference on Electronics Computer Technology, vol. 5, pp. 129–133. IEEE (2011)
19. Shen, D., Li, Z., Su, X., Ma, J., Deng, R.: Tinyvisor: an extensible secure framework on android platforms. Comput. Secur. **72**, 145–162 (2018)
20. Smalley, S., Craig, R.: Security enhanced (se) android: bringing flexible mac to android. NDSS **310**, 20–38 (2013)
21. Sun, Y., Safford, D., Zohar, M., Pendarakis, D., Gu, Z., Jaeger, T.: Security namespace: making linux security frameworks available to containers. In: 27th {USENIX} Security Symposium ({USENIX} Security 18), pp. 1423–1439 (2018)

Toward a Fine-Grained Evaluation of the Pwnable CTF

Sung-Kyung Kim(iD), Eun-Tae Jang(iD), and Ki-Woong Park$^{(\boxtimes)}$(iD)

Department of Information Security, Sejong University, Seoul, South Korea
jotun9935@gmail.com, euntaejang@gmail.com, woongbak@sejong.ac.kr

Abstract. In the untacted era of the recent COVID-19 virus outbreak, the pedagogic value of Capture the Flag (CTF) has grown even more as an effective means for students to learn knowledge about the overall computer system and information security through active participation without facing the teacher. However, in the process of successfully introducing CTF into the classroom, educators may suffer a high burden due to factors such as time and economy in the process of crafting problems and operating CTFs. Accordingly, various studies have been conducted to reduce this burden. On the other hand, in introducing CTF to the classroom, the burden of educators also exists in the aspect of an in-depth evaluation of students' academic achievement. This means that educators need to evaluate students' academic abilities in-depth so that educators can provide clear feedback on the factors that caused students to fail. Through this, educators can effectively increase student learning efficiency by helping students correct their own weaknesses. The need for such detailed evaluation can be said to be quite high in the pwnable field, one of the representative fields of CTF. This is because pwnable requires participants to have a comprehensive understanding of overall program analysis, vulnerability, mitigation bypassing techniques, systems, and so on. However, the evaluation manner of the existing CTF is not suitable for an in-depth evaluation of students' academic ability because they simply measure whether or not they solve problems in a pass and/or non-pass manner. Therefore, we designed a fine-grained evaluation CTF platform that aims to help educators provide precise evaluation and feedback on learners' failure factors in an attempt by educators to introduce CTF into the classroom to educate pwnable to reduce the burden on educators in properly evaluating student's Academic achievement.

Keywords: Capture the flag · CTF · Pwnable · Control flow hijack · Exploit

1 Introduction

Recently, various studies are attempting to increase the effectiveness of information security education [3,14,16]. Accordingly, pedagogics using the CTF (Cap-

Supported by the Institute for Information Communications Technology Promotion (IITP) of the Korea government (MSIT) [Grant No. 2018-0-00420, 2019-0-00273].

© Springer Nature Switzerland AG 2020
I. You (Ed.): WISA 2020, LNCS 12583, pp. 179–190, 2020.
https://doi.org/10.1007/978-3-030-65299-9_14

ture the Flag) manner in information security education has been recognized as a new paradigm. Besides, in the present era of the recent outbreak of COVID-19 virus, CTF is more valuable in that it is a pedagogical way of an untacted manner that enables active participation of students in a non-face-to-face. As the pedagogical value of CTF increases, various research and education platforms are being developed to help educators increase student access to CTF and increase learning efficiency [2, 4, 5, 7, 15, 16].

Representatively, some recent studies on CTFs suggest a manner such as automated problem creation to reduce the burden required for educators to introduce CTFs into the classroom [1, 8, 17]. However, the burden of educators in introducing CTF into the classroom also exists in the process of carefully evaluating students. This means that if an educator can evaluate a student's academic ability in detail, the educator can provide clear feedback on the factors that caused the student to fail in learning, and effectively improves the student's learning efficiency in a manner that corrects the student's weaknesses [14]. However, the evaluation manner of the CTF platform, which is used for the competition, evaluates the competency of participants in a pass and/or non-pass manner. For example, in CTF competitions, CTF organizers use some kind of computer science and information security knowledge to make problems. When the organizer makes a problem system. The flag (generally in the form of a string) is hidden so that it cannot be read without specific knowledge of programs and files. The participant successfully acquires the flag hidden by the organizer using the knowledge required by the problem and then submits it to the flag certification server of the CTF competition. At this time, whether or not the participant solves the problem is determined as whether or not the corresponding flag is successfully acquired.

As such, the CTF for existing competition purposes only evaluates the participant's problem-solving capacity in a pass and/or non-pass manner. Therefore, for problems that require comprehensive knowledge to solve a specific problem, it is difficult to identify the participant's failure point in this evaluation manner. These features can be burdensome for educators attempting to introduce CTF as an educational tool in the classroom. This is because if students are evaluated only in a pass and/or non-pass manner, educators must invest additional time and money to analyze the causes of learners' failures and provide appropriate feedback. A representative example of a field where the burden of educators is prominent is the pwnable field that requires a comprehensive understanding of binary and system knowledge and exploit technology and so on. For example, the control flow hijack type of problem frequently asked in pwnable is solved through the following complex process. First, the vulnerability of the program must be identified through static and dynamic analysis of the problem provided in the form of source code or binary file. Next, if you have successfully identified the vulnerability, you need to create the input data of the program that allows the program to trigger the vulnerability. Also, depending on the type of problem, a single and/or multiple vulnerabilities might be utilized to hijack the control flow of a program, and an appropriate payload must be configured to allow an

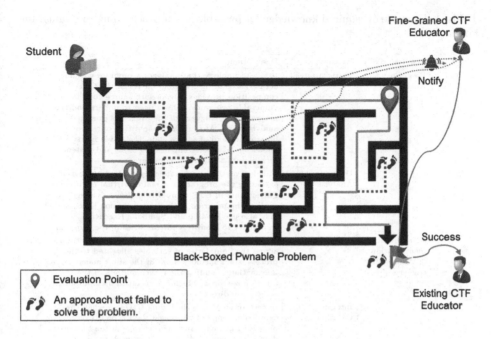

Fig. 1. Comparison of existing CTF and fine-grained CTF.

attacker to craft or execute existing code in the application address space. In some cases, when the mitigation policy is applied to the system and binary, a bypassing technique is used to bypass it. As such, pwnable problems generally require comprehensive knowledge of coding, system, attack, and defense, and program analysis skills, so learners need a comprehensive understanding of the overall process to solve single pwnable problem (see Table 1).

The existing CTF's pass and/or non-pass evaluation manner has limitations in accurately judging the learner's failure factors because it is judged that the problem itself has not been solved when a learner fails at some points in these processes. Therefore, this paper helps educators to accurately evaluate learners' failure factors in introducing CTF to the classroom, thereby reducing the burden on educators in appropriately evaluating student capabilities. To achieve this, we have defined a general problem solving process for control flow hijack type problems, and based on this, we designed a pwnable CTF platform that aims to enable precise evaluation and feedback on learners' failure factors.

The rest of this paper is organized as follows. Chapter 2 describes the general knowledge required to solve pwnable problems. Chapter 3 draws detailed evaluation points for the overall composition of a pwnable problem. Chapter 4 describe the design and implementation of fine-grained pwnable CTF. Finally, Chap. 4 presents the conclusions of this study.

Table 1. Example of required knowledge for pwnable learning according to Evaluation Points(EP)

EP	Required Skills	Example	Description
Ep1	Program Analysis	Static Analysis	It is a technology that analyzes a program without actually executing the program When the CTF competition provides solvers with source code for vulnerable programs, solvers need to understand the programming language of the programs provided to analyze them. Also, if the competition only provides binaries instead of source code, the solver needs knowledge of reverse engineering skills and system architecture to analyze the program
		Dynamic Analysis	This is a method to dynamically analyze a program by executing the program in a real or virtual environment. Participants in CTF competitions use a debugger to analyze the program during the execution process, and may also use Fuzzing and Symbolic Execution techniques to identify vulnerabilities in the program
	Vulnerability Identification & Vulnerability trigger	Stack Overflow	Stack overflow is a vulnerability that can inject data across the boundaries of variables allocated to the process' stack memory area. In the stack memory area, information including the return address of the function is stored, which can result in manipulating arbitrary indirect calls
		Integer Overflow	In certain languages, including C/C++, when the expression range of an integer data type is exceeds, undefined behavior such as a change in the sign of the data may occur. If the variable is used in conditional expressions or memory allocation size, it may cause fatal results
		Use After Free (UAF)	Most operating systems use their own memory management policy to reduce fragmentation of heap area. The UAF vulnerability can lead to information leaks, code execution, etc., depending on conditions when reusing freed memory
EP2	Control-Flow Hijacking	Indirect Call Overwrite	A skill that handles the program's control flow by manipulating data associated with the program's indirect call. The return address, function pointer, global offset table, etc. are subject to tampering
		Shellcoding	The skill of creating a small-sized program that executes specific instructions in the system, usually in machine code
EP3	Mitigation Bypassing	Return to Library	A method that bypasses protection by modulating the execution flow into a library code area that has execution authority. It is mainly used in situations where there is no write permission for the stack or heap area due to the protection techniques such as NX
		Return Oriented Programming	This method is used to bypass protection techniques such as NX, DEP, and ASLR. This skill uses a gadget in the program code area to control the call stack

2   Pwnable CTF Problem-Solving Workflow

In this study, we divide the required knowledge of the general pwnable problem into four stages based on the overall stage for exploitation: program analysis, vulnerability identification, control flow hijacking, and mitigation bypassing. This chapter describes the typical required knowledge for each step of solving pwnable problems (see Table 1).

2.1   Program Analysis

In general, pwnable systems are configured to acquire a flag by hijacking system permissions using a security vulnerability in a program running on a remote server. Accordingly, the attacker analyzes the program to identify the vulnerabilities of the program. Therefore, the knowledge required to solve the problem varies depending on the architecture of the server on which the vulnerable program is running. The process of analyzing the program is provided in competition problems. This process requires skills such as reverse engineering depending on whether the source code is provided and whether symbols and obfuscation are present [6,9,11,12].

2.2   Vulnerability Identification

Once the solver has successfully analyzed the program, the single and/or multiple vulnerabilities that exist within the given program are then identified to create the appropriate program inputs to trigger it. Therefore, at this stage, the solver must understand the various security vulnerabilities and sufficient programming knowledge to trigger the vulnerability [13].

2.3   Control Flow Hijacking

Most pwnable problems aim to hijack the control flow of the program as a final goal. To achieve this goal, attackers usually use the skill of manipulating areas where arbitrary manipulation is possible because write permission remains in the memory of application. For example, the return address of the function, function pointer, vtable, Global Offset Table (GOT) area, etc. can be a target. Therefore, the learner should understand the memory space and various techniques for handling control flow.

2.4   Mitigation Bypassing

The final step for the exploit is to take control of the program on the remote server. However, owing to mitigation policies developed over a long period of time, many CTF competitions require participants to understand the methods for bypassing these protection techniques. Accordingly, after control flow hijacking, it is necessary to understand the protection techniques applied to systems and binaries and various skills to bypass them.

3   Evaluation Point Derivation

The main idea of this study is as follows. If it is possible to automate and measure the main steps for solving typical pwnable problems, the cause of failure can be analyzed also through the learner's failure point. Therefore, in this study, four evaluation points were derived based on the general process of a control flow hijacking attack, which uses the memory corruption exploit to derive clear points of failure for learners: crash, control flow handling, mitigation bypassing, and full exploit.

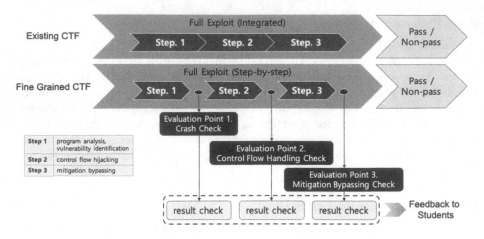

Fig. 2. Design concept comparison of existing CTF and fine-grained CTF.

3.1   Evaluation Point 1 – Crash Check

In the pwnable CTF competition, a program containing a vulnerable is generally provided to the solver by default, and in some cases, the source code of the corresponding program is also provided. Therefore, the student first goes through the static and dynamic analysis process in the problem solving process to identify the vulnerability of the program. Evaluation Point 1 evaluates students' ability to analyze programs and identify vulnerabilities. To cause a crash associated with a vulnerability in a running program for the solver, they must analyze the given program, find the vulnerability in that program, and craft an appropriate input payload that can trigger the vulnerability through programming. Accordingly, in this study, a student who can cause a crash related to a vulnerability in a running program is considered capable of analyzing basic problems. That is, if a student successfully passes Evaluation Point 1, the educator can judge that the student has the ability to analyze the program that contains the vulnerability, identify the program's vulnerability, and craft the input value that can trigger it through programming. At this stage, the student can identify bugs in the program by performing a source code auditing or reversing process to precisely analyze the program. In addition, bugs in the program can be identified by using dynamic testing techniques such as fuzzing and symbloic execution. Meanwhile, students who do not pass Evaluation Point 1 can be judged to have insufficient knowledge. Thus, educators can provide appropriate feedback to users to help students overcome this learning hurdle.

3.2   Evaluation Point 2 – Control Flow Handling Check

The pwnable problem usually requires the solver the ability to craft an exploit by exploiting single or multiple vulnerabilities in the program. To measure this, evaluation point 2 checks students' ability to exploit the program's vulnerability to manipulate the program's control flow. In other words, the evaluation point is a step of measuring the user's exploit capability in an environment where mitigation techniques are not applied. At this point, the student that successfully handles the instruction pointer of the program as an arbitrary value has successfully passed Evaluation Point 2. Such a student is judged to not only has knowledge of the preceding steps (program analysis), but also skills that can trigger potential vulnerabilities related to the instrument pointer by combining the vulnerabilities that exist within the program. Meanwhile, a student who passed Stage 1 but failed to pass the Evaluation Point 2 has the knowledge required in the previous stage, but he or she has insufficient knowledge for manipulating the instruction pointer as needed.

3.3   Evaluation Point 3 – Mitigation Bypassing Check

In the control flow hijacking scenario, a difference is observed between modulating the instruction pointer and seizing the complete control flow. This difference depends on whether the program and system are mitigated, so passing this stage requires the ability to bypass various mitigation techniques. For example, if a stack canary protection technique is applied to a program, the solver may need to utilize an information disclosure vulnerability such as leaking canary data inserted in the program stack to avoid the exploit code failure. In addition, when the program is executed in a system environment to which ASLR mitigation is applied, the solver can utilize an attack technique that can craft an exploit by using a code gadget with a fixed address such as ROP. To check this, evaluation point 3 reconstructs a given problem by partially applying various mitigation techniques applied to the problem. To sum up, evaluation point 3 measures whether a user has the ability to bypass exploit mitigation configured in various ways. Therefore, educators can judge that students who do not pass Evaluation Point 3 have insufficient understanding of protection techniques and the techniques to bypass them. Also, as with the previous evaluation point 2, if the student successfully passes the level, the student is considered to have the knowledge required for the previous evaluation point. Students who pass the evaluation point 2 but do not pass evaluation point 3 may be considered to have the necessary knowledge in previous steps, but not enough knowledge to bypass certain mitigation techniques.

3.4   Evaluation Point 4 – Full Exploit Check

Evaluation Point 4 verifies whether the student has succeeded in obtaining a flag of the remote system through a control flow hijacking exploit. This step is the same as the scoring method in the general CTF platform. Students who have completely passed the final evaluation point can be judged to have all the knowledge required for the problem.

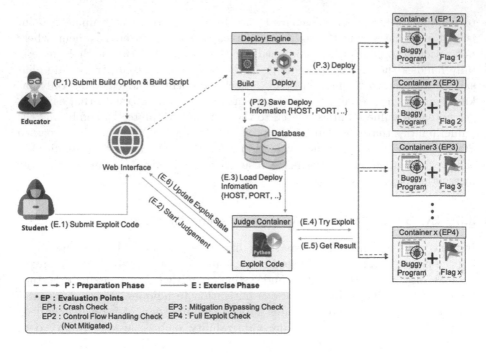

Fig. 3. Design of the fine-grained CTF.

4   Design and Implementation of the Fine-Grained CTF

In this section, we describe the design for implementing fine-grained pwnable CTF. Figure 3 shows the overall design overview of our fine-grained CTF architecture. The fine-grained CTF aims to automatically transform the evaluation of the pass/non-pass manner of the existing jeopardy-style pwnable CTF into a more fine-grained evaluation method. To achieve this, we used a method to build a separate evaluation container environment for each evaluation point derived in Sect. 3. For example, we configure a separate evaluation container environment that measures whether control flow has been tampered with in order to evaluate the user's control flow handling capabilities. We also constructed each evaluation container environment for all subsets of the mitigation technique applied to the pwnable problem, to verify the user's ability to bypass the various protection techniques used in the problem. Our evaluation system is largely composed of a preparation phase in which educators distribute problems and an exercise phase in which students solve problems. The rest of this section describes the process of deploying the pwnable problem by the educator in the preparation phase, and the process by which the user's exploit code is evaluated in our fine-grained CTF during the exercise phase.

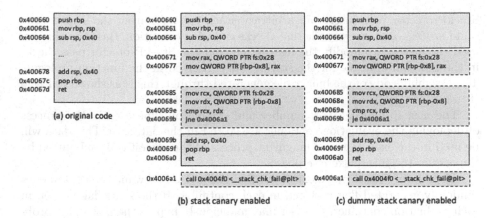

Fig. 4. Change of code address offset according to the application of the code instrumentation protection technique.

4.1 Preparation Phase

In the preparation phase, the educator first submits the source code of the pwnable problem, the build script which builds the source code, and the mitigation type to be applied to the problem through the web interface. Next, the Deploy Engine checks the available port information of the system and constructs an evaluation container corresponding to each port number. The container created in the process consists of a power set for mitigation specified by the user. For example, when the mitigation set for a specific container is $\{\emptyset\}$ (least mitigated), the container corresponds to Evaluation Point 2, which evaluates a user's control flow handling capability. In addition, when the mitigation is the same as the mitigation set specified by the user (most mitigated), the container refers to Evaluation Point 4. It means evaluating whether the user can bypass all mitigation techniques applied to the problem.

In each fine-grained evaluation container configuration, we reconstruct the binary file so that the built binary file always has the same code address offset and memory layout. A lot of memory corruption exploit techniques use code address offset and memory layout information of binary files in exploit code construction. The ROP is a representative exploit technique that uses a code gadget which is in the binary file. However, the binary file applied with mitigation technique through binary instrumentation such as stack canary has a difference in code address offset in the program as shown in (a) and (b) of Fig. 4. Also, in many exploit techniques such as buffer overflow and UAF, the memory layout of the program has an important effect on exploit reliability. For this reason, in a fine-grained evaluation system, it is necessary to reconstruct the problem binary files executed in each evaluation container to have the same code offset and memory layout. To achieve this, we implemented the dummy StackProtector Pass by modifying the code that generates the canary check instruction of the StackProtector Pass in the LLVM project [10]. As shown in Fig. 4, LLVM's

StackProtector pass inserts an arbitrary stack canary during the source code build process, and inserts code that checks it during execution. Based on this, we used the method to modify the instruction that the StackProtector pass checks in the function epilogue for the stack canary inserted in the function prologue. The assembly code of the binary file generated through this is as shown in Fig. 4 (b) and (c).

The host ip address, port number and evaluation type used in the process of deploying the evaluation container are stored in the database. This data will be used in the execution and judgment process of the exploit code submitted by the user in the future exercise phase.

Also, during the deployment of our fine-grained CTF evaluation container, a randomly generated flag is stored in each container. If the same flag is used in each evaluation container, the user may maliciously bypass the high stage problem by simply printing the flag obtained through solving the low stage problem. For example, consider the case where a malicious user submits exploit code that causes a program crash to the judgment server. Then the user successfully passes the evaluation point 1. Subsequently, a malicious scenario in which a malicious user simply prints the flag data string of evaluation point 1 obtained through the exploit code targeting evaluation point 1 to evaluation points other than evaluation point 1 may exist. Because of the existence of this malicious scenario, the flags existing in the containers constituting each evaluation point should not only be difficult for the user to infer, but also must use different flag values for each container. The flag strings of each evaluation container are also stored into the database for the user's exploit code judgment at a future exercise phase.

4.2   Exercise Phase

In the exercise phase, students submit exploit code through a web interface in the form of an online judge system. Unlike the usual jeopardy-style CTF method, which transmits an exploit payload over the network to remote servers where the vulnerable binaries are operating, our proposed fine-grained CTF gets an exploit code from users. This is because our fine-grained CTF is a system designed with educators as the main target. Our fine-grained CTF system allows educators to provide detailed feedback by investigating the exploit code written by the student, as well as the point of failure of the student derived through a series of evaluation processes.

Next, the exploit code submitted by the user is executed in an isolated container environment. This is to restrict malicious behavior that can occur when the user's code is executed directly in the host environment of the system where the fine-grained CTF is hosted. For example, if the exploit code uploaded by the user is not isolated and operates directly in the host environment, the user can directly perform various malicious actions such as reading flag information stored in the database directly on the host computer. Because of the high risk of executing code directly in the host computing environment, our fine-grained CTF design forces user-submitted code to run only in an isolated environment.

ALGORITHM 1: Evaluation process of the judgment container.

Input : N – problem number

E – exploit code submitted by the student

D – database

C – crash identifier ("SIGABRT", "SIGSEGV")

Output: S – exploit status

1 P ← getPortNums (D, N)   /* get the port numbers of evaluation containers. */
2 H ← getHost (D, N)   /* get the host IP of evaluation containers. */
3 **for** p ← P **do**
4   F← getFlags (p)   /* read the flag stored in the evaluation container. */
5   s ← tryExploit (E, H, p)   /* try exploit and save output stream */
6   **if** isContain (s, F) **then**
7 | S← updateExploitState (S, D, p)   /* Update Exploit status. */
8   **end**
9   **if** isContain (s, C) **then**
10 | S← updateExploitState (S, D, p)   /* Update Exploit status(Crashed). */
11   **end**
12 **end**

The exploit code submitted by the user in the judgment container is executed with the host ip address and port number stored in the database as arguments. Therefore, the exploit code submitted by the student must be crafted with the host ip address and port number as system arguments in our fine-grained CTF system.

The process in which the exploit code submitted by the student in the judgment container is evaluated in detail in a fine-grained manner is described in detail in Algorithm 1. At this stage, our fine-grained system was built in the ubuntu environment, so the characters "SIGABRT" and "SIGSEGV" are used as identifier strings to identify crash in the linux system. Also, deploying a separate container for crash check, which is the purpose of evaluation point 1, can cause unnecessary system overhead, so we have inserted a string matching process for crash check into the evaluation process without constructing a separate container.

5 Conclusions

Recently, CTF, which was mainly used for hackers to exchange technical expertise and engage in competition, has now been widely implemented as an educational platform in the field of information security. Accordingly, various research approaches have been applied to improve learning efficiency for beginners. In addition, research has been conducted to reduce the costs and educators' burdens for operation of a CTF. This study subdivides the pwnable CTF, which requires a comprehensive understanding of the entire system, into distinct evaluation points to improve the ability of educators to identify the failure factors of learners. However, for this approach to successfully relieve the educators' burden, it is necessary not only to propose evaluation points but also to automate the detection of these points. Therefore, we design a CTF platform that can automate the detection of learner failure points based on these evaluation points.

References

1. Burket, J., Chapman, P., Becker, T., Ganas, C., Brumley, D.: Automatic problem generation for capture-the-flag competitions. In: 2015 {USENIX} Summit on Gaming, Games, and Gamification in Security Education (3GSE 15) (2015)
2. Chapman, P., Burket, J., Brumley, D.: Picoctf: A game-based computer security competition for high school students. In: 2014 {USENIX} Summit on Gaming, Games, and Gamification in Security Education (3GSE 14) (2014)
3. Chothia, T., Novakovic, C.: An offline capture the flag-style virtual machine and an assessment of its value for cybersecurity education. In: 2015 {USENIX} Summit on Gaming, Games, and Gamification in Security Education (3GSE 15) (2015)
4. ctfd: Ctfd. https://ctfd.io. Accessed 29 May 2020
5. daehee: pwnable.kr. http://pwnable.kr/. Accessed 29 May 2020
6. gdb: gdb. https://www.gnu.org/software/gdb/
7. hackthebox: hack the box. https://www.hackthebox.eu/. Accessed 29 May 2020
8. Hulin, P., et al.: Autoctf: creating diverse pwnables via automated bug injection. In: 11th {USENIX} Workshop on Offensive Technologies ({WOOT} 17) (2017)
9. ida: ida. https://www.hex-rays.com/products/ida/. Accessed 29 May 2020
10. llvm: Llvm project. https://llvm.org/docs/index.html. Accessed 29 May 2020
11. microsoft: debugging tools for windows. https://docs.microsoft.com/en-us/windows-hardware/drivers/debugger/. Accessed 29 May 2020
12. pwndbg: pwndbg. https://github.com/pwndbg/pwndbg. Accessed 29 May 2020
13. pwntools: pwntools. http://docs.pwntools.com/en/stable/. Accessed 29 May 2020
14. Rege, A.: Multidisciplinary experiential learning for holistic cybersecurity education, research and evaluation. In: 2015 {USENIX} Summit on Gaming, Games, and Gamification in Security Education (3GSE 15) (2015)
15. rootme: root me. https://www.root-me.org/. Accessed 29 May 2020
16. Vykopal, J., Barták, M.: On the design of security games: From frustrating to engaging learning. In: 2016 {USENIX} Workshop on Advances in Security Education ({ASE} 16) (2016)
17. Wi, S., Choi, J., Cha, S.K.: Git-based {CTF}: A simple and effective approach to organizing in-course attack-and-defense security competition. In: 2018 {USENIX} Workshop on Advances in Security Education ({ASE} 18) (2018)

A Statistical Approach Towards Fraud Detection in the Horse Racing

Moohong Min[1], Jemin Justin Lee[2], Hyunbeom Park[3], Hyojoung Shin[4], and Kyungho Lee[2](✉)

[1] Korea Racing Authority, Gwacheon-si, Gyeonggi-do, Republic of Korea
moohong@kra.co.kr
[2] Korea University, Seongbok-gu, Seoul, Republic of Korea
{jeminjustinlee,kevinlee}@korea.ac.kr
[3] A3security, Yeongdeungpo-gu, Seoul, Republic of Korea
hyunbeom.park@a3sc.co.kr
[4] Elastic, Gangnam-gu, Seoul, Republic of Korea
hyojoung.shin@elastic.co

Abstract. With the inception of online betting in S. Korea, various foreigner professional gambling groups have exploited the betting regulations. This phenomenon has occurred mainly in Asia, because the regulations on gambling in these countries are complex and robust. Our study focuses on the horse racing in S. Korea, which is operated under the government funding. The foreigner gambling groups tried unlimited betting by modifying the official IoT (Internet of Things) based APP arbitrarily. We have checked that some abnormal transactions can occur by modifying this application. Our study proposes a fraud detection method that can help detecting abnormal activities and prevent them. Currently, the Korea Racing Authority (KRA) has been criticized for being ill-equipped to detect abnormal activities with the Walkerhill Incident. Our study presents a new anomaly detection model that uses a flexible window. In this study, we propose an idea that aims to detect abnormal betting transactions.

Keywords: IoT (Internet of Things) based applications · Big data · Horse racing · Horse racing information security · Anomaly detection · Fraud detection

1 Introduction

The horse racing bets can be classified into the 'Bookmaking' (fixed-odds) and "Pari-mutuel' (not fixed-odds) forms of betting. Bookmaking can be defined by determining the odds and paying off bets on the outcome of horse racing. Pari-mutuel odds are a competition method among bettors who participate in the game, and it is not fixed. During a pari-mutuel game, a computerized system usually calculates the real-time odds so that the gamblers can observe the updates on the odds and participate in the game. Typically, a pari-mutuel game has a

© Springer Nature Switzerland AG 2020
I. You (Ed.): WISA 2020, LNCS 12583, pp. 191–202, 2020.
https://doi.org/10.1007/978-3-030-65299-9_15

predefined, fixed maximal total dividend rates. The average rate in S. Korea is around 73%, and 75.1% in Hong Kong. Even if the commission is between 20% and 30%, bettors will continue to bet because they have the possibility of choosing "wins" and "winners" (two or three places). For this reason, the entity operating the pari-mutuel game systems will be able to gain profits by collecting the commissions.

To attract the gamblers to join the game, the expected dividend rates for a gambler should be more than 70%. If the expected dividend rates are too low, the gamblers will have no reason to join the pari-mutuel game. South Korea has burdensome regulations on horse racing compared to other countries. For example, there is a limit on the amount of bet per race and a controlled place to bet online.

Online betting is carried out through the official Internet of Things (IoT) based application in South Korea. The problem is the manipulation of the betting transaction by modifying the application. If they buy the same amount less or more, it can be an opportunity to avoid taxes, even if there is no change in overall sales. This has the problem of damaging the game of horse racing.

In this paper, we studied the types of problems in a Korean horse racing environment, which is more regulated than in other countries. Horse racing transaction data were analyzed to make this possibility stand out. Moreover, we have set a standard for judging unfair horse racing based on the number of bets. Lastly, the statistical method was applied to identify actual cases and reflect them in the testbed for periodic monitoring. It is impossible or may take much time in a real horse racing environment to develop an optimal system by implementing a complex algorithm. Therefore, we applied the anomaly detection idea newly using a statistical idea, which can be applied in a unique environment called transaction data with repeatability (periodic) to the actual work. Also, we would like to propose an idea to "flexible window" the periodic data. Finally, this paper designed the basis for unfair horse racing that could occur systemically.

2   Background

2.1   Official Online Betting Mobile App

The Korea Racing Authority (KRA) has developed and operated a mobile app for official online betting called MyCard. The Mycard app can be downloaded directly through the KRA's official website, not through the PlayStore or App-Store. Customers can bet within the 30 branch offices and three racetracks anytime, anywhere with the app. The MyCard app is an IoT based application that uses GPS and Bluetooth beacons to identify the current location and limit the betting position.

2.2   Walkerhill Incident

KRA is the only organization that can legitimately hold horse racing games in S. Korea. It operates three stadiums and 30 branches. In 2020, one of the

30 operating branches, Walker Hill, reported operating problems through the media [9]. The Walker Hill branch is operated exclusively for foreigners, thus the domestic citizen's entering is prohibited. The governor pointed out that the dividend rates are excessively high compared to other branches. The dividend rates set by country law is 73%, excluding tax and profit. The winners have to pay an additional 22% tax (other income tax and local income tax) when the dividends are over 2 million KRW (1,680 USD), or the odds for winning are exceeded 100 times.

Six international betting teams (27 people) from professional gambling groups bet 21 billion KRW (17.6 million USD) from June 2016 in South Korea. The number of foreigner's dividends received during the above period was 218.9 billion KRW (183.8 million USD), while the amount of 21.9 billion KRW (18.4 million USD) in profits was recorded at 197.9 billion KRW (166 million USD), excluding taxes. Foreign professional gambling group's dividend rates averaged 110%, far exceeding the overall average dividend rates of 70.3% [9].

The dividend rates are the percentage of the amount of money won by the winner in the game. Excluding the Walker Hill branch, the remaining 29 branches accounted for only 69.5%. The foreign gambling company used automatic betting programs and printers. They made money by concentrating on dozens to hundreds of high odds while avoiding taxes by making small and double bets. For Koreans can bet to 100,000 KRW (84 USD) per 1 race. However, foreigners do not have a bet limit. Foreigners bet the same amount on a minimum basis, such as 100 KRW (0.08 USD).

Foreigners in Walker Hill abused the exemption of income tax law, which is not subject to taxation if the dividends are under 100,000 KRW (84 USD) and bet a few hundred times 100 KRW (0.08 USD) to avoid taxes. In a game where the odds for winning does not exceed 100 times, the tax was avoided by distributing a small amount so that the dividends would not exceed 2 million KRW (1,680 USD). At this time, it was found that they used the MyCard app to purchase large quantities. Foreigners bet unlimitedly by modifying the MyCard app arbitrarily. It is easy to buy a large amount through the modified app rather than buying it at the window (counter).

2.3 Applying Fraud Detection to Horse Racing

Frauds have become a rather serious issue for banks [7]. Various studies have been conducted in the financial sector to detect these frauds. In particular, research on credit card fraud has been actively carried out [8]. Recently, there have been many kinds of research trying to detect card fraud using AI techniques [6].

For instance, credit cards are not usually used multiple times in a short duration of time at the same place. It is also not common for banks to send money to the same person dozens of times a minute. In this regard, there is a difference between financial and horse racing transactions. Horse racing can take place dozens to hundreds of times a day, such as dividends, bets, deposits, and withdrawals. Some people bet more the same number, and some people suddenly bet different numbers within a minute. Alternatively, they bet a large amount at the last minute. Thus, the form of fraud detection used in the existing financial sector is not suitable for the horse racing industry. Horse racing is likely to be linked to organized crime because turnover is over the 1 trillion KRW (839 million USD) [11]. For example, a typical organized crime may be money laundering [1]. Organized criminals also engage with horse race insiders to cause match-fixing [3]. Therefore, horse racing operators in each country need a Fraud Detection idea.

3   Approach

3.1   Previous Fraud Detection Idea

The fraud detection can be divided mainly into Misuse Detection and Anomaly Detection methods [10]. The misuse detection method is the way to identify cheating that matches the pattern in the past [4]. The anomaly detection is a method of detection at the moment of a radically different form of activity compared to a conventional transaction [5]. Horse racing is likely to be a particular private environment. Therefore, the Anomaly Detection method is more advantageous than the Misuse Detection method.

Cybercriminals heavily target Internet banking services. The transfer can be anomalous and existing researches find abnormal transactions by statistical methods. FraudBuster effectively detects fraud scam called salami-slicing fraud [2]. This detecting system consists of 2 parts. Firstly, the system finds a user's spending patterns to get time windows. This paper used Discrete Fourier Transformation and Bartlett Filter to find patterns in the time-series data. When the system finds a time window, features will be calculated in each time window, such as the number of transitions, the total amount of transactions, etc. Feature values from previous time windows will be calculated in one feature as average and deviation. This paper used a z-score to distance the new window and the model from previous windows. If the distance is considerable, it means that the new window's abnormality score is high.

3.2   Elastic Machine Learning Anomaly Detection Feature

The 'Elastic' is an open-source solution provider and solution name for big data processing. Anomaly detection is provided as a paid feature of elastic. There is a real-time detection method in the Application Performance Monitoring (APM) domain. The Bayesian formulation is used for previous research [12]. That research proposes a statistical model which is based on Bayesian methods to analyze performance data gathered for a real internet banking system. This model acts effectively for very high dimensionality, high overall data rates, and seasonality data.

The definition of outliers in the past is an observation that is far from the others, and the observation is treated as an outlier because it could be generated by a different situation than others. However, in the real-world outliers are not just a data point which is far from others. For example, some logs can be accruing all day long, but the arrival rate could differ for each time range. It means that each observation will not have any distance between each other because the type of log is the same. However, when the logging mechanism has changed, the logging frequency or behavior will be changed, and we can call it an abnormal behavior. In this case, the traditional anomaly detection approach will not work well. That research suggests a new definition of the outlier base of the p-value concept. To identify an outlier, a hypothesis of the data generation mechanism needs to be defined first. After that, each mechanism can be labeled as normal or abnormal.

The anomaly detection of elastic is a method of dividing periods into a constant division and creating an observation within those periods. In reality, however, it is rare for data to represent the same behavior within a specified period. Some events can occur quickly or slowly within the same period. In horse racing, for example, race time rarely starts on time due to weather, indoor conditions, etc. The start time is different for each race. Because there are occasional delays, most races have different start times and intervals. The anomaly detection of elastic does not reflect the meaning of period, and the data is divided into periods with an interval of a particular value. Then, after creating an observation, learn the probability, and make it a model. Therefore, it is difficult for this model to learn about normal data.

4   Fraud Detection Idea for the Horse Racing

4.1   Proposed Method

For the horse racing transmission data, repeated shapes appear over time. Therefore, we would like to propose a simpler approach, not an algorithm that requires a complex process.

We proposed a fraud detection idea, which is applicable in real-time in a very simple way in horse racing. Banking and horse racing have similar but slightly different types of business. Therefore, the considerations or data for designing fraud detection may differ from bank data. The betting transaction of horse racing data has the characteristic of an instant rush of traffic at a particular time of race end. Before anything else, the betting pattern data of horse racing is used to implement fraud detection idea dedicated to horse racing. The betting pattern of horse racing is the history of the bettor's bet. Every race betting pattern is almost the same.

Pattern Analysis and Data Set. The Fig. 1 shows the real-time number of bet each race (Blue line). An average of 13 to 17 races is held per day.

First of all, if we interpret the graph, the bets begin prior to the races. The betting amounts are close to zero until the first 10 min. But the bets will begin to surge as it approaches the end. The graph peaks at the last minute, as the betting reaches zero towards the end. The last minute within the betting period is crucial,

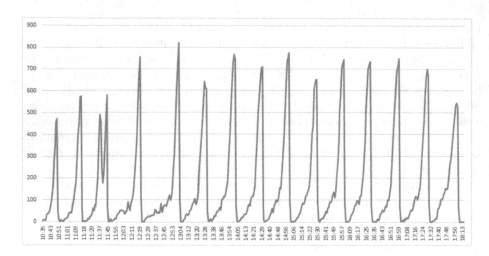

Fig. 1. A one-day Horse Racing betting data flow (Color figure online)

since the odds tends to match the end results. The bet has to consider many factors. There are various environmental factors, such as horse/rider grades, horse/rider conditions, weather, and competitors. The most important thing among them is the odds. The pari-mutuel game is not fixed but continues to change with people's bets amount. The win is a betting type that picks one thing. The win dividend rate formula is as follows.

$$WinOdds = \frac{Pool_T}{Pool_N} \tag{1}$$

$Pool_T$, win total turnover after takeout deduction, and $Pool_N$, a turnover of winning numbers help explains why the odds can be almost fixed, raising the betting money just before the release deadline, as shown in Eq. 1.

Therefore, the real-time odds are most similar to the final odds just before the deadline. If the bettor expects the horse to come in first with a 99% or higher probability, the odds will be lowered. If so, it will take the form of raising the betting money even if the odds of receiving the large dividends are low.

The number of bets does not affect the odds. Therefore, in situations where the betting amount is the same, increasing the numb er of bets does not change the flow of odds. Nevertheless, we focus on the number of bets to find bettor making split bets for various reasons, including tax benefits. It is assumable that if there is a large systemic operation, this can also affect the dividend rate. If it is approached in splitting it and bet a lot, it can cause well-meaning victims due to tax avoidance and changes in odds.

Pretest to Detect the Interval. We used pari-mutuel betting transaction data within 2017–2018. We conducted a simple experiment with the data.

Because it is difficult to define the time associated with the race, We collected the data at intervals of 15 min, 30 min, and 60 min to draw a graph.

Just before the end of the release time (just before the start of the race), the number of bets or the amount of money goes up quickly, and this pattern takes the same form on any day. Therefore, betting transaction data have the same pattern over a specific period. The problem is that the specific time is not same. The race time is not every hour, 15 min, or 30 min, but it changes little by little every time. If the data is grouped into one hour, and the race time is 10 min or 5 min are extended, a problem cannot be determined.

As a result of the experiment, problems were used if fixed intervals were used for anomaly detection because every race does not end in 15/30/60 min. For example, if the interval is fixed at 60 min, it splits into 1-to-2 h and 2-to-3 h (Orange line). If there is a race at 1:15 and two races at 1:45, it is not easy to find the exact buying pattern as two races will exist within an hour. Conversely, even if it is divided into 15 min, the unit will be difficult to analyze because the betting transaction data of a race is divided into several pieces. The Fig. 2 is a 30-min interval of Fig. 1. The races at later are similar, but the first four races do not match. So our goal is to pull forward the yellow lines of the four races.

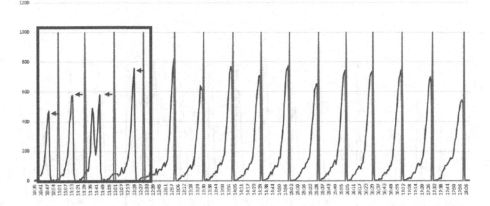

Fig. 2. A one-day Horse Racing betting data flow in a 30-min interval

Proposed the Flexible Window. We propose a new unit of time for anomaly detection called a flexible window. Due to its nature, the races have the following betting patterns depending on the schedule. Figure 1 shows the transaction data flow for a day (1 day) race.

As we can see in the Fig. 1 and 2, the betting transaction has a similar pattern in every race. Transactions are the most frequent just before the end of the race and drop rapidly when the release is closed and at the beginning of the race. Based on this data analysis, the start and endpoints where the betting climb changes rapidly were calculated as a window.

In this paper, a Flexible Window (FW) is proposed to determine the optimum collection interval. x_N is the sum of transactions at N-minute (1-min interval). The simple formula for checking the rate of change per minute is as follows:

$$y = x_{N+1} - x_N \qquad (2)$$

While if bets are increasing, the y-value is positive. y-value is negative just before the start of the race. At the moment, this y-value becomes positive, the next race begins. Figure 3 shows the process of determining Flexible Window.

To analyze data without splitting into fixed time to separate race intervals

- Step 1. [End Point] Find when the differential value of a transaction per minute shifts from positive to negative and more than half the value of last End Point (Red dot of top)
- Step 2. [Pre Start Point] Find when the y-value to change from negative to positive again (Red dot of bottom)
- Step 3. [Start Point] If positive is maintain several times and get to the half value of Step 1., the pre-start point of Step 2. is determined as the actual starting point.

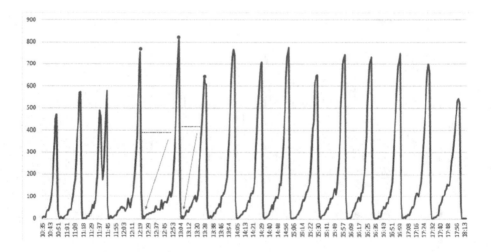

Fig. 3. The process of determining Flexible Window

This is an approach of finding inflection points through changes in the amount of change, or differential values. Through this process, it is possible to pinpoint repeated sections. The Flexible Window (FW) is the basic unit of the collection interval. This is to use a cycle of horse racing (from betting transaction data to termination) as a technique to find only through transaction analysis.

Proposed the Safe Zone. Defining fraud in horse racing betting transactions is a difficult problem. The betting transaction data can increase or decrease momentarily, depending on the form or type of race. Therefore, it is necessary to make predictions and a safe zone using historical statistical data through additional information.

This safe zone measures fraud, whether the actual value exceeds the safe zone. The safe zone generation Algorithm 1 is an important area for the Fraud Detection method.

Algorithm 1. SAFEZONE Generation algorithm

1: **procedure** SAFEZONE(F, R) ▷ F is a number of transactions per minute and R is a minutes that calculated FW size
2:    **while** $F \neq MAX$ **do**
3:        O = Overlap the group of F data cut into R size in one place
4:        S = Sort O to endpoint (right alignment)
5:    **end while**
6:    **while** $R \neq MAX$ **do**
7:        $a \leftarrow 0$
8:        $b \leftarrow 0$
9:        Check the max and min values every minute in S
10:        $a \leftarrow Maxvalue$
11:        $b \leftarrow Minvalue$
12:        To paint between a,b
13:    **end while**
14: **end procedure**

The period for training must be set first. If necessary, the data must be set as required betting transaction period such as one week, one month, three months, six months, one year, and so on. Then calculate Flexible Window (FW) and overlap it into one place. At this point, the starting point is unknown, so it sorts by the endpoint. The transaction data for each race is aggregated into one area based on the period set as Fig. 4(a). The max and min values are identified every minute, such as Fig. 4(b), which is used to create a safe zone.

4.2   Results

The horse racing data of January 2018 in a normal branch were used to check if it was out of the safe zone. The Fig. 5(a) is a safety zone made from one-year data in 2017, and the Fig. 5(b) uses one week data.

Based on the safe zone produced in five types, the experiment was conducted by reflecting the data in 2016–2017. In this experiment, it is regarded as Anomaly that the safe zone is out of range, as shown in Table 1.

The five safe zones are the last criteria. Inside the table is the total anomaly number. In parentheses, the left is the upward anomaly, and the right is the

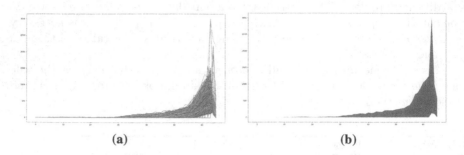

Fig. 4. (a) Overlapped 1 year's transaction data (b) Overlapped 1 year's transaction data and create a Safe Zone with maximum and minimum values

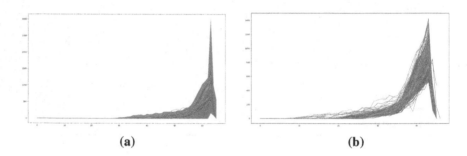

Fig. 5. (a) The Safe Zone using 12 months (b) The Safe Zone using 1 week

Table 1. The number of Anomalies detected (Normal branch)

	1 week	1 month	3 months	6 months	12 months
Sep 2017	483	56	52	40	4
Total: 6141	(482/1)	(56/0)	(52/0)	(40/0)	(4/0)
Sep–Oct 2017	800	88	83	61	4
Total: 10055	(792/8)	(88/0)	(83/0)	(61/0)	(4/0)
Sep–Nov 2017	1183	148	146	114	4
Total: 15375	(1173/10)	(148/0)	(146/0)	(114/0)	(4/0)
Sep–Dec 2017	1962	311	296	239	36
Total: 22165	(1937/25)	(310/1)	(296/0)	(239/0)	(36/0)

downward anomaly. As a result of the experiment, the least anomaly was identified when data were put into the Safe Zone made from the last 12 months of data in September 2017. On the other hand, if the safe zone is set to the previous week, its size is small, indicating most abnormalities. As seen in Fig. 5(a) and 5(b) and Table 1, a shorter period, narrower min-max height, is likely to be seen as an anomaly.

The next experiment was conducted on the Walkerhill branch that caused the problem, as shown in Table 2. Only the branch transaction data was changed to proceed in the same way as above.

Table 2. The number of Anomalies detected (Walkerhill branch)

	1 week	1 month	3 months	6 months	12 months
Sep 2017	963	234	162	125	113
Total: 4773	(159/804)	(80/154)	(79/83)	(50/75)	(38/75)
Sep–Oct 2017	1314	257	183	134	122
Total: 5913	(187/1127)	(82/175)	(80/103)	(50/84)	(38/84)
Sep–Nov 2017	1904	297	219	141	129
Total: 7676	(201/1703)	(82/215)	(81/138)	(50/91)	(38/91)
Sep–Dec 2017	2544	325	261	151	139
Total: 10177	(255/2289)	(85/240)	(83/178)	(52/99)	(40/99)

Compared to a normal branch, the Walkerhill branch detected a noticeably amount of anomalous activities. In the future, by reflecting each branch's data, it will be possible to check in real-time how far the current transaction of the branch is out of the safe zone. The safe zone interval was not modified arbitrarily, and the experiment was conducted only with the historical data.

5   Future Work and Conclusion

In this paper, experiments and detection techniques for introducing fraud detection idea was conducted. In this study, we implemented the flexible window is proposed to find the gap through inflection points for data that is repeated periodically with the same type of trend. This method is commonly used in the financial sectors, but we've also used for the horse racing. We also proposed a basis for designing a safe zone and reflecting it in testbed that finds singularities in fraud detection. In the future, we plan to evaluate the safety zone and conduct research to expand its flexibility. For instance, we are applying a Time-Series Prediction-based ML algorithm with statistical techniques. This method will make the safe zone stronger.

We proposed the base of the system for detecting anomalies in the cyclical repeatable horse racing betting transaction. Furthermore, we believe our study contributed to laying down the foundation for studying periodic data areas where a trend similar to research could occur in the future. This paper's fraud detection idea is specialized in the horse racing transactions but is flexible in repetitive transactions. It is also applicable to financial FDS as an additional factor in viewing the number of transactions. In addition to financial transactions, it applies to all areas where periodic transactions occur. Areas where data are collected repeatedly, such as IoT systems, can be a good example. In particular, data generated by IoT based applications such as MyCard has periodicity. We believe it will be advantageous to detect fraud of all periodic data generated by sensors, such as location and health information. Our study would contribute to the detection of a similar form of an anomaly in the future by proposing an algorithm to create a safe zone. The fraud detection idea proposed in this paper has the advantage of being able to systematize immediately. Through our study, the anomalous activities can be detected in real-time. For future studies, we recommend future researchers to focus on advanced statistical techniques to create safe zones.

References

1. Brooks, G.: Online gambling and money laundering: "views from the inside". J. Money Launder. Control **15**, 304–315 (2012)
2. Carminati, M., Baggio, A., Maggi, F., Spagnolini, U., Zanero, S.: FraudBuster: temporal analysis and detection of advanced financial frauds. In: Giuffrida, C., Bardin, S., Blanc, G. (eds.) DIMVA 2018. LNCS, vol. 10885, pp. 211–233. Springer, Cham (2018). https://doi.org/10.1007/978-3-319-93411-2_10
3. Carpenter, K.: Match-fixing–the biggest threat to sport in the 21st century? Int. Sports Law Rev. **2**(1), 13–24 (2012)
4. Garvey, T.D., Lunt, T.F.: Model based intrusion detection. In: Proceedings of the 14th National Computer Security Conference, vol. 10, pp. 372–385 (1991)
5. Ghosh, A.K., Schwartzbard, A.: A study in using neural networks for anomaly and misuse detection. In: USENIX Security Symposium, vol. 99, p. 12 (1999)
6. Halvaiee, N.S., Akbari, M.K.: A novel model for credit card fraud detection using artificial immune systems. Appl. Soft Comput. **24**, 40–49 (2014)
7. Hoffmann, A.O., Birnbrich, C.: The impact of fraud prevention on bank-customer relationships. Int. J. Bank Mark. **30**, 390–407 (2012)
8. Jha, S., Guillen, M., Westland, J.C.: Employing transaction aggregation strategy to detect credit card fraud. Expert Syst. Appl. **39**(16), 12650–12657 (2012)
9. NewsTAPA: Foreign horse racing problem...tens of billions of tax outflows. https://newstapa.org/42021
10. Richhariya, P., Singh, P.K.: A survey on financial fraud detection methodologies. Int. J. Comput. Appl. **45**(22), 15–22 (2012)
11. Riess, S.A.: The Sport of Kings and the Kings of Crime: Horse Racing, Politics, and Organized Crime in New York 1865–1913. Syracuse University Press, Syracuse (2011)
12. Veasey, T.J., Dodson, S.J.: Anomaly detection in application performance monitoring data. Int. J. Mach. Learn. Comput. **4**(2), 120 (2014)

On the Cost-Effectiveness of TrustZone Defense on ARM Platform

Naiwei Liu[1]([✉]), Meng Yu[2], Wanyu Zang[2], and Ravi Sandhu[1]

[1] Institute for Cyber Security,
University of Texas at San Antonio, San Antonio, TX 78249, USA
naiwei.liu@utsa.edu
[2] Roosevelt University, Chicago, IL 60605, USA

Abstract. In recent years, research efforts have been made to develop safe and secure environments for ARM platform. The ARMv8 architecture brought in security features by design. However, there are still some security problems with ARM. For example, on ARM platform, there are risks that the system is vulnerable to cache-based attacks like side-channel attacks. The success of such attacks highly depends on accurate information about the victim's cache accesses. Cortex-M series, on the other hand, have some design so that the side-channel attack can be prevented, but it also needs a security design to ensure the security of the users' privacy data. In this paper, we focus on TrustZone based approach to defend against cache-based attack on Cortex-A and Cortex-M series chips. Our experimental evaluation and theoretical analysis show the effectiveness and efficiency of FLUSH operations when entering and leaving TrustZone, which helps in design defense framework based on our research.

Keywords: ARM platform · TrustZone · IoT security

1 Introduction

In Recent years, many research papers have been focusing on security design on ARM platform. Some of security framework are designed and implemented making use of TrustZone, a secure enclave provided by ARM on both Cortex-A and Cortex-M series. These defense frameworks target to memory protection, process protection and even cache protection. For example, some of the malicious users can utilize the entry/exit of the TrustZone on ARM Cortex-A, launching a cache-based attack, and compromising the message channel between victim threads and the system. As a result, some research papers target to this problem using access control of entry/exit operations, and some papers use isolated cache protection design. The research papers and their implementations can cut down the bandwidth of cache-based attack, with various level of overhead on the whole system.

On the attacker side, many threats are threatening the IoT systems and devices. Some of them focus on systems and some of them are based on ARM

© Springer Nature Switzerland AG 2020
I. You (Ed.): WISA 2020, LNCS 12583, pp. 203–214, 2020.
https://doi.org/10.1007/978-3-030-65299-9_16

chips. Cache in these devices becomes the research focus on both single device environment and cloud with multiple devices, or even IoT network connecting smart devices. The attacks can be very effective on extracting the users' private and secured data, without the permissions and access to the protected enclaves. Side-channel attack among them is a research focus. Malicious hackers can collect performance data, power consumption data or even some 'trash' data to try retrieving useful information. Attackers derive users' information like cryptographic keys, protected or private data by launching attack on the cache, and analyze the information from what they get. Some attackers just try to collect the difference in access time with different memory blocks, and predict what is accessed frequently by the users. The difference in access time can be collected if the attacker and the victims are sharing data in the cache.

ARM platform, on the other hand, is a different environment from traditional x86 structures. It has different privilege levels and sets some instructions as privileged operations. For example, cache FLUSH operation on ARM is privileged. On ARMv8-M based on Cortex-M structures, there is a much simpler structure of instructions than other platforms. This is because that ARMv8-M is designed to use in small smart devices. They have limited energy input and are asked to work in a long duration. Some of the devices are powered even by some batteries we can find in grocery stores, so the performance limitation is a thing that must be considered when designing something about security and privacy.

In this paper, we investigate the defense effectiveness to cache based side-channel attacks on the ARM architecture. We design several tests based on TrustZone on both ARM cortex-A and cortex-M series chips and get the performance data. These can help in design and implementation of defense, while keeping the performance and effectiveness balanced. Overall, we have following contributions in this paper:

- We investigate the performance overhead of TrustZone related instructions. We analyze the percentage of TrustZone instructions in real life use cases and calculate the overhead brought by these instructions;
- We test FLUSH operation overhead and analyze clock cycles they take on different platforms. This helps in the evaluation of cost-effectiveness on both FLUSH-based attack and defense sides.
- We provide the best/worst case of defense performance based on our experimental results and analysis.

The structure of this paper is as follows: in Related Work section, we introduce previous research and recent research on this topic, analyzing their strong contribution and weaknesses; in Overview section, we introduce our environments of development, structure of design and security assumptions; in Implementation section, we provide some details about our design and experiment settings; in Evaluation section, we provide experimental results and discussion; and in Conclusion section we have our conclusions on the research topic.

2   Related Work

2.1   Cache-Based Attack

In a cloud computing system or a computer with multiple processes and threads, the Last Level Cache (LLC) is shared among multiple processor cores, making it vulnerable to LLC based side-channel attacks. Unlike L1 cache, LLC is much slower than L1 cache, leading to more difficult set up for side channels. There are different ways to launch side-channel attacks, e.g., FLUSH+RELOAD [6,17], PRIME+PROBE [6,7,11], and bus-locking [16].

For example, the FLUSH+RELOAD involves three steps. The attacker first flushes one or more of the desired cache contents using processor-specific instructions (e.g. clflush on x86 processors). Second, the attacker waits for sufficient time for the victim to use (or not to use) the flushed cache area. Finally, the attacker reloads previously flushed cache lines, measuring the reload time for each one of them to infer if it was touched by the victim. FLUSH+RELOAD strategy has been proven very effectively in many side channel attacks on x86 architecture. For example, Gulmezoglu et al. [6] recovered the AES key of OpenSSL within 15 s. Yarom and Falkner [17] recover a RSA encryption key across VMware VMs using FLUSH+RELOAD attack, and Irazoqui et al. [8] recovered AES keys using similar attack and exploiting the vulnerabilities in cache. For PRIME+PROBE attack, Work [11] recover AES keys in a cross-VM Xen 4.1 using PRIME+PROBE attack. Liu et al. [10] presented a PRIME+PROBE type side-channel attack model against the LLC, which is tested to be practical and threatens the system.

2.2   Hardware-Based Defense

Bernstein [2] suggested to add L1-table-lookup instruction to load an entire table in L1 cache, and also load a selected table entry in a constant number of CPU cycles. Page [12] investigated a partitioned cache architecture. Wang and Lee [13–15] proposed new security-aware cache designs to thwart the LLC side channel attack with low overhead. In [15], the Partition-Locked cache (PLcache) was able to lock a sensitive cache partition into cache, and Random Permutation cache (RPcache) randomized the mapping from memory locations to cache sets. In [10], a novel random fill cache architecture that replaces demand fetch with random cache fill within a configurable neighborhood window was proposed. While the hardware solutions provide strong isolations between the victim and the attacker, they require special hardware features that are not immediately available form commodity processors.

2.3   Software-Based Defense

Some researchers proposed to modify applications to better protect secrets from side-channel attacks. Brickell et al. [3] proposed three individual mitigation strategies: compact S-box table, frequently randomized tables, and pre-loading of relevant cache-lines. It compressed and randomized tables for AES. However, it requires manually rewriting the AES implementation and is specific to AES. Cleemput et al. [4] applied the mitigating code transformations to eliminate or minimize key-dependent execution time variations. Crane et al. [5] proposed a software diversity technique to transform each program unique. The approach offers probabilistic protection against both online and off-line side-channel attacks. In their work, using function or basic-block level dynamic control-flow diversity along with static cache noise results in a performance slowdown of 1.76x–2.02x compared to the baseline AES encryption when using 10%–50% cache noise insertion. Dynamic cache noise at 10%–50% has significantly impact on performance (2.39–2.87x slowdown). However, above software solutions are typically application specific or incur substantial performance overhead.

2.4 Recent Research on ARM TrustZone

In recent years, some papers have discussions and new research findings on ARM platform, especially focusing on TrustZone protection. Zhang et al. [18] proposed an Android protection framework using TrustZone on ARM, protecting VoIP phone calls. It enclaves privacy data so the phone calls cannot be intercepted easily by malicious eavesdropping. Amacher et al. [1] have evaluate the performance of ARM TrustZone using TEEs and different benchmarks, but the security concern is out of that paper's scope. Keystone defense framework proposed by Dayeol Lee and others [9] is a good example of defense framework based on TrustZone. It enclaves protected operations and disables sharing in TLBs and memory blocks so there's no side-channel attack based on the vulnerability here. However, the timing side-channel attack is out of that paper's scope. In our discussion, there are still risks of side-channels when exiting from TrustZone, so we need also investigate the vulnerability at the gate of security enclave.

3 Overview

3.1 Background

As multi-core processors become pervasive and the number of on-die cores increases, a key design issue facing processor architects is the security layers and policies for the on-die LLC. With LLC techniques, a CPU might only need to get around 5% data from main memory, which can improve the efficiency of CPU largely. In our implementations, we are using Intel i7-4790 processor, with 8 Mb SmartCache. On ARMv8 Cortex-A platform, we are using Juno r1 Development Platform which has one A57 and one A53 processors on the board. A57 has a 2M LLC on the processor. On Cortex-M platform, we are using ARM Cortex-M4 series chips, the development platform has 3 pipeline stages and no built-in cache.

With the increasing complexity of computing systems, as well as multiple level of memory access, some registers are designed to store some specific hardware events. These registers are usually called hardware performance counters.

We have many tools getting information from those performance counters, thus getting the performance information.

In our implementation, we use perf to collect the execution information of the programs. However, we cannot use perf for collecting timing information of memory access, since it cannot be accurate enough. On this paper we use inline assemblies and consult some related registers to measure time associated information with our side-channels.

3.2 Design on ARM Cortex-A

According to our evaluation on current on-the-market systems and applications, we find out that more and more Trusted Execution Environment (TEE) technologies are being used on the implementations of secure system. Besides, most of the implementations are utilizing ARM TrustZone to protect the memory access and critical data. As we are interested in the performance overhead of defending using FLUSH operations on exiting TrustZone, the experiments should start from the measurements of using TrustZone, like the time cost and performance overhead.

Our experiments on ARM Cortex-A are in three different steps. For the first step, we test the cost of entering and exiting from TrustZone. After we get the exact data (clock cycles) related to TrustZone, the next step is to measure how much it takes up for the TEEs to call TrustZone related instructions or operations. On the third step, we try to clean the cache every time the system exiting from TrustZone, and see the performance overhead by these FLUSH operations added to the system. As the cache gets FLUSHed every time after the using of TrustZone, the risk of being side-channel attacked can be theoretically cut down to non-exist.

3.3 Overview on ARM Cortex-M

Unlike ARM Cortex-A series chips, M-series chips have different structure, and with other limitations. Most IoT devices are based on Cortex-A platform, but still a rising trend that more products are using Cortex-M platform. As a result, it is still valuable to investigate the defense against malicious attackers with TrustZone. In this paper, we have similar tests on ARMv8-M platform, measuring the performance of TrustZone, as well as FLUSH operation overhead. Our experiments on Cortex-M are using ARM Versatile V2M-MPS2 Motherboard with ARM Cortex-M4 cores. It offers 8 Mb of single cycle SRAM, and 16 Mb of PSRAM. It supports the application of different ARM Cortex-M classes, from Cortex-M0, to M3, M4, and M7. Besides these support, the development board supports simulation of ARMv8-M.

As mentioned above, on Cortex-M4 series chips, there is no built-in cache. However, the memory structure on M4 is different from other structures like x86 and Cortex-A. On that platform, memory blocks are allocated in fixed order, taking their assigned responsibilities. It is quite different from dynamic allocation, and is to the consideration of power consumption and performance overhead. Among these memory blocks, some are acting as 'cache-in-memory', so we can still see them working like cache and operate some instructions to read the working status of it.

The experiments are in two different steps. First, we measure the time cost entering and exiting from TrustZone. Next, we implement a program with Trust-Zone entry/exit instructions, as well as protected running steps. We then test it with controlling of the frequency of entry/exit instructions. We measure the FLUSH operation overhead according to different frequencies, and discuss the defense using FLUSH when exiting from TrustZone.

3.4   Threat Model and Assumptions

In this paper, we assume that the operating system is not compromised so that the attackers are forced to use covert channels or side channels without explicitly violating access control policies enforced by the operating system or other protection mechanisms. We assume that the attacker has sufficient privilege to access the memory access time. This is also needed for the covert channel, and for the performance analysis of the covert channel.

4   Implementations

4.1   Process Structure on Cortex-A Platform

As mentioned above, the very first step for our experiment is to calculate the cost of entering and exiting from the TrustZone. On ARM Cortex-A Platform, an instruction smc is used for connecting the secure world and non-secure world. While in normal non-secure world, some code could call privileged smc instruction. Then, secure world monitor will be triggered after validation. After execution of secure code, the return of the execution also calls smc to get back to the normal world. There are many open-source test platform to measure the world switch latency, and in this experiment, we use the well-known QEMU to test. It had been developed since the first patch published in 2011, and been patched by many manufacturers including Samsung, utilizing ARM TrustZone for security design.

The process structure is show at Fig. 1. When there are smc instructions trigger the TrustZone entry/exit, we trap the instructions and start using perf and other time measurement tools to calculate clock cycles they take to finish switching between trust environment and outside memory. We also FLUSH cache every time when we exit from TrustZone and see the difference in performance overhead by different frequency of TrustZone related instructions.

4.2   Process Structure on Cortex-M Platform

On ARM-v8 platform, SG/BXNS instructions are used to enter and exit from TrustZone. As there were almost no proper TEEs for ARMv8-M on the market as we were testing, we use a testing program instead. SG (Secure Gate) instruction is called by non-secure world code that wants to trigger TrustZone protection. Unlike Cortex-A structure, on ARMv8-M, the page table is not used, so the memory is fully mapped with different regions. When SG instruction is called, the reserved regions for secure world are used to execute the protected part of the code. After the secure execution within TrustZone, the code has an exit called BXNS/BLXNS (Back to Non-Secure) that can lead the execution to other region besides protected ones by TrustZone. We make use of the mechanism of this, and the structure of the testing program is as Fig. 2 shows.

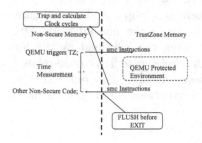

Fig. 1. Process structure on Cortex-A

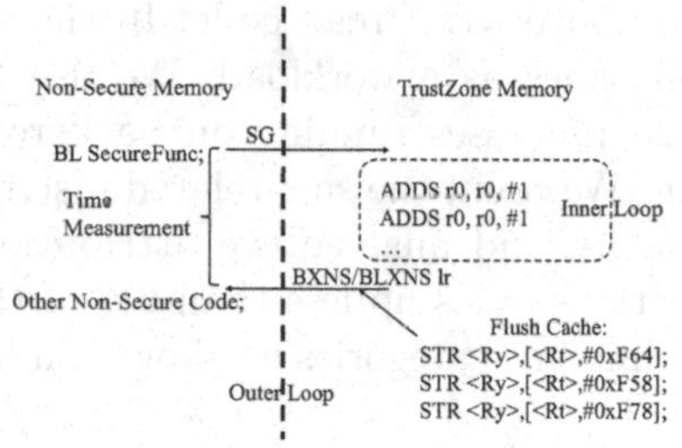

Fig. 2. Process structure on Cortex-M

The term 'cache' here on ARMv8-M is part of normal memory being set as 'cacheable'. In other words, it is a region set aside for possible cache using. On Cortex-A series chips or x86 chips, cache flush operations are just some instructions with privileges. However, the case are different on ARMv8-M. The allocation of a memory address to a cache address is defined by the designers of the applications. Because of the special structure of ARMv8-M, the cache FLUSH operations are sets of DSB (Data Synchronization Barrier) operations, with address-related instructions.

5   Evaluation

In this section, we introduce our experimental results and discussions, both on ARM Cortex-A and Cortex-M platforms.

5.1   Experimental Results

Cost of Entering and Exiting from TrustZone on Cortex-A. QEMU with ARM TrustZone provides us a variety of tests. The tests behave as we users initiating secure operations from user mode. The test functions validate the TrustZone features of QEMU, and utilizing the features of the functions themselves. We have tests on read/write from non-secure world to secure world and vice versa. The results are shown as Table 1 shows.

Table 1. TrustZone-related instruction cost on Cortex-A

Tests	Direction	Average cost (clock cycles)	Time on 800 Mhz
P0_nonsecure_check_register_access	Non-secure to Secure	1950	2.43 us
P0_secure_check_register_access	Secure to Non-secure	2200	2.75 us

Percentage of TrustZone-Related Instructions. We write a script based on the above write/read code. In the script, there is a loop called in and runs several times as a workload. We use Ubuntu 16.10 as the normal world OS, with 26 processes running on background, including the workload we use for testing. We count the smc-related instructions that belongs to TrustZone-related operations, and analyze the attributions of them. According to our test, the instructions takes up less than 6% of the total instructions running, with these three different categories as shown on Table 2.

Table 2. Different categories of TrustZone-related instructions

Type	Percentage
Non-secure to Secure Test R/W	2.87%
Secure to Non-secure Test R/W	2.91%
Others (Access from Background)	0.01%

In normal using conditions, however, the manufacturers are not using Trust-Zone that often. Thus, the test here can be the upper bound or 'worst case' of the utilization of TrustZone-Related instructions. Normally, the non-secure world does not have to call in the secure world too often.

Performance Overhead by FLUSH Operations. It is already known that ARM TrustZone on Cortex-A series are not going to clean the cache when exiting from the secure world to non-secure world. As a result, there are possibilities for the attackers to make the most of the last level cache and conduct cache-based attacks. For example, the side-channel attack of FLUSH+RELOAD, PRIME+PROBE are both found practical on the environment with TrustZone on ARM Cortex-A, some even with a fiercely high bandwidth. On the other hand, if we can FLUSH the cache every time on the 'exit' to the normal non-secure world, then it can be expected that the bandwidth of the side-channel attack can be limited to a number that is worthless to the attackers to gather the information possibly leaked by the smc operations.

We still test the performance using our test model. In this test, we are adding cache FLUSH operations on every smc instruction that calling exit from the secure world to non-secure world. On that situation, we measure the performance overhead by comparing the clock cycles of execution. At the same time, we change the percentage of TrustZone-related instructions to see the difference in the overhead. The results are shown on Fig. 3 and Fig. 4.

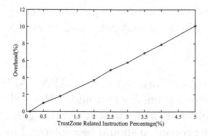

Fig. 3. TrustZone related instructions and their overhead

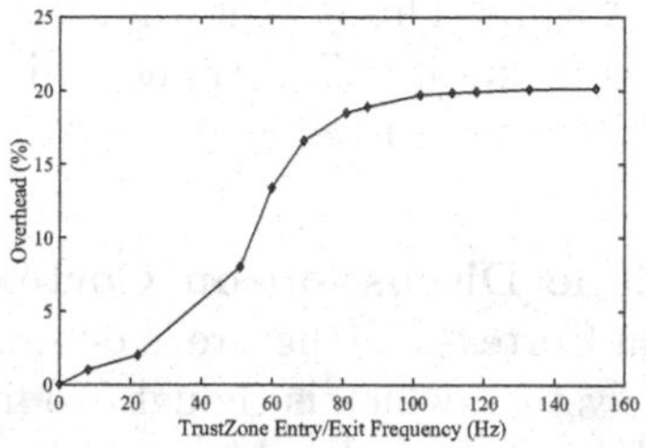

Fig. 4. TrustZone entry/exit frequency and FLUSH overhead

Experimental Results on ARMv8-M. According to our experiments, the testing case triggering TrustZone operations SG and BXNS. As every region is fixed in the memory, the costs of entering and exiting from TrustZone are surprisingly much lower than ARM Cortex-A series chips. The results are shown at Table 3.

Table 3. TrustZone-related instructions cost on ARMv8-M

Operation	Direction	Cost on average (clock cycles)
SG	Non-Secure to Secure	3.5
BXNS/BLXNS	Secure to Non-Secure	5.2

We measure the performance of the FLUSH operations using our testing program shown at Fig. 2. We add FLUSH operations before executing BXNS/BLXNS operations to ensure there is nothing left when exiting from TrustZone. We measure the overhead by the FLUSH operations, and we also change the outer loop to have different frequencies of TrustZone entries and exits. The results are shown at Fig. 5.

5.2   Discussions

TrustZone Usage Frequency and Flush Overhead. According to our experimental results, on ARMv8 platform, the system is connecting with Trust-Zone with very low frequency, taking up less than 10% of the instructions at most. Some specific instructions trigger the secure gate of TrustZone. However, when the contexts running in secured memory finish, TrustZone does not clean the cache before exit, leaving some risks here. Based on low frequency and overhead from TrustZone related instructions, we can FLUSH the cache every time when exiting from TrustZone, and still keep a low overhead of less than 20% on Cortex-A chips. This design will let the system manufacturer to put protected or private contexts into TrustZone and with no worries about side-channel attack when exiting from it.

TrustZone Discussion on Cortex-M. Unlike Cortex-A series, ARMv8-M based on Cortex-M structure is designed to have low energy cost and with much simpler system, which is thought to fit for mobile or home devices. At this case, the performance overhead brought by security protection should be controlled in a very low number. According to our experimental results, on Cortex-M structure, the secure gate instructions take much less clock cycles to execute, making it a good choice on the basis of security design. When we add FLUSH operations on exit instructions, we have even lower overhead comparing with Cortex-A chips, having less than 10% overhead at most. It is a practical design for the manufacturer to introduce and not hard to develop. On the other hand, they could put protected data and instructions into the secure enclave of TrustZone.

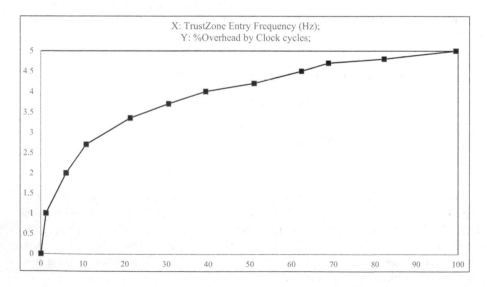

Fig. 5. TrustZone entry/exit frequency and FLUSH overhead on ARMv8-M

Cache Based Defense on ARM Platform. Though we have no perfect way to take the place of validating cache and cleaning the TLB entries, we still have some idea for possible solutions, because there are some potential for speeding up and getting better performance. For example, we can move the FLUSH operations out from the privileged level, and try implementing another framework to ensure the security of this type of operations, while maintaining low overhead. In this paper, we quantitatively discuss the security design for dealing with FLUSH operation requests, and there are still some more topics to research on.

6 Conclusion

In this paper, we have some discussion on the effectiveness and cost of attack and defense based on ARM platform. We start from investigating the cache-based attacks. Then we design and implement some tests on ARM platform, both on ARM Cortex-A and ARMv8-M series chips. It is shown that the side-channel attack and other types of exploitations are practical and serious, causing loss to users' privacy and security. From our experimental results, TrustZone can be utilized to help defending against side-channel and covert channel attacks, but it must have an adaptive ways to manage cache operations. On the other hand, it is practical to implement FLUSH based defense on ARM platform, with reasonable overhead and good effectiveness.

In the future, we need to develop some defense framework on ARM platform, based on FLUSH operations and secure gate entry/exit instructions. The challenge will be the difference in structures of ARMv8 platform, and real-life limitations like power consumption, portable needs and other challenges. However, it is promising that ARM platform can provide the users with an environment in balance of performance, privacy, security and good mobility as well.

Acknowledgements. This paper and research project are sponsored by NSF CREST Grant IIRD-1736209 and NSF Grant 1634441. The grants are for security research on cloud and systems. This research is performed in the Institute for Cyber Security (ICS) lab in University of Texas at San Antonio, and Computer Science Department in Roosevelt University.

References

1. Amacher, J., Schiavoni, V.: On the performance of ARM TrustZone. In: Pereira, J., Ricci, L. (eds.) DAIS 2019. LNCS, vol. 11534, pp. 133–151. Springer, Cham (2019). https://doi.org/10.1007/978-3-030-22496-7_9
2. Bernstein, D.J.: Cache-timing attacks on AES, Technical report (2005)
3. Brickell, E., Graunke, G., Neve, M., Seifert, J.-P.: Software mitigations to hedge AES against cache-based software side channel vulnerabilities (2006)
4. Cleemput, J.V., Coppens, B., De Sutter, B.: Compiler mitigations for time attacks on modern x86 processors. ACM Trans. Archit. Code Optim. **8**(4), 23:1–23:20 (2012)

5. Crane, S., Homescu, A., Brunthaler, S., Larsen, P., Franz, M.: Thwarting cache side-channel attacks through dynamic software diversity. In: 22nd Annual Network and Distributed System Security Symposium, NDSS 2015, San Diego, California, USA, 8–11 February 2014 (2015)
6. Gülmezoğlu, B., İnci, M.S., Irazoqui, G., Eisenbarth, T., Sunar, B.: A faster and more realistic *Flush+Reload* attack on AES. In: Mangard, S., Poschmann, A.Y. (eds.) COSADE 2014. LNCS, vol. 9064, pp. 111–126. Springer, Cham (2015). https://doi.org/10.1007/978-3-319-21476-4_8
7. Irazoqui, G., Eisenbarth, T., Sunar, B.: S$A: a shared cache attack that works across cores and defies VM sandboxing - and its application to AES. In: The Proceedings of 2015 IEEE Symposium on Security and Privacy, San Jose, CA, 17–21 May 2015, pp. 591–604. IEEE (2015)
8. Irazoqui, G., Inci, M.S., Eisenbarth, T., Sunar, B.: Wait a minute! A fast, cross-VM attack on AES. In: Stavrou, A., Bos, H., Portokalidis, G. (eds.) RAID 2014. LNCS, vol. 8688, pp. 299–319. Springer, Cham (2014). https://doi.org/10.1007/978-3-319-11379-1_15
9. Lee, D., Kohlbrenner, D., Shinde, S., Song, D., Asanović, K.: Keystone: a framework for architecting tees. arXiv preprint arXiv:1907.10119 (2019)
10. Liu, F., Lee, R.B.: Random fill cache architecture. In: 2014 47th Annual IEEE/ACM International Symposium on Microarchitecture, pp. 203–215, December 2014
11. Liu, F., Yarom, Y., Ge, Q., Heiser, G., Lee, R.B.: Last-level cache side-channel attacks are practical. In: 2015 IEEE Symposium on Security and Privacy, pp. 605–622, May 2015
12. Page, D.: Partitioned cache architecture as a side-channel defence mechanism (2005). Accessed 22 Aug 2005. page@cs.bris.ac.uk 13017
13. Shih, M.-W., Lee, S., Kim, T., Peinado, M.: T-SGX: eradicating controlled-channel attacks against enclave programs. In: Proceedings of the 2017 Annual Network and Distributed System Security Symposium (NDSS), San Diego, CA (2017)
14. Wang, Z., Lee, R.B.: A novel cache architecture with enhanced performance and security. In: 2008 41st IEEE/ACM International Symposium on Microarchitecture, pp. 83–93, November 2008
15. Wang, Z., Lee, R.B.: New cache designs for thwarting software cache-based side channel attacks. In: Proceedings of the 34th Annual International Symposium on Computer Architecture, ISCA 2007, pp. 494–505 (2007)
16. Wu, Z., Xu, Z., Wang, H.: Whispers in the hyper-space: high-bandwidth and reliable covert channel attacks inside the cloud. IEEE/ACM Trans. Netw. **23**(2), 603–614 (2015)
17. Yarom, Y., Falkner, K.: FLUSH+RELOAD: a high resolution, low noise, L3 cache side-channel attack. In: 23rd USENIX Security Symposium, USENIX Security 2014, San Diego, CA, August 2014, pp. 719–732. USENIX Association (2014)
18. Zhang, P., Liu, Z., Ma, C., Zhang, L., Han, D.: KPaM: a key protection framework for mobile devices based on two-party computation. In: 2019 IEEE Symposium on Computers and Communications (ISCC), pp. 1–6. IEEE (2019)

Detection on GPS Spoofing in Location Based Mobile Games

Shing Ki Wong$^{(\boxtimes)}$ (ID) and Siu Ming Yiu (ID)

The University of Hong Kong, Pokfulam, Hong Kong
{skwong,smyiu}@cs.hku.hk
http://www.hku.hk

Abstract. The widely used Global Positioning System (GPS) provides a handy way for electronic devices to locate their positions. Almost every mobile device nowadays has GPS module equipped inside. Apart from traditional location service applications, more and more eccentric applications are developed to utilize this functionality. Location based mobile games such as Pokémon GO are one of the examples which make use of location service to give players innovative experience. However, this kind of location based mobile games are vulnerable to Location Spoofing Attack (LSA), which malicious users can navigate freely in game using location spoofing applications without travelling themselves physically. Various approaches are being proposed to tackle this problem while none of them give good performance in detecting spoofing in local area. In this paper, we proposed a detection method on GPS spoofing in local area by making use of the gyroscope commonly equipped in most mobile devices. We compare the travelling direction of the GPS travelling path with the facing direction of the mobile device to check if they match well with each other. Experiment result shows that our method can efficiently differentiate between location spoofing behavior and normal behavior with easy implementation.

Keywords: Location spoofing · GPS spoofing · Spoofing attack · Mobile games

1 Introduction

The Global Positioning System (GPS) has been widely used nowadays. It provides geolocation data to GPS receivers to locate their position anywhere on the Earth when they are under the line of sights of four or more GPS satellites. The precise location data helps a lot in many industry scenarios such as aviation, marine and military. The development of the Global Positioning System has become so mature that it has now been commonly used in our daily lives. Almost every single mobile device nowadays has the GPS module equipped to provide location services for mobile applications such as map navigation and social platforms. In recent years, several mobile games are being developed utilizing the GPS data of the mobile device. Pokémon GO [1] and Jurassic World

© Springer Nature Switzerland AG 2020
I. You (Ed.): WISA 2020, LNCS 12583, pp. 215–226, 2020.
https://doi.org/10.1007/978-3-030-65299-9_17

Alive [2] are two famous location based augmented reality games that make use of the GPS data to provide an innovative gaming experience for gamers. They integrate virtual elements (i.e. Pokémon and Dinosaurs) with real live environment (i.e. the neighborhood) to give players a totally different experience from traditional mobile games. Player have to physically travel from place to place in order to navigate and catch virtual creatures in game. Such kind of games gained colossal popularity since launch and are continuously showing great success.

Although such kind of virtual reality gives some fun to players, playing the game walking around for a long period of time can be tiring. Not every single player has the ability, time or option to travel around physically. What's more, many people are not living in areas that are support by the games but would still like to get a taste of the new gaming experience. In location-based mobile games like Pokémon GO, players in-game are being located according to the GPS data provided by their device. Such kind of games which solely rely on GPS data for positioning are vulnerable to location spoofing attack (LSA). Cheater can simply modify their GPS locations before sending them to the game so that they can go to any place in game without travelling by themselves physically in the real world. Due to the abovementioned concerns, many application developers try to build applications that can spoof the location of the mobile device so that the user need not to be at the same location as its GPS location data indicates. Consequently, we can observe a flood of GPS Spoofing applications hitting app stores to accomplish the desire of these players. Even worse, selling these applications can lead to huge profit due to the large demand from the player base of these highly popular location-based mobile games. As a result, more and more spoofing applications with advanced features are developed, providing different heuristic for players to 'cheat' in the game with minimal effort. The abuse of these cheating applications would destroy the gaming experience of other legitimate players and finally ruin the game itself. What's more, currently there is no authenticating mechanisms to verify the genuineness of the GPS locations provided by the device. Malicious users can then easily spoof their locations using these applications to gain advantage over other users in the games. For instance, in Pokémon GO, cheaters can effortlessly travel from place to place in-game to catch rare appearing Pokémon, or hatch Pokémon eggs without moving physically in the real world.

To address this issue, Niantic [3] introduced several detection measures to prevent location spoofing in Pokémon GO, such as malicious application check, root detection, mock location application detection etc. Users can get shadow-banned (i.e. only be able to see common Pokémon nearby) or even get permanent banned on their accounts if they are found guilty on location spoofing. However, the problem persists upon the third year since the game launched, as cheaters can always find loopholes to bypass the detections by hiding the location spoofing application with the help of privilege escalation. The approach of system checking for potential spoofing behavior appears to be unable to solve the problem entirely.

In this paper, we focus on the detection for location spoofing using mobile devices in local area which involves relatively small displacement of the user as it is very difficult to tell whether a user spoofs on the location by looking solely on the little changes in the GPS coordinates. We proposed a novel detection method making use of the gyroscope equipped in mobile devices to verify the travel direction given by the GPS data from the user's device. Our detection method works in any device orientation assuming a fixed horizontal orientation of the device with respect to the user is maintained during the detection process.

The rest of the paper is organized as follow. Section 2 introduces some related work on location spoofing detection using various approaches in different aspects and directions. Section 3 discusses some prevention measures carried out by the gaming companies against location spoofing. Section 4 explains the mechanism of the GPS spoofing applications currently available in the market. Section 5 proposes and explains the idea of our detection method on location spoofing. Section 6 presents and explains the experiment results. Section 7 points out the limitation of our methodology and suggests possible future improvement. Section 8 gives conclusion in our work.

2   Related Work

Many location spoofing detection methods are being proposed while many of them make use of the network profile (e.g. IP address) during the detection process. [7] proposed a server-sided and network-based framework to detect location spoofing attack users. It tries to verify whether the location of the user's edge router's IP address matches with the GPS location provided by the user. This method is not applicable on detecting local area location spoofing which occurs only in the neighborhood within the range of one particular router. It also has the constraint of using IMCP packet only. [9] proposed a location validation scheme for participatory sensing (PS) systems without losing any quality of information (QoI) in the system. It assumes that users under the same Wi-Fi range of a mobile hotspot are directly connected with each other so that they can mutually validate their locations and can therefore, identify users who are spoofing their locations. [8] proposed a location validation system (LVS) which verifies user locations in location-based service systems. It is based on a similar idea that devices are practically sharing the same location if they are directly connected through the same Wi-Fi. Due to the limited range of the Wi-Fi, devices in the same Wi-Fi network can validate each other's location mutually. Malicious users would then be filtered out after multiple rounds of reputation updates. The system works well in Wi-Fi connection, while lacks practicability under cellular network due to the large signal range. [10] came up with location proofs which are issued to devices connecting to an access point after being signed by it. It acts as a digital certificate which can be verified later on by access points to prove the devices' current and previous locations. This approach is effective in theory while it requires implementation of the module in every access point, which is impractical in large scale.

We can see that all the above approaches take advantage of the location information provided by the Wi-Fi network for validations. Due to the wide effective range of a router, these methods may not be practical in detecting location spoofing in local area which occurs inside the range of the same router as the connected devices will always report the same single location as the router locates. Therefore, these approaches are not applicable in location-based mobile games and unfortunately, there exist no methodology at the moment that can tackle such situation.

3   Prevention Measures Against GPS Spoofing

Many different approaches are adopted to prevent GPS spoofing in mobile devices. These methods, although work well in specific scenarios, cannot solve the problem entirely. In this section, we summarize some common measures adopted against location spoofing.

3.1   Travel Viability Check

Although it is not easy to check whether the provided GPS location is genuine or not, it is still possible to check whether any two consecutive GPS locations are in fact physically reachable in a certain amount of time. If the time elapsed between two consecutive GPS locations is too short to be physically reachable, one can determine that the user is using location spoofing. However, such detection is not applicable for location spoofing in local area which only involves short distance travels, as the time elapsed are too short to be deterministic.

3.2   Mock Location App Detection

Android OS provides developer options for application developers. The mock location functionality is designed for devices without the GPS module to emulate GPS values. Mock location allows users to use produce fake information about the location of their devices by GPS and network operator. By setting a location spoofing application as mock location app, one can easily manipulate the GPS location through the application. Therefore, the mock location application setting should be checked to be disabled via the ALLOW_MOCK_LOCATION attribute in the system to prevent the possibility on location spoofing in this way. Nevertheless, cheater can convert the application into system application to escape from the detection.

3.3   Malicious App Detection

The Game application would try to detect any malicious app installed in the device during execution and prevent the game from running upon successful detection. However, a list of these malicious app is needed to be maintained and updated frequently with the rapid growth on the amount of location spoofing applications. Furthermore, applications can easily change their package name and hide themselves from the detection.

3.4   Emulator Detection

Emulators such as Bluestack [4] and Nox App Player [5] provide a wide range of functionalities for gaming including location modification and device rooting. Playing location-based games via emulators doubtlessly violate the terms and condition of the game, while it is difficult to check whether the system is running in a real device or via emulator. Generally, game developers can verify it by looking at the FINGERPRINT value of the system. However, with the help of privilege escalation, such value can be easily modified.

3.5   Jailbreak and Root Detection

By jailbreaking in IOS or rooting in Android, users can easily modify their GPS locations by gaining privilege in the OS. Thus, checking whether a mobile device is being jailbroken or rooted and prohibiting it from running the application is one of the solutions. However, there are applications that can help to hide the fact that the device is being jailbroken or rooted (e.g. magisk manager [6]). User can even make use of the escalated privilege to convert location spoofing applications into system applications to avoid the detection. This kind of hack is still unsolvable at the moment when this paper is being written.

4   GPS Spoofing Application

In this section, we are going to talk about the mechanism of GPS spoofing applications. In general, there are five variables that GPS spoofing applications can modify in the location details, which are latitude, longitude, altitude, speed and accuracy. It is sufficient for spoofing applications to perform GPS spoofing on the device by only modifying the latitude and longitude values. Therefore, for simplicity, most GPS spoofing applications available only update the latitude and longitude values when they are simulating movements, keeping the remaining three values constant. Figure 1 shows an example on a GPS spoofing application running along with Pokémon GO. Most of these GPS spoofing applications provide a joystick-like control in the user interface. By dragging on the joystick, users can easily simulate their desired movement through the application by modifying the corresponding GPS coordinates. As a result, users can move around from place to place in game effortlessly.

However, when the device receives real GPS values, apart from latitude and longitude which pinpoint the current location, the current altitude and speed would also be updated if the device is in motion, plus the accuracy (in meters) of how accurate the device believes those values are. That implies that all of the GPS values fluctuate every second even when the device is sitting still, as the GPS is constantly attempting to pinpoint our location and it changes slightly every other second. Therefore, by studying on such "incomplete" GPS data, it can be possible to tell whether a user is using location spoofing. Because of this, some advanced applications start emulating what a real GPS should report by adding random offsets to the GPS values and even provide customization on all of the values via settings, making the detection even harder.

Fig. 1. Location spoofing in Pokémon GO.

5 Proposed Method

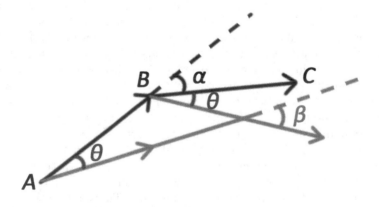

Fig. 2. Illustration of our detection idea.

We have learnt that it is quite impossible to detect GPS spoofing through system detections and GPS data behavioral analysis alone. In this section, we propose a detection method on GPS spoofing by making use of the gyroscope commonly equipped in most mobile devices. We focus on short walking distances where users walk around in the local area holding their phones on hand. To preserve consistency, we assume that the horizontal orientation of the mobile device with respect to the user remains the same throughout the whole detection process, that is, the back of the mobile device always faces at the same direction as the user does, which is a common scenario for a user using a phone. With such a fixed horizontal orientation, we can then accurately verify whether the user's travel direction matches the device's facing direction.

Figure 2 illustrates the idea with a scenario. Suppose the user is travelling from A to C via B. The black arrows indicate the travelling direction of the user from A to B and B to C, while the red arrows represent the facing direction of the mobile device from A to B and B to C. θ is the difference between the facing direction of the user and the mobile device. α is the angle of the change in travel direction from AB to BC and β is the change of the facing direction of the mobile device from AB to BC. If the user is legitimate, we would expect $\alpha \approx \beta$ as long as θ remains within a stable range. If the user is using GPS spoofing application to manipulate travelling paths moving in different directions with himself/herself actually stationary, β will not synchronize with α as the device will be most likely facing in one single direction. As a result, by keeping tracking of the change of α and β, we can differentiate legitimate users from users who use GPS spoofing.

5.1   Methodology

Our methodology collects two sets of data. The first set of data is the GPS coordinates provided by the GPS module of the device. The second set of data is the orientation of the device provided by the gyroscope of the device. To determine whether the travel direction of the user aligns with his/her facing direction, we first compute the horizontal directions of travel using the GPS data, and then compare it with the facing angles deduced from the orientation data. We then calculate the average of the differences between the two direction angles, denoted as Δ_θ, and compare it with the benchmark, which will be mentioned in the following section, to identify potential location spoofing behaviors. Below describes the detailed procedure of our algorithm.

Step 1. For each two consecutive GPS locations:

- Calculate the travel direction (in degree) with respect to the north from the GPS coordinates.
- Calculate the average rotation (in degree) around the z-axis with respect to the north in the same time interval between the two GPS coordinates are being recorded.
- Calculate the absolute value of the angle difference ($\leq 180°$) between the two angles obtained above.
- Repeat until all locations are done.

Step 2. Calculate the average of the differences obtained in step 1.

5.2   Benchmark

The efficiency of our detection algorithm is path dependent. If a user spoofs in a path with travel directions that coincidently aligns with the phone's facing directions, the spoofing may not be successfully detected. In this section, we set up a benchmark of Δ_θ for general spoofing behavior. We assume that in general, the travelling path of a user will be arbitrary, with equal probability in any direction in the long run. We can simulate it as a path with 361 GPS positions and 360 path fragments, where each path fragment travels with a direction ranging from 0° to 359° with respect to the north in random order. During spoofing, the facing direction of the mobile device is constant. Therefore, for such a path, the average of the angle differences between the device's GPS travel direction and facing direction in spoofing scenario would be

$$\Delta_\theta = \frac{0° + 1° + ... + 179° + 180° + 179° + ... + 1° + 0°}{360} = 90°$$

Claim. For a random spoofing path, the average of the angle differences between the device's GPS travel direction and facing direction with respect to the north during spoofing is 90°.

6   Evaluation

6.1   Experiment Setup

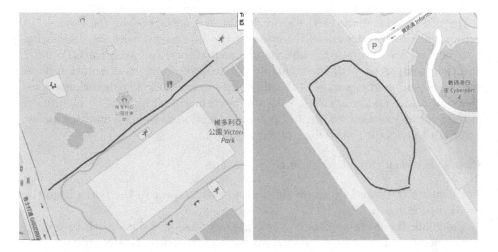

Fig. 3. Device moving in straight path.   **Fig. 4.** Device moving in circular path.

We conducted our experiment by making sample walks in open areas of Hong Kong. Figure 3 to 5 show the GPS mapping of walks with the mobile device

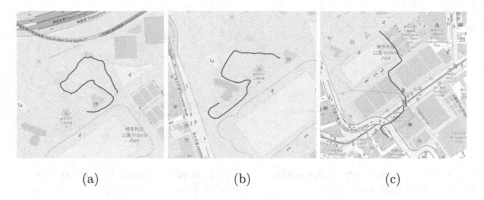

(a)   (b)   (c)

Fig. 5. Device moving in complex path.

moving in (i) straight path (Fig. 3), (ii) circular path (Fig. 4) and (iii) complex paths (Fig. 5). The mobile device is being handheld with its back facing forward throughout each walk. The GPS values are being recorded with minimal and desired update intervals of 5 and 10 s respectively and the facing angle direction of the device with respect to the north are being recorded with an update interval of 500 ms throughout the walk. In each interval between any two consecutive GPS values, the horizontal direction of travel of the device and the average value of the corresponding facing angle directions of the device in the same interval are computed for the subsequent calculation of Δ_θ. We also simulate the location spoofing scenarios of the walking paths by setting the device orientation at 0° all the time to obtain the corresponding Δ_θ when spoofing.

As we have assumed that the device orientation corresponding to the user remains stable throughout the walk, we can expect that the GPS direction of travel and the device's facing angle direction matches as their rotational change should be the same throughout the walk. If there exist notable difference between the angle of the two directions (i.e. $\Delta_\theta \geq 90°$), we can suspect that location spoofing occurs.

6.2 Results

Figure 6, 7 and 8 show the comparison between the bearings of the facing direction of the mobile device and the corresponding calculated bearings from the

Table 1. Average of the angle differences between the device's GPS travel direction and facing direction.

Path	Δ_θ	Δ_θ (spoofing)	No. of steps
Straight	12.5105°	51.9088°	343
Circular	14.3276°	92.3563°	593
Complex (a)	17.1231°	99.8231°	526
Complex (b)	15.8670°	107.9607°	500
Complex (c)	14.2551°	141.4167°	771

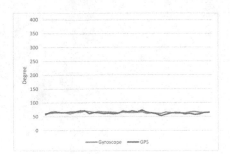

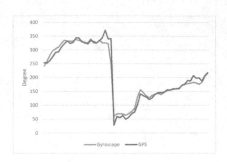

Fig. 6. Bearing comparison for device moving in straight path.

Fig. 7. Bearing comparison for device moving in circular path.

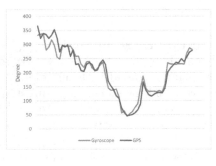

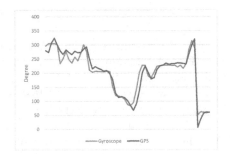

(a)

(b)

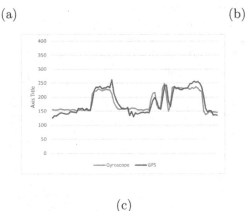

(c)

Fig. 8. Bearing comparison for device moving in complex path.

GPS values. Since the orientation of the mobile device will not align perfectly with the facing direction of the user most of the time, we calculate the average dispersion of the facing direction between the user and the device and apply a shift to align the two angles to give a better visual comparison in graphs. We can see that the bearings variate in similar trends, indicating that the device's movement matches with the user's movement. Table 1 summarizes the average of the angle differences between the device's GPS travel direction and facing direction for different paths. We can see that in real travelling scenarios, Δ_θ maintains at much lower values ($<15°$) compared to that in spoofing scenarios ($>90°$ except for straight path). As mentioned in Sect. 5.2, our methodology is path dependent. For straight paths which involve only very few direction changes, the corresponding Δ_θ on spoofing depends heavily on the dominant moving direction and can give relatively random results ($51.9088°$ in our case). However, for practical situations which involves more turning and changing in travelling direction, the corresponding Δ_θ on spoofing falls into our expectation. For circular path which involves even distribution in travelling directions (Fig. 4), Δ_θ on spoofing matches closely with our benchmark of $90°$ ($92.3563°$). For more complex paths in Fig. 5, the values of Δ_θ on spoofing are even higher ($99.8231°$, $107.9607°$ and $141.4167°$). Our methodology of the measurement with Δ_θ shows high competence in spotting location spoofing behavior.

6.3 Practicability

In our experiment, we retrieve the GPS coordinates and device's bearing via the android API (location service for GPS values and sensor service for bearings from gyroscope). The implementation is simple by calling respective functions provided by the API. The corresponding instructions are well documented in Android developer documentation. Energy consumption would be a concern for frequent update of GPS values and sensor readings so a good balance between updating and detection performance should be taken into consideration. However, it is totally adjustable depending on the need of the developer.

7 Limitation and Future Work

Although our detection method shows high competence in differentiating between GPS spoofer and legitimate users, the detection effectiveness is path dependent. Detection may fail if the travelling path simulated by location spoofing application coincidentally matches with the devices facing direction. What's more, our detection method does not take displacement into account. If an adversary performs GPS spoofing and at the same time turning himself to match the direction of movement of the fake GPS path, he may escape from the detection as our method only focuses on bearing comparison. To tackle these problems, more sensors should be taken into account to keep track of the displacement of the user. Footstep counting utilizing the accelerometer can give a good guideline on how far the user travels. It is being widely used in many health fitness applications and could possibly give a notable improvement after being implemented in our detection method. We will leave it to our future work with further investigation.

8   Conclusion

In this paper, we proposed a detection methodology by making use of the gyroscope commonly equipped in most mobile devices to detect GPS spoofing within local area which is difficult to be detected by detection methods using IP addresses in Wi-Fi networks. We calculate the travel direction of the user from the GPS data and compare it with the facing direction of the user's mobile device from the orientation data provided by the gyroscope. Experiment result shows that the average of the angle differences between the device's GPS travel direction and facing direction in real traveling cases and spoofing cases are highly differentiable ($<20°$ in real travels and $>90°$ in spoofing scenarios). We show that our method gives high competence in detecting location spoofing behavior and is easy to implement.

References

1. Pokemon GO Official Website. https://www.pokemongo.com/. Accessed 28 July 2020
2. Jurassic World Alive Official Website. https://www.jurassicworldalive.com/. Accessed 28 July 2020
3. Niantic Official Website. https://nianticlabs.com/. Accessed 28 July 2020
4. BlueStacks Official Website. https://www.bluestacks.com/. Accessed 28 July 2020
5. Nox App Player Official Website. https://www.bignox.com/. Accessed 28 July 2020
6. Magisk Manager Website. https://magiskmanager.com/. Accessed 28 July 2020
7. Chang, Y.-H., Hwang, Y.-L., Ou, C.-W., Hu, C.-L., Hsu, F.-H.: Fake GPS defender: a server-side solution to detect fake GPS. In: Proceedings of the 3rd International Conference on Advances in Computation, Communications and Services, pp. 36–41, Barcelona, Spain (2018)
8. Restuccia, F., Saracino, A., Das, S.K., Martinelli, F.: LVS: a WiFi-based system to tackle location spoofing in location-based services. In: Proceedings of the 2016 IEEE 17th International Symposium on A World of Wireless, Mobile and Multimedia Networks (WoWMoM), pp. 1–4, Coimbra, Portugal (2016). https://doi.org/10.1109/WoWMoM.2016.7523533
9. Restuccia, F., Saracino, A., Das, S.K., Martinelli, F.: Preserving QoI in participatory sensing by tackling location-spoofing through mobile WiFi hotspots. In: Proceedings of the 2015 IEEE International Conference on Pervasive Computing and Communication Workshops, pp. 81–86, St. Louis, MO, USA (2015) https://doi.org/10.1109/PERCOMW.2015.7133998
10. Saroiu, S., Wolman, A.: Enabling new mobile applications with location proofs. In: Proceedings of the 10th International Workshop on Mobile Computing Systems and Applications, pp. 1–6, Santa Cruz, CA, USA (2009)

Push for More: On Comparison of Data Augmentation and SMOTE with Optimised Deep Learning Architecture for Side-Channel

Yoo-Seung Won[✉], Dirmanto Jap, and Shivam Bhasin

Physical Analysis and Cryptographic Engineering, Temasek Laboratories at Nanyang Technological University, Singapore, Singapore
{yooseung.won,djap,sbhasin}@ntu.edu.sg

Abstract. Side-channel analysis has seen rapid adoption of deep learning techniques over the past years. While many paper focus on designing efficient architectures, some works have proposed techniques to boost the efficiency of existing architectures. These include methods like data augmentation, oversampling, regularization etc. In this paper, we compare data augmentation and oversampling (particularly SMOTE and its variants) on public traces of two side-channel protected AES. The techniques are compared in both balanced and imbalanced classes setting, and we show that adopting SMOTE variants can boost the attack efficiency in general. Further, we report a successful key recovery on ASCAD(desync=100) with 180 traces, a 50% improvement over current state of the art.

Keywords: Oversampling technique · Side-channel analysis · Deep learning

1 Introduction

The security of cryptograhic algorithm has been widely investigated. One of the possible vulnerabilities is due to the physical leakage from the implementation of the cryptographic algorithm itself, which is commonly referred to as side-channel analysis (SCA) [9]. Recently, many deep learning (DL) techniques have been introduced to SCA after the renaissance of machine learning to improve the performance of the attack. It can be naturally applied for profiled SCA, such as template attack [5] since DL frameworks can be divided to two fold; training and testing, similar to the framework of profiled SCA.

Related Works. The basic application of neural networks such as Multi-Layer Perceptron (MLP), Convolutional Neural Network (CNN), Recurrent Neural Network (RNN), Autoencoder were investigated by H. Maghrebi *et al.* [15] to enhance profiled SCA. More improvements have been proposed in later works.

© Springer Nature Switzerland AG 2020
I. You (Ed.): WISA 2020, LNCS 12583, pp. 227–241, 2020.
https://doi.org/10.1007/978-3-030-65299-9_18

By applying the data augmentation (DA) techniques, E. Cagli *et al.* [4] demonstrated that it can overcome the jitter and noise countermeasures. In the same manner, by adding the artificial noise to original traces, with application of VGG architecture and blurring technique, J. Kim *et al.* [10] proposed the general architecture for open datasets of SCA and improvement of the attack performance. G. Zaid *et al.* [7] recently suggested the efficient methodology on how to construct the neural network structure for open dataset of SCA and reported most efficient attacks in the current state of the art.

One of the recent work showed that, by adjusting the imbalanced data on Hamming weight (HW) model, the distribution of the HW classes can be balanced [16] and since the biased data is solved by oversampling technique from data analysis, it can outperform the previous works, in particular Synthetic minority oversampling technique (SMOTE). However, there are some restriction in [16] owing to the fact that they only handled two oversampling techniques and considered HW assumption. In other words, there are still open problems on how to expand the oversampling techniques for improving the performance in the SCA context.

Our Contributions. In this paper, we conduct in-depth investigation for oversampling techniques to enhance SCA. The main contributions of this work are as follows. We conduct a comparative study of previously proposed DA [4] and SMOTE [16] (and its variant) in context of SCA. The performance of DA and various SMOTE variants are compared in both balanced (256 classes) and imbalanced (9 classes) setting. Experimental validation is performed on two public databases with side-channel countermeasure (AES_RD and ASCAD). Finally, with optimised architectures as proposed in [7] and further adoption of SMOTE variants, we break ASCAD(desync=100) dataset in as low as 180 traces, which is a 50% improvements over the state of the art [7].

Paper Organization. This paper is organised as follows. Section 2 provides brief background on profiled SCA and security metric for adequately measuring the improvement. Afterwards, we explain the relationship between the oversampling technique and DA, and how imbalanced/balanced models for oversampling technique can affect SCA evaluation in Sect. 3. In Sect. 4, we highlight the experimental results for our suggestions and compared with the previous works. Finally, we provide the conclusion and further works in Sect. 5.

2 Preliminaries

2.1 Profiled Side-Channel Analysis

Profiled SCA [5] assumes a strong adversary with access to a clone of the target device. Adversary can query the clone device with known plaintext and key pairs while recording side-channel signature. These side-channel signature along with plaintext, key pair help to characterize a model for device leakage. Further, on the target device where key is unknown, the adversary queries a known plaintext to capture side-channel signature, which when queried with the characterized model can reveal the secret key. Ideally more than one query to target device might be needed to confidently recover the key due to presence of measurement noise and countermeasures.

In the following, we target side-channel protected software implementation of AES. The target operation is S-Box look up, which for a given plaintext t and secret key k^*, can be written as:

$$y(t, k^*) = \text{Model}(\text{Sbox}[t \oplus k^*]) \tag{1}$$

where Sbox$[\cdot]$ indicates S-box operation and Model$(\cdot)$ means the assumption for leakage model of side-channel information. We consider Hamming weight (HW) [1] and Identity as models, leading to 9 and 256 classes for y respectively. Classical profiled attacks use Gaussian templates [5], which are built for all values of $y(t, k^*)$.

2.1.1 Deep Learning Based Profiled Side-Channel Analysis

Novel profiled SCA have seen the adoption of deep neural networks (DNN [4,15]). The most commonly used algorithms are MLP and CNN. The use of DNN in side-channel evaluation has shown several advantages over classical templates. For example, they can overcome traditional SCA countermeasure, such as jitter [4] and masking [15], and they are also naturally incorporating feature selection. Owing to these advantages, a line of research has focused on improving the performance of SCA by techniques like DA [4], training set class balancing [16], noise regularization, [10], finding optimised network architectures [7,10] etc.

2.2 Security Metric

In order to quantify the effectiveness of profiled SCA with a security metric, the guessing entropy (GE) [12] is generally employed. Intuitively, the GE indicates the average number of key candidates needed for successful evaluation after the SCA has been performed. For measuring the GE, we repeat 100 times on randomly chosen test set in this paper. Additionally, Nt_{GE} [7] which implies the minimum number of traces when the GE reaches 1 is also utilized to compare the improvement.

3 Oversampling Versus Data Augmentation

In this section, we briefly discuss the oversampling and data augmentation techniques used in this paper.

3.1 Oversampling Techniques

Oversampling and undersampling are common data analysis techniques used to adjust the class distribution of a data set (i.e. the ratio between samples in different classes). Oversampling is deployed more often than undersampling due to scarcity of training data in a general context. Oversampling and undersampling are contrasted and roughly equivalent techniques. Oversampling is done through applying transformation to existing data instances to generate new data instances, in order to adjust the class imbalance.

3.1.1   Synthetic Minority Oversampling Technique

One of the main solution to adjust the balance for biased data is the synthetic minority oversampling technique (SMOTE) [3]. The core idea is that the artificial instance for minority instances is generated using k-nearest neighbors of sample. In the minority instance, k-nearest samples are selected from sample X. Afterward, the SMOTE algorithm selects n samples randomly and save them as X_i. Lastly, the new sample X' is generated based on the below equation.

$$X' = X + rand \times (X_i - X), \; i = 1, 2, ..., n \qquad (2)$$

where $rand$ follows a random number uniformly distributed in the range $(0, 1)$. By obtaining minority instances using SMOTE, the class imbalance is reduced thus allowing machine learning and deep learning algorithms to learn better. Naturally, it has been applied and shown working for SCA [16]. Picek et al. [16] study a very common case of SCA literature, i.e. the HW model. HW model is naturally biased. Considering one byte, the ratio of majority and minority class population for HW model is 70:1. In such cases, SMOTE balances the dataset improving the effectiveness of the DL based attack algorithm. In [16], authors study SMOTE and SMOTE-ENN, where SMOTE was shown to work better on the tested datasets. Recently, the candidates for SMOTE has increased quite a lot [8].

3.2   Data Augmentation

Data augmentation (DA [13]) is well-known in the field of DL and applied to overcome the overfitting issue while training phase. By applying artificial transformation to training data, the overfitting factor can be reduced and learning can be improved. In context of SCA, DA was applied as a solution to break jitter based countermeasures. Jitter causes horizontal shifts in side-channel trace resulting in misalignment which in turn reduces the attack efficiency. In [4], Cagli et al. used the translational invariance property of CNN to counter jitter based misalignment. Further, authors show that DA by applying small, random shift to existing traces can avoid overfitting, resulting in a better training of CNN. As S. Picek *et al.* [16] mentioned beforehand, this scheme can be considered as one of oversampling techniques.

While [4] use dedicated code to apply shifts to datasets and thus implement DA, we utilize the ImageDataGenerator[1] class in the Keras DL library to provide DA. Moreover, width_shift_range is only regarded as the variable for argument of ImageDataGenerator, due to the unidimensionality for side channel leakage.

---

[1] Refer to the Keras API description in https://www.tensorflow.org/api_docs/python/ tf/keras/preprocessing/image/ImageDataGenerator.

3.3 Case Study: Balanced (256) Classes Versus Imbalanced (9) Classes

Hamming weight (and distance) models are some of the most popular leakage models in side-channel literature, which are practically validated on range of devices including microcontroller, FPGA, GPU, ASIC etc. However, as stated earlier, this model follows a Binomial distribution and is highly imbalanced. It was shown in [16], how imbalanced model can negatively affect SCA evaluations [16]. As a result, most of DL based SCA consider the identity model. When considering a byte as in AES, HW and identity model result in 9 and 256 classes respectively.

While the main objective of SMOTE is minority class oversampling and DA is to reduce overfitting. Thus SMOTE is ideal for imbalanced setting (9 classes), however, balanced dataset should not have a negative impact. On the other hand, DA does not consider class imbalance as a parameter. This can help overcoming overfitting, however, augmentation preserve original distribution and does not improve any imbalance. Thus, DA is expected to work better in balanced dataset (256 classes). Note that, with limited size dataset even 256 classes might have minor imbalances and SMOTE may improve the imbalance.

In the following, we study the performance of different SMOTE variants and DA under 9 and 256 classes setting. The study is performed on two publicly available datasets of side-channel protected AES implementation.

4 Experimental Validation

In this section, we describe the experimental setting and target datasets. Further, experimental results on AES_RD and ASCAD datasets are reported in 256 and 9 classes setting.

4.1 Target Datasets and Network

We use two popular datasets, AES_RD[2] and ASCAD[3] containing side-channel measurements of protected AES implementations running on a 8-bit AVR microcontroller. The AES_RD contains traces for the software implementation AES with random delay countermeasure as described by J.-S. Coron et al. [6]. R. Benadjila et al. [2] introduced the open dataset ASCAD with traces corresponding to first order masking protected AES with artificially introduced random jitter. In particular we use the worst case setting with jitter up to 100 sample points (ASCAD(desync=100)).

The main motivation of this work is to investigate the effect of oversampling techniques on best known attacks so for. The work of G. Zaid et al. [7] recently published at CHES 2020, presents the best performing attacks and corresponding network choices to achieve those result. The following experiments takes the

---

[2] https://github.com/ikizhvatov/randomdelays-traces.
[3] https://github.com/ANSSI-FR/ASCAD.

result of G. Zaid *et al.* [7] as a benchmarking case to compare the affect of oversampling and DA techniques.

For the following experiments, the number of training traces used are 5,000 and 45,000 for AES_RD and ASCAD respectively. Moreover, 5,000 traces are used as validation set for all results and the number of epochs used are set as 20 (AES_RD) and 50 (ASCAD).

Furthermore, we investigate the effect of 256 and 9 classes for the open dataset. In the 256 classes, we accept the underlying network which is suggested by [7]. On the other hand, for the 9 classes, the only modification is the number of output layers. As all oversampling techniques in Appendix A and DA can be regarded as pre-processing scheme, the modification to neural network parameters is not required as we can use the networks proposed in [7] (except for output layer modification in case of 9 classes). For parameter setting of SMOTE variants, we employ the default setting because there are many SMOTE and setting value for each techniques. According to previous claim in [16], we do not provide the MCC, kappa, and G-mean results, since these values are not critical information in the context of SCA. Moreover, we only represent the best result in overall sampling techniques to definitely compare with the previous results. All results can be referred to Appendix A and B.

4.2   Result for AES_RD

As shown in Fig. 1, some variant SMOTE [8] and DA scheme [4] are outperforming the previous work [7], proposed in CHES 2020. DA(0.3)[4] which has the shift ratio 0.3 is best result in 256 classes. The attack needs only 11 traces to recover the correct key, although it is not enough to find the correct key in original scheme [7] where 15 traces are needed. CURE-SMOTE and Gaussian-based SMOTE also outperform original scheme by a small margin in Table 1. The main purpose of data augmentation and SMOTE schemes is to concentrate on noise removal. As mentioned earlier, this effect works well to AES_RD countermeasure. Unlike [7], the number of profiling traces is reduced to 5,000 for our experiments and thus our reported Nt_{GE} is more than what was reported in the original scheme. However, lower training set size allows us to evaluate the impact of data augmentation and oversampling. Sometimes the profiling sets can be restricted by the protocol effect. When considering it, our scheme can provide faster convergence than original scheme in limited profiling sets. Moreover, techniques like DA and oversampling become relevant when training set is limited in sample size.

In case of HW model (9 classes), we can observe that the performance of the method proposed by [7], is degrading. As such, several SMOTE techniques are now outperforming it because the difference between majority and minority is more distinguishable than 256 classes. In this case, more traces will be also required in general (>20× the traces required for 256 classes), since in HW

---

[4] DA(x) indicates that $x \times 100\%$ of the whole points is randomly shifted while training phase, which was suggested in [4].

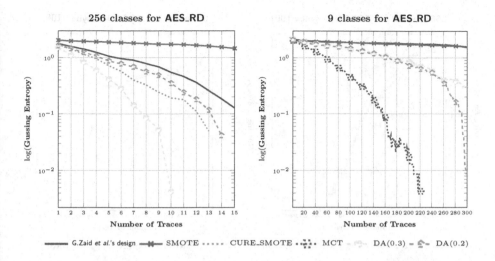

Fig. 1. Result for the best variant SMOTEs and DA against AES_RD

model, the adversary cannot directly infer the actual value of sensitive intermediate variables.

As shown in Table 1 for 256 and 9 classes, CURE-SMOTE and Gaussian-based SMOTE are useful oversampling techniques against AES_RD. Depending on the oversampling technique, the amount of traces added in the training set is variable. More precisely, the training dataset size is increased to $5,013(5,125)$ from $5,000$ for 256 classes (9 cases) in most of the oversampling techniques, which does not critically impact the learning time.

4.3 Result for ASCAD(desync=100)

In Fig. 2, the results are plotted for ASCAD dataset. In this case, the benchmarking attack of [7] performs better than the DA schemes. However, several SMOTE variants are performing better. As shown in Table 1, ASMOBD, MSMOTE, and SDSMOTE are especially ranked in top 10 results for all classes of ASCAD dataset. In the case of 256 classes, ASMOBD can recover the key in under 200 traces while the original scheme needs over 256 traces.

The size of training dataset is increased from 45000 traces by 10 and 400 traces when applying the oversampling techniques to 256 and 9 classes, respectively. When employing the HW model (9 classes), some oversampling techniques such as MOT2LD and Borderline_SMOTE2 have low GE, compared to original scheme.

4.4 Analysis and Discussion

We tested 85 variants of SMOTE and 3 variants of DA under 4 experiments. We have reported the best results in Table 1 for each datasets. In all the 4 cases, we

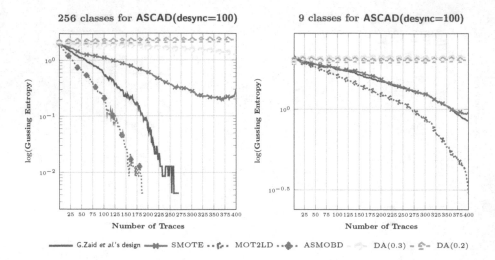

Fig. 2. Result for the best variant SMOTEs and DA against ASCAD(desync=100)

Table 1. Top 10 results for AES_RD and ASCAD(desync=100) datasets against variant SMOTEs and DA techniques, (∗): GE when the maximum number of traces is used

No.	AES_RD (256 classes)		AES_RD (9 classes)		ASCAD (256 classes)		ASCAD (9 classes)	
	Scheme	Nt_{GE}	Scheme	Nt_{GE}	Scheme	Nt_{GE}	Scheme	Nt_{GE}
–	Original	>15 (1.34)	Original	>300 (36)	Original	267	Original	>400 (7)
1	DA(0.3)	11	MCT	228	ASMOBD	190	MOT2LD	>400 (2)
2	CURE_SMOTE	14	CURE_SMOTE	243	MDO	193	Borderline_SMOTE2	>400 (4)
3	Gaussian_SMOTE	15	Gaussian_SMOTE	265	DEAGO	212	MSMOTE	>400 (5)
4	DA(0.2)	15	SMOTE_OUT	276	MSMOTE	224	Supervised_SMOTE	>400 (5)
5	distance_SMOTE	15	LLE_SMOTE	281	SMOTE_Cosine	234	LLE_SMOTE	>400 (6)
6	NoSMOTE	15	polynom_fit_SMOTE	283	SMOBD	242	polynom_fit_SMOTE	>400 (6)
7	SOI_CJ	15	Borderline_SMOTE1	285	SDSMOTE	242	ASMOBD	>400 (6)
8	SOMO	15	V_SYNTH	285	Stefanowski	245	SDSMOTE	>400 (6)
9	SMOTE_OUT	15	SMOTE_Cosine	286	SMOTE_RSB	248	SPY	>400 (6)
10	MCT	15	ASMOBD	295	SL_graph_SMOTE	249	cluster_SMOTE	>400 (6)

were able to report results better than best benchmarking results. However, it was not possible to identify one single oversampling method which would work best in all the cases. This is not surprising and in accordance with No Free Lunch theorems [18]. In general, we can make the following observations from the previously performed experiments.

– In general, SMOTE variants led to attack improvements in all the cases as compared to DA which only outperforms in one case. DA also shows negative impact in case of ASCAD, where the attack is worse than baseline benchmarking attack of G. Zaid *et al.*

- Dataset imbalance is a difficult problem for deep learning as already stated in [16] which results in better performance of SMOTE variants when used in 256 classes as compared to 9 class setting. The discrepancy is better highlighted in ASCAD dataset, as there are >20 variants which recovers the secret for 256 classes (though there are also a lot of methods which perform significantly worse) and only around 2 or 3 which have the correct key in top 5 rank candidates.
- Secondly, certain methods work better for a given dataset. For example, on AES_RD, CURE-SMOTE and Gaussian-based SMOTE are in top 3 in terms of performance for both 256 and 9 classes. For ASCAD, ASMOBD, polynom_fit_SMOTE and SDSMOTE are in top 10. However, there are no consistents techniques which work for all the dataset and the scenarios.
- Some SMOTE variants has a negative impact on training datasets represented to Appendix A. For example, in case of SMOTE-ENN, the training dataset is shrunk from 5000 to 38. Not to surprise, the technique performs much worse than benchmark case of CHES 2020, leave alone any improvement. SMOTE-ENN also reported training set shrinking in other 3 experiments as well. Similar observations were seen in other experiments too but not necessarily for all experiments. We hypothesize that oversampling considers some traces as noise and filters them out, resulting in shrinking of datasets. Note that SMOTE-ENN was also shown to perform worse in [16].

5   Conclusion and Further Works

In this paper, we investigate the effect of various SMOTE variants and previously proposed data augmentation against previously best known results. We outperform previous results with a decent margin. While DA improves the result in one case, different variants of SMOTE resulted in a general improvement across experiments. However, it was not possible to identify a single favorable SMOTE variant, it varied by experiments. We also reported that some oversampling techniques result in training set shrinking and thus lead to poor performance. Note that we tested various SMOTE variants in their default settings and there are other parameters to play with. Thus, a deeper investigations might help identify few candidates better suited for SCA application. Moreover, testing oversampling with more datasets could lead to better insights.

Acknowledgements. We gratefully acknowledge the support of NVIDIA Corporation with the donation of the Titan Xp GPU used for this research. The authors acknowledge the support from the 'National Integrated Centre of Evaluation' (NICE); a facility of Cyber Security Agency, Singapore (CSA).

A   Variants of Oversampling Techniques (SMOTE Variants)

Two approaches were already introduced in [16] (SMOTE and SMOTE-ENN). However, there are currently 85 variant of SMOTEs referring to [8]. To the best of our knowledge, the investigation for effectiveness of these schemes has not been properly conducted in terms of SCA.

The variant SMOTEs in Table 2 have developed to overcome the bias for imbalanced data for DL context. As mentioned previously, only SMOTE and SMOTE-ENN are utilized in [16]. Although the performance of SMOTE in [16] is better, many variant SMOTEs have not been utilized. Moreover, they mentioned that the role of SMOTE and SMOTE-ENN is to only increase the number of minority instance. However, in general, the oversampling techniques can be further used as compared to previous suggestion. Naturally, these techniques can be used beyond HW/HD model, because the data might be biased in practice. As such, variant SMOTEs provide benefit as preprocessing tool, which help smoothing the distribution of the data.

Moreover, as mentioned earlier, these techniques are worth investigated in the context of SCA, because there are several advantages offered by SMOTE variants, such as the change of majority and noise removal. Among 85 variant SMOTEs, we have conducted preliminary investigation on their effectiveness and only reported those who are quite successful for SCA.

B   Results for All Oversampling Techniques Against AES_RD and ASCAD(desync=100)

The legend of Fig. 3 and 4 is referred to Fig. 5.

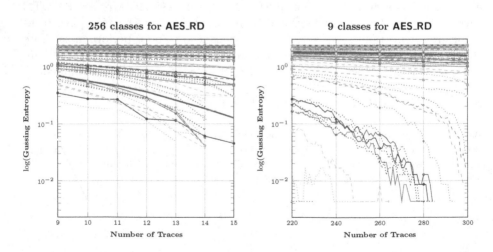

Fig. 3. Result for variant SMOTEs and DA against AES_RD

Table 2. API function list for variant SMOTEs in [8]. Table reports the number of training set for AES_RD(256 classes), AES_RD(9 classes), ASCAD(256 classes), and ASCAD(9 classes), respectively after applying each oversampling techniques. '-' indicates that we do not perform its oversampling techniques due to the time limit.

Scheme	#Training	Scheme	#Training	Scheme	#Training	Scheme	#Training	Scheme	#Training
SMOTE_TomekLinks	2787 3342 26568 31897	MSYN	5013 5126 - -	RWO_sampling	5013 5126 - -	Edge_Det_SMOTE	5013 5126 45010 46257	GASMOTE	5013 5126 45010 46257
SMOTE_ENN	38 1142 204 9569	SVM_balance	5013 5126 45010 46257	NEATER	5013 5126 45010 46257	CBSO	9985 10072 - -	A_SUWO	5000 5000 1001 30133
Borderline_SMOTE1	5013 5000 45010 46257	TRIM_SMOTE	5000 5000 45010 46257	DEAGO	5000 5000 45010 46257	E_SMOTE	5013 5126 45010 46257	SMOTE_FRST_2T	55 330 322 50
Borderline_SMOTE2	5013 5000 45010 46257	SMOTE_RSB	5017 5145 45020 47514	Gazzah	28 228 238 1939	DBSMOTE	28 228 238 1939	AND_SMOTE	5000 5000 45010 50
ADASYN	9972 9946 89698 89698	ProWSyn	5013 5125 45010 46257	MCT	5013 5126 45010 46257	ASMOBD	5013 5126 45010 46257	NRAS	5000 5000 45000 45000
AHC	54 206 462 1709	SL_graph_SMOTE	5013 5000 45010 46257	ADG	41 180 323 3567	Assembled_SMOTE	41 180 323 3567	AMSCO	72 684 326 2713
LLE_SMOTE	5013 5126 45010 46257	NRSBoundary_SMOTE	5000 5126 - -	SMOTE_IPF	27 289 170 2688	5DSMOTE	27 289 170 2688	SSO	5013 5126 45010 46257
distance_SMOTE	5013 5126 45010 46257	LVQ_SMOTE	5013 5126 45010 46257	KernelADASYN	5000 5000 45010 46257	DSMOTE	5000 5000 45010 46257	NDO_sampling	54 306 322 2816
SMMO	5000 5126 45010 46257	SOL_CJ	5000 5000 45000 45000	MOT2LD	5000 5000 44870 46115	G_SMOTE	5000 5000 44870 46115	DSRBF	5013 5126 45010 46257

(continued)

Table 2. (*continued*)

Scheme	#Training	Scheme	#Training	Scheme	#Training	Scheme	#Training	Scheme	#Training
polynom_fit_SMOTE	5013	ROSE	5013	V_SYNTH	5013	NT_SMOTE	5013	Gaussian_SMOTE	5013
	5135		5126		5126		5126		5126
	45151		45010		45010		45010		45010
	46208		46257		46257		46257		46257
Stefanowski	4973	SMOTE_OUT	5013	OUPS	5014	Lee	5013	kmeans_SMOTE	-
	4857		5126		5129		5126		-
	44845		45010		45010		45010		-
	43722		46257		46263		46257		
ADOMS	5013	SMOTE_Cosine	5013	SMOTE_D	5009	SPY	5013	Supervised_SMOTE	5013
	5126		5126		5127		5000		5126
	45010		45010		45014		45000		45010
	46257		46257		46245		45000		46257
Safe_Level_SMOTE	5001	Selected_SMOTE	5013	SMOTE_PSO	-	SMOTE_PSOBAT	-	SN_SMOTE	5013
	5006		5126		-		-		5126
	45001		45010		-		-		45010
	45036		46257		-		-		46257
MSMOTE	5000	LN_SMOTE	5000	CURE_SMOTE	5013	MDO	5000	CCR	5014
	5000		5126		5126		5000		5135
	45010		45000		45010		45000		45000
	4257		45000		46257		45000		46208
DE_oversampling	5013	MWMOTE	5000	SOMO	5000	Random_SMOTE	5013	ANS	5014
	5065		5000		5000		5126		5126
	45010		45010		45000		45010		45000
	46257		46257		45000		46257		46257
SMOBD	5013	PDFOS	5013	ISOMAP_Hybrid	-	ISMOTE	41	cluster_SMOTE	5014
	5126		5126		-		180		5126
	45010		45010		-		312		45010
	46257		46257		-		1559		46257
SUNDO	2501	IPADE_ID	-	CE_SMOTE	5013	VIS_RST	5013	NoSMOTE	5000
	2515		-		5126		5126		5000
	22502		-		45010		45010		45000
	22548		-		46257		46257		45000

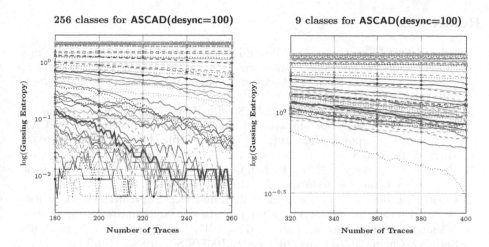

Fig. 4. Result for variant SMOTEs and DA against ASCAD(desync=100)

SMOTE		SMOTE_TomekLinks		SMOTE_ENN		Borderline_SMOTE1
Borderline_SMOTE2		ADASYN		AHC		LLE_SMOTE
distance_SMOTE		SMMO		polynom_fit_SMOTE		Stefanowski
ADOMS		Safe_Level_SMOTE		MSMOTE		DE_oversampling
SMOBD		SUNDO		MSYN		SVM_balance
TRIM_SMOTE		SMOTE_RSB		ProWSyn		SL_graph_SMOTE
NRSBoundary_SMOTE		LVQ_SMOTE		SOI_CJ		ROSE
SMOTE_OUT		SMOTE_Cosine		Selected_SMOTE		LN_SMOTE
MWMOTE		PDFOS		RWO_sampling		NEATER
DEAGO		Gazzah		MCT		ADG
SMOTE_IPF		KernelADASYN		MOT2LD		V_SYNTH
OUPS		SMOTE_D		CURE_SMOTE		SOMO
CE_SMOTE		Edge_Det_SMOTE		CBSO		DBSMOTE
ASMOBD		Assembled_SMOTE		SDSMOTE		DSMOTE
G_SMOTE		NT_SMOTE		Lee		SPY
MDO		Random_SMOTE		ISMOTE		VIS_RST
A_SUWO		SMOTE_FRST_2T		AND_SMOTE		NRAS
AMSCO		NDO_sampling		Gaussian_SMOTE		Supervised_SMOTE
SN_SMOTE		CCR		ANS		cluster_SMOTE
NoSMOTE		DA(0.3)		DA(0.2)		DA(0.1)
G.Zaid *et al.*'s design						

Fig. 5. The legend of Figs. 3 and 4

References

1. Brier, Eric., Clavier, Christophe, Olivier, Francis: Correlation power analysis with a leakage model. In: Joye, Marc, Quisquater, Jean-Jacques (eds.) CHES 2004. LNCS, vol. 3156, pp. 16–29. Springer, Heidelberg (2004). https://doi.org/10.1007/978-3-540-28632-5_2
2. Benadjila, Ryad., Prouff, Emmanuel., Strullu, Rémi., Cagli, Eleonora, Dumas, Cécile: Deep learning for side-channel analysis and introduction to ASCAD database. J. Cryptogr. Eng. **10**(2), 163–188 (2019). https://doi.org/10.1007/s13389-019-00220-8
3. Chawla, N.V., Bowyer, K.W., Hall, L.O., Kegelmeyer, W.P.: Smote: synthetic minority over-sampling technique. J. Artif. Int. Res. **16**(1), 321–357 (2002)
4. Cagli, Eleonora., Dumas, Cécile, Prouff, Emmanuel: Convolutional neural networks with data augmentation against jitter-based countermeasures. In: Fischer, Wieland, Homma, Naofumi (eds.) CHES 2017. LNCS, vol. 10529, pp. 45–68. Springer, Cham (2017). https://doi.org/10.1007/978-3-319-66787-4_3
5. Chari, Suresh., Rao, Josyula R., Rohatgi, Pankaj: Template attacks. In: Kaliski, Burton S., Koç, çetin K., Paar, Christof (eds.) CHES 2002. LNCS, vol. 2523, pp. 13–28. Springer, Heidelberg (2003). https://doi.org/10.1007/3-540-36400-5_3
6. Coron, Jean-Sébastien, Kizhvatov, Ilya: An efficient method for random delay generation in embedded software. In: Clavier, Christophe, Gaj, Kris (eds.) CHES 2009. LNCS, vol. 5747, pp. 156–170. Springer, Heidelberg (2009). https://doi.org/10.1007/978-3-642-04138-9_12
7. Zaid, G., Bossuet, L., Habrard, A., Venelli, A.: Methodology for efficient CNN architectures in profiling attacks. IACR Trans. Cryptographic Hardware Embed. Syst. **1**, 1–36 (2020)
8. Kovács, G.: smote_variants Documentation Release 0.1.0. https://readthedocs.org/projects/smote-variants/downloads/pdf/latest/, 03 February 2020
9. Kocher, Paul., Jaffe, Joshua, Jun, Benjamin: Differential power analysis. In: Wiener, Michael (ed.) CRYPTO 1999. LNCS, vol. 1666, pp. 388–397. Springer, Heidelberg (1999). https://doi.org/10.1007/3-540-48405-1_25
10. Kim, J., Picek, S., Heuser, A., Bhasin, S., Hanjalic, A.: Make some noise unleashing the power of convolutional neural netoworks for pofiled side-channel analysis. IACR Trans. Cryptographic Hardware Embed. Syst. **2019**(3), 148–179 (2019)
11. Lee, H., Kim, J., Kim, S.: Gaussian-based SMOTE llgorithm for solving Skewe class distributions. Int. J. Fuzzy Log. Intell. Syst. **17**(4), 229–237 (2017)
12. Standaert, François-Xavier., Malkin, Tal G., Yung, Moti: A unified framework for the analysis of side-channel key recovery attacks. In: Joux, Antoine (ed.) EUROCRYPT 2009. LNCS, vol. 5479, pp. 443–461. Springer, Heidelberg (2009). https://doi.org/10.1007/978-3-642-01001-9_26
13. Simard, P.Y., Steinkraus, D., Platt, J.C.: Best practices for convolutional neural networks applied to visual document analysis. In: 7th International Conference on Document Analysis and Recognition - Volume 2 (2003)
14. Ma, L., Fan, S.: CURE-SMOTE algorithm and hybrid algorithm for feature selection and parameter optimization based on random forests. BMC Bioinformatics **169**, 2017 (2017)
15. Maghrebi, Houssem., Portigliatti, Thibault, Prouff, Emmanuel: Breaking cryptographic implementations using deep learning techniques. In: Carlet, Claude, Hasan, M.Anwar, Saraswat, Vishal (eds.) SPACE 2016. LNCS, vol. 10076, pp. 3–26. Springer, Cham (2016). https://doi.org/10.1007/978-3-319-49445-6_1

16. Picek, S., Heuser, A., Jovic, A., Bhasin, S., Regazzoni, F.: The curse of class imbalance and conflicting metrics with machine learning for side-channel evaluations. IACR Trans. Cryptographic Hardware and Embed. Syst. **2019**(1), 209–237 (2019)
17. Wang, S., Li, Z., Chao, W., Cao, Q.: Applying adaptive over-sampling technique based on data density and cost-sensitive SVM to imbalanced learning. In: The 2012 International Joint Conference on Neural Networks (IJCNN), pp. 1–8 (2012)
18. Wolpert, D.H.: The lack of a prior distinctions between learning algorithms. Neural Comput. **8**, 1341–1390 (1996)

Cryptography

Identity-Based Unidirectional Proxy Re-encryption in Standard Model: A Lattice-Based Construction

Priyanka Dutta[✉], Willy Susilo, Dung Hoang Duong, Joonsang Baek, and Partha Sarathi Roy

Institute of Cybersecurity and Cryptology, School of Computing and Information Technology, University of Wollongong, Northfields Avenue, Wollongong 2522, Australia
{pdutta,wsusilo,hduong,baek,partha}@uow.edu.au

Abstract. Proxy re-encryption (PRE) securely enables the re-encryption of ciphertexts from one key to another, without relying on trusted parties, i.e., it offers delegation of decryption rights. PRE allows a semi-trusted third party termed as a "proxy" to securely divert encrypted files of user A (delegator) to user B (delegatee) without revealing any information about the underlying files to the proxy. To eliminate the necessity of having a costly certificate verification process, Green and Ateniese introduced an identity-based PRE (IB-PRE). The potential applicability of IB-PRE leads to intensive research from its first instantiation. Unfortunately, till today, there is no unidirectional IB-PRE secure in the standard model, which can withstand quantum attack. In this paper, we provide, for the first time, a concrete construction of unidirectional IB-PRE which is secure in standard model based on the hardness of learning with error problem. Our technique is to use the novel trapdoor delegation technique of Micciancio and Peikert. The way we use trapdoor delegation technique may prove useful for functionalities other than proxy re-encryption as well.

1 Introduction

Blaze, Bleumer and Strauss [5] introduced the concept of Proxy Re-encryption (PRE) towards an efficient solution that offers delegation of decryption rights without compromising privacy. PRE allows a semi-trusted third party, called a proxy, to securely divert encrypted files of one user (delegator) to another user (delegatee). The proxy, however, cannot learn the underlying message m, and thus both parties' privacy can be maintained. This primitive (and its variants) have various applications ranging from encrypted email forwarding [5], securing distributed file systems [4], to digital rights management systems [25]. In addition application-driven purposes, various works have shown connections between re-encryption with other cryptographic primitives, such as program obfuscation [8,9,14] and fully-homomorphic encryption [7]. Thus studies along this line are both important and interesting for theory and practice.

© Springer Nature Switzerland AG 2020
I. You (Ed.): WISA 2020, LNCS 12583, pp. 245–257, 2020.
https://doi.org/10.1007/978-3-030-65299-9_19

PRE systems are classified as unidirectional and bidirectional based on the direction of delegation. It is worth mentioning that the unidirectional constructions are much desirable because bidirectional construction easily implementable using a unidirectional one. Though the concept of PRE was initiated in [5], the first unidirectional PRE proposed by Ateniese et al. in [4], where following desired properties of a PRE are listed: *Non-interactivity* (*re-encryption key*, $rk_{A \to B}$, can be generated by A alone using B's public key; no trusted authority is needed); *Proxy transparency* (neither the delegator nor the delegatees are aware of the presence of a proxy); *Key optimality* (the size of B's secret key remains constant, regardless of how many delegations he accepts); *Collusion resilience* (it is computationally infeasible for the coalition of the proxy and user B to compute A's secret key); *Non-transitivity* (it should be hard for the proxy to re-delegate the decryption right, namely to compute $rk_{A \to C}$ from $rk_{A \to B}$, $rk_{B \to C}$). To achieve the aforementioned properties (partially) with improved security guarantee, there are elegant followup works which can be found in [6,8,9,14,17]. For quantum-safe version of PRE, Gentry [11] mentioned the feasibility of unidirectional PRE through fully homomorphic encryption scheme (FHE). However, FHE costs huge computation. Xagawa proposed construction of PRE in [26], but the construction lacks concrete security analysis. Further development of lattice-based PRE can be found in [8,10,16,21].

Certificate management problem is a crucial issue in the PKI based schemes. This crucial issue was addressed by Green et al. [13] in the area of PRE. For lattice-based construction, Singh et al. [23] proposed a bidirectional identity-based PRE. However, it is required to use secret key of both delegator and delegatee to generate re-encryption key, which lacks one of the fundamental properties of PRE. Further, they proposed unidirectional identity-based PRE [24], termed as IB-uPRE, secure in the random oracle model. However, the size of re-encrypted ciphertext blows up than the original encrypted one. Moreover, the schemes encrypt the message bit by bit. Later, there are some further attempts to construct lattice-based identity-based PRE, which are flawed[1] [15,27].

Our Contribution and Technique: It is an interesting open research problem to construct post-quantum secure IB-uPRE in the standard model. In this paper, we resolve this daunting task by constructing a concrete scheme based on the hardness of *learning with error* (LWE) problem. The proposed construction is capable of encrypting multi-bit message and enjoy the properties like non-interactivity, proxy transparency, key optimality, non-transitivity along with other properties follow generically from IB-PRE. To construct the IB-uPRE, we start with the construction of the identity-based encryption scheme by Agrawal et al. [1]. In non-interactive IB-uPRE, it is required to construct re-encryption key by the delegator alone. One of the feasible ways to adopt the non-interactive feature is to provide a trapdoor to the delegator as a secret key. But, this technique is not supported by the design of [1]. In [1], the trapdoor is the master

---

[1] In [15], authors claimed to proof IND-ID-CPA, but provide the proof for IND-CPA. In [27], authors assumed a universally known entity (**G** matrix; see Sect. 2.1) as a secret entity.

secret key and the secret key of user is sampled by the master secret key. We first trace the design of selective IBE, where the secret key of a user is also a trapdoor, by using the trapdoor delegation technique of [18]. Then extend the design to incorporate re-encryption feature based on the encryption scheme of [18]. Here, the secret key of a user is a tuple of trapdoor, where one is used for decryption and another one is used for re-encryption key (ReKey) generation. ReKey is generated as in [10,16] with a trick to resists proxy to get any information regarding the underlying message of the corresponding re-encrypted ciphertext. The underlying IBE of the proposed IB-uPRE may prove useful to design expressive cryptographic primitives other than IB-PRE as well.

2   Preliminaries

We denote the real numbers and the integers by $\mathbb{R}, \mathbb{Z}$, respectively. We denote column-vectors by lower-case bold letters (e.g. $\mathbf{b}$), so row-vectors are represented via transposition (e.g. $\mathbf{b}^t$). Matrices are denoted by upper-case bold letters and treat a matrix $\mathbf{X}$ interchangeably with its ordered set $\{\mathbf{x}_1, \mathbf{x}_2, \ldots\}$ of column vectors. We use $\mathbf{I}$ for the identity matrix and $\mathbf{0}$ for the zero matrix, where the dimension will be clear from context. We use $[*|*]$ to denote the concatenation of vectors or matrices. A negligible function, denoted generically by negl. We say that a probability is overwhelming if it is $1 - \mathsf{negl}$. The *statistical distance* between two distributions $\mathbf{X}$ and $\mathbf{Y}$ over a countable domain Ω defined as $\frac{1}{2} \sum_{w \in \Omega} |\Pr[\mathbf{X} = w] - \Pr[\mathbf{Y} = w]|$. We say that a distribution over Ω is ϵ-far if its statistical distance from the uniform distribution is at most ϵ. Throughout the paper, $r = \omega(\sqrt{\log n})$ represents a fixed function which will be approximated by $\sqrt{\ln(2n/\epsilon)/\pi}$.

2.1   Lattices

A *lattice* Λ is a discrete additive subgroup of $\mathbb{R}^m$. Specially, a lattice Λ in $\mathbb{R}^m$ with basis $\mathbf{B} = [\mathbf{b}_1, \cdots, \mathbf{b}_n] \in \mathbb{R}^{m \times n}$, where each $\mathbf{b}_i$ is written in column form, is defined as $\Lambda := \{\sum_{i=1}^n \mathbf{b}_i x_i | x_i \in \mathbb{Z}\ \forall i = 1, \ldots, n\} \subseteq \mathbb{R}^m$. We call n the rank of Λ and if $n = m$ we say that Λ is a full rank lattice. The dual lattice Λ^* is the set of all vectors $\mathbf{y} \in \mathbb{R}^m$ satisfying $\langle \mathbf{x}, \mathbf{y} \rangle \in \mathbb{Z}$ for all vectors $\mathbf{x} \in \Lambda$. If $\mathbf{B}$ is a basis of an arbitrary lattice Λ, then $\mathbf{B}^* = \mathbf{B}(\mathbf{B}^t\mathbf{B})^{-1}$ is a basis for Λ^*. For a full-rank lattice, $\mathbf{B}^* = \mathbf{B}^{-t}$.

In this paper, we mainly consider full rank lattices containing $q\mathbb{Z}^m$, called q-ary lattices, defined as the following, for a given matrix $\mathbf{A} \in \mathbb{Z}_q^{n \times m}$ and $\mathbf{u} \in \mathbb{Z}_q^n$: $\Lambda^\perp(\mathbf{A}) := \{\mathbf{z} \in \mathbb{Z}^m : \mathbf{A}\mathbf{z} = 0 \bmod q\}$; $\Lambda(\mathbf{A}^t) = \{\mathbf{z} \in \mathbb{Z}^m : \exists\, \mathbf{s} \in \mathbb{Z}_q^n\ s.t.\ \mathbf{z} = \mathbf{A}^t\mathbf{s}$ $\bmod\ q\}$; $\Lambda_{\mathbf{u}}^\perp(\mathbf{A}) := \{\mathbf{z} \in \mathbb{Z}^m : \mathbf{A}\mathbf{z} = \mathbf{u} \bmod q\} = \Lambda^\perp(\mathbf{A}) + \mathbf{x}$ for $\mathbf{x} \in \Lambda^\perp(\mathbf{A})$. Note that, $\Lambda^\perp(\mathbf{A})$ and $\Lambda(\mathbf{A}^t)$ are dual lattices, up to a q scaling factor: $q\Lambda^\perp(\mathbf{A})^* = \Lambda(\mathbf{A}^t)$, and vice-versa. Sometimes we consider the non-integral, 1-*ary* lattice $\frac{1}{q}\Lambda(\mathbf{A}^t) = \Lambda^\perp(\mathbf{A})^* \supseteq \mathbb{Z}^m$.

Gaussian on Lattices: Let $\Lambda \subseteq \mathbb{Z}^m$ be a lattice. For a vector $\mathbf{c} \in \mathbb{R}^m$ and a positive parameter $s \in \mathbb{R}$, define: $\rho_{\mathbf{c},s}(\mathbf{x}) = \exp\left(\pi \frac{\|\mathbf{x}-\mathbf{c}\|^2}{s^2}\right)$ and $\rho_{\mathbf{c},s}(\Lambda) =$

$\sum_{\mathbf{x}\in\Lambda}\rho_{\mathbf{c},s}(\mathbf{x})$. The discrete Gaussian distribution over Λ with center $\mathbf{c}$ and parameter σ is $\mathcal{D}_{\Lambda,\mathbf{c},s}(\mathbf{y}) = \frac{\rho_{\mathbf{c},s}(\mathbf{y})}{\rho_{\mathbf{c},s}(\Lambda)}, \forall \mathbf{y} \in \Lambda$.

Hard Problems on Lattices: There are two lattice-based one-way functions associated with matrix $\mathbf{A} \in \mathbb{Z}_q^{n\times m}$ for $m = poly(n)$:

- $g_{\mathbf{A}}(\mathbf{e},\mathbf{s}) = \mathbf{s}^t\mathbf{A} + \mathbf{e}^t \mod q$ for $\mathbf{s} \in \mathbb{Z}_q^n$ and a Gaussian $\mathbf{e} \in \mathbb{Z}^m$ and $f_{\mathbf{A}}(\mathbf{x}) = \mathbf{A}\mathbf{x} \mod q$, for $\mathbf{x} \in \mathbb{Z}^m$;
- The Learning With Errors (LWE) problem was introduced in [22]. The problem to invert $g_{\mathbf{A}}(\mathbf{e},\mathbf{s})$, where $\mathbf{e} \leftarrow \mathcal{D}_{\mathbb{Z}^m,\alpha q}$ is known as search-LWE$_{q,n,m,\alpha}$ problem and is as hard as quantumly solving Shortest Independent Vector Problem (SIVP) on n-dimensional lattices. The decisional- LWE$_{q,n,m,\alpha}$ problem asks to distinguish the output of $g_{\mathbf{A}}$ from uniform.
- The Small Integer Solution (SIS) problem was first suggested to be hard on average by Ajtai [2] and then formalized by Micciancio and Regev [20]. Finding a non-zero short preimage $\mathbf{x}'$ such that $f_{\mathbf{A}}(\mathbf{x}') = \mathbf{0}$, with $\|\mathbf{x}'\| \leq \beta$, is an instantiation of the SIS$_{q,n,m,\beta}$ problem. It is known to be as hard as certain worst-case problems (e.g. SIVP) in standard lattices [3,12,19,20].

Trapdoors for Lattices: Here, we briefly describe the main results of [18] and it's generalized version from [16]: the definition of **G**-trapdoor, the algorithms **Invert**$^{\mathcal{O}}$, **Sample**$^{\mathcal{O}}$ and **DelTrap**$^{\mathcal{O}}$.

A **G**-trapdoor is a transformation (represented by a matrix $\mathbf{R}$) from a public matrix $\mathbf{A}$ to a special matrix $\mathbf{G}$ which is called as gadget matrix. The formal definitions as follows:

Definition 1 ([18]). *Let* $\mathbf{A} \in \mathbb{Z}_q^{n\times m}$ *and* $\mathbf{G} \in \mathbb{Z}_q^{n\times w}$ *be matrices with* $m \geq w \geq n$. *A* $\mathbf{G}$-*trapdoor for* $\mathbf{A}$ *is a matrix* $\mathbf{R} \in \mathbb{Z}^{(m-w)\times w}$ *such that* $\mathbf{A}\begin{bmatrix}\mathbf{R}\\\mathbf{I}\end{bmatrix} = \mathbf{H}\mathbf{G}$, *for some invertible matrix* $\mathbf{H} \in \mathbb{Z}_q^{n\times n}$. *We refer to* $\mathbf{H}$ *as the tag of the trapdoor.*

Definition 2 ([16]). *The generalized version of a* $\mathbf{G}$-*trapdoor* : *Let* $\mathbf{A} = \begin{bmatrix}\mathbf{A}_0|\mathbf{A}_1|\cdots|\mathbf{A}_{k-1}\end{bmatrix} \in \mathbb{Z}_q^{n\times m}$ *for* $k \geq 2$, *and* $\mathbf{A}_0 \in \mathbb{Z}_q^{n\times\bar{m}}, \mathbf{A}_1,\ldots,\mathbf{A}_{k-1} \in \mathbb{Z}_q^{n\times w}$ *with* $\bar{m} \geq w \geq n$ *and* $m = \bar{m} + (k-1)\cdot w$ *(typically,* $w = n\lceil\log q\rceil$). *A* $\mathbf{G}$-*trapdoor for* $\mathbf{A}$ *is a sequence of matrices* $\mathbf{R} = \begin{bmatrix}\mathbf{R}_1|\mathbf{R}_2|\cdots|\mathbf{R}_{k-1}\end{bmatrix} \in \mathbb{Z}_q^{\bar{m}\times(k-1)w}$ *such that* :

$$\begin{bmatrix}\mathbf{A}_0|\mathbf{A}_1|\cdots|\mathbf{A}_{k-1}\end{bmatrix}\begin{bmatrix}\mathbf{R}_1 & \mathbf{R}_2 & \cdots & \mathbf{R}_{k-1}\\ \mathbf{I} & 0 & \cdots & 0\\ \vdots & \vdots & \ddots & \vdots\\ 0 & 0 & \cdots & \mathbf{I}\end{bmatrix} = \begin{bmatrix}\mathbf{H}_1\mathbf{G}|\mathbf{H}_2\mathbf{G}|\cdots|\mathbf{H}_{k-1}\mathbf{G}\end{bmatrix},$$

for invertible matrices $\mathbf{H}_i \in \mathbb{Z}_q^{n\times n}$ *and a fixed* $\mathbf{G} \in \mathbb{Z}_q^{n\times w}$.

Invert$^{\mathcal{O}}(\mathbf{R},\mathbf{A},\mathbf{b},\mathbf{H}_i)$ [16]: On input a vector $\mathbf{b}^t = \mathbf{s}^t\mathbf{A} + \mathbf{e}^t$, a matrix $\mathbf{A} = \begin{bmatrix}\mathbf{A}_0|-\mathbf{A}_0\mathbf{R}_1 + \mathbf{H}_1\mathbf{G}|\cdots|-\mathbf{A}_0\mathbf{R}_{k-1} + \mathbf{H}_{k-1}\mathbf{G}\end{bmatrix}$ and corresponding **G**- trapdoor $\mathbf{R} = \begin{bmatrix}\mathbf{R}_1|\mathbf{R}_2|\cdots|\mathbf{R}_{k-1}\end{bmatrix}$ with invertible tag $\mathbf{H}_i$, the algorithm computes

$$b'^t = b^t \begin{bmatrix} R_1 & R_2 & \cdots & R_{k-1} \\ I & 0 & \cdots & 0 \\ \vdots & \vdots & \ddots & \vdots \\ 0 & 0 & \cdots & I \end{bmatrix}$$

and then run the inverting oracle $\mathcal{O}(b')$ for G to get (s', e'). The algorithm outputs $s = H_i^{-1} s'$ and $e = b - A^t s$. Note that, $\textbf{Invert}^{\mathcal{O}}$ produces correct output if $e \in \mathcal{P}_{1/2}(q \cdot B^{-t})$, where B is a basis of $\Lambda^\perp(G)$; cf. [18, Theorem 5.4].

$\textbf{Sample}^{\mathcal{O}}(R, A, H, u, s)$ [18]: On input (R, A', H, u, s), the algorithm construct $A = [A' | -A'R + HG]$, where R is the G-trapdoor for matrix A with invertible tag H and $u \in \mathbb{Z}_q^n$. The algorithm outputs, using an oracle $\mathcal{O}$ for Gaussian sampling over a desired coset $\Lambda_v^\perp(G)$, a vector drawn from a distribution within negligible statistical distance of $D_{\Lambda_u^\perp(A), s}$. To sample a Gaussian vector $x \in \mathbb{Z}_q^m$ for $A = [A_0 | A_1 | \cdots | A_{k-1}] \in \mathbb{Z}_q^{n \times m}$ with the generalized trapdoor $R = [R_1 | R_2 | \cdots | R_{k-1}]$ and $k-1$ invertible H_i's given a coset $u \in \mathbb{Z}_q^n$, use generalized version of $\textbf{Sample}^{\mathcal{O}}$ from [16].

$\textbf{DelTrap}^{\mathcal{O}}(A' = [A | A_1], R, H', s)$[18]: On input an oracle $\mathcal{O}$ for discrete Gaussian sampling over cosets of $\Lambda = \Lambda^\perp(A)$ with parameter s, an extended matrix A' of A, an invertible matrix H', the algorithm will sample (using $\mathcal{O}$) each column of R' independently from a discrete Gaussian with parameter s over the appropriate coset of $\Lambda^\perp(A)$, so that $AR' = H'G - A_1$. The algorithm outputs a trapdoor R' for A' with tag H'.

2.2 Identity-Based Unidirectional Proxy Re-Encryption

Definition 3 (Identity-Based Unidirectional Proxy ReEncryption (IB-uPRE) [13]). *A unidirectional Identity-Based Proxy Re-Encryption (IB-uPRE) scheme is a tuple of algorithms* (**SetUp, Extract, ReKeyGen, Enc, ReEnc, Dec**) :

- $(PP, msk) \longleftarrow$ **SetUp**(1^n) : *On input the security parameter* 1^n, *the* **setup** *algorithm outputs* PP, msk.
- $sk_{id} \longleftarrow$ **Extract**(PP, msk, id) : *On input an identity id, public parameter* PP, *master secret key, output the secret key* sk_{id} *for id.*
- $rk_{i \to j} \longleftarrow$ **ReKeyGen**$(PP, sk_{id_i}, id_i, id_j)$: *On input a public parameter* PP, *secret key* sk_{id_i} *of a delegator i, and* id_i, id_j, *output a unidirectional re-encryption key* $rk_{i \to j}$.
- $ct \longleftarrow$ **Enc**(PP, id, m) : *On input an identity id, public parameter* PP *and a plaintext* $m \in \mathcal{M}$, *output a ciphertext ct under the specified identity id.*
- $ct' \longleftarrow$ **ReEnc**$(PP, rk_{i \to j}, ct)$: *On input a ciphertext ct under the identity i and a re-encryption key* $rk_{i \to j}$, *output a ciphertext ct' under the identity j.*

- $m \longleftarrow \mathbf{Dec}(PP, sk_{id_i}, ct)$: On input the ciphertext ct under the identity i and secret key sk_{id_i} of i, the algorithm outputs a plaintext m or the error symbol $\perp$.

An Identity-Based Proxy Re-Encryption scheme is called single-hop if a ciphertext can be re-encrypted only once. In a multi-hop setting proxy can apply further re-encryptions to already re-encrypted ciphertext.

Definition 4 (Single-hop IB-uPRE Correctness). *A single-hop* IB-uPRE *scheme* (SetUp, Extract, ReKeyGen, Enc, ReEnc, Dec) *decrypts correctly for the plaintext space* $\mathcal{M}$ *if*:

- *For all* sk_{id}, *output by* **Extract** *under id and for all* $m \in \mathcal{M}$, *it holds that* $\mathbf{Dec}(PP, sk_{id}, \mathbf{Enc}(PP, id, m)) = m$.
- *For any re-encryption key* $rk_{i \to j}$, *output by* **ReKeyGen**$(PP, sk_{id_i}, id_i, id_j)$ *and any* $ct = \mathbf{Enc}(PP, id_i, m)$, *it holds that* $\mathbf{Dec}(PP, sk_{id_j}, \mathbf{ReEnc}(PP, rk_{i \to j}, ct)) = m$.

Security Game of Unidirectional Selective Identity-Based Proxy Re-Encryption Scheme against Chosen Plaintext Attack (IND-sID-CPA): To describe the security model we first classify all of the users into honest (HU) and corrupted (CU). In the honest case an adversary does not know secret key, whereas for a corrupted user the adversary has secret key. Let $\mathcal{A}$ be the PPT adversary and $\Pi = $ (SetUp, Extract, ReKeyGen, Enc, ReEnc, Dec) be an IB-uPRE scheme with a plaintext space $\mathcal{M}$ and a ciphertext space $\mathcal{C}$. Let $id^*(\in HU)$ be the target user. Security game is defined according to the following game $\mathsf{Exp}_{\mathcal{A}}^{\mathsf{IND\text{-}sID\text{-}CPA}}(1^n)$:

1. **SetUp:** The challenger runs **SetUp**(1^n) to get (PP, msk) and give PP to $\mathcal{A}$.
2. **Phase 1:** The adversary $\mathcal{A}$ may make queries polynomially many times in any order to the following oracles:
   - $\mathcal{O}^{\mathbf{Extract}}$: an oracle that on input $id \in CU$, output sk_{id}; Otherwise, output $\perp$.
   - $\mathcal{O}^{\mathbf{ReKeyGen}}$: an oracle that on input the identities of i-th and j-th users: if $id_i \in HU \setminus \{id^*\}$, $id_j \in HU$ or $id_i, id_j \in CU$ or $id_i \in CU, id_j \in HU$, output $rk_{i \to j}$; otherwise, output $\perp$.
   - $\mathcal{O}^{\mathbf{ReEnc}}$: an oracle that on input the identities of i, j-th users, ciphertext of i-th user: if $id_i \in HU \setminus \{id^*\}$, $id_j \in HU$ or $id_i, id_j \in CU$ or $id_i \in CU, id_j \in HU$, output re-encrypted ciphertext; otherwise, output $\perp$.
3. **Challenge:** $\mathcal{A}$ outputs two messages $m_0, m_1 \in \mathcal{M}$ and is given a challenge ciphertext $ct_b \longleftarrow \mathbf{Enc}(PP, id^*, m_b)$ for either $b = 0$ or $b = 1$.
4. **Phase 2:** After receiving the challenge ciphertext, $\mathcal{A}$ continues to have access to the $\mathcal{O}^{\mathbf{Extract}}$, $\mathcal{O}^{\mathbf{ReKeyGen}}$ and $\mathcal{O}^{\mathbf{ReEnc}}$ oracle as in **Phase 1**.
5. $\mathcal{O}^{\mathbf{Decision}}$: On input b' from $\mathcal{A}$, this oracle outputs 1 if $b = b'$ and 0 otherwise.

The advantage of an adversary in the above experiment $\mathsf{Exp}_{\mathcal{A}}^{\mathsf{IND\text{-}sID\text{-}CPA}}(1^n)$ is defined as $|\mathrm{Pr}[b' = b] - \frac{1}{2}|$.

Definition 5. *An* IB-uPRE *scheme is* IND-sID-CPA *secure if all PPT adversaries* $\mathcal{A}$ *have at most a negligible advantage in experiment* $\mathsf{Exp}_{\mathcal{A}}^{\mathsf{IND\text{-}sID\text{-}CPA}}(1^n)$.

Remark 1. In [13], **ReKeyGen** query is allowed from id^* to HU to make the IB-uPRE collusion resilient (coalition of malicious proxy and delegetee to compute delegator's secret key). Here, we have blocked **ReKeyGen** query from id^* to HU and the proposed IB-uPRE scheme is not claimed to be collusion resilient.

3 Single-Hop Identity-Based Unidirectional Proxy Re-Encryption Scheme (IB-uPRE)

3.1 Construction of Single-Hop IB-uPRE

In this section, we present our construction of single-hop IB-uPRE. We set the parameters as the following.

- $\mathbf{G} \in \mathbb{Z}_q^{n \times nk}$ is a gadget matrix for large enough prime power $q = p^e = poly(n)$ and $k = O(\log q) = O(\log n)$, so there are efficient algorithms to invert $g_{\mathbf{G}}$ and to sample for $f_{\mathbf{G}}$
- $\bar{m} = O(nk)$ and the Gaussian $\mathcal{D} = D_{\mathbb{Z},r}^{\bar{m} \times nk}$, so that $(\bar{\mathbf{A}}, \bar{\mathbf{A}}\mathbf{R})$ is negl(n)-far from uniform for $\bar{\mathbf{A}}$
- the LWE error rate α for IB-uPRE should satisfy $1/\alpha = O(nk)^3 \cdot r^3$

To start out, we first recall encoding techniques from [1,18].

- **Message Encoding:** In the proposed construction, message space is $\mathcal{M} = \{0,1\}^{nk}$. $\mathcal{M}$ map bijectively to the cosets of $\Lambda/2\Lambda$ for $\Lambda = \Lambda(\mathbf{G}^t)$ by some function *encode* that is efficient to evaluate and invert. In particular, letting $\mathbf{E} \in \mathbb{Z}^{nk \times nk}$ be any basis of Λ, we can map $\mathbf{m} \in \{0,1\}^{nk}$ to $encode(\mathbf{m}) = \mathbf{Em} \in \mathbb{Z}^{nk}$ [18].
- **Encoding of Identity:** In the following construction, we use *full-rank difference* map (FRD) as in [1]. FRD: $\mathbb{Z}_q^n \to \mathbb{Z}_q^{n \times n}$; $id \mapsto \mathbf{H}_{id}$. We assume identities are non-zero elements in $\mathbb{Z}_q^n$. The set of identities can be expanded to $\{0,1\}^*$ by hashing identities into $\mathbb{Z}_q^n$ using a collision resistant hash. FRD satisfies the following properties: 1. $\forall$ *distinct* $id_1, id_2 \in \mathbb{Z}_q^n$, the matrix $\mathbf{H}_{id_1} - \mathbf{H}_{id_2} \in \mathbb{Z}_q^{n \times n}$ is full rank; 2. $\forall$ $id \in \mathbb{Z}_q^n \setminus \{\mathbf{0}\}$, the matrix $\mathbf{H}_{id} \in \mathbb{Z}_q^{n \times n}$ is full rank; 3. FRD is computable in polynomial time (in $n \log q$).

The proposed IB-uPRE consists of the following algorithms:

SetUp(1^n) : On input a security parameter n, do:

1. Choose $\bar{\mathbf{A}} \leftarrow \mathbb{Z}_q^{n \times \bar{m}}$, $\mathbf{R} \leftarrow \mathcal{D}$, and set $\bar{\mathbf{A}}' = -\bar{\mathbf{A}}\mathbf{R} \in \mathbb{Z}_q^{n \times nk}$.
2. Choose four invertible matrices $\mathbf{H}_1, \mathbf{H}_2, \mathbf{H}_3, \mathbf{H}_4$ uniformly random from $\mathbb{Z}_q^{n \times n}$.
3. Choose two random matrices $\mathbf{A}_1, \mathbf{A}_2$ from $\mathbb{Z}_q^{n \times nk}$.
4. Output $PP = (\bar{\mathbf{A}}, \bar{\mathbf{A}}', \mathbf{A}_1, \mathbf{A}_2, \mathbf{H}_1, \mathbf{H}_2, \mathbf{H}_3, \mathbf{H}_4, \mathbf{G})$ and the master secret key is $msk = \mathbf{R}$.

Extract(PP, msk, id) : On input a public parameter PP, master secret key msk and the identity of i-th user id_i, do:

1. Construct $\tilde{\mathbf{A}}_i = [\bar{\mathbf{A}}|\bar{\mathbf{A}}'+\mathbf{H}_{id_i}\mathbf{G}] = [\bar{\mathbf{A}}|-\bar{\mathbf{A}}\mathbf{R}+\mathbf{H}_{id_i}\mathbf{G}] \in \mathbb{Z}_q^{n\times m}$, where $m = \bar{m} + nk$. So, $\mathbf{R}$ is a trapdoor of $\tilde{\mathbf{A}}_i$ with tag $\mathbf{H}_{id_i}$.
2. – Construct $\mathbf{A}_{i1} = \mathbf{A}_1 + \mathbf{H}_3\mathbf{H}_{id_i}\mathbf{G} \in \mathbb{Z}_q^{n\times nk}$ and set $\mathbf{A}'_{i1} = [\tilde{\mathbf{A}}_i|\mathbf{A}_{i1}] \in \mathbb{Z}_q^{n\times(m+nk)}$.
   – Call the algorithm $\mathbf{DelTrap}^{\mathcal{O}}(\mathbf{A}'_{i1}, \mathbf{R}, \mathbf{H}_1, s)$ to get a trapdoor $\mathbf{R}_{i1} \in \mathbb{Z}^{m\times nk}$ for $\mathbf{A}'_{i1}$ with tag $\mathbf{H}_1 \in \mathbb{Z}_q^{n\times n}$, where $s \geq \eta_\epsilon(\Lambda^\perp(\tilde{\mathbf{A}}_i))$, so that $\tilde{\mathbf{A}}_i\mathbf{R}_{i1} = \mathbf{H}_1\mathbf{G} - \mathbf{A}_{i1}$.
3. – Construct $\mathbf{A}_{i2} = \mathbf{A}_2 + \mathbf{H}_4\mathbf{H}_{id_i}\mathbf{G} \in \mathbb{Z}_q^{n\times nk}$ and set $\mathbf{A}'_{i2} = [\tilde{\mathbf{A}}_i|\mathbf{A}_{i2}] \in \mathbb{Z}_q^{n\times(m+nk)}$.
   – Call the algorithm $\mathbf{DelTrap}^{\mathcal{O}}(\mathbf{A}'_{i2}, \mathbf{R}, \mathbf{H}_2, s)$ to get a trapdoor $\mathbf{R}_{i2} \in \mathbb{Z}^{m\times nk}$ for $\mathbf{A}'_{i2}$ with tag $\mathbf{H}_2 \in \mathbb{Z}_q^{n\times n}$, so that $\tilde{\mathbf{A}}_i\mathbf{R}_{i2} = \mathbf{H}_2\mathbf{G} - \mathbf{A}_{i2}$.
   Output the secret key as $sk_{id_i} = [\mathbf{R}_{i1}|\mathbf{R}_{i2}] \in \mathbb{Z}^{m\times 2nk}$. Notice that,

$$[\tilde{\mathbf{A}}_i|\mathbf{A}_{i1}|\mathbf{A}_{i2}]\begin{bmatrix}\mathbf{R}_{i1} & \mathbf{R}_{i2}\\ \mathbf{I} & \mathbf{0}\\ \mathbf{0} & \mathbf{I}\end{bmatrix} = [\mathbf{H}_1\mathbf{G}|\mathbf{H}_2\mathbf{G}].$$

Enc$(PP, id_i, \mathbf{m} \in \{0,1\}^{nk})$: On input a public parameter PP, the identity of i-th user id_i and message $\mathbf{m} \in \{0,1\}^{nk}$, do:

1. Construct $\tilde{\mathbf{A}}_i = [\bar{\mathbf{A}}|-\bar{\mathbf{A}}\mathbf{R}+\mathbf{H}_{id_i}\mathbf{G}] \in \mathbb{Z}_q^{n\times m}$.
2. Construct $\mathbf{A}_{i1}, \mathbf{A}_{i2}$ for id_i same as in **Extract** algorithm and set $\mathbf{A}_i = [\tilde{\mathbf{A}}_i|\mathbf{A}_{i1}|\mathbf{A}_{i2}]$.
3. Choose a uniformly random $\mathbf{s} \leftarrow \mathbb{Z}_q^n$.
4. Sample error vectors $\bar{\mathbf{e}}_0 \leftarrow D_{\mathbb{Z},\alpha q}^{\bar{m}}$ and $\mathbf{e}'_0, \mathbf{e}_1, \mathbf{e}_2 \leftarrow D_{\mathbb{Z},s'}^{nk}$, where $s'^2 = (\|\bar{\mathbf{e}}_0\|^2 + \bar{m}(\alpha q)^2)r^2$. Let the error vector $\mathbf{e} = (\mathbf{e}_0, \mathbf{e}_1, \mathbf{e}_2) \in \mathbb{Z}^{\bar{m}+nk} \times \mathbb{Z}^{nk} \times \mathbb{Z}^{nk}$, where $\mathbf{e}_0 = (\bar{\mathbf{e}}_0, \mathbf{e}'_0) \in \mathbb{Z}^{\bar{m}} \times \mathbb{Z}^{nk}$.
5. Compute $\mathbf{b}^t = (\mathbf{b}_0, \mathbf{b}_1, \mathbf{b}_2) = 2(\mathbf{s}^t\mathbf{A}_i \mod q) + \mathbf{e}^t + (\mathbf{0}, \mathbf{0}, encode(\mathbf{m})^t)$ $\mod 2q$, where the first zero vector has dimension $\bar{m} + nk$, the second has dimension nk and $\mathbf{b}_0 = (\bar{\mathbf{b}}_0, \mathbf{b}'_0)$.
6. Output the ciphertext $ct = \mathbf{b} \in \mathbb{Z}_{2q}^{\bar{m}+3nk}$.

Dec(PP, sk_{id_i}, ct) : On input a public parameter PP, the secret key of i-th user sk_{id_i} and ciphertext ct, do:

1. If ct has invalid form or $\mathbf{H}_{id_i} = \mathbf{0}$, output $\perp$. Otherwise,
   – Construct $\tilde{\mathbf{A}}_i = [\bar{\mathbf{A}}|-\bar{\mathbf{A}}\mathbf{R}+\mathbf{H}_{id_i}\mathbf{G}] \in \mathbb{Z}_q^{n\times m}$.
   – Construct $\mathbf{A}_{i1}, \mathbf{A}_{i2}$ for id_i same as in **Extract** algorithm and set $\mathbf{A}_i = [\tilde{\mathbf{A}}_i|\mathbf{A}_{i1}|\mathbf{A}_{i2}]$.
2. Call **Invert**$^{\mathcal{O}}([\mathbf{R}_{i1}|\mathbf{R}_{i2}], \mathbf{A}_i, \mathbf{b}, \mathbf{H}_2)$ to get $\mathbf{z} \in \mathbb{Z}_q^n$ and $\mathbf{e} = (\mathbf{e}_0, \mathbf{e}_1, \mathbf{e}_2) \in \mathbb{Z}^{\bar{m}+nk} \times \mathbb{Z}^{nk} \times \mathbb{Z}^{nk}$, where $\mathbf{e}_0 = (\bar{\mathbf{e}}_0, \mathbf{e}'_0) \in \mathbb{Z}^{\bar{m}} \times \mathbb{Z}^{nk}$ for which $\mathbf{b}^t = \mathbf{z}^t\mathbf{A}_i + \mathbf{e}^t$ $\mod q$. If the call to **Invert** fails for any reason, output $\perp$.

3. If $\|\bar{\mathbf{e}}_0\| \geq \alpha q \sqrt{\bar{m}}$ or $\|\mathbf{e}_0'\| \geq \alpha q \sqrt{2\bar{m}nk} \cdot r$ or $\|\mathbf{e}_j\| \geq \alpha q \sqrt{2\bar{m}nk} \cdot r$ for $j = 1, 2$, output $\perp$.

4. Let $\mathbf{V} = \mathbf{b} - \mathbf{e} \mod 2q$, parsed as $\mathbf{V} = (\mathbf{V}_0, \mathbf{V}_1, \mathbf{V}_2) \in \mathbb{Z}_{2q}^{\bar{m}+nk} \times \mathbb{Z}_{2q}^{nk} \times \mathbb{Z}_{2q}^{nk}$, where $\mathbf{V}_0 = (\overline{\mathbf{V}}_0, \mathbf{V}_0') \in \mathbb{Z}_{2q}^{\bar{m}} \times \mathbb{Z}_{2q}^{nk}$. If $\overline{\mathbf{V}}_0 \notin 2\Lambda(\bar{\mathbf{A}}^t)$, output $\perp$.

5. Output $encode^{-1}(\mathbf{V}^t \begin{bmatrix} \mathbf{R}_{i1} & \mathbf{R}_{i2} \\ \mathbf{I} & \mathbf{0} \\ \mathbf{0} & \mathbf{I} \end{bmatrix} \mod 2q) \in \{0,1\}^{nk}$ if it exists, otherwise output $\perp$.

ReKeyGen$(PP, sk_{id_i}, id_i, id_j)$: On input a public parameter PP, the secret key of i-th user sk_{id_i} and identity of j-th user id_j, do:

1. Construct $\mathbf{A}_i = \begin{bmatrix} \tilde{\mathbf{A}}_i | \mathbf{A}_{i1} | \mathbf{A}_{i2} \end{bmatrix}$, where $\tilde{\mathbf{A}}_i = \begin{bmatrix} \bar{\mathbf{A}} | \bar{\mathbf{A}}' + \mathbf{H}_{id_i} \mathbf{G} \end{bmatrix}$ and $\mathbf{A}_{i1}, \mathbf{A}_{i2}$ are same as in **Extract** algorithm .

2. Construct $\mathbf{A}_j = \begin{bmatrix} \tilde{\mathbf{A}}_j | \mathbf{A}_{j1} | \mathbf{A}_{j2} \end{bmatrix}$, where $\tilde{\mathbf{A}}_j = \begin{bmatrix} \bar{\mathbf{A}} | \bar{\mathbf{A}}' + \mathbf{H}_{id_j} \mathbf{G} \end{bmatrix}$ and $\mathbf{A}_{j1}, \mathbf{A}_{j2}$ are same as in **Extract** algorithm .

3. Using **Sample**$^{\mathcal{O}}$ with trapdoor $\mathbf{R}_{i1}$(from the secret key of ith user), with tag $\mathbf{H}_1$, we sample from the cosets which are formed with the column of the matrix $\bar{\mathbf{A}}' + \mathbf{H}_{id_j} \mathbf{G}$. After sampling nk times we get an $(\bar{m} + 2nk) \times nk$ matrix and parse it as three matrices $\mathbf{X}_{00} \in \mathbb{Z}^{\bar{m} \times nk}$, $\mathbf{X}_{10} \in \mathbb{Z}^{nk \times nk}$ and $\mathbf{X}_{20} \in \mathbb{Z}^{nk \times nk}$ matrices with Gaussian entries of parameter s. So,

$$\begin{bmatrix} \tilde{\mathbf{A}}_i | -\tilde{\mathbf{A}}_i \mathbf{R}_{i1} + \mathbf{H}_1 \mathbf{G} \end{bmatrix} \begin{bmatrix} \mathbf{X}_{00} \\ \mathbf{X}_{10} \\ \mathbf{X}_{20} \end{bmatrix} = \bar{\mathbf{A}}' + \mathbf{H}_{id_j} \mathbf{G}, \quad i.e. \begin{bmatrix} \tilde{\mathbf{A}}_i | \mathbf{A}_{i1} \end{bmatrix} \begin{bmatrix} \mathbf{X}_{00} \\ \mathbf{X}_{10} \\ \mathbf{X}_{20} \end{bmatrix} = \bar{\mathbf{A}}' + \mathbf{H}_{id_j} \mathbf{G}.$$

4. Continue sampling for the cosets obtained from the columns of the matrix $\mathbf{A}_{j1}$ from $\mathbf{A}_j$. This time, we increase the Gaussian parameter of the resulting sampled matrix up to $s\sqrt{\bar{m}/2}$: $\begin{bmatrix} \tilde{\mathbf{A}}_i | -\tilde{\mathbf{A}}_i \mathbf{R}_{i1} + \mathbf{H}_1 \mathbf{G} \end{bmatrix} \begin{bmatrix} \mathbf{X}_{01} \\ \mathbf{X}_{11} \\ \mathbf{X}_{21} \end{bmatrix} = \mathbf{A}_{j1}, \quad i.e. \begin{bmatrix} \tilde{\mathbf{A}}_i | \mathbf{A}_{i1} \end{bmatrix} \begin{bmatrix} \mathbf{X}_{01} \\ \mathbf{X}_{11} \\ \mathbf{X}_{21} \end{bmatrix} = \mathbf{A}_{j1}.$

For the last sampling, to get a correct re-encryption, we will use the cosets which are formed with the column of the matrix $\mathbf{A}_{j2} + \tilde{\mathbf{A}}_i \mathbf{R}_{i2} - \mathbf{H}_2 \mathbf{G}$:

$$\begin{bmatrix} \tilde{\mathbf{A}}_i | -\tilde{\mathbf{A}}_i \mathbf{R}_{i1} + \mathbf{H}_1 \mathbf{G} \end{bmatrix} \begin{bmatrix} \mathbf{X}_{02} \\ \mathbf{X}_{12} \\ \mathbf{X}_{22} \end{bmatrix} = \mathbf{A}_{j2} + \tilde{\mathbf{A}}_i \mathbf{R}_{i2} - \mathbf{H}_2 \mathbf{G}, \text{ where } \mathbf{X}_{01}, \mathbf{X}_{02} \in$$

$\mathbb{Z}^{\bar{m} \times nk}$, $\mathbf{X}_{11}, \mathbf{X}_{12}, \mathbf{X}_{21}, \mathbf{X}_{22} \in \mathbb{Z}^{nk \times nk}$ with entries distributed as Gaussian with parameter $s\sqrt{\bar{m}}$.

5. Output re-encryption key $rk_{i \to j} = \begin{bmatrix} \mathbf{I} & \mathbf{X}_{00} & \mathbf{X}_{01} & \mathbf{X}_{02} \\ \mathbf{0} & \mathbf{X}_{10} & \mathbf{X}_{11} & \mathbf{X}_{12} \\ \mathbf{0} & \mathbf{X}_{20} & \mathbf{X}_{21} & \mathbf{X}_{22} \\ \mathbf{0} & \mathbf{0} & \mathbf{0} & \mathbf{I} \end{bmatrix} \in \mathbb{Z}^{(m+2nk) \times (m+2nk)},$

which satisfies: $\mathbf{A}_i \cdot rk_{i \to j} = \mathbf{A}_j$.

ReEnc$(rk_{i \to j}, ct)$: On input $rk_{i \to j}$ and i-th user's ciphertext ct, Compute:
$\mathbf{b}'^t = \mathbf{b}^t \cdot rk_{i \to j} = 2\mathbf{s}^t \left[\tilde{\mathbf{A}}_j | \mathbf{A}_{j1} | \mathbf{A}_{j2} \right] + \tilde{\mathbf{e}}^t + (\mathbf{0}, \mathbf{0}, encode(\mathbf{m})^t)$, where $\tilde{\mathbf{e}} = (\tilde{\mathbf{e}}_0, \tilde{\mathbf{e}}_1, \tilde{\mathbf{e}}_2)$, $\tilde{\mathbf{e}}_0 = (\tilde{\bar{\mathbf{e}}}_0, \tilde{\mathbf{e}}'_0)$ and $\tilde{\bar{\mathbf{e}}}_0 = \bar{\mathbf{e}}_0$, $\tilde{\mathbf{e}}'_0 = \bar{\mathbf{e}}_0 \mathbf{X}_{00} + \mathbf{e}'_0 \mathbf{X}_{10} + \mathbf{e}_1 \mathbf{X}_{20}$, $\tilde{\mathbf{e}}_1 = \bar{\mathbf{e}}_0 \mathbf{X}_{01} + \mathbf{e}'_0 \mathbf{X}_{11} + \mathbf{e}_1 \mathbf{X}_{21}$, $\tilde{\mathbf{e}}_2 = \bar{\mathbf{e}}_0 \mathbf{X}_{02} + \mathbf{e}'_0 \mathbf{X}_{12} + \mathbf{e}_1 \mathbf{X}_{22} + \mathbf{e}_2$.
Then output $ct' = \mathbf{b}'$.

3.2 Correctness and Security

In this section, we analyze the correctness and security of the proposed scheme.

Theorem 1 (Correctness). *The* IB-uPRE *scheme with parameters proposed in Section 3.1 is correct.*

Proof. To show that the decryption algorithm outputs a correct plaintext, it is required to consider both original and re-encrypted ciphertext. The arguments for the original ciphertext follows from the Lemma 6.2 of [18]. For re-encrypted ciphertext, the main point is to consider the growth of error due to re-encryption. Argument for the controlled growth of error of re-encrypted ciphertext follows, with some modifications, from Lemma 15 of [16]. Details proof is omitted due to space constrained.

Theorem 2 (Security). *The above scheme is* IND-sID-CPA *secure assuming the hardness of decision-*LWE$_{q,\alpha'}$ *for* $\alpha' = \alpha/3 \geq 2\sqrt{n}/q$.

Proof. First, using the same technique in [18], we transform the samples from LWE distribution to what we will need below. Given access to an LWE distribution $\mathbf{A}_{s,\alpha'}$ over $\mathbb{Z}_q^n \times \mathbb{T}$, (where$\mathbb{T} = \mathbb{R}/\mathbb{Z}$) for any $\mathbf{s} \in \mathbb{Z}_q^n$, we can transform its samples $(\mathbf{a}, b = \langle \mathbf{s}, \mathbf{a} \rangle / q + e \mod 1)$ to have the form $(\mathbf{a}, 2(\langle \mathbf{s}, \mathbf{a} \rangle \mod q) + e' \mod 2q)$ for $e' \leftarrow D_{\mathbb{Z},\alpha q}$, by mapping $b \mapsto 2qb + D_{\mathbb{Z}-2qb,s} \mod 2q$, where $s^2 = (\alpha q)^2 - (2\alpha' q)^2 \geq 4n \geq \eta_\epsilon(\mathbb{Z})^2$, η_ϵ is smoothing parameter [18,20]. This transformation maps the uniform distribution over $\mathbb{Z}_q^n \times \mathbb{T}$ to the uniform distribution $\mathbb{Z}_q^n \times \mathbb{Z}_{2q}$. Once the LWE samples are of the desired form, we construct column-wise matrix $\mathbf{A}^*$ from these samples $\mathbf{a}$ and a vector $\mathbf{b}^*$ from the corresponding b. Let id_{i^*} be the target user. The proof follows by sequence of games.

Game 0: This is the original IND-sID-CPA game from definition between an attacker $\mathcal{A}$ against scheme and an IND-sID-CPA challenger.

Game 1: In **Game1**, we change the way that the challenger generates $\bar{\mathbf{A}}, \bar{\mathbf{A}}', \mathbf{A}_1$, $\mathbf{A}_2$ in the public parameters. In **SetUp** phase, do as follows:

- Set the public parameter $\bar{\mathbf{A}} = \mathbf{A}^*$, where $\mathbf{A}^*$ is from LWE instance $(\mathbf{A}^*, \mathbf{b}^*)$ and set $\bar{\mathbf{A}}' = -\mathbf{A}^* \mathbf{R} - H_{id_{i^*}} \mathbf{G}$, where $\mathbf{R}$ is chosen according to **Game 0**.
- Choose four invertible matrices $\mathbf{H}_1, \mathbf{H}_2, \mathbf{H}_3, \mathbf{H}_4$ uniformly random from $\mathbb{Z}_q^{n \times n}$.
- Choose $\mathbf{R}_{i^*1}, \mathbf{R}_{i^*2} \leftarrow \mathcal{D} = D_{\mathbb{Z},r}^{m \times nk}$; Set $\mathbf{A}'_1 = -\left[\mathbf{A}^* | -\mathbf{A}^* \mathbf{R} \right] \cdot \mathbf{R}_{i^*1}$ and $\mathbf{A}'_2 = -\left[\mathbf{A}^* | -\mathbf{A}^* \mathbf{R} \right] \cdot \mathbf{R}_{i^*2}$; Construct $\mathbf{A}_1 = \mathbf{A}'_1 - \mathbf{H}_3 H_{id_{i^*}} \mathbf{G}$ and $\mathbf{A}_2 = \mathbf{A}'_2 - \mathbf{H}_4 H_{id_{i^*}} \mathbf{G}$.
- Set $PP = (\bar{\mathbf{A}}, \bar{\mathbf{A}}', \mathbf{A}_1, \mathbf{A}_2, \mathbf{H}_1, \mathbf{H}_2, \mathbf{H}_3, \mathbf{H}_4, \mathbf{G})$ and send it to $\mathcal{A}$.

To answer secret key query against $id_i \in CU$, challenger will construct $\tilde{\mathbf{A}}_i = [\mathbf{A}^* | -\mathbf{A}^*\mathbf{R} - \mathbf{H}_{id_i}\mathbf{G} + \mathbf{H}_{id_i}\mathbf{G}] = [\mathbf{A}^* | -\mathbf{A}^*\mathbf{R} + (\mathbf{H}_{id_i} - \mathbf{H}_{id_{i*}})\mathbf{G}]$. So, $\mathbf{R}$ is a trapdoor of $\tilde{\mathbf{A}}_i$ with invertible tag $(\mathbf{H}_{id_i} - \mathbf{H}_{id_{i*}})$. Then using **Extract** algorithm, challenger gets the secret key $sk_{id_i} = [\mathbf{R}_{i1} | \mathbf{R}_{i2}]$ for id_i, sends sk_{id_i} to $\mathcal{A}$. Challenger will send $\perp$, against the secret key query for $id_i \in HU$.

Note that for id_{i*}, $\tilde{\mathbf{A}}_{i*} = [\mathbf{A}^* | -\mathbf{A}^*\mathbf{R}]$, so $\mathbf{A}'_1 = -\tilde{\mathbf{A}}_{i*}\mathbf{R}_{i*1}, \mathbf{A}'_2 = -\tilde{\mathbf{A}}_{i*}$ $\mathbf{R}_{i*2}$ and $\mathbf{A}_{i*} = [\tilde{\mathbf{A}}_{i*} | \mathbf{A}_{i*1} | \mathbf{A}_{i*2}] = [\tilde{\mathbf{A}}_{i*} | \mathbf{A}_1 + \mathbf{H}_3\mathbf{H}_{id_{i*}}\mathbf{G} | \mathbf{A}_2 + \mathbf{H}_4\mathbf{H}_{id_{i*}}\mathbf{G}]$ $= [\tilde{\mathbf{A}}_{i*} | \mathbf{A}'_1 | \mathbf{A}'_2] = [\tilde{\mathbf{A}}_{i*} | -\tilde{\mathbf{A}}_{i*}\mathbf{R}_{i*1} | -\tilde{\mathbf{A}}_{i*}\mathbf{R}_{i*2}]$.

For the re-encryption key query and re-encryption query, challenger maintain the restrictions as in Definition 5 and computes $rk_{i \to j}$, $\mathbf{ReEnc}(rk_{i \to j}, ct)$ according to the **ReKeyGen** and **ReEnc** algorithms to reply the adversary. Due to left-over hash lemma [1, Lemma 14], $(\mathbf{A}^*, -\mathbf{A}^*\mathbf{R}, -[\mathbf{A}^* | -\mathbf{A}^*\mathbf{R}] \cdot \mathbf{R}_{i*1}, -[\mathbf{A}^* | -\mathbf{A}^*\mathbf{R}] \cdot \mathbf{R}_{i*2})$ is statistically indistinguishable with uniform distribution. Hence, $(\mathbf{A}^*, -\mathbf{A}^*\mathbf{R} - \mathbf{H}_{id_{i*}}\mathbf{G}, -[\mathbf{A}^* | -\mathbf{A}^*\mathbf{R}] \cdot \mathbf{R}_{i*1} - \mathbf{H}_3\mathbf{H}_{id_{i*}}\mathbf{G}, -[\mathbf{A}^* | -\mathbf{A}^*\mathbf{R}] \cdot \mathbf{R}_{i*2} - \mathbf{H}_4\mathbf{H}_{id_{i*}}\mathbf{G})$ is statistically indistinguishable with uniform distribution. Since $\bar{\mathbf{A}}, \bar{\mathbf{A}}', \mathbf{A}_1, \mathbf{A}_2$ and responses to key queries are statistically close to those in **Game 0**, **Game 0** and **Game 1** are statistically indistinguishable.

Game 2: In **Game 2** we change the way that the challenger generates challenge ciphertext. Here Challenger will produce the challenge ciphertext $\mathbf{b}$ on a message $\mathbf{m} \in \{0,1\}^{nk}$ for id_{i*} as follows: Choose $\mathbf{s} \leftarrow \mathbb{Z}_q^n$ and $\bar{\mathbf{e}}_0 \leftarrow D_{\mathbb{Z},\alpha q}^m$ as usual, but do not choose $\mathbf{e}'_0, \mathbf{e}_1, \mathbf{e}_2$. Let $\bar{\mathbf{b}}_0^t = 2(\mathbf{s}^t\mathbf{A}^* \mod q) + \bar{\mathbf{e}}_0^t \mod 2q$ and $\mathbf{b}_0'^t = -\bar{\mathbf{b}}_0^t\mathbf{R} + \hat{\mathbf{e}}_0^t \mod 2q$, where $\hat{\mathbf{e}}_0 \leftarrow D_{\mathbb{Z},s'}^{nk}$. So, $\mathbf{b}_0 = (\bar{\mathbf{b}}_0, \mathbf{b}'_0)$. The last $2nk$ coordinates can be set as $\mathbf{b}_1^t = -\mathbf{b}_0^t\mathbf{R}_{i*1} + \hat{\mathbf{e}}_1^t \mod 2q$; $\mathbf{b}_2^t = -\mathbf{b}_0^t\mathbf{R}_{i*2} + \hat{\mathbf{e}}_2^t + encode(\mathbf{m}) \mod 2q$, where $\hat{\mathbf{e}}_1, \hat{\mathbf{e}}_2 \leftarrow D_{\mathbb{Z},s'}^{nk}$. Finally, replace $\bar{\mathbf{b}}_0$ with $\mathbf{b}^*$ in all the above expression, where $(\mathbf{A}^*, \mathbf{b}^*)$ is the LWE instance. Therefore, $\bar{\mathbf{b}}_0^t = \mathbf{b}^{*t}$; $\mathbf{b}_0'^t = -\mathbf{b}^{*t}\mathbf{R} + \hat{\mathbf{e}}_0^t \mod 2q$; $\mathbf{b}_1^t = -\mathbf{b}_0^{*t}\mathbf{R}_{i*1} + \hat{\mathbf{e}}_1^t \mod 2q$; $\mathbf{b}_2^t = -\mathbf{b}_0^{*t}\mathbf{R}_{i*2} + \hat{\mathbf{e}}_2^t + encode(\mathbf{m}) \mod 2q$. Set $\mathbf{b}_0^{*l} = (\mathbf{b}^{*l}, -\mathbf{b}^{*t}\mathbf{R} + \hat{\mathbf{e}}_0^t \mod 2q)$. Then the challenger output the challenge ciphertext $ct = \mathbf{b} = (\mathbf{b}_0^*, \mathbf{b}_1, \mathbf{b}_2)$.

We now show that the distribution of $\mathbf{b}$ is within negl statistical distance of that in **Game 1** from the adversary's view. Clearly, $\mathbf{b}^*$ have essentially the same distribution as in **Game 0** by construction. By substitution we have: $\mathbf{b}_0'^t = 2(\mathbf{s}^t(-\mathbf{A}^*\mathbf{R}) \mod q) + \bar{\mathbf{e}}_0^t\mathbf{R} + \hat{\mathbf{e}}_0^t \mod 2q$; $\mathbf{b}_1^t = 2(\mathbf{s}^t(-\tilde{\mathbf{A}}_{i*}\mathbf{R}_{i*1}) \mod q) + (\bar{\mathbf{e}}_0^t, \bar{\mathbf{e}}_0^t\mathbf{R} + \hat{\mathbf{e}}_0^t)\mathbf{R}_{i*1} + \hat{\mathbf{e}}_1^t \mod 2q$; $\mathbf{b}_2^t = 2(\mathbf{s}^t(-\tilde{\mathbf{A}}_{i*}\mathbf{R}_{i*2}) \mod q) + (\bar{\mathbf{e}}_0^t, \bar{\mathbf{e}}_0^t\mathbf{R} + \hat{\mathbf{e}}_0^t)\mathbf{R}_{i*2} + \hat{\mathbf{e}}_2^t + encode(\mathbf{m}) \mod 2q$.

By Corollary 3.10 in [22], the noise term $\bar{\mathbf{e}}_0^t\mathbf{R} + \hat{\mathbf{e}}_0^t$ of $\mathbf{b}'_0$ is within negl statistical distance from discrete Gaussian distribution $D_{\mathbb{Z},s'}^{nk}$. The same argument, also, applies for the noise term of $\mathbf{b}_1, \mathbf{b}_2$. Hence, **Game 1** and **Game 2** are statistically indistinguishable.

Game 3: Here, we only change how the $\mathbf{b}^*$ component of the challenge ciphertext is created, letting it be uniformly random in $\mathbb{Z}_{2q}^m$. Challenger construct the public parameters, answer the secret key queries, re-encryption queries and construct the last $3nk$ coordinates of challenge ciphertext exactly as in Game 2. It follows from the hardness of the decisional $\mathrm{LWE}_{q,\alpha'}$ that **Game 2** and **Game 3** are computationally indistinguishable.

Now, by the left-over hash lemma [1, Lemma 14], $(\mathbf{A}^*, \mathbf{b}^*, -\mathbf{A}^*\mathbf{R}, \mathbf{b}^{*t}\mathbf{R}, -\tilde{\mathbf{A}}_{i^*}\mathbf{R}_{i^*1}, \mathbf{b}_0^{*t}\mathbf{R}_{i^*1}, -\tilde{\mathbf{A}}_{i^*}\mathbf{R}_{i^*2}, \mathbf{b}_0^{*t}\mathbf{R}_{i^*2})$ is negl-uniform when $\mathbf{R}, \mathbf{R}_{i^*1}, \mathbf{R}_{i^*2}$ are chosen as in Game 2. Therefore, the challenge ciphertext has the same distribution (up to negl statistical distance) for any encrypted message. So, the advantage of the adversary against the proposed scheme is same as the advantage of the attacker against decisional $\mathrm{LWE}_{q,\alpha'}$.   □

References

1. Agrawal, S., Boneh, D., Boyen, X.: Efficient lattice (H)IBE in the standard model. In: Gilbert, H. (ed.) EUROCRYPT 2010. LNCS, vol. 6110, pp. 553–572. Springer, Heidelberg (2010). https://doi.org/10.1007/978-3-642-13190-5_28
2. Ajtai, M.: Generating hard instances of lattice problems. In STOC 1996, pp. 99–108. ACM (1996)
3. Ajtai, M.: Generating hard instances of the short basis problem. In: Wiedermann, J., van Emde Boas, P., Nielsen, M. (eds.) ICALP 1999. LNCS, vol. 1644, pp. 1–9. Springer, Heidelberg (1999). https://doi.org/10.1007/3-540-48523-6_1
4. Ateniese, G., Fu, K., Green, M., Hohenberger, S.: Improved proxy re-encryption schemes with applications to secure distributed storage. ACM Trans. Inf. Syst. Secur. 9(1), 1–30 (2006)
5. Blaze, M., Bleumer, G., Strauss, M.: Divertible protocols and atomic proxy cryptography. In: Nyberg, K. (ed.) EUROCRYPT 1998. Divertible protocols and atomic proxy cryptography, vol. 1403, pp. 127–144. Springer, Heidelberg (1998). https://doi.org/10.1007/BFb0054122
6. Canetti, R., Hohenberger, S.: Chosen-ciphertext secure proxy re-encryption. ACM CCS 2007, 185–194 (2007)
7. Canetti, R., Lin, H., Tessaro, S., Vaikuntanathan, V.: Obfuscation of probabilistic circuits and applications. In: Dodis, Y., Nielsen, J.B. (eds.) TCC 2015. LNCS, vol. 9015, pp. 468–497. Springer, Heidelberg (2015). https://doi.org/10.1007/978-3-662-46497-7_19
8. Chandran, N., Chase, M., Liu, F.-H., Nishimaki, R., Xagawa, K.: Re-encryption, functional re-encryption, and multi-hop re-encryption: a framework for achieving obfuscation-based security and instantiations from lattices. In: Krawczyk, H. (ed.) PKC 2014. LNCS, vol. 8383, pp. 95–112. Springer, Heidelberg (2014). https://doi.org/10.1007/978-3-642-54631-0_6
9. Chandran, N., Chase, M., Vaikuntanathan, V.: Functional re-encryption and collusion-resistant obfuscation. In: Cramer, R. (ed.) TCC 2012. LNCS, vol. 7194, pp. 404–421. Springer, Heidelberg (2012). https://doi.org/10.1007/978-3-642-28914-9_23
10. Fan, X., Liu, F.-H.: Proxy re-encryption and re-signatures from lattices. In: Deng, R.H., Gauthier-Umaña, V., Ochoa, M., Yung, M. (eds.) ACNS 2019. LNCS, vol. 11464, pp. 363–382. Springer, Cham (2019). https://doi.org/10.1007/978-3-030-21568-2_18
11. Gentry, C.: A fully Homomorphic Encryption Scheme, vol. 20. Stanford University Stanford, Stanford (2009)
12. Gentry, C., Peikert, C., Vaikuntanathan, V.: Trapdoors for hard lattices and new cryptographic constructions. ACM STOC 2008, 197–206 (2008)
13. Green, M., Ateniese, G.: Identity-based proxy re-encryption. In: Katz, J., Yung, M. (eds.) ACNS 2007. LNCS, vol. 4521, pp. 288–306. Springer, Heidelberg (2007). https://doi.org/10.1007/978-3-540-72738-5_19

14. Hohenberger, S., Rothblum, G.N., Shelat, A., Vaikuntanathan, V.: Securely obfuscating re-encryption. In: Vadhan, S.P. (ed.) TCC 2007. LNCS, vol. 4392, pp. 233–252. Springer, Heidelberg (2007). https://doi.org/10.1007/978-3-540-70936-7_13

15. Hou, J., Jiang, M., Guo, Y., Song, W.: Identity-based multi-bit proxy re-encryption over lattice in the standard model. J. Inf. Secur. Appl. **47**, 329–334 (2019)

16. Kirshanova, E.: Proxy re-encryption from lattices. In: Krawczyk, H. (ed.) PKC 2014. LNCS, vol. 8383, pp. 77–94. Springer, Heidelberg (2014). https://doi.org/10.1007/978-3-642-54631-0_5

17. Libert, B., Vergnaud, D.: Unidirectional chosen-ciphertext secure proxy re-encryption. In: Cramer, R. (ed.) PKC 2008. LNCS, vol. 4939, pp. 360–379. Springer, Heidelberg (2008). https://doi.org/10.1007/978-3-540-78440-1_21

18. Micciancio, D., Peikert, C.: Trapdoors for lattices: simpler, tighter, faster, smaller. In: Pointcheval, D., Johansson, T. (eds.) EUROCRYPT 2012. LNCS, vol. 7237, pp. 700–718. Springer, Heidelberg (2012). https://doi.org/10.1007/978-3-642-29011-4_41

19. Micciancio, D., Peikert, C.: Hardness of SIS and LWE with small parameters. In: Canetti, R., Garay, J.A. (eds.) CRYPTO 2013. LNCS, vol. 8042, pp. 21–39. Springer, Heidelberg (2013). https://doi.org/10.1007/978-3-642-40041-4_2

20. Micciancio, D., Regev, O.: Worst-case to average-case reductions based on gaussian measures. FOCS **2004**, 372–381 (2004)

21. Nishimaki, R., Xagawa, K.: Key-private proxy re-encryption from lattices revisited. IEICE Trans. Fundam. Electron. Commun. Comput. Sci. **98-A**(1), 100–116 (2015)

22. Regev, O.: On lattices, learning with errors, random linear codes, and cryptography. ACM STOC **2005**, 84–93 (2005)

23. Singh, K., Rangan, C.P., Banerjee, A.: Lattice based identity based proxy re-encryption scheme. J. Internet Serv. Inf. Secur. **3**(3/4), 38–51 (2013)

24. Singh, K., Rangan, C.P., Banerjee, A.K.: Lattice based identity based unidirectional proxy re-encryption scheme. In: Chakraborty, R.S., Matyas, V., Schaumont, P. (eds.) SPACE 2014. LNCS, vol. 8804, pp. 76–91. Springer, Cham (2014). https://doi.org/10.1007/978-3-319-12060-7_6

25. Smith, T.: DVD Jon: buy DRM-less tracks from apple Itunes (2005). https://www.theregister.co.uk/2005/03/18/itunes_pymusique/

26. Xagawa, D.K.: Cryptography with lattices, Ph.d. thesis, Tokyo Institute of Technology (2010)

27. Yin, W., Wen, Q., Li, W., Zhang, H., Jin, Z.P.: Identity based proxy re-encryption scheme under LWE. KSII Trans. Internet Inf. Syst. **11**(12), 6116–6132 (2017)

Efficient Algorithm for Computing Odd-Degree Isogenies on Montgomery Curves

Kenta Kodera[1]([✉]), Chen-Mou Cheng[2], and Atsuko Miyaji[1,3]

[1] Graduate School of Engineering, Osaka University,
2-1, Yamadaoka, Suita, Osaka, Japan
kodera@cy2sec.comm.eng.osaka-u.ac.jp
[2] Graduate School of Natural Science and Technology, Kanazawa University,
Kakumamachi, Kanazawa, Japan
[3] Japan Advanced Institute of Science and Technology, Nomi, Japan

Abstract. Isogeny-based cryptography, such as commutative supersingular isogeny Diffie-Hellman (CSIDH), has been shown to be promising candidates for post-quantum cryptography. However, their speeds have remained unremarkable. For example, computing odd-degree isogenies between Montgomery curves is a dominant computation in CSIDH. To increase the speed of this isogeny computation, this study proposes a new technique called the "2-ADD-Skip method," which reduces the required number of points to be computed. This technique is then used to develop a novel algorithm for isogeny computation. It is found that the proposed algorithm requires fewer field arithmetic operations for the degrees of $\ell \geq 19$ compared with the algorithm of Meyer *et al.*, which utilizes twisted Edwards curves. Further, a prototype CSIDH-512 implementation shows that the proposed algorithm can give a 6.7% speedup over the implementation by Meyer *et al.* Finally, individual experiments for each degree of isogeny show that the proposed algorithm requires the lowest number of clock cycles among existing algorithms for $19 \leq \ell \leq 373$.

Keywords: Montgomery curves · Isogeny · Post-quantum cryptography

1 Introduction

1.1 Overview

Post-quantum cryptography has been studied intensively in response to threats brought about by the rapid development of quantum computing. Isogeny-based cryptography, such as supersingular isogeny Diffie-Hellman (SIDH) [1] and commutative SIDH (CSIDH) [2], has been considered as promising candidates for post-quantum cryptography. In particular, supersingular isogeny key encapsulation (SIKE) [3], an SIDH-based key encapsulation algorithm, has recently

© Springer Nature Switzerland AG 2020
I. You (Ed.): WISA 2020, LNCS 12583, pp. 258–275, 2020.
https://doi.org/10.1007/978-3-030-65299-9_20

entered as an alternative algorithm the third round of the post-quantum cryptography standardization process promoted by the National Institute of Standards and Technology (NIST). Among all candidates in the competition, SIKE has the smallest public key size [4]. In 2018, CSIDH was proposed as a non-interactive key exchange protocol with an even smaller public key size than that of SIDH. However, its speed performance is not as impressive and leaves a lot of room for improvement.

There have been a series of research efforts attempting to tailor the CSIDH algorithm and its parameters to increase its speed [5–8]. Researchers have also focused on its two main subroutines, namely: scalar multiplication and odd-degree isogeny computation on Montgomery curves. For example, Cervantes-Vázquez et al. sped up the addition chain for scalar multiplication [9], while Meyer-Reith reduced the cost of isogeny computation by using twisted Edwards curves [5]. Specifically, for an elliptic curve E with a finite subgroup Φ, there exists an elliptic curve E' and an isogeny $\phi : E \longrightarrow E'$ satisfying $\ker(\phi) = \Phi$. Isogeny computation consists of computing points in the kernel Φ, E', and $\phi(P) \in E'$ for $P \in E$. Meyer and Reith have found that E' can be computed more efficiently by using the isomorphic curve in the twisted form of the Edwards curves. Additionally, Bernstein et al. have proposed a different sequence to compute points in Φ [10]. It is noted that their approach still requires to compute the same number of points in Φ.

The present work investigates the reduction of the cost of isogeny computation to realize compact and efficient post-quantum cryptography. While conventional algorithms precisely compute the points in Φ, this study focuses on reducing the number of points to be computed[1]. It may be noted that researches have also been exploring constant-time algorithms and their optimizations for protection against side-channel attacks [6,9,12]. The approach proposed herein is also applicable to these constant-time algorithms.

1.2 Contributions

This study focuses on the isogeny computation with odd degrees ℓ on Montgomery curves. The "2-ADD-Skip method" is proposed to reduce the number of points to be computed during isogeny computation. Specifically, a novel efficient algorithm to utilize the technique is presented, and its computational cost is analyzed in terms of the required amount of field multiplication, squaring, and addition. The proposed algorithm is compared with the combined algorithm by Costello et al. [13] and Castryck et al. [2]. The algorithm can reduce the computational cost and and lower the required number of field arithmetic operations when $\ell \geq 13$. Similarly, for the algorithm with twisted Edwards curves as shown in [5], the proposed technique can be also applied. It is seen that the proposed algorithm can reduce the computational cost and lower the required number of field arithmetic operations when $\ell \geq 19$. Experiments are conducted on an Intel

---

[1] A new paper by Bernstein et al. [11] is discussed in Sect. 5.2.

Core i7-8569U Coffee Lake processor by comparing a CSIDH-512 implementation whose isogeny computation is performed by the proposed algorithm with that in [5]. The proposed algorithm is found to be faster by approximately 6.7%. Furthermore, they also show that the proposed algorithm requires lower number of clock cycles than any other algorithms for $19 \leq \ell \leq 373$.

1.3   Organization

The reminder of this paper is organized as follows. Section 2 presents a brief review of elliptic curves, isogenies, and CSIDH. Section 3 summarizes algorithms for isogeny computation on Montgomery curves. Section 4 describes the proposed 2-ADD-Skip method as well as algorithms to utilize it. An analysis of the computational cost of the proposed method is then discussed in terms of the required number of field arithmetic operations. Section 5 reports the preliminary experimental results of increasing the speed of CSIDH using the proposed approach. Finally, Sect. 6 concludes this paper.

2   Preliminaries

2.1   Montgomery Curves

Let K be a field with char$(K) \neq 2$. A Montgomery curve [14] over K with coefficients $a, b \in K$, $b(a^2 - 4) \neq 0$ is given by

$$M_{a,b}: \quad by^2 = x^3 + ax^2 + x. \tag{1}$$

The scalar multiplication by k is denoted as $[k]P := \underbrace{P + \cdots + P}_{k}$.

Alternatively, following the work of Costello, Longa, and Naehrig [15], Montgomery curves can alternatively be written as

$$M_{A,B,C}: \quad BY^2Z = CX^3 + AX^2Z + CXZ^2,$$

where (A, B, C), $(X, Y, Z) \in \mathbb{P}^2(K)$, $C \neq 0$, $Z \neq 0$, $a = A/C$, $b = B/C$, $x = X/Z$ and $y = Y/Z$. Let

$$\varphi_x : \mathbb{P}^2(K) \longrightarrow \mathbb{P}^1(K), \ (X : Y : Z) \longmapsto (X : Z).$$

For the points $(X : Z) \in \mathbb{P}^1(K)$, Montgomery himself introduced efficient addition formulae as follows [14]. Let $P, Q \in M_{a,b}(K)$, $(X_P : Z_P) = \varphi_x(P)$, and $(X_Q : Z_Q) = \varphi_x(Q)$.

– When $P \neq Q$,

$$\begin{cases} X_{P+Q} = Z_{P-Q}(X_P X_Q - Z_P Z_Q)^2 \\ \qquad = Z_{P-Q}[(X_P - Z_P)(X_Q + Z_Q) + (X_P + Z_P)(X_Q - Z_Q)]^2, \\ Z_{P+Q} = X_{P-Q}(X_P Z_Q - Z_P X_Q)^2 \\ \qquad = X_{P-Q}[(X_P - Z_P)(X_Q + Z_Q) - (X_P + Z_P)(X_Q - Z_Q)]^2. \end{cases} \tag{2}$$

- When $P = Q$,

$$
\begin{cases}
X_{[2]P} = 4C(X_P + Z_P)^2(X_P - Z_P)^2, \\
Z_{[2]P} = (4X_P Z_P)(4C(X_P - Z_P)^2 + (A + 2C)(4X_P Z_P)), \quad (3) \\
4X_P Z_P = (X_P + Z_P)^2 - (X_P - Z_P)^2.
\end{cases}
$$

From these formulae in XZ-only coordinates, two functions are defined:

$$\text{ADD} : (\varphi_x(P), \varphi_x(Q), \varphi_x(P - Q)) \longmapsto \varphi_x(P + Q),$$
$$\text{DBL} : (\varphi_x(P), (A : C)) \longmapsto \varphi_x([2]P).$$

Let $\mathbf{M}, \mathbf{S}$, and $\mathbf{a}$ denote the computational costs of multiplication, squaring, and addition, respectively, in a field K. Then ADD requires $4\mathbf{M} + 2\mathbf{S} + 6\mathbf{a}$ operations, and DBL requires $4\mathbf{M} + 2\mathbf{S} + 8\mathbf{a}$ operations as in [5].

2.2 Twisted Edwards Curves

A twisted Edwards curve [16] over a field K with $\operatorname{char}(K) \neq 2$, $a_{tE}, d_{tE} \in K, a_{tE} d_{tE} \neq 0, a_{tE} \neq d_{tE}, d_{tE} \neq 1$ is given by

$$tE_{a_{tE}, d_{tE}} : \quad a_{tE} u^2 + v^2 = 1 + d_{tE} u^2 v^2.$$

A twisted Edwards curve $tE_{a_{tE}, d_{tE}}$ is birationally equivalent to a Montgomery curve $M_{a,b}$:

$$
\begin{cases}
a_{tE} = \dfrac{a+2}{b}, \quad d_{tE} = \dfrac{a-2}{b}, \quad (x, y) \longmapsto (u, v) = \left(\dfrac{x}{y}, \dfrac{x-1}{y+1} \right), \\
a = \dfrac{2(a_{tE} + d_{tE})}{a_{tE} - d_{tE}}, \quad b = \dfrac{4}{a_{tE} - d_{tE}}, \quad (u, v) \longmapsto (x, y) = \left(\dfrac{1+v}{1-v}, \dfrac{1+v}{(1-v)u} \right).
\end{cases}
$$

As Montgomery curves, twisted Edwards curves have efficient addition formulae in YZ-only coordinates [17]. A point $(X : Z)$ on the Montgomery curve over $\mathbb{P}^1(K)$ can be transformed to a point $(Y^{tE} : Z^{tE})$ on the corresponding twisted Edwards curve via

$$(X : Z) \longmapsto (Y^{tE} : Z^{tE}) = (X - Z : X + Z). \quad (4)$$

2.3 Isogenies

Let E and E' be elliptic curves. An isogeny from E to E' is a morphism $\phi : E \longrightarrow E'$ satisfying $\phi(\mathcal{O}_E) = \mathcal{O}_{E'}$. If ϕ is separable, then $\#\ker(\phi) = \deg \phi$. It is denoted as ℓ-isogeny for $\ell = \deg \phi$. Let Φ be a finite subgroup of E. Then, There exist a unique elliptic curve E' up to an isomorphism and a separable isogeny $\phi : E \longrightarrow E'$ satisfying $\ker(\phi) = \Phi$. For a given E and Φ, the Vélu's formula provides explicit equations for E' and ϕ [18]. Isogeny computation consists of computing points in the kernel Φ, computing the coefficients of the new curve E' by referring to *curve computation*, and computing $\phi(P) \in E'$ for $P \in E$ by referring to *image computation*.

2.4 CSIDH

CSIDH is a non-interactive key exchange protocol proposed by Castryck, Lange, Martindale, Panny, and Renes in 2018 [2]. Let p be a prime number, and $\mathcal{E}\ell\ell_p(\mathbb{Z}[\sqrt{-p}])$ be a set of $\mathbb{F}_p$-isomorphic classes of supersingular Montgomery curves defined over $\mathbb{F}_p$ whose endomorphism ring is isomorphic to $\mathbb{Z}[\sqrt{-p}]$. The ideal class group $\mathrm{Cl}(\mathbb{Z}[\sqrt{-p}])$ acts freely and transitively on the set $\mathcal{E}\ell\ell_p(\mathbb{Z}[\sqrt{-p}])$. Then, Castryck *et al.* construct a Diffie–Hellman-style key exchange protocol based on the Couveignes–Rostovtsev–Stolbunov scheme [19–21]. Let $E_0 \in \mathcal{E}\ell\ell_p(\mathbb{Z}[\sqrt{-p}])$. Alice chooses a secret $\mathfrak{a} \in \mathrm{Cl}(\mathbb{Z}[\sqrt{-p}])$ and generates her public key $E_a = \mathfrak{a} \cdot E_0$ by computing the action given by $\mathfrak{a}$. Bob also computes his public key E_b with his secret $\mathfrak{b}$. Now Alice and Bob can compute a shared secret $\mathfrak{a} \cdot \mathfrak{b} \cdot E_0 = \mathfrak{a} \cdot E_b = \mathfrak{b} \cdot E_a$ by the commutativity of $\mathrm{Cl}(\mathbb{Z}[\sqrt{-p}])$.

The action given by a class group element $\mathfrak{a} \in \mathrm{Cl}(\mathbb{Z}[\sqrt{-p}])$ is defined by an isogeny $\phi : E \longrightarrow E/E[\mathfrak{a}]$, where $E[\mathfrak{a}] = \cap_{\alpha \in \mathfrak{a}} \ker(\alpha)$. In CSIDH, a prime of the form $p = 4 \prod_{i=1}^{n} \ell_i - 1$ is used, where ℓ_i's are odd primes. The principal ideal (ℓ_i) splits into $\mathfrak{l}_i = (\ell_i, \pi - 1)$ and $\bar{\mathfrak{l}}_i = (\ell_i, \pi + 1)$ over $\mathbb{Z}[\sqrt{-p}]$, where π is the Frobenius endomorphism. Hence, the action given by $\mathfrak{l}_i$ corresponds to the ℓ_i-isogeny whose kernel is generated by a point over $\mathbb{F}_p$. Similarly, the action given by $\bar{\mathfrak{l}}_i$ corresponds to the ℓ_i-isogeny whose kernel is generated by a point over $\mathbb{F}_{p^2} \setminus \mathbb{F}_p$. We have $\bar{\mathfrak{l}}_i = \mathfrak{l}_i^{-1}$ in $\mathrm{Cl}(\mathbb{Z}[\sqrt{-p}])$. Then, an element in the class group is sampled by $\mathfrak{a} = \prod \mathfrak{l}_i^{e_i}$ for small integers e_i's. Hence, a secret key is represented by a vector $e = (e_1, \ldots, e_n)$. Therefore, given a secret vector e, the main computation in CSIDH is the evaluation of the class group actions. This requires $|e_i|$ operations to compute each ℓ_i-isogenies for all odd prime factors ℓ_i of $p+1$. Furthermore, public keys and shared secrets are elements in $\mathbb{F}_p$ because curves in $\mathcal{E}\ell\ell_p(\mathbb{Z}[\sqrt{-p}])$ can be represented by supersingular Montgomery curves of the form $E_a : y^2 = x^3 + ax^2 + x$ for $a \in \mathbb{F}_p$.

The high-level concept of the class group action evaluation is given in Algorithm 1. It can be seen that the scalar multiplications in lines 6 and 8 and the odd-degree isogeny computations in line 10 are the primary subroutines in this algorithm. Furthermore, the computational cost of evaluation of class group actions depends on the secret vector e, which can be a target in side-channel attacks. To protect against the attacks, Meyer, Campos, and Reith proposed a constant-time algorithm by constructing a dummy computation of ℓ_i-isogenies [6].

In a parameter set CSIDH-512, all e_i's are chosen from the interval $[-5, \ldots, 5]$. Further, $p+1$ has 74 odd prime factors: $\ell_1 = 3, \ell_2 = 5, \ldots, \ell_{73} = 373$, and $\ell_{74} = 587$. It is noted that ℓ_i happens to be the i-th smallest odd prime in all cases except the last ℓ_{74}. This parameter set is estimated to provide a security level of NIST-1.

3 Isogeny Computation on Montgomery Curves

This section summarizes algorithms for the isogeny computation on Montgomery curves with odd degree $\ell = 2d + 1$, where an isogeny is given by $\phi : M_{A,B,C} \longrightarrow M_{A',B',C'}$. These algorithms are constructed based on an explicit formula derived

Algorithm 1. Evaluation of the class group action

Input: $a \in \mathbb{F}_p, e = (e_1, \ldots, e_n)$
Output: $a' \in \mathbb{F}_p$ s.t. $E_{a'} = \mathfrak{a} \cdot E_a$ where $\mathfrak{a} = \prod_i \mathfrak{l}_i^{e_i}$
1: **while** $\exists e_i \neq 0$ **do**
2:    Sample a random $x \in \mathbb{F}_p$.
3:    $s \leftarrow +1$ if $x^3 + ax^2 + x$ is square in $\mathbb{F}_p$, else $s \leftarrow -1$
4:    $S \leftarrow \{i \mid e_i \neq 0, \operatorname{sign}(e_i) = s\}$
5:    **if** $S \neq \emptyset$ **then**
6:        $k \leftarrow \prod_{i \in S} \ell_i, Q \leftarrow [(p+1)/k](x:1)$
7:        **for** $i \in S$ **do**
8:            $R \leftarrow [k/\ell_i]Q$
9:            **if** $R \neq \mathcal{O}$ **then**
10:               ℓ_i-isogeny computation $\phi : E_a \rightarrow E_{a'}, \ker(\phi) = \langle R \rangle$
                   $a \leftarrow a', Q \leftarrow \phi(Q), k \leftarrow k/\ell_i, e_i \leftarrow e_i - s$
11:           **end if**
12:       **end for**
13:   **end if**
14: **end while**
15: **return** a

---

by Costello and Hisil. It is noted that given a generator $(X_1 : Z_1)$, where $(X_i : Z_i) := \varphi_x([i]P)$ for $\ker(\phi) = \langle P \rangle$, all points $(X_2 : Z_2), \ldots, (X_d : Z_d)$ are precisely computed using addition formulae. Moreover, a technique is described to speed up the curve computation by using twisted Edwards curves.

Hereinafter, $(X_i : Z_i)$ is denoted as a point in the $\ker(\phi)$, as given above. Further, $(X : Z) \in M_{A,B,C}$ and $(X' : Z') := \phi((X : Z)) \in M_{A',B',C'}$ are defined for image computation, and we denote $(A' : C')$ and $(A : C)$ are denoted as curve coefficients in curve computation.

3.1 Costello-Hisil Formula

Costello and Hisil derived an explicit formula for computing odd-degree isogenies between Montgomery curves [13]. Given a field K with $\operatorname{char}(K) \neq 2$, let P be a point of order $\ell = 2d+1$ on the Montgomery curve $M_{a,b} : by^2 = x^3 + ax + x$. We write $\sigma = \sum_{i=1}^d x_{[i]P}, \tilde{\sigma} = \sum_{i=1}^d 1/x_{[i]P}$ and $\pi = \prod_{i=1}^d x_{[i]P}$, where $x_{[i]P}$ denotes the x-coordinate of $[i]P$. The Montgomery curve $M_{a',b'} : b'y^2 = x^3 + a'x + x$ with

$$a' = (6\tilde{\sigma} - 6\sigma + a)\pi^2 \quad \text{and} \quad b' = b\pi^2 \tag{5}$$

is the codomain of ℓ-isogeny $\phi : M_{a,b} \longrightarrow M_{a',b'}$ with $\ker(\phi) = \langle P \rangle$, which is defined by the coordinate map

$$\phi : (x, y) \longmapsto (f(x), yf'(x)),$$

where

$$f(x) = x \cdot \prod_{i=1}^d \left(\frac{x \cdot x_{[i]P} - 1}{x - x_{[i]P}} \right)^2, \tag{6}$$

and $f'(x)$ is its derivative. It is noted that Renes gave a different proof and generalized the formula for any separable isogeny whose kernel does not contain $(0,0)$ [22].

In a projective space $\mathbb{P}^1(K)$, Eq. (6) leads to Eq. (7) for point computation:

$$(X' : Z') = (X \cdot (S_X)^2 : Z \cdot (S_Z)^2), \tag{7}$$

where

$$S_X = \prod_{i=1}^{d}(XX_i - Z_iZ) \text{ and } S_Z = \prod_{i=1}^{d}(XZ_i - X_iZ). \tag{8}$$

Similarly, Eq. (5) leads to equations for curve computation:

$$(A' : C') = (\tau(A - 3\sigma) : C),$$

where

$$\tau = \prod_{i=1}^{\ell-1} \frac{X_i}{Z_i}, \quad \sigma = \sum_{i=1}^{\ell-1} \left(\frac{X_i}{Z_i} - \frac{Z_i}{X_i} \right).$$

Castryck *et al.* defined T_i as $\sum_{i=0}^{\ell-1} T_iw^i = \prod_{i=1}^{\ell-1}(Z_iw + X_i)$ for efficient curve computation [2].

$$(A' : C') \left(AT_0T_{\ell-1} - 3C(T_0T_{\ell-2} - T_1T_{\ell-1}) : CT_{\ell-1}^2 \right), \tag{9}$$

where

$$\begin{cases} T_0 = \prod_i X_i, \quad T_1 = \sum_i (Z_i \prod_{j \neq i} X_j), \\ T_{\ell-2} = \sum_i (X_i \prod_{j \neq i} Z_j), \text{ and } T_{\ell-1} = \prod_i Z_i. \end{cases} \tag{10}$$

3.2 Conventional Algorithm for Isogeny Computation on Montgomery Curves

In a conventional algorithm for odd-degree isogeny computation on Montgomery curves, intermediate variables such as $S_X, S_Z, T_0, T_1, T_{\ell-2}$, and $T_{\ell-1}$ are computed first. As shown in Eqs. (8) and (10), all these variables are polynomial in $(X_i : Z_i)$ for $i = 1, \ldots, d$; hence, they are computed by iteration. To begin with, all intermediate variables are initialized with $(X_1 : Z_1)$ as follows: $S_X = (X-Z)(X_1+Z_1)+(X+Z)(X_1-Z_1)$, $S_Z = (X-Z)(X_1+Z_1)-(X+Z)(X_1-Z_1)$, $T_0 = X_1, T_1 = Z_1, T_{\ell-2} = Z_1$, and $T_{\ell-1} = X_1$. Then, for all $i = 2, \ldots, d$, a point $(X_i : Z_i)$ is computed using the addition formula, and intermediate variables are successively updated by following the formulae (11) and (12).

$$\begin{cases} S_X \leftarrow S_X \cdot ((X-Z) \cdot (X_i+Z_i) + (X+Z) \cdot (X_i-Z_i)), \\ S_Z \leftarrow S_Z \cdot ((X-Z) \cdot (X_i+Z_i) - (X+Z) \cdot (X_i-Z_i)); \end{cases} \tag{11}$$

$$\begin{cases} T_1 \leftarrow T_1 \cdot X_i + T_0 \cdot Z_i, \\ T_0 \leftarrow T_0 \cdot X_i, \\ T_{\ell-2} \leftarrow T_{\ell-2} \cdot Z_i + T_{\ell-1} \cdot X_i, \\ T_{\ell-1} \leftarrow T_{\ell-1} \cdot Z_i. \end{cases} \tag{12}$$

Here, the update formulae (11) and (12) require $4M+4a$ and $6M+2a$ operations, respectively; this is because $X+Z$ and $X-Z$ can be reused over several updates if they are computed once at the beginning of the algorithm. Finally, $(X' : Z')$ and $(A' : C')$ are computed by Eqs. (7) and (9).

Algorithm 2 summarizes the algorithm for $(\ell = 2d + 1)$-isogeny computation on Montgomery curves. It requires a total of $(14d-5)M + (2d+1)S + (12d-1)a$ operations.

Algorithm 2. Isogeny computation on Montgomery curves

Input: d, $(X : Z)$, $(X_1 : Z_1)$, and $(A : C)$
Output: $(X' : Z')$ and $(A' : C')$
1: $t^+ \leftarrow X + Z$, $t^- \leftarrow X - Z$ // 2a
2: $t_0 \leftarrow t^- \cdot (X_1 + Z_1)$, $t_1 \leftarrow t^+ \cdot (X_1 - Z_1)$ // $2M + 2a$
3: $(S_X : S_Z) \leftarrow (t_0 + t_1, t_0 - t_1)$ // 2a
4: $(T_0, T_1, T_{\ell-2}, T_{\ell-1}) \leftarrow (X_1, Z_1, Z_1, X_1)$
5: **for** $i = 2$ to d **do**
6:     **if** $i == 2$ **then**
7:         $(X_i : Z_i) \leftarrow \mathtt{DBL}((X_1 : Z_1), (A : C))$ // $4M + 2S + 8a$
8:     **else**
9:         $(X_i : Z_i) \leftarrow \mathtt{ADD}((X_{i-1} : Z_{i-1}), (X_1 : Z_1), (X_{i-2} : Z_{i-2}))$ // $4M + 2S + 6a$
10:    **end if**
11:    Update $(S_X : S_Z)$ by (11) with $(X_i : Z_i)$ // $4M + 4a$
12:    Update $(T_0, T_1, T_{\ell-2}, T_{\ell-1})$ by (12) with $(X_i : Z_i)$ // $6M + 2a$
13: **end for**
14: $(X' : Z') \leftarrow (X \cdot (S_X)^2 : Z \cdot (S_Z)^2)$ // $2M + 2S$
15: $(A' : C') \leftarrow (A \cdot T_0 \cdot T_{\ell-1} - 3C(T_0 \cdot T_{\ell-2} - T_1 \cdot T_{\ell-1}) : C \cdot T_{\ell-1}^2)$ // $5M + S + 4a$
16: **return** $(X' : Z')$ and $(A' : C')$

When $Z_1 = 1$ or $C = 1$, $\mathtt{ADD}$ or $\mathtt{DBL}$ requires fewer multiplication operations. Bernstein et al. pointed out that computing d points in the kernel in a different way reduces computational cost [10]. For example, Montgomery ladder-like iterations computes d points with more doubling ($\mathtt{DBL}$) operations. However, $Z_1 \neq 1$ and $C \neq 1$ are generally observed in CSIDH, unless inversion is computed with a certain amount of field arithmetic operations. The effect of normalization will not be considered as it is beyond the scope of this paper.

3.3 Curve Computation Through Twisted Edwards Curves

Meyer and Reith proposed a faster approach to curve computation by using twisted Edwards curves [5].

As per their approach, when $b = 1$, it is possible to convert a curve between its Montgomery form and twisted Edwards form at the cost of a only few field additions:

$$a' = A + 2C, \ d' = A - 2C,$$
$$(A : C) = (2(a' + d') : a' - d').$$

In the context of isogeny computation, the efficient conversion is always available due to an isomorphism between $by^2 = x^3 + ax^2 + x$ and $\tilde{y}^2 = \tilde{x}^3 + a\tilde{x}^2 + \tilde{x}$ given by $y = \tilde{y}/\sqrt{b}$. Furthermore, Moody and Shumow presented an explicit formula for isogeny computation on twisted Edwards curves [23]. Specifically, curve computation in YZ-only coordinates is given by Eq. (13):

$$a'_{tE} = a^\ell_{tE} \cdot \pi_Z^8, \ d'_{tE} = d^\ell_{tE} \cdot \pi_Y^8, \tag{13}$$

where

$$\pi_Z = \prod_{i=1}^d Z_i^{tE} \text{ and } \pi_Y = \prod_{i=1}^d Y_i^{tE}. \tag{14}$$

Considering Eq. (4), the update formula (12) for intermediate variables in curve computation on Montgomery curves can be replaced by the following formula (15):

$$\begin{cases} \pi_Y \leftarrow \pi_Y \cdot (X_i - Z_i), \\ \pi_Z \leftarrow \pi_Z \cdot (X_i + Z_i). \end{cases} \tag{15}$$

Therefore, the computational cost per update for curve computation is reduced from $6\mathbf{M} + 2\mathbf{a}$ to $2\mathbf{M}$ because $X_i - Z_i$ and $X_i + Z_i$ have already been computed in the point computation formula (11) for point computation. The bit length of ℓ is denoted as $\tilde{\ell}$, and $(\tilde{\ell}/2)\mathbf{M} + \tilde{\ell}\mathbf{S}$ is assumed to be required to compute the ℓ-th power. Isogeny computation on Montgomery curves can be sped up to $(10d + \tilde{\ell} - 4)\mathbf{M} + (2d + 2\tilde{\ell} + 6)\mathbf{S} + (10d + 3)\mathbf{a}$ field arithmetic operations. This requires $(4d - \tilde{\ell} - 5)\mathbf{M} + (-2\tilde{\ell} - 5)\mathbf{S} + (2d - 2)\mathbf{a}$ operations fewer than those in the Algorithm 2.

4   Proposed Approach

In this section, a novel technique called the "2-ADD-Skip method" is proposed, and its application to isogeny computation is discussed. Let us explain rough sketch of our strategy.

In Algorithm 2, given a point $(X_1 : Z_1)$, the points in the kernel $(X_i : Z_i)$ for $i = 2, \ldots, d$ are precisely computed by the addition formulae, and used for the corresponding update formulae. However, the coordinates of all d points are not necessarily required as long as the image $(X' : Z')$ and the new coefficient $(A' : C')$ can be computed. Hence, the 2-ADD-Skip method is proposed, in which new formulae for computing updates are shown in terms of two points, namely: $(X_{m+n} : Z_{m+n})$ and $(X_{m-n} : Z_{m-n})$; this is achieved by using only $(X_m : Z_m)$ and $(X_n : Z_n)$ for $m \neq n$. By this method, two additions that are required to compute $(X_m : Z_m)$ and $(X_n : Z_n)$ are skipped. To apply the 2-ADD-Skip method to isogeny computation, the notion of the complete chain is introduced, describing the update process. In conventional methods, the chain may be expressed as $1 \to 2 \to \cdots \to d$. Here, a chain fill-in using the 2-ADD-Step methods is proposed.

4.1 2-ADD-Skip Method

Equations for image computation (8) and curve computation (10) show that all intermediate variables such as S_X are symmetrical in terms of index i. For example, on expressing $T_1(X_1, Z_1, \ldots, X_n, Z_n)$ as a polynomial in $X_1, Z_1, \ldots, X_n, Z_n$, the relation $T_1(X_1, Z_1, \ldots, X_n, Z_n) = T_1(X_{\sigma(1)}, Z_{\sigma(1)}, \ldots, X_{\sigma(n)}, Z_{\sigma(n)})$ holds true for any $\sigma \in \mathfrak{S}_n$, where $\mathfrak{S}_n$ is the symmetric group of degree n. Additionally, the respective update formulae, (11) and (12), are expressed as linear combinations of X_i and Z_i. Therefore, if $X_i X_j, Z_i Z_j$, and $X_i Z_j + X_j Z_i$ exist for some indices i and j, updates can be performed in terms of $(X_i : Z_i)$ and $(X_j : Z_j)$ according to the new update formulae (16) and (17), respectively:

$$
\begin{cases}
S_X \leftarrow S_X \cdot ((X^2) \cdot X_i X_j - (XZ) \cdot (X_i Z_j + X_j Z_i) + (Z^2) \cdot Z_i Z_j), \\
S_Z \leftarrow S_Z \cdot ((X^2) \cdot Z_i Z_j - (XZ) \cdot (X_i Z_j + X_j Z_i) + (Z^2) \cdot X_i X_j);
\end{cases}
\tag{16}
$$

$$
\begin{cases}
T_1 \leftarrow T_1 \cdot X_i X_j + T_0 \cdot (X_i Z_j + X_j Z_i), \\
T_0 \leftarrow T_0 \cdot X_i X_j, \\
T_{\ell-2} \leftarrow T_{\ell-2} \cdot Z_i Z_j + T_{\ell-1} \cdot (X_i Z_j + X_j Z_i), \\
T_{\ell-1} \leftarrow T_{\ell-1} \cdot Z_i Z_j.
\end{cases}
\tag{17}
$$

The new formulae (16) and (17) require $7\mathbf{M} + 4\mathbf{a}$ and $6\mathbf{M} + 2\mathbf{a}$ respectively, as X^2, XZ and Z^2 can be reused if they are computed once at the beginning of the algorithm.

Furthermore, for any indices m and n with $m \neq n$, $X_{m+n} X_{m-n}, Z_{m+n} Z_{m-n}$ and $X_{m+n} Z_{m-n} + X_{m-n} Z_{m+n}$ can be computed from $(X_m : Z_m)$ and $(X_n : Z_n)$ as follows. As in [14], let $(x_3, y_3) = (x_1, y_1) + (x_2, y_2)$ and $(x_4, y_4) = (x_1, y_1) - (x_2, y_2)$, where $(x_1, y_1) \neq (x_2, y_2) \in M_{a,b}(K)$. By the addition law, $x_3 x_4$ and $x_3 + x_4$ can be expressed without using y-coordinates:

$$
x_3 x_4 = \frac{(1 - x_1 x_2)^2}{(x_2 - x_1)^2}, \quad x_3 + x_4 = \frac{2(x_1 + x_2)(x_1 x_2 + 1) + 4a x_1 x_2}{(x_2 - x_1)^2}.
\tag{18}
$$

Considering them over $\mathbb{P}^1(K)$, we have:

$$
\begin{cases}
X_{m+n} X_{m-n} = C(X_n X_m - Z_n Z_m)^2, \\
Z_{m+n} Z_{m-n} = C(X_n Z_m - X_m Z_n)^2, \\
X_{m+n} Z_{m-n} + X_{m-n} Z_{m+n} = 2C(X_n Z_m + X_m Z_n)(X_n X_m + Z_n Z_m) \\
\qquad\qquad\qquad\qquad\qquad\qquad + 4A X_n X_m Z_n Z_m.
\end{cases}
\tag{19}
$$

268   K. Kodera et al.

Equation (19) can be computed by $9\mathbf{M} + 3\mathbf{S} + 7\mathbf{a}$ field arithmetic operations using the following transformation:

$$4AX_nX_mZ_nZ_m = A\left((X_nX_m + Z_nZ_m)^2 - (X_nX_m - Z_nZ_m)^2\right).$$

In summary, if we have $(X_m : Z_m)$ and $(X_n : Z_n)$ for some $m \neq n$, then updates for curve and image computation in terms of $(X_{m+n} : Z_{m+n})$ and $(X_{m-n} : Z_{m-n})$ can be computed without using those points themselves. This technique is called the "2-ADD-Skip method" because two executions of ADD for $(X_{m+n} : Z_{m+n})$ and $(X_{m-n} : Z_{m-n})$ can be skipped.

Table 1 shows the computational cost of computing updates in terms of two points, $(X_i : Z_i)$ and $(X_j : Z_j)$, with and without the 2-ADD-Skip method.

Table 1. Computational cost of updates in terms of two points $(X_i : Z_i)$ and $(X_j : Z_j)$ with and without the 2-ADD-Skip method.

		(i) Conventional approach	(ii) 2-ADD-Skip method	Diff (ii)−(i)
Computing $(X_i : Z_i)$ and $(X_j : Z_j)$ or X_iX_j, Z_iZ_j and $X_iZ_j + X_jZ_i$		8M + 4S + 12a	9M + 3S + 7a	−1M + 1S + 5a
Updates for image computation		8M + 8a	7M + 4a	1M + 4a
Updates for curve computation	Mon	12M + 4a	6M + 2a	6M + 2a
	with tE	4M	2M + 3a	2M − 3a
Total	Mon	28M + 4S + 24a	22M + 3S + 13a	6M + 1S + 11a
	with tE	20M + 4S + 20a	18M + 3S + 14a	2M + 1S + 6a

Each time the proposed method is used for isogeny computation on Montgomery curves, $6\mathbf{M} + 1\mathbf{S} + 11\mathbf{a}$ operations can be saved. Therefore, increasing the usage of this method leads to a faster algorithm for isogeny computation.

4.2   An Efficient Algorithm with 2-ADD-Skip Method

To apply the 2-ADD-Skip method to correct isogeny computations, the following conditions should be satisfied:

- $(X_i : Z_i), (X_j : Z_j)$, and $(X_{i-j} : Z_{i-j})$ should be available before computing the point $(X_{i+j} : Z_{i+j})$;
- $(X_m : Z_m)$ and $(X_n : Z_n)$ should be available before computing updates in terms of $(X_{m+n} : Z_{m+n})$ and $(X_{m-n} : Z_{m-n})$ with 2-ADD-Skip method; and
- the result is equivalent to that when each update is executed *exactly once* in terms of $(X_i : Z_i)$ for $i = 2, \ldots, d$ without duplication nor omission.

Importantly, it is observed that for a point $(X_{m_i} : Z_{m_i})$ and n points $(X_1 : Z_1), \ldots, (X_n : Z_n)$, updates in terms of $2n+1$ points can be computed by using a single update in terms of $(X_{m_i} : Z_{m_i})$ and n 2-ADD-Skip methods as $\{(X_{m_i-1} : Z_{m_i-1}), (X_{m_i+1} : Z_{m_i+1})\}, \ldots, \{(X_{m_i-n} : Z_{m_i-n}), (X_{m_i+n} : Z_{m_i+n})\}$, as shown in Fig. 1.

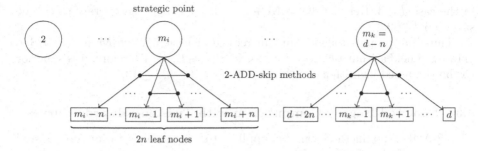

strategic point

Fig. 1. Complete chain with n-time 2-ADD-Skip methods

In this context, the pivot $(X_{m_i} : Z_{m_i})$ is called the i-th *strategic point*. Notably, the point addition that is required to compute points corresponding to leaf nodes can be skipped. If the $(i + 1)$-th strategic point is set as $m_i + 2n + 1$, updates can be computed in terms of the next $2n + 1$ points, which correspond to $m_i + n + 1, \ldots, m_i + 3n + 1$, without duplications nor omissions.

Consider a chain with nodes $\{2, \ldots, d\}$. When a chain ends with an nth 2-ADD-Skip method and covers all $d - 1$ nodes without duplications nor omissions, as shown in Fig. 1, it is defined as a *complete chain*. Essentially, in a complete chain, for the last strategic point m_k, $m_k + n = d$ is satisfied.

As an example, $n = 1$ is determined in advance, and a complete chain is constructed as follows. Firstly, $2n + 1 = 3$ points $(X_1 : Z_1), (X_2 : Z_2)$, and $(X_3 : Z_3)$ are prepared via DBL and ADD operations. Given a degree of isogeny $\ell = 2d + 1$, $d = 3k + r + 1$ can be expressed uniquely, with $k \geq 1$ and $0 \leq r < 3$. Starting from the first strategic point $(X_{m_1} : Z_{m_1})$ with $m_1 = 3 + r$, then $m_i = 3i + r$ holds for all strategic points. It is easy to verify that an update can be reached for $(X_d : Z_d)$ when the 2-ADD-Skip method is executed with $(X_1 : Z_1)$ and $(X_{m_k} : Z_{m_k})$. Hence, k 2-ADD-Skip methods can be expected to be utilized during a complete chain of updates for $2, \ldots, d$. Algorithm 3 provides an explicit sequence for the case of $n = 1$. Here, $d \geq 4$ is assumed because the 2-ADD-Skip method is not executed when $d \leq 3 = 2n + 1$.

As $6\mathbf{M} + 1\mathbf{S} + 11\mathbf{a}$ operations are saved each time the 2-ADD-Skip method is utilized, approximately $6k\mathbf{M} + k\mathbf{S} + 11k\mathbf{a}$ operations can be saved as compared to Algorithm 2. As shown in line 5, $\mathbf{M} + 2\mathbf{S}$ operations are additionally required at the beginning. Moreover, some overheads are involved when $r = 1$ and $r = 0$, where r satisfies $d = 3k + r + 1$. When $r = 1$, the first strategic point $m_1 = 4$, as shown in line 12. Hence, an update with (X_3, Z_3) is computed by the first 2-ADD-Skip method in lines 29–31, although we have (X_3, Z_3) in line 6. Therefore, $(6k - 5)\mathbf{M} + (k - 4)\mathbf{S} + (11k - 6)\mathbf{a}$ operations can be saved because $4\mathbf{M} + 2\mathbf{S} + 6\mathbf{a}$ operations cannot be saved, which is the cost of ADD to compute (X_3, Z_3). Similarly, when $r = 0$, an update with (X_2, Z_2) is computed by the first 2-ADD-Skip method, although it can be found in line 5. Furthermore, DBL is required instead of ADD, as in line 23, which requires an additional $2\mathbf{a}$ except in the case $d = 4$. Hence, $(6k - 5)\mathbf{M} + (k - 4)\mathbf{S} + (11k - 8)\mathbf{a}$ operations can be saved for $k \geq 2$.

Thus, the proposed algorithm can reduce at least $(6k - 5)\mathbf{M} + (k - 4)\mathbf{S} + (11k-8)\mathbf{a}$ field arithmetic operations for $k = \lfloor (\ell-2)/6 \rfloor$. Therefore, it is superior to the combined algorithm in [13] and [2] when $d \geq 6, \ell \geq 13$.

4.3 Renewed Isogeny Computation with Twisted Edwards Curves

The 2-ADD-Skip method can be applied to curve computation on twisted Edwards curves as follows.

$$\begin{cases} \pi_Y \leftarrow \pi_Y \left(X_i X_j + Z_i Z_j - (X_i Z_j + X_j Z_i) \right), \\ \pi_Z \leftarrow \pi_Z \left(X_i X_j + Z_i Z_j + (X_i Z_j + X_j Z_i) \right). \end{cases} \tag{20}$$

It is noted that $3\mathbf{a}$ additional operations are required here in contrast to the conventional iterative algorithm, in which $X_i \pm Z_i$ is obtained at no additional cost by reusing the point computation results. As mentioned earlier, Table 1 shows that $2\mathbf{M} + 1\mathbf{S} + 6\mathbf{a}$ operations can be saved each time the 2-ADD-Skip method is utilized. Because the same overheads are involved as in Sect. 4.2, this algorithm can avoid at least $(2k - 5)\mathbf{M} + (k - 4)\mathbf{S} + (6k - 8)\mathbf{a}$ field arithmetic operations for $k = \lfloor (\ell - 2)/6 \rfloor$ as compared to with the algorithm in [5]. Hence, the proposed algorithm is fast even with the curve computation with twisted Edwards curves, when $d \geq 9, \ell \geq 19$.

4.4 Constructing Dummy Isogenies for Constant-Time CSIDH

As mentioned in Sect. 2.4, CSIDH implementations can be protected against side-channel attacks by always computing a constant number of ℓ-isogenies while choosing appropriately between a dummy and a real isogeny computations. Because ℓ-isogeny inherently removes a factor of ℓ from the order of the image point $\phi(P)$, the dummy isogeny computation must perform scalar multiplication $[\ell]P$. Using the proposed approach, a dummy isogeny computation can also be performed with two extra ADD operations, resulting in similar overheads as in [6]. Specifically, for any d, $(X_{d-3n+1} : Z_{d-3n+1})$ and $(X_{d-n} : Z_{d-n})$ are obtained as the last two strategic points. We can obtain $(X_{d+n+1} : Z_{d+n+1})$ by $\mathtt{ADD}((X_{d-3n+1} : Z_{d-3n+1}), (X_{d-n} : Z_{d-n}), (X_{2n+1} : Z_{2n+1}))$. Then, $(X_{2d+1} : Z_{2d+1})$ can be computed by $\mathtt{ADD}((X_{d+n+1} : Z_{d+n+1}), (X_{d-n} : Z_{d-n}), (X_{2n+1} : Z_{2n+1}))$. Thus, the proposed approach can also increase the speed of constant-time CSIDH implementations.

5 Experimental Results

5.1 Results for CSIDH-512

To demonstrate the efficiency of the proposed method, it was applied to CSIDH-512, which involves ℓ_i-isogenies for $(\ell_1, \ldots, \ell_{74}) = (3, \ldots, 587)$, the first 73 smallest odd primes and 587. The proposed algorithm is implemented in C by replacing the xISOG function in the reference implementation https://zenon.cs.hs-rm.de/pqcrypto/faster-csidh [5]. It is noted that twisted Edwards curves were used for the curve computation in both cases. The experiments were performed using bench.c from the same repository, by taking an average of over 10000 runs on an Intel Core i7-8569U Coffee Lake processor running Ubuntu 16.04LTS for both case. Table 2 shows a comparison between the proposed algorithm and that in [5] with regard to the computational cost in clock cycles and wall-clock time for the evaluation of the class group action in CSIDH.

Table 2. Comparison of evaluation of class group action in CSIDH-512.

	Previous work	Proposed method	Ratio
Clock cycles $\times 10^6$	96.16	89.69	0.9327
Wall-clock time (ms)	48.20	44.97	0.9329

As seen in the table, the implementation of the proposed algorithm can increase the speed of CSIDH-512 by approximately 6.7% as compared to that in [5].

5.2   Comparison with Bernstein *et al.*'s Algorithm

Toward the end of March in 2020, Bernstein *et al.* proposed a new algorithm to compute ℓ-isogeny by $\tilde{O}(\sqrt{\ell})$ [11]. Isogeny computation was treated as a polynomial evaluation and performed in a systematic manner using the resultant computation. As a result, they successfully reduced the number of points to be computed in the kernel. Particularly, their biquadratic relation in [[3], Example 4.4] is essentially identical to Eq. (18), although both works are conducted individually.

Figures 2 and 3 compares the proposed algorithm, Bernstein *et al.*'s algorithm, and the previous algorithm [5] for isogeny computation with each degree in terms of required number of field multiplications and clock cycles, respectively.

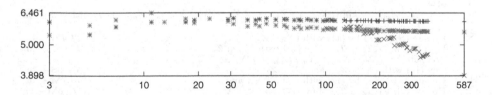

Fig. 2. Required numbers of field multiplications during ℓ-isogeny divided by $\ell + 2$ (Color figure online)

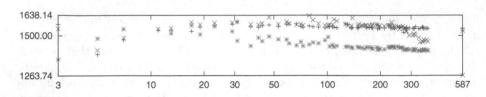

Fig. 3. Required numbers of clock cycles during ℓ-isogeny divided by $\ell+2$ (Color figure online)

These experiments were performed by referring implementation in https://velusqrt.isogeny.org [11]. Numbers of field multiplications and clock cycles were obtained by a median across 15 experiments on an Intel Core i7-8569U Coffee Lake processor running Debian 10.4 with Turbo Boost disabled. In these figures,

---

Algorithm 3. Isogeny computation on Montgomery curves with 2-ADD-Skip method

Input: $d \geq 4$, $(X : Z)$, $(X_1 : Z_1)$, and $(A : C)$
Output: $(X' : Z')$ and $(A' : C')$

1: $t^+ \leftarrow X + Z$, $t^- \leftarrow X - Z$ // 2a
2: $t_0 \leftarrow t^- \cdot (X_1 + Z_1)$, $t_1 \leftarrow t^+ \cdot (X_1 - Z_1)$ // 2M + 2a
3: $(S_X : S_Z) \leftarrow (t_0 + t_1, t_0 - t_1)$ // 2a
4: $(T_0, T_1, T_{\ell-2}, T_{\ell-1}) \leftarrow (X_1, Z_1, Z_1, X_1)$
5: $XX \leftarrow X^2$, $XZ \leftarrow X \cdot Z$, $ZZ \leftarrow Z^2$ // M + 2S
6: $(X_2 : Z_2) \leftarrow \text{DBL}((X_1 : Z_1), (A : C))$ // 4M + 2S + 8a
7: $(X_3 : Z_3) \leftarrow \text{ADD}((X_2 : Z_2), (X_1 : Z_1), (X_1 : Z_1))$ // 4M + 2S + 6a
8: $(r, k) \leftarrow ((d-1) \bmod 3, \lfloor (d-1)/3 \rfloor)$
9: **for** $i = 1$ to k **do**
10:     $m \leftarrow 3 * i + r$
11:     **if** $i == 1$ **then**
12:        **if** $r \equiv 1 \pmod 3$ **then**
13:           $(X_4 : Z_4) \leftarrow \text{ADD}((X_3 : Z_3), (X_1 : Z_1), (X_2 : Z_2))$ // 4M + 2S + 6a
14:           Update $(S_X : S_Z)$ by (11) with $(X_2 : Z_2)$ // 4M + 4a
15:           Update $(T_0, T_1, T_{\ell-2}, T_{\ell-1})$ by (12) with $(X_2 : Z_2)$ // 6M + 2a
16:        **else if** $r \equiv 2 \pmod 3$ **then**
17:           $(X_5 : Z_5) \leftarrow \text{ADD}((X_3 : Z_3), (X_2 : Z_2), (X_1 : Z_1))$ // 4M + 2S + 6a
18:           Update $(S_X : S_Z)$ by (11) with $(X_2 : Z_2)$ // 4M + 4a
19:           Update $(T_0, T_1, T_{\ell-2}, T_{\ell-1})$ by (12) with $(X_2 : Z_2)$ // 6M + 2a
20:           Update $(S_X : S_Z)$ by (11) with $(X_3 : Z_3)$ // 4M + 4a
21:           Update $(T_0, T_1, T_{\ell-2}, T_{\ell-1})$ by (12) with $(X_3 : Z_3)$ // 6M + 2a
22:        **end if**
23:     **else if** $m == 6$ **then**
24:        $(X_6 : Z_6) \leftarrow \text{DBL}((X_3 : Z_3), (A : C))$ // 4M + 2S + 8a
25:     **else**
26:        $(X_m : Z_m) \leftarrow \text{ADD}((X_{m-3} : Z_{m-3}), (X_3 : Z_3), (X_{m-6} : Z_{m-6}))$ // 4M + 2S + 6a
27:     **end if**
28:     Update $(S_X : S_Z)$ by (11) with $(X_m : Z_m)$ // 4M + 4a
29:     Update $(T_0, T_1, T_{\ell-2}, T_{\ell-1})$ by (12) with $(X_m : Z_m)$ // 6M + 2a
30:     Compute $t = (X_{m+1}X_{m-1}, X_{m+1}Z_{m-1} + X_{m-1}Z_{m+1}, Z_{m+1}Z_{m-1})$
       by (16) with $(X_m : Z_m)$ and $(X_1 : Z_1)$ // 9M + 3S + 7a
31:     Update $(S_X : S_Z)$ by (17) with t, XX, XZ and ZZ // 7M + 4a
32:     Update $(T_0, T_1, T_{\ell-2}, T_{\ell-1})$ by (17) with t, XX, XZ and ZZ // 6M + 2a
33: **end for**
34: $(X' : Z') \leftarrow (X \cdot (S_X)^2 : Z \cdot (S_Z)^2)$ // 2M + 2S
35: $(A' : C') \leftarrow (A \cdot T_0 \cdot T_{\ell-1} - 3C(T_0 \cdot T_{\ell-2} - T_1 \cdot T_{\ell-1}) : C \cdot T_{\ell-1}^2)$ // 5M + S + 4a
36: **return** $(X' : Z')$ and $(A' : C')$

the horizontal axis corresponds to degree ℓ for 74 primes used in CSIDH-512, which consists of the first 73 smallest odd primes and 587. The vertical axis corresponds to required clock cycles, which is obtained by a median across 15 experiments, divided by $\ell+2$ as in [11]. The figure are displayed on a logarithmic scale. Moreover, green, red, and blue dots represent the proposed algorithm, Bernstein *et al.*'s algorithm, and the previous algorithm, respectively. It is shown that the proposed algorithm has the lowest number of field multiplications and clock cycles for $19 \leq \ell \leq 157$ and $19 \leq \ell \leq 373$, respectively. It is noted that the proposed algorithm is not asymptotically faster than the Bernstein *et al.*'s algorithm.

6 Conclusion

In this study, efficient algorithms for isogeny computation were investigated to accelerate isogeny-based cryptography. A technique we call "2-ADD-Skip method" was proposed for isogeny computation on Montgomery curves. This method can reduce the amount of computation for points in the kernel $(X_i : Z_i)$. Furthermore, the method was used to construct explicit algorithms for isogeny computation with odd degree ℓ. This study also shows that 2-ADD-Skip method can also increase the speed of constant-time CSIDH implementations.

Moreover, the computational costs of the proposed algorithms were analyzed in terms of number of field multiplication $\mathbf{M}$, squaring $\mathbf{S}$, and addition $\mathbf{a}$. The results show that, compared with the combined algorithm by Costello *et al.* [13] and Castryck *et al.* [2], the proposed algorithm can save at least $(6k - 5)\mathbf{M} + (k - 4)\mathbf{S} + (11k - 7)\mathbf{a}$ field arithmetic operations for isogeny computation for $k = \lfloor(\ell - 2)/6\rfloor$. Hence, the proposed approach can enable a lower number of operations when $\ell \geq 13$. Even when the curve computation is performed with twisted Edwards curves, the proposed algorithm can save at least $(2k-5)\mathbf{M}+(k-4)\mathbf{S}+(6k-7)\mathbf{a}$ field arithmetic operations compared with the algorithm by Meyer *et al.* [5] In this case, it can enable a lower number of operations when $\ell \geq 19$. It was found that a CSIDH-512 implementation with the proposed algorithm for isogeny computation is approximately 6.7% faster than that obtained by Meyer *et al.* Although the proposed algorithm is not asymptotically faster than the Bernstein *et al.*'s algorithm [11], experiments showed that it requires still lower number of clock cycles for $19 \leq \ell \leq 373$. It is noted that the number of leaf nodes is fixed to $n = 1$ in the proposed algorithms, and exploring n will give more efficient algorithms.

Acknowledgments. This work was supported by JSPS KAKENHI Grant Number JP19J10400, enPiT (Education Network for Practical Information Technologies) at MEXT, and Innovation Platform for Society 5.0 at MEXT.

References

1. De Feo, L., Jao, D., Plût, J.: Towards quantum-resistant cryptosystems from supersingular elliptic curve isogenies. J. Math. Cryptol. **8**(3), 209–247 (2014)

2. Castryck, W., Lange, T., Martindale, C., Panny, L., Renes, J.: CSIDH: an efficient post-quantum commutative group action. In: Peyrin, T., Galbraith, S. (eds.) ASIACRYPT 2018. LNCS, vol. 11274, pp. 395–427. Springer, Cham (2018). https://doi.org/10.1007/978-3-030-03332-3_15

3. Jao, D., et al.: Supersingular isogeny key encapsulation. Submission to the NIST Post- Quantum Cryptography Standardization project. https://sike.org

4. Alagic, G., et al.: Status report on the first round of the NIST post-quantum cryptography standardization process. NISTIR 8240 (2019)

5. Meyer, M., Reith, S.: A faster way to the CSIDH. In: Chakraborty, D., Iwata, T. (eds.) INDOCRYPT 2018. LNCS, vol. 11356, pp. 137–152. Springer, Cham (2018). https://doi.org/10.1007/978-3-030-05378-9_8

6. Meyer, M., Campos, F., Reith, S.: On lions and elligators: an efficient constant-time implementation of CSIDH. In: Ding, J., Steinwandt, R. (eds.) PQCrypto 2019. LNCS, vol. 11505, pp. 307–325. Springer, Cham (2019). https://doi.org/10.1007/978-3-030-25510-7_17

7. Hutchinson, A., LeGrow, J.T., Koziel, B., Azarderakhsh, R.: Further optimizations of CSIDH: a systematic approach to efficient strategies, permutations, and bound vectors. IACR Cryptol. ePrint Arch. **2019**, 1121 (2019)

8. Nakagawa, K., Onuki, H., Takayasu, A., Takagi, T.: L_1-norm ball for CSIDH: optimal strategy for choosing the secret key space. IACR Cryptol. ePrint Arch. **2020**, 181 (2020)

9. Cervantes-Vázquez, D., Chenu, M., Chi-Domínguez, J.-J., De Feo, L., Rodríguez-Henríquez, F., Smith, B.: Stronger and faster side-channel protections for CSIDH. In: Schwabe, P., Thériault, N. (eds.) LATINCRYPT 2019. LNCS, vol. 11774, pp. 173–193. Springer, Cham (2019). https://doi.org/10.1007/978-3-030-30530-7_9

10. Bernstein, D.J., Lange, T., Martindale, C., Panny, L.: Quantum circuits for the CSIDH: optimizing quantum evaluation of isogenies. In: Ishai, Y., Rijmen, V. (eds.) EUROCRYPT 2019. LNCS, vol. 11477, pp. 409–441. Springer, Cham (2019). https://doi.org/10.1007/978-3-030-17656-3_15

11. Bernstein, D.J., De Feo, L., Leroux, A., Smith, B.: Faster computation of isogenies of large prime degree. IACR Cryptol. ePrint Arch. **2020**, 341 (2020)

12. Onuki, H., Aikawa, Y., Yamazaki, T., Takagi, T.: (Short paper) a faster constant-time algorithm of CSIDH keeping two points. In: Attrapadung, N., Yagi, T. (eds.) IWSEC 2019. LNCS, vol. 11689, pp. 23–33. Springer, Cham (2019). https://doi.org/10.1007/978-3-030-26834-3_2

13. Costello, C., Hisil, H.: A simple and compact algorithm for SIDH with arbitrary degree isogenies. In: Takagi, T., Peyrin, T. (eds.) ASIACRYPT 2017. LNCS, vol. 10625, pp. 303–329. Springer, Cham (2017). https://doi.org/10.1007/978-3-319-70697-9_11

14. Montgomery, P.L.: Speeding the Pollard and elliptic curve methods of factorization. Math. Comput. **48**, 243–264 (1987)

15. Costello, C., Longa, P., Naehrig, M.: Efficient algorithms for supersingular isogeny Diffie-Hellman. In: Robshaw, M., Katz, J. (eds.) CRYPTO 2016. LNCS, vol. 9814, pp. 572–601. Springer, Heidelberg (2016). https://doi.org/10.1007/978-3-662-53018-4_21

16. Bernstein, D.J., Birkner, P., Joye, M., Lange, T., Peters, C.: Twisted Edwards curves. In: Vaudenay, S. (ed.) AFRICACRYPT 2008. LNCS, vol. 5023, pp. 389–405. Springer, Heidelberg (2008). https://doi.org/10.1007/978-3-540-68164-9_26

17. Castryck, W., Galbraith, S.D., Farashahi, R.R.: Efficient arithmetic on elliptic curves using a mixed Edwards-Montgomery representation. IACR Cryptol. ePrint Arch. **2008**, 218 (2008)

18. Vélu, J.: Isogènies entre courbes elliptiques. C R Acad. Sci. Paris Sér. A-B **273**, A238–A241 (1971)
19. Couveignes, J.M.: Hard homogeneous spaces. IACR Cryptol. ePrint Arch. **2006**, 291 (2006)
20. Rostovtsev, A., Stolbunov, A.: Public-key cryptosystem based on isogenies. IACR Cryptol. ePrint Arch. **2006**, 145 (2006)
21. Stolbunov, A.: Constructing public-key cryptographic schemes based on class group action on a set of isogenous elliptic curves. Adv. Math. Commun. **4**(2), 215–235 (2010)
22. Renes, J.: Computing isogenies between montgomery curves using the action of (0, 0). In: Lange, T., Steinwandt, R. (eds.) PQCrypto 2018. LNCS, vol. 10786, pp. 229–247. Springer, Cham (2018). https://doi.org/10.1007/978-3-319-79063-3_11
23. Moody, D., Shumow, D.: Analogues of Vélu's formulas for isogenies on alternate models of elliptic curves. Math. Comput. **85**(300), 1929–1951 (2016)

An Efficient Implementation of AES on 8-Bit AVR-Based Sensor Nodes

YoungBeom Kim and Seog Chung Seo[✉][iD]

Department of Information Security, Cryptology, and Mathematics,
Kookmin University, Seoul, South Korea
{darania,scseo}@kookmin.ac.kr

Abstract. Recently, FACE-LIGHT was proposed on 8-bit AVR MCUs for fast AES encryption. FACE-LIGHT is an extended version of Fast AES-CTR mode Encryption (FACE) method which was firstly proposed for high-end processors and it is tailored for performance on 8-bit AVR MCUs. Even though it has achieved high performance, it has to suffer from the overhead caused by table generation. Thus, when the number of blocks is less than a certain number, the table generation overhead is greater than the gains from using the generated table in the process of encryption. In other words, FACE-LIGHT needs to generate new tables whenever the Initial Vector (IV) is changed. Thus, frequent table regeneration results in a significant performance degradation. In this paper, we present an efficient implementation of AES block cipher on 8-bit AVR Microcontrollers (MCUs). Our method combines ShiftRows, SubBytes, and MixColumns operations into one with column-wise fashion and makes full use of registers of AVR MCUs for high performance. With handcrafted assembly codes, our implementation has achieved 2,251, 2,706, and 3,160 clock cycles for 128-bit, 192-bit, and 256-bit security, respectively. Our implementation outperforms FACE-LIGHT with respect to overall performance including table generation and block encryptions until around 1,850 blocks (resp. 15,000 blocks) for 128-bit (resp. 192-bit) security. With respect to 256-bit security, our implementation always outperforms FACE-LIGHT without considering the table generation time. Our implementation operates in constant time and can be used for not only CTR mode, but also CBC mode differently from FACE-LIGHT.

Keywords: AES · Optimization · 8-bit AVR · Atmega · Embedded · WSN · Sensor node · Counter mode · CTR mode

1 Introduction

With development of Internet of Things (IoT) technology, Wireless Sensor Networks (WSNs) have been widely used for various applications such as smart

This work was supported by the National Research Foundation of Korea (NRF) grant funded by the Korea government (MSIT) (No. 2019R1F1A1058494).

I. You (Ed.): WISA 2020, LNCS 12583, pp. 276–290, 2020.
https://doi.org/10.1007/978-3-030-65299-9_21

factory, smart farm, military surveillance systems, and home automation systems. In WSNs, sensor nodes collect information at where they are deployed and transmit it to the server with wireless communication. Thus, the data needs to be encrypted in order to provide confidentiality of the sensitive data. However, applying encryption to transmitted data is challenging on WSNs because the sensor nodes are very resource-constrained. For example, MICAz mote is a popular sensor node in WSNs and it is equipped with 8-bit AVR Atmega128 microcontroller clocked at 7.3728 MHz and it has only 4 KB SRAM. Atmega328p, our target MCU, is also widely used for various types of sensor nodes.

AES cipher is widely used in several communication standards for data confidentiality in WSNs. Until now, many researchers have presented efficient implementations of AES on 8-bit AVR MCUs. Among them, recently FACE-LIGHT was proposed for fast AES CTR encryption on 8-bit AVR MCUs [11]. FACE-LIGHT is an extended version of FACE(Fast AES-CTR mode Encryption) [3], originally proposed for high-end processors. Its main idea is to build Lookup tables of 4 KB containing all possible values until Round 2, and to utilize them for fast computation of the first two rounds. Actually, it can encrypt a 128-bit data block in 2,218 clock cycles (cc) with 128-bit security. Although it has achieved high performance, it has to suffer from the overhead caused by Lookup table generation. Actually, FACE-LIGHT needs to rebuild the Lookup tables whenever the nonce value in the IV(initialization vector) changes (In our estimation, it requires around 61,440 cc for generating Lookup tables). Therefore, FACE-LIGHT is not suitable for environments where the communication session is frequently refreshed. In WSNs, the communication session can be frequently refreshed because the sensor nodes are usually deployed on harsh environments.

In this paper, we present an efficient implementation of AES on 8-bit AVR MCUs for data confidentiality in WSNs. Our method integrates ShiftRows, SubBytes, and MixColumns operations into one for fast round computation and makes full use of registers in the target MCU. Differently from FACE-LIGHT using 4 KB Lookup tables affected by IV value, our implementation utilizes constant Lookup tables of just 512 Bytes which is affordable in SRAM of 8-bit AVR MCUs. Furthermore, the table Lookup operations are optimized for high performance in our implementation. Therefore, with handcrafted assembly codes, our implementation can encrypt a 128-bit data block in 2,251 (resp. 2,706 and 3,160) cc with 128-bit (resp. 192-bit and 256-bit) security. Our implementation outperforms all existing AES implementations including FACE-LIGHT on 8-bit AVR with respect to overall performance including Lookup table generation and block encryption. In detail, our implementation provides improved performance compared with FACE-LIGHT until encrypting 1,850 blocks (resp. 15,000 blocks) for 128-bit (resp. 192-bit) security. Notably, our implementation always outperforms FACE-LIGHT without considering Lookup table generation time for 256-bit security. Our implementation executes in constant time, which provides the resistance against timing attack and it can be efficient executed with not only CTR mode, but also CBC mode differently from FACE-LIGHT.

Table 1. Notations

Symbol	Meaning
state	Internal State composed of 16 bytes (typically 4 by 4 matrix)
Nb	Number of Columns (32-bit words) comprising the *state*
Nk	Number of 32-bit words comprising the *state*
Nr	Number of rounds depending on key length
Subbytes()	Transformation using a non-linear byte substitution table (SBOX-Table)
ShiftRows()	Transformation cyclically Shifting the last three rows of the *state* by different offsets
MixColumns()	Transformation taking all of the columns of the *state* and mixing their data to produce new columns
AddRoundKey()	Transformation adding RoundKey to the *state* with XOR operation
KeyExpansion()	Routine generating a series of Round Keys from a master key

2   Overview of AES Block Cipher and 8-Bit AVR MCUs

2.1   Overview of AES Block Cipher

AES is the most widely used 128-bit block cipher providing 128, 192, and 256-bit security. Table 1 defines notations used in this paper. Each round of AES encryption except for the last round is composed of **Subbytes()**, **ShiftRows()**, **MixColumns()**, and **AddRoundKey()** functions. **MixColumns()** function is not executed in the last round. The number of rounds in the AES depends on the length of the key initially entered [1]. AddRoundKey updates the *state* by XORing the *state* with round key. Subbytes provides Confusion effect, and ShiftRows and MixColumns cause Diffusion effect during AES operation. Sub-Bytes is a single substitution operation for bytes. ShiftRows rotates the last three rows of the *state*. Equation 1 is MixColumns process mixing bytes in each columns. In the Eq. 1, each byte in a column is updated with Eq. 2.

$$\begin{bmatrix} S'_{0,c} \\ S'_{1,c} \\ S'_{2,c} \\ S'_{3,c} \end{bmatrix} = \begin{bmatrix} 02\ 03\ 01\ 01 \\ 01\ 02\ 03\ 01 \\ 01\ 01\ 02\ 03 \\ 03\ 01\ 01\ 02 \end{bmatrix} \begin{bmatrix} S_{0,c} \\ S_{1,c} \\ S_{2,c} \\ S_{3,c} \end{bmatrix} \tag{1}$$

$$S_{0,c}^{'} = (02 \cdot S_{0,c}) \oplus (03 \cdot S_{1,c}) \oplus S_{2,c} \oplus S_{3,c}$$
$$S_{1,c}^{'} = S_{0,c} \oplus (02 \cdot S_{1,c}) \oplus (03 \cdot S_{2,c}) \oplus S_{3,c}$$
$$S_{2,c}^{'} = S_{0,c} \oplus S_{1,c} \oplus (02 \cdot S_{2,c}) \oplus (03 \cdot S_{3,c}) \qquad (2)$$
$$S_{3,c}^{'} = (03 \cdot S_{0,c}) \oplus S_{1,c} \oplus S_{2,c} \oplus (02 \cdot S_{3,c})$$

In the above equation, $(02 \cdot S_{i,c})$ can be computed as a multiplication in $GF(2^8)$ with an irreducible polynomial $x^8 + x^4 + x^3 + x + 1$. $(03 \cdot S_{i,c})$ can be executed with a multiplication in $GF(2^8)$ and additional addition in $GF(2^8)$. Since all bytes in the *state* need to be updated with following Eq. 2, MixColumns causes the most computational load in AES.

2.2   Overview of 8-Bit AVR MCUs

Table 2. AVR Assembly Instructions

Instruction	Operands	Operation	Clocks
MOV	Rd, Rr	Copy register from R_r to R_d, $Rd \leftarrow Rr$	1
LD	Rd, X	Load memory data from X to R_d ,$Rd \leftarrow (X)$	2
LPM	Rd, Z	Load program memory from Z to R_d ,$Rd \leftarrow (Z)$	3
ST	Rr, X	Store memory from R_r to X ,$(X) \leftarrow Rr$	2
EOR	Rd, Rr	Exclusive-OR two register, $Rd \leftarrow Rd \oplus Rr$	1
LSL	Rd	Logical shift left, $Rd(n) \leftarrow Rd(n), Rd(0) \leftarrow 0$	1
BRCC	k	Branch if Carry cleared, $if\ (C = 0)\ then\ PC \leftarrow PC + k + 1$	1/2
SET	*None*	Set T in SREG, $T \leftarrow 1$	1
RJMP	k	Relative jump, $PC \leftarrow PC + k + 1$	2

8-bit AVR is the most widely used embedded MCU for low-priced embedded devices including sensor nodes in WSNs. The AVR's commands consist of operation codes and operand, which have more than 130 commands. operand can use registers, memory, and constant values as targets for the command, and sometimes, according to the command, it is included in the command code without an operation [5]. All AVR commands require less than 4 clock cycles to execute [7]. Table 2 shows operand and clock cycles of commands used in this paper [6]. Currently, there are various types of AVR microcontrollers, and they have various peripherals and memory sizes. AVR is divided into Flash memory, SRAM and EEPROM with a Harvard architecture. the AVR-MCU has 32 general-purpose resisters with an 8-bit size, which are used for various roles, including basic private operation and bit operation. In particular, the R26 - R31 registers can be combined into two each and used as three 16-bit registers, X, Y, and Z registers. They are used as pointers to indirectly specify a 16-bit address for data memory. There is also a SREG(Status Register) that show the status and result after ALU calculation.

3   Analysis of Existing Implementations on 8-Bit AVR

3.1   Analysis of Otte et al.'s Implementation

In Otte et al.'s AES implementation [2], the *state* are stored in general-purpose registers of AVR to minimize memory access time. SBOX-Table is stored in Flash Memory and its value is loaded with LPM instruction. KeyExpansion is executed before beginning encryption process and the generated round keys are stored in memory. Otte et al.'s implementation requires 3 clock cycles to load a value in SBOX-Table located at Flash memory. Since Arduino UNO, the most popular 8-bit embedded device, has 2 KB of SRAM, SBOX-Table of 256-bytes is affordable in SRAM. Therefore, storing SBOX-Table in SRAM could achieve performance improvement because accessing a value in SRAM costs 2 clock cycles .

Algorithm 1. MixColumns of Otte et al.[2]

1: `.irp row, in 0,1,2,3`	17: `EOR` $T1, 1B$
2: `MOV` $r0, ST\backslash row\backslash()2$	18: 3: `EOR` $T1, r0$
3: `EOR` $r0, ST\backslash row\backslash()3$	19: `EOR` $ST\backslash row\backslash()1, T1$
4: `MOV` $T2, r0$	
	20: `LSL` $T2$
5: `MOV` $T0, ST\backslash row\backslash()0$	21: `BRCC` $3f$
6: `EOR` $ST\backslash row\backslash()0, ST\backslash row\backslash()1$	22: `EOR` $T2, 1B$
7: `EOR` $r0, ST\backslash row\backslash()0$	23: 3: `EOR` $T2, r0$
8: `LSL` $ST\backslash row\backslash()0$	24: `EOR` $ST\backslash row\backslash()2, T2$
9: `BRCC` $3f$	
10: `EOR` $ST\backslash row\backslash()0, 1B$	25: `EOR` $T0, ST\backslash row\backslash()3$
11: 3: `EOR` $ST\backslash row\backslash()0, ro$	26: `LSL` $T0$
12: `EOR` $ST\backslash row\backslash()0, T0$	27: `BRCC` $3f$
	28: `EOR` $T0, 1B$
13: `MOV` $T1, ST\backslash row\backslash()1$	29: 3: `EOR` $T0, r0$
14: `EOR` $T1, ST\backslash row\backslash()2$	30: `EOR` $ST\backslash row\backslash()3, T0$
15: `LSL` $T1$	31: `.endr`
16: `BRCC` $3f$	

Algorithm 1 is the MixColumns implementation of Otte et al.'s. In Algorithm 1, $STij(i, j \in [0, 3])$ is a register for maintaining the byte located at i-th row and j-th column in the *state*. Otte et al.'s implementation make full use of $Ti(i \in [0, 3])$ register in order to recycle the computed values without memory accessing. Otte et al.'s implementation requires branch instruction and label depending on the value of carry flag C in SREG to compute a multiplication in $GF(2^8)$. In other words, if the result of LSL instruction makes the carry flag set, the result needs to be XORed with 0x1b. However, BRCC instruction requires a 2 clock cycles when the carry Flag is zero, and vice versa, 1 clock cycles occurs, which results in non-constant timing execution. Therefore, Otte et al.'s implementation provides additional information to the attackers in view of timing side channel analysis.

3.2 Analysis of FACE-LIGHT

FACE-LIGHT is an optimized AES-CTR implementation on 8-bit AVR MCUs by constructing Lookup tables related to IV and recycling them for performance improvement [4]. Actually, FACE-LIGHT is an extended version of FACE [3] which was proposed for general purpose CPU environments. Although FACE is fast, however, it has the disadvantage of updating the Lookup tables every 256 encryption times. Furthermore, it requires 5 KB memory for storing Lookup tables. FACE-LIGHT reduces the size of Lookup tables into 4 KB and does not require to renew the Lookup tables during encryption process.

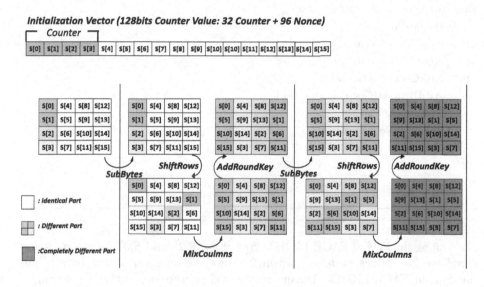

Fig. 1. Overview of FACE-LIGHT [4]

Figure 1 describes the process of FACE-LIGHT. It utilizes IV where first 4 bytes are used for counter value differently from the original CTR mode using last 4 bytes as the counter value. In Round 0, only operation is AddRoundKey. the plaintext and roundkey is XORed. Thus, as the counter value in IV increases, only 4 bytes of *state* changes. Round 1 performs SubBytes, ShiftRows, and Mix-Columns operations in the same way as a typical AES implementation. Through SubBytes operation, only 4 bytes differs from the previous block. Namely, the nonce parts in IV does not change (only counter parts change). This is the same as ShiftRows operation. However, in MixColumns operation, 8-bit data is mixed with 32-bit columns. Therefore, the counter value of IV is spread to the each column through MixColumns operation in Round 1. For example, $S[0]$ affects $S[5]$, $S[10]$ and $S[15]$. The same applies to other counters $S[1]$, $S[2]$ and $S[3]$. In addition, there are only 256 cases for each counter. As the counter value of IV changes, the difference from the previous block in the Round 0 is at most 4 bytes, and the difference in the Round 1 is at most 16 bytes from the previous block. However, even though the change of counter values updates each column, this result can be saved as a Lookup table. SubBytes and ShiftRows operations in Round 2 can be also optimized because the diffusion process does not take place unlike Mixcolumns operation. The Lookup table used in FACE-LIGHT includes the results up to the SubBytes in Round 2, and ShiftRows can be omitted by assigning the results directly to the register.

Algorithm 2. Generation of Lookup table for S[3] of IV in FACE-LIGHT

Require: byte $Counter[4]$, byte $key[4]$

Ensure: byte $Lookuptable[4][256]$

1: byte $state[4]$
2: **for** $i = 0$ to 255 **do**
3:     $state = Counter$
4:     **MixColumns**($state$)
5:     **AddRoundKey**($Counter, key$)
6:     **Subbyte**($state$)
7:     $Lookuptable[4][i] = state$
8:     $Counter = Counter + 1$
9:     $i = i + 1$
10: **end for**

Among the IV's of FACE-LIGHT, $S[0]$, $S[1]$, $S[2]$, and $S[3]$ are counters and can have 256 values each. Algorithm 2 shows the creation of 256 byte tables for $S[3]$ in FACE-LIGHT. During initial 256 encryptions, only $S[3]$ changes, and during AddRoundKey and Subbytes of Round 0, the difference from the previous block is only 1 byte. The ShifRows of 1 Round is implemented by direct means of bringing results, the actual necessary computations are MixColumns and AddRoundKey operation transformations, and the Subbytes of Round 2.

The FACE implementation requires updating some parts of Lookup tables after encryption 256 times. Furthermore, whole Lookup tables needs to be reconstructed whenever the IV is refreshed. In [3], the time for generating Lookup tables is almost same as time for encrypting 47 blocks on general purpose CPU environments. However, in view of cryptographic protocol, timing for generating Lookup tables needs to be included in the timing cost of whole encryption process. FACE-LIGHT basically follows the concept of FACE for optimizing the performance of AES-CTR on 8-bit AVR MCUs. Thus, it also requires huge timing for constructing Lookup tables of 4 KB. In other words, FACE-LIGHT needs to generate new Lookup tables whenever the IV is changed. Frequent regeneration of Lookup tables results in the significant performance degradation. Furthermore, 4 KB of Lookup tables needs to be located at the flash memory because it is larger than the size of SRAM in Arduino UNO which is the target of FACE-LIGHT [4]. Even though the source codes of FACE-LIGHT is open through github, the codes for generating Lookup tables are omitted [11]. Thus, we need to estimate the timing for Lookup table generation. In order to estimate the minimum timing of table generation, we have utilized the description of the table generation presented in FACE-LIGHT. In addition, from the open source codes of FACE-LIGHT, we have found out that FACT-LIGHT made use of Otte et al.'s implementation from Round 2 to the last Round. Therefore, the number of clock cycles for generating Lookup table is estimated based on the paper [4] and the implementation of Otte et al. [2]. Since our estimation is conservative (actually, we have excluded the timing for extra operations), it is likely that more clock cycles will be required if it is implemented in practice. Algorithm 2 shows the implementation of Look up table for S[3] of IV.

It takes 3 clocks cycles to perform LD and EOR commands for AddRoundKey operation of Round 0, and 4 clocks to perform MOV and LPM in the Subbytes operation of Round 1. In Otte et al.'s implementation, it takes 25 cc to calculate the each Columns [2]. The AddRoundKey in the Round 1 and Subbytes in the Round 2 require 28 clocks cycles, because all 4 bytes must be calculated. Therefore, a total of 15, 360 cc $((3 + 4 + 25 + 28) * 256 = 15,360)$ are required to make the Lookup table[4][256] corresponding to $S[3]$. In an AVR environment, FACE-LIGHT has the advantage of having a table of 4 KB and not renewing, which is done by creating a table for each counter. In other words, a total of 61, 440 $(15360 * 4 = 61,440)$ is required to make a table for S[0], S[1], S[2], and S[3]. The 4 KB Lookup table should be stored in the 32 KB Flash memory in Atmega328P which is the target MCU of FACE-LIGHT. Since the Look up table is stored during the encryption process, the boot-loader system must be used to generate the Lookup table of FACE-LIGHT. Therefore, it is necessary to read the pages in Flash memory, then change the data, and rewrite the entire page area. Therefore, This incurs additional costs. Considering that both the Otte et al. based on AES-128 bit implementation and the FACE-LIGHT implementation require 2, 600 cc or less, the table generation time for FACE-LIGHT requires a very large clock cycle. This is the same as the clock cycles that take about 24 encryption times.

Our estimation seems to be reasonable because the timing for Lookup table generation is almost same as encrypting 24 blocks on 8-bit AVR MCUs, which is less that that of FACE on conventional CPUs environments. Actually, 8-bit AVR MCUs have much less computing capabilities than conventional CPUs. Thus, it is more likely that Lookup table generation on 8-bit AVR MCUs requires more clock cycles than on conventional CPUs. However, since we have conservatively estimated the timing for Lookup table generation by omitting extra operations, our result of our estimation is less than that presented in FACE [3], which supports the rationale of our estimation.

In the next Section, we will present an efficient AES implementation techniques optimized on 8-bit AVR MCUs. Our implementation not only executes in constant time and but also provide fast encryption timing with only 512 bytes of constant Lookup table.

4 Proposed AES Implementation on 8-Bit AVR MCUs

4.1 Main Idea

Differently from implementation of Otte et al. and FACE-LIGHT, our implementation optimizes the process of encryption in a constant time manner. In addition, we propose a more generic AES implementation techniques which can be used for various mode of operations. Our main idea is to combine the transformations of SubBytes, ShiftRows, and Mixcolumns operations into one by column-wise fashion differently from row-wise implementations from the works of Otte et al. and FACE-LIGHT.

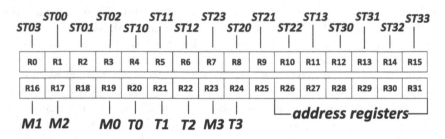

Fig. 2. Register scheduling for proposed implementation in the target AVR MCUs

In the row-wise implementation of Mixcolumns, it is effective to use branch instruction aforementioned in Sect. 3. However, this results in non-constant time execution. In addition, both works from Otte et al. and FACE-LIGHT locate SBOX-Table in Flash memory (Since the Lookup table in FACE-LIGHT is 4 KB it needs to be stored in Flash memory). However, in our implementation, we store SBOX-Table and MIX-Table in SRAM. We make use of MIX-Table containing the values of $(02 \cdot S_{i,c}, (i \in [0,3])$ in Eq. 2) rather than computing it. Thus, our implementation requires only 512 bytes of Lookup tables having constant values. The 512 bytes of SBOX-Table and MIX-Table is constant and does not change for each encryption session. Furthermore, we minimize the number of Lookup tables accesses in the MixColumns operation, which will be described in detail with Sect. 4.2. With this approach, we can optimize the performance of the MixColumns operation with a constant time manner.

For efficiency, we maintain the *state* of the encryption process in 16 general-purpose registers in AVR MCUs. Figure 2 shows the register scheduling of our implementation. Through this scheduling, we can use assembly instruction such as MOVW that can be only applicable on even-numbered registers, which can reduce by 1 clock cycle from 2 calls of MOV instructions. $R0$-$R15$ are used to maintain the values of the *state* in the encryption process. Thus, all *states* are updated in the register without memory accesses. Eight registers ($R16$-$R23$, aliased as $M0$, $M1$, $M2$, $M3$, $T0$, $T1$, $T2$, and $T3$) are used as temporary registers to recycle the intermediate values in MixColumns. ($R26$:$R27$) keeps the address value of the generated round keys required for the AddRoundKey operation, ($R28$:$R29$) keeps the address of MIX-Table, and ($R30$:$R31$) keeps the address of SBOX-Table.

4.2   Proposed Register Scheduling and Implementation

$$\bar{S}_{i,c} = SBOX(S_{i,c \ll i}) \ and \ \tilde{S}_{i,c} = MIX(S_{i,c \ll i}), \ for \ i \in [0,3]$$

$$\begin{bmatrix} S'_{0,c} \\ S'_{1,c} \\ S'_{2,c} \\ S'_{3,c} \end{bmatrix} = \underbrace{\begin{bmatrix} \tilde{S}_{0,c} \\ \bar{S}_{0,c} \\ \bar{S}_{0,c} \\ \tilde{S}_{0,c} \oplus \bar{S}_{0,c} \end{bmatrix}}_{A} \oplus \underbrace{\begin{bmatrix} \tilde{S}_{1,c} \oplus \bar{S}_{1,c} \\ \tilde{S}_{1,c} \\ \bar{S}_{1,c} \\ \bar{S}_{1,c} \end{bmatrix}}_{B} \oplus \underbrace{\begin{bmatrix} \bar{S}_{2,c} \\ \tilde{S}_{2,c} \oplus \bar{S}_{2,c} \\ \tilde{S}_{2,c} \\ \bar{S}_{2,c} \end{bmatrix}}_{C} \oplus \underbrace{\begin{bmatrix} \bar{S}_{3,c} \\ \bar{S}_{3,c} \\ \tilde{S}_{3,c} \oplus \bar{S}_{3,c} \\ \tilde{S}_{3,c} \end{bmatrix}}_{D} \quad (3)$$

In our implementation, for efficiency, we combine SubBytes, ShiftRows, and MixColumns on a column-wise operation as shown in Eq. 3.

The c-th column of *state* is updated with Eq. 3. In other words, for computing four bytes of the c-th column, the results of A, B, C, and D parts in Eq. 3 need to be XORed. We maintain the intermediate result of each part in $M0$, $M1$, $M2$, and $M3$ registers. Namely, the value of the first row in each part is maintained at $M0$. Likewise, the second, the third, and the fourth bytes of each part are maintained in $M1$, $M2$, and $M3$ registers, respectively. For optimizing the usage of limited registers in AVR MCUs, we accumulate the results of each part in Eq. 3 in four registers $M0$, $M1$, $M2$, and $M3$. In other words, at first, the four bytes result from the computation of the part A are stored in $M0$, $M1$, $M2$, and $M3$. Then, when computing the part B, C, and D, each byte result is directly accumulated into one of $M0$, $M1$, $M2$, and $M3$. Finally, the accumulated bytes in $M0$, $M1$, $M2$, and $M3$ are stored in ST registers holding *state* bytes. Our implementation processes SubBytes operation with Table Lookup by accessing SBOX-Table in RAM. In other words, a $\bar{S}_{i,c}$ corresponding to $S_{0,c}$ is retrieved from SBOX-Table. Similarly, $(02 \cdot S_{0,c})$ is efficiently computed with simple Table Lookup by accessing MIX-Table in RAM. $(03 \cdot S_{0,c})$ can be computed by XORing the result of SBOX-Table and the result of MIX-Table. For the efficiency of ShiftRows operation, we store the intermediate result of each part in Eq. 3 at the shifted position in the scheduled registers rather than actual shifting registers.

Algorithm 3 shows codes for computing the proposed Eq. 3 when $c = 0$ which is the combined operation for the first column of the *state*. The same logic can be used to compute columns of index $c \in 1, 3$. Note that the addresses for SBOX-Table and MIX-Table should be loaded Z and Y registers with LDI instruction.

Algorithm 3. Codes for proposed combined Subbytes, ShiftRows and Mix-Columns operations with equation 3 when $c = 0$

Part A Computation	Part C Computation
1: MOV $r30, ST00$	17: MOV $r30, ST22$
2: LD $M1, Z$	18: LD $T0, Z$
3: MOV $M2, M1$ // $M2 \leftarrow \bar{S}_{0,0}$	19: EOR $M0, T0$ // $M0 \leftarrow M0 \oplus \bar{S}_{2,0}$
4: MOV $M3, M2$	20: EOR $M1, T0$
5: MOV $r28, ST00$	21: EOR $M3, T0$ // $M3 \leftarrow M3 \oplus \bar{S}_{2,0}$
6: LD $M0, Y$ // $M0 \leftarrow \tilde{S}_{0,0}$	22: MOV $r28, ST22$
7: EOR $M3, M0$ // $M3 \leftarrow \tilde{S}_{0,0} \oplus \bar{S}_{0,0}$	23: LD $T0, Y$
	24: EOR $M2, T0$ // $M2 \leftarrow M2 \oplus \tilde{S}_{2,0}$
Part B Computation	25: EOR $M1, T0$ // $M1 \leftarrow M1 \oplus \tilde{S}_{2,0} \oplus \bar{S}_{2,0}$
8: MOV $r30, ST11$	
9: LD $T0, Z$	**Part C Computation**
10: EOR $M0, T0$	26: MOV $r30, ST33$
11: EOR $M2, T0$ // $M2 \leftarrow M2 \oplus \bar{S}_{1,0}$	27: LD $T0, Z$
12: EOR $M3, T0$ // $M3 \leftarrow M3 \oplus \bar{S}_{1,0}$	28: EOR $M0, T0$ // $M0 \leftarrow M0 \oplus \bar{S}_{3,0}$
13: MOV $r28, ST11$	29: EOR $M1, T0$ // $M1 \leftarrow M1 \oplus \bar{S}_{3,0}$
14: LD $T0, Y$	30: EOR $M2, T0$
15: EOR $M1, T0$ // $M1 \leftarrow M1 \oplus \tilde{S}_{1,0}$	31: MOV $r28, ST33$
16: EOR $M0, T0$ // $M0 \leftarrow M0 \oplus \tilde{S}_{1,0} \oplus \bar{S}_{1,0}$	32: LD $T0, Y$
	33: EOR $M3, T0$ // $M3 \leftarrow M3 \oplus \tilde{S}_{3,0}$
	34: EOR $M2, T0$ // $M2 \leftarrow M2 \oplus \tilde{S}_{3,0} \oplus \bar{S}_{3,0}$

At the beginning of Algorithm 3, *state* registers $ST0c$, $ST1c$, $ST2c$, and $ST3c$ contain the value of $S_{0,c}$, $S_{1,c}$, $S_{2,c}$, and $S_{3,c}$ where $c \in 0, 3$. Lines 1–7 compute the part A of Eq. 3. Lines 1–2 load $ST00$'s corresponding SBox value ($\bar{S}_{0,0}$) from SBOX-Table and store it in $M1$ register. Likewise, lines 5–6 load $ST00$'s corresponding value ($\tilde{S}_{0,0}$) from MIX-Table and store it in $M0$ register. With line 7, the result of XOR operation with $M3$ and $M0$ is stored in $M3$. Through lines 1–7, $M0$, $M1$, $M2$, and $M3$ maintain the result of $\tilde{S}_{0,0}$, $\bar{S}_{0,0}$, $\bar{S}_{0,0}$, and $\tilde{S}_{0,0} \oplus \bar{S}_{0,0}$ which are the result of the part A in Eq. 3, respectively. Lines 8–16 accumulate the result of the part B to $M0$, $M1$, $M2$, and $M3$ registers. Note that we load $ST11$ rather than actually computing ShiftRows. The operation sequences of lines 8–16 (for computing the part B), lines 17–25 (for computing the part C), and lines 26–34 (for computing the part D) are identical except for the related registers. After finishing Algorithm 3, $M0$, $M1$, $M2$, and $M3$ registers contain $S'_{0,0}$, $S'_{1,0}$, $S'_{2,0}$, and $S'_{3,0}$, respectively.

The implementations in row-wise fashion, as shown in Eq. 2, calculate $(S'_{i,c}, (i \in [0,3]))$ for each row, there are memory accesses for $S_{i,c}, (i \in [0,3])$ for each calculation of rows. Also, non-constant time execution occurs by calculating in both $(02 \cdot S_{i,c})$ and $(03 \cdot S_{i,c})$ directly with branch instruction. The proposed column-wise implementation focuses on optimizing memory accesses for each $(S_{i,c}, (i \in [1,3]))$ by reducing the duplicate memory accesses. Since our method requires only 512 bytes of Lookup Tables they can reside in SRAM, which enables fast access compared with accessing data in flash memory. In addition, the proposed combined round transformations execute in constant-time, which makes the proposed implementation secure against timing attacks.

4.3 CTR Optimization

Our implementation is not limited to a specific mode of operation differently from FACE-LIGHT. In addition, it's performance can be improved by using the characteristics of CTR mode like FACE and FACE-LIGHT. Similar to FACE-LIGHT, our implementation makes use of four bytes of the counter. Among 16 bytes of the *state*, 12 bytes are the same in the result of Round 0 (namely, AddRoundKey) of each block processing. Thus, we can store these 12 bytes as a Lookup table like [3]. When receiving a new nonce value, our implementation creates a Lookup table. The creation time for this Lookup table is negligible compared to generation time for Lookup table in FACE-LIGHT, and it contributes saving of clock cycles during Round 0.

Currently, 8-bit AVR MCUs are used for a variety of applications in WSNs (Wireless Sensor Networks) [8]. In WSN environments, since session-based cryptographic protocols require too much overhead for resource-constrained sensor nodes, broadcast-based communication protocols are mainly used. Therefore, using a long sequence of counter values is not easy for these protocols. In other words, encrypting many blocks sharing the same nonce value is not suitable for WSNs using 8-bit AVR MCUs [10]. In Sect. 3.2, we have shown that FACE-LIGHT requires a large number of clock cycles for creating a Lookup table. In environments where the nonce value is changed frequently, the overhead for creating a Lookup table surpasses the benefit of using the generated Lookup table.

5   Performance Analysis

Table 3. Comparison of AES implementations on AVR in terms of clock cycles

Security	Dinu et al. [9]	Otte et al. [2]	FACE-Light [4]	This work	This work (CTR)
AES-128	2,835	2,507	2,218	2,289	2,251
AES-192	N/A	2,991	2,702	2,746	2,706
AES-256	N/A	3,473	3,184	3,209	3,160

In this section, we compare our implementation with other existing implementations including FACE-LIGHT [4] on 8-bit AVR MCUs. Atmega328p is the target MCU and it is the most popular AVR MCU for Arduino UNO and various sensor nodes in WSNs. It equips Flash memory of 32 KB, EEPROM of 1 KB and internal SRAM of 2 KB. The measurement environment is Atmel Studio 7 and the source codes were compiled with -OS option. Table 3 represents a comparison of AES's clock cycles for each implementation. The implementation of both Otte et al. [2] and Dinu et al. [9] are AES-ECB, and the FACE-LIGHT implementation is AES-CTR. In this paper, we present an efficient AES implementation that can be used in various operating mode and AES-CTR with optimization of FACE in Round 0. Creation time of Lookup Table is not included in Table 3. Our implementation improves performance over implementation of both Dinu et al. and Otte et al. and the performance of our implementation increases more in the AES-CTR. In particular, in AES implementation for 256-bit security, our implementation has better performance than both Otte et al. and FACE-LIGHT. Our AES-CTR implementation is more efficient as the key bit length increases, because FACE-LIGHT optimizes only Round 0 and Round 1. However, in this work, we optimize AES with combining the three operations(SubBytes, ShiftRows, MixColumns) and apply to all Rounds except the Round 0 and 10 Round(resp. 12 and 14 Round) for 128-bit (resp. 192-bit and 256-bit) security. Thus, our implementation is effective rather than FACE-LIGHT as the number of encryption rounds increases.

Table 4. Running time comparison of AES implementations using 128-bit key (Timings are measured by clock cycles. NB means the number of blocks.)

NB	1	50	100	200	800	1,850
Otte et al. [2]	2,507	125,350	250,700	501,400	2,005,600	4,665,527
	(-)	(-)	(-)	(-)	(-)	(-)
FACE-Light. [4]	63,658	172,340	283,240	505,040	1,835,840	4,189,138
	(-2,439%)	(-37.49%)	(-12.98%)	(-0.73%)	(+8.46%)	(+10.2%)
This Work	2,251	112,550	225,100	450,200	1,800,800	4,189,111
(CTR)	(+10.2%)	(+10.2%)	(+10.2%)	(+10.2%)	(+10.2%)	(+10.2%)

Table 4 is a performance table of AES-CTR according to the number of encryption blocks. The value of the non-sets changes in all sessions. In the cryptographic protocol, the nonce value should change for each session. The table creation time must be considered in order to use FACE-LIGHT. In Github, the FACE-LIGHT code for the AVR environment exists [11], however no code for Lookup table generation exists, thus we estimate it based on the FACE-LIGHT implementation in Sect. 3. The estimated cost of generating the Lookup table is 61,440 clock cycles. The creation time of the Lookup table of proposed implementation in this paper is omitted because it is much smaller than the memory access time omitted during the estimation of generating the Lookup table of FACE-LIGHT. Table 4 shows that our implementation requires a lower clock cycles than the FACE-LIGHT up to 1,850 blocks for 128-bit security. The performance of our implementation and FACE-LIGHT are compared with the performance of Otte et al.'s implementation. Thus, our implementation always provides around 10.2% improvement performance compared with Otte et al.'s implementation. However, the entire performance of FACE-LIGHT is lower than

Otte et al.'s implementation until encryption 200 blocks. Based on Table 3, our implementation outperforms FACE-LIGHT until encrypting 15,000 blocks for AES-192. Regarding AES-256, our implementation is always faster than FACE-LIGHT without including table generation time based on Table 3.

6 Concluding Remarks

Due to the development of IoT technology, research to develop optimized performance in a limited environment is required. This is true not only for the basic performance of IoT, but also for encryption that needs to be additionally performed to protect personal information. Previously, a implementation such as FACE-LIGHT that optimizes AES in an 8-bit AVR MCUs has been proposed. In this paper, we present an AES implementation in an 8-bit AVR MCUs that is more efficient than FACE-LIGHT. We integrated major operations in AES and implemented them to make the most of the registers on the target MCU. Unlike FACE-LIGHT, the memory size used for the Lookup tables is reduced and optimized for use in SRAM. In addition, by using assembly instructions, we have completed an efficient implementation that eliminates unnecessary operations. Through the proposed optimization implementation, we obtained 2,251, 2,706, and 3,160 clock cycles for the key lengths of AES, 128-bit, 192-bit, and 256-bit, respectively. These results show up to 10.2% performance improvement over Otte et al. In this paper, only the optimization implementation for AES in the 8-bit AVR MCU is presented, but we will study various lightweight block encryption algorithms in various MCU in the future. This study can be used in a MCU in a constrained environment used in IoT devices.

References

1. NIST.: Announcing the ADVANCED ENCRYPTION STANDARD(AES). https://www.nist.gov/publications/advanced-encryption-standard-aes
2. Otte, D., et al.: AVR-crypto-lib (2009). http://www.das-labor.org/wiki/AVRCrypto-Lib/en
3. Park, J.H., Lee, D.H.: FACE: Fast AES CTR mode encryption techniques based on the reuse of repetitive data. In: IACR Transactions on Cryptographic Hard-ware and Embedded Systems, pp. 469–499 (2018)
4. Kim, K., Choi, S., Kwon, H., Liu, Z., Seo, H.: FACE–LIGHT: fast AES–CTR mode encryption for Low-End microcontrollers. In: Seo, J.H. (ed.) ICISC 2019. LNCS, vol. 11975, pp. 102–114. Springer, Cham (2020). https://doi.org/10.1007/978-3-030-40921-0_6
5. Z., Liu, H., J., Seo, J., Großschädl, H., W., Kim.: Efficient implementation of NIST-compliant elliptic curve cryptography for 8-bit AVR-based sensor nodes. In: IEEE Transactions Information Forensics and Security, pp. 1385–1397 (2016)
6. Atmel.: AVR Instruction Set Manual. http://ww1.microchip.com/downloads/en/-devicedoc/atmel-0856-avr-instruction-set-manual.pdf
7. Seo, S.C., Seo, H.: Highly efficient implementation of NIST-compliant koblitz curve for 8-bit AVR-based sensor nodes. IEEE Access 6, 67637–67652 (2018)

8. Tawalbeh, H., Hashish, S., Tawalbeh, L., Aldairi, A.: Security in wireless sensor networks using lightweight cryptography. In: ISSN Information Assurance and Security, pp. 118–123 (2017)
9. Dinu, D., Biryukov, A., Großschädl, J., Khovratovich, D., Le Corre, Y., Perrin, L.: FELICS-fair evaluation of lightweight cryptographic systems. In: NIST Workshop on Lightweight Cryptography, vol. 128 (2015)
10. Boneh, D., Gentry, C., Waters, B.: Collusion resistant broadcast encryption with short ciphertexts and private keys. In: Shoup, V. (ed.) CRYPTO 2005. LNCS, vol. 3621, pp. 258–275. Springer, Heidelberg (2005). https://doi.org/10.1007/11535218_16
11. Kim, K.H.: FACE-LIGHT (2019). https://github.com/solowal/DEVELOP/tree/master/Source%20Code

Revisiting the Minrank Problem on Multivariate Cryptography

Yacheng Wang[1(✉)], Yasuhiko Ikematsu[2], Shuhei Nakamura[3],
and Tsuyoshi Takagi[1]

[1] Department of Mathematical Informatics, University of Tokyo, Bunkyo City, Japan
{wang-yacheng,takagi}@g.ecc.u-tokyo.ac.jp
[2] Institute of Mathematics for Industry, Kyushu University, Fukuoka, Japan
ikematsu@imi.kyushu-u.ac.jp
[3] Department of Liberal Arts and Basic Sciences, Nihon University,
Chiyoda City, Japan
nakamura.shuhei@nihon-u.ac.jp

Abstract. The minrank problem is often considered in the cryptanalysis of multivariate cryptography and code-based cryptography. There have been many multivariate cryptosystems proven insecure due to their weakness against the minrank attack, which is an attack that transforms breaking a cryptosystem into solving a minrank problem instance.

In this paper, we review two existing methods, the Kipnis-Shamir method (KS), and minors modeling for solving a minrank instance, and then propose a mixed method that merges these two methods. Our method uses a bilinear subsystem from the KS method and a subsystem from minors modeling. It is at least as effective as the KS method, and does not require as many minors as minors modeling. Moreover, we consider applying the hybrid approach on multivariate polynomials solved in our mixed method to further improve our method. We then revisit the minrank attack on Rainbow and conclude the previous complexity analysis of the minrank attack on Rainbow is overestimated, and provide the correct complexity of the minrank attack on NIST PQC 2nd round Rainbow parameters.

Keywords: Minrank problem · Multivariate cryptography · Gröbner basis

1 Introduction

With currently widely used cryptosystems, RSA [30] and ECC [25], being threatened by the development of quantum computers because of Shor's quantum algorithm [31], research on the post-quantum cryptography has become more urgent. NIST [1,11] anticipated a realization of quantum computers that are capable enough of breaking 2048-bit RSA by the year of 2030, and they have taken actions on standardizing post-quantum cryptosystems.

© Springer Nature Switzerland AG 2020
I. You (Ed.): WISA 2020, LNCS 12583, pp. 291–307, 2020.
https://doi.org/10.1007/978-3-030-65299-9_22

Among all candidates of post-quantum cryptosystems, multivariate public key cryptosystems often face some challenges from a so-called minrank attack, that is an attack that transforms breaking a cryptosystem into solving a minrank problem instance. The rank metric decoding problem, which is the main problem considered in code-based cryptography, can be reduced to the minrank problem as well. The minrank problem $(\mathrm{MR}(q, n, m, r))$ asks one to find a linear combination of given $m + 1$ matrices $M_0, M_1, \ldots, M_m$ over a finite field of order q that has rank between 1 and r. This problem is proven to be an NP-complete problem [8], and in the field of multivariate cryptography, by far there are three different methods proposed for solving it, that are the Kipnis-Shamir (KS) method [24], minors modeling [5] and linear algebra search method [23].

In multivariate cryptography, many attempts on building secure cryptosystems failed due to their weakness against the minrank attack, for example, HFE [24], SRP [28], ZHFE [9], and TTM [23]. Techniques such as enlarging parameters or applying modifiers are applied to some multivariate cryptosystems such as Rainbow [16] and HFEv- [27,29] because of the minrank attack.

Unlike fairly well-understood minors modeling and linear algebra search method, there were not many results published on the complexity analysis of the KS method until Verbel et al. [33] gave their analysis. They gave a method of constructing non-trivial syzygies (see definition in Sect. 2.1) for super-determined minrank instances, and hence understanding the first fall degree (see definition in Sect. 2.1) of the polynomial system obtained from the KS method, which indicates a tighter complexity bound. This result is used on cryptanalysis on rank metric code-based cryptosystems [2]. As its advantage, the KS method gives low first fall degrees for super-determined minrank instances. As its drawback, it introduces many new variables and its analysis on using subsystems are not thorough. On the other hand, various analyses on the complexity of minors modeling are given [10,18,21]. This method does not introduce new variables but requires a heavy computation of many minors.

Contribution. The first contribution of this paper is to propose a new method of solving the minrank problem called the mixed method. It uses a bilinear subsystem (say S_μ) from the KS method and a subsystem (say T_μ) from minors modeling. When S_μ is an under-determined subsystem, adding T_μ to S_μ means adding more equations to S_μ without introducing any new variables, and it can possibly decrease the overall degree of regularity. Conversely, adding S_μ to T_μ significantly reduces the number of spurious solutions of T_μ. Therefore, when S_b is under-determined, the proposed mixed method possibly improves the KS method. When S_μ is an over-determined subsystem, T_μ is not needed, which means our mixed method reduces to the KS method.

Another contribution of this paper is to consider applying the hybrid approach [4] on multivariate polynomials solved in the mixed method. The hybrid approach is a combination of exhaustive search and Gröbner basis computation for solving a set of multivariate polynomials. The values of a few variables of a polynomial system are specified randomly before solving this system, the process terminates once the correct values are used. A bilinear subsystem is used in the mixed method, which means there are two sets of variables. The more significant set of variables being specified expects to bring more degree drops in the first fall degree of a polynomial system. For the mixed method, specifying every variable from the set that has fewer variables, according to our experiments, expects to decrease its first fall degree by 1. We also revisit the minrank attack on NIST PQC 2nd Rainbow proposal by considering the KS, minors modeling and the mixed method all together. We find that the previous complexity analysis of the minrank attack on Rainbow Ia, IIIc and Vc parameters [13] are overestimated, that are $2^{156.1}, 2^{578.0}$ and $2^{771.7}$. We update the new complexity to be $2^{138.1}, 2^{308.1}, 2^{405.4}$, and our investigation shows that the proposed parameters for Rainbow are secure from the minrank attack.

The paper is organized as follows. Section 2 explains about multivariate quadratic problem and bilinear systems. In Sect. 3, we review the minrank problem, the KS method and minors modeling. In Sect. 4, we propose a mixed method for solving the minrank problem and discuss the behavior of the mixed method coupling with the hybrid approach. In Sect. 5, we present experimental results on scaled-down Rainbow and application of our method on Rainbow. Finally, Sect. 6 gives a conclusion.

2 Multivariate Quadratic Problem and Bilinear Systems

2.1 Multivariate Quadratic Problem

Let $\mathbb{F}$ be a finite field of order q, $m, n \in \mathbb{N}$, and $R := \mathbb{F}[x_1, \ldots, x_n]$ be the polynomial ring in variables $x_1, \ldots, x_n$ over $\mathbb{F}$.

Problem 1 (Multivariate Qudratic Problem). *Given a set of quadratic polynomials $f_1, \ldots, f_m \in R$ and a vector $\mathbf{y} = (y_1, \ldots, y_m) \in \mathbb{F}^m$, find $\mathbf{z} \in \mathbb{F}^n$ such that $f_1(\mathbf{z}) = y_1, \ldots, f_m(\mathbf{z}) = y_m$.*

An effective method for solving this problem is through Gröbner basis computation [7]. Efficient algorithms for computing a Gröbner basis include XL [12], F4 [19] and F5 [20]. A good indicator of the complexity of computing a Gröbner basis is the *degree of regularity* (d_{reg}) [3], which is the maximal polynomial degree appeared during a process of computing a Gröbner basis. This complexity mainly comes from a computation of the row echelon form of a Macaulay matrix of degree d_{reg}. Suppose such a Macaulay matrix has size $R_{d_{reg}} \times C_{d_{reg}}$, then the complexity of the fast algorithm proposed in [32] for computing its row echelon form is given by $O(R_{d_{reg}} C_{d_{reg}}^{\omega-1})$, where $2 \leq \omega \leq 3$ is the linear algebra constant. The degree of regularity d_{reg} for random systems can be precisely evaluated, but hard to estimate for specific families of polynomial systems. Therefore, in cryptographical studies, d_{reg} is often approximated by the *first fall degree* (d_{ff}). To define the first fall degree, we need to be familiar with a notion called non-trivial syzygies.

Definition 1 (Syzygy). *Let* $\{h_1, \ldots, h_m\} \in R$ *be a set of polynomials. A syzygy of* $(h_1, \ldots, h_m)$ *is an m-tuple* $(s_1, \ldots, s_m) \in R^m$ *such that* $\sum_{i=1}^{m} s_i h_i = 0$. *The degree of a syzygy* $\mathbf{s} = (s_1, \ldots, s_m)$ *is defined as* $\deg(\mathbf{s}) = \max_{1 \leq i \leq m} \deg(s_i h_i)$.

The linear combinations of m-tuples $(s_1, \ldots, s_m) \in R^m$ with $s_i = h_j, s_j = -h_i$ for some i, j $(i \neq j)$ and $s_t = 0$ for $t \neq i, j$ are called *trivial syzygies*. The syzygies that are not linear combinations of the trivial syzygies are called *non-trivial syzygies*. Non-trivial syzygies of the homogeneous components of the highest degree of $h_1, \ldots, h_m$ account for the non-trivial degree falls during a Gröbner basis computation.

Definition 2 (First fall degree d_{ff}). *Let* $\{f_1, \ldots, f_m\} \subset R$ *be a set of polynomials and* $\{f_1^h, \ldots, f_m^h\} \subset R$ *be their homogeneous component of the highest degree. Its first fall degree is the smallest degree* d_{ff} *such that there exist nontrivial syzygies* $(s_1, \ldots, s_m) \in R^m$ *of* $(f_1^h, \ldots, f_m^h)$ *with* $\max_i(\deg(s_i f_i^h)) = d_{ff}$, *satisfying* $\deg(\sum_{i=1}^{m} s_i f_i) < d_{ff}$ *but* $\sum_{i=1}^{m} s_i f_i \neq 0$.

Many results on multivariate cryptosystems are based on analyzing d_{ff} [14, 15, 17], although it is not always true that d_{ff} and d_{reg} are very close, experimental and theoretical evidences in these results have shown it seems to be true for some cryptographic schemes.

2.2 Bilinear System

A bilinear polynomial is defined as follows.

Definition 3 (Bilinear polynomial). *Let* $\mathbf{x} = (x_1, \ldots, x_{n_1})$, $\mathbf{y} = (y_1, \ldots, y_{n_2})$ *be variables,* $\mathbb{F}[\mathbf{x}, \mathbf{y}]$ *be the polynomial ring in* $\mathbf{x}$ *and* $\mathbf{y}$ *over a field* $\mathbb{F}$. *A bilinear polynomial* $f \in \mathbb{F}[\mathbf{x}, \mathbf{y}]$ *is a quadratic polynomial, and linear in each set of variables, i.e.* $\deg_{\mathbf{x}}(f) = \deg_{\mathbf{y}}(f) = 1$.

Regarding a set of bilinear polynomials, there are some special properties, and we will use Jacobian matrices to explain these properties. The Jacobian matrix of a set of bilinear polynomials is defined as follows.

Definition 4 (Jacobian matrix). *Given a set of bilinear polynomials* $F = (f_1, \ldots, f_m) \in \mathbb{F}[\mathbf{x}, \mathbf{y}]^m$, *then the Jacobian matrices of* F *with respect to variables* $\mathbf{x}$ *and* $\mathbf{y}$ *are given by*

$$\mathrm{Jac}_{\mathbf{x}}(F) = \left[\frac{\partial f_i}{\partial x_j} \right]_{1 \leq i \leq m, 1 \leq j \leq n_1}, \quad \mathrm{Jac}_{\mathbf{y}}(F) = \left[\frac{\partial f_i}{\partial y_k} \right]_{1 \leq i \leq m, 1 \leq k \leq n_2}.$$

And we have the following proposition for a set of bilinear polynomials:

Proposition 1 *(See proof in Appendix). Let* $F = (f_1, \ldots, f_m) \in \mathbb{F}[\mathbf{x}, \mathbf{y}]^m$ *be a set of bilinear polynomials. For* $G = (g_1, \ldots, g_m) \in \mathbb{F}[\mathbf{y}]^m$, *it is a syzygy of* F *if* $G \cdot \mathrm{Jac}_{\mathbf{x}}(F) = 0$. *Moreover, if* G *is non-zero, then* G *is a non-trivial syzygy of* F. *Similar statement holds for* $\mathrm{Jac}_{\mathbf{y}}(F)$.

From the above proposition, we can construct some non-trivial syzygies of a set of homogeneous bilinear polynomials $F = (f_1, \ldots, f_m) \in \mathbb{F}[\mathbf{x}, \mathbf{y}]^m$ using its Jacobian matrices, which have linear polynomials as its entries, and we need to compute their left kernels. By Cramer's rule, see [22], we know the kernel of such matrices have elements in the span of its maximal minors (also see example 1 and 2 in Appendix). Here, maximal minor refers to determinants of square submatrices with the maximal size of a matrix.

3 The Minrank Problem

In this section, we introduce the minrank problem and two existing methods for solving the minrank problem, the KS method and minors modeling.

3.1 The Minrank Problem

The minrank problem is defined as follows.

Problem 2 (Minrank Problem). *Given a field $\mathbb{F}$ of order q, a positive integer $r \in \mathbb{N}$ and $n \times n$ matrices $M_0, M_1, \ldots, M_m \in \mathbb{F}^{n \times n}$, find $x_1, \ldots, x_m \in \mathbb{F}$ such that $\Delta = M_0 + \sum_{i=1}^{m} x_i M_i, 0 < Rank(\Delta) \le r$. A minrank instance is denoted by $MR(q, n, m, r)$.*

3.2 Minors Modeling

Minors modeling [5] is based on the fact that all $(r+1) \times (r+1)$ minors of $\Delta = M_0 + \sum_{i=1}^{m} x_i M_i$ vanish at $(x_1, \ldots, x_m)$ when Δ has rank no larger than r. This method gives a system of $\binom{n}{r+1}^2$ equations in m variables. The property of this polynomial system is related to the so-called determinantal ideal. In [10, 18, 21], intensive analyses on the property of the ideal generated by polynomials from minors modeling are given. Minors modeling, as its advantage, does not introduce any other variables except $x_1, \ldots, x_m$. But it requires a computation of as many as $\binom{n}{r+1}^2$ minors of a matrix with linear polynomial entries. If we consider the XL algorithm, there are $\binom{m+r+1}{r+1}$ monomials up to degree $r+1$, and we need $\binom{m+r+1}{r+1}$ independent equations to terminate the XL algorithm, which means the complete $\binom{n}{r+1}^2$ equations are unnecessary to achieve d_{reg} being $r+1$ when $\binom{n}{r+1}^2 > \binom{m+r+1}{r+1}$. Every minor is a degree $r+1$ polynomial in variables $x_1, \ldots, x_m$, which has $\binom{m+r+1}{r+1}$ terms at most. Suppose obtaining every coefficient takes complexity $O(1)$, computing $\min\{\binom{n}{r+1}^2, \binom{m+r+1}{r+1}\}$ minors requires a complexity of $O\left(\min\{\binom{n}{r+1}^2, \binom{m+r+1}{r+1}\} \cdot \binom{m+r+1}{r+1}\right)$. Note that when partial minors are used, d_{reg} turns to be higher and spurious solutions appear. Moreover, solving the polynomials obtained from making those minors vanish takes complexity $O\left(\binom{m+r+1}{r+1}^\omega\right)$, where $2 \le \omega \le 3$ is a linear algebra constant.

3.3   The Kipnis-Shamir Method

The KS method [24] was first used to break the HFE cryptosystem [26]. This method is based on the fact that the dimension of the right kernel of $M_0 + \sum_{i=1}^{m} x_i M_i$ should be no smaller than $n - r$, since it has rank no larger than r. There exists a canonical echelonized basis for this right kernel, we put these basis vectors into a matrix as column vectors, then this matrix should be in the form of $\begin{bmatrix} I_{n-r} \\ K \end{bmatrix}$, where I_{n-r} is the identity matrix of size $n - r$ and K is an $r \times (n - r)$ matrix. We denote the column vectors of $\begin{bmatrix} I_{n-r} \\ K \end{bmatrix}$ by $\hat{\mathbf{k}}_1, \hat{\mathbf{k}}_2, \ldots, \hat{\mathbf{k}}_{n-r}$. Then we have

$$\Delta \begin{bmatrix} I_{n-r} \\ K \end{bmatrix} = \Delta \left[\hat{\mathbf{k}}_1, \hat{\mathbf{k}}_2, \ldots, \hat{\mathbf{k}}_{n-r} \right] = 0. \tag{1}$$

If we regard the entries of K as new variables:

$$K = \begin{bmatrix} k_1 & k_{r+1} & \cdots & k_{r(n-r-1)+1} \\ k_2 & k_{r+2} & \cdots & k_{r(n-r-1)+2} \\ \vdots & \vdots & \ddots & \vdots \\ k_r & k_{2r} & \cdots & k_{r(n-r)} \end{bmatrix},$$

then we obtain a system of $n(n - r)$ bilinear equations in variables $\mathbf{x} = (x_1, \ldots, x_n)$ and $\mathbf{k} = (k_1, k_2, \ldots, k_{r(n-r)})$ from (1). Moreover, $n - r$ subsystems can also be obtained from (1), which are denoted by $S_1, S_2, \ldots, S_{n-r}$ as follows:

$$\underbrace{\Delta \cdot \hat{\mathbf{k}}_1 = 0}_{S_1}, \quad \underbrace{\Delta \cdot [\hat{\mathbf{k}}_1 \ \hat{\mathbf{k}}_2] = 0}_{S_2}, \quad \cdots, \quad \underbrace{\Delta \cdot [\hat{\mathbf{k}}_1 \ \hat{\mathbf{k}}_2 \cdots \hat{\mathbf{k}}_{n-r}] = 0}_{S_{n-r}}.$$

Solving a subsystem may take less time than solving the full system. However, the d_{ff} of a subsystem is no smaller than the d_{ff} of the full system, i.e. $d_{ff}(S_i) \geq d_{ff}(S_{n-r})$ for $i = 1, \ldots, n-r-1$. In [33], this is pointed out and they suggest using subsystems that are determined or over-determined since under-determined subsystems tend to have higher d_{ff} and give spurious solutions.

In [33], Verbel et al. gave a tight bound on the d_{ff} of S_{n-r}, and they experimentally showed the d_{reg} is close to their bound as well. As its advantages, the KS method can construct a polynomial system more easily compared to minors modeling, optionally determined or over-determined subsystems can be used, and for super-determined minrank instances, over-determined subsystems from the KS method have low d_{ff}. However, this method introduces more variables than minors modeling, i.e. variables $k_1, k_2, \ldots, k_{r(n-r)}$. Moreover, precise bounds on the d_{ff} of the subsystems $S_1, \ldots, S_{n-r-1}$ are not yet clear. According to [33], when S_{n-r} is used, by only multiplying monomials in variables from $\mathbf{k}$ in the XL algorithm, a complexity of $O\left(\left(\binom{\mu r + d_{ff}}{d_{ff}}\right)^{\omega}\right)$ can be achieved, where

$$d_{ff} = \min_{1 \leq d \leq r-1} \left\{ d \ \middle| \ \binom{r}{d} n > \binom{r}{d+1} m \right\} + 2.$$ And with high probability, d_{ff} remains the same when S_μ is used, where $\max\{\frac{m}{n-r}, d_{ff} - 1\} \leq \mu \leq n - r$.

4   Our Proposed Method

In this section, we propose a new method that combines the KS method and minors modeling.

4.1   The Mixed Method

Let $\mathbf{b}_1, \ldots, \mathbf{b}_n$ be the row vectors of Δ, i.e.

$$\Delta = \begin{bmatrix} \mathbf{b}_1^\top & \mathbf{b}_2^\top & \cdots & \mathbf{b}_{n-r}^\top & \mathbf{b}_{n-r+1}^\top & \mathbf{b}_{n-r+2}^\top & \cdots & \mathbf{b}_n^\top \end{bmatrix}^\top.$$

Since the rank of a matrix is the maximal number of linearly independent column vectors, we assume the last r rows $\mathbf{b}_{n-r+1}, \ldots, \mathbf{b}_n$ are linearly independent. Then $\{\mathbf{b}_i, \mathbf{b}_{n-r+1}, \ldots \mathbf{b}_n\}$ for each $i = 1, \ldots, n-r$ is linearly dependent, which gives us in total $n - r$ linear relations. We can translate the linear dependence of $\{\mathbf{b}_i, \mathbf{b}_{n-r+1}, \ldots, \mathbf{b}_n\}$ into either "find k_j for $\sum_{j=1}^r k_j \mathbf{b}_{n-r+j} = \mathbf{b}_i$" or "$(r+1) \times (r+1)$ minors of the matrix $\begin{bmatrix} \mathbf{b}_i^\top & \mathbf{b}_{n-r+1}^\top & \cdots & \mathbf{b}_n^\top \end{bmatrix}^\top$ vanish." The approach where new variables k_i are introduced corresponds to a subsystem in the KS method.

Let $1 \le \mu \le n - r$ be an integer, in the mixed method, we first realize the linear dependence of $\{\mathbf{b}_i, \mathbf{b}_{n-r+1}, \ldots, \mathbf{b}_n\}$ for $i = 1, \ldots, \mu$ by introducing new variables, the resulting polynomial system is the same with S_μ in the KS method. Then we compute $(r+1) \times (r+1)$ minors of the matrices $\begin{bmatrix} \mathbf{b}_i^\top & \mathbf{b}_{n-r+1}^\top & \cdots & \mathbf{b}_n^\top \end{bmatrix}^\top$ for $i = \mu + 1, \ldots, n - r$, we denote this system as T_μ. Finally we solve the S_μ and T_μ combined polynomial system.

As shown in [33], the more kernel vectors $\hat{\mathbf{k}}_1, \hat{\mathbf{k}}_2, \ldots, \hat{\mathbf{k}}_{n-r}$ are used in the KS method, the smaller its d_{ff} and d_{reg} will become, and when a subsystem S_μ is over-determined, its d_{ff} is smaller than $r+2$. In the mixed method, the S_μ and T_μ combined polynomial system is used, and polynomials in T_μ have degree $r + 1$, which means adding T_μ to an over-determined S_μ does not reduce the overall d_{ff}. Hence we only use an under-determined S_μ in our mixed method, i.e. $\mu = 1, \ldots, \lfloor \frac{m}{n-r} \rfloor$. The motivation of our method is, on one hand, adding T_μ to an under-determined S_μ to make all subsystems in the KS method usable and substantially reduces spurious solutions of those under-determined subsystems. On the other hand, mixing two methods to achieve the lowest d_{ff} possible without introducing many additional variables and computing many minors.

4.2   Complexity Analysis

In this subsection, we investigate the complexity of the mixed method.

I. Case $\mu = 1$

Since $F_1 = S_1 \cup T_1$, where S_1 is a bilinear polynomial system and T_1 has polynomials of degree $r + 1$. We first analyze the first fall degree of S_1, and we have the following proposition.

Proposition 2. *Let S_1^h be the homogeneous components of the highest degree of S_1. S_1^h has non-trivial syzygies in variables $\mathbf{k}$ of degree $m+2$ and non-trivial syzygies in variables $\mathbf{x}$ of degree $r+2$.*

Proof. Let S_1^h be the degree two homogeneous components of S_1, then the lowest degree of its non-trivial syzygies coincide with the d_{ff} of S_1. The left kernel of $\mathrm{Jac}_{\mathbf{k}}(S_1^h)$ gives non-trivial syzygies of S_1^h in variables $\mathbf{x}$. Since $\mathrm{Jac}_{\mathbf{k}}(S_1^h)$ is an $n \times r$ matrix, and has maximal minors of degree r, we know it gives us non-trivial syzygies of degree $r+2$. On the other hand, the left kernel of $\mathrm{Jac}_{\mathbf{x}}(S_1^h)$ gives non-trivial syzygies of S_1^h in variables $\mathbf{k}$. Since $\mathrm{Jac}_{\mathbf{x}}(S_1^h)$ is an $n \times m$ matrix, and it has maximal minors of degree $\min\{m, n\}$, and gives non-trivial syzygies of degree $\min\{m+2, n+2\}$. $\square$

From Proposition 2, we have the first fall degree d_{ff} of S_1 is no larger than $\min\{r+2, m+2\}$. Furthermore, we know the left kernel of $\mathrm{Jac}_{\mathbf{k}}(S_1^h)$ (resp. $\mathrm{Jac}_{\mathbf{x}}(S_1^h)$) are n-tuples with polynomial entries, which can be computed from the maximal minors of $\mathrm{Jac}_{\mathbf{k}}(S_1^h)$ (resp. $\mathrm{Jac}_{\mathbf{x}}(S_1^h)$), if there exist common divisors among those polynomial entries, we would have non-trivial syzygies with lower degrees. These common divisors are difficult to compute mathematically, but can be confirmed using experiments. We found that when $n \geq m+r$ holds, such common divisors appear, which means when $n \geq m+r$, there exists non-trivial syzygies of degree $\leq \min\{r+1, m+1\}$. Related experimental results are shown in Table 1, it verifies the correctness of using $\mathrm{Jac}_{\mathbf{x}}(S_1^h)$ and $\mathrm{Jac}_{\mathbf{k}}(S_1^h)$ to analyze the d_{ff} of S_1, and also confirms the existence of the aforementioned common divisors when $n \geq m+r$.

Table 1. Experiments on the d_{ff} and d_{reg} of S_1, and degrees of the non-trivial syzygies of S_1^h from the left kernel of $\mathrm{Jac}_{\mathbf{x}}(S_1^h)$ and $\mathrm{Jac}_{\mathbf{k}}(S_1^h)$. $\mathbf{ker}(\mathrm{Jac}_{\mathbf{x}}(S_1^h))$ (resp. $\mathbf{ker}(\mathrm{Jac}_{\mathbf{k}}(S_1^h))$) are computed on Magma using the function "Kernel", where the $F4$ algorithm is used. Note that when $n \geq m+r$ satisfies, we have $d_{ff} = d_{reg}$

(q,n,m,r)	$\mathbf{ker}_{\mathrm{left}}(\mathrm{Jac}_{\mathbf{x}}(S_1^h))$	$\mathbf{ker}_{\mathrm{left}}(\mathrm{Jac}_{\mathbf{k}}(S_1^h))$	$d_{ff}(S_1)$	$d_{reg}(S_1)$
$(7,6,5,3)$	7	5	5	7
$(7,7,5,3)$	7	5	5	7
$\mathbf{(7,8,5,3)}$	5	4	4	4
$(7,9,5,3)$	4	3 or 4	3 or 4	4
$(7,10,5,3)$	3 or 4	3	3	3
$(7,11,5,3)$	3	3	3	3

Therefore, we conclude with the following upper bounds for the d_{ff} of S_1 :

$$\begin{aligned} n < m+r, && d_{ff}(S_1) \leq \min\{r+2, m+2\}, \\ n = m+r, && d_{ff}(S_1) \leq \min\{r+1, m+1\}, \\ n > m+r, && d_{ff}(S_1) < \min\{r+1, m+1\}. \end{aligned} \qquad (2)$$

Regarding the first fall degree of F_1 and its relation to the first fall degree of S_1, we have the following proposition.

Proposition 3 *(See proof in Appendix). Let $d_{ff}(S_1)$ be the first fall degree of S_1, which depends on either the non-trivial syzygies in variables $\mathbf{k}$ of degree no larger than $m + 2$ or non-trivial syzygies in variables $\mathbf{x}$ of degree no larger than $r + 2$. From these non-trivial syzygies of S_1, non-trivial syzygies of F_1 can be constructed, and the first fall degree of F_1 is no larger than $d_{ff}(S_1)$.*

According to this proposition, we have Eq. (2) holds also for F_1.

II. Case $\mu = 2, \ldots, \lfloor \frac{m}{n-r} \rfloor$

When $1 < \mu \leq n - r$, our method solves a polynomial system $F_\mu = S_\mu \cup T_\mu$, where S_μ is an under-determined bilinear system and T_μ consists of polynomials of degree $r + 1$. Similarly, an upper bound for the d_{ff} of F_μ can be obtained by analyzing the first fall degree d_{ff} of S_μ and T_μ. Let S_μ^h be the degree two homogeneous components of S_μ, then we have

$$
\mathrm{Jac}_{\mathbf{k}}(S_\mu^h) = I_\mu \otimes \mathrm{Jac}_{\mathbf{k}}(S_1^h),
$$

$$
\mathrm{Jac}_{\mathbf{x}}(S_\mu^h) = \left(I_n \otimes \begin{bmatrix} k_1 & k_2 & \cdots & k_r \\ k_{r+1} & k_{r+2} & \cdots & k_{2r} \\ \vdots & \vdots & \ddots & \vdots \\ k_{(\mu-1)r+1} & k_{(\mu-1)r+2} & \cdots & k_{\mu r} \end{bmatrix} \right) \cdot L^\mu, \tag{3}
$$

where $L^\mu \in \mathbb{F}^{nr \times m}$ is a matrix derived from the matrices $M_1, \ldots, M_m$.

By (3), the non-trivial syzygies from the left kernel of $\mathrm{Jac}_{\mathbf{k}}(S_\mu^h)$ and $\mathrm{Jac}_{\mathbf{k}}(S_1^h)$ should have same degree, so $\mathrm{Jac}_{\mathbf{k}}(S_\mu^h)$ gives non-trivial syzygies of degree $r + 2$ when $n < m + r$ and less than or equal to r when $n \geq m + r$. Similarly, the left kernel of $\mathrm{Jac}_{\mathbf{x}}(S_\mu)$ also gives non-trivial syzygies of S_μ. But analyzing their precise degree is difficult as aforementioned common divisors have to be analyzed. Nevertheless, we know the d_{ff} and d_{reg} of S_μ should be decreasing with μ increasing from 1 to $\lfloor \frac{m}{n-r} \rfloor$ since S_μ becomes less under-determined. Therefore, the d_{ff} of the mixed method of $\mu = 2, \ldots, \lfloor \frac{m}{n-r} \rfloor$ is upper bounded by the first fall degree of the mixed method of $\mu = 1$ given in (2).

4.3 Further Improvement

In this section, we consider applying the hybrid approach [4] on the mixed method. That is to exhaustively guess a few variables before applying Gröbner basis computation algorithms on the polynomial system obtained by the mixed method. The question here is to guess which variables. In both the KS method and the mixed method, we have bilinear systems, which means there are two sets of different variables. We want to find the set of variables to guess that minimizes the total complexity. Table 2 presents results about applying the hybrid approach on S_1 under $(q, n, m, r) = (7, 13, 8, 5)$, which should have $d_{ff} \leq 6$ because of the non-trivial syzygies from $\mathrm{Jac}_{\mathbf{k}}(S_1^h)$. Note that specifying variables from $\mathbf{x}$ does not change the degree of polynomials in T_1, therefore its first fall degree will always be no smaller than $r + 1$.

Table 2. Results of hybrid approach on S_1 under $(q, n, m, r) = (7, 13, 8, 5)$, and $\ker(\mathrm{Jac}_{\mathbf{x}}(S_1^h))$ (resp. $\ker(\mathrm{Jac}_{\mathbf{k}}(S_1^h))$) are computed on Magma using the function "Kernel", where the $F4$ algorithm is used. $\lfloor x \rceil$ means the nearest integer to x.

# variables specified in $\mathbf{x}$	0	1	2	3	4	5	6	7	8	$0 \leq i \leq m$
deg of syzygies from $\mathbf{ker}_{\mathrm{left}}(\mathrm{Jac}_{\mathbf{x}}(S_1^h))$	8	6	5	4	3	3	2	2	-	$\approx 8 - \lfloor \frac{m \cdot i}{m} \rceil$
deg of syzygies from $\mathbf{ker}_{\mathrm{left}}(\mathrm{Jac}_{\mathbf{k}}(S_1^h))$	6	5	5	4	3	3	2	2	-	$\approx 6 - \lfloor \frac{r \cdot i}{m} \rceil$
d_{ff}	6	5	5	4	3	3	2	2	1	$\approx 6 - \lfloor \frac{r \cdot i}{m} \rceil$

# variables specified in $\mathbf{k}$	0	1	2	3	4	5	$0 \leq j \leq r$
deg of syzygies from $\mathbf{ker}_{\mathrm{left}}(\mathrm{Jac}_{\mathbf{x}}(S_1^h))$	8	6	5	3	2	-	$\approx 8 - \lfloor \frac{m \cdot j}{r} \rceil$
deg of syzygies from $\mathbf{ker}_{\mathrm{left}}(\mathrm{Jac}_{\mathbf{k}}(S_1^h))$	6	5	4	3	2	-	$\approx 6 - \lfloor \frac{r \cdot j}{r} \rceil$
d_{ff}	6	5	4	3	2	1	$\approx 6 - \lfloor \frac{r \cdot j}{r} \rceil$

The table tells us specifying every variable from $\mathbf{k}$ (resp. $\mathbf{x}$) brings -1 to the degree of syzygies from the left kernel of $\mathrm{Jac}_{\mathbf{k}}(S_1^h)$ (resp. $\mathrm{Jac}_{\mathbf{x}}(S_1^h)$), and this can be rationalized as this specification changes the size of $\mathrm{Jac}_{\mathbf{k}}(S_1^h)$ (resp. $\mathrm{Jac}_{\mathbf{k}}(S_1^h)$) to $n \times (r - 1)$ (resp. $n \times (m - 1)$), which gives non-trivial syzygies of 1 less degree. Moreover, specifying every variable from $\mathbf{k}$ (resp. $\mathbf{x}$) decreases approximately the degrees of the non-trivial syzygies from $\mathrm{Jac}_{\mathbf{x}}(S_1^h)$ (resp. $\mathrm{Jac}_{\mathbf{k}}(S_1^h)$) by $\lfloor \frac{m}{r} \rceil$ (resp. $\lfloor \frac{r}{m} \rceil$). Note that this technique can be applied to the mixed method and the KS method.

Practically, $F_\mu = S_\mu \cup T_\mu$ is used in the mixed method, T_μ is for decreasing the overall d_{ff} and reducing spurious solutions. When either variables in $\mathbf{x}$ or $\mathbf{k}$ are specified, S_μ may turn into a less under-determined or an over-determined system. In this case, less polynomials or no polynomials from T_μ are needed. Moreover, specifying either m variables from $\mathbf{x}$ or r variables from $\mathbf{k}$ leads to a complete solve of a minrank instance.

Summarizing the discussion, we assume using XL algorithm and only multiplying by monomials from variables $\mathbf{k}$ or $\mathbf{x}$, let $d_{\mathbf{x}}$ (resp. $d_{\mathbf{k}}$) be the lowest degree of the non-trivial syzygies from $\mathrm{Jac}_{\mathbf{x}}(S_\mu^h)$ (resp. $\mathrm{Jac}_{\mathbf{k}}(S_\mu^h)$), then the complexity of our mixed method is bounded by[1]

$$m \geq r \ O\left(\min_{1 \leq k < r} \left\{ q^k \cdot \left(\min \left\{ \binom{r\mu - k + d_{\mathbf{x}} - \lfloor \frac{km}{r} \rceil}{d_{\mathbf{x}} - \lfloor \frac{km}{r} \rceil} \right)^\omega, \binom{m + d_{\mathbf{k}} - k}{d_{\mathbf{k}} - k}^\omega \right\} + knm \right) \right\} \right)$$

$$m < r \ O\left(\min_{1 \leq k < r} \left\{ q^k \cdot \left(\min \left\{ \binom{m - k + d_{\mathbf{k}} - \lfloor \frac{rk}{m} \rceil}{d_{\mathbf{k}} - \lfloor \frac{rk}{m} \rceil} \right)^\omega, \binom{r\mu + d_{\mathbf{x}} - k}{d_{\mathbf{x}} - k}^\omega \right\} + kn^2 \right) \right\} \right) 4$$

where $2 \leq \omega \leq 3$ is the linear algebra constant. Note that the complexity given above are for polynomial solving only. For computing minors, suppose S_μ after specifying k variables is under-determined, $(n - r - \mu)\binom{n}{r+1}$ minors will be used in the mixed method, which requires a complexity of

---

[1] Note that the computation involving kn^2 and kmn can be done in parallel.

$O\left((n - r - \mu)\binom{n}{r+1}\binom{m-k+r+1}{r+1}\right)$ when k variables from $\mathbf{x}$ are specified, and
$O\left((n - r - \mu)\binom{n}{r+1}\binom{m+r+1}{r+1}\right)$ when k variables from $\mathbf{k}$ are specified. This computation of minors can be done in parallel and its complexity is neglectable compared to that of polynomial solving.

5 Experiments and Application

5.1 Experiments

The parameters we choose to run experiments on proportionally coincide with Rainbow [16], which is $(q, v, o_1, o_2) = (16, 5, 5, 5)$. Note that the first layer of Rainbow central map polynomials have rank $v + o_1$, and second layer polynomials have full rank. Its public key has $o_1 + o_2$ polynomials. Therefore, we can recover some first layer Rainbow central map polynomials by solving some minrank instances $MR(q, v + o_1 + o_2, o_1 + o_2, v + o_1)$. However, the span of the low rank polynomials hidden in Rainbow, say $\mathcal{S}_c$ (dimension o_1), is a subspace of the span of the public key, say $\mathcal{S}_p$ (dimension $o_1 + o_2$). The intersection of $\mathcal{S}_c$ with any dimension $o_2 + 1$ subspace of $\mathcal{S}_p$ is a subspace of dimension no smaller than 1. Therefore, using $o_2 + 1$ polynomials $p_1, \ldots, p_{o_2+1}$ from the public key of Rainbow, we are able to recover partial Rainbow secret key by solving $MR(q, v + o_1 + o_2, o_2 + 1, v + o_1)$. Moreover, if we fix the variable x_1 from $x_1, \ldots, x_m$ in the minrank problem to be 1, with probability $\frac{q-1}{q}$, we can still obtain a solution. Therefore, breaking Rainbow is almost equivalent to solving $MR(q, v + o_1 + o_2, o_2, v + o_1)$.

Table 3. Experimental results on $MR(16, 15, 5, 10)$, which is equivalent to breaking $Rainbow(q, v, o_1, o_2) = (16, 5, 5, 5)$. The best complexity is $2^{23.4}$, which is when we use S_1 with hybrid approach of specifying 3 variables out of $x_1, \ldots, x_m$. $d_{\mathbf{x}}$ (resp. $d_{\mathbf{k}}$) denotes the lowest degree of the non-trival syzygies derived from the Jacobian matrix of S_1 w.r.t variables $\mathbf{x}$ (resp. $\mathbf{k}$), and t denotes the total time for computing minors and solving the obtained polynomials with $F4$ algorithm

MR(16, 15, 5, 10)		d_{ff}	d_{reg}	$d_{\mathbf{k}}$	$d_{\mathbf{x}}$	t [s]	Complexity ($\omega = 2.8$)
Method							
Minors		11	11	–	–	*a	$\binom{m+r+1}{r+1}^{\omega} = \binom{5+11}{11}^{\omega} \approx 2^{33.9}$
KS	S_2	5	5	–	–	615.57	$\binom{2 \cdot r+5}{5}^{\omega} = \binom{2 \cdot 10+5}{5}^{\omega} \approx 2^{44.0}$
	S_3	4	4	–	–	30.49	$\binom{3 \cdot r+4}{4}^{\omega} = \binom{3 \cdot 10+4}{4}^{\omega} \approx 2^{43.4}$
New S_1		6	6	$10 = r$	6	67.20	$\min\{\binom{m+10}{10}^{\omega}, \binom{r+6}{6}^{\omega}\} \approx 2^{32.3}$
	fix x_1	5	5	8	5	10.80	$q \cdot \left(\min\{\binom{m-1+10-2}{10-2}^{\omega}, \binom{r+6-1}{6-1}^{\omega}\} + n^2\right) \approx 2^{29.1}$
	fix x_1, x_2	4	4	6	4	5.12	$q^2 \cdot \left(\min\{\binom{m-2+10-4}{10-4}^{\omega}, \binom{r+6-2}{6-2}^{\omega}\} + 2n^2\right) \approx 2^{25.9}$
	fix $x_1, \ldots, x_3$	3	3	4	3	4.73	$q^3 \cdot \left(\min\{\binom{m-3+10-6}{10-6}^{\omega}, \binom{r+6-3}{6-3}^{\omega}\} + 3n^2\right) \approx 2^{23.4}$
	fix $x_1, \ldots, x_4$	2	2	2	2	4.34	$q^4 \cdot \left(\min\{\binom{m-4+10-8}{10-8}^{\omega}, \binom{r+6-5}{6-5}^{\omega}\} + 4n^2\right) \approx 2^{25.8}$
	fix $x_1, \ldots, x_5$	–	–	–	–	–	$q^m \cdot (5n^2 + \frac{n^3}{6}) \approx 2^{30.7}$

a Due to the limited computation resources, we were not able to obtain this timing. The computation of minors did not finish in 2 days, which is the maximal time limit for our platform.

All of our experiments are executed on a 2.10 GHz Intel® Xeon® Gold 6130 Processor with Magma V2.24-8 [6], where F4 algorithm [19] is implemented. We run 5 experiments for each set of parameter.

Table 3 shows results on breaking Rainbow$(16, 5, 5, 5)$ by solving a minrank instance $\mathrm{MR}(q, n, m, r) = \mathrm{MR}(16, 15, 5, 10)$. Since $m + r = n$ satisfies, S_1 in KS and the mixed method is determined, no extra minors are needed. Hence, in the mixed method, we only consider using S_1 coupling with the hybrid approach. Namely, we randomly specify variables from $x_1, \ldots, x_m$ in S_1, and try to solve S_1. Note for this scaled down Rainbow parameter with $m \leq r$ and $n = m + r$, when only S_1 is used, the degree of the non-trivial syzygies from the Jacobian matrix of S_1 w.r.t variables $\mathbf{x}$ is $r = 10$, and the degree of the non-trivial syzygies from the Jacobian matrix of S_1 w.r.t variables $\mathbf{k}$ is $m + 1 = 6$. Comparing to the KS method and minors modeling, specifying 3 variables in S_1 gives the best complexity, $2^{23.4}$.

To testify that our mixed method is indeed efficient, we also conduct experiments on $\mathrm{MR}(16, 9, 6, 6)$ and $\mathrm{MR}(16, 11, 6, 8)$. The results are shown in Table 4. For minors modeling and the mixed method, computing minors are necessary, and they are computed on Magma in our experiments, the timings are recorded under the label t_{minors} in Table 4. t_{F4} means timings for polynomial solving using $F4$ algorithm with graded reverse lexicographical monomial order. This table shows that minors modeling requires a long time on computing all the minors needed, but takes shorter time on polynomial solving compared to the KS and mixed method. As for the KS method, computations of minors are not required, but it can take a considerably long time on polynomial solving for some minrank instances, such as parameters presented in Table 4. As for the mixed method, not as many minors as minors modeling are needed, and it is faster in polynomial solving than the KS method for certain parameters such as ones shown in Table 4.

Table 4. Experimental results on solving minrank instances with minors modeling (see Sect. 3.2), the KS method (see Sect. 3.3) and the mixed method (see Sect. 4.1)

(q, n, m, r) $(16, 9, 6, 6)$	method		d_{ff}	d_{reg}	t_{minors} [s]	t_{F4} [s]	$t_{minors} + t_{F4}$ [s]
	minors		7	7	39.01	1.56	40.57
	KS	S_2	5	6	0	234.42	234.42
		S_3	4	5	0	114.29	114.29
	mixed	$\mu = 1$	8	8	2.17	8.54	**10.71**
		$\mu = 2$	5	6	1.08	247.88	248.96

(q, n, m, r) $(16, 11, 6, 8)$	method		d_{ff}	d_{reg}	t_{minors} [s]	t_{F4} [s]	$t_{minors} + T_{F4}$ [s]
	minors		9	9	1183.59	14.40	1197.99
	KS	S_2	6	6	0	13375.86	13375.86
		S_3	5	5	0	3296.61	3296.61
	mixed	$\mu = 1$	8	10	43.04	395.57	**438.61**
		$\mu = 2$	6	6	21.52	16823.13	16844.65

5.2 Application on Multivariate Cryptography

Rainbow. A public key from $\text{Rainbow}(q, v, o_1, o_2)$ gives an $\text{MR}(q, n, m, r) = \text{MR}(q, v+o_1+o_2, o_2, v+o_1)$. For example, $\text{Rainbow}(16, 32, 32, 32)$, which achieves NIST type I security, gives us $\text{MR}(q, n, m, r) = \text{MR}(16, 96, 32, 64)$. If we use minors modeling, d_{ff} is estimated to be 65, assuming $\omega = 2.8$ gives us a complexity $\binom{m+r+1}{r+1}^{\omega} = 2^{238.5}$. Note that computing minors has a complexity of $\min\{\binom{m+r+1}{r+1}^2, \binom{n}{r+1}^2 \binom{m+r+1}{r+1}\} = \min\{2^{170.39}, 2^{337.59}\} = 2^{170.39}$. If we use KS method considering [33] with $n - r = 32$ kernel vectors, d_{ff} is estimated to be 18 and we assume using $d_{ff} - 1 = 17$ out of 32 kernel vectors and multiply only by monomials from kernel variables in the XL algorithm still has $d_{ff} = 18$, then we have a complexity $\binom{17r+d_{ff}}{d_{ff}}^{\omega} = 2^{362.0}$. Using exhaustive search on variables $x_1, \ldots, x_m$ and verifying the solution cost a complexity of $q^m \cdot \left(mn^2 + \frac{n^3}{6}\right) \approx 2^{146.8}$, here mn^2 accounts for the computation of $\sum_{i=1}^{m} x_i M_i$, which can be done in parallel and $\frac{n^3}{6}$ accounts for verifying the rank of $M_0 + \sum_{i=1}^{m} x_i M_i$ using Gaussian elimination. Since for the given minrank instance, $m + r = n$ satisfies, we only need to use S_1 in the mixed method. Similar to the results in Table 3, by specifying $k = 30$ variables from $x_1, \ldots, x_m$, non-trivial syzygies from $\text{Jac}_k(S_1)$ will have degree $64 - 30 \cdot 2 = 4$, namely we have $d_k = 4$, which gives us a complexity of $q^k \cdot \left(\binom{m-k+r-2k}{r-2k}^{\omega} + kn^2\right) \approx 2^{138.1}$. It is much lower than the claimed value $2^{156.1}$ presented in NIST PQC Rainbow proposal [13] (see Table 5).

For parameter IIIc, $\text{Rainbow}(256, 68, 36, 36)$, there is a minrank instance $\text{MR}(q, n, m, r) = \text{MR}(256, 140, 36, 104)$. Exhaustive search on variables $x_1, \ldots, x_m$ and verifying the correctness of the solution require a complexity $q^m \cdot \left(mn^2 + \frac{n^3}{6}\right) = 2^{308.1}$. Minors modeling has a complexity of $\binom{m+r+1}{r+1}^{\omega} \approx 2^{313.2}$. When $n - r = 36$ kernel vectors are used in the KS method, its d_{ff} is expected to be 23. Assuming using $d_{ff} - 1 = 22$ kernel vectors also has $d_{ff} = 23$ gives a complexity of $\binom{22r+23}{23}^{\omega} \approx 2^{510.7}$. When the mixed method is used, since $m + r = n$ satisfies, we only need to use S_1. The non-trivial syzygies from $\text{Jac}_x(S_1)$ have degree $m + 1$ and ones from $\text{Jac}_k(S_1)$ have degree r considering experiment results in Table 3. Moreover, since the cardinality of the field is 256, applying the hybrid approach will not bring any benefit. Therefore, the mixed method has a complexity of $\min\{\binom{m+r}{r}^{\omega}, \binom{r+m+1}{m+1}^{\omega}\} \approx 2^{312.0}$, which is also much lower than the claimed complexity $2^{578.0}$ given in [13].

Similarly, for parameter Vc, $\text{Rainbow}(256, 92, 48, 48)$, its complexities of minrank attack using exhaustive search on variables $x_1, \ldots, x_m$ and verifying the correctness of the solution, minors modeling, the KS method and the mixed method are $2^{405.4}, 2^{421.7}, 2^{705.8}$ and $2^{420.5}$, respectively.

From the above-mentioned discussions, we know the previous complexity analysis on the minrank attack presented in the NIST PQC standardization 2nd round Rainbow proposal is overestimated, but the minrank attack is not enough to break Rainbow.

Table 5. Complexity of the minrank attack on NIST PQC standardization 2nd round Rainbow proposal with different methods, minrank exhaustive represents the attack that exhaustively searches the values of $x_1, \ldots, x_m$, and verify whether the solution gives a matrix of the target rank

Security	(q, v, o_1, o_2)	$MR(q, n, m, r)$	Complexity in [13]	Minrank exhaustive	Minors	KS	Mixed
Ia	$(16, 32, 32, 32)$	$(16, 96, 32, 64)$	$2^{156.1}$	$2^{146.8}$	$2^{238.5}$	$2^{362.0}$	$\mathbf{2^{138.1}}$
IIIc	$(256, 68, 36, 36)$	$(16, 140, 36, 104)$	$2^{578.0}$	$\mathbf{2^{308.1}}$	$2^{313.2}$	$2^{510.7}$	$2^{312.0}$
Vc	$(256, 92, 48, 48)$	$(256, 188, 48, 140)$	$2^{771.7}$	$\mathbf{2^{405.4}}$	$2^{421.7}$	$2^{705.8}$	$2^{420.5}$

6   Conclusion

In this paper, methods for solving the minrank problem were considered. We reviewed two of the existing methods, the KS method and minors modeling, and some results on their complexities. We proposed a mixed method that combined the KS method and minors modeling. The new system used an under-determined bilinear subsystem from the KS and a subsystem from the minors modeling. When the bilinear subsystem is under-determined, the mixed method possibly outperforms the KS method and minors modeling. When the bilinear subsystem is over-determined, the mixed method has the same complexity as the KS method.

We also considered applying the hybrid approach on multivariate polynomials solved in our mixed method. A bilinear subsystem is used in the mixed method, so we considered specifying the set of variables that could minimize the complexity, which is the set that had fewer variables, and every variable specified at least reduced the first fall degree by 1. Finally we revisit the minrank attack on NIST PQC 2nd round Rainbow proposal, and found that originally estimated complexities of the minrank attack on Rainbow Ia, IIIc and Vc, which are $2^{156.1}, 2^{578.0}, 2^{771.7}$, are overestimated. We updated them to be $2^{138.1}, 2^{308.1}, 2^{405.4}$, and concluded Rainbow is secure from the minrank attack.

Acknowledgement. This work was supported by JSPS KAKENHI Grant Number JP18J20866, JP19K20266, JP20K19802 and JST CREST Grant Number JPMJCR14D6.

1. Proof of Proposition 1

Proof. By the definition of the Jacobian matrix, we have $Jac_{\mathbf{x}}(F)\mathbf{x} = F^\top$. Given $G \cdot Jac_{\mathbf{x}}(F) = 0$, we easily obtain $\sum_{i=1}^{m} g_i f_i = G \cdot Jac_{\mathbf{x}}(F)\mathbf{x} = 0$. Therefore, G is a syzygy, and it also lies in the left kernel of $Jac_{\mathbf{x}}(F)$.

Since the trivial syzygies of F contains variables $\mathbf{x}$ and $\mathbf{y}$, and G can only contain variables $\mathbf{x}$, we know if G is non-zero, it is a non-trivial syzygy.

Similar proof can be applied to $Jac_{\mathbf{y}}(F)$ case.   □

2. Examples

Example 1. Let $\mathbb{Q}$ be the field of rational numbers. We consider solving $\begin{bmatrix} a_1 & a_2 & a_3 \\ b_1 & b_2 & b_3 \end{bmatrix} \cdot \begin{bmatrix} x_1 \\ x_2 \\ x_3 \end{bmatrix} = 0$ for x_1, x_2, x_3 over the field $\mathbb{Q}(a_1, a_2, a_3, b_1, b_2, b_3)$.

We convert it to the echelon form: $\begin{bmatrix} a_1 & a_2 & a_3 \\ 0 & \frac{b_2 a_1 - b_1 a_2}{a_1} & \frac{b_3 a_1 - b_1 a_3}{a_1} \end{bmatrix} \cdot \begin{bmatrix} x_1 \\ x_2 \\ x_3 \end{bmatrix} = 0$. Let $x_3 = t$ for any $t \in \mathbb{Q}$ then $x_2 = -t\left(\frac{b_3 a_1 - b_1 a_3}{b_2 a_1 - b_1 a_2}\right)$, $x_1 = t\left(\frac{b_2 a_3 - b_3 a_2}{b_2 a_1 - b_1 a_2}\right)$. If we reparametrize $x_3 = t \begin{vmatrix} a_1 & a_2 \\ b_1 & b_2 \end{vmatrix}$, we finally obtain $\dfrac{x_1}{\begin{vmatrix} a_3 & a_2 \\ b_3 & b_2 \end{vmatrix}} = \dfrac{-x_2}{\begin{vmatrix} a_1 & a_3 \\ b_1 & b_3 \end{vmatrix}} = \dfrac{x_3}{\begin{vmatrix} a_1 & a_2 \\ b_1 & b_2 \end{vmatrix}} = t$.

Example 2. Consider solving $\begin{bmatrix} a_1 & a_2 & a_3 & a_4 \\ b_1 & b_2 & b_3 & b_4 \end{bmatrix} \cdot \begin{bmatrix} x_1 \\ x_2 \\ x_3 \\ x_4 \end{bmatrix} = 0$ for $x_1, \ldots, x_4$ over the field $\mathbb{Q}(a_1, a_2, a_3, a_4, b_1, b_2, b_3, b_4)$.

We convert it to the echelon form : $\begin{bmatrix} a_1 & a_2 & a_3 & a_4 \\ 0 & \frac{b_2 a_1 - b_1 a_2}{a_1} & \frac{b_3 a_1 - b_1 a_3}{a_1} & \frac{b_4 a_1 - b_1 a_4}{a_1} \end{bmatrix} \cdot \begin{bmatrix} x_1 \\ x_2 \\ x_3 \\ x_4 \end{bmatrix} = 0$. Let $x_3 = t, x_4 = s$ for any $t, s \in \mathbb{Q}$. Then we have $x_1 = -\begin{vmatrix} a_2 & a_4 \\ b_2 & b_4 \end{vmatrix} s - \begin{vmatrix} a_2 & a_3 \\ b_2 & b_3 \end{vmatrix} t$, $x_2 = \begin{vmatrix} a_1 & a_4 \\ b_1 & b_4 \end{vmatrix} s + \begin{vmatrix} a_1 & a_3 \\ b_1 & b_3 \end{vmatrix} t$, $x_3 = -\begin{vmatrix} a_1 & a_2 \\ b_1 & b_2 \end{vmatrix} t$, $x_4 = -\begin{vmatrix} a_1 & a_2 \\ b_1 & b_2 \end{vmatrix} s$.

3. Proof of Proposition 3

Proof. Suppose $(s_1, \ldots, s_n)$ is a non-trivial syzygy of degree d. Then we can construct a syzygy of degree d for F_1^h, which is $(s_1, \ldots, s_n, 0, \ldots, 0)$, where F_1^h consists of the homogeneous components of the highest degree of F_1.

If $(s_1, \ldots, s_n)$ is a non-trivial syzygy in variables $\mathbf{k}$, $s_i (1 \leq i \leq n)$ are polynomials of degree no larger than m, then $(s_1, \ldots, s_n, 0, \ldots, 0)$ is a non-trivial syzygy of F_1^h by Proposition 1. On the other hand, if $(s_1, \ldots, s_n)$ is in variables $\mathbf{x}$, $s_i (1 \leq i \leq n)$ will have degree no larger than r. Since T_1 consists of polynomials of degree $r + 1$, we know $(s_1, \ldots, s_n, 0, \ldots, 0)$ can only be a non-trivial syzygy of F_1^h by Proposition 1. According to the definition of d_{ff}, we know the d_{ff} of F_1 is at most d since there may exist other non-trivial syzygies of F_1^h that have a smaller degree than d. Therefore, the statement is proved. ∎

References

1. Alagic, G., et al.: Status report on the first round of the NIST post-quantum cryptography standardization process. NIST Internal Report 8240, National Institute of Standards and Technology (2018)
2. Bardet, M., et al.: An algebraic attack on rank metric code-based cryptosystems (2019, preprint)
3. Bardet, M., Faugère, J.-C., Salvy, B., Yang, B.-Y.: Asymptotic behavior of the index of regularity of quadratic semi-regular polynomial systems. In: 8th International Symposium on Effective Methods in Algebraic Geometry - MEGA 2005 (2005)
4. Bettale, L., Faugère, J.-C., Perret, L.: Hybrid approach for solving multivariate systems over finite fields. J. Math. Cryptol. **3**, 177–197 (2009)
5. Bettale, L., Faugère, J.-C., Perret, L.: Cryptanalysis of HFE, multi-HFE and variants for odd and even characteristic. Des. Codes Crypt. **69**(1), 1–52 (2013)
6. Bosma, W., Cannon, J., Playoust, C.: The Magma algebra system. I. The user language. J. Symb. Comput. **24**(3–4), 235–265 (1997)
7. Buchberger, B.: Ein Algorithmus zum Auffinden der Basiselemente des Restklassenringes nach einem nulldimensionalen Polynomideal. PhD thesis, Universitat Innsbruck (1965)
8. Buss, J.F., Frandsen, G.S., Shallit, J.O.: The computational complexity of some problems of linear algebra. J. Comput. Syst. Sci. **58**(3), 572–596 (1999)
9. Cabarcas, D., Smith-Tone, D., Verbel, J.A.: Key recovery attack for ZHFE. In: Lange, T., Takagi, T. (eds.) PQCrypto 2017. LNCS, vol. 10346, pp. 289–308. Springer, Cham (2017). https://doi.org/10.1007/978-3-319-59879-6_17
10. Caminata, A., Gorla, E.: The complexity of minrank. arXiv:1905.02682 [cs.SC] (2019)
11. Chen, L., et al.: Report on post-quantum cryptography. NIST Interagency Report 8105, National Institute of Standards and Technology (2016)
12. Courtois, N., Klimov, A., Patarin, J., Shamir, A.: Efficient algorithms for solving overdefined systems of multivariate polynomial equations. In: Preneel, B. (ed.) EUROCRYPT 2000. LNCS, vol. 1807, pp. 392–407. Springer, Heidelberg (2000). https://doi.org/10.1007/3-540-45539-6_27
13. Ding, J., Chen, M.-S., Petzoldt, A., Schmidt, D., Yang, B.-Y.: Rainbow. NIST PQC Submission, University of Cincinnati (2017)
14. Ding, J., Hodges, T.J.: Inverting HFE systems is quasi-polynomial for all fields. In: Rogaway, P. (ed.) CRYPTO 2011. LNCS, vol. 6841, pp. 724–742. Springer, Heidelberg (2011). https://doi.org/10.1007/978-3-642-22792-9_41
15. Ding, J., Kleinjung, T.: Degree of regularity for HFE-. Cryptology ePrint Archive, Report 2011/570 (2011). https://eprint.iacr.org/2011/570
16. Ding, J., Schmidt, D.: Rainbow, a new multivariable polynomial signature scheme. In: Ioannidis, J., Keromytis, A., Yung, M. (eds.) ACNS 2005. LNCS, vol. 3531, pp. 164–175. Springer, Heidelberg (2005). https://doi.org/10.1007/11496137_12
17. Ding, J., Yang, B.-Y.: Degree of regularity for HFEv and HFEv-. In: Gaborit, P. (ed.) PQCrypto 2013. LNCS, vol. 7932, pp. 52–66. Springer, Heidelberg (2013). https://doi.org/10.1007/978-3-642-38616-9_4
18. Faugeère, J.-C., El Din, M.S., Spaenlehauer, P.-J.: Computing loci of rank defects of linear matrices using gröbner bases and applications to cryptology. In: Proceedings of the 2010 International Symposium on Symbolic and Algebraic Computation, ISSAC 2010, pp. 257–264. ACM (2010)

19. Faugère, J.-C.: A new efficient algorithm for computing Gröbner bases (F4). J. Pure Appl. Algebra **139**(1), 61–88 (1999)
20. Faugère, J.C.: A new efficient algorithm for computing Gröbner bases without reduction to zero (F5). In: ISSAC 2002, pp. 75–83. ACM (2002)
21. Faugère, J.-C., Din, M.S.E., Spaenlehauer, P.-J.: On the complexity of the generalized minrank problem. J. Symb. Comput. **55**, 30–58 (2013)
22. Faugère, J.-C., Din, M.S.E., Spaenlehauer, P.-J.: Gröbner bases of bihomogeneous ideals generated by polynomials of bidegree (1,1): algorithms and complexity. J. Symb. Comput. **46**(4), 406–437 (2011)
23. Goubin, L., Courtois, N.T.: Cryptanalysis of the TTM cryptosystem. In: Okamoto, T. (ed.) ASIACRYPT 2000. LNCS, vol. 1976, pp. 44–57. Springer, Heidelberg (2000). https://doi.org/10.1007/3-540-44448-3_4
24. Kipnis, A., Shamir, A.: Cryptanalysis of the HFE public key cryptosystem by relinearization. In: Wiener, M. (ed.) CRYPTO 1999. LNCS, vol. 1666, pp. 19–30. Springer, Heidelberg (1999). https://doi.org/10.1007/3-540-48405-1_2
25. Koblitz, N.: Elliptic curve cryptosystems. Math. Comput. **48**, 203–209 (1987)
26. Patarin, J.: Hidden fields equations (HFE) and isomorphisms of polynomials (IP): two new families of asymmetric algorithms. In: Maurer, U. (ed.) EUROCRYPT 1996. LNCS, vol. 1070, pp. 33–48. Springer, Heidelberg (1996). https://doi.org/10.1007/3-540-68339-9_4
27. Patarin, J., Courtois, N., Goubin, L.: QUARTZ, 128-bit long digital signatures. In: Naccache, D. (ed.) CT-RSA 2001. LNCS, vol. 2020, pp. 282–297. Springer, Heidelberg (2001). https://doi.org/10.1007/3-540-45353-9_21
28. Perlner, R., Petzoldt, A., Smith-Tone, D.: Total break of the SRP encryption scheme. In: Adams, C., Camenisch, J. (eds.) SAC 2017. LNCS, vol. 10719, pp. 355–373. Springer, Cham (2018). https://doi.org/10.1007/978-3-319-72565-9_18
29. Petzoldt, A., Chen, M.-S., Yang, B.-Y., Tao, C., Ding, J.: Design principles for HFEv- based multivariate signature schemes. In: Iwata, T., Cheon, J.H. (eds.) ASIACRYPT 2015. LNCS, vol. 9452, pp. 311–334. Springer, Heidelberg (2015). https://doi.org/10.1007/978-3-662-48797-6_14
30. Rivest, R.L., Shamir, A., Adleman, L.: A method for obtaining digital signatures and public-key cryptosystems. Commun. ACM **21**(2), 120–126 (1978)
31. Shor, P.: Polynomial-time algorithms for prime factorization and discrete logarithms on a quantum computer. SIAM J. Comput. **26**(5), 1484–1509 (1997)
32. Stothers, A.: On the complexity of matrix multiplication. PhD thesis, University of Edinburgh (2010)
33. Verbel, J., Baena, J., Cabarcas, D., Perlner, R., Smith-Tone, D.: On the complexity of "Superdetermined" minrank instances. In: Ding, J., Steinwandt, R. (eds.) PQCrypto 2019. LNCS, vol. 11505, pp. 167–186. Springer, Cham (2019). https://doi.org/10.1007/978-3-030-25510-7_10

Paid and Anonymous Usage of Cloud Software

Kun Peng$^{(\boxtimes)}$

Huawei Technology, Shenzhen, China
dr.kun.peng@gmail.com

Abstract. A solution is proposed in this paper to implement paid and anonymous use of cloud software. It addresses a popular cloud computing service, cloud software, and considers the requirement of some users to protect their privacy. It enables a software user to access a paid cloud software anonymously such that his input to the software and the output of the software to him cannot be linked to his identity. Firstly, a software user buys an anonymous token from a software provider. The anonymous token proves the user's access privilege to the software and does not reveal his identity. Then the user communicates with the software provider anonymously through a two-way onion routing network, submitting his input and anonymous token and obtaining the output from the software. The two-way onion routing network employs symmetric encryption and decryption and an efficient key exchange mechanism and so does not compromise efficiency of the new scheme.

1 Introduction

In the era of cloud computing, it is very popular for software users to rent the softwares they need and use them on-line instead of buying them and installing them locally. After paying the renting cost to a software provider, a user can use the rented cloud software on-line in two steps. Firstly, he sends the software provider his input to the software. Then, the software provider runs the software with the input and returns the user the output. Software renting in the cloud has some obvious advantages as the user does not need to care about the software (e.g. its secure execution environment) except knowing that it runs somewhere securely in the cloud. Firstly, renting a software is cheaper than buying it. Secondly, the users do not need to provide local hardware (computing power) to run the software. Thirdly, the users do not need to worry about system maintains and software update. Fourthly, the software provider does not need to worry for copyright violation. However, this new trend raises some security concerns. One of them is privacy of the users as both their inputs to the software and the software' outputs to them are transmitted on-line between the users and the software providers. Many users do not want to reveal their inputs to the software and the returned outputs to other parties as they may be sensitive information. For example, users of financial management software will not reveal their financial data and users of market analysis software will not reveal the analysis result. Privacy of users of cloud rent software has the following two requirements.

© Springer Nature Switzerland AG 2020
I. You (Ed.): WISA 2020, LNCS 12583, pp. 308–320, 2020.
https://doi.org/10.1007/978-3-030-65299-9_23

- Their inputs to the software and the software's outputs to them are confidential when being transmitted on the Internet.
- Their inputs to the software and the software's outputs to them are confidential to the software providers. At least the software providers cannot link the identities of the users to their inputs and outputs. Even if a software provider receives an input and process it in plaintext to obtain an output, he has no idea which user they belong to.

The first requirement is not hard to satisfy: encrypting the inputs and outputs when they are transmitted on the Internet is enough. Of course, key exchange between the software users and software providers is needed. The second requirement is harder to satisfy. A software provider has to inject an input into the software and extract an output from it. The only way to hide the input and the output from the software provider is to design a software able to process encrypted input and returns an encrypted output. Although in theory secure computation techniques [1, 2, 7–9, 14, 15, 22, 23] can process inputs in ciphertext and calculate their functions, in practice there are some difficulties in applying them to private usage of cloud software. Practical software usually carries out complex computations and implementing them through secure computation is complex and costly, especially when fully homomorphic encryption [17–21, 24] must be employed. So, to the best of our knowledge, no cloud software provider employ the inefficient whole-course-encrypted computation to process users' inputs in practical software services.

A practical solution to private usage of cloud software is anonymising the users. Namely, although a software provider receives an input from a user, runs it on the software and returns an output to the user, he cannot link the input and the output to the user as the user is anonymous. More precisely, although the software provider knows the input and the output in plaintext, he cannot link them to their owners, who accesses the software service anonymously. Privacy protection of personal data through anonymisation is an effective method and even strict legislation like GDPR [11] recognises that it is not necessary to limit processing and transfer of anonymised data. However, anonymity of the software users raises another question: how to authenticate the anonymous users and guarantee that only qualified users can access the software. An obvious solution for anonymous authentication is pseudonym. In private usage of cloud software, pseudonym technique must cooperate with a billing system as very often paid usage to a cloud software is not permanent. A legal user usually buys a certain times of usage of a software such that his access to the software is permitted until his credits run out. Therefore, anonymous authentication for a limited number of times must be supported.

After anonymous authentication for a limited number of times is implemented, there is another practical consideration: the software users' network connection to the software providers must be anonymous and not traceable. Otherwise, even if a user uses a pseudonym to access a software, he can still be traced through his network connection (e.g. his IP address). So an anonymous communication network is needed. The most common anonymous communication network is onion routing [3, 12, 13], whose most popular real-world instance is Tor [10]. However, application of onion routing to private usage of cloud software faces a challenge: onion routing is usually present as a one-way channel and only deals with a transmit from a sender to a receiver where the receiver does not respond to the sender. More precisely, although a software user can submits his pseudonym and input to a software provider through onion routing, the software provider still need additional support to return the output of the software to the software user as the user is anonymous and his whereabout is unknown. Therefore, a two-way anonymous communication network is needed.

In this paper two new techniques are designed to support anonymous usage of cloud software. Firstly, an anonymous token technique is proposed to enable the software users to buy tokens from the software providers and use them anonymously. A token from a software provider permits a software user to use the software of the software provider once. A special mechanism prevents the users to tamper with their tokens or reuse them. Secondly and more importantly, a two-way onion routing technique is implemented to support two-way anonymous communication between the software providers and the software users. As efficiency of onion routing deteriorates after being extended to two-way, a new key exchange technique is proposed as an efficiency improvement mechanism to prevent efficiency of onion routing from being compromised.

2   Preliminaries

Background knowledge and symbol denotions to be used in this paper are introduced and recalled in this section.

2.1   Onion Routing

Anonymous communication network is a very useful tool in e-commerce, e-finance, e-government and other cryptographic applications, which often require anonymity and privacy. In an anonymous communication network, the messages are untraceable, so can be transmitted anonymously. A common method to implement anonymous networks is onion routing [3,12,13], which employs multiple nodes to route a message. A node in an onion routing communication network can send a message to any node in the network. The sender can flexibly choose any route from all the connection paths between him and the receiver. Each message is contained in a packet called an onion. In the packet, a message is encrypted layer by layer using the encryption keys of all the routers on its route and the receiver. Each layer of encryption is just like a layer of onion bulb. In onion routing, given a message packet, each router unwraps a layer of encryption by decrypting the message packet using its decryption key, finds out the identity of the next router and forwards the partially unwrapped message packet to the next router. Unless gaining collusion of all the routers on the routing path of his received message, the receiver cannot trace the message back to the sender, who then obtains anonymity. When a packet is routed together with a large number of other packets, onion routing prevents it from being traced, even if the traffic in the whole onion routing network is monitored.

Tor [10] is the second generation of onion routing. It proposes a few optimisations for onion routing. A suggested optimisation in Tor is to replace asymmetric cipher with much more efficient symmetric cipher to improve efficiency of onion routing. It is a common sense that symmetric cipher is much more efficient than asymmetric cipher in encryption and decryption. The key point in using symmetric cipher is how to distribute the session keys using public key operations, while a simple solution to the key-exchange problem in application of symmetric ciphers is the Diffie-Hellman key exchange protocol recalled in Sect. 2.3. So it is suggested in Tor [10] to employ "Diffie-Hellman handshake" to implement key changes and generate session keys for the routers and the receiver. Although more efficient symmetric cipher is employed in TOR, it does not provide an efficient implementation of key distribution, which is necessary to make full use of the advantage of symmetric cipher. It is only simply mentioned in [10] that the secret key for every router is generated by the sender and the router using a separate Diffie-Hellman handshake and the communication between them is routed by the routers between them on the route of the transfered message. This key distribution mechanism greatly increases communicational cost.

2.2 Parameter Setting and Symbols

The following symbols are used in this paper.

- p and q are large primes and q is a factor of $p - 1$. G is the cyclic subgroup with order q in Z_p^*. g is a generator of G.
- Encryption of m using key k is denoted as $E_k(m)$ where a block cipher (e.g. AES) is employed.
- Encryption chain of m using block cipher and key $k_1, k_2, \ldots, k_i$ is denoted as $E_{k_1,k_2,\ldots,k_i}(m)$. The encryptions are performed layer by layer. k_1 is the the key used in the most outer layer; k_2 is the key used in the second most outer layer; $\ldots$; k_i is the the key used in the most inner layer.
- In onion routing, the routers and receiver are denoted as $P_1, P_2, \ldots,$.
- The private key of P_i is x_i, which is randomly chosen from Z_q. The corresponding public key is $y_i = g^{x_i} \bmod p$.

2.3 Diffie-Hellman Key Exchange

Symmetric ciphers like block cipher are very efficient in encryption and decryption. However, unlike asymmetric cipher they depend on key exchange protocols to distribute keys. The most common key exchange protocol is Diffie-Hellman key exchange protocol. Two parties A and B can cooperate to generate a session key as follows.

1. A randomly chooses α from Z_q and sends his key base $\mu = g^\alpha \bmod p$ to B.
2. B randomly chooses β from Z_q and sends his key base $\nu = g^\beta \bmod p$ to A.
3. A can calculate the session key $k = \nu^\alpha \bmod p$, while B can calculate the session key $k = \mu^\beta \bmod p$.

Security of this key exchange protocol depends on hardness of the famous Diffie-Hellman problem as recalled in the following.

Definition 1 *(Diffie-Hellman problem defined in Page 28 of Chapter 3 of [16]). Given μ and ν, it is difficult to calculate k if the discrete logarithm problem is hard.*

3   How to Obtain Anonymous Usage Permit of a Cloud Software: Anonymous Token

The main idea in [5] about blind signature is adopted to generate the anonymous token permitting the clients to anonymously buy and use the cloud software. Suppose a software provider wants to sell online usage permit of a cloud software, he can act as follows.

– He publishes detailed information about the software like its functionality and performance. He publishes the price of online usage permit of the software as well.
– He choose an RSA composite $N = pq$ where p and q are large primes. He chooses his RSA private key d and publishes his public key $e = d^{-1} \bmod N$.

A user wanting to buy the usage permit of the cloud software can buy an anonymous token as his access privilege to the software as follows.

1. He employs a one-way and collision-resistent hash function $H()$ from Z_l to Z_N where l is a security parameter.
2. He randomly chooses an integer t from Z_l and calculates $t' = H(t)$.
3. He randomly chooses another integer r from Z_N and calculates $T = t'r^e \bmod N$.
4. He pays the price for the software to the software provider and asks the software provider to sign T.
5. The provider receives the money and returns the user $T' = T^d \bmod N$.

The user can extract an anonymous token from T' and employ it to use the cloud software anonymously as follows.

1. He calculate $\kappa = T'/r \bmod N$.
2. When he wants to use the cloud software, he submits (t, κ) as his anonymous token to the software provider together with his input to the software.
3. The software provider verifies validity of the token as follows.
   (a) He firstly checks his database, which stores the used tokens. The received token cannot exist in the database.
   (b) He verifies $\kappa = H(t)^d \bmod N$, which must be satisfied.
   If and only if both verifications are passed, the user has the access privilege to the software. When the verifications are passed, the software provider runs the software with the user's input and sends the output of the software to the user. Otherwise, the user's request is rejected.

4. The software provider inserts the used token into his database and it cannot be used any longer.

Hardness to factorize N and thus find d given e and onewayness and collision-resistence of the employed hash function guarantees that anonymous token cannot be forged or malleated. This security assumption is similar to the popular security assumption for the hash-and-sign technology in digital signature (Chapter 11 of [16]), which assume that when a digital signature is the hash function of the message to sign raised to the power of an RSA private key it cannot be forged if RSA assumption is solid and the employed hash function is one way and collision-resistent. So under the security assumption no polynomial adversary can forge an anonymous token or malleated a used token into a new token. Moreover, as a random integer r is involved in generation of T and its influence is removed when the anonymous token, (t, κ), is extracted, the software provider cannot link the anonymous token (t, κ) to the corresponding T he signs earlier. So anonymity of the software user is achieved.

Any user can buy multiple tokens for multiple-time usage of a cloud software. A software provider can sell a permanent token to users frequently using a software. When buying a permanent token, the software user and the software provider use a special public/private key pair different from (e, d). When a permanent token is used, the software user and the software provider employ the special public/private key pair to generate and verify the token and there is no database to record the used tokens.

So far we have not discussed how the software users and the software providers communicate to each other when purchasing and consuming anonymous tokens. When a software user buys an anonymous token, he can visit the software provider in person and make the payment in the normal way. Alternatively, the software user can buy the token online using credit card or e-cash [4,6]. Choice of the employed communication network for the purchase communication depends on whether the software user wants to hide his identity completely. If a software user wants to buy a token using his real identity and use it anonymously later, he can buy it through normal network connections. If a software user does not want to reveal his identity when buying a token, he needs to employ the anonymous communication network proposed in Sect. 4 to communicate with the software provider and pay by anonymous e-cash [4,6]. Communication network for the software accessing communication must be anonymous in this paper and so must employ the anonymous communication network proposed in Sect. 4.

A main difference of our anonymous token from anonymous e-coin (e-cash) is that the receiver of any anonymous token is unique, its issuer, while an e-coin is issued by a finance institute (e.g. bank) and may be received by any vender. So the database of used e-coins is maintained by their issuing bank and needed to be checked by any vender. Therefore, to detect invalid e-coin in real time a vender needs to have a real time network connection to the bank. In our design of anonymous token every software provider can maintain his own database and does not need any help from any third party. Another difference is that our anonymous token is simpler than e-coin as it does not need to contain information like issuing party and value etc.

4 How to Communicate with a Cloud Software Anonymously: Efficient Two-Way Onion Routing

As mentioned before, even if a software user has an anonymous token to access a cloud software he still needs an anonymous communication network to communicate with the software provider. As the most popular anonymous communication network, onion routing network, usually only supports one-way anonymous communication, it is extended to a two-way communication pattern in this section. The new design adopts two ideas. Firstly, two-way onion routing is implemented such that the initial sender of an onion packet can fetch some information from a receiver of the onion. More precisely, an onion packet is routed back to its initial sender after obtaining some information from the router in the end of its route. Secondly, like in Tor symmetric cipher is employed in encryption and decryption of the onion layers, while every router's secret session key is distributed by the sender using Diffie-Hellman handshakes. The new protocol describes a more detailed implementation of symmetric cipher operations and the supporting key distribution mechanism in onion routing as key distribution for symmetric cipher is not implemented in detail in the description of TOR in [10].

To avoid efficiency compromise in two-way communication, its efficiency is optimised by employing a more efficient key exchange mechanism than that in Tor. We notice that direct application of Diffie-Hellman key exchange in multiple separate instances to onion routing like in Tor cannot achieve satisfactory advantage in efficiency. To reduce the additional communication cost and additional encryption and decryption operations in the key exchange mechanism in Tor, a novel technique, compact Diffie-Hellman handshakes, is designed. It seals the Diffie-Hellman key bases for all the routers and the software provider in a single integer. For each router, to generate his session key, he needs his private key and a key base initially sealed by the software user and then recovered by cooperation of all the previous routers in the course of routing. As only one single integer is needed in each onion packet to commit to all the Diffie-Hellman key bases, a very small amount of additional communication is employed and very few additional encryption (decryption) operations are needed.

In the efficient two-way onion routing, an onion packet consists of three parts: message, route list and key base, where Route list contains the identities of all the nodes on the route. Key base is the base to generate the session keys distributed to the routers. The message part in the efficient two-way onion routing is similar to that in most onion routing schemes. The message is encrypted in a encryption chain using the sessions keys of all the routers. An efficient block cipher is employed in the encryption chain. In the efficient two-way onion routing, the route list is similar to that in other onion routing schemes. It consists of all the routers' identities. One block cipher encryption chain is used to seal each router's identity using the session keys of the all the routers before it.

The most important novel technique is generation and update of the key base, which enables key exchanges for all the routers' session keys. Each router builds his session key on the base of the key base using his private key and updates the key base for the next router. The key generation function employs the principle of Diffie-Hellman assumption, but it does not employ separate Diffie-Hellman handshakes to distribute the session keys to the routers. Instead the key base updating mechanism actually generates a key base chain and so all the session keys and their generation functions are linked in a compact chain structure. So the key exchange technique is called compact Diffie-Hellman key exchange. After obtaining his session key, each router extracts the identity of the next router from the route list using his session key, removes one layer of encryption from the message and the route list using his session key and then forwards the onion packet to the next router. Compact Diffie-Hellman key exchange only needs the bandwidth of one integer, and thus is much more efficient than separate key exchanges in communication.

For simplicity of description, in description of the efficient two-way onion routing protocol simple denotations are employed. Suppose an inquiry package m (which contains at least the input to a cloud software and an anonymous token enabling him to use the software) is sent by a software user S through n routers $P_1, P_2, \ldots, P_n$ to a software provider P_{n+1}. Encryption of the inquiry package may actually contain multiple symmetric ciphertext blocks as the inquiry package may be long and is divided into multiple blocks when being encrypted. For convenience of description encryption of the inquiry package is still denoted as a single variable and the readers should be aware that it is the encryption of the whole inquiry package and may contain multiple blocks. Although a different number of routers can be chosen to route the inquiry result (output of the software) back to the software user, for simplicity of description, we suppose that it is sent by the software provider back to the software user through n routers $P_{n+2}, P_{n+3}, \ldots, P_{2n+1}$. In practice it is very probable that the number of routers to transfer the inquiry result is different from the number of routers to transfer the inquiry package. The two sets of routers are not necessary to be completely different and some routers may be employed in both transfers. The efficient two-way onion routing protocol is as follows.

1. Firstly, the software user generates the session keys $k_1, k_2, \ldots, k_{2n+1}$ respectively for $P_1, P_2, \ldots, P_{2n+1}$ as follows.
   (a) The software user randomly chooses an integer s_1 from Z_q.
   (b) The software user calculates P_1's session key $k_1 = y_1^{s_1} \bmod p$.
   (c) The software user calculates $s_2 = s_1 + k_1 \bmod q$.
   (d) The software user calculates P_2's session key $k_2 = y_2^{s_2} \bmod p$.
   $\ldots\ldots$

   $\ldots\ldots$
   (e) The software user calculates $s_{2n+1} = s_{2n} + k_{2n} \bmod q$.
   (f) The software user calculates P_{2n+1}'s session key $k_{2n+1} = y_{2n+1}^{s_{2n+1}} \bmod p$.
   Generally speaking, for $i = 1, 2, \ldots, 2n + 1$, the software user
   (a) if $i > 1$ then calculates $s_i = s_{i-1} + k_{i-1} \bmod q$ as his secret seed to generate k_i;

(b) calculates $k_i = y_i^{s_i} \bmod p$

where s_1 is randomly chosen from Z_q. In summary, the software user uses the sum of the previous router's session key and his secret seed in generating the previous router's session key as his secret seed to generate a router's session key. The other secret seed to generate the router's session key is the router's own private key.

2. The software user generates an onion packet containing an inquiry package, a key base and a route list. The inquiry package m contains at least the input to a cloud software and an anonymous token enabling him to use the software and is encrypted into $e = E_{k_1, k_2, \ldots, k_{n+1}}(P_{n+1}, m)$. The key base is g^{s_1}. The route list consists of $p_1, p_2, \ldots, p_{2n+2}$ where $p_i = E_{k_1, k_2, \ldots, k_i}(P_{i+1})$ for $i = 1, 2, \ldots, 2n + 1$ and $P_{n+2} = S$. The initial onion

$$O_1 = (a_1, b_1, c_{1,1}, c_{1,2}, \ldots, c_{1,2n+1}) = (e, g^{s_1}, p_1, p_2, \ldots, p_{2n+1})$$

is sent to P_1.

3. Generally, for $i = 1, 2, \ldots, n$ each P_i receives $O_i = (a_i, b_i, c_{i,1}, c_{i,2}, \ldots, c_{i,2n+1})$ and operates as follows.
   (a) P_i generates his session key $k_i = b_i^{x_i} \bmod p$.
   (b) P_i uses k_i to decrypt $c_{i,1}$ and obtains $P_{i+1} = D_{k_i}(c_{i,1})$.
   (c) P_i calculates the new key base $b_{i+1} = b_i g^{k_i} \bmod p$.
   Finally, P_i sends

$$O_{i+1} = (a_{i+1}, b_{i+1}, c_{i+1,1}, c_{i+1,2}, \ldots, c_{i+1,2n+1})$$

to P_{i+1} where $a_{i+1} = D_{k_i}(a_i)$ and $c_{i+1,j} = D_{k_i}(c_{i,j+1})$ for $j = 1, 2, \ldots, 2n$ and $c_{i+1,2n+1}$ is a random ciphertext in the ciphertext space of the employed symmetric encryption algorithm.

4. After the routing by $P_1, P_2, \ldots, P_n$, the software provider P_{n+1} receives

$$O_{n+1} = (a_{n+1}, b_{n+1}, c_{n+1,1}, c_{n+1,2}, \ldots, c_{n+1,2n+1})$$

and operates as follows.
   (a) P_{n+1} generates his session key $k_{n+1} = b_{n+1}^{x_{n+1}} \bmod p$.
   (b) P_{n+1} uses k_{n+1} to decrypt $c_{n+1,1}$ and obtains P_{n+2}.
   (c) P_{n+1} uses k_{n+1} to decrypt a_{n+1} and obtains the inquiry package m and his own identity P_{n+1}. He knows that he himself is the software provider as P_{n+1} is its own identity. So he verifies validity of the anonymous token, runs the software using the input in m, obtains an output R and generates $a_{n+2} = (E_m(R), H(m))$ where $E_m()$ denotes symmetric encryption using key m and $H()$ is a one-way and collision-free hash function.

5. For $i = n+1, n+2, \ldots, 2n+1$ each router P_i routes the onion packet as follows where the onion he receives is in the form $O_i = (a_i, b_i, c_{i,1}, c_{i,2}, \ldots, c_{i,2n+1})$.
   (a) P_i generates his session key $k_i = b_i^{x_i} \bmod p$.
   (b) P_i uses k_i to decrypt $c_{i,1}$ and obtains $P_{i+1} = D_{k_i}(c_{i,1})$.
   (c) P_i calculates the new key base $b_{i+1} = b_i g^{k_i} \bmod p$.

Finally, P_i sends

$$O_{i+1} = (a_{i+1}, b_{i+1}, c_{i+1,1}, c_{i+1,2}, \ldots, c_{i+1,2n+1})$$

to P_{i+1} where $a_{i+1} = D_{k_i}(a_i)$ and $c_{i+1,j} = D_{k_i}(c_{i,j+1})$ for $j = 1, 2, \ldots, 2n$ and $c_{i+1,2n+1}$ is a random ciphertext in the ciphertext space of the employed symmetric encryption algorithm.

6. After the routing by $P_{n+2}, P_{n+3}, \ldots, P_{2n+1}$, the software user S receives

$$O_{2n+2} = (a_{2n+2}, b_{2n+2}, c_{2n+2,1}, c_{2n+2,2}, \ldots, c_{2n+2,2n+1})$$

and operates as follows.

(a) S calculates $k = b_{2n+2}^x \bmod p$ where x is his own private key.

(b) S tries to use k to decrypt $c_{2n+2,1}$ but does not obtain a legal identity. He knows that he is not a router or software provider of the onion packet. The only possibility is that his own onion packet is returned by the software provider.

(c) S calculates $(\rho, \tau) = E_{k_{n+2}, k_{n+3}, \ldots, k_{2n+1}}(a_{2n+2})$. If $\tau = H(m)$, he is ensured that the software provider P_{n+1} returns him an encrypted inquiry result. He can extract the inquiry result as $R = D_m(\rho)$ where $D_m()$ denotes symmetric decryption using key m.

Note that although the encryption chain for the next router's identity is completely decrypted and discarded by each router, the length of the encrypted route list is kept unchanged in the routing protocol for the sake of untraceability. If an onion packet becomes shorter after each router's routing, its change in length can be observed and exploited to trace it. So we keep the length of the encrypted route list constant to maintain the size of an onion packet. This is implemented in the routing protocol by inserting a random tag into the onion packet after an encryption chain is discarded. The new key exchange mechanism improves efficiency of the two-way onion routing technique. As most of its operations depend on symmetric encryptions and decryptions and employ small (in comparison with the large integers in asymmetric cipher operations) integers and the number of asymmetric cipher operations is minimized, efficiency of onion routing is not compromised after it is extended to support two-way anonymous communication.

5   Security Analysis

Security of the efficient two-way onion routing scheme depends on hardness of Diffie-Hellman problem as its key exchange mechanism is an extension of Diffie-Hellman key exchange. Its main trick is combining key exchanges into a compact chain such that every router can obtain his session key with the help the previous routers. As security of Diffie-Hellman key exchange has been formally proved and hardness of Diffie-Hellman problem is widely accepted, no further proof of security is needed except for Theorem 1, which shows that the session keys can be correctly exchanged.

Theorem 1. *For $i = 1, 2, \ldots, 2n + 1$, the same session key k_i is generated, respectively by the software user as $k_i = y_i^{s_i} \bmod p$ and by P_i as $k_i = b_i^{x_i} \bmod p$.*

To prove Theorem 1, a lemma has to be proved first.

Lemma 1. *For $i = 1, 2, \ldots, 2n + 1$, $b_i = g^{s_i} \bmod p$.*

Proof: Mathematical induction is used.

1. When $i = 1$, $b_1 = g^{s_1} \bmod p$.
2. Suppose when $i = j$ and $j \geq 1$ it is still satisfied that $b_i = g^{s_i} \bmod p$. Then a deduction can be made in next step.
3. When $i = j + 1$, $b_{j+1} = b_j g^{k_j} = g^{s_j} g^{k_j} \bmod p$ as it is supposed in last step that $b_i = g^{s_i}$ when $i = j$. So

$$b_{j+1} = g^{s_j} g^{k_j} = g^{s_j + k_j} = g^{s_{j+1}} \bmod p$$

Therefore, $b_i = g^{s_i} \bmod p$ for $j = 1, 2, \ldots, 2n + 1$ as a result of mathematical induction. □

Proof of Theorem 1:
According to Lemma 1,
$$y_i^{s_i} = g^{x_i s_i} = b_i^{x_i} \bmod p$$

for $i = 1, 2, \ldots, 2n + 1$. □

6   Conclusion

The new solution proposed in this paper allows users caring about their privacy to use paid cloud software online anonymously. The users buy anonymous tokens to access the software they need and employ an efficient two-way onion routing network to communicate with the software providers.

References

1. Beerliová-Trubíniová, Z., Hirt, M.: Efficient multi-party computation with dispute control. In: Halevi, S., Rabin, T. (eds.) TCC 2006. LNCS, vol. 3876, pp. 305–328. Springer, Heidelberg (2006). https://doi.org/10.1007/11681878_16
2. Bogetoft, P., et al.: Secure multiparty computation goes live. In: Dingledine, R., Golle, P. (eds.) FC 2009. LNCS, vol. 5628, pp. 325–343. Springer, Heidelberg (2009). https://doi.org/10.1007/978-3-642-03549-4_20
3. Camenisch, J., Lysyanskaya, A.: A formal treatment of onion routing. In: Shoup, V. (ed.) CRYPTO 2005. LNCS, vol. 3621, pp. 169–187. Springer, Heidelberg (2005). https://doi.org/10.1007/11535218_11
4. Chan, A., Frankel, Y., Tsiounis, Y.: Easy come - easy go divisible cash. Updated version with corrections (1998). http://www.ccs.neu.edu/home/yiannis/

5. Chaum, D.: Blind signatures for untraceable payments. In: Chaum, D., Rivest, R.L., Sherman, A.T. (eds.) Crypto 1982, pp. 199–203. Springer, Boston (1983). https://doi.org/10.1007/978-1-4757-0602-4_18

6. Chaum, D., Fiat, A., Naor, M.: Untraceable electronic cash. In: Goldwasser, S. (ed.) CRYPTO 1988. LNCS, vol. 403, pp. 319–327. Springer, New York (1990). https://doi.org/10.1007/0-387-34799-2_25

7. Cramer, R., Damgård, I., Nielsen, J.B.: Multiparty computation from threshold homomorphic encryption. In: Pfitzmann, B. (ed.) EUROCRYPT 2001. LNCS, vol. 2045, pp. 280–300. Springer, Heidelberg (2001). https://doi.org/10.1007/3-540-44987-6_18

8. Damgård, I., Geisler, M., Krøigaard, M., Nielsen, J.B.: Asynchronous multiparty computation: theory and implementation. In: Jarecki, S., Tsudik, G. (eds.) PKC 2009. LNCS, vol. 5443, pp. 160–179. Springer, Heidelberg (2009). https://doi.org/10.1007/978-3-642-00468-1_10

9. Damgård, I., Ishai, Y., Krøigaard, M., Nielsen, J.B., Smith, A.: Scalable multiparty computation with nearly optimal work and resilience. In: Wagner, D. (ed.) CRYPTO 2008. LNCS, vol. 5157, pp. 241–261. Springer, Heidelberg (2008). https://doi.org/10.1007/978-3-540-85174-5_14

10. Dingledine, R., Mathewson, N., Syverson, P.F.: Tor: the second-generation onion router. In: USENIX Security Symposium, pp. 303–320 (2004)

11. GDPR Recital 26. In: General Data Protection Regulation. https://gdpr.eu/recital-26-not-applicable-to-anonymous-data/

12. Goldreich, O., Micali, S., Wigderson, A.: How to play any mental game or a completeness theorem for protocols with honest majority. In: STOC 1987, pp. 218–229 (1987)

13. Goldschlag, D.M., Reed, M.G., Syverson, P.F.: Onion routing for anonymous and private internet connections. Commun. ACM 42(2), 84–88 (1999)

14. Jakobsson, M., Juels, A.: Mix and match: secure function evaluation via ciphertexts. In: Okamoto, T. (ed.) ASIACRYPT 2000. LNCS, vol. 1976, pp. 162–177. Springer, Heidelberg (2000). https://doi.org/10.1007/3-540-44448-3_13

15. Juels, A., Szydlo, M.: A two-server, sealed-bid auction protocol. In: Blaze, M. (ed.) FC 2002. LNCS, vol. 2357, pp. 72–86. Springer, Heidelberg (2003). https://doi.org/10.1007/3-540-36504-4_6

16. Menezes, A., van Oorschot, P., Vanstone, S.: Handbook of Applied Cryptography. CRC Press Inc., Boca Raton (1996)

17. Alperin-Sheriff, J., Peikert, C.: Faster bootstrapping with polynomial error. In: Garay, J.A., Gennaro, R. (eds.) CRYPTO 2014. LNCS, vol. 8616, pp. 297–314. Springer, Heidelberg (2014). https://doi.org/10.1007/978-3-662-44371-2_17

18. Brakerski, Z., Vaikuntanathan, V.: Efficient fully homomorphic encryption from (standard) LWE. SIAM J. Comput. 43(2), 831–871 (2014)

19. Brakerski, Z., Vaikuntanathan, V.: Lattice-based FHE as secure as PKE. In: Conference on Innovations in Theoretical Computer Science, vol. 14, pp. 1–12 (2014)

20. Cheon, J.H., Kim, A., Kim, M., Song, Y.: Homomorphic encryption for arithmetic of approximate numbers. In: Takagi, T., Peyrin, T. (eds.) ASIACRYPT 2017. LNCS, vol. 10624, pp. 409–437. Springer, Cham (2017). https://doi.org/10.1007/978-3-319-70694-8_15

21. Chillotti, I., Gama, N., Georgieva, M., Izabachène, M.: Faster fully homomorphic encryption: bootstrapping in less than 0.1 seconds. In: Cheon, J.H., Takagi, T. (eds.) ASIACRYPT 2016. LNCS, vol. 10031, pp. 3–33. Springer, Heidelberg (2016). https://doi.org/10.1007/978-3-662-53887-6_1

22. Hastings, M., Hemenway, B., Noble, D., Zdancewic, S.: Sok: general purpose compilers for secure multi-party computation. In: IEEE S&P 2019, pp. 1220–1237 (2019)
23. Lindell, Y., Pinkas, B., Smart, N., Yanai, A.: Efficient constant-round multi-party computation combining BMR and SPDZ. J. Cryptol. **32**(3), 1026–1069 (2019)
24. Yagisawa, M.: Fully homomorphic encryption without bootstrapping. IACR Cryptology ePrint Archive 2015:474 (2015)

Optimization of PBKDF2-HMAC-SHA256 and PBKDF2-HMAC-LSH256 in CPU Environments

Hojin Choi and Seog Chung Seo[✉][iD]

Department of Information Security, Cryptology, and Mathematics,
Kookmin University, Seoul, South Korea
{ondoli0312,scseo}@kookmin.ac.kr

Abstract. Password-Based Key-Derivation Function 2 (PBKDF2) is commonly employed to derive secure keys from a password in real life such as file encryption and implementation of authentication systems. Nevertheless, owing to the limited entropy of the password, the security of the generated keys is lower than that of the normally generated keys. To address this, issue increase the number of iterative operations during the PBKDF2 may increase. However, the higher the number of iterative operations, the more time it takes to generate the key. This paper presents various techniques for optimizing the performance of PBKDF2. The main idea of our proposed methods is to reduce redundant block operations and to optimize Pseudo Random Function (PRF) itself by combining operations and making full use of fixed values within PBKDF2. As the underlying hash function in PRF, we utilize two algorithms: Hash-based Message Authentication Code-Secure Hash Algorithm 256 (HMAC-SHA256) and HMAC-Lightweight Secure Hash 256 (HMAC-LSH256) (SHA256 is the most widely used hash function and LSH256 was recently developed hash function in South Korea). With the proposed techniques, the proposed implementation of PBKDF2-HMAC-SHA256 provides a performance enhancement of about 135.27% over the reference implementation provided by Korea Internet & Security Agency (KISA) and about 80.21% over OpenSSL. Concerning PBKDF2-HMAC-LSH256, the proposed implementation provides a huge performance enhancement of about 330.48% over the reference implementation provided by KISA. With the proposed implementation, more iteration operations can be possible for higher security. Furthermore, we can use the proposed techniques to optimize PBKDF2 performance on embedded MCUs.

Keywords: PBKDF2 · HMAC · SHA256 · LSH256 · Optimization

This work was supported by the National Research Foundation of Korea (NRF) grant funded by the Korea government (MSIT) (No. 2019R1F1A1058494).

I. You (Ed.): WISA 2020, LNCS 12583, pp. 321–333, 2020.
https://doi.org/10.1007/978-3-030-65299-9_24

1   Introduction

Although the development of Internet of Things (IoT) and Cloud computing technologies enable users to utilize various convenient services, users' data has become more easily exposed. To protect users' data, many secure applications or services depend on the knowledge of one or more secrets. Passwords are common examples of these secrets. Even if short and predictable passwords can be easier to remember, they can be more effectively attacked by exhaustive search and dictionary attacks. To avoid the use of user-chosen passwords as a secret key to cryptographic systems, several techniques have been developed. Among them, Password-Based Key Derivation Function 2 (PBKDF2) [2] is widely used for generating secret keys from a user-chosen password and for several applications including file encryption software, authentication systems, and Android data backup systems. As an example, when we backup the data in Android file system, the system requires a user's password. The entered password is used to generate secret keys for encrypting the data in the Android system.

Typically, the entropy of password entered into PBKDF2 is much lower than the typical random secret. Thus, PBDKF2 utilizes a random salt and iteration counts to prevent the construction of dictionary table. The iteration count needs to be at least 1,000 and it needs to be scaled to 10,000,000 for applications requiring higher security. In other words, more iterations needs to be executed for higher security. However, increasing the iteration counts causes performance degradation. Therefore, it is required to optimize the performance of PBKDF2 to apply the increased number of iteration counts for higher security.

Unlike other crypto algorithms like symmetric and public key algorithms, the importance of PBKDF2 optimization has recently been recognized. Until now, some studies have been performed to enhance the performance of PBKDF2 [4,5]. The works from [4,5] presented several techniques for PBKDF2 using Hash-based Message Authentication Code - Secure Hash Algorithm 160 (HMAC-SHA160) as the underlying Pseudo Random Function (PRF). However, in 2017, Marc Stevens et al. published a paper on finding collision pairs of SHA-1 [6]. Furthermore, PBKDF2 algorithm in the approved algorithm list of Korean Cryptographic Module Validation Program (KCMVP) limits the use of HMAC-SHA-2 family and HMAC-Lightweight Secure Hash (LSH) (LSH is a hash function developed in South Korea in 2014) as its PRF [14].

This paper presents several optimization techniques to enhance the performance of PBKDF2-HMAC-SHA256 and PBKDF2-HAMC-LSH256 on general purpose Central Processing Unit (CPU). The main idea of our proposed optimization techniques is to reduce the redundant operations and omit the unnecessary operations in the process of PBKDF2 operation. For PBKDF2-HMAC-SHA256, we present a total of four optimization techniques: two for HMAC and two for SHA256. By applying the proposed optimization techniques, our optimized PBKDF2-HMAC-SHA256 outperformed the reference implementation provided by Korea Internet & Security Agency (KISA) (resp. OpenSSL 1.1.1d) by 135.27% (resp. 80.21%). For PBKDF2-HMAC-LSH256, we propose a total of five optimization techniques. By applying the proposed methods, our optimized PBKDF2-HMAC-LSH256 implementation provides 330.48% of performance enhancement compared with the naive implementation.

2 Overview of PBKDF2 and Existing Results

In this section, we firstly define notations used throughout this paper and introduce what PBKDF2 and its operational process. The existing implementations of PBKDF2 will be also described in this section.

2.1 Introduction to PBKDF2

Table 1. PBKDF2 parameters

Parameter	Meaning
PRF	Pseudo random function to be used in PBKDF2
p, s, c	Input password, salt, and iteration count
$dklen$	the length of derived Key
$hlen$	the length of PRF Output
DK	Derived key of length $dklen$

The high entropy of cryptographic keys is essential in cryptographic applications. For some applications requiring data encryption, passwords may be the only input that users can access data. However, typically the entropy of users' passwords much lower than that of the secret keys generated from Deterministic Random Bit Generator (DRBG). Thus, the passwords need not directly be used as cryptographic keys for security. PBKDF is widely used to solve this problem.

PBKDF is a kind of key derivation function that generates a series of secure keys using PRF from input parameters such as a user password, random salt, and iteration count. There are mainly two versions of PBKDF: PBKDF1 (PBKDF version 1) and PBKDF2 (PBKDF version 2) [2]. PBKDF1 uses SHA-1 or Message Digest 5 (MD5) as its PRF. However, recently, many researchers have questioned the security of MD5, and SHA-1 as well as and their applications. Actually, PBKDF1 is deprecated and is only recommended for compatibility with legacy systems. Therefore, currently PBKDF2 is recommended for generating keys from a use password for secure applications [2,3].

Table 1 defines the parameters used in PBKDF2. Based on Table 1, PBKDF2 can be expressed as $DK = PBKDF2(PRF, p, s, c, dklen)$. Since PBKDF2 generated a series of internal T_i blocks and the block length of T_i is the same as $hLen$, DK can be expressed as $DK = T_1||T_2||T_3||\cdots||T_{\lceil dklen/hlen \rceil}$. PBKDF2 makes use of HMAC with any one of approved hash functions as it PRF. In PBKDF2, HMAC function is executed $c \times len$ and the number of iteration count c needs to be large enough to provide security of the generated keys (c needs to be at least 1,000 and for higher security it needs to be 10,000,000) [2,3].

2.2   Existing Results of PBKDF2 Implementation on CPU Side

In 2018, A. Visconti and F. Gorla presented some techniques for optimizing the performance of PBKDF2-HMAC-SHA-1 on CPU environment [4]. They suggested how to reduce unnecessary XOR operations in SHA-1 and how to reduce redundant operations in the structure of HMAC-SHA-1. In 2019, A. Francesco and A. Visconti presented the extended idea from [4] in their work [5]. They explained a total of six optimization methods (two for HMAC optimization, three for SHA-1 optimization, one for optimization in the certification process) in the context of the CPU/Graphics processing unit. They compared their implementation with OpenSSL 1.1.0e version on AMD FX-8320 8 cores 4 GHz as parameters of $c = 1,000$ and $dklen = 32$ bytes and their implementation achieved 2.1 times enhancement compared with OpenSSL.

NIST deprecated the use of SHA-1 in 2011, and disallowed its use for digital signatures at the end of 2013 [9]. Thus, governmental institutions and companies have been using stronger hash algorithms, SHA-2 and SHA-3, instead of SHA-1. In 2017, M. Stevens et al. presented how to generate a collision of SHA-1 hash values [6]. As a result of this, Google, Microsoft, and Mozilla published the termination of SHA-1 support on their browsers. This requires the use of hash function providing higher security levels such as SHA-2 and SHA-3. Moreover, KCMVP in South Korea allows only HMAC-SHA-2 and HMAC-LSH families as PBKDF's PRF. Therefore, we have chosen SHA-2 and LSH hash functions providing higher hash security level than SHA-1 as hash function in PRF, and presented optimized PBKDF2-HMAC-SHA256 and PBKDF2-HMAC-LSH256.

3   Proposed Techniques for PBKDF2-HMAC-SHA256

In this section, we propose four optimization techniques for PBKDF2-HMAC-SHA256:a Block-Reduction (BR) technique and a technique using known Input Size (IS) in HMAC, and a technique of Zero-Based optimization (ZB) and a Block Operation (BO) technique in SHA256. The HMAC optimization, techniques are merely extension of the concept of optimization techniques from [4,5], while those of SHA256 are new.

3.1   Proposed HMAC Optimization Techniques

This section proposes two techniques—a BR technique and a technique using known-IS—that can reduce redundant and unnecessary operations during HMAC process in PBKDF2-HMAC-SHA256. In HMAC optimization techniques $U_1 = \text{HMAC}(p, s \,\|\, i)$ is excluded.

Block-Reduction in HMAC (BR). DK consists of T_i with $\|$ operation. To create a single T_i, a total of c iterations should be executed for generating intermediate $U_1, \ldots U_c$ values. According to [8], c needs to be at least 1,000. And for systems requiring strong security, c needs to be 10,000,000. The computation speed of PBKDF2-HMAC-SHA256 is closely related to the speed of computing

U_i where $1 \leq i \leq c$. Therefore, it is necessary to optimize the performance of computing U_i value in order to enhance the overall performance of PBKDF2-HMAC-SHA256.

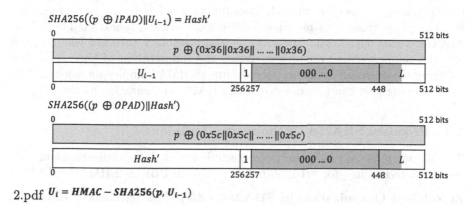

Fig. 1. U_i value computation process in PBKDF2-HMAC-SHA256 ($IPAD$ = 0x36 $OPAD$ = 0x5c. L: Message length info.) (Color figure online)

The BR technique uses the fact that the input password p does not change during PBKDF2-HMAC-SHA256 operation. Figure 1 shows the process of generating a single U_i value. In the process of PRF generating U_i value, SHA256 hash functions are executed twice. In each hash function, two 512-bit blocks need to be processed. The first and second blocks in the first hash function contains $p \oplus IPAD$ and the concatenation of U_{i-1} and padded length information (L), respectively. Similarly, the first and the second blocks in the second hash function contains $p \oplus OPAD$ and the concatenation of $hash'$ and padded length information (L), respectively. Since the ($p \oplus IPAD$) and ($p \oplus OPAD$) do not change in the process of PBKDF2, their intermediate hash values also do not change. Thus, we can compute the intermediate hash values of ($p \oplus IPAD$) and ($p \oplus OPAD$) when computing U_1 and reuse them for computing $U_2, \ldots, U_c$. In other words, in Fig. 1, the blocks represented in gray rectangles do not need to be computed by recycling the values computed from the process of U_1.

With the proposed BR technique, the number of processed blocks decreases from ($4 \times c$) to ($2 \times c + 2$), where c is the number of the iteration count. In other words, in our implementation, U_1 requires computing four blocks (each of the two hash function processes two 512-bit blocks) and a total of ($2c - 2$) (each of the two hash function reuses the precomputed value and processes only one 512-bit block) are required for computing $U_2, \ldots, U_c$.

Using Known Input Size (IS). The IS technique uses the fact that the second block of each hash function during the computation of U_i value in Fig. 1 is a 256-bit data, namely either $hash'$ or U_{i-1}. With the BR technique, since the first block of each hash function in U_i computation except for U_1 can be processed by reusing the precomputed value from the U_1 process, we need to manage only the second block of each hash function for efficiency. The size of the second block in each hash function is always 256-bit (either $hash'$ or U_{i-1}), We have not divided the message for the block operation. In addition, the length of the padding in each hash function is fixed (orange rectangles in Fig. 1) and the value of 64-bit input length information L is also fixed as 768-bit. Therefore, this optimization provides us the possibility to avoid length checks and the chunk splitting operations during the computation of $U_2, \ldots, U_c$, thus reducing the overhead necessary to compute an HMAC implementation and the fixed padding part can be extended with SHA256 optimization method [10].

3.2   Proposed SHA256 Optimization Technique

This section presents two optimization techniques—a ZB optimization and a BO reduction technique—for SHA256 function used in PBKDF2-HMAC-SHA256.

Zero-based Optimization in SHA256 (ZB). This technique uses the fact that a specific part becomes zero during PBKDF2-HMAC-SHA256 operation. Algorithm 1 is SHA256 $WordExpansion$ process.

Algorithm 1. SHA256 Word Expansion Process [7]

Require: Message $M = (M[0], M[1], \ldots\ldots, M[15])$
Ensure: Expansion Data $W = (W[0], W[1], \ldots\ldots, W[63])$
1: Define $Ch(x, y, z) = (x \wedge y) \oplus (\neg x \wedge z)$
2: Define $Maj(x, y, z) = (x \wedge y) \oplus (x \wedge z) \oplus (y \wedge z)$
3: Define $\sum_0^{256}(x) = ROTR^2(x) \oplus ROTR^{13}(x) \oplus ROTR^{22}(x)$
4: Define $\sum_1^{256}(x) = ROTR^6(x) \oplus ROTR^{11}(x) \oplus ROTR^{25}(x)$
5: Define $\sigma_0^{256}(x) = ROTR^7(x) \oplus ROTR^{18}(x) \oplus (x \gg 3)$
6: Define $\sigma_1^{256}(x) = ROTR^{17}(x) \oplus ROTR^{19}(x) \oplus (x \gg 10)$
7: **for** i=0 to 15 **do**
8:     $W[i] = M[i]$;
9: **end for**
10: **for** i=16 to 63 **do**
11:     $W[i] = \sigma_1^{256}(W[i-2]) \boxplus W[i-7] \boxplus \sigma_0^{256}(W[i-15]) \boxplus W[i-16]$
12: **end for**
13: **return** W

According to Algorithm 1, if $W[i]$ is zero, it does not affect the computation of the other $W[t]$. In Fig. 1, the rectangles in orange color are represented with six 32-bit word expansion data (from $W[9]$ to $W[14]$), and the values are always fixed as zero. Thus, they can be excluded from actual computation during SHA256 word expansion process. With the proposed ZB technique, when $16 \leq t \leq 30$, 19 of 45 $\boxplus$ operations, six of 30 σ_0^{256} operations, and one of 30 σ_1^{256} operations can be reduced in SHA256 $WordExpansion$ process.

Reduction of Block Operation in SHA256 (*BO*). This technique combines multiple rounds in the process of hash block computation into one to reduce redundant operations for efficiency.

Algorithm 2. SHA256 Block operation process [7]

Require: Expansion Data $W = (W[0], ..., W[63])$
Require: Working variables (a, b, c, d, e, f, g, h) in hash state
Ensure: Updated working variables (a, b, c, d, e, f, g, h) in hash state
1: **for** t =0 to 63 **do**
2:     $T_1 = h + \sigma_1^{256}(e) \boxplus Ch(e, f, g) \boxplus K_t^{256} \boxplus W[t]$
3:     $T_2 = \sigma_0^{256}(a) \boxplus Maj(a, b, c)$
4:     $h = g,$
5:     $g = f,$
6:     $f = e,$
7:     $e = d \boxplus T_1,$
8:     $d = c,$
9:     $c = b,$
10:    $b = a,$
11:    $a = T_1 \boxplus T_2$
12: **end for**
13: **return** Hash value (a, b, c, d, e, f, g, h)

Table 2. Changes of intermediate values in eight working Variables in block operation process of Algorithm 2 ($T(m, n)$ is the T_m value of n-th round in Algorithm 2.)

Variables	0R	1R	2R	3R
a	$T(0,1) + T(0,2)$	$T(1,1) + T(1,2)$	$T(2,1) + T(2,2)$	$T(3,1) + T(3,2)$
b	a	$T(0,1) + T(0,2)$	$T(1,1) + T(1,2)$	$T(2,1) + T(2,2)$
c	b	a	$T(0,1) + T(0,2)$	$T(1,1) + T(1,2)$
d	c	b	a	$T(0,1) + T(0,2)$
e	$d + T(0,1)$	$c + T(1,1)$	$b + T(2,1)$	$a + T(3,1)$
f	e	$d + T(0,1)$	$c + T(1,1)$	$b + T(2,1)$
g	f	e	$d + T(0,1)$	$c + T(1,1)$
h	g	f	e	$d + T(0,1)$

Algorithm 2 describes the block computation process in SHA256. In Algorithm 2, $\sigma_1^{256}(x)$, $\sigma_0^{256}(x)$, $\sum_0^{256}(x)$, $\sum_1^{256}(x)$, $Ch(x, y, z)$, and $Maj(x, y, z)$ are same as in Algorithm 1 and K_t^{256} is the round constant given in [7]. Algorithm 2 updates hash state consisting of eight working variables (a, b, c, d, e, f, g, and h) through 64 rounds.

Table 2 shows that the change of intermediate values in the eight working variables $a \sim h$ during the first four iterations ($0R \sim 3R$) of the block computation process. Since the computation of these four round iterations are repeated 16 times in Algorithm 2, we can combine the four iterations into one. Therefore, the proposed BO technique directly computes the fourth round computation ($3R$ in Table 2), omitting the first three rounds computation ($0R \sim 2R$ in Table 2), resulting in saving of redundant operations and memory accesses. With the proposed BO technique, the number of block rounds can be reduced from 64 to 16 rounds also, the redundant operations can be reduced.

4   Proposed Techniques for PBKDF2-HMAC-LSH256

We propose six optimization techniques for PBKDF2-HMAC-LSH256. We have utilized the concept of BR technique in HMAC-LSH256 presented in Sect. 3 and newly proposed four techniques for LSH256 itself.

4.1   Proposed HMAC-LSH256 Optimization Technique

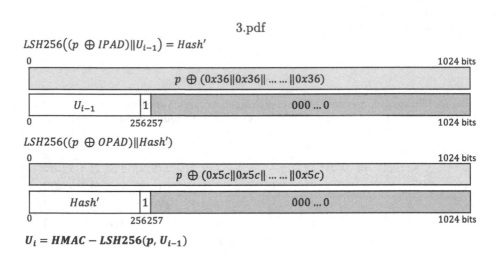

$U_i = HMAC - LSH256(p, U_{i-1})$

Fig. 2. U_i value computation process in PBKDF2-HMAC-LSH256v (Color figure online)

Figure 2 shows the process for computing U_i value in PBKDF2-HMAC-LSH256. There are two differences between HMAC-LSH256 and HMAC-SHA256. The first is that the block size of hash function changed from 64 to 128 bytes, and the second is that LSH256 does not require the information of message length (L in Fig. 1).

The optimization techniques are the same as those of HMAC-SHA256 (BR and IS techniques). In other words, when computing U_1 value, we precalculate the first block of each hash function (gray rectangles in Fig. 2) and reuse the values in all the subsequent HMAC invocations. Then, whenever a U_i operation ($2 \leq i \leq c$) is required, the precalculated values are set to the initial hash value of the second block of each hash function (*BR* technique). Since the second block of each hash function always inputs 256-bit data, the length of padded data in the second block is fixed (orange rectangles in Fig. 2) (*IS* technique). In addition, LSH256 does not require message length information. Thus, the number of padded zero values increases in LSH256 optimization compared to SHA256 optimization.

4.2   Proposed LSH256 Optimization Techniques

There are a total of four methods to optimize LSH256 (*ZB* optimization in LSH256 and three optimization methods of LSH256 itself). The Compression function in LSH256 consists of three stages: *Message Expansion*, *Mix*, and *WordPerm*.

Zero-Based Optimization in LSH256 (*ZB*). In Fig. 2, the second block of hash function is allocated 767 bits of 1024 bits as a fixed value of zero (orange rectangles). That is, 23 words of 32-bit are allocated as zero, and these are stored in $W[10]$–$W[31]$. Zero words can exclude operations from the LSH *Message Expansion*. The LSH256's *Message Expansion* is executed as follows:

$$M_0^i \leftarrow (M^{(i)}[0], M^{(i)}[1], M^{(i)}[2], \cdots, M^{(i)}[15])$$
$$M_1^i \leftarrow (M^{(i)}[16], M^{(i)}[17], M^{(i)}[18], \cdots, M^{(i)}[31])$$
$$M_j^{[I]} = (M_{j-1}^{(i)}[I] \boxplus M_{j-2}^{(i)}[\tau[I]]) \; where \; (0 \leq I \leq 15, \quad 2 \leq j \leq 15) \qquad (1)$$

$W[i]$ containing zero value can be excluded from the operation. The proposed technique reduces $\boxplus$ operations by 32 times and τ by 22 times.

Reduction of Compression Process in LSH256. Here, we propose three optimization techniques in LSH256 Compression function. In detail, we propose optimization techniques in *Mix* and *WordPerm* operations. Figure 3 shows *Mix* function process.

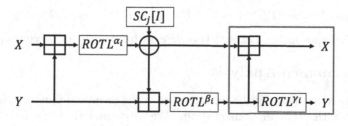

Fig. 3. LSH256 *Mix* function process[1]

The first technique is to precalculate SC values because SC values are constant values calculated by $\oplus$ in Mix function. The SC value expansion formula is as follows [1]:

$$SC_j[I] \leftarrow SC_{j-1}[l] \boxplus SC_{j-1}[l]^{\lll 8}, \ for \ (0 \le l \le 7, \ 1 \le j \le N_s - 1) \quad (2)$$

Subsequent SC values in each round can be precalculated with the initial SC values and the above formula. The precalculated SC values are stored in a lookup table, and at each round, the SC values are loaded from the table and used in Mix function. Using this proposed technique, the operational cost for computing SC values in Mix function can be removed.

The second technique is to divide the entire rounds into odd and even rounds. The values of α_j and β_j are different depending on whether the round is even or odd. In Fig. 3, α and β are assigned as follows [1]:

$$\alpha_j = \begin{cases} 29 \ \text{if } j \text{ is even} \\ 5 \ \ \text{if } j \text{ is odd} \end{cases} \beta_j = \begin{cases} 1 \ \ \text{if } j \text{ is even} \\ 17 \ \text{if } j \text{ is odd} \end{cases} \quad (3)$$

Except for the actual values of α and β, the structure of the even and odd rounds in Mix function are identical. Using this, Mix function is implemented by separating the even and odd rounds. With the proposed technique, there is no need to check whether the current round is odd or even in Compression function.

Table 3. LSH256 $WordPerm$ process[1]

I	0	1	2	3	4	5	6	7	8	9	10	11	12	13	14	15
$\sigma[I]$	6	4	5	7	12	15	14	13	2	1	0	3	8	11	10	9

The third technique is to combine Mix and $WordPerm$ functions during LSH256 operation. The $WordPerm$ function is the last process of LSH256 Compression function. It is a function that permutes the output of Mix function. Table 3 shows $WordPerm$ process among the Compression function. Subsequent Mix and $WordPerm$ functions can be combined by directly storing the output of Mix function at the permuted output location. The final computation of Mix function, represented by the blue rectangle in Fig. 3, is defined as follows:

$$output[I] = X[\sigma[I]] \boxplus Y[\sigma[I]] \quad (0 \le I \le 3 \quad or \quad 8 \le I \le 11)$$
$$output[I] = ROTL^{\gamma_i}(Y[\sigma[I] - 8]) \quad (4 \le I \le 7 \quad or \quad 12 \le I \le 15)$$

With this approach, Mix and $WordPerm$ functions can be combined.

5   Performance Analysis

In this section, we measure the performance of the proposed implementation and compare it with other implementations. We used Intel(R) Core(TM) i7-8750H 2.20 GHz, 2.21 GHz CPU for the measurement environment, and Release x64 mode. The measurement unit is clock cycles (average of 1,000 executions).

Table 4. Performance of LSH256 and SHA256

Hash function	Message byte length			
	1,600	576	64	8
KISA-SHA256	13,819	7,177	1,615	864
KISA-LSH256	26,866	17,221	3,328	2,609

Table 5. Parameters used for measuring the performance of PBKDF2-HMAC-SHA256

parameter byte length						
	case1	case2	case3	case4	case5	case6
p (byte)	32	64	128	32	64	128
s (byte)	32	64	128	32	64	128
c	1	1,024	2,048	1,000,000	1,000,000	10,000,000
$dkLen$ (byte)	32	64	128	32	64	128

Table 6. Running time of PBKDF2-HMAC-SHA256 (figures in bracket are the performance improvement compared with *Naive*)

Case	*Naive*	*OpenSSL*	*All version*
Case 1	2,888(−)	12,074(−76.08%)	2,408(+19.93%)
Case 2	4,956,071(−)	3,781,868(+31.04%)	2,245,814(+120.68 %)
Case 3	19,755,982(−)	15,132,401(+30.55%)	8,397,092(+135.27%)
Case 4	24,468,430(−)	18,707,809(+30.79%)	11,287,813(+116.76%)
Case 5	47,931,052(−)	37,638,738(+27.34%)	22,196,116(+115.94%)
Case 6	95,190,746,667(−)	75,665,227,762(+25.80%)	43,869,999,588(+116.98%)

Performance of LSH256 and SHA256. In [1], LSH performs more than twice better than SHA-256 in single instruction multiple data (SIMD) environments [1]. In other words, the structure of LSH is suitable for parallel processing with SIMD instructions. However, the performance of LSH256 is lower than that of SHA256 on general CPU without using the SIMD instructions. Table 4 shows the running time of LSH256 and SHA256 on our target CPU. In Table 4, *KISA-SHA256* and *KISA-LSH256* used the SHA256 and LSH256 open-source codes provided by KISA[11,12]. Based on the open-source codes from KISA, SHA256 performs more than twice better than LSH256 on the target CPU without using the SIMD instructions.

Performance of PBKDF2-HMAC-SHA256. We used three versions for PBKDF2-HMAC-SHA256 performance measurement. *Naive* is KISA HMAC-SHA256 Open Code [11], *OpenSSL* is OpenSSL version 1.1.1d version [13], *All Version* is proposed implementation with all proposed techniques. For measurement, different input parameters are used as Table 5. Table 6 shows the running time of each implementation. It shows that the performance of openSSL is much slower than other implementations when c is 1. Except case 1, for each case, if c is small, *All version* programs about 68.39% (resp. 120.68%) and 80.21% (resp. 135.27%) performance measures combined with *OpenSSL* (resp. *Naive*). If c is increased to a practical size, *All version* programs about 65.73% (resp. 116.76%), 69.57% (resp. 115.94%) and 72.47% (resp. 116.98%) performance measures combined with *OpenSSL* (resp. *Naive*).

Table 7. Parameters used for measuring the performance of PBKDF2-HMAC-LSH256

parameter Length						
	case1	case2	case3	case4	case5	case6
p (byte)	32	64	128	32	256	256
s (byte)	32	64	128	32	256	256
c	1	1,024	2,048	1,000,000	1,000,000	10,000,000
$dkLen$ (byte)	32	64	128	32	128	128

Table 8. Performance of PBKDF2-HMAC-LSH256 (figures in bracket are the performance improvement compared with *Naive-LSH256*)

Case	Naive-LSH256	LSH-OP	LSH-ALL-version
Case 1	14,496(−)	5,202(+178.66%)	4,512(+221.27%)
Case 2	19,209,253(−)	9,023,197(+112.88%)	4,588,082(+318.67%)
Case 3	77,250,239(−)	36,232,054(+113.20%)	18,823,101(+310.40%)
Case 4	9,944,714,429(−)	4,510,556,803(+120.47%)	2,310,098,377(+330.48%)
Case 5	38,185,287,325(−)	18,166,313,812(+110.19%)	9,194,434,665(+315.30%)
Case 6	383,772,203,768(−)	182,129,663,126(+110.71%)	92,000,036,153(+317.14%)

Performance of PBKDF2-HMAC-LSH256. We used three versions for PBKDF2-HMAC-LSH256 performance measurement. *Naive-LSH256* is KISA-HMAC-LSH256 open code [12], *LSH-OP* is proposed implementation with LSH2-56 optimization and *LSH-All-version* is proposed implementation with HMAC optimization and LSH256 optimization. Table 7 shows the parameters used for measuring the performance of PBKDF2-HMAC-LSH256. From Table 7, *LSH-All-verion* provides about 318.67% and 310.40% performance improvements compared with *Naive-LSH256* for case 2 and case 3, respectively. [2,3] proposes 10,000,000 or more c sizes in a higher security system. For each case in which c is applied a practical size, *LSH-All-verion* provides about 330.48%, 315.30% and 317.14% performance improvements compared with *Naive-LSH256* for case 4, case 5 and case 6, respectively (Table 8).

6   Concluding Remarks

In this paper, we have presented several optimization techniques for PBKDF2-HMAC-SHA256 and PBKDF2-HMAC-LSH256. The proposed PBKDF2-HMAC-SHA256 outperforms openSSL over 80.21% which is a significant improvement and the proposed PBKDF2-HMAC-LSH256 provides more than 330.48% of performance improvement compared with naive implementation. With the proposed PBKDF2 implementations, the iteration counter can be increased for higher security. The proposed techniques can be applied for embedded devices MCUs including 8-bit AVR, 16-bit MSP430, and ARM. In the future, we will extend our optimization techniques in embedded deivces and SIMD environments.

References

1. Kim, D.-C., Hong, D., Lee, J.-K., Kim, W.-H., Kwon, D.: LSH: a new fast secure hash function family. In: Lee, J., Kim, J. (eds.) ICISC 2014. LNCS, vol. 8949, pp. 286–313. Springer, Cham (2015). https://doi.org/10.1007/978-3-319-15943-0_18
2. RFC2898.: PKCS #5 : Password-Based Cryptography Specification Version 2.0. https://dl.acm.org/doi/book/10.17487/RFC2898
3. RFC8018.: PKCS #5 : Password-Based Cryptography Specification Version 2.1. http://www.rfc-editor.org/info/rfc8018
4. Visconti, A., Gorla, F.: Exploiting an HMAC-SHA-1 optimization to speed up PBKDF2. In: IEEE Transactions on Dependable and Secure Computing (Early Access). https://ieeexplore.ieee.org/document/8514806
5. Iuorio, A.F., Visconti, A.: Understanding optimizations and measuring performances of PBKDF2. In: Woungang, I., Dhurandher, S.K. (eds.) WIDECOM 2018. LNDECT, vol. 27, pp. 101–114. Springer, Cham (2019). https://doi.org/10.1007/978-3-030-11437-4_8
6. Stevens, M., Bursztein, E., Karpman, P., Albertini, A., Markov, Y.: The first collision for full SHA-1. In: Katz, J., Shacham, H. (eds.) CRYPTO 2017. LNCS, vol. 10401, pp. 570–596. Springer, Cham (2017). https://doi.org/10.1007/978-3-319-63688-7_19
7. FIPS PUB 180-4.: Secure Hash Standard (SHS). https://nvlpubs.nist.gov/nistpubs/FIPS/NIST.FIPS.180-4.pdf
8. NIST: Special Publication 800–132, Recommendation for Password-Based Key Derivation Part 1: Storage Applications. https://nvlpubs.nist.gov/nistpubs/Legacy/SP/nistspecialpublication800-132.pdf
9. NIST: Research Results on SHA-1 Collisions. https://csrc.nist.gov/News/2017/Research-Results-on-SHA-1-Collisions
10. Steube, J.: Optimising computation of hash-algorithms as an attacker. https://hashcat.net/events/p13/js-ocohaaaa.pdf
11. Korea Internet & Security Agency (KISA): KISA-SHA256 Open Source Code. https://seed.kisa.or.kr/kisa/Board/21/detailView.do
12. Korea Internet & Security Agency (KISA): KISA-LSH256 Open Source Code. https://seed.kisa.or.kr/kisa/Board/22/detailView.do
13. OpenSSL: OpenSSL 1.1.1d version. https://www.openssl.org/source/old/1.1.1/openssl-1.1.1d.tar.gz
14. The List of Approved Cryptographic Algorithm List. https://www.nis.go.kr:4016/AF/1_7_3_2.do

Cryptanalysis of Two Fully Anonymous Attribute-Based Group Signature Schemes with Verifier-Local Revocation from Lattices

Yanhua Zhang[1]($\boxtimes$), Ximeng Liu[2], Yupu Hu[3], Qikun Zhang[1], and Huiwen Jia[4]

[1] Zhengzhou University of Light Industry, Zhengzhou 450001, China
{yhzhang,qkzhang}@zzuli.edu.cn
[2] Fuzhou University, Fuzhou 350108, China
snbnix@gmail.com
[3] Xidian University, Xi'an 710071, China
yphu@mail.xidian.edu.cn
[4] Guangzhou University, Guangzhou 510006, China
hwjia@gzhu.edu.cn

Abstract. Attribute-based group signature (ABGS) is a new variant of group signature, and it allows any group member with certain specific attributes to sign a message on behalf of the whole group anonymously, without revealing the member's identity or attributes information; once a dispute arises, an opening authority (OA) can effectively reveal the anonymity and track the real identity and attributes of the signer. In order to support for membership revocation and resist against quantum computers, Perera et al. (NSS 2019, WISA 2019) recently proposed two (traceable or not) fully anonymous ABGS schemes with verifier-local revocation (VLR) from lattices. Unfortunately, in this paper we show that their two constructions do not satisfy the *full-anonymity* and present an improved scheme which obtains the strongest security, *full-anonymity*, in a relatively simple manner.

Keywords: Attribute-based group signature · Lattices · Verifier-local revocation · Full-anonymity · Random oracle model

1 Introduction

GROUP SIGNATURE. Group signature (GS), first introduced by Chaum and van Heyst [8], is accepted as a central cryptographic primitive, which enjoys two key privacy-preserving properties: *anonymity* and *traceability*. For the former, it means that any member can sign a message on behalf of the whole group, meanwhile, without divulging the signer's identity information; for the latter, it means that there exists an opening authority (OA) who owns certain secret-key to reveal the anonymity and track the signer's real identity efficiently. With these two appealing properties, GS has found several applications in real-life, such as in

© Springer Nature Switzerland AG 2020
I. You (Ed.): WISA 2020, LNCS 12583, pp. 334–346, 2020.
https://doi.org/10.1007/978-3-030-65299-9_25

the trusted computing, anonymous online communications, e-commerce systems, and much more.

ATTRIBUTE-BASED GROUP SIGNATURE. Attribute-based group signature (ABGS), first put forward by Khader [10] in 2007, is a subgroup of GS. In this new cryptosystem, each member possesses a secret signing key depending on his identity and attributes information, and the member is only allowed to sign a message on behalf of the whole group if and only if his attributes set satisfies the signing policy (frequently expressed as predicates). Of course, unlike the traditional GS schemes, in ABGS, the members do not enjoy the same signing privileges, instead, the group member can sign a message only if he possesses the sufficient attributes required by the signing predicates. Compared with traditional GS [8], ring signatures (RS) [16] and attribute-based signatures (ABS) [14], the signer in ABGS needs to anonymously prove to verifiers that he is indeed a valid member, meanwhile owning certain attributes or signing privileges, and the generated signature can also obtain traceability. Therefore, ABGS is more suitable for the environment that needs to provide anonymous authentication and fine-grained access control simultaneously.

At a theoretical level, to design such an efficient ABGS scheme, three relatively independent cryptographic ingredients are required and within some sophisticated combinations, these key building blocks include: a digital signature (DS) scheme, a public-key encryption (PKE) scheme and an efficient noninteractive zero-knowledge proof (NIZKP) protocol. Since it was first introduced by Khader [10], much progress have been made for the design of ABGS over the nearly fifteen years, and some creative constructions based on different mathematical hardness assumptions and with different levels of operating efficiency are proposed (e.g., [2–4,11,17–19]).

LATTICE-BASED ABGS. As the conventional number-theoretic problems (such as big integer factoring problem or discrete logarithm problem) and ABGS schemes based on these hardness assumptions are vulnerable to quantum computers, it is urgent to construct a secure and efficient ABGS in post-quantum cryptography (PQC) era. Believed to be one of the promising candidates for PQC, lattice-based cryptography enjoys some competitive advantages over number-theoretic cryptography: security reduction in the *worst-case* hardness assumptions, simpler arithmetic operations, provision of rich cryptographic functionality and services. The first lattice-based ABGS scheme was introduced by Kuchta et al. [11] in 2017, however their construction can only handle the candidate members enrollment, and the members cannot be revoked once they join the group.

As a flexible revocation approach for group-type cryptographic constructions, the verifier-local revocation (VLR) mechanism [6] is quite practical because it only requires verifiers to download the up-to-date revocation information for signature verification, and no signer is required. So Zhang et al. [19] creatively adopted this technique to ABGS construction, and they proposed the first lattice-based ABGS scheme with VLR in 2018, and thus, the first lattice-based ABGS scheme supporting for membership revocation, an orthogonal problem of members enrollment. However one main flaw in [19] is that it only achieves the *selfless-anonymity*, a weaker anonymity as in all lattice-based VLR group-type schemes.

MOTIVATIONS AND CONTRIBUTIONS. Recently, Perera et al. [17, 18] proposed two (traceable or not) fully anonymous lattice-based ABGS schemes with VLR, which aimed at achieving the following goals simultaneously: achieving *full-anonymity* and supporting *explicit-traceability* (only for their traceable construction [17]). They claimed that their two new designs are proven secure under two well-known hardness assumptions of lattice problems: learning with errors (LWE) and short integer solution (SIS). But in this paper we show that their both lattice-based ABGS schemes are not fully anonymous, only achieving the *selfless-anonymity* as in [19], the reason is that one of their core building blocks, the group member revocation token (RT) is not secure, that is to say, in the *full-anonymity* proof, once the members signing secret-keys are compromised, the adversary can easily calculate the members RTs to trace the real identity and attributes information for the signature. Furthermore we propose an improved design for the members RTs and an improved Stern-type ZKP protocol for our new construction.

ORGANIZATION. Our paper is organized as follows, we first recall the background knowledge on lattice-based cryptography in Sect. 2. Section 3 turns to review the definition and *full-anonymity* for Perera et al.'s lattice-based ABGS schemes with VLR. In Sect. 4, we review Perera et al.'s members RTs design. In Sect. 5, we give our detailed attacks to show that their members RTs and Stern-type ZKP protocols are not secure and cannot fulfill the *full-anonymity* they claimed. Our improvement is constructed and analyzed in Sect. 6.

2   Preliminaries

NOTATIONS. Let $\mathcal{S}_k$ denote the set of all permutations of k elements, $\|\cdot\|$ and $\|\cdot\|_\infty$ denote Euclidean norm and infinity norm respectively. $\log e$ denotes the logarithm of e with base 2, and PPT stands for "probabilistic polynomial-time".

For integers n, m, $q \geq 2$, a random matrix $\mathbf{A} \in \mathbb{Z}_q^{n \times m}$, the m-dimensional q-ary lattice $\Lambda_q^\perp(\mathbf{A})$ is defined as: $\Lambda_q^\perp(\mathbf{A}) = \{\mathbf{e} \in \mathbb{Z}^m \mid \mathbf{A} \cdot \mathbf{e} = \mathbf{0} \bmod q\}$.

Lemma 1. ([1, 5, 15]). *Let $n \geq 1$, $q \geq 2$, $m = 2n\lceil \log q \rceil$, there is a PPT algorithm* TrapGen(q, n, m) *outputting $\mathbf{A} \in \mathbb{Z}_q^{n \times m}$ and $\mathbf{R_A}$, such that $\mathbf{A}$ is statistically close to a uniform matrix in $\mathbb{Z}_q^{n \times m}$ and $\mathbf{R_A}$ is a trapdoor for lattice $\Lambda_q^\perp(\mathbf{A})$.*

Lemma 2. ([9, 15]). *Let $n \geq 1$, $q \geq 2$, $m = 2n\lceil \log q \rceil$, given $\mathbf{A} \in \mathbb{Z}_q^{n \times m}$, a trapdoor $\mathbf{R_A}$ of $\Lambda_q^\perp(\mathbf{A})$, a Gaussian parameter $s = \omega(\sqrt{n \log q \log n})$ and $\mathbf{u} \in \mathbb{Z}_q^n$, there is a PPT algorithm* SamplePre$(\mathbf{A}, \mathbf{R_A}, \mathbf{u}, s)$ *returning a short vector $\mathbf{e} \in \Lambda_q^{\mathbf{u}}(\mathbf{A})$ sampled from a distribution statistically close to $\mathcal{D}_{\Lambda_q^{\mathbf{u}}(\mathbf{A}), s}$, where $\Lambda_q^{\mathbf{u}}(\mathbf{A}) = \{\mathbf{e} \in \mathbb{Z}^m \mid \mathbf{A} \cdot \mathbf{e} = \mathbf{u} \bmod q\}$ is a coset of $\Lambda_q^\perp(\mathbf{A})$.*

Definition 1. *The* $\text{SIS}_{n,m,q,\beta}^\infty$ *problem is defined as follows: given a uniformly random $\mathbf{A} \in \mathbb{Z}_q^{n \times m}$ and a real $\beta > 0$, to get a vector $\mathbf{e} \in \mathbb{Z}^m$ such that $\mathbf{A} \cdot \mathbf{e} = \mathbf{0} \bmod q$ and $0 < \|\mathbf{e}\|_\infty \leq \beta$.*

The ISIS problem is an variant of SIS, additionally given a random syndrome $\mathbf{u} \in \mathbb{Z}_q^n$, the $\text{ISIS}_{n,m,q,\beta}^\infty$ problem is asked to get a vector $\mathbf{e} \in \mathbb{Z}^m$ such that $\mathbf{A} \cdot \mathbf{e} = \mathbf{u} \bmod q$ and $\|\mathbf{e}\|_\infty \leq \beta$. For both problems, they are as hard as certain *worst-case* lattice problems, such as shortest independent vectors problem (SIVP).

Lemma 3 ([9]). *For m, $\beta = poly(n)$, $q \geq \beta \cdot \tilde{\mathcal{O}}(\sqrt{n})$, the average-case $\text{SIS}_{n,m,q,\beta}^\infty$ and $\text{ISIS}_{n,m,q,\beta}^\infty$ problems are at least as hard as the $\text{SIVP}_{\beta \cdot \tilde{\mathcal{O}}(n)}$ problem in the worst-case.*

Definition 2. *The $\text{LWE}_{n,q,\chi}$ problem is defined as follows: given a random $\mathbf{s} \xleftarrow{\$} \mathbb{Z}_q^n$, a probability distribution χ over $\mathbb{Z}$, let $\mathcal{A}_{\mathbf{s},\chi}$ be a distribution obtained by sampling $\mathbf{A} \xleftarrow{\$} \mathbb{Z}_q^{n \times m}$, $\mathbf{e} \xleftarrow{\$} \chi^m$, output $(\mathbf{A}, \mathbf{A}^\top \mathbf{s} + \mathbf{e})$, and make distinguish between $\mathcal{A}_{\mathbf{s},\chi}$ and uniform distribution $\mathcal{U} \xleftarrow{\$} \mathbb{Z}_q^{n \times m} \times \mathbb{Z}_q^m$.*

Let $\beta \geq \sqrt{n} \cdot \omega(\log n)$, and for a prime power q, given a β-bounded distribution χ, the $\text{LWE}_{n,q,\chi}$ problem is at least as hard as $\text{SIVP}_{\tilde{\mathcal{O}}(nq/\beta)}$.

3 Definition and Security Model

We review the definition and *full-anonymity* model for Perera et al.'s two ABGS schemes with VLR mechanism introduced into GS by Boneh and Shacham [6].

3.1 Definition

Perera et al.'s traceable lattice-based ABGS scheme [17] consists of the following six polynomial-time algorithms: Setup, KeyGen, Sign, Verify, Open and Revoke. For their untraceable design [18], the fifth algorithm, Open, as in [19], is replaced by an implicit tracing algorithm as in any group-type signatures, thus no tracing secret-key Gmsk is generated in KeyGen.

Setup(1^λ): A PPT algorithm takes as input security parameter λ, and it outputs the system's public parameters pp which contains universe of attributes Att.

KeyGen(pp, N): A PPT algorithm takes as input pp and group size N, and it outputs the group public-key Gpk, the tracing secret-key Gmsk, a set of group members secret-keys Gsk= ($\text{gsk}_0, \text{gsk}_1, \cdots, \text{gsk}_{N-1}$) and members revocation tokens Grt= ($\text{grt}_0, \text{grt}_1, \cdots, \text{grt}_{N-1}$).

Sign(pp, $\mathcal{T}$, Gpk, id, gsk_i, grt_i, S_i, m): A PPT algorithm takes as input pp, Gpk, a predicate $\mathcal{T}$, a signing secret-key gsk_i and a revocation token grt_i of a member id with an index $i \in \{0, 1, \cdots, N-1\}$ and an attributes set $\text{S}_i \subseteq$ Att satisfying $\mathcal{T}$, a message m $\in \{0,1\}^*$, and it outputs a signature σ.

Verify(pp, $\mathcal{T}$, Gpk, RL, σ, m): A deterministic algorithm takes as input pp, Gpk, a list of revocation tokens RL $\subseteq$ Grt, a predicate $\mathcal{T}$, a signature σ on a message m $\in \{0,1\}^*$, and it outputs either 0 or 1. The output 1 indicates that σ is a valid signature on m, the signer and its corresponding attributes set have not been revoked.

Open(pp, Gpk, Gmsk, σ, m): A PPT algorithm takes as input pp, Gpk, Gmsk and a
message-signature pair (m, σ), and it outputs an index $i \in \{0, 1, \cdots, N-1\}$,
a list of attributes or $\perp$. The output $\perp$ indicates that the tracing is failure.

Revoke(pp, Gpk, RL, j, S_r $\subseteq$ Att): A deterministic algorithm takes as input pp,
Gpk, RL, a revoking member $j \in \{0, 1, \cdots, N-1\}$ and a revocation attributes
set $S_r \subseteq$ Att, and it outputs an updated RL.

3.2   Security Model

Perera et al. claimed that their two lattice-based ABGS schemes with VLR [17,18]
are fully anonymous following the experiment given below (For the definition of
selfless-anonymity, the readers can refer to [19]).

In this experiment, an adversary $\mathcal{A}$'s goal is to determine which of the two
adaptively chosen members id_0 with an index i_0 and an attributes set $S_{i_0} \subseteq$ Att,
id_1 with an index i_1 and an attributes set $S_{i_1} \subseteq$ Att, both of which satisfying $\mathcal{T}^*$,
generated the signature σ^* on $m^* \in \{0, 1\}^*$. $\mathcal{A}$ is given all the members secret-
keys, $\mathcal{A}$ can make opening queries for any message-signature pair (m, σ) except
for the challenge one $(m^*, \sigma^*) \neq (m, \sigma)$ and the revoking queries for member
revocation token of any member id except for the challenge ones id_0 and id_1.

a. Initialization: The challenger $\mathcal{C}$ runs the Setup and KeyGen algorithms to obtain
(pp, Gpk, Gmsk, Gsk, Grt), in Perera et al.'s untraceable construction [18] no
Gmsk is generated, and only provides (pp, Gpk, Gsk) to $\mathcal{A}$.

b. Query phase: $\mathcal{A}$ adaptively makes a polynomially bounded number of queries
as follows:
  - Opening: Request for an identity and an attributes set of a message-
    signature pair (m, σ), the opening oracle returns Open(pp, Gpk,
    Gmsk, m, σ) or uses the implicit-tracing algorithm to $\mathcal{A}$.
  - Revoking: Request for a revocation token of member id with an index i
    and an attributes set $S_i \subseteq$ Att, $\mathcal{C}$ returns grt_i to $\mathcal{A}$.

c. Challenge: $\mathcal{A}$ outputs a message $m^* \in \{0, 1\}^*$, a predicate $\mathcal{T}^*$, two members
id_0 with index i_0 and attributes set S_{i_0}, id_1 with index i_1 and attributes set
S_{i_1}, both of whose attributes set satisfying $\mathcal{T}^*$. $\mathcal{C}$ chooses a bit $b \xleftarrow{\$} \{0, 1\}$,
computes $\sigma^* \leftarrow$ Sign(pp, $\mathcal{T}^*$, Gpk, gsk_{i_b}, grt_{i_b}, S_{i_b}, m^*) as a signature on m^* by
id_b and returns it to $\mathcal{A}$.

d. Restricted query: Once obtain a challenge signature σ^*, $\mathcal{A}$ can still make queries
as before, but with the restrictions that it is not allowed to make revoking
query for id_0 or id_1, and opening query for (m^*, σ^*).

e. Guessing: $\mathcal{A}$ outputs a bit $b' \in \{0, 1\}$, and it wins if $b' = b$.

The advantage of $\mathcal{A}$ wining the fully anonymous experiment described above
is defined as

$$\mathsf{Adv}_{\mathcal{A}}^{\mathsf{full\text{-}anon}} = |\Pr[b' = b] - 1/2|$$

Thus, a ABGS with VLR satisfies the *full-anonymity* if $\mathsf{Adv}_{\mathcal{A}}^{\mathsf{full\text{-}anon}}$ is negligible.

4   Review of Perera et al.'s Revocation Token

Perera et al.'s (traceable or not) fully anonymous lattice-based ABGS schemes supporting for membership revocation are with VLR mechanism [6], and consist of 6 algorithms: Setup, KeyGen, Sign, Verify, Open (for untraceable construction [18], this algorithm is not needed) and Revoke. Here we only focus on KeyGen, in Perera et al.'s two schemes this algorithm is same, for it is the core of not being fully anonymous. Concretely it is the following KeyGen algorithm:

KeyGen(pp, N): Take as input the public parameters pp = (param, Att, list, $\mathcal{H}, \mathcal{G}$) and group size $N = 2^\ell = poly(\lambda)$, here λ is the security parameter, param defines these parameters: $n = poly(\lambda)$, modulus $q = \mathcal{O}(\ell n^2)$, dimension $m = 2n\lceil \log q \rceil$, Gaussian parameter $s = \omega(\log m)$, norm bound $\beta = \widetilde{\mathcal{O}}(\sqrt{\ell n})$, number of universal attributes $u = poly(\lambda)$; attributes set Att $= \{\mathbf{u}_1, \mathbf{u}_2, \cdots, \mathbf{u}_u\}$, where $\mathbf{u}_i \in \mathbb{Z}_q^n$ is a random vector, each attribute att_i is associated to $\mathbf{u}_i$ via an attribute list list $= \{(\mathsf{att}_i, \mathbf{u}_i)\}_{i \in \{1,2,\cdots,u\}}$, two hash functions, $\mathcal{H} : \{0,1\}^* \to \{1,2,3\}^{\kappa = \omega(\log n)}$, $\mathcal{G} : \{0,1\}^* \to \mathbb{Z}_q^{n \times m}$, to be modeled as random oracles, and this PPT algorithm works as follows:

1. Generate $\ell + 2$ matrices $\mathbf{A}, \mathbf{A}_0, \cdots, \mathbf{A}_\ell \in \mathbb{Z}_q^{n \times m}$ as the verification key and a trapdoor $\mathbf{R_A}$ as a signing key for the modified Boyen's signature scheme proposed in [15].

2. For a member id $= d_1 d_2 \cdots d_\ell \in \{0,1\}^\ell$, a binary representation of its index $i \in \{0, 1, \cdots, N-1\}$ and with an attributes set $\mathsf{S}_i = \{\mathbf{u}_{j_1}, \mathbf{u}_{j_2}, \cdots, \mathbf{u}_{j_p}\} \subseteq$ Att, the group manager does the following steps:

   (a). Let $\mathbf{A_{id}} = [\mathbf{A} | \mathbf{A}_0 + \sum_{i=1}^\ell d_i \cdot \mathbf{A}_i] \in \mathbb{Z}_q^{n \times 2m}$.

   (b). Sample $\mathbf{e}_{i,j_a} = (\mathbf{e}_{i,j_a,1}, \mathbf{e}_{i,j_a,2}) \in \mathbb{Z}^m \times \mathbb{Z}^m$ such that $\mathbf{A_{id}} \cdot \mathbf{e}_{i,j_a} = \mathbf{A} \cdot \mathbf{e}_{i,j_a,1} + (\mathbf{A}_0 + \sum_{i=1}^\ell d_i \cdot \mathbf{A}_i) \cdot \mathbf{e}_{i,j_a,2} = \mathbf{u}_{j_a} \bmod q$, $\|\mathbf{e}_{i,j_a}\|_\infty \leq \beta$ for $a \in \{1, 2, \cdots, p\}$, i.e., $\mathbf{u}_{j_a} \in \mathsf{S}_i$. (*Note:* these short vectors can be got by using SamplePre($\mathbf{A_{id}}, \mathbf{R_A}, \mathbf{u}_{j_a}, s$).)

   (c). Sample $\mathbf{e}_{i,j_a} = (\mathbf{e}_{i,j_a,1}, \mathbf{e}_{i,j_a,2}) \in \mathbb{Z}_q^m \times \mathbb{Z}_q^m$ such that $\mathbf{A_{id}} \cdot \mathbf{e}_{i,j_a} = \mathbf{A} \cdot \mathbf{e}_{i,j_a,1} + (\mathbf{A}_0 + \sum_{i=1}^\ell d_i \cdot \mathbf{A}_i) \cdot \mathbf{e}_{i,j_a,2} = \mathbf{u}_{j_a} \bmod q$, $\|\mathbf{e}_{i,j_a}\|_\infty > \beta$ for $a \in \{p+1, p+2, \cdots, u\}$, i.e., $\mathbf{u}_{j_a} \in$ Att$\backslash \mathsf{S}_i$. (*Note:* these vectors, not short, can be got by using basic linear algebra algorithm.)

   (d). Let $\mathbf{A'_{id}} = [\mathbf{0} | \sum_{i=1}^\ell d_i \mathbf{A}_i]$ and $\mathbf{v}_{j_a} = \mathbf{A'_{id}} \cdot \mathbf{e}_{i,j_a} \bmod q$, $a \in \{1, 2, \cdots, u\}$.

   (e). Sample $\mathbf{f}_{i,j_a} \in \mathbb{Z}^m$ such that $\mathbf{A} \cdot \mathbf{f}_{i,j_a} = \mathbf{u}_{j_a} - \mathbf{v}_{j_a} \bmod q$, $\|\mathbf{f}_{i,j_a}\|_\infty \leq \beta$ for $a \in \{1, 2, \cdots, u\}$, i.e., $\mathbf{u}_{j_a} \in$ Att. (*Note:* these short vectors can be got by using SamplePre($\mathbf{A}, \mathbf{R_A}, \mathbf{u}_{j_a} - \mathbf{v}_{j_a}, s$).)

   (f). Let id's signing secret-key be $\mathsf{gsk}_i = \{\mathbf{e}_{i,a}\}_{a \in \{1,2,\cdots,u\}}$ and its revocation token be $\mathsf{grt}_i = \{\mathbf{r}_{i,a} = \mathbf{A} \cdot \mathbf{f}_{i,a} \bmod q\}_{a \in \{1,2,\cdots,u\}}$.

3. Output the group public-key Gpk $= (\mathbf{A}, \mathbf{A}_0, \mathbf{A}_1, \cdots, \mathbf{A}_\ell)$, the members secret-keys Gsk $= (\mathsf{gsk}_0, \cdots, \mathsf{gsk}_{N-1})$ and revocation tokens Grt $= (\mathsf{grt}_0, \cdots, \mathsf{grt}_{N-1})$.

5   Our Attacks

In this section, we show that Perera et al.'s two lattice-based ABGS schemes with VLR are not fully anonymous, only achieving the *selfless-anonymity* as Zhang et al.'s lattice-based ABGS scheme [19].

We define a function bin to denote the binary representation of the member index, i.e., the member id $= \mathsf{bin}(i) \in \{0,1\}^{\ell}$ for $i \in \{0, 1, \cdots, N-1\}$, where $N = 2^{\ell} = poly(\lambda)$ is the maximum number of members. The detailed attacks are as follows:

(1). For a specific case, i.e., the member id with an index $i = 0$.

In this case, id $= \mathsf{bin}(i) = \mathbf{0}^{\ell}$, for id with an attributes set $\mathsf{S}_0 \subseteq \mathsf{Att}$, we have:

(a). $\mathbf{A}_{\mathsf{id}} = [\mathbf{A}|\mathbf{A}_0 + \sum_{i=1}^{\ell} d_i \cdot \mathbf{A}_i] = [\mathbf{A}|\mathbf{A}_0] \in \mathbb{Z}_q^{n \times 2m}$.

(b). Let id's signing secret-key be $\mathsf{gsk}_0 = \{\mathbf{e}_{0,a}\}_{a \in \{1,2,\cdots,u\}}$.

(c). $\mathbf{A}'_{\mathsf{id}} = [\mathbf{0}| \sum_{i=1}^{\ell} d_i \cdot \mathbf{A}_i] = \mathbf{0}^{n \times 2m}$, $\mathbf{v}_a = \mathbf{A}'_{\mathsf{id}} \cdot \mathbf{e}_{0,a} = \mathbf{0}$, $a \in \{1, 2, \cdots, u\}$.

(d). $\mathbf{f}_{0,a} \in \mathbb{Z}^m$ satisfies $\mathbf{A} \cdot \mathbf{f}_{0,a} = \mathbf{u}_a - \mathbf{v}_a = \mathbf{u}_a \bmod q$ and $\|\mathbf{f}_{0,a}\|_{\infty} \leq \beta$, $a \in \{1, 2, \cdots, u\}$.

(e). id's revocation token $\mathsf{grt}_0 = \{\mathbf{r}_{0,a} = \mathbf{A} \cdot \mathbf{f}_{0,a} = \mathbf{u}_a \bmod q\}_{a \in \{1,2,\cdots,u\}}$.

According to the above analysis, for member id $= \mathbf{0}^{\ell}$, its revocation token grt_0 is exactly equivalent to universal attributes set Att. And for member id $\neq \mathbf{0}^{\ell}$, $\mathbf{A}'_{\mathsf{id}} \neq \mathbf{0} \bmod q$ and $\mathbf{e}_{i,a} \neq \mathbf{0} \bmod q$, $i \in \{1, \cdots, N-1\}$, $a \in \{1, \cdots, u\}$, then $\mathbf{v}_a = \mathbf{A}'_{\mathsf{id}} \cdot \mathbf{e}_{i,a} \bmod q$ is uniform over $\mathbb{Z}_q^n$, i.e., $\mathbf{v}_a \neq \mathbf{0} \bmod q$ is with a high probability $1 - 1/q^n$, so as for $\mathsf{grt}_i = \{\mathbf{r}_{i,a} = \mathbf{A} \cdot \mathbf{f}_{i,a} = \mathbf{u}_a - \mathbf{v}_a \neq \mathbf{u}_a \bmod q\}_{a \in \{1,2,\cdots,u\}} \neq \mathsf{Att}$. Therefore, we have the following conclusions:

(i). If a universal attribute vector, e.g., $\mathbf{u}_i \in \mathsf{Att}$, is included in RL, we can infer that the corresponding attribute vector for id $= \mathbf{0}^{\ell}$ is revoked. Therefore, *attribute-anonymity* for Perera et al.'s two schemes is unavailable.

(ii). If a given message-signature pair, e.g., (m, σ), is rejected by Verify for an attribute vector in RL, we can infer that the signature is indeed issued by id $= \mathbf{0}^{\ell}$. Therefore, *identity-anonymity* for Perera et al.'s schemes is unavailable.

Therefore, for the case id $= \mathsf{bin}(i) = \mathbf{0}^{\ell}$, Perera et al.'s ABGS schemes [17,18] are completely not fully anonymous, even not selfless-anonymous.

(2). For a more general case, i.e., member id with an index $i \in \{0, 1, \cdots, N-1\}$.

In this case, id $= \mathsf{bin}(i) = d_1 d_2 \cdots d_{\ell} \in \{0,1\}^{\ell}$, thus for id with an attributes set $\mathsf{S}_i \subseteq \mathsf{Att}$, we have:

(a). $\mathbf{A}_{\mathsf{id}} = [\mathbf{A}|\mathbf{A}_0 + \sum_{i=1}^{\ell} d_i \cdot \mathbf{A}_i] \in \mathbb{Z}_q^{n \times 2m}$.

(b). Let id's secret-key be $\mathsf{gsk}_i = \{(\mathbf{e}_{i,a,1}, \mathbf{e}_{i,a,2})\}_{a \in \{1,2,\cdots,u\}}$, so $\mathbf{A} \cdot \mathbf{e}_{i,a,1} + (\mathbf{A}_0 + \sum_{i=1}^{\ell} d_i \cdot \mathbf{A}_i) \cdot \mathbf{e}_{i,a,2} = \mathbf{u}_a \bmod q$.

(c). $\mathbf{A}'_{\mathsf{id}} = [\mathbf{0}| \sum_{i=1}^{\ell} d_i \mathbf{A}_i] \in \mathbb{Z}_q^{n \times 2m}$, $\mathbf{v}_a = \mathbf{A}'_{\mathsf{id}} \cdot \mathbf{e}_{i,a} = \sum_{i=1}^{\ell} d_i \cdot \mathbf{A}_i \cdot \mathbf{e}_{i,a,2} \bmod q$, $a \in \{1, 2, \cdots, u\}$.

(d). $\mathbf{f}_{i,a} \in \mathbb{Z}^m$ satisfies $\mathbf{A} \cdot \mathbf{f}_{i,a} = \mathbf{u}_a - \mathbf{v}_a = \mathbf{A} \cdot \mathbf{e}_{i,a,1} + \mathbf{A}_0 \cdot \mathbf{e}_{i,a,2} \bmod q$, $\|\mathbf{f}_{i,a}\|_{\infty} \leq \beta$, $a \in \{1, 2, \cdots, u\}$.

(e). id's token $\mathsf{grt}_i = \{\mathbf{r}_{i,a} = \mathbf{A} \cdot \mathbf{f}_{i,a} = \mathbf{A} \cdot \mathbf{e}_{i,a,1} + \mathbf{A}_0 \cdot \mathbf{e}_{i,a,2} \bmod q\}_{a \in \{1,2,\cdots,u\}}$.

According to the above analysis, for $\mathsf{id} = \mathsf{bin}(i) \in \{0,1\}^\ell$, its revocation token grt_i is exactly dependent on its secret-key $\mathsf{gsk}_i = \{(\mathbf{e}_{i,a,1}, \mathbf{e}_{i,a,2})\}_{a \in \{1,2,\cdots,u\}}$, and once i's secret-key gsk_i is compromised, anyone (including adversary) can compute its revocation token grt_i with the public matrices $\mathbf{A}$ and $\mathbf{A}_0$ in a polynomial-time. Therefore we have the following conclusions:

(i). If the secret-key for challenge one is provided, for each universal attribute vector, the corresponding revocation token can be computed, such as $\mathbf{u}_i \in \mathsf{Att}$, we can infer that the corresponding attribute vectors for member $\mathsf{id} = \mathsf{bin}(i)$ are used for the challenge signature generating by using Verify for these two different attributes subsets satisfying the predicate. Therefore, *attribute-anonymity* for Perera et al.'s two schemes is unavailable.

(ii). If the secret-keys for challenge ones are provided, for a universal attribute vector, the corresponding revocation token can be computed, such as $\mathbf{u}_i \in \mathsf{Att}$, given a valid message-signature pair (m, σ), rejected by Verify for these two challenge ones, we can infer that the signature is issued by a corresponding member $\mathsf{id} = \mathsf{bin}(i)$. Therefore, *identity-anonymity* for Perera et al.'s two schemes is unavailable.

To avoid the above flaws, not giving the secret-keys for the challenge ones is a better measure. Therefore, for the case $\mathsf{id} = \mathsf{bin}(i) \in \{0,1\}^\ell$, Perera et al.'s both constructions are only selfless-anonymous (i.e., completely not fully anonymous).

To summarize, by showing the detailed attacks for a specific case $\mathsf{id} = 0^\ell$ and a more general case $\mathsf{id} = \mathsf{bin}(i) \in \{0,1\}^\ell$ of the members revocation tokens design for Perera et al.'s two lattice-based ABGS schemes with VLR, it indicates that these two constructions cannot obtain the *full-anonymity*, and only achieve the *selfless-anonymity* as in [19].

6   Improved Revocation Token and Stern-Type Protocol

In this section, we give an improved revocation token to achieve the *full-anonymity*. Furthermore, an improved shorter group public-key and the corresponding Stern-type ZKP protocols for the new members tokens are also provided.

6.1   Improved Revocation Token Design

We add the $\ell + 3$-th matrix $\mathbf{A}_{\ell+1} \xleftarrow{\$} \mathbb{Z}_q^{n \times m}$, whose columns can generate $\mathbb{Z}_q^n$, to Gpk, and $\ell + 2$ others all stay the same, i.e., $\mathsf{Gpk} = (\mathbf{A}, \mathbf{A}_0, \cdots, \mathbf{A}_\ell, \mathbf{A}_{\ell+1})$. Then we can obtain the member signing secret-key as in Perera et al.'s original schemes following (a), (b) (given in Sect. 4), and obtain the member RT following (c), (d) and (e) (given in Sect. 4), while modifying (f) to (f'), where

(f'). Let member id's secret-key be $\mathsf{gsk}_i = \{\mathbf{e}_{i,a}\}_{a \in \{1,2,\cdots,u\}}$ and its new member RT be $\mathsf{grt}_i = \{\mathbf{r}_{i,a} = \mathbf{A}_{\ell+1} \cdot \mathbf{f}_{i,a} \bmod q\}_{a \in \{1,2,\cdots,u\}}$.

The improved member revocation token can resist our attacks since the adversary can no longer compute RTs or get any useful information on RTs from the given member secret-keys, and further, grt_i is statistical close to a uniform distribution over $\mathbb{Z}_q^n$. Therefore, the *full-anonymity* for lattice-based ABGS scheme with VLR is really achieved.

In addition, we notice that Perera et al.'s both lattice-based ABGS schemes with VLR are within the structure of Bonsai Tree [7], which feature the bit-size of group public-key proportional to $\log N$, and thus for a large group Perera et al.'s both constructions are not that efficient. By adopting a creative idea introduced by Zhang et al. [20], we utilize identity-encoding technique to encode the identity index and obtain a shorter key-size, that is, saving a $\mathcal{O}(\log N)$ factor for bit-size of group public-key. Our improvement is as follows:

KeyGen(pp, N): Take as input the public parameters pp as in original schemes (we restate, in this present paper, the group size $N = 2^\ell = poly(\lambda)$), and this PPT algorithm works as follows:

1. Sample $\mathbf{A} \in \mathbb{Z}_q^{n \times m}$ and a trapdoor $\mathbf{R_A}$. (*Note*: these matrices can be got by using TrapGen(q, n, m).)

2. Sample 3 matrices $\mathbf{A}_0, \mathbf{A}_1, \mathbf{A}_2 \xleftarrow{\$} \mathbb{Z}_q^{n \times m}$.

3. For member id with an index $i \in \{0, 1, \cdots, N-1\}$ and an attributes set $S_i = \{\mathbf{u}_{j_1}, \mathbf{u}_{j_2}, \cdots, \mathbf{u}_{j_p}\} \subseteq$ Att, the group manager does the following steps:

   (a). Let $\mathbf{A}_{id} = [\mathbf{A}|\mathbf{A}_0 + i\mathbf{A}_1] \in \mathbb{Z}_q^{n \times 2m}$.

   (b). Sample $\mathbf{e}_{i,j_a} = (\mathbf{e}_{i,j_a,1}, \mathbf{e}_{i,j_a,2}) \in \mathbb{Z}^m \times \mathbb{Z}^m$ such that $\mathbf{A}_{id} \cdot \mathbf{e}_{i,j_a} = \mathbf{A} \cdot \mathbf{e}_{i,j_a,1} + (\mathbf{A}_0 + i \cdot \mathbf{A}_1) \cdot \mathbf{e}_{i,j_a,2} = \mathbf{u}_{j_a} \bmod q$, $\|\mathbf{e}_{i,j_a}\|_\infty \leq \beta$ for $a \in \{1, 2, \cdots, p\}$, i.e., $\mathbf{u}_{j_a} \in S_i$. (*Note*: these short vectors can be got by using SamplePre($\mathbf{A}_{id}, \mathbf{R_A}, \mathbf{u}_{j_a}, s$).)

   (c). Sample $\mathbf{e}_{i,j_a} = (\mathbf{e}_{i,j_a,1}, \mathbf{e}_{i,j_a,2}) \in \mathbb{Z}_q^m \times \mathbb{Z}_q^m$ such that $\mathbf{A}_{id} \cdot \mathbf{e}_{i,j_a} = \mathbf{A} \cdot \mathbf{e}_{i,j_a,1} + (\mathbf{A}_0 + i \cdot \mathbf{A}_1) \cdot \mathbf{e}_{i,j_a,2} = \mathbf{u}_{j_a} \bmod q$, $\|\mathbf{e}_{i,j_a}\|_\infty > \beta$ for $a \in \{p+1, p+2, \cdots, u\}$, i.e., $\mathbf{u}_{j_a} \in$ Att$\backslash S_i$. (*Note*: these vectors, not short, can be got by using basic linear algebra algorithm.)

   (d). Let $\mathbf{A}'_{id} = [\mathbf{0}|i\mathbf{A}_1] \in \mathbb{Z}_q^{n \times 2m}$, $\mathbf{v}_{j_a} = \mathbf{A}'_{id} \cdot \mathbf{e}_{i,j_a} \bmod q$, $a \in \{1, 2, \cdots, u\}$.

   (e). Sample $\mathbf{f}_{i,j_a} \in \mathbb{Z}^m$ such that $\mathbf{A} \cdot \mathbf{f}_{i,j_a} = \mathbf{u}_{j_a} - \mathbf{v}_{j_a} \bmod q$, $\|\mathbf{f}_{i,j_a}\|_\infty \leq \beta$ for $a \in \{1, 2, \cdots, u\}$, i.e., $\mathbf{u}_{j_a} \in$ Att. (*Note*: these short vectors can be got by using SamplePre($\mathbf{A}, \mathbf{R_A}, \mathbf{u}_{j_a} - \mathbf{v}_{j_a}, s$).)

   (f). Let id's signing secret-key be $gsk_i = \{\mathbf{e}_{i,a}\}_{a \in \{1,2,\cdots,u\}}$ and its revocation token be $grt_i = \{\mathbf{r}_{i,a} = \mathbf{A}_2 \cdot \mathbf{f}_{i,a} \bmod q\}_{a \in \{1,2,\cdots,u\}}$.

4. Output the group public-key Gpk $= (\mathbf{A}, \mathbf{A}_0, \mathbf{A}_1, \mathbf{A}_2)$, the members secret-keys Gsk $= (gsk_0, \cdots, gsk_{N-1})$ and revocation tokens Grt $= (grt_0, \cdots, grt_{N-1})$.

From the above new design, we can construct a (traceable or not) fully anonymous lattice-based ABGS scheme with VLR, meantime, with a constant number of public matrices in Gpk to encode the member's identity index and attributes.

6.2   Improved Fully Anonymous Stern-Type ZKP Protocol

We first summarize our main idea of Stern-type ZKP protocol corresponding to the new design of RTs and Bonsai Tree structure, and then turn to a new protocol with identity-encoding technique.

Given a vector $\mathbf{e} = (e_1, e_2, \cdots, e_n) \in \mathbb{R}^n$, we define $\mathsf{Parse}(\mathbf{e}, k_1, k_2)$ to denote a vector $(e_{k_1}, \cdots, e_{k_2}) \in \mathbb{R}^{k_2-k_1+1}$ for $1 \leq k_1 \leq k_2 \leq n$. Let $k = \lfloor \log \beta \rfloor + 1$, $\beta_1 = \lceil \frac{\beta}{2} \rceil$, $\beta_2 = \lceil \frac{\beta-\beta_1}{2} \rceil$, $\beta_3 = \lceil \frac{\beta-\beta_1-\beta_2}{2} \rceil, \cdots, \beta_k = 1$. Given a threshold predicate $\mathcal{T} = (t, \mathsf{S} \subseteq \mathsf{Att})$ and $1 \leq t \leq |\mathsf{S}|$, member $\mathsf{id} = d_1 d_2 \cdots d_\ell \in \{0,1\}^\ell$ with index i and attributes set $\mathsf{S}_i \subseteq \mathsf{Att}$ satisfying $\mathcal{T}$, i.e., there exists an attributes set $\mathsf{S}_t \subseteq \mathsf{S} \cap \mathsf{S}_i$, $t = |\mathsf{S}_t|$. For convenience of describing our idea, define $\mathsf{S}_t = \{\mathbf{u}_1, \mathbf{u}_2, \cdots, \mathbf{u}_t\} \subseteq \mathsf{Att}$, $\mathsf{S} = \{\mathbf{u}_1, \mathbf{u}_2, \cdots, \mathbf{u}_p\} \subseteq \mathsf{Att}$. Obviously, $t \leq p \leq u$.

(1). For Bonsai Tree structure.

In this case, we proof the following 4 relations:

(a). $\mathbf{A}_{\mathsf{id}} \cdot \mathbf{e}_{i,a} = \mathbf{u}_a \bmod q$, $\|\mathbf{e}_{i,a} = (\mathbf{e}_{i,a,1}, \mathbf{e}_{i,a,2})\|_\infty \leq \beta$, $a \in \{1, 2, \cdots, t\}$.

(b). $\mathbf{A}_{\mathsf{id}} \cdot \mathbf{e}_{i,a} = \mathbf{u}_a \bmod q$, $\|\mathbf{e}_{i,a} = (\mathbf{e}_{i,a,1}, \mathbf{e}_{i,a,2})\|_\infty > \beta$, $a \in \{t+1, \cdots, p\}$.

(c). $\mathbf{A} \cdot \mathbf{f}_{i,a} = \mathbf{A} \cdot \mathbf{e}_{i,a,1} + \mathbf{A}_0 \cdot \mathbf{e}_{i,a,2} \bmod q$, $\|\mathbf{f}_{i,a}\|_\infty \leq \beta$, $a \in \{1, 2, \cdots, p\}$.

(d). $\mathbf{r}_{i,a} = \mathbf{A}_{\ell+1} \cdot \mathbf{f}_{i,a} \bmod q$, $a \in \{1, 2, \cdots, p\}$.

For (a), we utilize the classical Dec-Ext, Mat-Ext techniques first introduced in [13] on short vectors $\mathbf{e}_{i,a}$ for $a \in \{1, 2, \cdots, t\}$ and $\mathbf{A}_{\mathsf{id}} = [\mathbf{A}|\mathbf{A}_0 + \sum_{i=1}^{\ell} d_i \mathbf{A}_i] \in \mathbb{Z}_q^{n \times 2m}$, then do the followings:

(a_1). $\mathsf{id} \to \mathsf{id}^* = (\mathsf{id}, \mathsf{id}')$, a vector enjoying the Hamming weight ℓ.

(a_2). $\mathbf{A}_{\mathsf{id}} \to \mathbf{A}^* = [\mathbf{A}|\mathbf{0}^{n \times 2m}|\mathbf{A}_0|\mathbf{0}^{n \times 2m}|\cdots|\mathbf{A}_\ell|\mathbf{0}^{n \times 2m}|\mathbf{0}^{n \times 3m\ell}] \in \mathbb{Z}_q^{n \times (2+2\ell)3m}$.

(a_3). $\mathbf{e}_{i,a} \to \mathbf{e}'_{i,a} = (\mathbf{e}_{i,a,1}, \mathbf{e}_{i,a,2}, d_1 \mathbf{e}_{i,a,2}, \cdots, d_\ell \mathbf{e}_{i,a,2}) \in \mathsf{Sec}_\beta(\mathsf{id})$, a set owning special form and norm.

(a_4). $\mathbf{e}'_{i,a} \to \mathbf{e}'^1_{i,a}, \mathbf{e}'^2_{i,a}, \cdots, \mathbf{e}'^k_{i,a} \in \mathsf{SecExt}(\mathsf{id}^*)$, a set owning a special form (for precise definition, refer to [20]).

(a_5). $\mathbf{A}^* \cdot (\sum_{j=1}^{k} \beta_j \mathbf{e}'^j_{i,a}) = \mathbf{u}_a \bmod q$.

(a_6). Sample tk vectors $\mathbf{r}^j_{i,a} \xleftarrow{\$} \mathbb{Z}_q^{(2\ell+2)3m}$ to mask $\mathbf{e}'^j_{i,a}$, thus

$$\mathbf{A}^* \cdot (\sum_{j=1}^{k} \beta_j (\mathbf{e}'^j_{i,a} + \mathbf{r}^j_{i,a})) - \mathbf{u}_a = \mathbf{A}^* \cdot (\sum_{j=1}^{k} \beta_j \mathbf{r}^j_{i,a}) \bmod q, \ a \in \{1, \cdots, t\}.$$

For (b), we first decompose and extend $\mathbf{e}_{i,a}$ for $a \in \{t+1, t+2, \cdots, p\}$ to $\mathbf{e}'^1_{i,a}, \mathbf{e}'^2_{i,a}, \cdots, \mathbf{e}'^k_{i,a} \in \mathbb{Z}_q^{(2\ell+2)3m}$, and others stay the same, then do the followings:

(b_1). $\mathbf{e}'^1_{i,a}, \mathbf{e}'^2_{i,a}, \cdots, \mathbf{e}'^k_{i,a} \notin \mathsf{SecExt}(\mathsf{id}^*)$.

(b_2). $\mathbf{A}^* \cdot (\sum_{j=1}^{k} \beta_j \mathbf{e}'^j_{i,a}) = \mathbf{u}_a \bmod q$.

(b_3). Sample $(p - t)k$ vectors $\mathbf{r}^j_{i,a} \xleftarrow{\$} \mathbb{Z}_q^{(2\ell+2)3m}$ to mask $\mathbf{e}'^j_{i,a}$, thus

$$\mathbf{A}^* (\sum_{j=1}^{k} \beta_j (\mathbf{e}'^j_{i,a} + \mathbf{r}^j_{i,a})) - \mathbf{u}_a = \mathbf{A}^* (\sum_{j=1}^{k} \beta_j \mathbf{r}^j_{i,a}) \bmod q, a \in \{t+1, \cdots, p\}.$$

(b_4). Sample 4 permutations $\pi, \varphi \xleftarrow{\$} \mathcal{S}_{3m}, \tau \xleftarrow{\$} \mathcal{S}_{2\ell}, \phi \xleftarrow{\$} \mathcal{S}_p$, it can be checked that: $\mathcal{F}_{\pi,\varphi,\tau}(\mathbf{e}'^j_{i,\phi(a)}) \in \mathsf{SecExt}(\tau(\mathsf{id}^*))$ is valid for at least t sets of vectors and for all $j \in \{1, 2, \cdots, k\}$, where $\mathcal{F}_{\pi,\varphi,\tau}(\mathbf{e}'^j_{i,\phi(a)}) = \mathcal{F}_{\pi,\varphi,\tau,\phi}(\mathbf{e}'^j_{i,a})$ is a composition of 4 permutations as described in [19].

For (c), we utilize the classical Dec-Ext, Mat-Ext techniques on short vectors $\mathbf{f}_{i,a}$ for $a \in \{1, 2, \cdots, p\}$, and matrix $\mathbf{A}, \mathbf{A}_0 \in \mathbb{Z}_q^{n \times m}$, then do the followings:

(c_1). $\mathbf{A} \to \hat{\mathbf{A}}^* = [\mathbf{A}|\mathbf{0}^{n \times 2m}] \in \mathbb{Z}_q^{n \times 3m}$.

(c_2). $\mathbf{f}_{i,a} \to \mathbf{f}_{i,a}^1, \mathbf{f}_{i,a}^2, \cdots, \mathbf{f}_{i,a}^k \in \mathsf{B}_{3m}$, a set owning a special form (for precise definition, refer to [18–20]).

(c_3). Define $\mathbf{e}_{i,a}'^{j_0} = \mathsf{Parse}(\mathbf{e}_{i,a}'^j, 1, m)$, $\mathbf{e}_{i,a}'^{j_1} = \mathsf{Parse}(\mathbf{e}_{i,a}'^j, 3m+1, 4m)$.

(c_4). Define $\mathbf{r}_{i,a}^{j_0} = \mathsf{Parse}(\mathbf{r}_{i,a}^j, 1, m)$, $\mathbf{r}_{i,a}^{j_1} = \mathsf{Parse}(\mathbf{r}_{i,a}^j, 3m+1, 4m)$.

(c_5). Pick pk vectors $\mathbf{f}_{i,a}^{(j)} \xleftarrow{\$} \mathbb{Z}_q^{3m}$ to mask $\mathbf{f}_{i,a}^j$, thus $\hat{\mathbf{A}}^* \cdot (\sum_{j=1}^k \beta_j(\mathbf{f}_{i,a}^j + \mathbf{f}_{i,a}^{(j)})) - \mathbf{A} \cdot (\sum_{j=1}^k \beta_j(\mathbf{e}_{i,a}'^{j_0} + \mathbf{r}_{i,a}^{j_0})) - \mathbf{A}_0 \cdot (\sum_{j=1}^k \beta_j(\mathbf{e}_{i,a}'^{j_1} + \mathbf{r}_{i,a}^{j_1})) = \hat{\mathbf{A}}^* \cdot (\sum_{j=1}^k \beta_j \mathbf{f}_{i,a}^{(j)}) - \mathbf{A} \cdot (\sum_{j=1}^k \beta_j \mathbf{r}_{i,a}^{j_0}) - \mathbf{A}_0 \cdot (\sum_{j=1}^k \beta_j \mathbf{r}_{i,a}^{j_1}) \bmod q$, $a \in \{1, 2, \cdots, p\}$.

(c_6). Sample a permutation $\zeta \xleftarrow{\$} \mathcal{S}_{3m}$, it can be checked that $\zeta(\mathbf{f}_{i,a}^j) \in \mathsf{B}_{3m}$.

For (d), we utilize the creative idea introduced in [12] to bound the revocation token grt_i to a one-way and injective LWE function described in Definition 2. As in [12], draw a matrix $\mathbf{B}_{i,a} \in \mathbb{Z}_q^{n \times m}$, $a \in \{1, 2, \cdots, p\}$, from the random oracle $\mathcal{G}$, then do the followings:

(d_1). Sample $\mathbf{e}_{i,a,0} \xleftarrow{\$} \chi^m$.

(d_2). Define $\mathbf{C}_{i,a} = \mathbf{B}_{i,a}^\top \cdot \mathbf{A}_{\ell+1} \in \mathbb{Z}_q^{m \times m}$, $\mathbf{b}_{i,a} = \mathbf{C}_{i,a} \cdot \mathbf{f}_{i,a} + \mathbf{e}_{i,a,0} \bmod q \in \mathbb{Z}_q^m$.

(d_3). $\mathbf{e}_{i,a,0} \to \mathbf{e}_{i,a,0}^1, \mathbf{e}_{i,a,0}^2, \cdots, \mathbf{e}_{i,a,0}^k \in \mathsf{B}_{3m}$.

(d_4). $\mathbf{C}_{i,a} \to \mathbf{C}_{i,a}^* = [\mathbf{C}_{i,a}|\mathbf{0}^{n \times 2m}|\mathbf{I}_m|\mathbf{0}^{n \times 2m}]$, $\mathbf{b}_{i,a} = \mathbf{C}_{i,a}^* \cdot (\sum_{j=1}^k \beta_j(\mathbf{f}_{i,a}^j, \mathbf{e}_{i,a,0}^j))$.

(d_5). Pick $\mathbf{r}_{i,a,0}^j \xleftarrow{\$} \mathbb{Z}_q^{3m}$ to mask $\mathbf{e}_{i,a,0}^j$, $\mathbf{C}_{i,a}^* \cdot (\sum_{j=1}^k \beta_j(\mathbf{f}_{i,a}^j + \mathbf{f}_{i,a}^{(j)}, \mathbf{e}_{i,a,0}^j + \mathbf{r}_{i,a,0}^j)) - \mathbf{b}_{i,a} = \mathbf{C}_{i,a}^* \cdot (\sum_{j=1}^k \beta_j(\mathbf{f}_{i,a}^{(j)}, \mathbf{r}_{i,a,0}^j)) \bmod q$, $a \in \{1, 2, \cdots, p\}$,

(d_6). Sample a permutation $\psi \xleftarrow{\$} \mathcal{S}_{3m}$, it can be checked that $\psi(\mathbf{e}_{i,a,0}^j) \in \mathsf{B}_{3m}$.

Putting the above creative techniques together, we can obtain a new Stern-type interactive statistical ZKP protocol, and then transformed to a non-interactive one by using *Fiat-Shamir* heuristic in the random oracle model.

(2). For identity-encoding technique.

In this case, we proof the following 4 relations:

(a). $\mathbf{A}_{\mathsf{id}} \cdot \mathbf{e}_{i,a} = \mathbf{u}_a \bmod q$, $\|\mathbf{e}_{i,a} = (\mathbf{e}_{i,a,1}, \mathbf{e}_{i,a,2})\|_\infty \le \beta$, $a \in \{1, 2, \cdots, t\}$.

(b). $\mathbf{A}_{\mathsf{id}} \cdot \mathbf{e}_{i,a} = \mathbf{u}_a \bmod q$, $\|\mathbf{e}_{i,a} = (\mathbf{e}_{i,a,1}, \mathbf{e}_{i,a,2})\|_\infty > \beta$, $a \in \{t+1, \cdots, p\}$.

(c). $\mathbf{A} \cdot \mathbf{f}_{i,a} = \mathbf{A} \cdot \mathbf{e}_{i,a,1} + \mathbf{A}_0 \cdot \mathbf{e}_{i,a,2} \bmod q$, $\|\mathbf{f}_{i,a}\|_\infty \le \beta$, $a \in \{1, 2, \cdots, p\}$.

(d). $\mathbf{r}_{i,a} = \mathbf{A}_2 \cdot \mathbf{f}_{i,a} \bmod q$, $a \in \{1, 2, \cdots, p\}$.

The main differences from (1) are: in (a) and (b), $\mathbf{A}_{\mathsf{id}}$ is replaced to $\mathbf{A}_{\mathsf{id}} = [\mathbf{A}|\mathbf{A}_0 + i\mathbf{A}_1] \in \mathbb{Z}_q^{n \times 2m}$; in (d), $\mathbf{A}_{\ell+1}$ is replaced to $\mathbf{A}_2$ since we only need 4 matrices to encode member's identity index.

For (a) and (b), we only need to replace $\mathbf{A}_{\mathsf{id}} \to \mathbf{A}^*$, and others stay the same, where the new $\mathbf{A}_{\mathsf{id}} \to \mathbf{A}^*$ transformation is $\mathbf{A}_{\mathsf{id}} \to \mathbf{A}^* \in \mathbb{Z}_q^{n \times (2+2\ell)3m}$, where

$$\mathbf{A}^* = [\mathbf{A}|\mathbf{0}^{n \times 2m}|\mathbf{A}_0|\mathbf{0}^{n \times 2m}|\cdots|2^{\ell-1}\mathbf{A}_1|\mathbf{0}^{n \times 2m}|\mathbf{0}^{n \times 3m\ell}].$$

For (c), all operations remain the same.

For (d), we replace $A_{\ell+1}$ with A_2 and other operations remain the same.

Similarly, a new Stern-type statistical ZKP protocol can be achieved by combining the above transformations ideas with the Stern-extension argument system also adopted in [18–20]. This concludes the whole ZKP protocol design.

7   Conclusion

In this paper, we showed that two recent attribute-based group signature schemes with verifier-local revocation from lattices do not satisfies *full-anonymity* they claimed, the main reason is that one core building block of their constructions, the member revocation token is not secure. Finally we proposed an improved design for member revocation token and an improved Stern-type zero-knowledge proof protocol for a new fully anonymous lattice-based attribute-based group signature scheme with verifier-local revocation.

Acknowledgments. The authors would like to thank the anonymous reviewers of WISA 2020 for their helpful comments, and this research is supported by the National Natural Science Foundation of China (Nos. 61772477, 61702230 and 61802075), the Science and Technology Development of Henan Province (Nos. 20210222210356 and 20210222210382) and Guangxi Key Laboratory of Cryptography and Information Security (No. GCIS201907).

References

1. Ajtai, M.: Generating hard instances of lattice problems (extended abstract). In: STOC, pp. 99–108. ACM (1996). https://doi.org/10.1007/978-3-642-13190-5_28

2. Ali, S.T., Amberker, B.B.: Dynamic attribute based group signature with attribute anonymity and tracing in the standard model. In: Gierlichs, B., Guilley, S., Mukhopadhyay, D. (eds.) SPACE 2013. LNCS, vol. 8204, pp. 147–171. Springer, Heidelberg (2013). https://doi.org/10.1007/978-3-642-41224-0_11

3. Ali, S.T., Amberker, B.B.: Short attribute-based group signature without random oracles with attribute anonymity. In: Thampi, S.M., Atrey, P.K., Fan, C.-I., Perez, G.M. (eds.) SSCC 2013. CCIS, vol. 377, pp. 223–235. Springer, Heidelberg (2013). https://doi.org/10.1007/978-3-642-40576-1_22

4. Ali, S.T., Amberker, B.B.: Dynamic attribute-based group signature with verifier-local revocation and backward unlinkability in the standard model. Int. J. Appl. Cryptogr. **3**(2), 148–165 (2014). https://doi.org/10.1504/IJACT.2014.062736

5. Alwen, J., Peikert, C.: Generating shorter bases for hard random lattices. Theory Comput. Syst. **48**(3), 535–553 (2011). https://doi.org/10.1007/s00224-010-9278-3

6. Boneh, D., Shacham, H.: Group signatures with verifier-local revocation. In: CCS, pp. 168–177. ACM (2004). https://doi.org/10.1007/978-3-540-30574-3_11

7. Cash, D., Hofheinz, D., Kiltz, E., Peikert, C.: Bonsai trees, or how to delegate a lattice basis. In: Gilbert, H. (ed.) EUROCRYPT 2010. LNCS, vol. 6110, pp. 523–552. Springer, Heidelberg (2010). https://doi.org/10.1007/978-3-642-13190-5_27

8. Chaum, D., van Heyst, E.: Group signatures. In: Davies, D.W. (ed.) EUROCRYPT 1991. LNCS, vol. 547, pp. 257–265. Springer, Heidelberg (1991). https://doi.org/10.1007/3-540-46416-6_22

9. Gentry, C., Peikert, C., Vaikuntanathan, V.: Trapdoor for hard lattices and new cryptographic constructions. In: STOC, pp. 197–206. ACM (2008). https://doi.org/10.1145/1374376.1374407

10. Khader, D.: Attribute based group signatures. http://eprint.iacr.org/2007/159

11. Kuchta, V., Sahu, R.A., Sharma, G., Markowitch, O.: On new zero-knowledge arguments for attribute-based group signatures from lattices. In: Kim, H., Kim, D.-C. (eds.) ICISC 2017. LNCS, vol. 10779, pp. 284–309. Springer, Cham (2018). https://doi.org/10.1007/978-3-319-78556-1_16

12. Ling, S., Nguyen, K., Roux-Langlois, A., Wang, H.: A lattice-based group signature scheme with verifier-local revocation. Theor. Comput. Sci. **730**, 1–20 (2018). https://doi.org/10.1016/j.tcs.2018.03.027

13. Ling, S., Nguyen, K., Stehlé, D., Wang, H.: Improved zero-knowledge proofs of knowledge for the ISIS problem, and applications. In: Kurosawa, K., Hanaoka, G. (eds.) PKC 2013. LNCS, vol. 7778, pp. 107–124. Springer, Heidelberg (2013). https://doi.org/10.1007/978-3-642-36362-7_8

14. Maji, H.K., Prabhakaran, M., Rosulek, M.: Attribute-based signatures. In: Kiayias, A. (ed.) CT-RSA 2011. LNCS, vol. 6558, pp. 376–392. Springer, Heidelberg (2011). https://doi.org/10.1007/978-3-642-19074-2_24

15. Micciancio, D., Peikert, C.: Trapdoors for lattices: simpler, tighter, faster, smaller. In: Pointcheval, D., Johansson, T. (eds.) EUROCRYPT 2012. LNCS, vol. 7237, pp. 700–718. Springer, Heidelberg (2012). https://doi.org/10.1007/978-3-642-29011-4_41

16. Rivest, R.L., Shamir, A., Tauman, Y.: How to leak a secret. In: Boyd, C. (ed.) ASIACRYPT 2001. LNCS, vol. 2248, pp. 552–565. Springer, Heidelberg (2001). https://doi.org/10.1007/3-540-45682-1_32

17. Perera, M.N.S., Nakamura, T., Hashimoto, M., Yokoyama, H.: Traceable and fully anonymous attribute based group signature scheme with verifier local revocation from lattices. In: Liu, J.K., Huang, X. (eds.) NSS 2019. LNCS, vol. 11928, pp. 675–684. Springer, Cham (2019). https://doi.org/10.1007/978-3-030-36938-5_42

18. Perera, M.N.S., Nakamura, T., Hashimoto, M., Yokoyama, H.: Zero-knowledge proof system for fully anonymous attribute based group signatures from lattices with VLR. In: You, I. (ed.) WISA 2019. LNCS, vol. 11897, pp. 126–140. Springer, Cham (2020). https://doi.org/10.1007/978-3-030-39303-8_10

19. Zhang, Y., Gan, Y., Yin, Y., Jia, H.: Attribute-based VLR group signature scheme from lattices. In: Vaidya, J., Li, J. (eds.) ICA3PP 2018. LNCS, vol. 11337, pp. 600–610. Springer, Cham (2018). https://doi.org/10.1007/978-3-030-05063-4_46

20. Zhang, Y., Hu, Y., Zhang, Q., Jia, H.: On new zero-knowledge proofs for lattice-based group signatures with verifier-local revocation. In: Lin, Z., Papamanthou, C., Polychronakis, M. (eds.) ISC 2019. LNCS, vol. 11723, pp. 190–208. Springer, Cham (2019). https://doi.org/10.1007/978-3-030-30215-3_10

Advances in Network Security
and Attack Defense

Analysis on Malicious Residential Hosts Activities Exploited by Residential IP Proxy Services

Akihiro Hanzawa[✉] and Hiroaki Kikuchi

School of Interdisciplinary Mathematical Sciences, Meiji University,
Nakano, Tokyo, Japan
{cs192013,kikn}@meiji.ac.jp

Abstract. A *residential IP Proxy* is a proxy service that provides a traffic relay using hosts on residential networks. Although the service providers claim that hosts voluntarily participate in the service and use it for various high-quality applications, in fact, the service provides avoiding detection and blocking by pretending as apparently benign users, they exploited the residential hosts to perform malicious acts such as DoS attacks. In 2019, Mi et al. studied that malicious hosts participating in the Residential IP Proxy service, and profiled the hosts, and clarified the infrastructure, scale, and malignancy of the such services. They found that most malicious activities were sending SPAMs and hosting fake websites that were performed by routers and WAP devices. However, residential WAP devices are commonly inside of firewall and these are not likely to be feasible in well managed residential networks. To answer to the concern, in this paper, we analyze datasets of Residential-IP-Proxy hosts, collected by Mi et al. and report an analysis of the communication that Residential IP Proxies perform in Japan. We use NONSTOP, the analysis platform, provided by the Information Technology Research Organization, in the analysis. Our analysis found that most of devices used in Japan were mobile laptop PCs and port-scanning was the most frequent malicious activity. Consequently, more RESIP hosts are becoming involved in serious threat and we need countermeasures aimed at minimizing the abuse of RESIP hosts.

1 Introduction

Recently, a new service called *Residential IP Proxy as a Service* (RPaaS) have been provided in the market of proxy Internet connection via proxy hosts. Table 1 lists the major RPaaS service providers. RPaaS plays a useful role in enabling users access to arbitrary sites without any restriction. For example, Luminati, the largest Residential IP Proxy (RESIPs) service provider, is located in the United States, but has many clients who reside in Turkey, and who may be trying to avoid Turkey's network censorship. Web proxy services are studied for many researchers. Chung et al. studied a paid proxy services to be manipulating contents [13]. A measurement to reveal the purpose of proxy services was conducted by Weaver et al. in [14].

© Springer Nature Switzerland AG 2020
I. You (Ed.): WISA 2020, LNCS 12583, pp. 349–361, 2020.
https://doi.org/10.1007/978-3-030-65299-9_26

In [1], Mi et al. reported that the presence of likely compromised hosts as residential IPs, identified from 6.18 million unique IPs, distributed over 238 countries and 52,905 ISPs. Among the hosts, they identified 237,029 IoT devices and 4,141 hosts running PUP networks. The traffic relayed via the RESIP involved ad clicking, SPAM messaging, and malicious IP hosting activities. They found that these malicious activities were performed by routers and WAP devices in residential networks. However, residential WAP devices are commonly inside of firewall and are not vulnerable to be compromised if these are under control.

Hence, our analysis of this study is motivated by the following questions.

1. What kinds of networks do RESIPs belong to (residential, institutional, or academic networks?)
2. How are RESIPs distributed geometrically in Japan, countryside, or metropolitan regions?
3. Who are the major RPaaS providers?
4. What is the impact of malicious RESIPs?
5. For what purposes are the RESIPs abused (advertisement, phishing, port scanning, or exploring)?

Our objective is to answer above research questions by investigating up-to-date RESIP activities.

To answer questions (1) and (2), we investigate the detailed properties of the RESIP addresses. For each of the IP addresses detected by Mi et al. [1] in 2017, we examine the geolocation query using the GeoLite2 city database [3] from MaxMind, Inc. We use the Registration Data Access Protocol (RDAP) service provided by the Asia–Pacific Network Information Center (APNIC)[4] to identify the domain and registry to which RESIP addresses belong.

To answer questions (3) to (5), we need to observe the malicious packets sent from the RESIP addresses. We, therefore, use the darknet database, NONSTOP [6], serviced by the National Institute of Information and Communications Technology (NICT). Using NONSTOP, we examine whether suspicious addresses detected as RESIPs had performed port-scanning to NICT's darknet. Since a darknet is unknown and unused network segment, we regard any packets designated for the darknet as malicious.

Our contributions of this work are as follows.

We have found new trends in RESIP host activities based on the darknet traffic observed in Japan. Our new findings is that the main devices used in Japan were mobile laptop PCs, whereas router, firewall and WAP devices were identified from the profiles in the previous study [1].

- We have identify the malicious activities performed by RESIP hosts. Our analysis shows that the most frequent activity was port-scanning to look for vulnerable hosts, whereas the heaviest traffic was associated with SPAM-related activities, according to Mi et al.'s work [1].

- Our analysis reveals that the RESIP hosts are distributed widely across all regions in Japan. The statistics for RESIP hosts show that hosts are mainly associated with residential and mobile ISPs.

Table 1. RESIP service providers and basic specifications

RESIP Provider	Fee (2017)	Fee (2019)	IPs[1]
Proxies Online (United States)	$25/Gb	certificate expired	1,257,418
Geosurf (Netherlands)	$300/month	$450–2000/month	432,975
ProxyRack (United States)	$40/month	$60–120/month	857,178
Luminati (United States)	$500/month	$12.5/GB+$500/month	4,033,418
IAPS Security	$500/month	site unavailable	

2   Residential IP Proxy

Residential IP proxy services are a new business. The RESIP providers control a large number of residential hosts to proxy their customers' communication with any destination on the Internet.

Figure 1 illustrates how the RESIP service model works. Three parties are involved here, namely, the RESIP client, the Proxy gateway and the Residential hosts. Once a client signs up with a RESIP service, it receives a gateway's IP address or URL for the service. The gateway forwards the client's requests to one of residential hosts, which sends the request to the target hosts that the client wishes to visit. The responses are sent back to the client via the same routing arrangements. The forwarding proxies are assigned randomly and are periodically updated to confound analysis of traffic.

According to the study [1], the followings were discovered from their crawling, and analysis.

A total of 6,183,876 unique RESIP addresses were collected. Their classifier estimated that 95.22% of RESIPs were residential addresses and that 237,029 addresses (43.2%) were assigned to IoT devices.

- RESIP service providers claimed that their proxies were all common users who willingly join their network. However, none of the five major providers operated a completely consent-based proxy system.
- The new RESIP service became a booming business. Table 1 shows that most providers have increased their service fees in the two years from 2017 [1] to our work (2019). On the other hand, some providers have already abandoned the business.

3   Investigation Methodology

3.1   Datasets

Table 2 lists the four databases examined in this study.

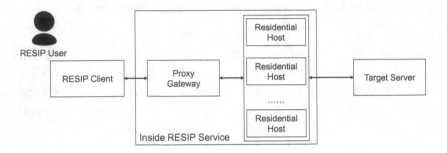

Fig. 1. RESIP service overview

Rpaas Dataset This comprises records containing of the detected RESIP address, and the duration of its activities for the five major RESIP providers: Proxies Online (PO)[1] Geosurf (GO)[2], ProxyRack (PR)[3], Luminati (LU)[4] IAPS Security (IS)[5] The dataset of RESIP addresses and the source code of the profiling tools used are available at [2].

NICTER Darknet Dataset NICT provides the source IP addresses sent to the NICT darknet of /20 block. Their analysis infrastructure, NONSTOP, provides the remote access to the attributes stored in packet headers, including capturing time, source and destination of the address and port, and the countries involved.

GeoLite2 City Dataset This is a geolocation database provided by MaxMind Inc. The attribute information includes countries, region, latitude and longitude.

APNIC Whois Dataset APNIC is one of the five Regional Internet Registries (RIRs) offering a Whois directory service to resources of IP addresses and domain names, and Autonomous System number (ASN). These information are provided in JSON format object from Registration Data Access Protocol (RDAP)[7].

---

[1] Proxies Online. http://proxies.online.
[2] Geosurf: Residential and data center proxy network. https://www.geosurf.com/.
[3] Proxyrack. https://proxyrack.
[4] Luminati: largest business proxy service.
[5] IAPS security.

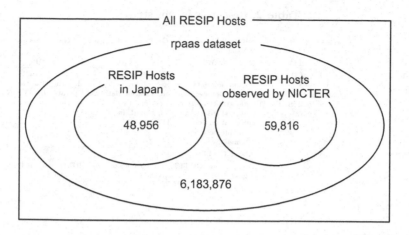

Fig. 2. Relationships among some subsets of RESIP addresses

3.2 Attributes of RESIP Hosts

To investigate the attributes of RESIP hosts, we focus on those RESIP addresses that are under the management of Japanese organizations for which we know the region, name of organization, and address blocks used. The steps were as follows.

1. Lookup GeoLite2 city dataset for RESIP addresses to identify the addresses belonging to Japanese regional networks (JP). Estimate the prefecture names for the addresses.
2. Perform `nslookup` query to the extracted address to find the domain information.
3. Use RDAP query to obtain the CIDR block information and the registration organization.

3.3 Suspicious Traffic from RESIP Hosts

Assume that any host whose source address has been captured in the NICT darknet is performing port scans to look for new vulnerable hosts. We use the NICT NONSTOP service on the first and last days for which a RESIP address has been detected. We examine if the target RESIP address has been observed. Of so, we identify the corresponding port numbers that indicate the type of service the host is interested in.

Table 2. Resources in this study

	rpaas dataset	NICTER Darknet dataset	GeoLite2 City dataset	APNIC whois dataset
Year	2017	2017	2019	2019
Details	The list of IP addresses participating RESIP service collected in [1]	Source and destination data of packets observed on /20 darknet by the National Institute of Information and Communications Technology	IP address and geographic information database provided by MaxMind, Inc.	IP address and domain database operated by APNIC registry
Records	6,183,876	About 150 billion		
Usage	Published	Access from NICTER NONSTOP	Datebase access from Python	RDAP request from Python

4   Results

4.1   Attributes of RESIP Hosts in Japan

Figure 2 illustrates the relationships between address subsets, RPaas datasets, and the target addresses; in a Venn diagram. Among the RESIP addresses (RPaas dataset), we found 48,956 IP addresses managed by Japanese organizations.

Table 3 lists the top 10 prefectures (states) as well as the numbers of RESIP addresses with regard to RESIP providers. Tokyo is the greatest in the number of RESIP addresses. The most common RESIP provider in Japan is ProxyRack (18,502 addresses).

Tables 4 and 5 shows the top ten domains (with third level) and the ISPs, respectively. The biggest RESIP owner was NTT Communication Corp. , which is known as the largest IPS under which the greatest RESIP domain ocn.ne.jp is management of.

Table 6 shows the numbers of RESIP addresses classified by the type of network. Following the domestic convention in Japan, the second level of a domain indicates the characteristics of the network, e.g., "ne" (**ne**twork service), "or" (**or**ganization), "ad" (**ad**ministrative) and so on. Table shows that the "ne" domain (usually used for residential networks) has the greatest number of RESIP addresses in Japan.

Note that 91 addresses are for "ac" (academic network, such as universities), nine are for "co" (companies), and one is for "go" (government). Obviously, these addresses are not residential and have not yet detected via Mi et al.'s analysis [1].

We should comment on the accuracy of the datasets. First, the estimated country is not always consistent. For example, 43 domains with a .ru top-level domain were estimated with Tokyo in the GeoLite2 City database. The undetermined domain (**pinspb.ru**) has some webpages written in Russian and was classified as Russian in [10] but Israel in [11].

Table 3. List of top 10 prefectures for RESIP hosts with service providers. PO: Proxies Online, GS: Geosurf, PR: ProxyRack, LU: Luminati, IS: IAPS Security

Prefecture	RESIPs	%	PO	GS	PR	LU	IS	Fraction of mobile phone and PHS users(%)[8]
Tokyo	12,766	26.1	2,709	84	4,442	5,027	4	26.0
Kanagawa	3,094	6.3	721	17	1,145	1,087	0	6.4
Aichi	2,940	6.0	715	15	1,163	942	0	5.2
Osaka	2,917	5.9	769	17	1,148	880	1	6.7
Saitama	2,544	5.1	605	14	1,082	754	0	4.7
Tiba	1,912	3.9	484	32	726	557	0	4.0
Hyogo	1,722	3.5	460	21	693	493	0	3.5
Hukuoka	1,266	2.5	426	9	436	320	0	4.0
Sizuoka	1,083	2.2	251	7	484	308	0	2.2
not found	6,619	13.5	1,741	52	2,108	2,507	8	
Total	48,956	100	11,918	304	18,502	16,325	13	100

Table 4. List of TOP 10 TLD+2 domains for RESIP hosts

TLD+2	RESIPs	%
ocn.ne.jp	7,468	15.2
au-net.ne.jp	5,616	11.4
plala.or.jp	2,900	5.9
dion.ne.jp	2,528	5.1
not found	2,441	4.9
so-net.ne.jp	1,966	4.0
mesh.ad.jp	1,935	3.9
eonet.ne.jp	1,305	2.6
home.ne.jp	1,209	2.4
nttpc.ne.jp	1,116	2.2
Total	48,956	100

4.2 Traffic from RESIPs

Figure 4 shows the daily numbers of packets observed in the NICTER darknet. There were a total 1,683,440 packets sent from 59,816 RESIP addresses. The results show that the durations detected in Mi et al.'s analysis [1] has the intersection with the NICTER datasets.

Table 7 lists the top 10 RESIP addresses in terms of the cumulative observed packets. Note that the very busy activities (62,669 scans) were performed by only a few RESIP hosts. The durations of port-scanning from these 10 hosts are plotted in Fig. 5, where the scans are indicated at the IP addresses along the Y-axis.

Table 8 shows the top 10 destination port numbers specified by RESIP hosts. The corresponding services are given in the table. For example, the Telnet service

Table 5. Top 10 domains for RESIP hosts

Organization	Domains	RESIPs	%	Share of FTTH users (%)[9]
NTT Communication Corporation	ocn.ne.jp, plala.or.jp	10,941	22.3	34.2
KDDI CORPORATION	au-net.ne.jp, dion.ne.jp	8,301	16.9	12.8
Japan Nation-wide Network of Softbank Corp.	bbtec.net, access-internet.ne.jp	7,781	15.8	
Japan Network Information Center	nttpc.ne.jp, mesh.ad.jp	4,756	9.7	
Sony Network Communications Inc.	so-net.ne.jp, ap.nuro.jp	2,544	5.1	
OPTAGE Inc.	eonet.ne.jp	1,274	2.6	5.4
BIGLOBE Inc.	mesh.ad.jp	1,230	2.5	
Jupiter Telecommunication Co.,Ltd	home.ne.jp	1,209	2.4	
Chubu Telecommunications Co.,Inc.	commufa.jp	1,125	2.2	
ARTERIA Networks Corporation	ucom.ne.jp, vectant.ne.jp	965	1.9	2.3
Total		48,956	100	

designated for the well-known port number 23 was observed in 613,606 packets, which accounts for 36.4% of the total.

Any possible relationship between the designated port number and the duration of the scan would be brought out by the scatterplot of Fig. 6. Note that no significant correlation between the target of the service and its duration can be seen. However, major services MSSQL and SMTP are constantly observed.

4.3 Discussion

Let us remark each of questions.

Table 6. Counts of RESIP hosts for the various network types (second-level domains)

2LD	RESIPs	%
ne	28,824	74.1
or	4,340	11.1
ad	2,208	5.6
ac	91	0.2
co	9	
go	1	
gr	1	
ed	1	
Total(.jp)	38,946	100

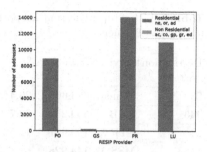

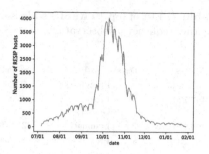

Fig. 3. Number of RESIP addresses for network types (second-level domains)

Fig. 4. Daily counts of RESIP hosts observed in NICTER darknet

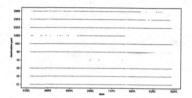

Fig. 5. Active durations for RESIP source addresses

Fig. 6. Active durations for destination port numbers

(1) For the various kinds of networks, we found that 90.8% of the RESIP hosts could be classified as residential, based on Table 6 and Fig. 3. The subdomains "ne", "ad", and "or" were the most used in RESIP proxies. According to the domain name convention, these are known to be residential. Note that some exceptions "ac" and "co" domains, assigned for academic and company business, were also found. We consider that, for mobile laptop computers with a RESIP library installed, the installation was without consent of their owners and was being operated for malicious purposes.

(2), (3) Tables 3, 4 and 5 confirm that the RESIPs are distributed widely in all prefectures (regions) and that the distribution matches the statistics for cell phone users. This implies that residential and mobile ISPs are the main RESIP hosts in Japan, which differs with the earlier observation [1] that most RESIP devices (69.8%) could be identified as routers, firewalls, or WAP devices. Table 5 shows no skew in the relationship between RESIP hosts and the number of ISPs.

(4) Tables 7, Figs. 4 and 5 demonstrate that constant port-scanning was performed from RESIP hosts. In contrast to the report [12], there are now many cyberattacks form identified RESIP hosts. Therefore, we can infer that the threat from RESIP service is becoming more serious.

Table 7. List of top 10 RESIP addresses for the frequency of observations in darknet

Address	Days	RESIP provider	# Packets
43.249.57.255	8	ProxyRack	62,669
187.120.17.2	34	Proxies Online Geosurf	35,353
200.170.223.50	7	Luminati	21,676
103.29.97.2	8	Proxies Online Geosurf Luminati	17,004
165.73.122.29	14	Luminati	16,127
212.90.62.209	5	Luminati	15,142
43.248.73.6	90	Proxies Online Geosurf Luminati	13,425
190.57.236.230	18	Luminati	13,388
112.196.77.202	27	Proxies Online Geosurf	13,061
125.99.100.22	10	Proxies Online Luminati	12,952

Table 8. List of top 10 destination port numbers in frequencies

Destination port	Service	# Packets	%
23	Telnet	613,606	36.4
445	SMB	399,250	23.7
21	FTP	193,917	11.5
1433	MSSQL	144,928	8.6
80	HTTP	97,780	5.8
22	SSH	49,767	2.9
2323	(Telnet)	43,310	2.5
25	SMTP	21,732	1.3
2222	(SSH)	16,838	0.1
3389	RDP	9,782	0.5

(5) Table 8 shows that the major RESIP activities were related to port-scanning. This observation is not consistent with the result from Mi et al.'s work [1], which claimed that the most frequent activity was ad mail (SPAM) at 36.55%. Our analysis shows that the SPAM traffic accounts for only 1.3 % of activity and that its duration is limited, as shown in Fig. 6.

This may be a feature of Japanese networks, where ad messages are shifting from email to SNSs. Another possible reason might be limitations in the observation. Our estimations were based on the darknet, which carries only a small fraction of the Internet traffic. We need additional investigations to be able to distinguish clearly between the objectives of RESIP hosts.

5   Conclusions

We have studied RESIP host activities detected from networks under the control of organizations in Japan, which accounts for 0.79% of the all Internet RESIP hosts. Our analysis of 1,683,550 RESIP packets observed from the darknet revealed that 90.8% RESIP residential and the RESIP proxies were distributed evenly across all prefectures and IPSs. New finding is that most of devices that became RESIP hosts in Japan were mobile, whereas routers, firewalls and WAP devices were identified from the profiles in the previous study [1]. Another distinct aspect of the RESIP behavior is the distribution of malicious activities. In [1], the SPAM and malicious website hosting were the most common (36.5% and 32.7%, respectively), whereas the SPAM traffic accounted for only 1.3% of all traffic in our analysis. We found that port-scanning was the most frequent malicious activity. Despite these evolving trends, we conclude that more RESIP hosts are becoming involved in serious threat and we need countermeasures aimed at minimizing the abuse of RESIP hosts.

A   47 prefectures for RESIP

Table 9 shows the number of RESIP addresses for each of 47 prefecture of Japan, with numbers for major five service providers.

Table 9. List of 47 prefectures for RESIP hosts with service providers. PO: Proxies Online, GS: Geosurf, PR: ProxyRack, LU: Luminati, IS: IAPS Security

Prefecture	RESIPs	PO	GS	PR	LU	IS
Tokyo	12,766	2,709	84	4,442	5,027	4
Kanagawa	3,094	721	17	1,145	1,087	0
Aichi	2,940	715	15	1,163	942	0
Osaka	2,917	769	17	1,148	880	1
Saitama	2,544	605	14	1,082	754	0
Chiba	1,912	484	32	726	557	0
Hyogo	1,722	460	21	693	493	0
Hukuoka	1,266	426	9	436	320	0
Sizuoka	1,083	251	7	484	308	0
Hokkaido	1,061	324	9	448	225	0
Kyoto	997	213	0	438	310	0
Mie	638	115	1	300	208	0
Hiroshima	589	168	2	257	138	0
Gifu	584	118	1	299	139	0
Ibaragi	568	107	1	264	179	0
Okinawa	543	89	3	153	284	0
Tochigi	473	125	1	186	134	0
Gunma	432	112	1	144	158	0
Nagano	418	80	0	172	144	0
Niigata	409	95	0	200	100	0
Shiga	380	99	1	131	135	0
Miyagi	372	104	5	150	97	0
Okayama	316	89	0	129	97	0
Nara	302	74	1	121	85	0
Kumamoto	297	98	1	108	82	0
Ehime	271	94	0	97	68	0
Yamaguchi	242	79	0	97	57	0
Fukushima	241	72	0	113	42	0
Kagawa	227	60	2	128	27	0
Toyama	216	57	0	92	56	0
Ishikawa	210	61	0	65	73	0
Yamanashi	201	54	0	81	62	0

(continued)

Table 9. (*continued*)

Prefecture	RESIPs	PO	GS	PR	LU	IS
Oita	186	48	1	77	52	0
Wakayama	177	51	0	88	34	0
Aomori	168	34	0	85	46	0
Fukui	159	36	1	57	61	0
Kagoshima	157	41	1	72	38	0
Kouchi	154	53	0	67	27	0
Yamagata	148	31	1	68	38	0
Iwate	139	36	0	61	32	0
Akita	131	36	0	60	31	0
Nagasaki	128	25	0	49	52	0
Saga	126	38	0	54	28	0
Tokushima	125	37	0	46	33	0
Miyazaki	124	33	0	51	36	0
Tottori	94	38	0	37	14	0
Shimane	90	13	0	30	43	0
not found	6,619	1,741	52	2,108	2,507	8
Total	48,956	11,918	304	18,502	16,325	13

References

1. Mi, X., Feng, X., Liao, X., Liu, B., Wang, X., Qian, F., Li, Z., Alrwais, S., Sun, L., Liu, Y.: Resident evil: understanding residential IP proxy as a dark Service. IEEE Symp. Secur. Priv. (SP) **1**, 170–186 (2019)
2. RPaaS: Characterizing Residential IP Proxy as a Service. https://rpaas.site/
3. MAXMIND: GeoLite2 Free Downloadable Databases. https://dev.maxmind.com/geoip/geoip2/geolite2/
4. APNIC: Whois search. https://www.apnic.net/about-apnic/whois_search/
5. Inoue, D., Eto, M., Yoshioka, K., Baba, S., Suzuki, K., Nakazato, J., Ohtaka, K., Nakao, K.: "nicter: an incident analysis system toward binding network monitoring with malware analysis. In: WOMBAT Workshop on Information Security Threats, Data Collection, and Sharing, WISTDCS 2008, pp. 58–66. IEEE (2008)
6. Takehisa, T., Kamizono, M., Kasama, T., Nakazato, J., Eto, M., Inoue, D., Nakao, K.: Utilization of secure remote analysis platform for cybersecurity information (NONSTOP). Comput. Secur. Symp. **2**, 207–214 (2014). (in Japanese)
7. APNIC: Registration Data Access Protocol. https://www.apnic.net/about-apnic/whois_search/about/rdap/
8. Telecom data book 2018. (Compiled by TCA)
9. Statistics on Internet traffic in Japan, MIC. http://www.soumu.go.jp/main_content/000523384.pdf
10. IPInfoDB. https://ipinfodb.com/
11. RIPE NCC: whois Database. https://www.ripe.net/manage-ips-and-asns/db/support/documentation/glossary/whois-database
12. National Institute of Information and Communications Technology NICTER Observation report 2017. https://www.nict.go.jp/cyber/report/NICTER_report_2017.pdf. (in Japanese)

13. Chung, T., Choffnes, D., Mislove, A.: Tunneling for transparency: a large-scale analysis of end-to-end violations in the internet. In: Proceedings of the 2016 ACM on Internet Measurement Conference, pp 199–213. ACM (2016)
14. Weaver, N., Kreibich, C., Dam, M., Paxson, V.: Here be web proxies. In: Faloutsos, M., Kuzmanovic, A. (eds.) PAM 2014. LNCS, vol. 8362, pp. 183–192. Springer, Cham (2014). https://doi.org/10.1007/978-3-319-04918-2_18

Insights into Attacks' Progression: Prediction of Spatio-Temporal Behavior of DDoS Attacks

Ahmed Abusnaina[1]([⊠]), Mohammed Abuhamad[2], DaeHun Nyang[3], Songqing Chen[4], An Wang[5], and David Mohaisen[1]

[1] University of Central Florida, 32816 Orlando, FL, USA
ahmed.abusnaina@knights.ucf.edu
[2] Loyola University Chicago, 60660 Chicago, IL, USA
[3] Ewha Womans University, Incheon, South Korea
[4] George Mason University, 22030 Fairfax, VA, USA
[5] Case Western Reserve University, 44106 Cleveland, OH, USA

Abstract. DDoS attacks are an immense threat to online services, and numerous studies have been done to detect and defend against them. DDoS attacks, however, are becoming more sophisticated and launched with different purposes, making the detection and instant defense as important as analyzing the behavior of the attack during and after it takes place. Studying and modeling the Spatio-temporal evolvement of DDoS attacks is essential to predict, assess, and combat the problem, since recent studies have shown the emergence of wider and more powerful adversaries. This work aims to model seven Spatio-temporal behavioral characteristics of DDoS attacks, including the attack magnitude, the adversaries' botnet information, and the attack's source locality down to the organization. We leverage four state-of-the-art deep learning methods to construct an ensemble of models to capture and predict behavioral patterns of the attack. The proposed ensemble operates in two frequencies, hourly and daily, to actively model and predict the attack behavior and evolvement, and oversee the effect of implementing a defense mechanism.

Keywords: DDoS Attacks Prediction · Deep learning

1 Introduction

Distributed Denial-of-Service (DDoS) attacks are explicit malicious attempts to prevent legitimate users from accessing a service by sending an overwhelming amount of traffic to the service server. According to Netscout's annual worldwide infrastructure security report [15], the traffic generated for launching DDoS attacks exceeded 1 TBPS in size in 2019. On a more recent event, an attack of size 1.7 TBPS has been recorded. These attacks, if successful, result in a service shutdown that costs a provider an average of $221,836 per attack [15].

© Springer Nature Switzerland AG 2020
I. You (Ed.): WISA 2020, LNCS 12583, pp. 362–374, 2020.
https://doi.org/10.1007/978-3-030-65299-9_27

The growing threat of DDoS attacks has inspired many recent research studies to contribute to the efforts toward the analysis and characterization of the attacks [16,17], including methods for the attacks detection and prediction [6,14]. These efforts have made the field of detecting DDoS attacks widely-explored and resulting in highly-accurate detection systems [8,10,18]. However, there are limited studies that explore behavioral patterns and characteristics of the DDoS attacks during the progression of the attack and after the detection. Understanding the Spatio-temporal behavior and characteristics of the attack is crucial for defending against the attack, limiting its impact, and planing countermeasures to prevent it from occurring in the future. This study aims to contribute to this area by providing in-depth analyses and insights for modeling seven behavioral characteristics of DDoS attacks using deep learning-based methods. This analysis and modeling task takes place after the detection of the attack and continues as the attack progresses (in space and time). The Spatio-temporal analysis of DDoS behavior can be done by addressing various characteristics, such as the attack magnitude, botnet information, and attack source location.

This paper is dedicated to investigating several Spatio-temporal characteristics of the DDoS attacks, namely, attack magnitude, botnet family and ID, attack source locations including countries, ASNs, cities, and organizations. Due to the underlying nature of patterns to be extracted for separate characteristics, we leverage current state-of-the-art machine learning methods, including Deep Neural Networks (DNN), Long Short Term Memory (LSTM), Transformer, and Convolutional Neural Networks (CNN), to model separate characteristics and construct an ensemble of models to predict at different frequencies the behavioral patterns of DDoS attacks. The ensemble incorporates 14 different models, two for each characteristic, and operates in two frequencies, hourly-based, and daily-based frequencies, to actively monitor and account for the latest status of the attack while in progress. The ensemble is built and evaluated on a large-scale real-world dataset that includes 50,704 verified DDoS attacks launched by eleven botnet families and 674 botnet IDs on 9,026 targets from August 2012 to March 2013. This work sheds light on different aspects and patterns of DDoS attacks.

Contribution. This work presents an ensemble of models to predict the Spatio-temporal behavioral patterns of DDoS attacks. The contribution is as follows:

- **Modeling Spatio-temporal Characteristics:** Predicting seven different characteristics of the ongoing DDoS attacks using Spatio-temporal behavioral patterns of the attack, namely: *attack magnitude, botnet family, botnet ID, attack source country, ASN, city,* and *organization,* using large-scale real-world dataset of approximately nine million records of verified DDoS attacks.
- **Constructing Predictive Ensemble:** Implementing an ensemble of seven models based on four machine learning architectures, namely, DNN, LSTM, Transformer, and CNN, to actively predict the attack behavior on different operational frequencies (hourly and daily bases).
- **Addressing Unseen Attacks and Targets:** Evaluate the performance of the ensemble on a real-world large-scale dataset of known and unseen targets

and DDoS attacks. The ensemble offers high accuracy over targets with no attacking history, and new represented DDoS attacks.

– **Addressing the Cold Start Problem:** We investigate the effect of cold start problem, i.e., modeling with insufficient information such as at the beginning of the attack. We show that the ensemble can achieve high accuracy even under the cold start situation.

2   Dataset Overview

2.1   Dataset Collection

The dataset is provided by the monitoring unit of a DDoS mitigation company [3]. Traces of malicious infected hosts were collected by collaborating with over 300 major Internet Service Providers (ISPs) globally monitoring attacks launched by specific malicious actors worldwide across America, Europe, Asia, Africa, and Australia. The activities of the participating hosts in the given botnet attacks, by either communicating with the infected infrastructure or launching the actual DDoS attack on the monitored targets, were monitored and analyzed over time. To this end, the traces of the traffic associated with various botnets were collected using different sensors on the Internet, in corporation with several ISPs, where the source of the collected traffic is an infected host participating in botnet attacks, and the destination is a verified targeted client. Afterward, malware botnets used in launching various attacks were reverse engineered and labeled to a known malware family using best practices (i.e., AMAL, a fully automated system for analysis, classification, and clustering of malware samples) [12,13]. The dataset consists of 50,704 verified DDoS attacks collected in the period of 08/29/2012 to 03/24/2013, a total of 207 days, targeting 9,026 clients, represented as hourly snapshots of each family activities over the monitored period, including the botnet information, targeted client IP, and the IPs of the hosts associated with the botnet attack.

2.2   Behavioral Characteristics of DDoS Attacks

We focus on three groups of characteristics: attack magnitude, botnet information, and attack source location. The following is a description of each group.

Attack Magnitude (AM). This attribute refers to the number of DDoS attacks launched by infected hosts on a specific target over a period of time, regardless of their malicious families and attack objectives. It is important to understand the magnitude of the attack to estimate and allocate a suitable amount of resources to counter the attack.

Botnet Information. The importance of knowing the attacking botnet families lies in implementing the correct defense against the attack since popular botnets have well-known attack patterns. Therefore, two characteristics have been extracted: *botnet family (BF)* and *ID*. The DDoS attacks reported in our dataset originated mainly from eleven popular botnet families: *dirtjumper, darkshell, ddoser, nitol, pandora, blackenergy, optima, aldibot, yzf, colddeath,* and *armageddon*. Botnet families may evolve over time. Therefore, new botnet generations are marked by their unique MD5 and SHA-1 hashes. We consider the botnet ID as a standalone characteristic, as the behavior of the botnet may change over several generations. Table 1 shows the number of botnet IDs associated with DDoS attacks for each family. Note that the eleven botnet families have a total of 674 different botnet IDs, indicating the continuous evolvement of botnets over time. The number of records represents the instances of recorded DDoS attacks associated with infected hosts from a malicious botnet family.

Table 1. Distribution of the botnet IDs over botnet families.

Family	# Botnet IDs	# Records
dirtjumper	251	6, 902, 882
darkshell	166	80, 129
ddoser	102	37, 172
nitol	43	20, 411
pandora	41	1, 397, 027
blackenergy	28	95, 330
optima	25	41, 321
aldibot	9	269
yzf	6	113, 923
colddeath	2	28, 259
armageddon	1	906
Total	674	8, 717, 629

Attack Source Location. It has been shown that botnets have strong geographical and organizational localities [2]. Therefore, such information can be used to predict future attack source locations and the shifting patterns of attackers across geographical locations to help in planning defenses and countermeasures. To this end, the hosts IP addresses were used to extract the attack source country *(CN)*, city *(CT)*, organization *(OG)* and *(ASN)*, using the IP-to-region dataset and MaxMind online database [11]. In the monitored duration in which the dataset is collected, the attack source locations were distributed over 186 countries, 2,996 cities, 4,036 organizations, and 4,375 ASNs, The distribution of the infected hosts indicates the existence of worldwide botnet infections.

2.3   Dataset Splitting

The dataset is split into three parts as follows. ① *Training dataset:* The training dataset contains the traces and records of 80% (7220) of DDoS attacks' victims (i.e., targeted clients). For the purpose of predicting the behavioral patterns of the attacks during the attack progression, we considered the records that occurred at the first 80% of the attack duration for each victim (*target*) as the actual training dataset. ② *Known targets testing dataset:* This dataset contains the remaining records that occurred during the last 20% of the attack duration per target. This sub-dataset is used to evaluate the prediction models in modeling the behavioral pattern of DDoS attacks on targets with known history (by observing the earlier 80% of the attack duration). ③ *Unseen targets testing dataset:* This dataset consists of DDoS attack records of the remaining 20% (1806) of targeted clients that are not considered in the training dataset. The aim of this dataset is to evaluate the prediction models over targets with no attack history available to our model. Table 2 shows the distribution of the dataset characteristics over each partition of the dataset.

Table 2. Overall characteristics of the dataset distribution.

Partition	# Targets	# Families	# IDs	# IPs	# Countries	# ASN	# Cities	# Org.
① Train Dataset	7,220	11	605	841,471	186	4,150	2,877	3,831
② Known Targets	7,220	11	606	158,230	179	3,275	2,275	3,024
③ Unseen Targets	1,806	10	248	234,113	151	2,571	1,800	2,382
Overall	9,026	11	674	880,451	186	4,375	2,996	4,036

3   System Design

The proposed design aims to predict the seven different characteristics of the DDoS attack. The system design is shown in Fig. 1.

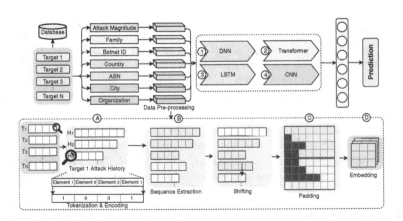

Fig. 1. The general flow of the DDoS attacks prediction design. Here, T refers to the attacked target, whereas H represents one hour in the attack duration.

3.1   Operational Frequency and Data Pre-processing

We adopted two operational frequencies to model and analyze behavioral patterns of DDoS attacks. The data pre-processing and handling follows the same manner in both approaches with slight modifications.

Operational Mode. For studying attack behavior manifested with the considered characteristics, data records were aggregated at different frequencies (i.e., *Agile* with hourly frequency and *Passive* with daily frequency). The agile mode requires six hours of data to be fully-functional at an hourly frequency, while the passive mode requires three days of information to be full-functional in modeling behavioral patterns at a daily frequency.

Data Processing and Sequence Generation. Addressing different characteristics of DDoS attacks captured by their records, the data is represented as $\Phi_{\mathcal{X}} = \{\phi_1, \phi_2, \ldots, \phi_t\} \in \mathbb{R}^{N \times T}$, where $\phi_\alpha \in \mathbb{R}^{1 \times T}$ is a vector of the attribute in hand (Φ) for the attack targeting $\mathcal{X}$ at a given time step α (e.g., ϕ_1 and ϕ_t represent the vectors of the first and last time step), T is the maximum length of the reported attacks, and N is the total number of targeted clients. For instance, addressing the *botnet ID* of an attack targeting $\mathcal{X}$, the data is represented as a matrix $ID_{\mathcal{X}} = \{id_1, id_2, \ldots, id_t\} \in \mathbb{R}^{N \times T}$, where $id_\alpha \in \mathbb{R}^{1 \times T}$ is a vector of botnet IDs targeting $\mathcal{X}$ at a given time step α. We achieve such representation by the following steps. Ⓐ *Tokenization and Encoding:* We assign identifiers for unique elements (e.g., botnet IDs are assigned to unique identifiers when processing the *ID* attribute). Assuming an attack at target $\mathcal{X}$ in a time step α, the *ID* attribute is represented with a vector of all unique botnet IDs identifiers occurring in the attack record within α. For example, assuming the IDs appear in a certain attack record at the first time step are $\{id_{32}, id_{105}, id_{12}\}$, then, we present the vector as $\mathrm{ID}_0 = \{id_{12}, id_{32}, id_{105}\}$. Ⓑ *Sequence Extraction:* The sequence of attribute behavior of DDoS attacks is extracted with different frequencies. Sequence extraction refers to the length of the previous time steps required to predict future steps. In the agile approach, we chose six-time steps (i.e., six hours) to be a sufficient time needed to predict future behaviors based on our experiment. For example, IDs sequences are generated as follows: $\mathrm{Seq}_1 = \{\mathrm{ID}_1, \mathrm{ID}_2, \ldots, \mathrm{ID}_6\}$, $\mathrm{Seq}_2 = \{\mathrm{ID}_2, \mathrm{ID}_3, \ldots, \mathrm{ID}_7\}$, and so on. Operating with the passive approach, we chose three time steps (three days) as sufficient information to predict daily future behavior. Ⓒ *Attribute Vector Padding:* The input data for each attribute are presented with different lengths based on the attribute magnitude at each time step. To allow efficient processing and tensor calculation, all vectors are padded to the maximum length enabling the packing of several attribute vectors in one sequence as well as packing several sequences in one batch. Ⓓ *Attribute Vector Embedding:* Attribute vectors are forwarded to an embedding layer in all deep learning-based models in our ensemble, to enable the compact representation of vectors. Vectors represented with attribute identifiers $\phi_\alpha \in \mathbb{R}^T$, where T is the maximum occurrence of unique identifiers in an attack, will be embedded to $\gamma_\alpha \in \mathbb{R}^{128}$, where 128 is the size of the vector embedding. We chose the size of the embedding based on several experiments that showed

128 is adequate to incorporate the information present in the attribute vector. Sequences are then viewed as matrices of $\Gamma_\alpha \in \mathbb{R}^{t_s \times 128}$, where t_s is the number of time steps.

Attack Magnitude. The approach to predict and study attack magnitude is different from the one adopted for other characteristics. The magnitude of the attack is calculated per targeted client at each time step and presented as one real value (instead of attribute vector). Thus, only step Ⓑ is required from the aforementioned approach, which aims to generate sequences of the calculated value of magnitude at each time step. To present the values of magnitude to the deep learning model, we normalize the values in the range of zero to one.

3.2   Prediction Models Architectures

Our approach adopts an ensemble of powerful classifiers to predict different behaviors of DDoS attacks including DNN, Transformer, LSTM, and CNN. We chose different model architectures for modeling different tasks (i.e., characteristics behaviors) since certain architectures are proven to work better than the others in certain circumstances. In particular, the best performing deep learning architecture in predicting each DDoS attack characteristic is reported.

DNN for Attack Magnitude. The model architecture consists of four dense layers of size 1,000 units with ReLU activation function. Each dense layer is followed by a dropout operation with a rate of 30%. The last layer is connected to a sigmoid layer of size one signaling the normalized number of the attack magnitude (i.e., the scale of the magnitude from zero to one).

Transformer for Botnet Information. The model is adopted from the model proposed by Vaswani et al. [19]. It consists of stacked layers in both encoder and decoder components. Each layer has eight sub-layers comprising multi-head attention layers. The prediction is done by conducting a beam search with a length penalty ($\lambda = 0.6$). The Transformer is used to train two models performing two separate tasks, predicting botnet family and ID.

LSTM for Wide Attack Locality. The model consists of one LSTM layer with a size of 128 units. The LSTM layer is followed by a dense layer of size 128 and a dropout operation with a rate of 20%. Then, a dense layer with a sigmoid activation function is used to output the prediction of attack source locality. The LSTM is used to predict attack source country and ASN.

CNN for Specific Attack Locality. The model architecture consists of one convolutional layer with 64 kernels of size 1×3 convolving over the input vector, followed with a sigmoid output layer of size equals to the size of the addressed attribute vector (i.e., to predict the future status of the attack). The CNN architecture is used to predict the specific attack locality (i.e., city and organization).

4   Evaluation and Discussion

We report our results using two evaluation metrics, namely True Positive Rate (TPR) and True Negative Rate (TNR). TPR represents the number of correctly predicted elements over all the elements that occurred within the duration of the prediction. For instance, if the DDoS attack launched from four countries, of which, the prediction model predicts three correctly, the TPR is equal to 75% (3/4). TNR is referred to as $1 - (FP/N)$ where FP is the number of the incorrectly predicted elements and N represents all the elements that did not occur within the duration of the prediction. For instance, if the DDoS attack launched from four countries out of 186, and the prediction model incorrectly predicts two elements, the TNR is equal to 98.90% $(1-(2/182))$. Note that TPR and TNR are preferred metrics in evaluating the systems as true indicators of performance in different scenarios. For example, achieving a TNR of 100% means zero false alarms. On the other hand, TPR indicates the precision of predicting attack behavior. Therefore, it's important for all models to maintain high TPR and TNR to ensure the usefulness of the classifier prediction.

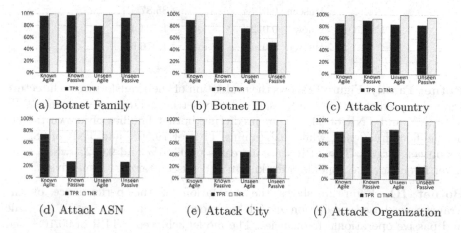

Fig. 2. Evaluation of the prediction models over known and unseen targets.

4.1   Attack Characteristics Evaluation

Figure 2 summarizes the results of six attack characteristics using both *known* and *unseen* test targets when adopting the agile and passive approaches. The seventh attribute (i.e., the attack magnitude) is evaluated separately due to the data nature of the attribute. Two models were implemented for each attribute, one for each operational frequency (agile and passive operational modes), and evaluated on known and unseen targets.

Attack Magnitude. We evaluate the DNN model for predicting the attack magnitude using the *mean error* metric. Since the data observations were normalized, the output of the model indicates the magnitude as a fraction of the maximum recorded magnitude. Then, to calculate the magnitude, we multiply the model's output by the maximum magnitude rounded to the decimal point. We report the results in Table 3. Here, the shift error is reported by the actual number of attacking hosts contributed to the attacks. For instance, the error rate of the agile model on *unseen* data is 0.0014% which is off by roughly 86 hosts from the actual number of the attacking hosts. Even though this number might seem large at first, it appears to be a good estimate knowing that the average attack magnitude on the agile data sampling rate (i.e., per the hour) equals 551 hosts (15.60% deviation). Similarly, the average shift rate for the passive approach is roughly 1,977 hosts for predicting the magnitude of *unseen* targets, which is also acceptable estimation knowing the average of magnitude is 15,394 hosts per day (12.97% deviation).

Table 3. Attack magnitude prediction evaluation.

Approach	Target	Mean Error Rate	Avg. Shift Error
Agile	Known	0.015%	$\mp$88.64
	Unseen	0.014%	$\mp$85.87
Passive	Known	0.012%	$\mp$1,734.40
	Unseen	0.014%	$\mp$1,976.65

Botnet Family. Figure 2a shows the evaluation of the Transformer architecture trained to predict botnet family using different settings. The models achieve TPR of 95.97% and TNR of 99.65% for predicting botnet families of known targets on one-hour frequency, while maintaining TPR of 79.50% and TNR of 98.94% for unseen targets. The TPR score increases to 96.97% and 93.62% when using lower frequency (i.e., one-day) for known and unseen targets, respectively.

Botnet ID. Figure 2b shows the evaluation of the performance of the Transformer-based prediction model on known and unseen targets for agile and passive operational frequencies. The model achieved a TPR of 90.16% and 76.42% for predicting known targets, and unseen targets with a TNR of 99.97% and 99.95%, respectively, using agile operational frequency. For passive operational frequency, the model achieved a TPR of 62.96% and 52.74% for predicting known targets, with a TNR of 99.95% and 99.93% for unseen targets, respectively.

Attack Source Country. Figure 2c shows the performance of the LSTM-based model on known and unseen targets for agile and passive operational frequencies. Using the agile approach, we achieved a TPR and TNR of 85.26% and 98.62% for known targets, and 83.83% and 99.95% for unseen targets, respectively. Similarly, the model achieved a TPR and TNR of 90.19% and 93.21% in predicting known targets attack source countries using passive frequency, and a TPR and TNR of 82.60% and 95.39% in predicting unseen target attack source countries.

Attack Source ASN. Figure 2d shows the evaluation of the LSTM-based models in predicting the attack source ASNs operating in two frequencies, agile and passive. The model achieved a TPR and TNR of 73.59% and 99.41% on known targets, and 65.68% and 99.96% on unseen targets, respectively, operating in agile frequency. Similarly, the model achieved a TPR and TNR of 27.06% and 97.53% on known targets, and 26.66% and 97.60% on unseen targets, respectively, on the passive approach. While the passive frequency-based LSTM model performance is low, it maintains a high TNR, reducing the false alarms.

Attack Source City. Using the agile frequency-based CNN model to predict the attack source city, we achieved a TPR and TNR of 72.23% and 99.72% for known targets, and 44.61% and 99.98% for unseen targets, respectively. For daily-based frequency, we achieved a TPR and TNR of 62.81% and 99.02% for known targets, and 17.39% and 99.34% for unseen targets, respectively. Figure 2e shows evaluation results of the CNN-based models. The high TNR (low false alarms) makes it possible to utilize the provided information by the model to implement a proper defense with high confidence.

Attack Source Organization. Figure 2f shows the evaluation of the performance of the prediction models on known and unseen targets for both operational frequencies. We achieved a TPR and TNR of 80.42% and 99.40% on known targets, and 84.48% and 99.72% on unseen targets, respectively, using agile frequency operational mode.

4.2 Discussion and Limitation

DDoS Attack Behavior Prediction. This work focuses on predicting the DDoS attack behavioral patterns after the detection of the attack. Therefore, the ensemble operates on top of the DDoS attack detection system. The purpose of the ensemble is to provide critical information and insights to help the targeted victims in designing and planning a proper defense mechanism.

- *Magnitude driven defenses:* DDoS attacks with a low magnitude will unlikely result in total denial of service, while high magnitude attacks can cause shutting down the service. Understanding the ongoing attack magnitude within a continuous time window allows a better decision making process and allocating resources to combat and mitigate the attack.
- *Botnet-based driven defenses:* Certain botnet families have repetitive attacking patterns. In addition, botnet families can collaborate to conduct a DDoS attack. Understanding the attack nature and behavior through its associate botnet families and IDs create a better awareness of how the attack will progress, and better defend against it.
- *Region-based driven defenses:* DDoS attacks have regional dependencies, as the infected hosts may be originated from the same region, or related regions. Understanding the regional distribution of the infected hosts, and the over-time shifting will provide better insights to implement region-based defenses.

First-Hour Attack: The Cold Start. We implemented the ensemble to operate on the specified frequency using the available information aggregated using the sampling time while padding the unavailable sequence steps with zero-vectors. For example, assume an attack with only two-hours information is available, the agile approach will process the two-hours vectors and pad four-steps of zero-vectors to predict the third hour. This approach has shown to be effective in our experiments, especially for predicting botnet families and attack source countries. For instance, using six-hours information, the agile approach predicts the attack source cities with TPR of 72.23% and 44.61%, for known and unseen targets; while using only one-hour information results in TPR of 65.56% and 17.49% for the same settings, while maintaining a high TNR ($\approx$99%).

5   Related Work

DDoS Attacks Detection. DDoS attacks detection is well explored in different environments. Sekar et al. [18] proposed LADS, a triggered, multi-stage in-network DDoS detection system to overcome the scalability issues in detecting DDoS attacks over the large-scale monitored network. In addition, Chang et al. [1,2] performed an in-depth analysis of botnet behavior patterns. Their analysis showed that different botnets start to collaborate when launching DDoS attacks. Similarly, they conducted an in-depth analysis measurement study showing that bots recruitment has strong geographical and organizational locality. Lu et al. [9] clustered botnet traffic into C&C channels using the K-mean clustering algorithm on large-scale network traffic payload signatures. In more recent work, Doshi et al. [4] distinguished normal traffic from DDoS traffic using limited packet-level features.

DDoS Attacks Behavior Prediction. Recent studies predicted different aspects of the attack behavior, such as Gupta et al. [7], where they estimated the number of bots involved in a flooding DDoS attack with high accuracy by calculating various statistical performance measures. In addition, Fachkha et al. [5] proposed a systematic approach for inferring DDoS activities, predicting DDoS attack characteristics, and clustering various targets to the same DDoS campaign. Furthermore, Wang et al. [20] designed three DDoS attacks models from temporal (attack magnitudes), spatial (attacker origin), and Spatio-temporal (attack inter-launching time) perspectives by analyzing 50,000 verified DDoS attacks. Even though recent studies investigated the attack detection and behaviors, only a few of them provided information that would assist the client in implementing a proper defense on the spot. Our design provides the victim with essential information that can be utilized to properly implement a magnitude-, region-, and malware-based DDoS attacks mitigation techniques and defenses.

6   Conclusion

This work proposes an ensemble approach for studying and predicting the behavioral characteristics of DDoS attacks. Toward this, we built an ensemble of deep learning models to predict seven behavioral characteristics of DDoS attacks, providing insights for handling such attacks. Evaluating our approach on a large-scale real-world dataset that contains records of more than fifty thousand verified attacks, the results of our approach show remarkable performance when operating on different sampling frequencies and under different settings. This success of efficient and accurate modeling of DDoS attack characteristics can help to implement proper defenses for mitigating the attack.

Acknowledgement. This work was supported by NRF grant 2016K1A1A2912757, NIST grant 70NANB18H272, and NSF grant CNS-1524462 (S. Chen), and by the Institute for Smart, Secure and Connected Systems at CWRU (A. Wang).

References

1. Chang, W., Mohaisen, A., Wang, A., Chen, S.: Measuring botnets in the wild: Some new trends. In: Proceedings of the 10th ACM Symposium on Information, Computer and Communications Security, ASIA CCS, pp. 645–650 (2015)
2. Chang, W., Mohaisen, A., Wang, A., Chen, S.: Understanding adversarial strategies from bot recruitment to scheduling. In: Proceedings of the 13th International Conference on Security and Privacy in Communication Networks - SecureComm, pp. 397–417 (2017)
3. Cymru, T.: Cymru (2019).https://www.team-cymru.com/
4. Doshi, R., Apthorpe, N., Feamster, N.: Machine learning DDOS detection for consumer internet of things devices. In: 2018 IEEE Security and Privacy Workshops (SPW), pp. 29–35. IEEE (2018)
5. Fachkha, C., Bou-Harb, E., Debbabi, M.: On the inference and prediction of DDOS campaigns. Wirel. Commun. Mob. Comput. **15**(6), 1066–1078 (2015)
6. Gong, D., Tran, M., Shinde, S., Jin, H., Sekar, V., Saxena, P., Kang, M.S.: Practical verifiable in-network filtering for DDoS defense. In: 39th IEEE International Conference on Distributed Computing Systems, ICDCS 2019, Dallas, TX, USA, July 7–10, 2019, pp. 1161–1174 (2019)
7. Gupta, B., Joshi, R., Misra, M.: Prediction of number of zombies in a DDoS attack using polynomial regression model. J. Adv. Inform. Technol. **2**(1), 57–62 (2011)
8. Lee, K., Kim, J., Kwon, K.H., Han, Y., Kim, S.: DDoS attack detection method using cluster analysis. Exp. Syst. App. **34**(3), 1659–1665 (2008)
9. Lu, W., Rammidi, G., Ghorbani, A.A.: Clustering botnet communication traffic based on n-gram feature selection. Comput. Commun. **34**(3), 502–514 (2011)
10. Ma, X., Chen, Y.: DDoS detection method based on chaos analysis of network traffic entropy. IEEE Commun. Lett. **18**(1), 114–117 (2014)
11. MaxMind: Maxmind (2019). https://www.maxmind.com/
12. Mohaisen, A., Alrawi, O.: Av-meter: An evaluation of antivirus scans and labels. In: Proceedings of the 11th International Conference on Detection of Intrusions and Malware, and Vulnerability Assessment - DIMVA, pp. 112–131 (2014)
13. Mohaisen, A., Alrawi, O., Mohaisen, M.: AMAL: high-fidelity, behavior-based automated malware analysis and classification. Comput. Secur. **52**, 251–266 (2015)
14. Najafabadi, M.M., Khoshgoftaar, T.M., Calvert, C., Kemp, C.: A text mining approach for anomaly detection in application layer DDoS attacks. In: Proceedings of the Thirtieth International Florida Artificial Intelligence Research Society Conference, FLAIRS, pp. 312–317 (2017)

15. Netscout: Netscout 14th annual worldwide infrastructure security report (2019). https://www.netscout.com/report/
16. Rasti, R., Murthy, M., Weaver, N., Paxson, V.: Temporal lensing and its application in pulsing denial-of-service attacks. In: Proceedings of the IEEE Symposium on Security and Privacy, SP, pp. 187–198 (2015)
17. Rossow, C.: Amplification hell: Revisiting network protocols for DDoS abuse. In: Proceedings of the 21st Annual Network and Distributed System Security Symposium, NDSS (2014)
18. Sekar, V., Duffield, N.G., Spatscheck, O., van der Merwe, J.E., Zhang, H.: LADS: large-scale automated ddos detection system. In: Proceedings of the 2006 USENIX Annual Technical Conference, Boston, MA, USA, May 30–June 3, 2006, pp. 171–184 (2006)
19. Vaswani, A., Shazeer, N., Parmar, N., Uszkoreit, J., Jones, L., Gomez, A.N., Kaiser, L., Polosukhin, I.: Attention is all you need. In: Advances in Neural Information Processing Systems 30: Annual Conference on Neural Information Processing Systems, pp. 5998–6008 (2017)
20. Wang, A., Mohaisen, A., Chen, S.: An adversary-centric behavior modeling of ddos attacks. In: Proceedings of the 37th IEEE International Conference on Distributed Computing Systems, ICDCS, pp. 1126–1136 (2017)

Methods to Select Features for Android Malware Detection Based on the Protection Level Analysis

Chaeeun Lee, Eunnarae Ko, and Kyungho Lee[✉]

Institute of Cyber Security and Privacy (ICSP), Korea University, Seoul 02841, Korea
{katey95415,eun13,kevinlee}@korea.ac.kr

Abstract. Android's permission system is asked to users before installing applications. It is intended to warn users about the risks of the app installation and gives users opportunities to review the application's permission requests and uninstall it if they find it threatening. However, not all android permissions ask for the user's decision. Those who are defined as 'Dangerous' in the permission protection level are only being confirmed by the users in Android Google Market. We examine whether the 'Dangerous permissions' are actually being a main component of detection when it comes to defining the app as malicious or benign. To collect important features and to investigate the correlation between the malicious app and the permission's protection level, feature selection and deep learning algorithms were used. The study evaluates the feature by using the confusion matrix. We used 10,818 numbers of malicious and benign applications, and 457 permission lists to investigate our examination, and it appeared that 'Dangerous' permissions may not be the only important factor, and we suggest a different perspective of viewing permissions.

Keywords: Android application · Permission · Protection level · Malware detection · Feature selection · Classification · Deep learning

1 Introduction

An investigation report by International Data Corporation (IDC) expects that the overall smartphone market will reach to 1.511 billion units in 2024. In the same year, the Android market will still be in the first place of the OS Market with 87% share, while Apple's iOS will be accounted for second place with 13% share [11]. As of December 2019, the Google Play Store consists of 2.87 million applications which are consisting of a wide range of contents, such as music, magazines, books, film, games, and TV [18].

Permissions are divided into four levels of protection level. Among them, dangerous level permissions are defined as higher-risk permissions, which is required to be confirmed by an Android user since they can cause harmful impact to the user and device. In our paper, we performed a research to examine how effective dangerous level permissions are when detecting malware applications. Therefore, we made a feature selection of our dataset to see which permissions are being important factors. 70 different types of permissions were selected via the Weka tool to detect malware applications. We used

© Springer Nature Switzerland AG 2020
I. You (Ed.): WISA 2020, LNCS 12583, pp. 375–386, 2020.
https://doi.org/10.1007/978-3-030-65299-9_28

four different deep learning algorithms to see the accuracy of the detection and calculated them with the confusion matrix. All of the selected features resulted in a high score; all of them were above 90% accuracy. We now look in-depth to see what kind of permissions were being selected to be important and figured out what particular protection level was considered more when detecting malware applications.

2 Background

2.1 The Android Permission System

Android uses permission to protect an Android user's privacy, so all Android apps must request permission to alert users about the risks that applications can contain [8]. Permissions that are asked must be approved by the user in order to access to user's sensitive data. Android provides API framework for applications to interact with the Android system, and API is consisted of packages and classes [15]. If the device's API level is 23 or higher, app permissions are notified to users at runtime, and if the device is running under API level 22, app permissions are automatically asked to users at install-time. Therefore, users can choose whether they want to accept or deny the permissions request [1]. Permissions that are reviewed by users are defined as "Dangerous" permissions, according to the Android Developer's protection level. Permissions are categorized into four threat levels [3], [6]:

Normal permissions are default values. They are lower-risk permissions that are automatically granted by the system without needing the user's approval. However, if needed, users can review these permissions before installing them.

Dangerous permissions are higher-risk permissions that are needed to be reviewed by the user. These permissions request access to the user's private data or can control the device. Since these permissions can cause a negative impact on the user, they are not automatically granted by the system which means that they are asked for a review before proceeding. Dangerous permissions potentially have harmful API calls that are related to the user's private information. These permissions, for instance, can read and send user's text messages.

Signature permissions are granted by the system only if the requesting application has the same certificate as the application that declared the permission. Permissions are automatically granted without asking for the user's review when the certificates match.

SignatureOrSystem permission is an old synonym for signature|privileged which was deprecated in API level 23. These permissions are used in some special cases and are granted only to applications in the dedicated folder of the Android system image or to applications signed with the same certificate as those that have declared permissions. Since this protection level is sufficient to most cases, permissions in this protection level can be activated regardless of the exact area of installation.

2.2 Feature Selection

When using machine learning, large data can be redundant or irrelevant. These data can cause overfitting, increase run time and model complexity, and mislead the learning algorithm. In order to run files in an efficient way, reducing unnecessary features can help the program perform well with a higher level of accuracy. In particular, permission-based analysis require feature selection methods with classification algorithms. However, choosing the right feature selection method is a challenge because the result of feature selection can be impacted with not only the characteristic of the dataset but also the interaction with the classification algorithms [17].

The feature selection method is consisted of three types of methods; filter, wrapper, and embedded method. The filter method removes the least important features one by one, the wrapper method finds which feature subset has the best performance in running the algorithm, and the embedded method adds itself a feature selection function [4], [20].

In our paper, to reduce the dimension size of the dataset, we performed a feature selection method with the Weka tool. 16 different algorithms were used to get the best feature set, and with the selected features, we were able to perform permission-based malware application detection.

3 Related Work

Barrera et al. performed an empirical analysis of the permission-based security models by analyzing 1,100 popular Android apps with the SOM algorithm. The study was to find what permissions were used by the Android developers. They found out that out of many permissions, only a small amount of numbers of permissions are used by them. Also, they found that permissions do not exactly matter or correlate with the category of the application [2]. Jesse Obiri-Yeboah et al. discussed how people relate their privacy issues with the Android permission system, and studied about security issues that come along [12]. Ontang et al. [14] propose access control policy infrastructure to prevent applications. They also propose that Android permissions should be in more detail with notifying some specific requirements for configurations or software versions for instance. Felt et al. conducted a usability study on the effectiveness of the Android permissions. The study came up with the result that permissions do not help users to be informed about the malware threat that could impact their security [7]. Aung et al. detected malware applications by extracting permission-based applications at Google's Play market. They extracted the data from AndroidManifest.xml files. In order to calculate the accuracy of their detection method, they compared the performances with true positive, false positive, precision, and recall rates. J48 and Random Forest outperformed CART [21]. Enck et al. paper proposes Kirin security service to check on the permissions when installing applications to reduce the risks of malware applications. The study is relied on developer's perspective of requesting permissions [5].

4 Data

In order to conduct this research, 6414 benign apps and 4404 malware apps were used. These applications were collected from 2017 to 2019 by NSHC and Google. Out of 457 lists of permission that were provided by Android API features, we have figured out what permissions were being used for each application that we have. For those permissions that were being used, we marked them as "1", and "0" for those that weren't being used, and saved as a CSV file. In order to perform various algorithms for Feature Selection, we used all of 457 permissions for features.

10,818 applications that we have collected used 182 different kinds of permissions. We have matched all of used permissions with protection levels. 23 dangerous permissions, 54 normal permissions, 49 signature permissions, and 56 signature|privileged permissions were used.

We wanted to check how many protection levels existed in each benign and malware app in total. We counted the actual numbers of permissions by its protection level. Out of 6,414 benign applications, and 4,404 malware applications, 10,699 and 22,283 dangerous permissions were used respectively, and the detailed numbers are in Table 1.

Table 1. Percentage of Dangerous Protection Level Permissions

	Dangerous	Normal	signature	signature|privileged
Benign App (6,414)	10,699	17,286	800	1,391
Malware App (4,404)	22,283	37,460	8,386	8,829

5 Methodology

5.1 Weka Attribute Selection

To perform Feature Selection, we used WEKA's Attribute Selection, which is great for measuring the utility of attributes and finding the subsets that are predictive of the data [9], [10]. Both wrapper and filter approaches are included in Attribute Selection. For Attribute Evaluator, for example, correlation-based feature selection, chi-square statistic, gain ratio, information gain, symmetric uncertainty, and support vector machine-based criterion is provided. For search methods, the best-first search, ranker method, and random search methods are provided, for example.

In this paper, we have used 16 algorithms for Feature Selection that were provided in Weka's interface, and 3 search methods. We are to select those that are the main features to detect malware applications. The following Table 2 shows which algorithms and methods were used in Feature Selection.

12 out of 16 algorithms were required to use the ranker method for the search methods in Weka. Ranker methods rank all the features by their individual evaluations. Therefore, they ranked all 457 features, which were not intended, so we made another experiment with python to select the right features for malware detection. We calculated the accuracy of the first ranked feature. Then, the next ranked feature was added to calculate the accuracy, and then the next ranked feature was added, and so on until the program calculates all 457 features. We continued this for 12 algorithms. After all the features were calculated, we figured out the best feature selection for each algorithm by the accuracy that they have reached (see Fig. 1).

Table 2. Algorithms used for Feature Selection in Weka.

Attribute Evaluator	Search Method
CfsSubsetEval	BestFirst
ChiSquaredAttributeEval	Ranker
ClassifierAttributeEval	Ranker
ClassifierSubsetEval	GreedyStepwise
CorrelationAttributeEval	Ranker
FilteredAttributeEval	Ranker
GainRatioAttributeEval	Ranker
InfoGainAttributeEval	Ranker
OneRAttributeEval	Ranker
ReliefAttributeEval	Ranker
ConsistencySubsetEval	GreedyStepwise
SignificanceAttributeEval	Ranker
SVMAttributeEval	Ranker
FilteredSubsetEval	GreedyStepwise
SymmetricalUncertAttributeEval	Ranker
WrapperSubsetEval	GreedyStepwise

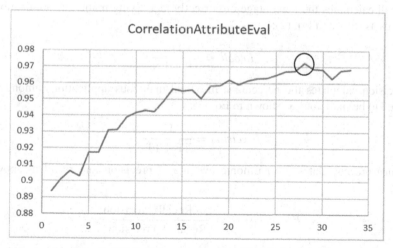

Fig. 1. An example of Ranker Method feature selection. The circle shows the peak of accuracy. We selected all features until this point.

In Fig. 1, we are showing one example of how we performed a feature selection for the ranker method. This figure is about the CorrelationAttributeEval algorithm. The circle that surrounds the peak of the graph is the 28th feature. It was the highest peak, which eventually means that 28 features all together scored the highest accuracy. We used this 28 features as a feature set to perform malware detection.

After the peak, when we continue to add permissions to calculate its accuracy, some do reach up to the point where we first considered to be the highest accuracy. However, we considered all the results after the peak to be overfitting, so they were not reviewed in our study.

5.2 Deep Learning Algorithms

After selecting all the features that are relevant to detect malware applications, we now put it into practice to see the accuracy of detection by using deep learning algorithm. This method was intended to check if selected features are actually being meaningful when detecting malware applications. The detection rate could differ by the dataset and algorithm's characteristics; we chose four different deep learning algorithms to see the detection rate; MLP (Multilayer Perceptron), CNN (Convolutional Neural Networks), LSTM (Long Short-Term Memory), and DBN (Deep Belief Network) [16].

Performance Evaluation Criteria. To evaluate the performance of our features, we used a confusion matrix, which is a summary of prediction results that are used in the field of machine learning. We used recall, precision, f-measure, and accuracy [19].

Accuracy calculates the percentage of correctly identified applications as shown in Eq. (1):

$$Accuracy = \frac{TP + TN}{TP + TN + FP + FN} \tag{1}$$

Recall calculates the percentage of correctly identifying malicious applications as malicious as shown in Eq. (2):

$$Recall = \frac{TP}{TP + FN} \tag{2}$$

Precision calculates the percentage of actual malicious applications among those predicted to be malicious as shown in Eq. (3):

$$Precision = \frac{TP}{TP + FP} \tag{3}$$

F-measure calculates the harmonic average of precision and recall as shown in Eq. (4):

$$F - measure = \frac{2 * Recall*Precision}{Recall + Precision} \tag{4}$$

6   Results and Evaluation

6.1   Accuracy of Malware Detection

With selected features from Weka's attribution selection, we evaluated its efficiency with deep learning algorithms. According to Table 3, all of the detection rates are above

90% which scored a high percentage of malware detection. This percentage proves that the selected features are meaningful to determine malware applications. Selected features included all protection levels, and 324 permissions were used, with 70 types of permissions. The confusion matrix was used to calculate the accuracy, and we only scored the accuracy part on our Table 3.

Table 3. Malware application detection results

	CNN (%)	MLP (%)	LSTM (%)	DBN (%)
CfsSubsetEval	94.4778	94.5779	94.2814	92.7911
ChiSquaredAttributeEval	95.5869	96.1799	95.7139	94.4778
ClassifierAttributeEval	94.9399	96.5496	95.0439	93.2070
ClassifierSubsetEval	95.1017	95.1325	94.9168	95.0323
CorrelationAttributeEval	96.7421	97.2274	96.8807	94.8013
FilteredAttributeEval	96.3725	97.0425	95.9681	94.7551
GainRatioAttributeEval	94.9630	96.1491	95.2403	93.7384
InfoGainAttributeEval	96.1414	96.4571	96.1183	94.5702
OneRAttributeEval	96.0259	96.1183	95.9681	93.6922
ReliefAttributeEval	97.2505	97.0425	97.3198	95.6099
ConsistencySubsetEval	97.0425	96.9808	96.9039	95.6099
SignificanceAttributeEval	95.1248	96.2723	95.8872	94.4778
SVMAttributeEval	95.4251	95.0708	95.3905	94.1312
FilteredSubsetEval	94.4547	94.3931	94.0850	92.4445
SymmetricalUncertAttributeEval	97.0656	97.1965	96.6266	94.9399
WrapperSubsetEval	96.7190	97.2581	96.8115	95.5175

From the process of selecting features that are important to detect malware applications, MLP's accuracy was all above 94% which performed better than the other three methods. The highest detection rate was conducted with a combination of ReliefAttributeEval and LSTM methods.

Out of selected permissions, that were consisted of 370 permissions with 70 different types, we counted each protection level to see which one was more used to detect malware applications. Table 4 shows exactly counted numbers of protection levels, and it appears that the normal protection level is more used than a dangerous level. This is based on permissions.

Out of 70 types of permissions, 19 were dangerous, 22 were normal, 10 were signature, and 19 were signature|privileged (Table 5). We divided 70 types of permissions into four protection levels to use for malware application detection.

Four different deep learning algorithms were used for the detection, and the confusion matrix was used to calculate the accuracy. Table 6 shows the accuracy.

Table 4. Total number of Protection Levels in Selected Features via Weka

	Dangerous	Normal	Signature	signature|privileged
# of Protection Levels	119	147	54	50

Table 5. Protection Level counted for 70 types of permissions in Feature Selection

	Dangerous	Normal	Signature	signature|privileged
# of Protection Levels	19	22	10	19

Table 6. Malware application detection with protection level

	CNN (%)	MLP (%)	LSTM (%)	DBN (%)
Dangerous	92.4676	92.2982	92.3406	89.2329
Normal	94.0619	94.3007	94.1774	90.5961
Signature	89.2791	88.3240	88.5166	88.3318
signature|privileged	91.1275	91.5280	91.5434	90.1571

When we detected malware applications with protection levels, CNN's overall performance was good, but the highest accuracy was detected with LSTM, 94.1774%, with Normal protection level. This would let us assume that permissions with normal protection are important factors to consider when detecting malware applications.

6.2 Classification

With the accuracy results from what we performed with various feature selection algorithms and deep learning methods, it appeared that Relief Attribute Evaluator and LSTM method detects higher accuracy. Relief Attribute Evaluator repeatedly samples the instance and evaluates the value of the attribute by taking the value into account of the given attribute for the nearest instance of the same and different classes. It can perform on both discrete and continuous class data [13].

Out of 70 types of permissions that were selected with feature selection, we wanted to investigate which are more important to consider when detecting malware applications, and figure out what kinds of protection levels exist. Therefore, we chose to follow the steps we made in 5.1, and used Relief Attribute Evaluator and LSTM for detection.

Relief Attribute Evaluator uses Ranker for the search method, and Fig. 2 shows the peak of accuracy; 94.66%. 11 permissions as a set scored the highest accuracy when we ran it through LSTM. 11 permissions are listed in Table 7. We also counted how many applications have used them, and counted them in two ways; malware applications, and both malware and benign applications. It appears that selected permissions are way more used in malware applications.

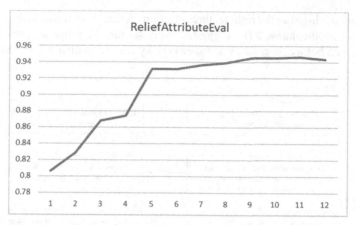

Fig. 2. ReliefAttributeEval's accuracy. 11 permissions together scored highest.

Table 7. Relief Attribute Evaluator Feature Selection results

ReliefAttributeEval	Protection Level	Malware/Total
android.permission.BIND_DEVICE_ADMIN	signature	2012/2032
android.permission.GET_TASKS	normal	2638/2965
android.permission.VIBRATE	normal	1780/3420
android.permission.WRITE_SETTINGS	signature	2343/2564
android.permission.SEND_SMS	dangerous	3668/4055
android.permission.RECEIVE_SMS	dangerous	3436/3729
android.permission.READ_SMS	dangerous	2832/2960
android.permission.WRITE_SMS	normal	2308/2384
android.permission.WRITE_EXTERNAL_STORAGE	dangerous	3793/6025
android.permission.READ_PHONE_STATE	normal	4077/6073
android.permission.RECEIVE_BOOT_COMPLETED	normal	3572/4284

Permissions that were selected again with Relief Attribute Evaluator algorithm consists of 4 dangerous, 5 normal, and 2 signature levels. These selected permissions represent important factors in determining malware applications. Once again here, the normal protection level was the most. While dangerous permissions are to ask users to review their usage, other levels in these selected features are not notified to a user unless users intend to look up for them. Permissions in Table 7 are all related to user's privacy and security, and many permissions were related to SMS and the device. Not only dangerous level permissions are important factors that users should be noticed and be aware of, but also all other permission levels. Therefore, we will name lastly selected permissions to be "Risky", and other remaining ones rather "Safe".

The result of choosing the right feature selection method with the right deep learning study varies with the dataset. The suggested study set that we propose is not definitely the right answer, but we propose a way to select risky features with a way to follow along (see Fig. 3).

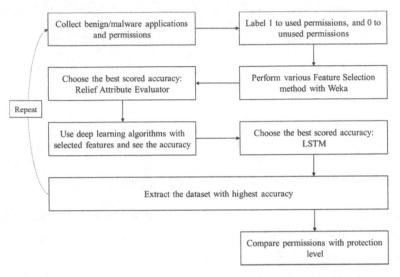

Fig. 3. How to choose risky features when detecting malware applications.

7 Conclusion

As Android has defined each permission with its permission levels, some are required to be reviewed by the user, and some are not. Dangerous permissions are correlated with user's privacy issues, which we would all consider it being a really dangerous factor when it comes up to detecting malware applications. In our research, we wanted to find out what features are being considered to be the main elements to detect malware applications, and proposed a way to follow. To detect malware applications, feature selection and a way to evaluate it needs to be done. With our data, feature selection was well done with the Relief Attribute Evaluator method, and malware detection was done well with LSTM. However, we emphasize that this combination varies with the character of the dataset. Selected features were closely related to the user's privacy and device, but most of the permissions were not required to be reviewed by the user. Four levels of protection level are classified by the Android Google Homepage, but they are divided into developer-friendly ways. Users must understand that other levels can also be dangerous, and change their view of understanding the protection level. Therefore, in our perspective, we view selected features as the same level, and define it "Risky".

Our study was to investigate important features and see how these feature's protection level was organized by the developer's view. How we defined some permissions as

"Risky" is just a start of defining them in the user's view. In future work, some user-friendly views should be made, and we would like to categorize the views in more detail. Usability studies and empirical analysis should be conducted to fully understand the user's view. Dividing up permissions with the user's view would be another challenge coming up.

Acknowledgements. "This research was supported by the MSIT (Ministry of Science and ICT), Korea, under the ITRC (Information Technology Research Center) support program (IITP-2020-2015-0-00403) supervised by the IITP (Institute for Information &communications Technology Planning &Evaluation)"

"This study was supported by a grant of the Korean Heath Technology R&D Project, Ministry of Health and Welfare, Republic of Korea. (HI19C0866)"

References

1. Android Developers Homepage. https://developer.android.com/guide/topics/permissions/overview. Accessed 28 May 2020
2. Barrera, D., Kayacik, H.G., van Oorschot, P.C., Somayaji, A.: A methodology for empirical analysis of permission-based security models and its application to android. In: Proceedings of the 17th ACM Conference on Computer and Communications Security, CCS 2010, pp. 73–84 (2010)
3. Chin, E., Felt, A. P., Greenwood, K., Wagner, D.: Analyzing inter-application communication in Android. In Proceedings of the 9th International Conference on Mobile systems, Applications, and Services, pp. 239–252 (2011)
4. DAS, Sanmay.: Filters, wrappers and a boosting-based hybrid for feature selection. In: ICML, pp. 74–81 (2001)
5. Enck, W., Ongtang, M., McDaniel, P.: On lightweight mobile phone application certification. In Proceedings of the 16th ACM Conference on Computer and Communications Security, pp. 235–245 (2009)
6. Enck, W., Ongtang, M., McDaniel, P.: Understanding android security. IEEE Secur. Priv. **7**(1), 50–57 (2009)
7. Felt, A. P., Finifter, M., Chin, E., Hanna, S., & Wagner, D.: A survey of mobile malware in the wild. In Proceedings of the 1st ACM Workshop on Security and Privacy in Smartphones and Mobile Devices, pp. 3–14 (2011)
8. Felt, A. P., Ha, E., Egelman, S., Haney, A., Chin, E., Wagner, D.: Android permissions: user attention, comprehension, and behavior. In Proceedings of the Eighth Symposium on Usable Privacy and Security, pp. 1–14 (2012)
9. Frank, E., et al.: WEKA-a machine learning workbench for data mining. In: Maimon, O., Rokach, L. (eds.) Data Mining And Knowledge Discovery Handbook, pp. 1269–1277. Springer, Boston, MA (2009)
10. Hall, M., et al.: The WEKA data mining software: an update. ACM SIGKDD Explorations Newsletter 11.1 (2009)
11. IDC Homepage. http://www.idc.com/prodserv/smartphone-os-market-share.jsp. Accessed 02 April 2020
12. Obiri-Yeboah, J., Man, Q.: Data security of android applications. In: 2016 12th International Conference on Natural Computation, Fuzzy Systems and Knowledge Discovery (ICNC-FSKD). IEEE (2016)

13. Kononenko, I.: Estimating attributes: analysis and extensions of RELIEF. In: Bergadano, F., De Raedt, L. (eds.) ECML 1994. LNCS, vol. 784, pp. 171–182. Springer, Heidelberg (1994). https://doi.org/10.1007/3-540-57868-4_57
14. Ongtang, M., McLaughlin, S.E., Enck, W., McDaniel, P.D.: Semantically rich application-centric security in android. In: ACSAC, IEEE Computer Society, pp. 340–349 (2009)
15. Peiravian, N., Zhu, X.: Machine learning for android malware detection using permission and API calls. In: 2013 IEEE 25th International Conference on Tools with Artificial Intelligence, pp. 300–305. IEEE (2013)
16. Samira, P., et al.: A survey on deep learning: algorithms, techniques, and applications. ACM Comput. Surv. (CSUR) **51**(5), 1–36 (2018)
17. Shabtai, A., et al.: "Andromaly": a behavioral malware detection framework for android devices. J. Intell. Inf. Syst. **38**(1), 161–190 (2012)
18. Statista Homepage. https://www.statista.com/statistics/266210/number-of-available-applications-in-the-google-play-store/. Accessed 28 May 2020
19. Story, M., Congalton, R.G.: Accuracy assessment: a user's perspective. Photogramm. Eng. Rem. Sens. **52**(3), 397–399 (1986)
20. Lei, Y., Liu, H.: Feature selection for high-dimensional data: a fast correlation-based filter solution. In: Proceedings of the 20th International Conference on Machine Learning (ICML 2003), pp. 856–863 (2003)
21. Zarni Aung, W.Z.: Permission-based android malware detection. Int. J. Sci. Technol. Res. **2**(3), 228–234 (2013)

Cyber Security

Filtering-Based Correlation Power Analysis (CPA) with Signal Envelopes Against Shuffling Methods

Youngbae Jeon and Ji Won Yoon[✉]

School of Cybersecurity, Institute of Cyber Security and Privacy (ICSP),
Korea University, Seoul, South Korea
{jyb9443,jiwon_yoon}@korea.ac.kr

Abstract. The Correlation Power Analysis (CPA) is one of the powerful Side-Channel Analysis (SCA) methods to reveal the secret key using linear relationship between intermediate values and power consumption. To defense the analysis, many crypto-systems often embed the shuffling implementation which shuffles the order of operations to break the relationship between power consumption and processed information. Although the shuffling method increases the required number of power traces for deploying the CPA, it is still vulnerable if an attacker can classify or group the power traces by operations. In this work, we propose a new CPA technique by efficiently clustering the power traces using signal envelopes. We demonstrate theoretically reduced time complexity and tested our approach with the eight-shuffling AES implementations.

Keywords: Side-Channel Analysis · Correlation Power Analysis (CPA) · Shuffling method · Envelope · Clustering algorithm

1 Introduction

Nowadays many crypt-analysts use the Side-Channel Analysis (SCA) in order to reveal secret keys. The analysis does not explore the theoretical defects of cipher algorithms but analyzes side signals which can be obtained from hardware or systems. Therefore, SCA becomes a robust and practical approach to analyzing even highly secure crypto-systems which are extremely impossible to understand or break in theory.

The Correlation Power Analysis (CPA) is one of the well known SCA methods with electrical power signals [4,13,15]. In CPA, the attacker gathers a sufficient amount of power traces while randomly changing plain texts as inputs. Based on electrical power consumption model such as Hamming weight or Hamming distance, CPA estimates the power ratios between the gathered power traces for

This work was supported as part of Military Crypto Research Center (UD170109ED) funded by Defense Acquisition Program Administration (DAPA) and Agency for Defense Development (ADD).

© Springer Nature Switzerland AG 2020
I. You (Ed.): WISA 2020, LNCS 12583, pp. 389–402, 2020.
https://doi.org/10.1007/978-3-030-65299-9_29

each guessed key. By computing the correlation between estimated power ratio and gathered power traces, we can infer that the most correlated power trace is obtained from correctly guessed key [4].

Compared to the brute-force analysis, CPA does not guess the whole keys simultaneously but each single byte and this reduces the computational complexity of crypto-system. To prevent this cryptanalysis, *shuffling* techniques are used to randomize the execution time of operations to break the linear relationship between the power traces. To apply the CPA to crypto-system against *shuffling*, an attacker needs more electrical power traces than original AES implementation to deal with the noise. Let us assume that the simple crypto-system, which does not embed *shuffling* scheme, needs at least M power traces for analyzing. If $1/K$ is the probability that there exists the same operation appears in the *shuffling* based approaches, we statistically need at least MK^2 power traces [5,7,11] which make attackers to spend more time to obtain sufficient power traces to analyze the crypto-system.

However, we find that attackers can identify and analyze the used crypto-system with reduced computational complexity although the *shuffling* technique is applied. In this paper, we introduce the outline patterns of signals for identifying and analyzing the crypto-system and they are called *envelope* in signal processing domain. Using the *envelope*, we demonstrate the vulnerability of the *shuffling* approach. We show that attackers can save a lot of time to identify and analyze the crypto-system by efficiently clustering the signals with the *envelope*. Our contributions are listed as follows:

- We demonstrate that the practical execution time to analyze the *shuffling* based crypto-system is much shorter than its expected time because our proposed method reduces the minimum number of power traces from MK^2 to MK. We discovered that the power *envelope* can be used as powerful feature for distinguishing the power traces of macro-scale shuffling techniques.
- We also applied our CPA approach to the eight-shuffling AES implementations [1]. We found that the time complexity of the eight-shuffling AES implementation is reduced from $O\left(K \sum_k M_k\right)$ to $O\left(K \min(M_1, M_2, \cdots, M_K)\right)$ if our proposed SCA is used. Here, K is the number of implementations and M_i is the minimum number of power traces of the ith implementation to be analyzed.

2   Background

2.1   Correlation Coefficient

The correlation coefficient is a general method to investigate the quantitative similarity between two signals. The Pearson correlation coefficient (PCC), which normalizes the coefficient values between -1 and 1 using standard deviation, can be defined as:

$$pcc(X, Y) = \frac{E[(X - \mu_x)(Y - \mu_y)]}{\sigma_x \sigma_y} \qquad (1)$$

where X and Y are two real-valued random variables, while μ_x and μ_y are means and σ_x and σ_y are standard deviations of X and Y, respectively. The numerator of Eq. (1) is also known as covariance of X and Y. By Cauchy-Schwarz inequality, we can ensure that the PCC value always locates between -1 and 1.

2.2 Correlation Power Analysis (CPA) for AES Algorithm

The basic idea of CPA is guessing the secret key using the linear relationship between measured power traces and hypothetically expected power consumption [4]. The following procedure is the detailed explanation of exploiting the First-Order CPA to obtain the secret key ν of original AES algorithm.

- **Power traces measurement.** First of all, we measure a number of power traces $x_{n,t}$ for CPA and record them with corresponding plain texts P_n where t is the time index from 1 to T and n is the index of power traces from 1 to N. The power traces should be aligned in time sequence since CPA uses the concurrent information of power trace. The power amplitude fluctuates as the encryption module runs. The number of encryption rounds in AES can be 10, 12 or 14 which depends on key size [6]. In each round except the initial and final rounds, all *SubBytes, ShiftRows, MixColumns* and *AddRoundKey* steps are operated.
- **Power consumption model.** In the phase of *AddRoundkey*, AES performs the XOR in each byte of the plain texts and secret key [6,9], which is $P_n \oplus \nu$. Then it substitutes XOR's values with *S-box* in the phase of *SubBytes* such as $S(P_n \oplus \nu)$. At the moment the module uses this output value of *SubBytes*, we can expect the power consumption with a specific power consumption model. One of the general power consumption models is Hamming weight [4,14]. It assumes the power consumption is proportional to the number of '1's in the operating byte sequence. Let HW be a Hamming weight function which calculates the number of '1's in the byte sequence and then $HW(0xa3)$ is 4 because $0xa3 = 10100011_2$.
- **Power analysis of guessing each key.** Since all operations are byte-wise, we can estimate the power trace followed by the operation of each single byte. Firstly, we guess the ith byte of secret key ν_i from 0 to 255 and then we have the power consumption as

$$y_n^{(i)}(\nu^{(i)}) = HW(S(P_n^{(i)} \oplus \nu^{(i)})).$$

At the time of the operation of S-box, the estimated power consumption is proportional to the real power. To find the most likely correct key, we measure the correlation between estimated power consumption and actual power amplitude for each guessed key, which can be represented as $pcc(\boldsymbol{y}_{1:N}^{(i)}, \boldsymbol{x}_{1:N,t})$ where $\boldsymbol{y}_{1:N}^{(i)}(\nu^{(i)}) = [y_1^{(i)}(\nu^{(i)}), y_2^{(i)}(\nu^{(i)}), \cdots, y_N^{(i)}(\nu^{(i)})]$ and $\boldsymbol{x}_{1:N,t} = [x_{1,t}, x_{2,t}, \cdots, x_{N,t}]$.
- **Monitoring PCC values for a whole period.** In the aligned sequences of the power traces, we have to compare the estimated power ratio with actual

power ratio for all period of the sequences since the starting time of the operation is not known. Summing up, we can obtain a correct secret key by calculating the PCCs for a whole period of the sequences with each guessing key $\nu^{(i)}$, which is expressed as:

$$(\hat{\nu}^{(i)}, \hat{t}) = \arg\max_{\nu^{(i)}, t} pcc\left(\boldsymbol{y}^{(i)}(\nu^{(i)}), \boldsymbol{x}_{1:N,t}\right). \tag{2}$$

If the bytes of the key have been correctly guessed, relatively high correlation coefficient will appear at a specific time. Otherwise, we will not be able to find such trace.

If we guess the whole key of 16 bytes (128 bits) of AES algorithm, the time complexity will be 2^{128}. However, if we can guess every single byte of the key, it will decrease the time complexity to $16 \times 2^8 = 2^{12}$. To guess the key with the method, we need a sufficient number of power trace as correlation coefficient is covered by observation error. The minimum number of power traces for analyzing is considered as one of the criteria of time complexity of the CPA attack since the measuring power traces is the most laboring task [1,4].

2.3 Shuffling Techniques

As we mentioned in the previous section, the feasibility of exploiting CPA comes from linear relationship between power consumption and intermediate value. To break this linear relationship, several countermeasures appeared such as *masking* and *shuffling* [1,5,7,8,11,16,18]. Masking shades the intermediate information with other values and shuffling randomizes the execution time of functional operations. Let us assume that the *shuffling* method has K different operations with equal probability of $1/K$. It is known that at least MK^2 power traces are needed to succeed the CPA against the *shuffling* method [5,7,11], where M is the minimum number of power traces to deploy the CPA to original crypto-system.

The Eight-shuffling AES (Advanced Encryption Standard) implementations [1] is one of the shuffling methods. In the eight-shuffling AES, it executes the AES algorithm with 8 different types of implementations while operating the encryption module, which are listed in Table 1. The traces gathered from the encryption modules look different as shown in Fig. 1. The shape of traces varies as experimental setup changes.

3 Proposed Approach

In this section, we propose the efficient CPA algorithm using *envelope* to break the eight-shuffling AES implementations. In general, the traditional approach applies CPA to whole mixed-up signals. It seems like we need a myriad of power traces to reveal the secret key in the implementation but we can eventually obtain the key value in a practical time since the same types of traces will be repeatedly gathered. In spite of using whole power traces for analysis, we can classify all

Table 1. Eight-shuffling AES implementations

No	AES Implementation method	Feature
(1)	Original 1	S-Box Lookup Table 256×1
(2)	Original 2	S-Box Lookup Table 16×16
(3)	Bertoni	Suggested method by Bertoni
(4)	T-Table	The Round Transformation
(5)	Original 1 Macro	AES Original 1 Macro Implementation
(6)	Original 2 Macro	AES Original 2 Macro Implementation
(7)	Bertoni Macro	AES Bertoni Macro Implementation
(8)	T-Table Macro	AES T-Table Macro Implementation

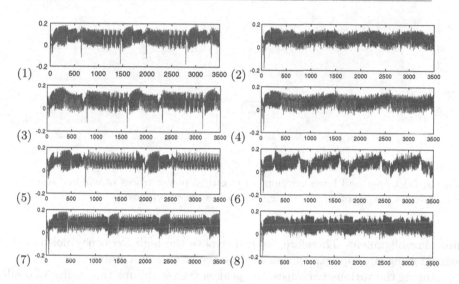

Fig. 1. Eight types of electrical power traces extracted from the eight-shuffling ΛES implementations using the experimental setup described in Sect. 4.1. Each signal from (1) to (8) is listed in Table 1, respectively.

signals which are gathered from the same implementation method. Therefore, we do not need to process the whole signals but focus to analyze only related signals which are extracted using power envelop with clustering algorithms. The overall process is well depicted in Fig. 2.

3.1 Extracting Envelopes

The *envelopes* are outlines which cover the extrema of fluctuating signal. The frequency of power signal will basically follows the clock rate of the integrated circuit. Since the signal rapidly fluctuates, measuring the similarity with the only raw signals is unstable since it is sensitive to the high frequency noise and

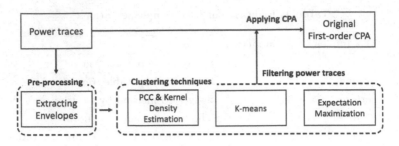

Fig. 2. Overall process of proposed approach.

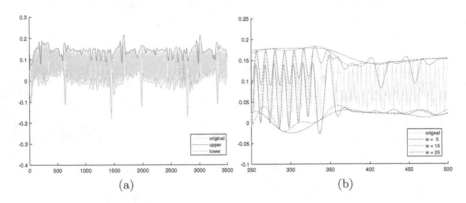

(a)   (b)

Fig. 3. (a) Upper and lower envelope of electrical power traces of window size of 16. (b) Different shapes of envelopes depend on the size of window.

fine time-alignment. Therefore, we can remove the high frequency noise of the signals using envelopes so we can analyze the signals in a stable way.

Among the various *envelope*s, the peak envelope obtains the outline of oscillating signals. It uses local maxima or minima within the given window size w. Figure 3-(a) demonstrates both upper and lower envelopes obtained from one signal. We use local maxima to find upper envelope, and local minima to get lower envelope. To extract the envelopes from original power trace, we should find peaks of each extrema and applies spline interpolation. The time indexes of the peaks from maxima and minima of the nth power trace $\mathbf{x}_{n,1:T}$ with the window size w are defined as:

$$\Gamma_{upper}(\mathbf{x}_{n,1:T}) = \{m \mid \max(x_{n,m-j}, x_{n,m-j+1}, ..., x_{n,m-j+w}) = x_{n,m}, \exists j \in W\}$$
$$\Gamma_{lower}(\mathbf{x}_{n,1:T}) = \{m \mid \min(x_{n,m-j}, x_{n,m-j+1}, ..., x_{n,m-j+w}) = x_{n,m}, \exists j \in W\}$$

where $W = \{0, 1, ...w - 1\}$ and $m = 1, 2, \cdots, T$. After extracting the upper and lower peaks, we applied cubic spline interpolation [12] to those selected peaks. Cubic spline interpolation provides the smooth curve connecting the selected peaks with third degree polynomial piecewise function $S(x)$. As the properties of cubic spline, $S(x)$ passes all peaks and $S(x)$, $S'(x)$ and $S''(x)$ are continuous for interval between all peaks points. As setting the second derivative of the first and last piece of $S(x)$ to be zero, $S(x)$ is unique which is called natural spline [12]. The upper envelope $u_t(x)$ and lower envelope $l_t(x)$ of sequence x_t at time t can be defined as $u_t(\mathbf{x}_{n,1:T}) = S(\Gamma_{upper}(\mathbf{x}_{n,1:T}))$, and $l_t(\mathbf{x}_{n,1:T}) = S(\Gamma_{lower}(\mathbf{x}_{n,1:T}))$.

3.2   Filtering Power Traces

If the attacker can classify the power traces, the expected time complexity of CPA can be significantly reduced. Considering current shuffling techniques use big number of K [7], reduced amount of time complexity can be regarded as quite critical issue. To filter/group the whole power traces from the same implementation method, we need to measure the similarities. There are two scenarios depending on whether the number of implementation methods is known or not. If we do not know the number of implementation methods K, we choose any power trace from a specific implementation method and refine the other power traces which seemed to be gathered from the same implementation method. Kernel Density Estimation (KDE) is one of the possible methods for this case which is well described in Sect. 3.2. However, if K is known, we can directly apply the parametric clustering algorithms to envelopes, such as K-means and Expectation-Maximization (EM) algorithm, which is described in Sect. 3.2.

Kernel Density Estimation (KDE) with PCC. Clustering with the kernel density estimation (KDE) [17] method is based on measuring similarities between traces. First, we choose a power trace as a template signal for classification. As we mentioned in Sect. 2.1, we can estimate the similarities between the power traces from the chosen implementation method and those from the other implementation methods by calculating PCCs of envelopes. That is, we can define the similarity between two aligned signals $\boldsymbol{x}$ and $\boldsymbol{y}$ as

$$d_{sim}(\boldsymbol{x}, \boldsymbol{y}) = \frac{pcc(u(\boldsymbol{x}), u(\boldsymbol{y})) + pcc(l(\boldsymbol{x}), l(\boldsymbol{y}))}{2}.$$

where $u(\cdot)$ and $l(\cdot)$ are the whole upper and lower envelops of the given signal respectively. As the result of pcc is locating in range from -1 to 1, the two metrics of similarity are scalar values between -1 and 1. The higher value indicates the target signal has higher probability of being extracted from same implementation method.

With these calculated one-dimensional similarity scores of length N, we can set the threshold and classify the target trace. To decide the threshold, we estimate the probability density with KDE and use derivative to find the local minimum. KDE uses specific kernel function ϕ such as normal distribution or rectangle. Those functions have their bandwidth, which are standard deviation and width of rectangle respectively. For the ith data $\mathbf{x}^{(i)}$, probability density function $p(\mathbf{x})$ can be estimated by summing all the kernel function of mean of $\mathbf{x}^{(i)}$ and given bandwidth, which is $\sum_i^N \phi(\mathbf{x} - \mathbf{x}^{(i)})$. The only parameter which decides the shape of the $p(\mathbf{x})$ is the bandwidth. Low bandwidth makes $p(\mathbf{x})$ rough

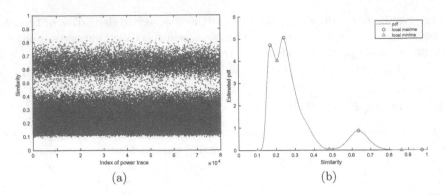

(a)   (b)

Fig. 4. (a) Similarity scores obtained from envelope between the power trace from *Bertoni Macro* method and others. (b) Estimated probability density function by adaptive KDE.

and empirical, and high bandwidth makes it smooth and conjectural. Moreover, optimal bandwidth can be chosen by minimizing the expected integrated squared error of $\mathbf{x}^{(i)}$ [3]. Figure 4-(a) is the similarity scores between an envelope from *Bertoni Macro* and rest of the traces. With normal distribution kernel function and optimally obtained bandwidth, we can obtain the probability distribution as Fig. 4-(b). As shown in the figure, we can observe a few local minima and maxima. We can simply infer that the biggest local minimum value cannot be appropriate as plotted in Fig. 4-(b) so we choose the threshold which takes a sufficient number of power traces as 1% of the total number of traces.

K-Means. K-means algorithm is a well-known clustering approach using similarity with K centroids when the number of cluster K is known [2]. As the high frequency noise in the original power traces is removed by extracting envelope, we can use the envelope data itself rather than raw power traces. K-means searches for the optimal solutions to find appropriate clusters by minimizing the sum of all distances between the means of the clusters and the assigned data. It initially sets K random centroids of clusters. Then, all data are assigned to the closest cluster. For all data in each assumed cluster, we calculate the means of the clusters again and reassign the data to the newly calculated cluster, and repeat these tasks iteratively. Finally, K-means searches for the optimal K clusters until the number of iteration reaches the configured maximum number, which is 1000 in this work. To measure similarity, we use $1 - pcc(\mathbf{c}_k, \mathbf{x}_{n,1:T})$ as distance metric, where $\mathbf{c}_k$ is the centroid of the kth cluster and $\mathbf{x}_{n,1:T}$ is the nth power trace.

Expectation-Maximization (EM) Algorithm. Expectation-Maximization (EM) algorithm for Gaussian mixture model is based on maximum likelihood estimation [2]. Similar to K-means algorithm, EM assumes the parameters for clusters and update the parameters to find a optimal solutions of clusters by maximizing the sum of log likelihood. While K-means algorithm only uses the distances between the means of clusters and involved data, EM uses the prior, mean and covariance which has higher computational cost. As we also use the envelope itself as a data to find a cluster, the nearby data point on the envelopes are correlated each other. Thus, we can expect the higher performance of clustering than K-means algorithm.

4   Evaluation

4.1   Experimental Setup

We use CW1173 Chip Whisperer Lite board for extracting power trace. It is generally used for side-channel analysis. It is based on FPGA and uses AVR/Xmega programming. The power traces are extracted by Chip Whisperer Capture V2 and sampling rate is 7.38 MS/s. We measure the power trace for 2 or 3 rounds of each AES, and the number of collected power traces was 80,000. Each traces have 3,500 points with about 0.47 ms long. To analyze the performance of our proposed method, we used the computer equipped with Intel(R) Xeon(R) CPU E5-2609 0 @ 2.40 GHz, 32 GB RAM, and Ubuntu 18.04 LTS (64-bit) operating system. We used MATLAB as a programming language. Any multiprocessing or parallelization techniques are not used. We apply our proposed approaches into Eight Shuffling AES implementation.

4.2   Filtering Performance

As we mentioned in Sect. 3.2, we filtered the power traces with three different clustering algorithms (KDE, K-means and EM clustering) with envelopes. Total 80,000 power traces are used to evaluate the filtering performance. We extract the envelopes from all power traces with a fixed window size ($w = 16$). We picked sample template traces in each algorithm. Based on chosen template traces, we applied our three different filtering methods and measure precision, recall and accuracy. We repeat this whole process 30 times and calculate the mean of obtained those metrics.

Table 2 demonstrates the results of our proposed approaches with the power traces which are generated from the 8-shuffling AES implementations. Compared to other filtering methods, KDE is deterministic since we fixed the bandwidth of the kernel. Other algorithms have several probabilistic factors such as random initial means and covariances. Thus, we repeated evaluation process for those algorithms and averaged. First of all, KDE has roughly high performance of precision while recall is relatively low for *Original 1* and *T-Table*. Meanwhile, K-means and EM algorithm have relatively high recall. Since the distance of power trace gathered from *Original 2* and *T-Table* is close to each other, it is hard to distinguish the two power traces. It is obvious that the appropriate method for each implementation is different so we need to select proper approach to obtain high precision and recall. For all implementation methods, at least one filtering method exists that can have perfect precision and recall. Furthermore, t-Distributed Stochastic Neighbor Embedding (t-SNE) [10] shows the distances of raw traces and envelopes between them as we can see in Fig. 5. We can also observe the effect of envelope which removes the high frequency components and makes signals from the same implementation method to get closer.

Table 2. Precision, recall and accuracy of three filtering methods (KDE, K-means, EM) using envelopes conduct on the implementation method of eight-shuffling AES.

Implementation Method	KDE			K-means			EM		
	Prec.	Rec.	Acc.	Prec.	Rec.	Acc.	Prec.	Rec.	Acc.
Original 1	1.0000	0.4406	0.9299	1.0000	1.0000	1.0000	0.7991	1.0000	0.9494
Original 2	1.0000	1.0000	1.0000	1.0000	1.0000	1.0000	0.6178	1.0000	0.8498
Bertoni	1.0000	1.0000	1.0000	1.0000	0.4481	0.9318	0.7649	1.0000	0.9244
T-Table	1.0000	1.0000	1.0000	1.0000	1.0000	1.0000	0.5334	1.0000	0.8493
Original 1 Macro	1.0000	1.0000	1.0000	1.0000	0.5796	0.9483	1.0000	0.8968	0.9873
Original 2 Macro	1.0000	1.0000	1.0000	0.4983	1.0000	0.8736	0.8004	0.9080	0.9384
Bertoni Macro	0.9999	0.9768	0.9971	1.0000	1.0000	1.0000	1.0000	0.8255	0.9784
T-Table	1.0000	0.4626	0.9318	1.0000	1.0000	1.0000	0.8866	0.6211	0.9268

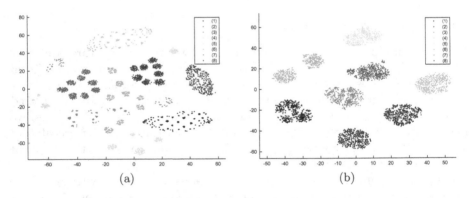

(a)   (b)

Fig. 5. t-SNE results of 8,000 samples of (a) original power traces and (b) upper envelopes of window size 15, gathered from eight-shuffling AES implementations. The data labels from (1) to (8) are listed in in Table 1. The figure is best viewed in color. (Color figure online)

4.3   CPA Performance

To compare the CPA performance of our approach to original CPA for eight-shuffling AES algorithm, we first measure the required minimum number of power traces for the original CPA, which is well depicted as Fig. 6. The metrics for measuring CPA is accuracy, which is the ratio of the number of two correct

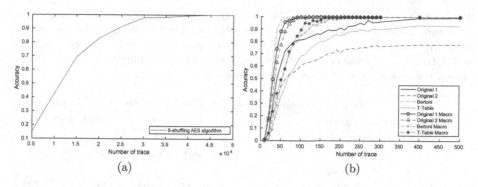

Fig. 6. Accuracy of First-order CPA vs The used number of power traces of (a) eight-shuffling AES and (b) each of the implementation method in eight-shuffling AES.

bytes of guessed key to those of real secret key. To obtain the valid results, we repeat the test for 30 times and take the average of all accuracy. Since we can use more power correlation information from the large number of power traces, the accuracy increases as the number of power trace increases. To obtain high accuracy applying only CPA to whole mixed-up power traces, we need at least 45,000 power traces as we can see in Fig. 6-(a). Meanwhile, if we apply the CPA to perfectly refined power traces for each implementation method, we can dramatically reduce the required number of power traces as shown in Fig. 6-(b) and column *pure* in Table 3. It is ideal to be perfectly refined that the wrong power traces are not mixed up among the analyzed traces and also any power trace is not excluded from analyzed traces. The minimum numbers of power traces in ideal case for each implementation method are also written in Table 3 in column *ideal*, which is simple 8 times to *pure* column since the probability of each implementation appearance is equally distributed which is 1/8.

To measure the performance of ours, we filtered the power traces with our three approaches for each target implementation and applies CPA to refined power traces. We also repeat the procedure 30 times. The evaluation results for our approaches are filled in Table 3. Corresponding to Table 2, the accuracy of CPA is high as the filtering performance increases. We can also see how much precision and recall affects to the CPA performance by comparing the performances conduct on each approach. Observing the cases of perfect precision and low recall such as *Original 1* of *KDE*, we can infer that the CPA performances are dropped in inverse proportioned to recall. The performance drop is due to the shuffling complexity, which makes the probability of certain power traces lower. While low recall drops the probability of appearance, precision pollute the power traces with those from the other implementation method which can be inferred in case of *Original 2* of *K-means*. However, we could see the huge performance improvement compared to the only CPA. We could also obtain the sufficiently low complexity for each implementation method using at least one approach compared to ideal case when the traces are perfectly refined.

Table 3. The minimum numbers of power trace for analyzing eight-shuffling AES algorithm in our approaches and ideal case. The hyphen (-) indicates the case which needs the power traces more than 45,000 or cannot be analyzed with one round of power traces. The numbers of bold face indicate the lowest number of power traces among the clustering algorithms for exploiting CPA.

	Target implementation method	KDE	K-means	EM	ideal	pure
Proposed approach	Original 1	15,000	5,000	**4,200**	4,800	600
	Original 2	–	–	–	–	–
	Bertoni	**600**	1,500	700	560	70
	T-Table	–	–	–	–	–
	Original 1 Macro	1,000	1,500	**900**	800	100
	Original 2 Macro	1,000	–	**900**	880	110
	Bertoni Macro	**2,400**	**2,400**	**2,400**	2,240	280
	T-Table Macro	3,300	1,800	**1,400**	1,760	220
Original First-Order CPA			45,000			

5   Discussion

We showed that our approach can extremely reduce the required minimum number of power traces against shuffling from MK^2 to MK. Our approaches can be used even when we do not know the number of implementation methods. The *shuffling* techniques are commonly used to avoid the vulnerability from CPA since it have relatively low cost for computation compared to *masking* techniques. In this case, the filtering techniques using envelopes and several clustering algorithms simply exploits the shuffling algorithm.

In case of the eight-shuffling AES implementation, each implementation has different required number of power traces. In addition, it is known that the 8-shuffling AES implementation has complexity with $O\left(\frac{\sum_{k=1}^{K} M_k}{K} K^2\right) = O\left(K \sum_{k=1}^{K} M_k\right)$. However, as we can observe from the experiment, if an attacker can effectively distinguish and group the power traces, the complexity significantly decreased to $O\left(K \min(M_1, M_2, \cdots, M_k, \cdots, M_K)\right)$ where M_k is the minimum number of power trace to analyze the kth implementation. The vulnerability is derived from the exposure of the weakest implementation among the shuffled operations.

6   Conclusion

In this paper, we proposed a novel technique to exploit the vulnerability of the shuffling technique by using envelopes and clustering algorithms. The main idea of our proposed approaches is to refine the power traces gathered from the target implementation to reduce the minimum number of power traces to apply CPA. We used the envelopes to avoid and filter the high frequency noise. In addition, we found that the envelops is robust to temporal lags and it results in raising the filtering performance. The proposed approach can be easily used in the case where the number of implementation methods is known. However, even in case the number is not known, we can still use our proposed algorithm in non-parametric way.

With our approach, the required minimum number of power trace can be reduced from MK^2 to MK. Especially for eight-shuffling AES implementations, it decreases from $K \sum_{k=1}^{K} M_k$ to $K \min(M_1, M_2, \cdots, M_K)$. For shuffling implementations to be used safely, we recommend to use implementations with sufficiently high complexity for the shuffling technique for the attacker not to group the power traces.

References

1. Baek, S.S., Won, Y.S., Han, D.G., Ryou, J.C.: The effect of eight-shuffling AES implementations techniques against side channel analysis. Indian J. Sci. Technol. **8**, 91 (2015)
2. Bishop, C.M.: Pattern Recognition and Machine Learning. Springer, Heidelberg (2006)
3. Bowman, A.W., Azzalini, A.: Applied Smoothing Techniques for Data Analysis: The Kernel Approach with S-Plus Illustrations, vol. 18. OUP Oxford, Oxford (1997)
4. Brier, E., Clavier, C., Olivier, F.: Correlation power analysis with a leakage model. In: Joye, M., Quisquater, J.-J. (eds.) CHES 2004. LNCS, vol. 3156, pp. 16–29. Springer, Heidelberg (2004). https://doi.org/10.1007/978-3-540-28632-5_2
5. Clavier, C., Coron, J.-S., Dabbous, N.: Differential power analysis in the presence of hardware countermeasures. In: Koç, Ç.K., Paar, C. (eds.) CHES 2000. LNCS, vol. 1965, pp. 252–263. Springer, Heidelberg (2000). https://doi.org/10.1007/3-540-44499-8_20
6. FIPS, P.: 197: Advanced Encryption Standard (AES). National Institute of Standards and Technology 26 (2001)
7. Herbst, C., Oswald, E., Mangard, S.: An AES smart card implementation resistant to power analysis attacks. In: Zhou, J., Yung, M., Bao, F. (eds.) ACNS 2006. LNCS, vol. 3989, pp. 239–252. Springer, Heidelberg (2006). https://doi.org/10.1007/11767480_16
8. Kocher, P., Jaffe, J., Jun, B.: Differential power analysis. In: Wiener, M. (ed.) CRYPTO 1999. LNCS, vol. 1666, pp. 388–397. Springer, Heidelberg (1999). https://doi.org/10.1007/3-540-48405-1_25
9. Lo, O., Buchanan, W.J., Carson, D.: Power analysis attacks on the AES-128 s-box using differential power analysis (DPA) and correlation power analysis (CPA). J. Cyber Secur. Technol. **1**(2), 88–107 (2017)
10. Maaten, L.V.D., Hinton, G.: Visualizing data using t-SNE. J. Mach. Learn. Res. **9**(Nov), 2579–2605 (2008)
11. Mangard, S.: Hardware countermeasures against DPA–a statistical analysis of their effectiveness. In: Okamoto, T. (ed.) Hardware countermeasures against dpa-a statistical analysis of their effectiveness. LNCS, vol. 2964, pp. 222–235. Springer, Heidelberg (2004). https://doi.org/10.1007/978-3-540-24660-2_18
12. McKinley, S., Levine, M.: Cubic spline interpolation. Coll. Redwoods **45**(1), 1049–1060 (1998)

13. Messerges, T.S.: Using second-order power analysis to attack DPA resistant software. In: Koç, Ç.K., Paar, C. (eds.) Using second-order power analysis to attack dpa resistant software. LNCS, vol. 1965, pp. 238–251. Springer, Heidelberg (2000). https://doi.org/10.1007/3-540-44499-8_19

14. Messerges, T.S., Dabbish, E.A., Sloan, R.H.: Investigations of power analysis attacks on smartcards. Smartcard **99**, 151–161 (1999)

15. Moradi, A., Mischke, O., Eisenbarth, T.: Correlation-enhanced power analysis collision attack. In: Mangard, S., Standaert, F.-X. (eds.) CHES 2010. LNCS, vol. 6225, pp. 125–139. Springer, Heidelberg (2010). https://doi.org/10.1007/978-3-642-15031-9_9

16. Rivain, M., Prouff, E.: Provably secure higher-order masking of AES. In: Mangard, S., Standaert, F.-X. (eds.) CHES 2010. LNCS, vol. 6225, pp. 413–427. Springer, Heidelberg (2010). https://doi.org/10.1007/978-3-642-15031-9_28

17. Silverman, B.W.: Density Estimation for Statistics and Data Analysis. Routledge, Melbourne (2018)

18. Veyrat-Charvillon, N., Medwed, M., Kerckhof, S., Standaert, F.-X.: Shuffling against side-channel attacks: a comprehensive study with cautionary note. In: Wang, X., Sako, K. (eds.) ASIACRYPT 2012. LNCS, vol. 7658, pp. 740–757. Springer, Heidelberg (2012). https://doi.org/10.1007/978-3-642-34961-4_44

Security Problems of 5G Voice Communication

Seongmin Park[1], HyungJin Cho[1], Youngkwon Park[1], Bomin Choi[1],
Dowon Kim[1], and Kangbin Yim[2(✉)]

[1] Korea Internet & Security Agency, Seoul, Korea
{smpark,hjcho86,young6874,bmchoi,kimdw}@kisa.or.kr
[2] Department of Information Security Engineering,
Soonchunhyang University, Asan, Korea
yim@sch.ac.kr

Abstract. In April 2019, the world's first 5G mobile communication was commercialized in South Korea. 5G mobile communication aims to provide 20 Gbps transmission speed which is 20 times faster than 4G mobile communication, connection of at least 1 million devices per 1 km^2, and 1 ms transmission delay which is 10 times shorter than 4G. To meet this, various technological developments were required, and various technologies such as Massive MIMO (Multiple-Input and Multiple-Output), mmWave, and small cell network were developed and applied in the area of 5G access network. However, in the core network area, the components constituting the LTE (Long Term Evolution) core network are utilized as they are in the NSA(Non-Standalone) architecture, and only the changes in the SA(Standalone) architecture have occurred. Also, in the network area for providing the voice service, the IMS (IP Multimedia Subsystem) infrastructure is still used in the SA architecture. Here, the issue is that while 5G mobile communication is evolving openly to provide various services, security elements are vulnerable to various cyber-attacks because they maintain the same form as before. Therefore, in this paper, we will look at what the network standard for 5G voice service provision consists of, and what are the vulnerable problems in terms of security. We also want to consider whether these problems can actually occur and what is the countermeasure.

Keywords: 5G Voice communication · Voice over 5G · Mobile network · IMS · SIP · 5G Security

1 Introduction

In April 2019, the world's first 5G mobile communication was commercialized in South Korea. 5G mobile communication aims to provide 20 Gbps transmission speed which is 20 times faster than 4G mobile communication, connection of at least 1 million devices per 1 km^2, and 1 ms transmission delay which is 10 times shorter than 4G. To meet this, various technological developments were

I. You (Ed.): WISA 2020, LNCS 12583, pp. 403–415, 2020.
https://doi.org/10.1007/978-3-030-65299-9_30

required, and various technologies such as Massive MIMO (Multiple-Input and Multiple-Output), mmWave, and small cell network were developed and applied in the area of 5G access network.

Meanwhile, the voice service of the conventional mobile communication network was provided using circuit switch-based network (2G and 3G), and the packet switch-based network at the time was used for data communication purposes and from the 4th generation mobile communication, it began to provide voice services with packet switch-based network by supporting the ALL-IP structure of the mobile communication network. The 4th generation mobile communication voice service based on VoIP(Voice over IP) is called VoLTE(Voice over LTE) and currently provides stable voice service in 4th generation mobile communication.

As the competition for commercialization of 5G mobile communication has been increasing, voice services in 5G mobile communication are expected to be commercialized soon. Voice service in 5th generation mobile communication is called Vo5G(Voice over 5G), and it uses VoIP related technologies such as VoLTE. VoIP is widely used through online voice chat, internet phone, and mobile communication voice services. Research on related vulnerabilities has been actively conducted since long time ago and security measures have been developed [8–14].

VoIP is also used in 5G mobile communication, and 3GPP(Third Generation Partnership Project) has defined security measures for mobile communication networks and voice services. However, despite the definition of security measures in the standard, there may be still vulnerabilities caused by implementation errors, and occurred by the non-forced security items in the standard and the resulting loose security level. In this paper, we examine the security vulnerability of SIP(Session Initiation Protocol)/RTP(Real-Time Transport Protocol) according to the application of mobile voice service in traditional VoIP and security vulnerability according to non-forced security items in the standard from three perspectives. First, SIP protocol, which is a representative session control protocol of VoIP, allows easy manipulation of headers based on text. Second, the traffic of the RTP protocol, which is a data transmission protocol of VoIP, is easy to be reproduced. Third, in the 3GPP standard, LTE or 5G voice communication is defined to be encrypted through IPSec(IP Security), but it is defined as a non-forced item and can be selectively operated as required by the manufacturer or carrier. Therefore, we want to check whether there are any vulnerabilities that can occur based on these weaknesses, and to find out the countermeasures.

In this regard, Sect. 2 in this paper examines the standards and status related to 5G mobile communication. Section 3 identifies problems related to 5G voice service and presents test methods. Section 4 tries to derive problems based on the test results. Section 5 proposes countermeasures to problems. The final Sect. 6 makes a conclusion.

2 Mobile Communication Network Standards and Status

2.1 5G Mobile Communication Network Status

5G mobile communication network is a next generation mobile communication technology led by 3GPP standardization group. Currently, technology competition for 5G commercialization is actively taking place worldwide, and 5G mobile communication service to public is in progress, starting with commercialization services in China, Korea, the United States, and Japan in 2019 [1]. Starting from the NSA structure, the 5G mobile communication network is currently commercializing the SA structure (see Fig. 1). When it is commercialized, the 5G voice communication might be serviced by 5GC(5G Core) which is the SA core network and is called Vo5G [5] (see Fig. 2).

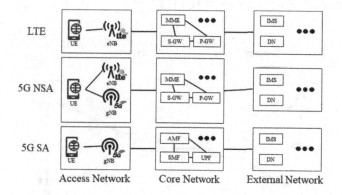

Fig. 1. Evolution of 5G mobile communication network (Simplification)

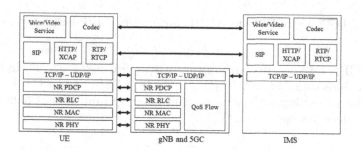

Fig. 2. 5GC Vo5G Protocol Stack

2.2   3GPP IMS Security Standard

In 3GPP, IMS security standards specify security-related matters in TS 33.210, TS 33.328, and TS 33.203 standard documents. In 3GPP, the IPSec-based security mechanism is applied all control plane IP communication to the external network through the Security Gateway (SEG). IPSec has so many options, therefore it is difficult to provide full interoperability, and the options of IPSec has reduced in 3GPP. Communication with the different network domain is performed through SEG, and the Za interface, which is an external network connection section, must be implemented with IPSec, and is optional in the Zb interface which is an internal network connection section. In the Zb interface, authentication must always be provided, but encryption is optional (see Fig. 3). In addition to Z-interface, the Gm interface is defined as interface of UE and P-CSCF of IMS. In case of the Gm interface, use of IPsec is not depends on network domain but local policy of the P-CSCF.

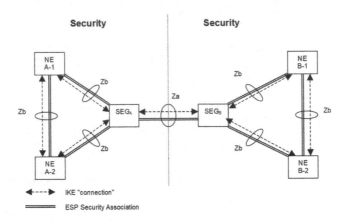

Fig. 3. NDS(Network Domain Security) architecture for IP-based protocols. [4]

The 3GPP IMS security architecture is specified in TS 33.203. In the IMS security architecture, four entities (UE, P-CSCF, I-CSCF, and S-CSCF) interact and aim for subscriber authentication and integrity protection. Confidentiality protection does not apply to IMS [2,3].

2.3   SIP/RTP Protocol

The SIP protocol is defined in IETF(Internet Engineering Task Force) RFC(Request for Comments) 3261 [6] and is an application layer signaling protocol. The 3GPP standard has been adopted in the IMS(IP Multimedia Subsystem) architecture since November 2000 and is still in use. The RTP protocol is a protocol for end-to-end, real-time transmission of streaming media and is defined in IETF RFC 3550 [7], and is used for the purpose of voice data transmission with SIP protocol in mobile communication networks.

The SIP protocol is a text-based message, and the SIP message format consists of Starting Line, Header Field, Separator, and Message Body. For basic SIP session connection, when the caller sends an Invitation message, the Callee responds with 100 Trying, 180 Ringing, and 200 OK messages. When the caller sends an ACK message, a session is established and voice data is exchanged. When the call ends, the callee sends a BYE message, and the caller responds with a 200 OK message [6] (see Fig. 4). Voice data is transmitted through RTP which is for real-time delivery and multitasking [7].

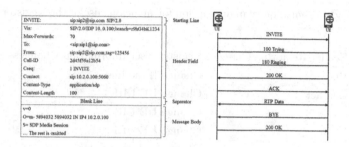

Fig. 4. SIP Message Format and SIP Call Flow

3 Problems and Test Methods

3.1 Related Work

Several related studies have been conducted about VoIP and SIP attacks and countermeasures. For example, there are billing bypass [8], man-in-the-middle attack [9], and authentication neutralization [10]. If 5G mobile communication using SIP/RTP protocol was not considered, these attacks could also be a potential threat to Vo5G.

According to the VoLTE attack paper published in CCS'15 ACM, attacks such as DoS(Denial of Service), overcharge, free video calls, and sender forgery are possible through the VoLTE hidden channel [14].

In 5G mobile communication, voice calls are supported in the form of Vo5G. If Vo5G is implemented without complementing VoLTE-related attacks, these attacks can be a potential threat in Vo5G.

3.2 Problems of 5G Voice Communication (The Proposed Approach)

This section shows the problem of IMS, a network that provides 5G voice communication. The problems of the IMS standard can be divided into three categories.

Easy Manipulation of Text-Based SIP Protocol Headers. The SIP packet has a header name and a header value in text format, so a malicious attacker can easily change the text if desired. In particular, the Initial Register message for registering a user device on the IMS server is delivered before the encryption setting even if it uses IPSec encryption, so it can be easily obtained through a packet dump on the device. Among them, an attacker can manipulate several header values to change the information of the user who delivers the message. The headers of Contact, To, From, and Authorization can be changed to the subject's IMSI or URI, and the Expire value can be changed to set up or cancel the registration (see Table 1).

Table 1. Headers that require manipulation for malicious use of the Register message.

Header Requiring Change	Register User Information Changes
Via	Change IP address
Contact	Change UE URI
To	Change UE URI
From	Change UE URI
Cseq	Change to higher value
Expires	Change to 3600 or 0
Authorization	IMSI or UE Calling Number

Subscribe messages used to provide real-time PTT(Push to Talk) services, such as RCS(Rich Communication Services) services, can also be used maliciously. Like the Register, the Subscribe message requires the manipulation of several header values to change user information (see Table 2).

Table 2. Headers needed to change user information in Subscribe message.

Header Requiring Change	Subscribe User Information Changes
Request URI	Change IP address
Via	Change IP address
Contact	Change UE URI
To	Change UE URI
From	Change UE URI
Cseq	Change to higher value
P-Preferred-Identity	IMSI or UE Calling Number

Easy Reproduction of RTP Traffic. RTP traffic is exposed through sniffing when SRTP(Secure Real-time Transport Protocol) is not used. The exposed RTP traffic can be reproduced through Wireshark. When going to the RTP, RTP Streams menu on the Telephony tab, information about RTP packets is summarized and displayed. If you request Analyze by selecting the desired source and destination, you can show the Stream Analysis result between specific peers and request Play Streams. Wireshark can output audio for PCMU(Pulse Code Modulation Mu-Law)/PCMA(Pulse Code Modulation A-Law) codec and for AMR(Adaptive Multi-Rate) or AMR-WB(Adaptive Multi-Rate Wideband) codec, a separate program is required together with file dump. File dumps can be created using tshark -nr rtp.pcap -R rtp -T fields -e rtp.payload, and audio playback can be played through AMRPlayer [15].

Non-mandatory for IPSec Encryption. As described above, the interface for using IPSec SAs(Security Associations) is divided into Gm interface and Z-interface. The Za interface is used for different network domain entities, therefore the use of IPSec is mandatory in the Za interface. The Zb interface is used for same network domain entities, therefore the use of IPSec is optional in the Zb interface. In 3GPP, the use of IPSec on Za is defined as mandatory, while reducing the range of options related to IPSec configuration to ensure compatibility. In this case, the operation mode is divided into transport and tunnel mode. In the case of using the tunneling mode, the entire original IP packet can be encrypted to maintain the confidentiality of the origin and destination. However, IPs of two IPSec VPN(Virtual Private Network) Nodes are exposed through the new IP header. In the transmission mode, only data is encrypted, and confidentiality of the traffic flow is not provided (see Table 3).

Table 3. Requirements on Za interface for IPSec SAs settings for 5G voice communication.

Requirements	Setting value
Protocol (prot)	Use EPS only
Operation mode (mod)	Always use Tunnel Mode
Integrity Algorithm	HMAC-SHA-1
Encryption Algorithm	3DES

In the Zb interface, the process for using IPSec in a 5G voice service terminal is as follows. First, in order to use IPSec, the device inserts the Security-Client header with the Require header and sends it to the first Register message. The Require header is a request for the use of IPSec encryption, and the Security-Client header contains configuration requests for setting various IPSec encryption (see Table 4).

However, in the Gm interface, whether UE and P-CSCF is in the same network domain or not, the use of IPSec is depends on local policy of the P-CSCF.

Table 4. Requirements on Zb interface for IPSec SAs settings for 5G voice communication.

Requirements	Setting value
Protocol (prot)	EPS
Operation mode (mod)	Transport
spi-c, port-c	Client Index & Port Number
spi-s, port-s	Server Index & Port Number
Integrity Algorithm	HMAC-MD5-96 or HMAC-SHA-1-96
Encryption Algorithm	AES-CBC or AES-GCM

Therefore, if the IMS uses IPSec on Gm interface as optional, even if an UE located in different network domain is registered to IMS without using IPSec at the device, communication is performed in decrypted text if authentication is made [4].

3.3   Test Method (Implementation)

The IMS network that provides 5G voice communication supports IPSec and uses the IPSec mechanism for user registration of the device. If IPSec is not used, it can be very vulnerable to threats such as Rogue base stations, and it is possible to manipulate the outgoing number by capturing SIP messages that communicate in plain text. 5G Android devices released so far have been developed to use IPSec, and if you dump the packet of the device, you can see that in addition to the first Register message and 401 Un-authorization message. And next messages are encrypted using IPSec ESP(Encapsulating Security Payload). However, there is a hidden menu for developers on the device to disable IPSec SAs and communicate without that. We tested using the representative 5G device, Galaxy S10, and the test devices used are as follows (see Table 5).

Table 5. Security Testing device information for 5G Voice Communication

Testing Components	Components Details
Test device	Galaxy S10 (SM-G977N)
Android OS version	9(Pie)
Kernel version	4.14.85

IPSec Disable. When accessing the hidden menu of the test device, there is a 'VoLTE Settings' menu, and there are context menus that can change the IMS service settings of the device. Among them, if you access the 'VoLTE Profile' by entering the 'IMS Profile' setting, there is SIP menu with CSCF(Call Session

Control Function) settings. In the SIP menu, there are sub-menus for setting the SIP port, IP version, etc. Among them, you can see that the option, Enable IPSec is checked. If you disable this option and reboot the device, the setting is completed.

Packet Sniffing. When the IPSec disabling process of the device is finished, procedure for sniffing the terminal packet should be performed. Packets can be sniffed with tcpdump from the device and must be rooted in advance. The rooting process using Odin is divided into 4 steps. The first step is to prepare for rooting. Download and install and run the Magisk Manager app on the device. The second is the Un-LOCK stage of the bootloader, which unlocks OEM(Original Equipment Manufacturing) lock in the developer options of the device. The third step is to install custom recovery. Flashing the device through Odin program and installing custom recovery. Last step is acquiring root authority. Afer factory reset in recovery mode, the root authority is acquired using the Magisk patch created using the Magisk Manager app. Linux OS and open sources such as tcpdump were installed on the rooted device as follows (see Table 6).

Table 6. Installation elements on Security Testing device for 5G Voice Communication

Installed Components	Components Details
Linux OS	Distributor ID: Ubuntu
	Description: Ubuntu 16.04 LTS
	Release: 16.04
	Codename: xenial
tcpdump	4.7.4
libpcap	1.7.4
OpenSSL	1.0.2 g

Packet Analysis. Dumped packets from the device can be analyzed by moving to PC. Wireshark is used, and the header value inside the SIP packet can be checked through SIP filtering. We conducted this process using two Operators' USIM(Universal Subscriber Identify Module)s and compared the differences.

4 Test Results and Problem Identification

Test Result. Packets can be captured by using tcpdump in the environment where the device is rooted. When the captured packets are checked with Wireshark, SIP messages and RTP traffic in plain text can be viewed.

As a result of testing the USIMs of the two operators, IPSec is disabled when using the first Operator(A)'s USIM, and it is decrypted. However, when using the

USIM of the other Operator(B), IPSec is not disabled, and voice communication is performed with encryption even though we set off for the IPSec configuration on the testing devices.

Comparing the packets for the two Operators' USIMs, you can see that the Initial Register message is different. In the case of Operator A (see Fig. 5), there is no Require, Supported and Security-Client header in the Initial Register message, and if you send a SIP message, you can see that it is sent in plain text.

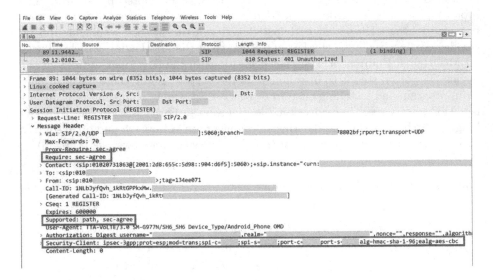

Fig. 5. SIP decryption testing on IPSec disabled device with Operator A's USIM.

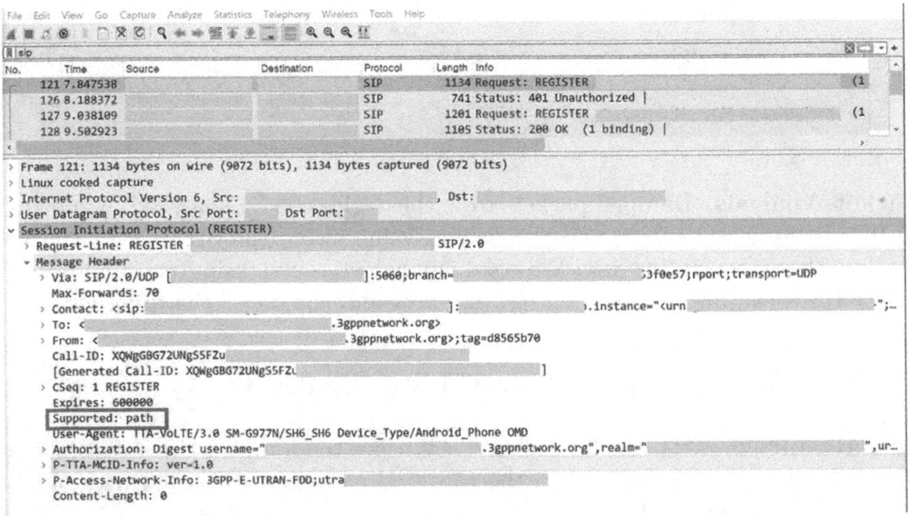

Fig. 6. SIP decryption testing on IPSec disabled device with Operator B's USIM.

However, in the case of Operator B (see Fig. 6), you can clearly see that Require, Supported and Security-Client headers were added to the Initial Register message and transmitted. Which means, when using B Operator's USIM, it can be assumed that security settings for use in 5G voice communication are obtained from the network, not from the device. A packet captured in the test using Operator A's USIM can be altered using open source such as HxD. In addition, by using an open source such as sendip, it is possible to generate a threat such as forgery of the originating number by sending an altered packet (see Table 7).

Table 7. Characteristics of 5G Voice Communication on tested Operators.

Type	Operator A	Operator B
Network Protocol	IPv6	IPv6
Transport protocol	UDP	UDP
Use of IPSec	V	V
Integrity Algorithm	AES-CBC	AES-CBC
Encryption Algorithm	HMAC-SHA-1-96	HMAC-SHA-1-96
IPSec disable by UE	V	X

5 Countermeasures

There are various ways to respond to these threats. We considered approach to countermeasures for 5G Voice Security Threats at total of four levels.

Countermeasures at Security Appliance Level. You can think of introducing physical system such as IPS(Intrusion Prevention System) at the security device level. Packets flowing into the core network are monitored using a dedicated IPS capable to detect voice communication protocol such as SIP or RTP, and then detected and blocked in the case of an attacking or manipulated packet. Depending on the policy, it may be possible to alert the operator after detection without blocking it immediately to secure the availability of the voice service. However, in this case, the cost of investing in security equipment will be considerable and the efficiency of the investment must be considered.

Countermeasures at IMS Server Level. Among the IMS servers, CSCF or SBC(Session Border Controller) might be able to play a role of SEG. When manipulating SIP packets by disabling IPSec, CSCF or SBC can be supplemented to go through the verification procedure on the mismatch between the IP of the terminal and the manipulated field value, and the manipulated packet would be able to be blocked. In this case, there is no need to invest in additional security equipment, but performance degradation in CSCF or SBC can be expected.

Countermeasures at IPSec Configuration Level. There may be a way to prevent 5G users from essentially disabling IPSec. That is, when a terminal accesses a 5G network, it receives information such as IPSec settings from a separate server and communicates without depending on the IPSec setting values set in the terminal. This method must satisfy two conditions; Development of server to send IPSec configuration information and IPSec configuration control through USIM. If the operator is equipped with DM (Device Management) system, it will be very effective method against the investment to block IPSec disabling in advance. However, if you need to build new server, you will need to consider the operator's point of view.

Countermeasures at 3GPP Standard Level. In 3GPP, the application of IPSec on Gm interface is depends on local policy of the P-CSCF. However, it is necessary to review at the 3GPP standard level for the change to compulsory by making the IPSec on Gm interface mandatory. However, it is considered that the 3GPP standard revision is very time consuming and requires lots of efforts and there must be a reason to define the IPSec on Gm interface as optional. Therefore, it can be expected that it will be difficult to respond at the 3GPP standard level.

6   Concluding Remarks and Future Work

Through this study, we can see that there is security problems with voice communication in 5G networks, and it is very easy to access the problem with a device. First, security problems for 5G voice communication can be divided into three categories, easy operation, easy RTP traffic reproduction, and non-force of IPSec encryption due to text-type SIP protocol header. This paper focused on two problems, and further research seems to be needed for the other. Besides, the procedure for 5G voice communication security test can be divided into three steps. The first is the process of disabling the IPSec of the device, and it was easy to enter through the hidden menu. The second is to make it sniff-able by rooting the device. The third step is to analyze the actual 5G voice packet by sniffing it. Here, it is necessary to take further action to analyze the third voice packet analysis process by dividing it into SIP, RTP protocols and reproducing threats such as bugging or tampering. However, since 5G mobile communication network is a private communication network, it is obviously illegal to threaten or bug on the network. Therefore, it is desirable to proceed it by using test network. In the future, operators will build 5G SA environment that has never existed before, and provide customers with new and convenient services that utilize its advantages. However, before launching a service, it is also necessary to think about what security threats exist in new services and countermeasures.

Acknowledgment. This work was supported by the Institute of Information & Communications Technology Planning & Evaluation (IITP) grant funded by the Korea government(MSIT) (No.2019-0-00793, Intelligent 5G Core Network Abnormal Attack Detection & Countermeasure Technology Development.

References

1. CTIA. https://www.ctia.org/national-spectrum-strategy. Accessed 12 June 2020
2. 3GPP TS 23.228, IP Multimedia Subsystem (IMS) Stage 2 (2011)
3. 3GPP TS 33.203, Access Security for IP-Based Services (2011)
4. 3GPP TS 33.210, Network Domain Security (NDS); IP Network Layer Security (2011)
5. Huawei, Vo5G Technical White Paper (2018)
6. IETF, RFC 3261, SIP: Session Initiation Protocol
7. IETF, RFC 3550, RTP: A Transport Protocol for Real-Time Applications
8. Zhang, R., Wang, X., Yang, X., Jiang, X.: Billing attacks on SIP-based VoIP systems. WOOT **7**, 1–8 (2007)
9. Zhang, R., Wang, X., Farley, R., Yang, X., Jiang, X.: On the feasibility of launching the man-in-the-middle attacks on VoIP from remote attackers. In: Proceedings of the 4th International Symposium on Information, Computer, and Communications Security, pp. 61–69. ACM (2009)
10. Beekman, J., Thompson, C.: Breaking cell phone authentication: vulnerabilities in AKA, IMS, and android. In: WOOT (2013)
11. Ferdous, R.: SIP Malformed Message Detection. University of Trento, Italy, SIP LEX (2012)
12. Seo, D., Lee, H., Nuwere, E.: SIPAD: SIP/VoIP anomaly detection using a stateful rule tree. Comput. Commun. **36**, 562–574 (2013)
13. Sengar, H., Wijesekera, D., Jajodia, S.: Detecting VoIP floods using the Hellinger distance. IEEE Trans. Parallel Distrib. Syst. **19**(6), 794–805 (2008)
14. Kim, H.: Breaking and fixing VoLTE: exploiting hidden data channels and mis-implementations. In: CCS 2015, pp. 328–339. ACM (2015)
15. CloudShark. https://www.cloudshark.org/captures/71c1b394bbbf. Accessed 12 June 2020

Author Index

Printed in the United States
By Bookmasters